OTHER A TO 7
THE SCARECR

C000138189

The A to Z of Spain

Angel Smith

The A to Z Guide Series, No. 238

The Scarecrow Press, Inc.
Lanham • Toronto • Plymouth, UK
2010

Published by Scarecrow Press, Inc.
A wholly owned subsidiary of
The Rowman & Littlefield Publishing Group, Inc.
4501 Forbes Boulevard, Suite 200, Lanham, Maryland 20706
http://www.scarecrowpress.com

Estover Road, Plymouth PL6 7PY, United Kingdom

British Library Cataloguing in Publication Information Available

Library of Congress Cataloging-in-Publication Data

The hardback version of this book was cataloged by the Library of Congress
as follows:

Smith, Angel, 1958–
  Historical dictionary of Spain / Angel Smith.
    p. cm. — (Historical dictionaries of Europe ; no. 65)
  Includes bibliographical references.
  1. Spain–History–19th century–Dictionaries. 2. Spain–History–20th century–
Dictionaries. I. Title.
DP12.S59 2008
946.003–dc22   2008022770

ISBN 978-0-8108-7217-2 (pbk. : alk. paper)

♾ TM The paper used in this publication meets the minimum requirements of
American National Standard for Information Sciences—Permanence of Paper
for Printed Library Materials, ANSI/NISO Z39.48-1992.
Printed in the United States of America

Contents

Editor's Foreword

A relative backwater not so long ago, Spain has moved vigorously into the European mainstream in recent decades. It plays a prominent role in the European Union and is now seeking to become a link with countries south of the Mediterranean. Its economy has been substantially revamped and is gradually coming to terms with globalization. It participates significantly in cultural and social activities and its people thoroughly enjoy this opening after a dismal period of closure. During recent decades, Europeans and others have gotten to know Spain much better, and probably better than many other countries. This is partly due to tourism, but also to an intriguing history and fascinating culture. However, despite the increasing familiarity, Spain is a very complicated country, and it takes some digging to understand the variations from one region to the next and also among various segments of the population.

The A to Z of Spain helps to deepen our knowledge by providing a broad view of Spain as a whole, but also some of its regions, and a range of essential variations on the common themes. This is done primarily in the dictionary section, which includes several hundred entries on leading figures of earlier times and today, crucial events that have shaped the nation, the major institutions and organizations, and other essential aspects of its politics, economy, society, and culture. The overall situation can be grasped from the introduction and the many twists and turns of its history become much clearer on reading the chronology and referring to the useful appendixes. For those who want to know more, and they should be numerous, there is an extensive bibliography broken down by subject and historical period.

This volume was written by Angel Smith who lived in Barcelona during most of the 1980s. He gained his first academic post in 1990 and is presently Reader in Modern Spanish History at the University of Leeds. His main areas of specialization are crucial ones, namely social and labor history and nationalisms and national identities, especially those of Catalonia. During this period, Dr. Smith has visited Spain frequently and at length and has lectured and written on a broad range of topics. He has also written, edited, or coedited a growing number of books. The most recent of these is *Anarchism, Revolution and Reaction: Catalan Labour and the Crisis of the Spanish State*. This is a very solid foundation for writing an essential guide to Spain, which is not only informative but an amazingly good read for a reference work.

Jon Woronoff
Series Editor

Reader's Note

Several issues raised their heads when writing the dictionary. A first question is the language in which the entries should be written. Entries for the names of parties and other organizations and bodies have been written in the foreign language rather than English (for languages spoken in Spain, see below). I have also used the foreign language for movements, events, and the like, when this is common in the English literature. However, in these cases I have also used cross-references to avoid confusion. Most place names have also been written in the foreign language. I have, however, excepted a number of such names when it is common to use the English translation (for example, Andalusia, Castile, Catalonia, and Navarre).

There are four main languages spoken in Spain: Castilian (often referred to simply as Spanish), Catalan, Galician, and Basque. In the case of parties and other organizations covering the whole country, I have used Castilian-Spanish. However, with respect to parties and organizations based in Catalonia and Galicia and events that took place in these territories, I have used the autochthonous languages. Regarding Basque organizations and events in the Basque Country, I have adopted a more eclectic approach, basing my choice of language on common usage. The names of persons born in Catalonia, Galicia, and the Basque Country have normally been written in these languages. However, in some cases in which the person in question normally wrote their name in Castilian-Spanish, and had no sympathy for local regionalist/nationalist movements, I have made an exception.

A second major issue is the sometimes-confusing usage of surnames in Spain. This requires some clarification. Spaniards inherit both their father's and mother's surnames (though they only pass their father's surname on to their children). Their father's surname comes first and their mother's surname second. Most people only use their father's surname in everyday contexts, but if it is very common they will frequently be referred to by both surnames (and, on occasion, only their mother's surname). For example, the leader of the opposition party is normally referred to as "Mariano Rajoy," but the Spanish prime minister is called "José Luis Rodríguez Zapatero," rather than "José Luis Rodríguez." In the dictionary entries I have almost always included both the individual's surnames (except in rare instances in which the person has repudiated one of their surnames or in which it has been impossible for me to find the mother's surname). However, in the text itself I have generally followed common usage. The only exception is when an individual is frequently referred to by only his or her mother's surname (for example, the prime minister is sometimes called "Zapatero"). In order to avoid additional confusion, in these cases I use the mother's and father's surnames throughout ("Rodríguez Zapatero"). There is one further source of difficulties. Castilian-Spanish speakers used to insert a "y" between their surnames. This is not now usually the case. However, Catalans continue to insert an "i" between their surnames. In the dictionary a "y" or "i" has been inserted if this is what the person did or does. Throughout the text, terms in bold are cross-references.

List of Acronyms and Abbreviations

AC	Acción Católica/Catholic Action
ACNP	Asociación Católica Nacional de Propagandistas/ National Association of Catholic Propagandists
AP	Alianza Popular/People's Alliance
ASO	Asociación Sindical Obrera/Workers' Trade Union Alliance
AVT	Asociación de Víctimas del Terrorismo/ Association of Terrorist Victims
BOC	Bloc Obrer i Camperol/Workers and Peasants' Bloc
BNG	Bloque Nacionalista Galego/Galician Nationalist Bloc
CC.OO	Comisiones Obreras/Workers Commissions
CDS	Centro Democrático y Social/Democratic and Social Center
CEDA	Confederación Española de Derechas Autónomas/ Spanish Confederation of Autonomous Right-Wing Groups
CEOE	Confederación Española de Organizaciones Empresariales/Spanish Confederation of Employers' Organizations
CiU	Convergència i Unió/Convergence and Union
CNCA	Confederación Nacional Católica Agraria/ National Catholic Agrarian Confederation
CNT	Confederación Nacional del Trabajo/National Labor Confederation
EA	Eusko Alkartasuna/Basque Solidarity

ERC	Esquerra Republicana de Catalunya/Catalan Republican Left
EE	Eukadiko Esquerra/Basque Left
ETA	Euskadi ta Askatasuna/Basque Homeland and Freedom
EC	European Community
EEC	European Economic Community
EU	European Union
FAI	Federación Anarquista Ibérica/Anarchist Iberian Federation
FET y de las JONS	Falange Española Tradicionalista y de las Juntas de Ofensiva Nacional Sindicalista/Traditionalist Spanish Falange and the Juntas of the National Syndicalist Offensive
FLP	Frente de Liberación Popular/Popular Liberation Front
FNTT	Federación Nacional de Trabajadores de la Tierra/National Land Laborers' Federation
FOC	Front Obrer de Catalunya/Catalan Workers' Front
FRAP	Frente Revolucionario Antifascista Patriótico/Revolutionary Antifascist Patriotic Front
FRE	Federación Regional Española de la Asociación Internacional de Trabajadores/Spanish Regional Federation of the International Working Men's Association
FTRE	Federación de Trabajadores de la Región Española/Federation of Workers of the Spanish Region
GAL	Grupos Antiterroristas de Liberación/Antiterrorist Liberation Groups
GRAPO	Grupo Revolucionario Antifascista Primero de Octubre/Revolutionary Antifascist Group First of October
HB	Herri Batasuna/People's Unity
HOAC	Hermandad Obrera de Acción Católica/Workers' Brotherhood of Catholic Action

ILE	Institución Libre de Enseñanza/Independent Educational Institute
INI	Instituto Nacional de Industria/National Institute of Industry
IU	Izquierda Unida/United Left
JOC	Juventud Obrera Católica/Catholic Workers' Youth
Lliga	Lliga Catalana/Catalan League and Lliga Regionalista/Regionalist League
NATO	North Atlantic Treaty Organization
OSE	Organización Sindical Española/National Syndical Organization
PASOC	Partido de Acción Socialista/Party of Socialist Action
PC	Partido Conservador/Conservative Party
PCE	Partido Comunista de España/Spanish Communist Party
PL	Partido Liberal/Liberal Party
PNV	Partido Nacionalista Vasco/Basque Nationalist Party
POUM	Partido Obrero de Unificación Marxista/Unified Marxist Workers' Party
PP	Partido Popular/People's Party
PRR	Partido Republicano Radical/Radical Republican Party
PSC	Partit dels Socialistes de Catalunya/Party of the Catalan Socialists
PSOE	Partido Socialista Obrero Español/Spanish Socialist Workers' Party
PSOE-H	Partido Socialista Obrero Español-Histórico/Historic Spanish Socialist Workers' Party
PSP	Partido Social Popular/People's Social Party
PSUC	Partit Socialista Unificat de Catalunya/Unified Socialist Party of Catalonia
SEU	Sindicato Español Universitario/Spanish University Syndicate
SF	Sección Feminina/Women's Section

SO	Solidaridad Obrera/Worker Solidarity
TCV	Tres Clases de Vapor/Three Steam Classes
UCD	Unión del Centro Democrático/Union of the Democratic Center
UGT	Unión General de Trabajadores/General Workers' Union
UPG	Unión do Pobo Galego/Union of the Galician People
USO	Unión Sindical Obrera/Workers' Trade Union Alliance

Chronology

1469 **18 October**: Marriage of Fernando of Aragón and Isabel of Castile, the former heir to the throne of the Crown of Aragón, the latter disputed heir to the Crown of Castile.

1474 **13 December**: Isabel is crowned Isabel I, queen of the Crown of Castile.

1479 **9 January**: Death of Juan II of Aragón. His son is crowned Fernando II of Aragón. This results in the unification of the Crowns of Castile and Aragón.

1480 The Spanish Inquisition begins to operate.

1492 **2 January**: The Moorish city of Granada falls to Christian forces, bringing to an end the "Reconquest." **31 March**: The decision is taken to expel Jews who have not converted to Christianity from Spain. **12 October**: Christopher Columbus "discovers" America.

1494 **7 June**: The Treaty of Tordesillos is signed between Spain and Portugal.

1516 **13–14 June**: Charles of Gant is proclaimed King Carlos I of Castile and Aragón.

1519 **28 June**: Carlos I is also crowned Charles V, Holy Roman Emperor.

1521 **23 April**: The *Comuneros*' revolt suffers a decisive setback at the battle of Villalar.

1555 **25 September**: The Peace of Augsburg. Carlos I accepts the equality of Protestantism and Catholicism in his German dominions. **25 October**: Carlos I abdicates in the name of his son, Prince Felipe.

1556 16 January: Prince Felipe is proclaimed Felipe II, king of Castile, Aragón, Sicily, and America. **August**: The new king faces a rebellion against his rule in the Low Countries.

1559 2 April: Treaty of Canteen-Cambrésis brings peace with France.

1567 December: The *morisco* population in the Alpujarras (Granada) revolts against Christian rule.

1571 7 October: The Battle of Lepanto. A fleet of papal, Venetian, and Spanish ships inflicts a major defeat on the Ottoman Empire.

1579 17 May: A peace treaty is signed with the southern provinces of the Low Countries (the Unión of Arras).

1580 May: Spanish forces invade Portugal and incorporate the kingdom into Felipe II's Spanish Habsburg Empire.

1588 8 August: The Spanish Armada is dispersed off the coast of England.

1598 13 September: Felipe II dies. Prince Felipe is proclaimed Felipe III.

1604 18 August: The Treaty of London brings peace between England and Spain.

1609 9 April: Treaty of La Haya. Felipe III signs a 12-year truce with the Dutch United Provinces. **4 April**: The decision is taken to expel the *moriscos* from Spain.

1621 21 March: Felipe III dies. His son is proclaimed Felipe IV. War against the United Provinces is resumed.

1635 19 May: France declares war on Felipe IV's Spanish Habsburg Empire.

1640 February: The monarchy faces a rebellion in Catalonia. **7 June**: Catalan rebels enter the city of Barcelona and murder the viceroy. **1 December**: The revolt spreads to Portugal, where the Duke of Braganza is declared King João IV.

1643 24 January: The Count-Duke of Olivares is stripped of power and confined to his estates. **19 May**: Felipe III suffers a major defeat at the hands of the French army at Rocroi.

1648   30 January: The Treaty of Munster. Felipe III recognizes the independence of the United Provinces.

1652   October: Barcelona falls and Catalonia is reincorporated in the Spanish Habsburg Empire.

1659   14 January: Spanish forces are defeated by the Portuguese army at Elvas. **7 November**: The Treaty of the Pyrenees achieves long-term peace with France. However, the Crown of Aragón loses Roussillon and part of Cerdagne to France.

1660   6 June: Consequent upon the Treaty of the Pyrenees, the Infanta, María Teresa, marries the king of France, Louis XIV.

1665   September: Felipe IV dies. His remaining son is proclaimed Carlos II, but Queen Mariana of Austria rules as regent until his coming of age.

1668   13 February: Treaty of Lisbon. Spain recognizes Portuguese independence.

1675   6 November: Carlos II comes of age.

1678   17 September: Peace Treaty of Nijmagen. Spain cedes the France Compté, most of Artois, Ypes, and Cambrai to France.

1700   3 October: The testament of Carlos II confirms the succession of Philippe of Anjou, the grandson of Louis XIV. **1 November**: Carlos II dies. **24 November**: Philippe of Anjou is proclaimed Felipe V.

1701   7 September: England, Holland, and the German Habsburg Empire support the succession of Archduke Charles of Austria to the Spanish throne.

1702   15 May: The War of Succession begins.

1707   25 April: The Allied forces are defeated by the Duke of Berwick at Almansa. **29 June**: Felipe V issues a decree abolishing the Aragonese and Valencian *fueros*.

1710   10 December: The pro-French forces score a major victory at the battle of Villaviciosa.

1713   11 April: Utrecht Settlement. Felipe V is confirmed as the ruler of Spain (Crowns of Aragón and Castile) and of the American colonies, but loses the rest of the Spanish Habsburg Empire. Gibraltar and Minorca fall into British hands.

1714 **7 March**: Peace of Rastaat between France and the German Habsburgs. France agrees to hand over Spain's Italian possessions. **11 September**: Felipe V's forces enter Barcelona. The Catalan *fueros* are subsequently abolished.

1716 **16 January**: Nueva Planta Decrees. The laws of Castile are applied to Catalonia.

1746 **9 July**: Felipe V dies. His son is proclaimed Fernando VI.

1753 **11 January**: A concordat is signed between Spain and the Vatican.

1759 **10 August**: Fernando VI dies. His stepbrother is crowned Carlos III.

1766 **31 July**: The Jesuit order is expelled from Spain.

1778 **February–March**: The colonial monopoly of the port of Cádiz with the American colonies is abolished. **14 December**: Carlos III dies.

1779 **17 January**: His son is crowned Carlos IV.

1792 **November**: The court favorite, Manuel de Godoy, becomes secretary of state.

1796 **19 August**: Through the Treaty of San Ildefonso, Spain allies with France against Great Britain.

1805 **21 October**: The Battle of Trafalgar. The Spanish and French fleets are defeated by the British fleet under Lord Horatio Nelson.

1807 **December**: Napoleon gives the order to occupy Spain.

1808 **17–18 March**: The Aranjuez revolt: Carlos IV is forced to abdicate, putting sovereign power in the hands of his son, Fernando. **2 May**: A popular uprising in Madrid against the French troops is put down. **5–6 May**: Carlos IV and Fernando VII are forced by Napoleon to renounce the Bourbon claim to the throne and agree to his brother Joseph becoming king. **6 July**: The Napoleonic constitution is approved in Bayonne. **9 July**: Napoleon's brother is proclaimed King José I of Spain.

1809   24 September: The anti-Napoleonic Spanish Cortes meets on the Isla de León off Cádiz.

1812   19 March: Proclamation of a new liberal constitution by the Cádiz Cortes.

1813   21 June: The French army is defeated at Vitoria and retires from Spain.

1814   24 March: Fernando VII triumphantly reenters Spain. **4 May**: Fernando VII repudiates the Cádiz Constitution of 1812 and reestablishes absolutism.

1820   1 January: General Rafael de Riego launches a *pronunciamiento* (military coup) in favor of the Constitution of 1812. **7 March**: Fernando VII has to accept the Cádiz Constitution and appoint liberal ministers.

1823   7 April: French troops under the orders of the anti-liberal Holy Alliance invade Spain. **1 October**: Fernando VII is restored to absolute power.

1833   29 September: Death of Fernando VII. The king's daughter Isabel is proclaimed queen but until her coming of age, his wife, María Cristina of Naples, takes over as the queen regent. **6 October**: A Carlist rebellion begins in northern Spain.

1834   15 January: Francisco de Paulo Martínez de la Rosa is chosen as prime minister. **10 April**: The new constitutional text, the Royal Statute, is sanctioned by the queen regent.

1835   August: *Pronunciamientos* are accompanied by the formation of revolutionary juntas in southern Spain. **14 September**: The queen regent calls on Juan Álvarez Mendizábal to head a new government.

1836   February–March: Several decrees set in motion the *desamortización* (disentailment) of church, aristocratic, and municipal landholdings. **15 May**: Álvarez Mendizábal is forced out of government by the queen regent. **13 August** : Following the La Granja rebellion, the queen regent is forced to accept the 1812 Cádiz Constitution. **15 August**: Álvarez Mendizábal (as treasury minister) returns to office.

1837   28 June: Proclamation of the Constitution of 1837. **31 August**: The Vergara Treaty, signed by generals Baldomero Espartero and Rafael Maroto, signifies the virtual end of the First Carlist War.

1839   1 September: *Pronunciamiento* in Madrid against the queen regent, María Cristina. **12 October**: General Baldomero Espartero takes power and María Cristina abdicates.

1841   9 May: General Baldomero Espartero is proclaimed regent.

1843   11–12 June: A series of Moderate and Progressive *pronunciamientos* are launched against General Espartero. **30 July**: Espartero is forced to flee the country. **29 September**: The queen regent's daughter comes of age and is proclaimed Queen Isabel II of Spain. **5 December**: General Luis González Bravo takes office, consolidating the Moderates' grip on power.

1845   24 May: Proclamation of the Moderate Constitution.

1851   16 March: Signature of a concordat with the Vatican.

1854   28 June: Generals Leopoldo O'Donnell and Domingo Dulce launch a new anti-Moderate *pronunciamiento*. **6 July**: The generals issue the Manzanares Manifesto. **19 July**: General Baldomero Espartero returns to power.

1855   1 May: The Madoz Law extends the scope of the *desamortización*. **2 July**: A general strike is called in Barcelona.

1856   13 July: A successful *pronunciamiento* by General Leopoldo O'Donnell against Espartero and the Progressives. The Moderates return to power.

1861   6 July: A peasant uprising takes place in the town of Loja.

1864   10 April: The Night of San Daniel. Student protest in Madrid is brutally suppressed.

1866   16 August: The Ostend Pact, aimed at overthrowing the government, is signed by the Progressives and Democrats.

1868   18 September: The "Glorious Revolution" removes the Moderates from power. Queen Isabel II is forced into exile. **10 October**: The "Grito de Yara" launches a separatist uprising in Cuba.

1869 **6 June**: The Spanish Parliament, the Cortes, proclaims a new liberal-monarchist constitution. **15 June**: General Francisco Serrano is named regent.

1870 **18–25 June**: The founding congress of the anarchist-inspired labor confederation the Federación Regional Española (FRE) is held in Barcelona. **16 November**: The Cortes elects Amadeo de Saboya king of Spain.

1872 **21 April**: Carlist uprisings are launched throughout the country. The Third Carlist War begins.

1873 **11 February**: Amadeo de Saboya abdicates leading to the proclamation of a republic. **11 April**: Francisco Pi i Margall forms a new government. **July–August**: Radical-liberal Cantonalist revolts take place in southern Spain. **18 July**: Nicolás Salmerón takes over the premiership. **7 September**: Salmerón is replaced by the more conservative figure of Emilio Castelar.

1874 **3 January**: General Manuel Pavia launches a coup and disbands the Republican Cortes. **29 December**: The Bourbon monarchist, General Arsensio Martínez Campos, carries out a successful *pronunciamiento* against the Republic. **31 December**: Antonio Cánovas del Castillo's Conservative Party takes power and proclaims Isabel II's son King Alfonso XII. These events usher in the Cánovas Restoration.

1876 **28 February**: The Carlist rebellion is defeated. **30 June**: A new, more conservative, constitution is approved by the Cortes.

1879 **2 May**: Foundation of the Spanish Socialist Party, the Partido Socialista Obrero Español (PSOE), in Madrid.

1881 **6 February**: The Liberal Party is called to power for the first time. **21–25 September**: The founding congress of the proanarchist labor confederation the Federación de Trabajadores de la Región Española (FTRE) is held in Barcelona.

1883 **Spring**: The supposed discovery of the "Mano Negra" in Andalusia is used to repress the anarchist labor confederation, the FTRE.

1885 **25 November**: Death of Alfonso XII. His wife, María Cristina de Habsburgo, becomes the queen regent. **27 November**: A new Liberal government takes office. The "long Liberal parliament" will last until 1890.

1888 **13–14 August:** The founding congress of the Socialist labor confederation, the Unión General de Trabajadores (UGT), is held in Barcelona.

1891 **14 July:** New tariff barriers signify the beginning of an era of protectionism.

1892 **8 January:** A peasant uprising takes place in Jerez de la Frontera.

1893 **7 November:** The anarchist bombing of the Liceo Opera House in Barcelona spreads panic in middle-class circles.

1895 **24 February:** The "Grito de Baire" launches a new separatist uprising in Cuba. **31 July:** Sabino de Arana founds the Basque nationalist party, the Partido Nacionalista Vasco (PNV).

1897 **8 August:** The prime minister, Antonio Cánovas del Castillo, is assassinated by an anarchist gunman.

1898 **25 April–18 July:** The Spanish-American War results in a rapid defeat for Spain. **10 December:** Treaty of Paris: Spain renounces her American and Pacific colonies.

1899 **4 March:** The "regenerationist" Francisco Silvela government takes office.

1901 **24 May:** The Catalan regionalist/nationalist party, the Lliga Regionalista, is founded in Barcelona.

1902 **16–24 February:** A one-week general strike takes place in Barcelona. **17 May:** The end of the regency. The queen regent's son is proclaimed Alfonso XIII.

1906 **15 January:** Formation of the antigovernment Catalan coalition Solidaritat Catalana. **3 March:** New tariffs mean that Spanish tariff barriers are now nominally the highest in Europe.

1909 **16–23 July:** In Barcelona a weeklong general strike escalates into several days of church burning. The events are subsequently known as the Tragic Week.

1910   30 October–1 November: The Spanish anarchist-syndicalist confederation, the Confederación Nacional del Trabajo (CNT), is founded in Barcelona.

1913   18 December: The government approves the constitution of the Catalan Mancomunitat.

1915   World War I brings economic prosperity but also rapid inflation to Spain.

1916   18 July: A one-day general strike is called by the UGT and CNT against rising prices.

1917   9 July: The "Assembly of Parliamentarians" calls for the democratization of the constitution. **19 August**: A general strike is called by the PSOE-UGT and CNT against the Restoration regime.

1921   13 April: Following an Extraordinary Party Congress, dissidents break away from the PSOE to form the Communist Party (Partido Comunista de España [PCE] from November). **22 July**: Nine thousand Spanish troops lose their lives in the military disaster of Annual in Morocco.

1923   13 September: General Miguel Primo de Rivera launches a successful coup d'etat against the Restoration regime.

1927   26 July: Anarchist activists form their own organization, the Federación Anarquista Ibérica (FAI).

1930   28–30 January: Miguel Primo de Rivera resigns. **17 August**: Anti-monarchist forces sign the San Sebastián Pact. **12–14 December**: The pro-Republican Jaca uprising fails. Captains Fermín Galán and Ángel García Hernández are executed.

1931   12 April: Defeat of the monarchist candidates in the Spanish municipal elections. **14 April**: Proclamation of the Second Republic. King Alfonso XIII goes into exile and a provisional government is formed. **28 June**: Left-wing victory in the general elections. **9 December**: A new constitution is approved by the Cortes.

1932   10 August: General José Sanjurjo heads a failed anti-Republican coup. **9 September**: The Catalan autonomy statute is approved by the Cortes. **10 September**: The Agrarian Reform Law is approved by the Cortes.

1933   1 January: Anarchists launch their first insurrection against the Republic. **11–12 January**: Proanarchist peasants die at the hands of the Republican Assault Guard in the village of Casas Viejas. **12 September**: Fall of the republican-Socialist coalition government. **19 November**: Right-wing victory in the general elections.

1934   5 October: The PSOE-UGT calls a general strike, which is seconded by other left-wing groups. The strike becomes a full-blown uprising in Asturias.

1935   15 January: Signing of the Popular Front electoral pact by republican and other leftist forces.

1936   16 February: The Popular Front wins the general elections. **26 June**: Galicians vote for autonomy in a plebiscite. **13 July**. The leading right-wing politician, José Calvo Sotelo, is assassinated. **17–18 July**: An attempted coup d'etat against the Republic provokes civil war. **5 September**: Formation of the Popular Front Republican government headed by Francisco Largo Caballero. **27 September**: General Francisco Franco is declared head of the Nationalist forces. **1 October**: The Republican Cortes approves the Basque autonomy statute. **8 November**: Arrival of the first International Brigades in Madrid. **7 November–1 December**: Republicans repel the Nationalist onslaught on Madrid.

1937   19 April: The Falange and Carlists are forcibly united by Franco and form a new single party, the Falange Española Tradicionalista y de las Juntas de la Ofensiva Nacional Sindicalista (FET y de las JONS). **3–7 May**: "May Events." Fighting breaks out between anarchists and members of the Partido Obrero de Unificación Marxista (POUM), on the one hand, and republicans, Socialists, and Communists, on the other, on the streets of Barcelona. **17 May**: Largo Caballero falls and is replaced as prime minister by Juan Negrín.

1938   30 January: Francisco Franco forms his first government. Ramón Serrano Suñer becomes the minister of the interior. **July–August**: The Republican forces are defeated in the decisive battle of the Ebro.

1939   4 March: The anti-Communist Casado coup is launched in Madrid against the Republican authorities. **28 March**: The Francoist forces march into Madrid. The Spanish Civil War is at an end. **3 September**: Great Britain and France declare war on Germany. World War II begins.

1940   16 October: Serrano Suñer is also appointed foreign minister by Franco. **20 October**: Franco meets Adolf Hitler at Hendaye and after discussions decides not to enter the war on the side of the Axis.

1942   3 September: Serrano Suñer is dismissed as foreign minister and loses all positions of power. Spain subsequently takes a less overtly pro-Axis stance.

1945   7 May: Germany surrenders unconditionally. **17 July**: Proclamation of the Francoist "bill of rights," the Fuero de los Españoles.

1946   9 February: Spain is excluded from the United Nations (UN).

1953   27 August: A concordat is signed between the Franco regime and the Vatican. **20 September**: The Military Bases Agreement is signed with the United States.

1955   14 September: Spain is admitted into the UN.

1957   25 February: Opus Dei technocrats enter Franco's sixth government and plan a major liberalization of the Spanish economy.

1959   22 July: The government announces the Stabilization Plan, signifying the end of economic autarky. **31 July**: The Basque nationalist group Euskadi ta Askatasuna (ETA) is founded.

1962   9 April: Spain requests admittance to the European Economic Community (EEC). **April–June**: Worker and student protest. States of emergency are declared in the Basque Country and Asturias.

1963   20 April: The Communist activist, Julián Grimau, is executed.

1966   18 March: Approval by the Cortes of the Fraga Press Law. **14 December**: The Organic Law of State is approved in a referendum.

1968   22 July: Admiral Luis Carrero Blanco is appointed vice president of the cabinet.

1969 **22 July**: Franco names Juan Carlos his successor.

1970 **1 October**: The EEC signs a preferential trade agreement, the Luxembourg Accord, with Spain.

1973 **8 June**: Carrero Blanco takes over from Franco as prime minister. **16 October**: The first major oil price rise by the Organization for Petroleum Exporting Countries (OPEC) is announced. **20 December**: Carrero Blanco is assassinated by ETA.

1974 **31 January**: Franco names Carlos Arias Navarro as prime minister. **12 February**: Arias Navarro announces the reform of the regime. **11–13 October**: The PSOE holds its key Suresnes Congress. Felipe González is elected first secretary. **29 October**: Hopes of reform are dashed with the dismissal of the minister of information, Pío Cabanillas.

1975 **21 September**: Five activists linked to ETA and the Frente Revolucionario Antifascista and Patriótico (FRAP) are executed. **20 November**: Franco dies. **22 November**: Juan Carlos is crowned king. **13 December**: Carlos Arias Navarro forms a new government that includes regime reformers.

1976 **26 March**: Socialists and Communists lead the formation of the antiregime front, the Coordinación Democrática. **1 July**: Arias Navarro is forced to resign by the king. **3 July**: The king appoints Adolfo Suárez as prime minister. **10 September**: The government announces the Law of Political Reform, signaling its support for democracy. **9 October**: Foundation of Manuel Fraga's coalition, Alianza Popular (AP). **12 November**: The leftist opposition launches a one-day general strike against the government. **16 November**: The Law of Political Reform is approved in the Cortes, thereby opening the way to democratization. **15 December**: The Law of Political Reform is approved in a referendum.

1977 **1 April**: The state's single party, the Movimiento, is dismantled and unions legalized. **9 April**: The PCE is legalized. **15 June**: Adolfo Suárez's coalition, the Unión del Centro Democrático (UCD), wins the first democratic elections since 1936. **25–27 October**: Signing of the Moncloa Pacts.

1978 ETA's offensive against the armed forces intensifies. The strike wave reaches a crescendo. **27 April**: The radical Basque nationalist coalition Herri Batasuna (HB) is founded. **September**: The centrist Catalan nationalist coalition Convergéncia i Unió (CiU) is set up in Barcelona. **31 October**: The new constitution is approved by Congress and the Senate. **6 December**: The constitution is supported in a national referendum.

1979 **1 March**: New general elections. The UCD remains in power. **28–30 September**: An Extraordinary Party Congress affirms Felipe González's leadership and downgrades the place of Marxism in the PSOE's principles.

1980 **11 January**: The Basque and Catalan autonomous governments begin to operate.

1981 **29 January**: Suárez resigns the premiership. **23 February**: A coup (the "Tejerazo") is launched in a failed attempt to overthrow the new democratic institutions. **9 December**: Spain rapidly joins the North Atlantic Treaty Organization (NATO).

1982 **28 October**: The PSOE wins an overall majority in the general elections. Felipe González becomes prime minister. **11 November**: Santiago Carrillo resigns as PCE general secretary.

1983 **2 February**: The bankrupt RUMASA holding company is confiscated by the government.

1984 **26 June**: Approval of the government's Conversion and Re-industrialization Law in the Cortes. **9 October**: Signing of the Economic and Social Agreement (AES), the last of the tripartite economic pacts between the UGT, the government, and the employers' federation, the Confederación Española de Organizaciones Empresariales (CEOE). **1 November**: The Cortes approves the new education law (LODE) in the teeth of right-wing opposition.

1985 **12 June**: The EEC formally agrees to Spanish membership. **20 June**: The Communists lead a one-day general strike against the government's program to restructure Spanish industry. **3 July**: The "super-minister" Miguel Boyer is forced to resign after clashes with the PSOE vice president, Alfonso Guerra.

1986 1 January: Spain becomes a full member of the EEC. **12 March**: After an intensive government campaign, continued membership of NATO is narrowly ratified in the referendum called by the PSOE. **29 April**: The PCE, along with other left-wing groups, form the electoral coalition Izquierda Unida (IU). **22 June**: The PSOE wins the general elections with a decreased majority. **1 December**: Manuel Fraga resigns as president of AP.

1987 February: Antonio Hernández Mancha is elected the new president of AP at an extraordinary party congress. **10 October**: The labor confederations, the UGT and Comisiones Obreras (CC.OO) agree to carry out joint demonstrations against government economic policy.

1988 12 January: The Ajurea Enea Pact against terrorist violence is signed by all the parliamentary parties in the Basque Country, except HB. **22 February**: The PCE elects Julio Anguita as its new general secretary. **14 December**: A successful one-day general strike is called by CC.OO and the UGT against the government's economic policy.

1989 20 January: AP changes its name to Partido Popular (PP) at its ninth congress. **7 February**: Negotiations held between the government and unions to reach a "social pact" breakdown. **6 April**: ETA breaks off negotiations with the government in Algeria. **19 June**: Spain joins the Exchange Rate Mechanism (ERM) of the European Monetary System. **29 October**: The PSOE loses votes but retains an overall majority in the general elections.

1990 1 April: José María Aznar is elected president of the PP. **9 April**: The PP's treasurer, Rosendo Naseiro, is detained on bribery charges.

1991 12 January: Alfonso Guerra is forced to resign as vice president of the government following a corruption scandal involving his brother, Juan Guerra. **25 June**: Spain signs the Schengen agreement abolishing frontier controls between eight EEC countries. **19 September**: The former policemen José Amedo and Michel Domínguez are sentenced to 100 years in prison for their part in organizing the anti-ETA terrorist group, the Grupos Antiterroristas de Liberación (GAL).

1992 7 February: The Spanish government signs the Maastricht Treaty, committing it to meeting the convergence criteria of the EEC (European Union [EU] from 1993) for Economic and Monetary Union

(EMU). **21 March**: The governor of the Bank of Spain, Mariano Rubio, is forced to resign over insider trading involving the Ibercorp industrial group. **29 March**: ETA's leadership is detained in the town of Bidart near Biarritz. **25 June**: The opening ceremony of the Barcelona Olympic games is held. **29 October**: The Spanish parliament approves the Maastricht Treaty.

1993   6 June: The PSOE wins the general election but loses its overall majority in parliament. **30 June**: CiU decides to support the Socialist government, allowing it to remain in power. **30 August**: Under pressure from CiU the government agrees in principle to cede 15 percent of direct taxes (IRPF) to the autonomous communities. **11 September**: In San Sebastián, a demonstration of 80,000 people calls for the liberation of a Basque industrialist, Julio Iglesias Zamora, kidnapped by ETA. **6 October**: Nicolás Redondo steps down as head of the UGT. **3 December**: Ferran Cardenal replaces Luis Roldán, under suspicion of corruption, as director general of the Civil Guard. **27 December**: The Bank of Spain takes over the running of the banking group Banesto and dismisses its president, Mario Conde.

1994   27 January: The UGT and CC.OO call a further one-day general strike against the government. **March**: The "*guerristas*" are defeated by the "renovators" in the PSOE's 33rd Congress. **10 April**: Cándido Méndez is elected as the new head of the UGT. **29 April**: The former director general of the Civil Guard, Luis Roldán, accused of corruption, flees Spain. **30 April**: The minister of the interior, Antoni Asunción, is, as a result, forced to resign. **4 May**: The former governor of the Bank of Spain, Mariano Rubio, is arrested on charges of corruption. **22 June**: The PP wins the elections to the European Parliament. **17 October**: The financier with close links to CiU, Javier de la Rosa, is detained on fraud charges. **23 December**: Mario Conde, the former president of Banesto, is imprisoned on fraud charges.

1995   23 January: ETA assassinates Gregorio Ordóñez, the leader of the PP in Galicia, provoking anti-ETA demonstrations in the Basque Country. **19 March**: ETA attempts unsuccessfully to assassinate the future Spanish prime minister, José María Aznar, in Madrid. **13 June**: The vice president, Narcís Serra, is forced to resign after the revelation that the intelligence agency, the Centro Superior de Información de la

Defensa (Higher Defense Intelligence Center—CESID), had engaged in illegal phone tapings of conversations involving the king and leading politicians. **18 October**: The Senate agrees by one vote (with the PSOE and CiU opposed) to set up a commission to investigate the anti-ETA terrorist group, the GAL.

1996   6 January: ETA assassinates the Socialist politician Fernando Múgica. **19 February**: A demonstration by 850,000 in Madrid calls for an end to ETA assassinations. **3 March**: The PP wins the general elections but fails to gain an overall majority in parliament. **26 April**: A pact between the PP and CiU opens the way for the investiture of José María Aznar as prime minister.

1997   20 March: Mario Conde is sentenced to six years in prison for embezzling 600 million pesetas. **8 April**: Employers and unions pact the reform of Spain's labor laws. **20 June**: Felipe González announces at the PSOE's 34th Congress that he will not seek reelection as party leader. **22 June**: Joaquín Almunia is elected new PSOE general secretary. **1 July**: The Civil Guard rescues the prison functionary José Ortega Lara, who had been held by ETA for 532 days. **10 July**: ETA captures the PP local councilor, Miguel Angel Blanco, and threatens to kill him within 48 hours if its demand that ETA prisoners be moved to the Basque Country is not met. **12 July**: ETA carries out its threat. **14 July**: Massive anti-ETA demonstrations are held throughout Spain. **26 September**: Pascual Maragall steps down as mayor of Barcelona in order to run for the presidency of the Generalitat. **19 October**: Elections to the Galician parliament. The PP is victorious, but the Galician nationalist Bloque Nacionalista Galego (BNG) becomes the second largest party. **1 December**: The Herri Batasuna leadership is imprisoned for seven years for collaborating with ETA. **2 December**: Spain joins NATO's military structure.

1998   26 February: The former head of the Civil Guard, Luis Roldán, is sentenced to 28 years in prison. **24 April**: José Borrell defeats Joaquín Almunia in the PSOE's "primary elections" to choose the party's candidate for prime minister. **25 April**: An ecological disaster occurs in the Doñana National Park following a chemical spill. **16 July**: CiU, the PNV, and BNG sign the Declaration of Barcelona, demanding the Spanish state recognize Spain's "plurinational" nature. **17 July**: Julio

Anguita suffers a second heart attack. **12 September**: The "Declaration of Lizarra," or "Pact of Estella," is signed by PNV, EA, HB, IU, and the Basque unions ELA and LAB, calling for the revision of the Statute of Guernika and affirming the right to independence. **16 September**: ETA declares a ceasefire. **25 October**: Elections to the Basque autonomous parliament. The PNV remains the largest party, but statewide parties close the gap. **29 December**: Juan José Ibarretxe is elected *lehendakari* (president) of the Basque parliament.

1999   1 January: The euro replaces the peseta on currency exchange boards. **14 May**: Borrell resigns as PSOE candidate for the forthcoming general elections. **5 July**: Joaquín Almunia agrees to take over as the PSOE's candidate for the general elections. **28 September**: The Constitutional Tribunal annuls the prison sentences imposed on the leadership of Herri Batasuna. **17 October**: CiU wins most seats in the elections to the Catalan parliament but suffers a significant decline in support. **28 November**: ETA brings its ceasefire to an end.

2000   21 January: ETA assassinates the Civil Guard lieutenant colonel Pedro Antonio Blanco García. **23 January**: Anti-ETA demonstrations are held throughout Spain. **24 January**: Joaquín Almunia offers Izquierda Unida a pact in the forthcoming general elections. **6 February**: Immigrant workers are attacked in the town of El Ejido in Almería. **22 February**: ETA assassinates the leading Basque Socialist, Fernando Buesa. **12 March**: The PP gains an overall majority in the general elections. **22 July**: José Luis Rodríguez Zapatero is elected the new general secretary of the PSOE. **29 October**: Izquierda Unida elects Gaspar Llamazares as general coordinator in its VI Assembly. **11 November**: Jordi Pujol confirms Artur Mas as his successor in Convergència Democràtica de Catalunya's party congress. **21 November**: ETA assassinates the former Socialist minister Ernest Lluch in Barcelona, provoking mass demonstrations in Catalonia. **12 December**: The PP and the PSOE sign an "antiterrorist pact."

2001   20 March: ETA assassinates the Socialist councilor Froilán Elespe de Lasarte in San Sebastián. **6 May**: ETA assassinates Manuel Giménez Abad, president of the PP in Aragón. **11 May**: ETA explodes a car bomb in the center of Madrid. **13 May**: The PNV/EA nationalist coalition wins the elections to the Basque autonomous parliament.

11 June: The EU agrees to continue providing Spain with structural funding through to 2013. **13 June**: The Senate approves the National Hydraulic Plan (PHN). **28 October**: Morocco withdraws its ambassador from Spain. **7 November**: A one-day strike is called in Spanish universities against the PP's proposed Organic University Law (LOU).

2002 **1 January**: Euro notes and coins are introduced. **1 March**: The peseta loses its legal tender status. **14 June**: The Spanish parliament approves the government's labor and unemployment legislation. **20 June**: Unions hold a one-day strike in protest. **27 June**: Parliament approves the Ley Orgánica de Partidos, aimed at illegalizing parties with links to terrorist organizations. **11 July**: Morocco occupies the uninhabited rocky outcrop of Perejil. **7 November**: The Gibraltarian population overwhelmingly rejects the Spanish-British proposal for joint sovereignty in a referendum. **19 November**: The oil tanker *Prestige* sinks, leading to a large spill affecting, above all, the Galician coast.

2003 **16 March**: George W. Bush, Tony Blair, and José María Aznar meet on a U.S. base in the Azores. **20 March**: The U.S.-led invasion of Iraq leads to mass demonstrations throughout Spain. **6 April**: The U.S. State Department agrees to include Herri Batasuna on its list of terrorist organizations after a meeting between Aznar and Bush. **16 May**: The Spanish cultural center (Casa de España) in Casablanca is bombed by Islamic terrorists; 44 people are killed, including two Spaniards. **25 May**: Municipal and regional elections are held. There is a swing toward the PSOE, but the PP vote holds up well. **16 November 2003**: Following elections to the Catalan autonomous parliament, CiU loses it grip on power for the first time since 1980.

2004 **17 January**: The PNV elects Josu Jon Imaz as its new president. **11 March**: Several trains on route between Alcalá de Henares and Madrid are bombed by Islamic extremists, killing 191 people three days before the general election. **14 March**: The general election produces a surprise victory for the PSOE. José Luis Rodríguez Zapatero becomes prime minister. **18 April**: Rodríguez Zapatero makes the decision to withdraw Spanish troops from Iraq.

2005 **2 February**: The Spanish parliament rejects the "Plan Ibarretxe." **20 February**: The proposed new European constitution is approved (though only 42 percent of the electorate votes). **25 April**: The PNV loses seats in the Basque elections, but is able to maintain a minority coalition government. **17 May**: Despite the opposition of the Partido Popular, the Spanish parliament agrees to a dialogue with ETA as long as it renounces violence. **4 June**: Hundreds of thousands of demonstrators march in Madrid calling for no dialogue with ETA. **19 June**: The PP loses its overall majority in the elections to the Galician parliament. The PSG-PSOE and BNG subsequently form a coalition government. **21 July**: Negotiations between ETA and the government begin in Geneva. **30 September**: The Catalan parliament backs a new Catalan autonomy statute. **3–12 December**: Further negotiations between the government and ETA in Oslo.

2006   **21 January**: José Luis Rodríguez Zapatero and Artur Mas reach an agreement on the new Catalan autonomy statute. **22 March**: ETA declares a cease-fire. **7 April**: José Bono steps down as minister of defense. In the subsequent cabinet reshuffle Alfredo Pérez Rubalcaba becomes minister of the interior. **6 July**: Mariano Rajoy withdraws PP backing for negotiations with ETA. **29 July**: José Luis Rodríguez Zapatero announces in parliament that negotiations will take place with ETA, aimed at bringing violence in the Basque Country to an end. **1 November**: Elections to the Catalan parliament. CiU gets most votes, but the left-wing *tripartit* pact is subsequently reformed. **30 December**: ETA plants a bomb in Madrid Barajas airport, killing two Colombian migrant workers. **31 December**: Rodríguez Zapatero confirms that the "peace process" is over.

2007   **6 June**: ETA officially breaks its cease-fire. **31 October**: Twenty-one men are convicted at the end of the trial of the Madrid train bombers. **2 December**: ETA shoots dead two civil guards in the French Basque Country. **30 December**: The Catholic Church holds a large meeting in Madrid "in defense of the Christian family."

2008   **17 January**: A radical Islamic cell is broken up in Barcelona. **30 January**: The permanent commission of the Spanish Episcopal Conference issues a statement tacitly calling for voters not to support the PSOE. **8 February**: The investigative magistrate, Baltazar Garzón, suspends the activities of the radical Basque nationalist parties the Partido Comunista de las Tierras Vascas and Acción Nacionalista Vasca because of their suspected links with ETA. **7 March**: The political parties suspend the final meetings of the election campaign after the former Socialist local councilor Isaias Carrasco is murdered by ETA in the Basque Country. **9 March**: The PSOE wins the general election but fails to gain an overall majority.

Introduction

Since the Middle Ages, Spain has been a land of extremes. In the early Middle Ages, much of the Iberian Peninsula fell into Moorish hands. Yet shortly after the "Reconquest" was completed in 1492 it would be at the center of the Christendom's most powerful empire. Key moments in this journey were the "discovery" of the American continent by Christopher Columbus, again in 1492, and incorporation into the Habsburgs' European dominions in 1516. During the 16th century, the Castilian-Spanish language was exported to Spain's American colonies, and Castilian troops would play a leading role in the Habsburgs' struggle to maintain their empire intact and ward off the Turkish Ottoman threat. The 15th and 16th centuries would also witness the end of the Peninsula's multiethnic heritage, with the imposition of an intolerant Catholic faith. At home the large Jewish and Moorish populations were expelled, while Spain would also be the bulwark of the Counter-Reformation against the Protestant "heresy." A conservative, militant Church would be a key legacy of this period.

However, the country proved economically too weak and divided to maintain a leading role in world affairs and from the end of the 16th century went into relative decline. Indeed, in the 19th and early 20th centuries, it lost its empire at a time when the major powers were building theirs. And until the 1960s, Spain was viewed by many in the West as something of a backwater. Indeed, in the 1800s, there were claims that "Africa began at the Pyrenees" and that culturally Spain did not belong to Europe at all. And in Spain itself, especially after military defeat at the hands of the United States in 1898, fears were expressed that it could not adapt to the modern world as successfully as the Anglo-Saxon "races." These fears were accompanied by the growth of social and political divisions within Spain. As in the European continent as a whole, conflict between left and right intensified between the 1900s and

1

1930s. These years would also see the "national question" raise its head, with sectors of the Basque, Catalan, and Galician populations calling for either home rule or independence. These tensions would explode into open conflict during the civil war of 1936–1939.

Racial theories were discredited in the aftermath of World War II, and the vision of Spain as a quaint backwater has subsequently been dispelled by the spectacular transformation in its economic and political fortunes over the last 35 years. The archconservative dictatorship of General Francisco Franco, which took the reins of power in 1939, fell apart following Franco's death in November 1975, to be replaced by a constitutional monarchy under King Juan Carlos I. Under Juan Carlos a parliamentary democracy has been reinstalled, and Spain's linguistic and cultural diversity recognized through the granting of autonomy statutes to the "regions and nationalities." This has been accompanied by total integration within the Western European bloc, with Spain's accession to the European Economic Community (EEC) in 1986. Since this date the Spanish economy has also grown extremely rapidly, with the result that it has to a significant degree caught up with the major European economic powers. Furthermore, from the mid-1990s in particular, accelerated economic development has triggered wide-scale immigration. In December 2007, the Italian media was dumbstruck when the statistical office of the European Union (EU), Eurostat, announced the Spanish gross domestic product per capita had surpassed that of Italy.

This has been accompanied by something of a cultural renaissance. Barcelona's *modernista* architectural heritage came into fashion in the 1980s and has helped turn the city into a premier weekend tourist destination. Present-day architects, most notably Santiago Calatrava, have also made their mark, and cities like Valencia and Bilbao have used iconic building projects to spearhead economic renewal. Spain has also developed a cinema industry with a global reach, and now has a talented crop of directors, such as Pedro Almodóvar and Alejandro Almenábar, who have become international figures, while actors like Antonio Banderas, Penelope Cruz, and Javier Bardem have made the jump to Hollywood and are now household names. Yet the new sense of pride and well-being has been accompanied by the onset of problems common to other Western societies. There is concern about the degradation of the environment, while wide-scale migration from north Africa has raised the issue of multiculturalism. "Culture wars" have also erupted between

Catholic conservatives and the secularizing left. And to an extent unparalleled in the rest of Western Europe (with the possible exception of Great Britain), the "national question" has the potential to create grave divisions.

LAND AND PEOPLE

Spain is located in the Iberian Peninsula in southwestern Europe. On its eastern border, it is separated from France (along with the tiny Principality of Andorra) by the Pyrenean mountain range. It is bordered by the Atlantic Ocean to the north and the Mediterranean Sea to the south. To the west is Portugal, which forms a long strip of land on the Atlantic coast. The only other sovereign territory on the peninsula is Gibraltar, which is a British colony. The Balearic Islands and other minor islands and rocky outcrops in the Mediterranean, the African enclaves of Ceuta and Melilla, and the Canary Islands, located in the Atlantic Ocean off the northwest coast of Africa, also form part of Spain.

At 504,645 square kilometers, Spain is the second-largest Western European country after France. It is also the most mountainous country in Europe after Switzerland. Apart from the Pyrenees, a series of mountain ranges cut across its territory (the European Peaks, the Central, Betican, Catalan and Iberian Mountain Ranges, Sierra Morena, the Baetic Mountains, and the Sierra Nevada). Central Spain comprises a large plateau, which is divided up into the southern and northern plateaus (*mesetas*), separated by the Central Mountain Range. This helps explain the country's extreme geographical variations. It has three major climate systems: the Mediterranean system along its southeastern and southern seaboard, including the Guadalquivir Valley in Andalusia; the continental system of the central plateau; and the Atlantic system along its northern coastal strip. The northern coast (often referred to as "Green Spain") is marked by moderate temperatures (an average of 9°C in winter and 18°C in summer), and quite heavy rainfall (between 800 and 1,500 mm a year). The continental system is much more varied, with relatively low rainfall (under 400 mm a year), low temperatures in winter and higher temperatures in summer (averaging 24°C). The Mediterranean system is more temperate, but the southern Mediterranean is parched semidesert (especially the area around Alicante and

Almería), and the Guadalquivir valley is very hot in summer (Seville has been known to hit 47°C). Average temperatures are 11°C in winter and 23°C in summer and the average yearly rainfall varies between 250 mm and 600 mm.

In Western European terms the country is relatively sparsely populated, with a population density of 89.6 per square kilometer in 2007. However, very rapid immigration has begun to change this. The population grew from 38.9 million in 1995 to 45.2 million in 2007. During this period, the number of immigrants has risen from under 1 million to over 4.5 million. An important percentage of the legal immigration is made up of rich Westerners who have been buying up property, above all on or near the Mediterranean coast, but the majority are young men and women in search of work (with Moroccans, Ecuadorians, Colombians, and Rumanians the most numerous). This population is concentrated above all along the littoral and around Madrid. Large parts of central Spain remain very lightly populated.

This rapid increase in immigration has greatly benefited the economy but also led to social and cultural tensions. Yet, as noted previously, ethnic tension is not limited to newly arrived immigrant workers. Spain is unusual in Western European terms in that from the 19th century on attempts by the state to impose a more homogeneous "national culture" have to a degree failed, with the result that the country has maintained a high degree of linguistic diversity. The reasons behind this failure will be explored in subsequent sections. Suffice it to note for now that four major languages are spoken in the country. Almost all Spaniards speak Castilian-Spanish, the official language of the entire territory; Galician is widely spoken in the northwestern territory of Galicia; Catalan, and its variant Valencian, are spoken in Catalonia, Valencia, the Balearic Islands, and a narrow strip of Aragón; while a significant percentage of the population in the Basque Country and northern Navarre speak Basque. Since the promulgation of the State of the Autonomies in 1978 Catalan, Valencian, Galician, and Basque have become co-official languages in their autonomous communities (and Basque is also taught in schools in northern Navarre). There, however, remains a serious culture clash between Spaniards in Castilian-Spanish-only speaking areas, where a majority of people feel Spain to be a single nation and harbor some hostility toward the other languages (especially Catalan), and a significant proportion of the inhabitants in the multilingual territories, who claim that their area is in fact the nation and who defend what they see as their own linguistic and cultural traditions. This is especially the case in the Basque Country, Catalonia, and Galicia. What sociologists have called "multiple identities" provide some common ground (with most inhabitants of the multilingual territories regarding themselves as part Spanish), but conflict over the reform of the State of the Autonomies between 2004 and 2007 has heightened political and cultural tensions.

THE RISE AND FALL OF
THE SPANISH EMPIRE, 1479–1898

Spain's path to modernity has been, in many respects, a particularly difficult one, and some of the issues which arose in the Middle Ages still reverberate in Spain today. The country's modern contours were not established until the years between 1479 and 1492. In the former year, the Crown of Aragón and Crown of Castile came together under the Catholic Monarchs Isabel and Fernando; in the latter, the last Moorish stronghold in the peninsula, Granada, was recaptured, bringing to an end the Christian "Reconquest." Soon after, in 1516, Spain integrated into the European Habsburg Empire under King Carlos V (from 1519 he became the Holy Roman Emperor Charles I). The country would remain under Habsburg rule until 1700.

Unification and then integration into the Habsburg dominions would have a number of consequences. The pious Isabel I, concerned by the supposed threat posed by Jews who had converted to Christianity, but who were, it was widely believed, practicing the Jewish faith in secret, convinced the pope to issue a bull setting up the Spanish Inquisition. This was the beginning of a push to assert Catholic uniformity in Spain, by compelling Jews and Moors to conform to the Christian faith, expelling Jews who refused to convert in 1492, launching a counteroffensive against the threat of Protestantism from the 1520s, and expelling the Moorish population of Spain in 1609. In the process, the Spanish Catholic Church became a highly conservative institution, with the Inquisition policing Christian morality and banning works which were deemed to question the faith.

Along with the capture of Granada, 1492 also witnessed the "discovery" of the American continent by Christopher Columbus, who had been financed by the Catholic Monarchs to find a new route to the Far East. As a result, Spain quickly built an empire on the continent on the ruins of the Aztec and Inca civilizations. At the same time, integration into the Habsburg Empire meant that the country would be involved in almost constant warfare, the aim of which was to contain the threat of the Ottoman Empire, counter the growing power of France, and maintain the Habsburgs' dominions intact. From the reign of Felipe II, Spain (and above all the Crown of Castile) would be very much at the center of the empire. The Castilian economy was not, however, up to the task. Agricultural productivity was relatively low and the country's manufacturing base weak. Heavy taxes were raised on the Castilian townsfolk and peasantry, but these served to deter economic development. Further resources were mobilized through the import of great quantities of silver bullion from the New World, but this led to inflation at home, making Spanish products increasingly expensive on the European market and encouraging imports.

In these circumstances, France emerged as the major European power in the 17th century. After the establishment of a new Bourbon dynasty under Felipe V, in 1713 Spain was forced to relinquish its European possessions. This proved a blessing in disguise as it was able to concentrate on internal reconstruction. And the Bourbon monarchs were, in subsequent years, to check the power of the conservative Church and encourage moderate Enlightenment reforms in the economic and social sphere.

TRADITION AND MODERNITY: THE TRANSITION FROM ABSOLUTISM TO LIBERALISM, 1789–1845

Yet from the early 19th century, the country found it hard to respond to the challenge posed by the more dynamic economic powers of Western Europe and the United States. As the century progressed several problems became apparent: industrial development was very localized, the armed forces had become archaic, and governments were weak and indebted. The continuing decline of Spain's status as a world power was demonstrated between 1808 and 1823, when it quickly succumbed to an invasion at the hands of the forces of Napoleon Bonaparte and then failed to quell separatist revolts in its American colonies. The coup de grace came between 1895 and 1898, when, unable to deal with a separatist Cuban rebellion, it was then comprehensively defeated in a short-lived war with the United States, losing its remaining colonial possessions—most importantly Cuba and the Philippines—in the Americas and the Pacific. Hence, in the early 20th century it was left to fight over the arid scrubland of northern Morocco with the tribesmen of the Riff Mountains.

This perceived backwardness led to claims that Spain did not really belong to Europe at all, and that "Africa began at the Pyrenees." And Western travelers in search of the exotic felt they had no farther to go than Iberia. Spaniards themselves were not adverse to cataloging and bemoaning perceived traits in the Spanish character which prevented them from adapting to the modern world. Writers of the "Generation of 1898," most notably Miguel de Unamuno, combined a nostalgic portrayal of the Castilian countryside with much hand-wringing regarding the country's apparent inability to Europeanize. And yet, from a historical perspective, it is clear that Spain has, since the French Revolution, been fully immersed in the broad economic, social, and cultural movements which have shaped the development of the European continent, belonging—like Italy, Greece, and Poland—to that group of less powerful states, which were not at the forefront of economic development, and which were, as a result, largely on the receiving end of moves to redraw national boundaries and/or redivide colonial spoils.

Spain found it difficult to respond to the twin shocks of the late 18th-century French political revolution and British economic revolution. The combined result of these revolutions would, throughout Europe, be the destruction of the old system of noble and Church privileges and economic regulation, and the birth of a new liberal economic, social, and political order. They had two major facets. At an economic level they led to the sweeping away of restrictions on the free sale and purchase of land (mortmain, or to use the Spanish terms, *mayorazgos* and *senoríos*), of feudal and semifeudal dues, and guild restrictions on industry. In the political sphere, they resulted in the introduction of checks on the power of the monarch (or even, in the most extreme case, a republic) and the replacement of occasional parliaments (or Cortes, to use the Spanish term) by a national parliament, which to a greater or lesser degree oversaw the work of government. These transformations were accompanied by the advance of capitalist relations of production in manufacturing, with the growth of factory-based production, the decline of the petty artisanal trades, and the transfer of labor and capital from the countryside to the rapidly expanding towns and cities.

Spain's weak economic growth could, in part, be put down to its low agricultural yields. As noted, this was already a problem in the Middle Ages. Spain has never been blessed with a favorable climate. In the center and south of the country, rainfall is low and land in some areas is subject to serious soil erosion. Moreover, the amount of high-quality land subject to cultivation has been limited by the abrupt nature of much of the terrain. Just as important in retarding agricultural development has been landholding structures. In Andalusia, Extremadura, and southern Castile, during the "Reconquest" between the 8th and 15th centuries, great tracts of land, which became known as *latifundia*, were given over by the crown to the nobility, Church, and military orders. These great estates, which specialized in the production of wheat and olives, were worked by a vast army of land-hungry, poverty-stricken peasants, known as *braceros* or *jornaleros*. The surplus of cheap labor meant that there was little incentive to mechanize. Hence, the *latifundia*'s productivity tended to be low and workers' spending power was limited, with the result that during the 19th century the south provided only a limited stimulus to economic development. As we shall see, these estates would also be a source of great social tension. In parts of northern Spain, particularly in Galicia and the north of Old Castile, the opposite problem existed. Here landholding was enormously subdivided into units called minifundia. This tended to lock peasants into subsistence or near-subsistence farming, with the consequence that they could hardly contribute to the creation of a national market.

Low internal demand handicapped the expansion of Spanish industry. The only region to undergo an industrial transformation from the first half of the 19th century was Catalonia, where a modern factory-based cotton textile industry grew up. This was followed, in the second half of the century, by the development of coal mining in Asturias and an iron and steel industry in the Basque region of Vizcaya. Yet at the beginning of the 20th century, with around 70 percent of Spain's active population still living off the land, the Spanish economy was both poorer and more agrarian-based than those of the major European powers.

At the same time, resistance to liberalism in Spain was especially strong. Throughout Europe, the ideals of the French Revolution had been propagated by the urban middle classes, along with intellectual elites and reforming landowners, who realized that only an overhaul of economic and political structures could channel the new social and political forces. It was viewed with alarm if not outright hostility by the Catholic Church, monarchs, and much of the nobility, who feared losing their land and feudal dues and their place as key interlocutors in the nation's political and social life. In Spain, these groups were extremely powerful. The Church and nobility owned vast tracts of land and were firmly enmeshed in and enjoyed a privileged status under the ancien régime. The Church had played a particularly important ideological role. The "Reconquest" had been justified as a crusade against the infidel, and the subsequent conquest of the Americas was seen as a holy mission to Christianize the New World. Subsequently, as noted, the Spanish Church became the bulwark of the Counter-Reformation against Protestantism. In the 18th century, a group of reforming churchmen emerged, known as Regalists or Jansenists, but the majority of the clergy were antimodernizing conservatives. From the 1780s, therefore, much of the Church was quick to denounce liberalism, with its talk of political pluralism and the sovereignty of the citizenship, as an unholy aberration that threatened the central role it should have in state and society in order to spread the word of God.

The political and ideological conflicts that had racked Europe over the previous 20 years swept into Spain on the back of the Napoleonic invasion of 1808. The subsequent occupation would deal Spain a large blow by undermining its ability to defeat revolts in the Americas. Napoleon crowned his brother King Joseph I, but for the first time large sectors of the populace entered the political stage, launching a war which for some was a religious crusade and for others a struggle for national independence. It was in this context that, in 1812, the anti-Napoleonic Cortes of Cádiz proclaimed the first liberal constitution in Spanish history.

The Cádiz constitution was the work of the urban populace and the commercial and mercantile classes, centered on the Mediterranean littoral, for whom liberalism meant greater economic freedom and a say in the country's political affairs, along with a new class of intellectuals, who realized that only through liberalization could Spain hope to march to the beat of the new Europe. Yet the forces of reaction were far stronger. Hence, in 1814, after the Napoleonic army had abandoned the peninsula, the returning Bourbon king, Fernando VII, reimposed absolutist rule and purged liberals from the administration. Over the next 20 years absolutists and liberals vied for power. The line of fracture divided Church, nobility, and monarchy on the one hand, and the urban populace on the other. A great ideological gulf opened between the Traditionalist/Catholic and liberal vision of Spain, the former harking back to the "Reconquest" and the imperial glories of the Catholic Monarchs and Habsburgs, the latter emphasizing Spain's Europeanist vocation and the need to adapt and learn in order to keep abreast in the modern world. The social composition of the groups in conflict would be much modified, but key elements in these two discourses would remain remarkably constant right through to the 1940s. While the Spanish right continued to draw inspiration from the imperial past and pressed for authoritarian rule under the ideological tutelage of the Catholic Church, the left fought for democratic reform and for the defenestration of the Church, which it saw as one of the main obstacles to political and cultural modernization. The bitterness of this confrontation would lead the poet Antonio Machado to talk of "two Spains" pulled irreconcilably apart, and the image of the two antithetical Spains would maintain a powerful hold over the Spanish psyche through to the Spanish Civil War in the 1930s.

After Fernando VII's assumption of power, the liberals, unable to fight back by any other means, turned to the military. The Spanish army had already been a powerful institution in ancien-régime Spain, and, constantly in action during the War of Independence and the colonial campaigns in the Americas, it continued to play a key role in politics during the early 19th century. The liberals could rely on the backing of many army officers, who came from a nonaristocratic background and who had come to prominence during the War of Independence. Between 1814 and 1833, such officers were behind several attempted coups, or, to use the Spanish word, *pronunciamientos*, which aimed to impose liberal institutions. Typically, these *pronunciamientos* were followed by urban revolts, the setting up of popular committees or *juntas*, and the formation of a city-based National Militia. The archetypal coup in this respect was the *pronunciamiento* by General Rafael de Riego in 1820, which ushered in three years of liberal rule. This period would, therefore, see the birth of the figure of the soldier-politician, who, over the next 30 years, in a context of bitter political rivalries, weak and unstable government, and a constant mobilization of military forces, would come to play a key role in Spanish public life.

The so-called Constitutional Triennium was overthrown by a French army at the orders of the Holy Alliance in 1823. To the delight of clergy and nobility Fernando VII once again imposed absolutist rule, while the liberals were subject to harsh reprisals. Yet by the late 1820s the king had come to realize that his attempt to maintain the structures of the old order was doomed to failure. Faced with the American colonial rebellion, the government had accumulated an enormous public debt, and under the structures of the old regime there was no chance of raising sufficient revenues to balance the books. Hence, from the late 1820s, the king began to reach out to more conservative liberals. These liberals were by no means avid revolutionaries. They were men of substantial wealth and social position who wished, if possible, to reach a political and ideological compromise with the absolutists in order to carry out a bloodless, controlled transition to a liberal regime. Conservative liberals tried to maintain a middle course between the left- and right-wing discourses outlined above. They would play the leading role in the construction of a liberal social order that took place between the 1830s and 1850s, and would, subsequently, largely dominate the country's political life up to 1923.

The transition to liberalism appeared, in political terms, enormously complex, but a major element underlying this complexity was a compromise between the monarchy and the majority of the nobility, on the one hand, and more conservative sections of the liberal intellectual elite, nonnoble landowners, urban elites, and the wealthy urban middle classes, on the other. These social groups would come to see the new liberal order as broadly protecting their interests. The nobility, in particular, was assuaged by the support for the transition of the throne, and feared the populist, revolutionary implications of the antiliberal movement, known as Carlism, which burst into life in the 1830s.

At an economic level the compromise was forged by the so-called *desamortización* or disentailment that began in 1836. By abolishing feudal dues and entails, it created a free market in property, and, by putting municipal and Church property onto the market, gave new money the chance to buy a slice of the country's landed wealth, but it also allowed the nobility largely to keep—and on occasion extend—the amount of property under its control. In political terms, it was marked by a highly restrictive franchise—epitomized by the Constitution of 1845—and by the maintenance of a repressive, militarized, state apparatus. Indicative in this respect was the creation of the Civil Guard in 1844.

THE RISE AND FALL OF
OLIGARCHIC LIBERALISM, 1845–1923

During this period, the country was, with the exception of brief radical interludes, run by oligarchic parties such as the Partido Moderado, the Unión Liberal, and, from the Cánovas Restoration of 1875, the Partido Conservador and Partido Liberal. These were not modern mass parties but groupings of notables, who ensured their candidates were elected through the relations they established with local elites (the landowner or his administrator, the merchants and usurer, followed by the parish priest and doctor) known as *caciques*. In rural areas, these *caciques*, either through economic muscle or deference, had an enormous influence over the population, and even after the establishment of universal male suffrage in 1890 could usually ensure their favored candidate was elected. This model of politics became closely identified with the Bourbon monarchs Isabel II, Alfonso XII, and Alfonso XIII, who were seen by elites as guarantors of social order.

The new political ruling class showed itself to be highly conservative. It was powerfully influenced by noble, old-regime values, and sought to reach a compromise with the Catholic Church hierarchy, which it saw as a brake on social disorder and revolutionary doctrines. The Church had at first rejected any understanding with the liberals. Accordingly, when Fernando VII began to reach out to conservative liberalism the Church hierarchy put its weight behind his reactionary brother, Carlos María Isidoro Benito de Borbón y Borbón-Parma. Following Fernando VII's death in 1833 it backed Carlos's armed revolt against the new liberal Spain, which was championed by the former king's wife and now regent, María Cristina of Naples (until the coming of age of their daughter, Isabel). The movement, which in deference to its founder became known as Carlism, enjoyed mass support among the smallholding Catholic peasantry of northern Spain. Between 1833 and 1876, the Carlists were to launch three civil wars against the liberal order. The First Carlist War (1833–1840) in particular was a full-blown civil war. The Church's attitude hardened anticlerical feeling in liberal progressive circles, with the result that measures taken against it were harsher than had previously been contemplated. Thus, though the nobility suffered not one iota from the first *desamortización*, engineered by Juan Álvarez Mendizábal in 1837, a process was begun by which Church land was confiscated and sold on the open market and the male religious orders dissolved.

Yet the attitude of the dominant *moderado* liberal tradition to a large extent made possible a compromise between the Church hierarchy and liberal state from the mid-19th century (though most priests maintained a Traditionalist ideology and sympathized with Carlism). A key moment was the concordat between the Vatican and the Spanish state in 1851, by which, on the one hand, the Spanish state was declared confessional, and, on the other, the Vatican accepted past land sales. With the exception of the revolutionary interlude of 1868–1873 this was largely the basis of Church-state relations until 1931. It was not that the Church now accepted liberalism. Its ultimate goal was still some kind of theocratic autocracy in which it would dominate state and civil society. But the facilities the state provided enabled it to reconquer lost terrain within civil society, particularly through a massive expansion of the religious orders, which, following the establishment of the Cánovas Restoration (1875–1923), were increasingly to educate the sons and daughters of the well-to-do. At the same time, many elements of the Church's conservative message were to the liking of elites and the wealthy conservative middle classes. From the pulpit, priests anathematized democracy, justified inequality as natural and inevitable, and exhorted the poor to accept their sorrows in the knowledge of the happiness that the afterlife would bring.

The post-1833 settlement would lead a new divide quickly to open up between satisfied, conservative liberalism, on the one hand, and more radical, democratic liberal currents, on the other. Socially, the latter movement encompassed the urban lower-middle and working classes, much of the liberal intelligentsia, and the southern peasantry. These groups had a number of pressing grievances. Most obviously, with the exception of revolutionary interludes, until 1890 highly restrictive franchises excluded all but the wealthiest from power, and, even after this date, through the operation of *caciquismo*, elections were falsified. Moreover, Spain's limited economic development made it difficult for the new authorities (who were also reluctant to significantly tax social elites) to generate sympathy through effective social reforms. Nor would it be possible for the state to dissipate internal tensions through successful colonial wars. From the late 19th century, Spain's colonial campaigns produced little glory at the expense of a heavy loss of life.

At first the urban populace rallied behind the Partido Progresista, which wished somewhat to extend the franchise and civil liberties. Then, from the late 1840s, more radical currents emerged: first the Partido Demócrata and then the Partido Republicano Federalista. Finally, from the 1870s, sections of the working class enrolled in anarchist and socialist labor federations and industrial strife escalated. There were also economic reasons behind worker and peasant discontent. High tariff barriers on food imports combined with the slow pace of economic growth resulted in a very low standard of living. And the state, landowning, and manufacturing elites were hostile to trade unionism, undermining worker and peasant labor unions between the 1850s and 1890s. Finally, in rural Spain there was great anger among the peasantry because under the *desamortización*, land, which peasants saw as rightfully theirs, was sold off to the rich. In northern Spain, where the Church was at the center of community life and the structure of landholding more dispersed, this peasant anger bolstered support for Carlism. In the south, where landownership was more concentrated, and where, therefore, the landless and land-hungry peasantry could more clearly identify a bourgeois or noble enemy, the peasantry gravitated toward republicanism, anarchism, and socialism.

The urban and rural malcontents had to resort to violence in order to try and dislodge the conservative liberals from power. Hence they continued the liberal tradition of the military *pronunciamiento*. The most far-reaching of these attempts was the Glorious Revolution of September 1868. It was made possible because increasingly reactionary *moderado* administrations had stimulated the formation of a wide-ranging coalition of liberal and popular forces determined to unseat the monarchy of Isabel II and introduce democratic reform. Between 1868 and 1874, during the so-called Democratic Sexennium (Sexenio Democrático), Spain became a great laboratory for political and constitutional experimentation, with the proclamation of a constitutional monarchy in 1869 and a republic in 1873.

Yet it soon became apparent that more separated the constitutional forces than held them together. While promonarchist moderates, under the leadership of Práxedes Mateo Sagasta, desired only a degree of democratization, the Partido Republicano Federalista, captained by Francesc Pi i Margall, called for a total overhaul of the state and a massive devolution of power to the municipalities, while the anarchist labor federation, the Federación Regional Española, strove for social revolution. The result was growing chaos, especially after revolts by more leftist republicans, known as Intransigents, in July 1873 (the so-called Cantonalist uprisings). This allowed the conservative liberals to strike back, and, following the coup by General Manuel Pavia in January 1874, and then the *pronunciamiento* by General Arsensio Martínez Campos in December 1874, reinstall the Bourbon monarchy.

The architect of this restoration was Antonio Cánovas del Castillo. In order to achieve political stability Cánovas made an attempt to integrate the various promonarchist liberal tendencies into the regime, though the conservative tradition still predominated. He formed the Partido Conservador and convinced Práxedes Mateo Sagasta to group together the liberal monarchist center, which had been traumatized by the revolutionary upheaval of the Democratic Sexennium, into an opposition Partido Liberal. To bring the Liberals onboard, Cánovas deferred to their religious sensibilities and accepted the right of non-Catholics to practice their faith in private. This led to serious tensions with the Catholic Church. In the late 19th century, the Liberals were to introduce reforms extending civil liberties and establishing universal male suffrage. Yet they were fully integrated into *caciquista* networks and their opposition, from 1900, to the growing influence of the Church was timid and ineffectual.

In its favor, until 1898 the regime provided Spain with a period of social peace unknown since the 18th century, and this facilitated the country's slow but seemingly inexorable economic modernization. Yet, it showed little real will to democratize Spanish political life, and so the country's subaltern urban and rural classes remained marginalized from the political process. Indeed, the Cánovas Restoration saw a degree of cooperation between the central government and local *caciques* previously unknown. Moreover, despite integrating the Partido Liberal the regime was steeped in religious imagery. For all these reasons, it was slow to foster a modern integrative nationalist ideology that, rhetorically at least, stressed the equality of all its citizens in the nation's quest for economic power and imperial aggrandizement.

REVOLUTION, REACTION, AND
DICTATORSHIP, 1898–1939

The chickens came home to roost after Spain's defeat in the Spanish-American War in 1898. This shattering blow produced, in educated circles, a generalized belief that Spain had to reform in order to compete within the modern world. Extremely influential was a group of intellectuals known as the regenerationists, the most famous of whom was Joaquín Costa. Their remedies for reform varied, but they were all agreed that Spain's corrupt and inefficient political structures had to be overhauled. Political discontent also permeated literary and artistic circles, as could be seen with respect to the Catalan *modernistes* and Madrid-based "Generation of 1898." In was in this atmosphere that the "disaster" triggered a political mobilization on a scale unknown since 1868–1873. There were two major beneficiaries.

On the one hand, nationalist ideologues in Catalonia and the Basque Country took advantage. The Catalan and Basque nationalist movements were in character and intensity very different, but their emergence confirmed the partial failure of the attempt to create a unified Spanish nation-state. There were several important factors in the rise of the "peripheral nationalisms." First, from the early 18th century, administrations had tried to centralize the country, largely on the French Bourbon model. However, the previous Habsburg monarchy had been based on a federal structure. Until the reign of Felipe V, the Crown of Aragón (composed of Catalonia, Valencia, and Aragón) had enjoyed a high degree of independence, with its own parliaments, which could both legislate and block attempts to raise taxes by the king. Moreover, in Catalonia and Valencia, Catalan and its regional variant Valencian, rather than Castilian-Spanish, were the official languages. Indeed, the Habsburg monarchs did not enjoy the title of kings of Spain at all, but, in theory at least, ruled over each of the separate crowns and kingdoms that made up the Habsburg Empire separately. Furthermore, within the Crown of Castile, the Basque territories and Navarre had their own special privileges. These rights and privileges were known as *fueros*. Felipe V swept away the Crown of Aragón's separate administrative structures, but the Basque and Navarre *fueros* were not abolished until 1876. And, as the Romantic cultural movements of the mid-19th century were to show, regional sentiments remained intense.

Second, a peculiarity of Spanish political development during the 19th century was that the center of power was located in the economically backward city of Madrid, and that (again, with the exception of revolutionary interludes) political elites from Barcelona, the country's most dynamic industrial center, tended to be excluded from the levers of power. This was a consequence of the dominance of the Crown of Castile within the Spanish state since the unification of 1479, and was reflected in the fact that Spanish national identity in the 19th century was based on the Castilian-Spanish language and prioritized Castilian-Andalusian national-cultural stereotypes. Finally, the state's poverty and lack of democratic credentials, and the country's relative backwardness, hampered the nationalization of the populace. A particularly important example of this was the grossly underfunded state education system.

It was this weakness of Spanish nation-building, together with the country's anti-centralist heritage, that encouraged social groups who felt marginalized from power to express their discontent in anti-Spanish nationalist terms. This was particularly the case in Catalonia, the Basque Country, and Galicia, where distinct languages continued to be spoken. It was in these first two territories that strong nationalist movements grew up.

In Catalonia, a key element in the growth of nationalism (or Catalanism) was a sense of injustice among elites and the middle classes. From the 1880s in particular, there was a growing feeling that while their territory was economically and culturally the most advanced in Spain, power was concentrated in Madrid, and Madrid-based politicians were leading them on the road to ruin. The crisis of 1898 served enormously to amplify this sentiment, which would be channeled through a new party, the Lliga Regionalista. Basque nationalism was in its origins more archaic. It emerged in the 1890s as a reaction of the lower-middle-class urban populace against the influx of "foreign" (i.e., Spanish) migrants, which had been stimulated by rapid industrialization, and it combined racist xenophobia with exultant Catholicism. But from the turn of the century the major nationalist party, the Partido Nacionalista Vasco (PNV), would incorporate more pro-industrializing middle-class and manufacturing interests, whose outlook was closer to that of the Catalan Lliga.

In addition, the post-1898 mobilization led to a growth in the strength of the Spanish left. In the cities of Barcelona, Valencia, and Madrid, republicans would mount a powerful challenge to the representatives of the "official" Conservative and Liberal parties at election time. At the turn of the century increasing numbers of workers also joined socialist and anarchist organizations. This tendency accelerated rapidly after the onset of World War I in 1914, when the anarchist-syndicalist Confederación Nacional del Trabajo (CNT), and the Marxist Partido Socialista Obrero Español (PSOE) and Unión General de Trabajadores (UGT), grew rapidly in size. The anarchists-syndicalists, in particular, showed themselves to be highly radicalized, adopting the French syndicalist strategy of attempting to overthrow capitalism through a revolutionary general strike.

The growth in opposition precipitated the breakup of the Cánovas Restoration from 1914. During the Crisis of 1917, the Lliga Regionalista, with the support of most of the left, led an attempt to overthrow the regime and put in its place a more democratic monarchy. It ended in failure after intervention by the army, but demonstrated the regime's isolation. This was followed, between 1919 and 1922, by a massive upsurge of strikes and social unrest in both urban Spain and in the rural south. Labor protest produced a powerful counterreaction. Much of the more conservative and wealthy urban middle classes, manufacturing interests, and substantial landowners increasingly feared social revolution (especially given events in Russia in October 1917), and felt that the Restoration regime was no longer sufficiently protecting their interests. A key feature of these years was therefore a growing divide between the regime and much of its social base. In this atmosphere, some conservative political and economic elites, inspired, from 1922, by the rise to power of Benito Mussolini in Italy, began to consider replacing the Restoration regime by a more authoritarian monarchy. This was most notably the case of the Catalan-led Spanish Employers' confederation and within much of the so-called Maurista movement. It was an attitude with which much of the Catholic Church would sympathize.

Among the military such attitudes also resonated. Under the Cánovas Restoration an attempt had been made to exclude the army from political power in return for giving it almost complete institutional autonomy. During these years, it had become more conservative as officer recruitment from the lower classes dried up. It also became increasingly cut off from civil society, with the officers isolated in their own living and sleeping quarters. This produced a specific corporate mentality within the officer corps. In the future, they would act less at the behest of particular political groupings and more to defend their own interests and ideology. By the early 20th century, the major coordinates of their rather simplistic ideological universe were order, hierarchy, and discipline.

Moreover, given the predominance of Castilian and Andalusian officers and the emphasis on the imperial struggle for Spanish aggrandizement, there was a powerful aversion to "anti-Spanish" nationalisms. Consequently, the growth of leftist and peripheral nationalist movements from 1900 was viewed with preoccupation. Finally, following the defeat of 1898, there was growing anger at what was seen as the inability of weak and vacillating liberal politicians to effectively back the army. This was greatly intensified in July 1921, when 9,000 Spanish troops were massacred by Moroccan tribesmen at Annual. In its aftermath, colonial officers based in Morocco (the so-called *africanistas*) were furious that while the military was put on trial little was being done to look into responsibilities in political circles, and that, under pressure from public opinion, governments were reluctant to put into practice the aggressive "forward policy" they favored in Morocco. It was an attitude with which King Alfonso XIII sympathized. In the run-up to his coup of September 1923, the captain general of Barcelona, General Miguel Primo de Rivera, was to act as a hinge, gaining the support of both the Catalan right and *africanista* officers.

Given this ideological baggage, it is not surprising that the coup enjoyed widespread sympathy in Spanish conservative circles and also had the tacit support of the king. Although Primo de Rivera at first claimed he was going to hand back power to the people, he quickly set about establishing a corporatist dictatorship. The regime would only last until 1930, undermined by economic crisis and squabbling within the ranks of the army. Yet it was the first clear sign that, faced with large-scale social unrest, conservative Spain would resort to an antiliberal, right-wing dictatorship. In the meantime, in 1930 the aftermath of the dictatorship's demise provided the first opportunity since 1868–1873 for the left to fashion a regime in its image. The moment was propitious because the military was divided and political elites were disoriented and unsure how to proceed. This made possible the establishment of a new republic under a democratic constitution.

The Second Republic was to last from 1931 through to 1936. During this time, Socialists, republicans, and Catalan nationalists would attempt to forge a new decentralized state and a more egalitarian social order. Key elements of the reform process were an autonomy statute for Catalonia (which was extended to the Basque Country during the civil war), an agrarian reform law to redistribute *latifundista* estates to the peasantry, a military reform (the goal of which was to depoliticize the army), Church reform aimed at separating Church and state and drastically reducing the Church's role in Spanish life, and equal legal status for women. This final policy meant women were given voting rights for the first time and laws allowing civil marriage and divorce were promulgated.

As a result of these measures the country became increasingly polarized. Faced with the reforms initiated by the 1931–1933 republican-Socialist coalition government, the right quickly mobilized its supporters, presenting them as an attempt to bolshevize and dismember Spain. A new right-wing coalition, the Confederación Española de Derechas Autónomas, was founded in 1933 to fight the reform process in parliament, while other more extreme right-wing groupings, most notably the Carlists, the Fascist Falange Española, and Renovación Española, began to conspire to bring about the Republic's downfall. The Church, political and social elites, and sectors of the Spanish army were all behind this campaign, but it would also find strong popular backing within the rural and small-town populaces in the Catholic heartlands of Castile and Navarre. From the left, the conflict was presented as a life-and-death struggle between the forces of "progress" and democracy, and those of obscurantism and Fascism. Given the degree of social and political tension it would have taken enormous political acumen to avoid armed conflict. This was particularly the case given the international context of the Great Depression and the rise of Fascism. Conciliation proved impossible, with the attempted military coup of 17–18 July 1936 precipitating civil war.

The Spanish Civil War raged across the country for nearly three years. It was a total war in which the annihilation of the opponent was sought. It was to a significant degree a class war, in which the urban working class, land-hungry peasantry, and the liberal urban petty bourgeoisie lined up against social elites, the prosperous middle classes, and conservative small-town and rural Spain. There were also elements of a national struggle, with more wide-ranging middle-class support for the Republic in both Catalonia and the Basque Country. Finally, it pitted two antithetical cultural and ideological visions of Spain against one another, with the right claiming Spain should look to its imperial Catholic past for salvation, and the left, on the contrary, stressing its need to secularize Spanish society in order to build a freer society. As a result, the left gained the support of most Spanish intellectuals, including figures of international standing like Pablo Picasso and Federico García Lorca.

On the international plain, the war can be seen as marking a landmark in a broader early 20th-century Europe-wide social and ideological battle. From the beginning, Fascist Italy and Nazi Germany were quick to aid the rebels (or Nationalists as they were often referred to). The British Conservative administration, wishing to maintain its policy of appeasement and fearful of the consequences of social revolution in the Republican zone, did nothing to help the Republicans (and indeed covertly favored the Nationalists), while the Soviet Union finally decided to aid the Republic, thereby greatly strengthening the Spanish Communist Party, the Partido Comunista de España (PCE). At first the Republicans controlled most of industrial Spain, but the better organization of the Nationalist forces—which from September 1936 were under the command of General Francisco Franco—and greater German and Italian aid, quickly turned the war in the Nationalists' favor. Victory was finally achieved in March 1939 when the Nationalists marched into Madrid virtually unopposed.

THE FRANCO REGIME AND THE
TRANSITION TO DEMOCRACY, 1939–1982

The new regime was, like the Primo de Rivera dictatorship, organized on corporatist lines, though it was both more repressive and determined to wipe out all signs of cultural and political pluralism. The rebel's leader, General Francisco Franco, was proclaimed head of state and *generalísimo*, and a single party, the Falange Española Tradicionalista y de las Juntas de Ofensiva National Sindicalista (FET y de las JONS), an amalgam of the Falange Española and Carlists, was created to run the administration. At the same time, the confessional nature of the Spanish state was asserted, and the Church given total control over education. This signified an attempt to carry through a cultural counterrevolution, with the imposition of traditional Catholic patriarchal and family values. The 1940s, known as the "hunger years," were a bleak period of mass executions, economic stagnation, and food shortages. After the defeat of the Axis, the West treated the regime as an authoritarian relic of the interwar period and cut it off from the new international political order. But in any case, from 1939 it had adopted an inward-looking, autarkic policy, which hampered economic development and, post-1945, further isolated Spain from the outside world.

The regime portrayed itself as taking up the mantle of El Cid, the medieval Castilian nobleman who had supposedly led the offensive against the Moors, and of the Catholic Monarchs, and claimed that it was destined to revive Spanish greatness after a century and a half of decadent liberalism. Yet by the 1950s economic failure and continued international ostracism finally forced the regime to change its stance and begin to open up to the West. The opportunity came because of the Cold War, with the United States prepared to accept the staunchly anticommunist Franco into the Western fold in exchange for military bases on the peninsula and economic reform. The major stages of this process were the military pacts with the United States in 1951, a new concordat with the Vatican in 1953, and admission into the United Nations in 1955.

Spain's economic liberalization, combined with loans from the international banking system, allowed its to take advantage of the Western economic boom, which was gathering pace by the late 1950s. Foreign businesses began to invest in Spain because of low labor costs, tourists flocked to the country, and Spanish emigrants poured into France and Germany in search of job opportunities, thereby providing the country with much-needed foreign currency in the form of remittances. The result was that Spain experienced an unprecedented economic transformation in the 1960s. This transformation would have profound social and political implications. First, there was a rapid transfer of population from agriculture to industry, combined with a technological revolution in the agricultural sector of the economy. As a result, old social relations, marked by the divide between *latifundistas* and their *braceros*, would be recast. Meanwhile, in northern and central Spain, the conservative Catholic heartlands also emptied of population. The combined effect of these changes would be to smooth over the social and ideological cleavages that had rent Spain apart earlier in the 20th century.

This process was also aided by a quite generalized improvement in living standards. A new working class was born, which through the clandestine labor movement, Comisiones Obreras, vociferously defended its interests. But workers themselves, though suffering relative deprivation, were slowly integrated into the new consumerist culture from the 1960s, and, unlike their republican and anarchist predecessors, they were little disposed to mount the barricades in the name of revolution. The regime itself had to transform. Repression eased and became more selective, while the Catholic and imperialist rhetoric of the postwar years was replaced by an emphasis on efficient technocratic management of the economy. Divisions also began to open up within the regime itself. Most notably, sectors of the Catholic Church, profoundly affected by the Second Vatican Council of the early 1960s, began to call for political liberalization. By the early 1970s, the Vatican had ensured that these reformers formed a majority of the hierarchy.

All of these factors made easier a successful transition to democracy after the death of General Franco on 20 November 1975. By the early 1970s, the regime's social base was shrinking. Social elites were concerned that the continuance of the dictatorship would not permit a full integration into Western economic structures, in particular the European Economic Community (EEC), and that some paternalist aspects of the regime (especially, high levels of job security, instituted in order to recompense workers for the loss of trade-union and political freedoms) conflicted with the needs of enterprise in an ever-more competitive capitalist world market. Moreover, post-1945 Western experience had shown that elite and conservative middle-class fears that democracy was the anteroom to communism were groundless. The defection of the Church robbed the regime of ideological cover and made it difficult for the hardliners (the Bunker, as they were called by 1975) once again to take up the cudgel in order supposedly to save Christian civilization. And, finally, the growing secularization of Spanish society meant that the regime's backward-looking Catholic rhetoric was increasingly out of touch with broad sectors of society. This could be seen in the critical acclaim with which the work of writers and filmmakers who anathematized the stultified cultural climate of Franco's Spain, such as Juan Goytisolo and Luis Buñuel, was received. And following Franco's death, avant-garde youth culture was quick to make its mark, most notably in the case of the *movida madrileña*. It was in this atmosphere that a militant feminist movement raised its head for the first time. It was only to encompass a small minority of women, but the 1978 Constitution swept away the most glaring aspects of female inequality enshrined in Francoist law, and the extension of women's rights would subsequently be taken up by the Spanish left.

The transition was also made easier because by the mid-1970s, Socialists (PSOE) and Communists (PCE) were willing to drop calls for a new republic and provisional government of opposition forces. This reflected a realistic assessment of the balance of political power and of public opinion. The majority of the Spanish population—the Spanish Civil War still very much in the back of people's minds—had no stomach for a bloody confrontation. And with the death of Franco it became clear that his successor, King Juan Carlos I, would put his weight behind a constitutional monarchy. This combined set of factors made possible, between 1976 and 1978, the negotiation of a controlled transition to democracy by regime reformers and the democratic opposition. The key figures were the king, the former regime bureaucrat Adolfo Suárez, and the leaders of the PSOE and PCE, Felipe González and Santiago Carrillo. Essentially, the opposition had to pardon the Francoist apparatus and accept that the transition would be undertaken from above by Adolfo Suárez, who held the post of prime minister from July 1976.

The new arrangements were not to the liking of everyone. The Bunker did everything it could to block the reforms. Civilian *ultras* and far-rightists within the armed forces began conspiring from 1977, and launched an attempted coup—the so-called Tejerazo—in February 1981. In the Basque Country, where the situation had become enormously radicalized in the last years of the Franco regime, a Basque nationalist-terrorist group called ETA, which had emerged in the 1960s, demanded total Basque independence, and, between 1977 and 1979, stepped up its campaign of assassinations of civil guards and prominent military figures. Its overt aim was to provoke the military into attempting a coup, which the *etarras* believed would lead to further radicalization in the Basque Country and an unstoppable movement in favor of independence.

If these challenges did not derail the democratic process, it was because of a quite generalized conviction that democracy should be brought about without the civil strife suffered by previous generations. Suárez and the king moved quickly in order to wrong-foot the Bunker and satisfy opposition demands. Between July 1976 and June 1977, the Francoist Cortes were wound up, leftist parties and unions were legalized, and, finally, the first democratic elections in over 40 years were called. Suárez quickly put together a coalition of regime reformers, the Unión del Centro Democrático (UCD), in order to fight the elections under his leadership, and was able to achieve a majority in parliament. The PSOE came in a comfortable second, with the Communists and the right-wing Alianza Popular (AP) (captained by the former Francoist minister of information and tourism, Manuel Fraga) trailing in a rather distant third and fourth.

The new government, with the collaboration of the democratic opposition, set about elaborating a new constitution. Perhaps the most innovative element was the decision to try to incorporate demands for autonomy, which, as a result of Franco's centralizing and ineffecient rule, had extended beyond Catalonia, the Basque Country, and Galacia to other areas by decentralizing power throughout Spain. A new administrative map, the State of the Autonomies, was drawn up, with 16 "autonomous communities." Furthermore, for the first time the government seriously turned its attention to the economic crisis that had engulfed Spain following the oil price hike of 1973. Again the emphasis was on cooperation. In the October 1977 Moncloa Pacts, government and opposition worked out a package of measures aimed at bringing down inflation through wage control, while introducing income tax and extending social benefits.

These optimistic beginnings turned rather sour between 1979 and 1982. The UCD government was faced with rising unemployment, ETA terrorism, and continuous rumors of planned military intervention. Most seriously, the governing coalition itself began to fall apart in a welter of mutual recrimination. The nadir was reached with the attempted military coup of 1981. Only after its failure, following the decisive intervention of the king in favor of Spain's new democratic institutions, was the corner turned.

THE SPAIN OF FELIPE GONZÁLEZ: BUILDING A WESTERN EUROPEAN DEMOCRACY, 1982–1996

In the October 1982 elections a united, confident Socialist Party, under the charismatic leadership of Felipe González, swept to power. The

PSOE had come a long way since the mid-1970s, when it called for wide-ranging nationalizations and espoused an anti-imperialist, third-worldist ideology. By 1982, in contrast, it presented itself as a center-left party, dedicated to economic modernization and social reform. With respect to foreign policy, its successful negotiation of EEC membership in 1986 helped to maintain its popularity in the polls. More controversially, under pressure from the United States and Western governments, it went back on a commitment to take Spain out of the North Atlantic Treaty Organization (NATO), backing continued membership in the 1986 referendum.

In the economic sphere it followed a cautious monetary and fiscal policy that aimed to keep down inflation and restore the profitability of Spanish industry, while incentives were given to transfer capital and labor out of obsolete heavy industry (the Reconversion Plan). This was combined with efforts to make Spanish industry more competitive by reducing job security and making it easier to hire workers on temporary contracts. With economic revenue buoyed up by the post-1985 European economic boom, it slowly built a welfare state, but did not wish to alienate the middle classes by massive tax hikes. At the same time, it put large sums of money into the modernization of the country's transport infrastructure, in particular through a large road-building program. This was given a massive boost by European Union (EU) structural and cohesion funds, especially from the early 1990s. A particularly important year was 1992, which saw the holding of the Olympic Games in Barcelona and an international exhibition in Seville. These events were accompanied by the opening of Spain's first high-speed rail link from Madrid to Seville. Economic modernization generated a sense of pride among the population. Spain was catching up with the rest of Western Europe and showing it could be dynamic and innovative. Barcelona, in particular, took advantage of the Games, which it used as a platform for an innovative program of urban renewal, to become a major tourist destination.

The Socialists dominated the political scene throughout the 1980s. However, from 1988 the party became racked by internal problems. There was increasing union discontent at economic policies that were perceived as favoring capital over labor. In 1987, this led to a break between the Socialist government and its traditional ally, the UGT. This, combined with a slow decline in electoral support, produced increasingly bitter divisions between the more leftist supporters of the party's number-two politician, Alfonso Guerra, and centrists loyal to Felipe González. Moreover, from 1989 the government had to contend with a new economic downturn and was rocked by a series of corruption scandals. This revealed a darker side of Spanish political life. Despite the democratic transition, it had failed to stamp out the culture of political favors and backhanders.

At the same time, continued electoral defeat stimulated the main opposition party AP (renamed Partido Popular [PP] in 1989), under the youthful leadership of José María Aznar, to cast off its Francoist vestiges and present itself as a modern, democratic, neoliberal party. Not everyone was convinced. It still retained close links with the Catholic Church and Aznar's style was highly abrasive. Nevertheless, when combined with the growing crisis of the government, its efforts were enough to make it electable. The government lost its overall majority in the June 1993 elections and had to govern with the support of the center-right Catalanist coalition Convergència i Unió (CiU) to survive. In 1996, it was then defeated at the polls by the PP.

GLOBALIZATION, ECONOMIC, AND CULTURAL MODERNIZATION: 1996 TO THE PRESENT

The PP government instituted a number of major policy changes. With respect to economic policy, it speeded up the program of privatizations initiated by the PSOE. This led to the emergence of several major new Spanish companies, most notably the phone company, Telefónica, and the petrochemical giant Repsol. These years also saw the emergence of two powerful banking groups, Banco de Bilbao Vizcaya Argentaria (BBVA) and Banco de Santander Central Hispano (BSCH). The rise of these businesses was closely related to the rapid growth of the Spanish economy, which made it possible for well-placed companies to invest abroad (especially in Latin America) and acquire an international profile. In the area of foreign policy, the government was more Atlanticist than its predecessor and was willing to more aggressively pursue perceived Spanish interests. In home affairs, though Aznar respected the State of the Autonomies he wished to reassert Spanish national identity and was opposed to any further decentralization. In his first government, between

1996 and 2000, he did not have an overall majority in parliament and had to rely on CiU and PNV support. This very much moderated his stance.

However, at the March 2000 elections the PP gained an overall majority and this made it possible for him to more forcefully pursue his program. The legislature was dominated by two major issues: foreign policy and the "national question." Aznar backed the U.S.-led invasion of Iraq, despite the unpopularity of the war in Spanish public opinion. At the same time, the government's Spanish nationalist rhetoric became more strident. This was exacerbated by calls by the PNV, from 1998, for an autonomy statute that recognized the Basque Country's right to self-determination (which it linked to a process of negotiation with ETA), and demands from within Catalonia for a new, more generous, autonomy statute. Faced with what it saw as the danger of centrifugal forces undermining Spanish unity, in several areas the government tried to reassert central control, while also making clear that it would not reform the State of the Autonomies. This produced fierce polemic between the government and its supporters, and the "peripheral nationalists." The government launched a ferocious assault on the PNV, accusing it of helping to perpetuate terrorism through the soft line it took with ETA. The PP's tone was taken up in the Spanish right-wing press, producing significant ethnic and cultural tensions. The government also groomed two of its leading figures, Jaime Mayor Oreja and Josep Piqué, to capture (or at least take a share of) power in the Basque and Catalan governments themselves. Yet a Basque nationalist coalition won the crucial May 2001 elections in the Basque Country, and in Catalonia the PP remained the third party.

This was the background to the elections of March 2004. Since 2000, under the leadership of José Luis Rodríguez Zapatero, the PSOE had once again become an electable force. Rodríguez Zapateros's measured style was attractive. He was also able to present a clear alternative. On the home front, he was culturally liberal and favorable to the federalization of Spain and dialogue with the "peripheral nationalisms." With respect to foreign policy, he supported withdrawal from Iraq and the reestablishment of Spain's tacit alliance with the "European Axis" of France and Germany. From 2002, the PSOE began to make ground on the PP, but given the buoyant economic climate and Rodríguez Zapatero's lack of experience it still seemed that the PP (under Aznar's anointed successor, Mariano Rajoy) would win the elections. Then, on the morning of 11 March 2004, three days before the general elections, 13 terrorists planted satchel bombs on four trains traveling from Alcalá de Henares to Madrid, killing 191 people. The government claimed that ETA was to blame, but evidence quickly emerged that Islamic extremists were behind the attack. This was bad news for the PP because it shone a light on its unpopular support for the Iraq War. The opposition would immediately argue that by irresponsibly following George W. Bush the PP had placed the Spanish population in harm's way. It seems that this was why the government continued to insist that ETA was behind the bombings until the day of the elections (though this is strenuously denied by the PP). This led to a big popular mobilization against the PP between 12–13 March under the slogan "Who was it?" Dramatically, on 14 March, the PP lost the elections. The bombings clearly had a large impact, bringing the Iraq War to the forefront of people's minds.

The PSOE therefore came to power in a highly changed atmosphere, with the PP bitter that it had been "robbed" of victory. The new government's legislative program included a reform of the State of the Autonomies, extension of the welfare state, and culturally liberal reforms, such as gay civil marriage and rapid divorce, and a new state education law potentially reducing the weight of religious teaching. After ETA declared a cease-fire in March 2006, it also tried to bring an end to terrorism through dialogue. However, these measures produced a right-wing offensive. The PP accused the government of threatening the unity of Spain and giving in to ETA terrorism. It was supported by other sectors of the right, which then launched vociferous demonstrations against government policy. Dialogue with ETA was contested by mobilizations led by a terrorist victims' association, the Asociación de Víctimas del Terrorismo, and the Church held demonstrations against gay marriage and "in defense of the Christian family." (*El País*, 31 December 2007) This reflected the conservative turn within the Church since the election of Cardinal Wojtila as Pope John Paul II in 1978. The offensive was also backed by sectors of the media, notably the daily newspaper *El Mundo*, the radio station COPE (owned by the Church's Episcopal Conference), and the Internet newspaper *Libertad Digital*, which propagated wild theories of a PSOE-ETA conspiracy to unseat the PP with the complicity of sectors of the security apparatus, and apocalyptic warnings of the death of Spain. In part, the intensity of this confrontation was related to the way in which the PP lost the 2004 general election. However, the dominant right wing of the PP should be viewed as forming part of a wider "neoconservative" reaction in the West. Elements such as the aggressive denunciation of opposition, pronounced patriotic fervor, and a crusading culturally conservative spirit are common themes within the movement.

Yet the problem for the PP was that while such mobilizations might enthuse its core supporters, they could alienate more moderate voters. Moreover, its attack on the Catalan statute was likely to provoke an unfavorable reaction within the Catalan electorate. During 2007, the PP's leader, Mariano Rajoy, tried to steer a somewhat more moderate course, tacitly distancing himself from hardliners in the Church and in the PP's media entourage. It came into the campaign for the March 2008 elections trailing the Socialists by about 3 percent in the opinion polls. It was buoyed by the rapidly deteriorating economic climate and attacked the Socialists for supposedly allowing an "avalanche" of immigrants to enter the country. However, it only made up a little ground. The PSOE again failed to gain an overall majority but should be able to govern relatively comfortably over the next four years. Early indications are that Rajoy believes that the PP must recapture a more centrist image, but this is likely to lead to tensions both within the party and, possibly, with the Catholic Church and also alienate powerful right-wing media figures like Pedro J. Ramírez and Federico Jiménez Losantos.

PROSPECTS AND PROGNOSIS

As noted in the introductory comments, the areas of greatest success since the transition to democracy have been rapid economic modernization and a cultural renaissance. As a result, for the first time since the 19th century Spaniards can look toward the West without any sense of inferiority. It has also meant that Spain's profile in the Western media has become much higher, especially since the 1990s. This can be seen in a whole range of areas, from concerns at Spanish business takeovers, to profiles of Spanish cities, and information on Spanish food and drink. Spain also has an increased weight on the world political stage and, for the first time, from the 1990s its armed forces have begun to play a significant role in NATO and UN military and humanitarian missions.

Nevertheless, there are still concerns on the economic front. First, very significant economic imbalances remain, with the south still much poorer than the north. Second, the hectic pace of change has taken its toll on the environment. The overdevelopment of the coastline and destruction of Mediterranean marine environments have recently spread to the Atlantic coast, most notably Galicia. Third, Spain's economic model has to a significant degree been based on undercutting costs in other Western European countries, and this has involved a proliferation of temporary contracts. At the same time, governments have been slow to invest heavily in research and development, and the state university system is significantly underfunded. This means the country is not that well prepared to train highly qualified individuals who can compete at the level of quality rather than cost. Fourth, though Spain now has a number of major companies, and multinationals have invested heavily, there are still large numbers of small undercapitalized firms, which can only compete in local markets. Finally, the rapid growth in immigration into the country since 1995 has led to serious social tension and to the rise of immigrant ghettos in cities like Barcelona and Madrid. Nevertheless, recent governments have been very aware of the challenges faced and have begun investing considerably more in research and development. The 2004–2008 PSOE government also showed a willingness to take environmental issues more seriously than its predecessors and take more effective action to prevent unauthorized and illegal building work.

Other problems that face the country can at least in part be seen as hangovers from the past. During the transition to democracy, there was no revolutionary transformation, with the result that the civil and military bureaucracies remained largely unchanged, and in many areas of public and private administration and in the field of business, norms of conduct varied little. One of the major drawbacks in this respect, inherited from both the Moderate liberal tradition and Francoism, would be the continued prevalence of nepotistic practices (the figure of the *enchufe*—literally, the friend one needs to be plugged into the system—remains of key importance) and corruption within the state machine. Left-wing parties have not been above being drawn into this web, as was shown by the corruption scandals which rocked the ruling PSOE administration between 1990 and 1996. The big construction boom from the 1990s has exacerbated the problem of corruption at both local and regional levels, with politicians receiving kickbacks from the big construction firms. Added to this, the massive distance that has, historically, separated the state and civil society has meant that the citizenry has been slow to accept the responsibility demanded by democratic institutions, with the result that tax evasion and fraud and the use of black market labor have remained rife. Finally, the state machine (though improvements began in the 1960s and have continued) and police forces remain inefficient. Nevertheless, accountable democratic institutions have given Spain the opportunity to tackle these problems. That corruption has come into the open, ministers have had to resign, and the practice is censored in public debate are indicators of changing attitudes. Since the fall of the PSOE in 1996 governments have to a significant degree cleaned up their act, and since 2006 there has been an offensive against corrupt local councils.

Old problems which it seemed that the transition to democracy had "solved" have also reappeared. The State of the Autonomies represented a compromise between Spain's centralist tradition and the demands of the anti-Spanish nationalists and regionalists. Until the mid-1990s, it appeared to offer a stable solution to the "national question." However, competing national identities did not go away and the potential for conflict always remained. Matters came to a head after the PP victory in 1996, when, in the slipstream of Spain's economic modernization and growing international presence, it sought to reassert a more self-confident, aggressive, Spanish national identity. At the same time (and in the Basque case partly as a reaction), the "peripheral nationalisms" began demanding greater autonomy. This has occurred in a context in which the issue of the rights of "small nations" has once again raised its head on the international stage, with Western support for the dismemberment of the former Yugoslavia having particular resonance in Spain. The two extremes were represented by the PP's push to defeat the nationalists in their backyard and in the PNV's desire for a Greater Basque Country to have associate status with Spain. The 2004–2008 PSOE government seemed to have found a compromise acceptable to most people. However, the right was opposed and reported the Catalan autonomy statute to the Constitutional Tribunal to try and get it annulled. The PP's defeat in the March 2008 general election may force it to take a more accommodatory stance.

Over the past decade cultural divisions have also raised their heads. In this sphere, the transition again represented a compromise. While political and cultural pluralism was embraced, the Catholic Church retained a privileged position within the state (most notably through state subsidies for the salaries of the clergy and grants for private Church schools). The hope was that the Church would administer its flock while showing understanding for legislation catering to the demands of "soft" and non-Catholics. This has proved not to be the case. Legislation enshrining women's rights and measures contradicting Catholic doctrine—most notably divorce, civil and gay marriage, multifaith education, and abortion (though it should be noted, Spain has one of the most restrictive abortion laws in the West)—have produced a powerful Catholic counterreaction. Once again on the table is the question of whether the Church has the right to exercise a degree of moral tutorship over society. This is not, however, an issue that only affects Spain. "Culture wars" have broken out throughout the West, and while the Spanish right feels it has a common purpose with George W. Bush's neoconservative agenda, the left shows great affinity for the U.S. Democratic party.

Nevertheless, it is probably unwise to overdramatize these conflicts. Spain has the seventh largest economy in the world and much of its population is relatively wealthy and self-satisfied. And unlike the situation in the past, with the exception of ETA and its base, verbal radicalism is not generally accompanied by physical violence. Spain also shares many of the problems described above with other Western countries. And often (particularly in the area of Christian morality), the shrill tone of debate is not matched by intense concern among the majority of the population. Nevertheless, its political leaders do have to be careful to debate rationally and reach compromises. Otherwise, the "national question" in particular does have the potential to spiral out of control.

The Dictionary

– A –

ABC. *ABC* is a Madrid-based daily founded by the journalist and businessman Torcuato Luca de Tena (1861–1929) in 1903. At the outset it was politically independent but adopted a conservative-monarchist stance. By 1919, with a readership of 170,000, it had the highest circulation in Spain. As the **Cánovas Restoration** entered into crisis, from 1914, like much of the right, it became critical of the regime, seeing it as too weak in its dealings with the working-class left. It sympathized with the **Maurista** movement from 1913 and was favorably disposed to the coup by General **Miguel Primo de Rivera** in 1923. During the **Second Republic**, it was close to the **Alfonsoist monarchists**, welcoming the **Nationalist** uprising of 17–18 July 1936 with open arms.

Under the **Franco regime**, given its powerful monarchist backers, it was allowed to take a somewhat independent line. After the **transition to democracy**, it was close to **Alianza Popular/Partido Popular**, and, between 1993 and 1996, played a key role in the right-wing offensive against the scandal-ridden government of the **Partido Socialista Obrero Español** (PSOE). However, since the PSOE's return to power in 2004 it has taken a somewhat less partisan line. It forms part of the Prensa Española Group, which is largely owned by several Spanish **banks**. With a circulation of 230,000 in 2007, it was Spain's third most widely read (non free) daily, behind *El País* and *El Mundo*. Most of its readers are concentrated in central and southern Spain.

ABERTZALE. The name *abertzale* is used to refer to radical Basque nationalists who seek independence for the **Basque Country**. *See* *also* ARANA I GOIRI, SABINO DE; ETA; HERRI BATASUNA; PARTIDO NACIONALISTA VASCO.

ABRIL, VICTORIA (1959–). Victoria Abril (real name Victoria Mérida Rojas) is probably Spain's most versatile actress of recent decades. She first made a name for herself in **Vicente Aranda**'s 1976 film, *Cambio de sexo* (*Change of Sex*), in which she played a young man who had undergone a change of sex operation. Since then she has continued to work with Aranda in a variety of roles, including *Amantes* (*Lovers*, 1990), a critical hit in Europe and the United States. Her appearance in two successful **Pedro Almodóvar** films, ¡*Átame!* (*Tie Me Up, Tie Me Down!*, 1989) and *Tacones Lejanos* (*High Heels*, 1992) cemented her international reputation and facilitated a Hollywood debut in *Jimmy Hollywood* (1993). During the 1990s, she continued to work with Almodóvar and Aranda, winning the best actress award at the San Sebastián film festival for her role in Aranda's *Libertarias* (*Libertarians*, 1996).

ABSOLUTISM. *See* CARLISM; CATHOLIC CHURCH; FELIPE V; FERNANDO VII; FERNANDO RESTORATIONS; FRENCH REVOLUTION; MONARCHY.

ACCIÓ CATALANA/CATALAN ACTION. This was a political party formed in June 1922 by the **Lliga Regionalista** youth and liberal **Catalanists**. It was constituted as a reaction against what was seen as a betrayal by the Lliga of its Catalanist principles, as evidenced by its decision to participate in a number of coalition governments between 1918 and 1922. Acció Catalana was immediately able to gain considerable middle-class support and hence defeat the Lliga in the **Barcelona** provincial elections of June 1923. During the **Primo de Rivera dictatorship**, it was hit by divisions between a more radical, republican wing, led by Antoni Rovira i Virgili (1882–1949), and a more conservative, "accidentalist" wing. Both groups were to reunite under the title Acció Catalana Republicana once the **Second Republic** had been proclaimed. However, the party was never able to fulfill its early promise, failing to mobilize outside its base in the liberal middle class. As a result, it could not compete with the new left-wing Catalanist party **Esquerra Republicana de**

Catalunya (ERC). Nevertheless, it was to participate in the elaboration of the Catalan autonomy statute and formed part of the ERC-dominated autonomous governments.

ACCIÓN CATÓLICA (AC)/CATHOLIC ACTION. AC was a lay association launched in 1888 to propagate Catholic values within civil society. Until the 1950s, it was in tune with the dominant conservative tradition in the **Catholic Church** and was close to the Church hierarchy. Hence, when a central junta was formed in 1894, the reactionary **Second Marquis of Comillas** (a Catalan shipping magnate) became its first president, a position he was to hold until his death in 1925. AC was, however, largely to preach to the converted. This could be seen in the failure of the association of **Catholic unions** it founded in 1894 and, more generally, in the inability of the Catholic Church to gain a significant following among the urban working class and land-hungry southern peasantry. Its one great success was the formation, under its auspices, of the federation of agrarian syndicates, the **Confederación Nacional Católica Agraria**, which integrated the smallholders and tenant farmers of northern and central Spain.

Like the rest of the Church hierarchy, AC strongly supported the **Confederación Española de Derechas Autónomas** during the **Second Republic**, and in the aftermath of the **Spanish Civil War** it greeted the **Franco regime** with open arms. Yet, from the 1950s it was from within AC that Church opposition to the regime first manifested itself. Following the war it was reorganized in order to propagate the faith more effectively and set up specialist youth and working-class organizations, the **Juventud Obrera Católica** and **Hermandad Obrera de Acción Católica**, from which criticism was voiced at the Church's identification with authoritarian rule and with the rich and powerful in society. AC and the Church hierarchy were able to undermine these groups between 1967 and 1969, but AC was then carried along in the general tide of reform that swept through the Spanish Church in the early 1970s.

ACCIÓN NACIONAL/NATIONAL ACTION. Acción Nacional was a political organization formed on 26 April 1931—shortly after the proclamation of the **Second Republic**—by the Spanish right. It was born out of the Catholic agrarian confederation, the **Confederación Nacional Católica Agraria**, which was linked to the Catholic pressure groups, **Acción Católica** and the **Asociación Católica Nacional de Propagandistas**, along with other figures close to the **Catholic Church**. The party's main ideological planks were the defense of antiliberal Catholicism and the "social order," and the fight against socialism and Marxism. In the June 1931 elections, the party fought under the banner of the struggle to save Spain from Soviet communism. In the constituent **Cortes**, the party's deputies centered their efforts on combating the clauses of the **constitution** dealing with Church and land reform. Thereafter their rallying cry would become constitutional reform. In April 1932, it was renamed Acción Popular (Popular Action), and a year later, in February 1933, after negotiations with the Derecha Regional Valenciana (Valencian Regional Right), it founded a new rightist coalition, the **Confederación Española de Derechas Autónomas**.

ACCIÓN POPULAR. *See* ACCIÓN NACIONAL.

ACCIÓN REPUBLICANA. *See* AZAÑA DÍAZ, MANUEL.

ACEBES PANIAGUA, ÁNGEL (1958–). Ángel Acebes is a leading **Partido Popular** politician. He was born in Ávila and studied law at the University of Salamanca. He first made his mark in the party in the Ávila town hall, holding the post of town mayor between 1991 and 1995. During this time, he established a close alliance with **José María Aznar**. After the election, he was put in charge of the overall coordination of government policy and was subsequently to serve as minister of justice (January 1999–March 2000) and minister of public administration (March 2000–July 2002). In the former post, he was seen as a sound administrator, reaching agreement over reform to the judiciary with the opposition **Partido Socialista Obrero Español** (PSOE). He then became minister of the interior in the July 2002 reshuffle, where he proved effective in combating **ETA** terrorism, but came under pressure because of the rise of violent and petty crime. After the party's defeat in the 2004 elections, he held the post of secretary general, and, along with **Eduardo Zaplana**, effectively operated as **Mariano Rajoy**'s number two between 2004 and the March 2008 general elections. Both belong to the populist right of the party and have played a major role in policy formation since the PP's 2004 electoral defeat at the hands of the PSOE. However, the fact that the PP's defeat in the March 2008 elections is widely put down to it presenting too right-wing an image is likely to weaken his position.

AFGHANISTAN. Under the Atlanticist government of **José María Aznar**, Spain was the first European government to offer military assistance to the United States in 2001 in order to overthrow the Taliban regime. Only U.S. and British troops were finally employed, but from December 2001 Spain then participated in the airlift of humanitarian supplies and also sent close to 500 troops and four helicopters to Kabul, where they operated under British command. After the **Partido Socialista Obrero Español** (PSOE) had won the March 2004 elections, the previous government's plans to increase troop numbers were confirmed by the Spanish parliament (in part, one suspects, to compensate for the PSOE's decision to withdraw Spanish troops from **Iraq**). In September, 500 paratroops were sent to Mazar-i-Sharif in the north, to ensure stability in the area in the run-up to the 9 October presidential elections. These additional troops were subsequently withdrawn. However, in May 2005 the 540 troops stationed in Kabul were moved to Herat and Qal-i-Naw in the east of Afghanistan and were reinforced between August and September in anticipation of the parliamentary and provisional council elections. In 2008, 690 Spanish troops were based in the country.

AFRANCESADOS. This was the name given to those who collaborated with the Napoleonic regime of **José I** between 1808 and 1813. They were generally men of some social standing. Some collaborated simply to keep their jobs. Leading *afrancesados*, however, were identified with the tradition of "enlightened despotism" practiced under **Carlos III**. They favored reform and yet also feared the implications of a revolutionary uprising in Spain. At the same time, they believed (at least at first) that it would be impossible to overthrow the Napoleonic regime and that in the circumstances it provided the best opportunity for an orderly liberalization of Spanish society. With the defeat of the French forces, about 12,000 *afrancesados* had to seek exile in France.

AFRICANISTA. The term *africanista* was used in the early 20th century to refer to soldiers who had pursued most of their careers fighting in **Morocco**. This was far more dangerous than being posted on the mainland, but offered rapid promotion. A colonial army was built up in Morocco from 1909. From 1920, it also included a volunteer force, under *africanista* officers, known as the Tercio or **Legión Española**. *Africanistas* were possessed of a fierce *esprit de corps*, and, because of their involvement in an anti-insurgency war against the Riff tribesmen, they were renowned for their ruthlessness and attachment to discipline. This was especially the case among Legión officers because of the need to keep control of mercenary regiments. The most famous *africanista* to emerge in the 1920s was General **Francisco Franco**.

Like other sectors of the military, they generally maintained conservative social values and were highly critical of the political elite of the **Cánovas Restoration**. Resentment was intensified in the aftermath of the **Annual** defeat of July 1921, when the government agreed to name a commission to look into the military aspects of the debacle. To the *africanistas* it seemed that the political class was trying to pass the blame onto them. Further anger was generated by the government's reluctance to pursue a more aggressive military strategy in Morocco and by debates in the Spanish parliament, the **Cortes**, in which the inefficiency of the colonial forces was exposed. It reached a crescendo from the spring of 1923, in the face of the plan by **Santiago Alba** (minister of state in the **Partido Liberal** coalition government of **Manuel García Prieto**) to create a civil protectorate in Morocco (thereby taking power out of the hands of the military) and of the planned meeting of the Supreme Council of War and the Navy to decide on military responsibilities for Annual. In response to these threats, in June pro-*africanista* generals (the *cuadrilátero*) began conspiring with General **Miguel Primo de Rivera**, and the *africanistas* strongly supported the latter's 13 September coup d'etat. They would subsequently be among the most fervent backers of his dictatorship. They were also the group within the army most hostile to the **Second Republic** in the 1930s and participated in the July 1936 military rebellion in great numbers.

AGRARIAN REFORM LAW. The question of agrarian reform was one of the most important, if not the most important, problems that faced the **Second Republic**. In southern Spain, during the early 20th century, over 1.5 million half-starved, land-hungry peasants (*braceros* or *gañones*) worked large estates, known as *jorualeros*, either for powerful absentee landowners or large tenant farmers. Their principal demand was the redistribution of land that they felt had been stolen from them during the 19th-century *desamortización*. This problem fed into national politics during the Second Republic, when large numbers of these peasants joined the **Unión General de Trabajadores**'s peasants' union, the **Federación Nacional de Trabajadores de la Tierra**. Members of the provisional government of April–June 1931 affiliated with the **Partido Socialista Obrero Español** were behind a number of decrees in favor of the southern peasantry, and, after having won the June 1931 elections, introduced an agrarian reform bill to satisfy their demands. This is where the problems began. Their coalition partners, the left republicans, were more interested in institutional than social reform. Hence, the bill took a long time to draft, and, once it was introduced into the **Cortes**, the republicans' frequent failure to turn up to the parliamentary debates on the question allowed the right to filibuster it. During the pro-government backlash that followed the attempted right-wing coup d'etat of August 1932, it was finally able to secure rapid passage through the House. However, the law was extremely complicated and it soon became clear that it would take a long time to implement. Full compensation was to be paid to the expropriated landowners, while only 1 percent of the state budget was to be devoted to land reform. As a result, in the year after its promulgation only about 12,000 families were settled. In any case, following the right's victory in the November 1933 elections, the law was largely allowed to fall into disuse and a new agrarian law, passed in July 1935, essentially reestablished the pre-1931 status quo. After the **Popular Front**'s success in the February 1936 elections, the 1932 law was again put into effect, and land now transferred more rapidly than before. More important however, peasants tired of waiting began simply to take over the estates. This process accelerated at the outset of the **Spanish Civil War** in those areas that did not fall under **Nationalist** control. However, the landowners' rights were brutally reasserted by the forces of General **Francisco Franco** once they established control. *See also* AGRICULTURE.

AGRICULTURE. Spain has been a largely agrarian country until relatively recently, with over 50 percent of the country's active **population** still working on the land in the 1920s. As a result, through to the **Second Republic**, the productivity of the land, social relations, and landholding structures, were a major concern for Spanish politicians and essayists.

Agriculture has usually been seen as the Cinderella of the Spanish economy. By the latter Middle Ages a prosperous pastoral economy had developed, based on the export of high-quality wool by the **Mesta**. However, agricultural production was hampered by, in relative European terms, low productivity. In part, the problems were climatological. Much of Spain suffered (and suffers) from deficient rainfall, and parts of the territory are too rocky to be cultivated. These drawbacks were, however, exacerbated by landholding structures. In the south, by the 16th century, great estates known as *latifundia* dominated the scene. In central and northern Spain, on the other hand, plots of land were smaller, and were cultivated by smallholders, tenant farmers, and sharecroppers. In **Galicia**, tiny plots, known as *minifundia*, were predominant. The staple crops were the Mediterranean triad of wheat, olives, and vines. Neither the southern nor northern landholding structures encouraged the development of a dynamic agrarian sector of the economy. Southern agriculture was dogged by the low productivity of the great estates, with their vast armies of pauperized land-hungry laborers (*braceros*). Much of the center and north also suffered low levels of productivity, most notably the *minifundia* areas, in which peasants were locked into a largely subsistence economy.

In the 16th century in the **Crown of Castile** these problems were further exacerbated by inflation and rising direct taxation, leading to the import of increasing quantities of grain. The *desamortización* of the early 19th century brought a growth in production as new land was brought under the plough, and as the century progressed the slow improvement in roads, the construction of the **railways**, and increasing demand from urban Spain led to a further growth in agricultural production as something approaching a national market began to be constructed. Yet the rise in production was to a significant degree the result of an extension of cultivated area rather than improvements in productivity. Only in the irrigated plains of the **Valencian** littoral was there an agricultural revolution, with, from the 1870s, producers specializing to a greater degree in horticulture and citrus fruits. The system entered into crisis in the 1880s when the Spanish market was flooded by Russian and American grains, but rather than adapt to the new conditions, Castilian and Andalusian wheat producers were able to lobby the state successfully for higher **tariffs** on imported wheat. As a result, though there were modest improvements in agricultural yield between the 1900s and 1930s, these were not accompanied by a major transformation of either agrarian structures or the crops produced.

The varieties of landholding structures also conditioned social and political movements in rural Spain. In smallholding central and northern Spain, the peasantry tended to gravitate toward the **Catholic Church** and, in the 19th century, many peasants gave their support to **Carlism**. In addition, from the 1900s, in **Castile** above all, through the **Confederación Nacional Católica Agraria**, elements closely linked to the Catholic hierarchy were able to improve the lot of the peasantry and bind many to their cause. In *latifundia* Spain, on the other hand, social conflict between the landlords and *braceros* drew the peasants into the hands of the leftist **Confederación Nacional del Trabajo** and **Partido Socialista Obrero Español** (PSOE)-**Unión General de Trabajadores**.

During the 1920s and 1930s, there were two attempts to address the economic and social problems that beset the land. In the 1920s, as part of its ambitious public works program, the **Primo de Rivera dictatorship** extended the amount of land under irrigation. Overall the results were modest, though considerable headway was made in the Ebro Valley. Then, with the proclamation of the Second Republic, the progressive **republican**-PSOE coalition instituted a far more ambitious **Agrarian Reform Law**, the main element of which was the transfer of a part of the *latifundistas'* land in the south to the peasantry. This, it was hoped, would calm social tensions and improve productivity.

All experiments with land redistribution were, however, abruptly terminated with the consolidation of the **Franco regime** after the **Spanish Civil War**. The regime eulogized the Castilian peasant as the essence of **Nationalist** values and set as one of its main aims the attainment of self-sufficiency in agriculture. This, however, soon proved counterproductive. During the 1940s, both the U.S. economic boycott and the regime's policy of **autarky** ensured that, starved of imports of fertilizers and agricultural machinery, productivity on the land would remain low. Furthermore, subsidies to wheat and olive producers only served to discourage diversification into high-productivity export crops like citrus fruits.

The whole face of Spanish agriculture rapidly changed from the early 1950s, when the regime began to liberalize the economy and adopt a strategy of economic development at any cost. As a result, industry grew at an unprecedented rate. New opportunities for agricultural laborers opened up both at home and in the boom economies of western Europe, leading to a rapid increase in wage rates. Moreover, from the 1960s, consequent upon rising real incomes, the demand for bread began to decline. These factors combined to produce an unprecedented technological revolution on the land. In the face of rising wages, landowners rapidly mechanized cereal production by introducing large numbers of tractors and combine harvesters. The secondary effect of this was that smaller peasants could no longer compete and had to emigrate to the cities. Hence, by the mid-1960s only around 30 percent of the active population worked on the land.

At the same time, the new patterns of demand at last encouraged significant diversification, with both livestock farming and horticultural production growing rapidly in importance (though this transformation was slowed by continuing wheat subsidies). By the early 1990s, each of these sectors accounted for over one-third of the total final value of agricultural production. Exports of citrus fruits and horticultural produce accelerated after Spain joined the **European Economic Community** (EEC) in 1986. Valencian orange groves and the greenhouses of the southern Mediterranean coastline, between Almería and Huelva, constitute the fastest growing and most dynamic sectors of Spanish agriculture (though, in the case of the latter in particular, at a significant ecological cost). This tendency has been further encouraged by the efforts put into extending the area of land irrigated by Spanish governments since the 1940s, and by the growing availability of cheap **immigrant** labor and financial support for modernization by the EEC after Spain had become a member state. EEC subsidies allowed more marginal producers to survive, slowing the contraction of the agricultural sector. Nevertheless, rising productivity and the fall in cereal production have meant that the percentage of the active population employed on the land has continued to decline. By 2006 it was 4.6 percent of the active population (less than one million people), though this figure is still relatively large in comparative western European terms.

AGUIRRE GIL DE BIEDMA, ESPERANZA (1952–). Esperanza Aguirre is a controversial **Partido Popular** (PP) politician. She was born in an upper-class **Madrid** family and studied law at the Complutense University of Madrid. During the 1970s, she became a high-ranking official in the ministries of tourism and culture. At the same time, she showed an interest in politics, entering the small Partido Liberal (Liberal Party), led by the economist, Pedro Schwartz (1935–). In 1983, she became a Partido Liberal councilor in the Madrid town hall (as part of an **Alianza Popular**-led coalition). She subsequently joined the PP in 1987 and in 1995–1996 became the party's spokesperson in the Madrid local administration. She was elected to the Senate in the 1996 elections and became minister of education and culture in **José María Aznar**'s first government. From the outset, she identified with the populist right of the party, represented by those closest to Aznar (**Francisco Álvarez-Cascos, Ángel Acebes, Eduardo Zaplana**), and she gained a reputation for being a straight-talking politician, not afraid to speak her mind, but also liable to cause offense and make mistakes. Her major initiative was the introduction of a bill that signified a major reform of the education system (the Plan de Humanidades), above all giving central government greater control over the curriculum. This aroused great opposition in **Catalonia** and the **Basque Country** in particular, where it was seen as an attempt to impose a **Castilian**-Spanish version of the country's history, and, with all the opposition united against the initiative, it was finally defeated in parliament. At the same time, the proposed reform produced at times violent polemics in the press on the question of Spanish history and national identity.

In January 1999, she took over the presidency of the Senate and subsequently, in 2003, became president of the Madrid regional government, the Comunidad de Madrid, in anticipation of forthcoming regional elections. She was offered the post by the PP president, José María Aznar, much to the disgust of the previous incumbent, the more centrist PP politician, **Alberto Ruiz-Gallardón**. After two close-run and controversial election contests during the year, her position as president of the autonomous government was confirmed. Subsequently, she has built up a seemingly impregnable position. From the end of 2004, she then fought off a challenge by Ruiz-Gallardón to take over as Madrid party president, and in the run-up to the March 2008 elections blocked an attempt by Ruiz-Gallardón to stand as a PP deputy for Madrid. She is talked of as a possible successor to **Mariano Rajoy**.

ALAS URENA, LEOPOLDO ("CLARÍN") (1852–1901). "Clarín" was, along with Pérez Galdós, the greatest realist writer in late 19th-century Spain. From the 1880s, he stood out as both a novelist and as a literary critic. He was a **republican** anticleric and freethinker, and explicitly combined literature and social commentary. His greatest work, *La Regenta* (*The Regent*, 1885), was a penetrating critique of the stifling, traditional world of provincial Spain.

ALBA Y BONIFAZ, SANTIAGO (1872–1942). Alba was a major figure in Spanish politics between 1898 and 1923. He was born in Zamora into a merchant family and would remain close to Castilian agrarian interests throughout his political career. He first made his mark in the **regenerationist** movement after the **Spanish-American War** of 1898, playing an important role in the foundation of the **Unión Nacional** in 1900. However, the party's failure convinced him that reform would only be possible within the bounds of the **Cánovas Restoration**, leading him to join the **Partido Liberal** (PL) in 1905. Alba then developed his own variant on the "**revolution from above.**" In the first place, he wanted to open the party up to the nondynastic left. Second, following in the footsteps of **Joaquín Costa**, he argued that the modernization of Spain should be spearheaded from the country's agrarian center, via a program of irrigation and public works. He also favored free trade over protectionism and emphasized the need to reform **education**. In the second decade of the century, this led him into a direct confrontation with **Francesc Cambó** and the **Lliga Regionalista**, for whom it was **Catalonia**'s job to spearhead Spanish industrialization. The crunch came in the spring of 1916 when, as minister of the treasury (*hacienda*) in the

Count of Romanones' PL government, he introduced a national reconstruction plan, which involved taxing industrial war profits. Faced with bitter opposition from Cambó, who had mobilized Spain's manufacturing interests against the bill (and some obstruction by Romanones himself, who did not want Alba to become to become too powerful), he was forced to withdraw the plan in August. Henceforth, the rivalry with Cambó would further weaken the regime (most notably, bringing down the coalition government presided over by **Antonio Maura** in October 1918).

Alba formed his own left-liberal grouping within the PL in late 1917. Subsequently, his most important cabinet post would be that of minister of state in the 1923 PL coalition government headed by **Manuel García Prieto**. From this post, he reached trade agreements with Great Britain and France and made clear his aim of setting up a civilian protectorate in **Morocco**, thereby reducing the power of the **military**. This gained him both the enmity of *africanista* officers and induced howls of protest from manufacturing interests. Hence, when General **Miguel Primo de Rivera** launched his coup d'etat in September 1923, sensing that he was in danger, he quickly crossed the border to France. Bitter at his treatment at the hand of King **Alfonso XIII**, after the dictator's fall in 1930, he rejected his offer to form a government that would try to resurrect the Restoration regime.

ALBERTI, RAFAEL (1903–1999). Rafael Alberti was born into a middle-class family in the town of Santa María del Mar (Cádiz). He began to frequent artistic circles following his move to **Madrid** in 1917, taking up first painting and then poetry. Linked to the famous Residencia de los Estudiantes, he made friends, among others, with **Federico García Lorca** and **Luis Buñuel**. He shot to prominence in 1925 when he won the National Literature Prize (Premio Nacional de Literatura) for his first work, *Marinero en tierra* (*Sailor on Land*). At the same time, he moved in a left-wing direction, visiting the Soviet Union in 1932 and joining the **Partido Comunista de España**. During the **Spanish Civil War**, he was secretary of the Anti-Fascist Intellectual Alliance, and, following the **Nationalist** victory, went into exile, first in Argentina and then in Italy. He was not to return to Spain until 1977.

ALBORCH BATALLER, MARÍA DEL CARMEN (1947–). María del Carmen Alborch is an important figure in the **Partido Socialista Obrero Español** (PSOE) and also, more generally, on the Spanish cultural scene. She was born in Castelló de Rugat (**Valencia**), studied law at the University of Valencia, and went on to hold the positions of dean in the university's law faculty and director general of culture in the Valencian **Generalitat**. She was recruited by **Felipe González** as his minister of culture in 1993, even though she was not, at the time, a PSOE member. She became well known for her **feminist** views and her efforts to raise the profile of the arts. She entered parliament as a PSOE deputy in 1996 and is at present the Socialist (Partit Socialista del País Valencià (PSPV)-PSOE) spokesperson in the Valencia local administration and president of the control commission of Spanish state **television** (RTVE). On 27 May 2007, she stood as the PSPV-PSOE candidate for mayor of Valencia, but was beaten by the rival **Partido Popular** candidate, Rita Barberá. From 1997, she also began writing on the place of **women** in contemporary society and culture, publishing *Solas* (*The Solitary Ones*, 1997), *Malas* (*The Bad Ones*, 2002), and *Libres* (*The Free Ones*, 2004).

ALCALÁ ZAMORA Y CASTILLO, NICETO (1877–1949). Alcalá Zamora was the best-known member of the **Cánovas Restoration** political elite, who, after the proclamation of the **Primo de Rivera dictatorship**, abandoned King **Alfonso XIII** and went on to serve under the **Second Republic**.

He was born in Priego (Córdoba) and, like most ambitious young men of his generation, studied law at university. He joined the **Partido Liberal** and went on to serve in two cabinets between 1917 and 1923. He was known, in particular, for his centralist views, which led him to cross swords on more than one occasion with **Francesc Cambó** in the Spanish parliament. After the fall of the Primo de Rivera dictatorship, he rejected any attempt to resuscitate the Restoration regime and instead tried to build a liberal-conservative **republican** base, which would act as a counterweight to the socialist and republican left. Hence, in August 1930 he signed the **San Sebastián Pact** and presided over its central revolutionary committee while helping to found a new political party, the Derecha Liberal Republicana (Republican Liberal Right). He was then chosen by his fellow conspirators as prime minister of the provisional government, formed after the April 1931 municipal elections, in order to present a moderate image. He retained the post after the June 1931 elections but, like the minister of the interior, Miguel Maura, he was bitterly opposed to Article 26 of the new **constitution**, separating Church and state, and the anticlerical reforms promoted by the left-republican parties. For this reason he resigned the premiership on 14 October, though he did accept the post of president of the Republic in December 1931.

Until his replacement in May 1936, this was a position he was to carry with dignity. He hoped to promote a middle way between the **Confederación Española de Derechas Autónomas** (CEDA) on the right, and **Partido Socialista Obrero Español** (PSOE) on the left, and tried to defuse the growing social conflict that was to tear the Republic apart. Following the conservative victory in the November 1933 elections, he refused to consent to the CEDA forming a government because of their dubious republican credentials, and, when the **Partido Republicano Radical** disgraced itself through a series of **corruption** scandals during 1935, he preferred to hold elections to make sure that the Spanish public approved of the decidedly rightist turn politics would take should the CEDA take power. This earned Alcalá Zamora the enmity of the right, but he was not to be rewarded by the left. In May 1936, after the **Popular Front** elections, he lost the presidency to **Manuel Azaña** in an unsuccessful maneuver to try to bring the leader of the more moderate wing of the PSOE, **Indalecio Prieto**, into government. Álcala Zamora retired to Paris but remained a committed Republican, a fact that meant that at the end of the **Spanish Civil War** he could not return to Spain. He set up residence in Argentina, where he lived until his death in 1949.

ALFONSO XII (1857–1885). The future king was born to Queen **Isabel II** on 28 November 1857. He was forced to abandon the country along with the queen following the 1868 **Glorious Revolution** and thereafter faced an uncertain few years. Isabel II abdicated in his favor in June 1871, and in June 1873 the conservative politician **Antonio Cánovas del Castillo** became the official representative of the so-called **Alfonsoist** camp. The pretender received strong support from the country's social elite, avid for the social peace they felt could only be brought by a **Bourbon** restoration. They did not have long to wait. Following the ***pronunciamiento*** of General Arsensio Martínez Campos (1831–1900) at Sagunto in December 1874, Alfonso triumphantly entered Madrid on 14 January 1875.

Through the **Constitution of 1876**, the king was vested with great power should he wish to exercise it. He appointed the prime minister and dissolved the Spanish parliament, the **Cortes**, thereby leaving in his hands the decision as to whether the prime minister could call elections, "make" the parliament, and consolidate his position in power. In order to try to keep the **military** out of politics, Cánovas also made Alfonso a "soldier-king": the commander-in-chief of the army and representative of its interests. This, he believed, would ensure its allegiance to the regime. Future events (under his son **Alfonso XIII**) revealed the danger that the king and armed forces might ally against parliament. This was never to be a problem under Alfonso XII. As his mentor, Cánovas exercised a strong personal influence over him throughout his life. And he encouraged the king to see himself as a constitutional monarch who would accept the decisions of his prime minister as the representative of the will of the Cortes. As a result, despite his own pro-German sentiments and a preference for conservative-liberalism, he did not oppose the accession to power of the **Partido Liberal** in 1881.

The king married his cousin, María de Mercedes de Orleans, despite personal and political opposition, but she died six months later, after which, in 1879, he entered into an arranged marriage with the Austrian archduchess, María Cristina de Habsburgo (1858–1929). In **Madrid** circles, he became something of a folk hero because of his many affairs and nightly escapades. He died of tuberculosis on 25 November 1885.

ALFONSO XIII (1886–1941). The future King Alfonso XIII was born on 17 May 1886, several months after the death of his father, **Alfonso XII**. He was immediately proclaimed king, but his mother, María Cristina de Habsburgo (1858–1929), acted as regent until his coming of age in May 1902.

He married Queen Victoria's granddaughter, Princess Victoria Eugenia of Battenberg (1879–1969), in May 1906. It was his misfortune to begin his reign just as the **Cánovas Restoration** was entering into crisis following defeat in the **Spanish-American War** of 1898.

He largely tried to follow the rules of the *turno pacífico*, but he was more interventionist than his father. In particular, he had received a highly militaristic education and saw one of his key roles as the defense of **military** interests. This was first manifested when in 1905, after the *Cu-Cut!* **incident**, he supported the military, thereby forcing the resignation of the **Partido Liberal** (PL) administration of Eugenio Montero Ríos (1832–1914). It was replaced by another PL government under **Segismundo Moret**, which then approved the Jurisdictions Law, making any public criticism of the army an offense that could be tried in a military court. This represented the first clear example of renewed military intervention in Spanish public life during the Restoration regime.

Alfonso XIII was further pushed into the political fray by the growing splits within the official parties and by the escalating political and social conflicts within Spanish society. Most dramatically, after the harsh repression of the **Tragic Week** by Antonio Maura's **Partido Conservador Antonio Maura** government in 1909, the king, fearful that the international protests might call the Spanish monarchy into question, refused to renew his confidence in Maura in October. From this date, both main parties were split and it became increasingly difficult to form administrations. The crisis reached its apogée between 1917 and 1923, when social conflict escalated, political opposition to the regime grew, and, following the military disaster of **Annual**, policy in **Morocco** took center stage. In the aftermath of the fall of the Russian monarchy, in February 1917 the king moved to the right, fearing that democratization would endanger his throne. As a result, in April 1917 he engineered the fall of the PL government of the **Count of Romanones**, because he saw its foreign policy as too pro-Allied. His fears were further intensified by the Bolshevik Revolution and rapid rise of the Spanish working-class left. In these circumstances, he sympathized with claims in business and military circles that the Restoration parties were weak in the face of subversion. Furthermore, he wearied of the difficulties faced in forming administrations. And in the aftermath of Annual he also lent his ear to *africanista* complaints that civilian politicians were trying to pin the blame on them and were not willing to take an aggressive enough stance in Morocco. For these reasons, the king tacitly supported the military coup by the captain general of Barcelona, **Miguel Primo de**

Rivera, in September 1923, thereby temporarily bringing to an end almost 100 years of **liberal** rule.

It was a decision that would cost him his crown. When in 1930 the dictator fell, Alfonso XIII and his collaborators tried to resuscitate the Cánovas Restoration. It was like trying to breathe life into a corpse. There was no popular support for the *caciquista* politics of the *turno pacífico*, and many Restoration politicians, bitter at the king's actions in 1923, now refused to lend a hand. Furthermore, sections of the army had been alienated by attempted reforms during the dictatorship. Hence, when the left-wing forces, the **Partido Socialista Obrero Español** and the **republicans**, won an outright victory in urban Spain in the municipal elections of 12 April 1931, Alfonso XIII fled the country. However, he did not abdicate and hoped one day to return. The **Nationalists'** victory in the **Spanish Civil War** seemed to hold out this prospect, but it was dashed by General **Francisco Franco**'s determination to consolidate his own personal rule. Alfonso finally abdicated in favor of his son, **Juan de Borbón y Battenberg**, shortly before his death on 28 February 1941.

ALFONSOIST MONARCHISTS. The name refers to those monarchists who at various times during the 19th and 20th centuries pushed for a return of the **Bourbon monarchy** to Spain. The first two occasions were during the **Democratic Sexennium** (1868–1874) and the **Second Republic** (1931–1936). During both periods, they enjoyed the support of elites and sections of the army, both of which were alarmed by the social discontent that had been unleashed by the extension of democratic freedoms. Between 1868 and 1873, their main rallying cry was opposition to the abolition of slavery in the colonies, which was seen as an attack on private property. Their leading figure during these years was **Antonio Cánovas del Castillo**, who was to become the architect of the 1875 Restoration regime. During the Second Republic, Alfonsoist monarchists conspired in order to engineer a coup. They were well connected and had large funds at their disposal. Their spokesman became **José Calvo Sotelo**, who founded the party Renovación Española (Spanish Renovation) in 1933. During the **Franco regime**, the nature of Alfonsoist monarchism changed considerably. Within the military establishment, leading generals such as Antonio Aranda (1888–1979) and Alfredo Kindelán (1879–1962) were convinced monarchists, who were dismayed by **Francisco Franco**'s attempt to consolidate his own personal power base. They were also afraid that his pro-Axis policies would result in an Allied intervention in Spain. During the 1940s, therefore, they launched a campaign for the restoration of the monarchy under the pretender **Juan de Borbón y Battenberg**. As in previous periods, wide sections of the upper classes also retained monarchist sympathies. Franco, however, easily swept them aside. Finally, under the watchful eye of **Luis Carrero Blanco**, it became official regime policy for Don Juan's son, **Juan Carlos**, to take over the reins of power. This was to be not as a substitute for Franco but as his replacement—in order to guarantee the regime's continuation—after his death or incapacitation. Only after the dictator's death would the future king escape this straightjacket.

ALIADÓFILOS. Despite the fact that Spain remained neutral during **World War I** the fighting generated bitter political divisions. The sectors of society that favored democratization and secularization identified with the Allies and became known as *aliadófilos*, while those who put the values of order, stability, and religion first sympathized with the Germans and were referred to as *germanófilos*. This divide led to fierce polemics in the press and helped mobilize broad sectors of the urban populace. Support for the Allies was widespread in working and lower middle-class circles, and dominant in **Catalonia**. In political terms, all **republicans** and much of the **Partido Liberal** were pro-Allied. Most activists in the **Partido Socialista Obrero Español** also supported the Allies, though there was a minority wing of the party and union that maintained that the war was an imperialist struggle of no interest to the working class. This was also the view of most **anarchists**, though there was a small grouping within the anarchist camp, led by Ricardo Mella (1861–1921) and Eleuterio Quintanilla (1886–1966), that was pro-Allied.

ALIANÇA SINDICAL OBRERA (ASO)/WORKERS' TRADE UNION ALLIANCE. *See* MOVIMENT SOCIALISTA DE CATALUNYA.

ALIANZA POPULAR (AP)/POPULAR ALLIANCE. AP was formed in September 1976 by several clans of former Francoists, who hoped to build a right-wing coalition strong enough to win the forthcoming elections. From the start, the leader of the coalition was **Manuel Fraga**, and until his resignation in 1986 it was very much with his image that AP was associated. AP tried to present itself as a modern, democratic, neoliberal party, but the high profile of many of its leaders within the **Franco regime** and its defense of traditional family and religious values, law and order, and centralism, meant that for the majority of the electorate it came to be seen as a right or extreme right-wing party, which offered a continuation of policies pursued under Francoism. This image would be reinforced when half the party's deputies refused to vote in favor of the **Constitution of 1978**, largely because of their opposition to the **State of the Autonomies**. At a political level this proved a serious handicap in a context in which, because of the Franco regime, the term "right-wing" had acquired strong negative connotations, and the largest segment of the electorate defined itself as in the center. Moreover, the party's stress on traditional values seemed out of place in the new predominantly urban Spanish society, which had over the previous 20 years become far more secularized and culturally liberal.

The combined result of these factors was that in the June 1977 elections AP limped home in fourth place with only 8 percent of the vote. In the March 1979 elections (in which it allied with a number of liberal and Christian-democrat notables under the title Coalición Democrática [Democratic Coalition]), it did even worse, receiving just under 6 percent of the vote. It was, however, slow to learn from these mistakes. In its third national congress, held in December 1979, it adopted a more presidential structure under the undisputed leadership of Fraga, though it still remained a loose federation. At the same time, the theory was developed that the majority of the Spanish electorate was naturally right-wing, and that the main task at hand was to undermine the centrist governing coalition, the **Unión del Centro Democrático** (UCD). Over the next two years, as the UCD fell apart, the future looked brighter. There was an influx of younger members into the party and sectors of the UCD's base also transferred across.

In the October 1982 elections (in alliance with the small conservative Christian-democrat party that had broken with the UCD, the

Partido Democrático Popular [Popular Democratic Party—PDP]), AP increased its vote from one to five million and became the main opposition party. However, it was still a long way behind the victorious **Partido Socialista Obrero Español** (PSOE). AP still suffered from the stigma of association with Francoism, and there remained a generalized fear that should it come to power, social reforms and democratic liberties would be at risk. Hence, commentators talked of AP having a "ceiling" of votes, which was at most 30 percent of the electorate. AP tried to present a more centrist image by allying with virtually nonexistent groupings such as the PDP and the Partido Liberal (Liberal Party), formed in 1985, but few people were convinced. Center-left and center-right electors generally voted for the PSOE, **Adolfo Suárez**'s Centro Democrático y Social (Social and Democratic Center), and the nationalist parties, the **Partido Nacionalista Vasco** and **Convergència i Unió**. This was confirmed in the 1986 elections, when AP (along with the PDP and Partido Liberal) failed to close the gap on the PSOE.

This provoked a party crisis, which culminated in the resignation of Manuel Fraga in December 1986. A struggle followed to fill the fallen leader's shoes. At an extraordinary congress held in February 1987, a young senator from Andalusia, Antonio Hernández Mancha (1951–), took over. A fresh face was meant to provide a new image, but people were still not convinced that the party had really changed, and Hernández Mancha lacked both charisma and oratorical power. Hence, at the party's ninth congress, in January 1989, Fraga returned along with a new protégé, **José María Aznar**, finally convinced that the party had to be restructured and centralized. Fraga was reelected president, but Aznar became his vice president and the party's candidate in the forthcoming general elections. AP also changed its name to **Partido Popular** in order to present a more unified and coherent image. *See also* TABLE 10.

ALIANZAS OBRERAS/WORKERS' ALLIANCES. The idea that the various working-class parties and unions ally and set up Alianzas Obreras in the face of the right-wing threat was launched by the Catalan dissident Marxist party, the **Bloc Obrer i Camperol** (BOC) during 1933. They were seen as a way of uniting the working class to counter the threat of **Fascism** and prepare for revolutionary action, and also as a means for the BOC to raise its profile within the labor movement. In **Catalonia**, most of the smaller parties and unions opposed to the anarcho-syndicalist **Confederación Nacional del Trabajo** (CNT) joined. The Catalan CNT, on the other hand, refused to sign a pact with political parties in what it saw as a Marxist project. Outside Catalonia, at first the **Partido Comunista de España** (PCE) refused to become involved, calling for "unity from the grassroots up" (in reality from within the PCE), but gave greater support after the autumn of 1934, when the Comintern decided to call for the formation of popular front alliances. The **Largo Caballero** wing of the **Partido Socialista Obrero Español** (PSOE)-**Unión General de Trabajadores** was more interested than the PCE because of the extra support the Alianzas would provide in the case of the need to call a revolutionary general strike against the rightist government, but counseled their formation only in areas in which it felt it could control the resulting committee. Only in Asturias was an agreement signed by the PSOE-UGT and CNT to form a united Alianza Obrera. The unity achieved in Asturias was reflected in the fact that during the **October 1934 revolution** it was the only zone in which a full-blooded insurrection took place. After October, enthusiasm for the Alianzas cooled. The events of this month seemed to show that the road to revolution was blocked, and that in order to win back power the left would have to form a new alliance with the **republicans**. Hence the PSOE backed away, and by 1936 the movement had entered into decline.

ALMIRALL I LLOZER, VALENTÍ (1841–1904). Valentí Almirall was the leading **Catalanist** intellectual of the 19th century. He was born in **Barcelona** into a wealthy merchant family. He studied law at university and was soon attracted to **federalist republican** politics. In 1868, he helped set up the **Partido Republicano Federalista** in **Catalonia** and during the **Democratic Sexennium** was on the hard-line, intransigent wing of the party. From the 1870s, however, Almirall took an increasingly Catalanist stance. In 1879, he began to publish the first daily newspaper written in **Catalan**, *El Diari Català*, and in 1880, he organized the First Catalanist Congress. The following year he broke with federal republicanism and in 1882 he set up his own group, the Centre Català (Catalan Center). This represented an attempt to develop an interclass Catalanist movement that would stretch from the **republican** left to the monarchist right. Over the next decade, Almirall was to be at the forefront of Catalanist protest. In 1885, he helped draw up the so-called *Memorial de Greuges* (*Petition of Complaints*), a call addressed to King **Alfonso XII** for Catalan autonomy, and in 1886 he wrote the essay *Lo catalanisme* (*Catalanism*), which represented the first systematic exposition of Catalanist doctrine. Almirall, however, was criticized by more conservative Catalanists such as **Enric Prat de la Riba**, who went on to form the Unió Catalanista (Catalanist Union) in 1891. As these intellectuals increasingly dominated the Catalanist movement in the 1890s, Almirall found himself marginalized.

ALMODÓVAR CABALLERO, PEDRO (1949–). Almodóvar is easily Spain's best-known film director as well as a leading media personality. He shot to prominence in the late 1970s within the context of the so-called *movida madrileña*, a broad-ranging movement of sectors of post-Francoist youth who challenged the **Franco regime**'s Catholic conservatism, explored their sexuality more freely, and embraced new musical and artistic trends. In this vein, Almodóvar's films dealt with and provided an ironic and amusing commentary on contemporary urban concerns (including sexual and national identity) and satirized conservative Spanish institutions. But he was also able to reach a more mainstream audience through his incorporation of popular Spanish traditions, through the emotional intensity of his films, and through the fast-moving plots. His first film, *Pepi, Luci, Bom, y otras chicas del montón* (*Pepi, Luci, Bom, and Other Girls on the Heap*, 1978), was produced on a shoestring. In 2000, *Todo sobre mi madre* (*All about My Mother*) won an Oscar for the best foreign language film. His most commercially successful film to date is *Mujeres a borde de un ataque de nervios* (*Women of the Edge of a Nervous Breakdown*, 1988).

ALMUNIA AMANN, JOAQUÍN (1943–). Joaquín Almunia was a leading **Partido Socialista Obrero Español** (PSOE) politician in the 1980s and 1990s. He was born in Bilbao and studied economics and law at the University of Duesto. He then became linked to the PSOE-**Unión General de Trabajadores** (UGT) socialist movement as the UGT's economic advisor between 1976 and 1979. After **Felipe**

González's victory in the 1982 elections, he was brought onboard to mediate between the party and unions and held the posts of minister of labor and social security (1982–1986) and minister of public administration (1986–1991). After Felipe González stepped down as PSOE general secretary in June 1997, Almunia was elected to lead the party. He recognized the need for renewal but was handicapped by his image as the old guard's candidate. In order to gain legitimacy, he instituted a system of primary elections within the party to decide the next party candidate for the premiership, but this backfired when in April 1998 he was beaten by **Josep Borrell**. There followed an awkward period in which the PSOE had a dual leadership. When Borrell resigned in May 1999 Almunia took over sole control, but the general election was only 10 months away and the instability of the previous year had cost the party credibility. In the run-up to the election, trailing behind the ruling **Partido Popular**, Almunia offered the leftist coalition **Izquierda Unida** (IU) an electoral pact (which, after negotiations, was limited to only the Senate). However, it was not widely understood or welcomed (Felipe González and the president of IU, **Julio Anguita**, had been at daggers drawn) and it helped mobilize the right-wing vote. Following the electoral defeat Almunia resigned as secretary general. In April 2004, he replaced another Socialist, **Pedro Solbes**, as the **European Union**'s commissioner for economic and monetary affairs.

AL-QAEDA (OPERATIONS IN SPAIN). With a significant **immigrant** population of Muslim origin, Spain has emerged, from 2001, as an important center of Islamic **terrorism**. During investigations into the attack on the Twin Towers, it was discovered that while it had been planned above all in Germany, Spain had also been a center of operations. Mohamed Atta had been in Spain in July 2001 and held meetings in Madrid and Tarragona. Given the government of **José María Aznar**'s firm backing for the U.S.-led "war on terror," from 2002 reports emerged that it was now one of the Western countries most at risk of an Islamic terrorist attack.

A first warning came in May 2003 when the Spanish cultural center (Casa de España) in Casablanca (**Morocco**) was bombed and 44 people were killed including two Spaniards. Much more dramatic in their impact were the **Madrid train bombings** of 11 March 2004 (three days before the Spanish general elections). Ten satchel-bombs exploded on four trains carrying passengers from Alcalá de Henares to Madrid, leaving 191 dead and over 1,500 injured. At first the **Partido Popular** government stated that **ETA** was responsible, and its attempts to maintain ETA's authorship through to the date of the election led to an increasingly polarized political climate in Spain and was a key factor in the government's fall. From early on, evidence emerged that Islamic terrorists were to blame. The bombers were still at large and dangerous, and on 2 April would attempt, unsuccessfully, to blow up high-speed trains on the Madrid-Lleida and Madrid-Seville routes. On 3 April, the police surrounded seven members of the cell in the Madrid district of Leganés, who rather than surrender blew themselves up (also killing a member of Spain's elite antiterrorist police). Eighty arrests were to follow, decapitating the organization. A four-month trial of the remaining suspects began in July 2007. When the verdicts were read out at the end of October, 21 of the 28 defendants were found guilty of varying degrees of complicity. During the trial it was established that while the defendants were inspired by Al-Qaeda there was no actual funding or operational link.

Despite these detentions, Islamic radicals have tried to carry out further attacks in Spain. Important in this respect have been links established between Islamic radicals in Spain and terrorist training camps on the Pakistan-**Afghanistan** border. Militants have been particularly active in Barcelona, where there is an immigrant Pakistani community. Since 2004, around 400 Islamists have been detained. In 2005, the police intercepted a plot, initiated by imprisoned Islamist terrorists, to launch a suicide bomb attack on the High Court (Audiencia Nacional), and broke up an Islamist network that financed and supported terrorist activities and a cell that sent terrorists to fight for al-Qaeda in **Iraq**. Then, in January 2008, police broke up another cell in Barcelona and arrested 15 individuals (13 from Pakistan and 2 from India). Explosives were found at the scene.

ÁLVAREZ-CASCOS FERNÁNDEZ, FRANCISCO (1947–). Between 1989 and 2004, Álvarez Cascos was a leading figure within the **Partido Popular** (PP). He was a member of the older generation of PP activists, close to **Manuel Fraga**, who supported **José María Aznar**'s rise to power. At the time of the PP's foundation in 1989 he became its general secretary, a post he held until 1999. Following the party's victory in the 1996 elections he also became one of Aznar's two vice presidents. However, his raucous, aggressive style meant that he was never popular in broad sections of the electorate. Moreover, his attempt to build a pro-PP **telecommunications** empire via the formation of the digital service Vía Digital (while the government tried to stop Canal Satélite Digital—in which the **PRISA Group**, which was close to the **Partido Socialista Obrero Español**, had a key stake—from setting up an alternative) and through the acquisition of the private **television** station Antena 3 by the former state telephone monopoly, Telefónica, was so obvious that it lost him credibility. From 1998, he was excluded from the PP's inner circle, and after the 2000 elections given the lower-profile post of minister of economic development (*ministro de fomento*). He ran into further difficulty when his department played a key role in the mistaken decision to tow the leaking petrol tanker, called the ***Prestige***, away from the Galician coast, and over the problems facing the construction of the high-speed **rail** network (AVE) from **Madrid** to **Barcelona**. In January 2004, he made the decision to retire from active politics.

ÁLVAREZ GONZÁLEZ-POSADA, MELQUÍADES (1864–1936). Melquíades Álvarez was born in Oviedo, studied law at university, and at an early age became involved in **republican** politics, showing considerable journalistic talent and great oratorical powers. On the more moderate wing of the republican movement, when he formed part of the **Unión Republicana** in 1903, he rejected revolutionary agitation and tried to establish contacts with the **Partido Liberal (PL)**. He was, therefore, a strong supporter of the **Left Bloc**, formed by the PL and moderate republicans in 1908 in opposition to the prime minister, **Antonio Maura**. In April 1912, he took this policy a stage further, forming his own Partido Reformista (Reformist Party), along with **Gumersindo de Azcárate**. In 1914 the party declared itself "accidentalist" on the question of the form of government (Republic or monarchy). In reality, this meant that Melquíadez Álvarez was prepared to participate in the governments of the **Cánovas Restoration** in order, as he saw it, to push them down a more liberal path. In 1923, he effectively integrated into the regime when a member of his party entered the PL coalition government of **Manuel García Prieto**

and he became speaker of the Lower House of the Spanish parliament. This experience was, however, cut short by the coup d'etat of that September. With the proclamation of the **Second Republic**, Melquíadez Álvarez formed a new organization, the Partido Republicano Liberal Demócrata (Liberal Democrat Republican Party). The party began supporting the republican-Socialist coalition government but, frightened by its radical reforms, pulled away, and by 1935, Melquíadez Álvarez sympathized with the **Partido Republicano Radical-Confederación Española de Derechas Autónomas** right-wing coalition government. As a result, he was arrested in Madrid by the Republican government at the outset of the **Spanish Civil War** and assassinated when a leftist mob invaded the prison in August.

ÁLVAREZ MENDIZÁBAL, JUAN (1790–1853). Born in Cádiz, Álvarez Mendizábal rose to become both a rich merchant and one of the key figures in the liberalization of Spain's social structure during the early 19th century. He first entered liberal politics during the **War of Independence** and played a key role in organizing the 1820 *pronunciamiento* by General Rafael de Riego (1785–1823), which ushered in the **Constitutional Triennium**. During the Triennium, he became one of the leading figures in the more radical *exaltado* liberal camp. With the regime's fall, he sought exile in Great Britain, but following the death of **Fernando VII** and to the backdrop of popular urban protest for radical liberal reform, the queen regent, **María Cristina of Naples**, was forced to request his return to Spain to take over the reins of government. His assumption of power on 14 September 1835 signified a sharp turn to the left. He vigorously pursued the war against the forces of **Carlism** and in January 1936 approved a new electoral law that gave the industrial and commercial bourgeoisie the vote. Then, most important of all, in February and March he issued a series of decrees that set in motion the *desamortización* process. He was briefly forced out of office by the queen regent in May 1836, but following the **La Granja rebellion** of August 1836 he returned to power, under the old 1812 **Cádiz Constitution**, as treasury minister in a government headed by José María Calatrava (1781–1847). During the year, he issued further *desamortización* decrees, and was, moreover, a key figure in the elaboration of the **Constitution of 1837**. He was in the future only briefly again to attain high office, but remained a highly influential figure in what came to be known as the **Partido Progresista**.

AMADEO I (1845–1890). Amadeo Fernando María de Saboya was the second son of the king of Italy, Victor Emmanuel II. Most of the forces behind the **Glorious Revolution** favored a constitutional **monarchy**, and in order not to upset the balance of power in Europe Amadeo was, after a vote of the **Cortes** on 16 November 1870, offered the crown. He reluctantly accepted and was proclaimed King Amadeo I of Spain on 2 January 1871. His reign was, however, to be short-lived. He was plagued by divisions within the ruling parties and boycotted by elite **Madrid** society, who feared social unrest and wished a return to **Bourbon** rule. In response, he used the excuse of a dispute between the government and artillery corps (the so-called Hidalgo Affair) to abdicate on 11 February 1873. This led to the proclamation of the **First Republic**.

ANARCHISM. Between the late 19th century and the **Spanish Civil War**, anarchism captured the hearts and minds of large numbers of Spanish workers and peasants. It was first introduced into the country by Mikhail Bakunin's Italian disciple Giuseppi Fanelli in late 1868, and Bakunism became the guiding principle of the Spanish branch of the First International, the **Federación Regional Española** (FRE) in the early 1870s. This was the first of a number of anarchist-oriented labor confederations—the **Federación de Trabajadores de la Región Española** (FTRE), which operated between 1882 and 1888, the Pacto de Union y Solidaridad (Pact of Unity and Solidarity), active in the late 1880s, the **Federación Regional Española de Sociedades de Resistencia**, which briefly functioned at the turn of the century, and finally, the **Confederación Nacional del Trabajo** (CNT), which was founded in **Barcelona** in 1910. Thereafter, anarchists and Marxist socialists affiliated to the **Partido Socialista Obrero Español (PSOE)** and **Unión General de Trabajadores** formed the two major wings of the Spanish labor movement through to the 1930s.

The anarchists were antistatist and "antipolitical" (in the sense that they did not believe that political parties had any useful role to play in the fight for socialism) and laid stress on the need for the individual to discover his or her road to freedom. Most anarchists agreed that a key to attaining personal and collective freedom was **education**. The history of Spanish anarchism is, therefore, littered with initiatives to set up schools and institutes for the workers. The most famous is probably **Francisco Ferrer**'s **Escuela Moderna**, founded at the turn of the century in **Barcelona**. However, the emphasis on the individual inevitably meant that, as in other countries, the anarchists were plagued by divisions over questions of philosophy and strategy. Between 1870 and 1923, one can distinguish at least two main currents within the movement. On one side were to be found the union activists (subsequently often referred to as syndicalists), who believed in the need to build up the labor organization and argued that it was the unions that, through a general strike, would carry out the revolution. This wing was strongest within the Catalan labor federations, its best-known figures being Rafael Farga Pellicer (1844–1890) in the 1870s and 1880s and **Salvador Seguí** between 1914 and 1923. The other tendency may be referred to as the insurrectionaries (subsequently also known as anarcho-communists). They believed that it was up to the dedicated groups of revolutionaries to set off working-class and peasant revolt. Often they argued in favor of "propaganda by the deed," that is to say, acts of "reprisal" against the bourgeoisie. This was supposed to show the vulnerability of the oppressors and give confidence to the oppressed. In Barcelona, they tended to be strongest in periods of repression, when the trade unionists were driven underground. Their high point came in the 1890s when there were a number of **terrorist** outrages committed against the authorities and bourgeoisie, the most sensational the lobbing of a bomb onto spectators in the Barcelona opera house, the Liceo, in 1893, and the assassination of the architect of the Restoration regime, **Antonio Cánovas del Castillo**, by an Italian anarchist, Michele Angiolillo, in 1897. In **Andalusia**, from the 1880s they gained support because of the difficulty of forming labor unions, which only left open protest through such activities as crop burning and individual acts of violence.

However, even among the trade unionists differences were to emerge. In the early 1870s and early 1880s, the Catalan leadership of the FRE and FTRE showed itself to be quite cautious. It favored strike funds and argued that strikes should only be carried out if the chances of victory were high; otherwise, the organization would be put in jeopardy. But from the mid-1880s this practice was challenged by a more leftist group of anarchists, led by Federico Urales (pseudonym of Joan Montseny, 1864–1942) and Leopoldo Bonafulla (pseudonym of Joan Baptista Esteve), who argued that this system was bureaucratic and centralist, and therefore the antithesis of anarchist principles. Instead, workers should be encouraged to take strike action against the bourgeoisie whenever possible. From the mid-1890s, in line with syndicalist ideas being developed in France, this strategy became known as "direct action." Workers were to be mobilized against the bourgeoisie, and it was hoped that strikes and protest would finally culminate in a general strike that would overthrow capitalism.

This radical strategy became the hallmark of Spanish anarchism (as from the 1920s referred to anarcho-syndicalism). With the growth of the labor movement from the turn of the century it was the trade unionists who were dominant. Nevertheless, tensions remained between the out-and-out revolutionaries who were virulently "antipolitical" and others who laid more stress on union building and were more willing to cooperate with left-wing political forces. Between 1907 and 1919, the second group—led, from 1915, by Salvador Seguí—was in the ascendancy, but in the context of the severe social strife of the years 1919–1923, the hard-liners came to the fore. They were to be found in the "action groups," founded by people like **Buenaventura Durruti** to carry out attacks on representatives of the bourgeoisie and authorities. In 1927, the **Federación Anarquista Ibérica**, the purpose of which was to coordinate the actions of the revolutionary elite and ensure that the CNT did not stray from its anarchist principles, was founded. In this way, men like Durruti, though protrade unionists, also took onboard the insurrectionary and terrorist currents within the anarchist movement.

The growing divisions between these moderates and radicals was to be of key importance during the 1930s, with the organization at one point expelling the moderates, who then set up their own *treintista* organization. Tensions would live on during the Spanish Civil War, especially after the decision taken by the CNT leadership to join the Catalan and Spanish Republican governments. At the heart of the polemics was the question of the relationship of the anarchist movement and the CNT to the Spanish state and political parties. While the "antipolitical" current tried to maintain the traditional anarchist position that all governments should be combated at all times and that all parties were by their nature not to be trusted, pragmatists (who on this occasion included the firebrand orator **Federica Montseny**) could not ignore the advantages to be gained from collaboration with other leftist forces, from negotiations with the state, and, during the civil war, participation in state institutions.

These divisions lived on after the war. The various anarchist groups in exile formed the Movimiento Libertario Español (Spanish Libertarian Movement, MLE-CNT) in February 1939, but antagonism remained. In the south of France, the "collaborationists" dominated, participating in the noncommunist Republican alliance the Alianza Nacional de Fuerzas Democráticas (National Alliance of Democratic Forces), and establishing close relations with the PSOE left. In 1945, they even went so far as to enter the José Giral (1879–1962) Republican **Cortes** in exile. This produced an outright split with the "purists," under the leadership of Federica Montseny. Increasingly, however, these divisions between the anarchist exiles were becoming irrelevant in the postwar West. Within Spain, the CNT was from the 1960s rapidly outstripped by **Comisiones Obreras**. In exile, the anarchists found they could muster little support from a world that to a large degree viewed their ideas as an anachronism. In the 1970s, a strong libertarian current emerged among the radicalized student population in Spain, but this had more to do with personal freedom than the collective struggles that had fired the CNT. In these circumstances, the anarchists could never regain their former strength and have remained a lively but marginalized current in Spanish political life.

ANDALUCISMO. *See* ANDALUSIA.

ANDALUSIA. Andalusia is by far the largest region in Spain, covering much of the south of the Iberian Peninsula. It totals 87,268 square kilometers and in 2007 its total **population** was 8,059,461. The region encompasses eight provinces: Almería, Granada, Málaga, Cádiz, Huelva, Seville, Córdoba, and Jaén. It is marked by high summer temperatures (which can reach over 45°C in Seville and Córdoba), but there are significant variations. The region is divided by three mountain ranges: the Sierra Morena range (which runs from Huelva past Seville), the Baetic Mountains (which stretch from Huelva to Almería), and the Sierra Nevada between Granada and Almería.

The territory (the name of which comes from the Arab Ál-Ándalus, the territories governed by the **Moors** between 711 and 1492) was incorporated into the **Crown of Castile** during the Christian "**Reconquest**" between the 8th and 15th centuries. As the Christian armies pushed forward, vast tracts of land were given by the monarchs to powerful noble families, the Church, and military orders as a reward for their support, hence the rise of great landed estates known as *latifundia*, which were worked by armies of landless and land-hungry peasants.

Since the 19th century, Andalusia has been one of Spain's poorest regions. The years between 1830 and 1860 had seen the growth of an indigenous **iron industry**, but the region has no **coal**, and from the 1870s the charcoal furnaces proved unable to compete with coal-fired plants in Asturias, the **Basque Country**, and abroad. From the second half of the 19th century, large foreign-owned mining company towns grew up at Río Tinto, Tharsis, and Almadén, but these tended to be enclaves with limited linkages to the rest of the community. Hence, Andalusia's rural status was confirmed. Indeed, the latifundia were consolidated during the *desamortización* between the 1830s and 1850s. The great social divide this produced between the peasantry and the wealthy landlords and administrators was quickly to lead to severe social tensions. From the 1870s, the **anarchists**, and later the Marxist **Partido Socialista Obrero Español** (PSOE) and **Unión General de Trabajadores** (UGT), were to recruit heavily among the poor, calling for the redistribution of the great estates. The years 1903–1906 saw an upsurge of rural discontent with large numbers of strikes. This was, however, as nothing to the protest movement that surged through Andalusia in the wake of the Russian Revolution of October 1917 (and that, therefore, became known as the **Bolshevik Triennium**). The land question quickly came onto the agenda once more during the first years of the **Second Republic**. The PSOE now had ministers in government and pushed through an **Agrarian Reform Law**, which was meant to give the peasants new land. However, it soon proved slow and cumbersome to operate, leading to rising peasant discontent.

In the early 20th century, as in many parts of Spain, Andalusia also witnessed the growth of an anticentralist regionalist-nationalist movement known as *andalucismo*. A number of folklorists and anthropologists looked back to the centuries of Moorish domination as a time when arts, culture, and civilization had flourished, which, they maintained, had been brought to an end by the brutal Castilian conquest (not **Reconquest** as in the Spanish nationalist narrative). From 1910, the leading political activist was Blas Infante (1885–1936), who came from a **republican**-federalist background. Under Infante, the movement allied with the Spanish left and during the Second Republic agitated for an autonomy statute. New symbols of the motherland were agreed on: the green and white **flag**, the coat of arms (Hercules and the lion), and an anthem (based on the traditional peasant song *Santo Dios*). However, the fact that Andalusian and Spanish national identity were so closely interlinked, that Andalusian elites backed the Spanish right, and that the working-class left had made such strong inroads, limited its political and cultural space and it never made a big impact.

During the **Spanish Civil War**, in those areas in which the Republic held on, the peasantry pressed home a social revolution and collectivized the land, but they faced severe repression as the territory fell to the advancing Francoist forces. Under the **Franco regime**, the voice of the Andalusian peasantry fell silent. Their condition was to be transformed by Spain's rapid economic development from the 1960s. Points in the region began to industrialize: large petrochemical installations were built outside Huelva and a heavy engineering and chemical industry was established in Seville. Of greatest importance, however, was the fact that in the wake of Spain's economic boom the *latifundia* began to mechanize. This and the new opportunities for industrial work both in urban Spain and further afield led to a massive migration of peasants from the land and from Andalusia as a region.

The **transition to democracy** in the 1970s witnessed a rapid political mobilization of Andalusia's urban population. General Franco's corrupt centralist rule had led nationalist and regionalist sentiment to grow in strength beyond its key centers of **Catalonia**, the Basque Country, and, to a lesser extent, **Galicia**. Hence, from the mid-1970s, Andalusians called not only for democracy but also for home rule. On the Day of Andalusia, 4 December 1977, one million demonstrators took to the streets to demand an autonomy statute, and in the March

1979 elections five members of the *andalucista* Partido Socialista de Andalucía (Andalusian Socialist Party) were elected to parliament. Attempts by the ruling **Unión del Centro Democrático** government to put a brake on the pace of decentralization during 1980–1981 backfired, the government was defeated, and powers had to be transferred to the new Andalusian autonomous government at the same pace as its **Catalan** and **Galician** counterparts. The new Andalusian authority instated the *andalucista* symbols of identity, but once autonomy had been achieved, nationalist/regionalist sentiment died down. The PSOE, led by the Seville team of **Felipe González** and **Alfonso Guerra**, won a commanding victory in the October 1982 general elections and the autonomous Andalusian parliament has been in Socialist hands ever since. Since 1990, Manuel Chaves (1942–) has been the president of the autonomous government (the Junta de Andalucía).

During the 1980s and 1990s, the PSOE tried to combine efforts to modernize the Spanish **economy** with support for poorer regions, especially Andalusia. The Plan de Empleo Rural (PER), established in 1984, provided temporary work on infrastructural projects for unemployed rural laborers. Once they had worked at least 60 days they were also entitled to six months of unemployment benefits. In the same year, the Socialist administration also set up a Fondo de Compensación Interterritorial to correct regional imbalances and provide funds for investment in poorer areas. And the government ensured that in 1992 Spain's first high-speed **railway** line connected **Madrid** and Seville. Andalusia has also benefited greatly from **European Union** (EU) funds, especially from 1994. The results have, however, been disappointing, with the distance between Andalusia and Spain's richest regions growing from the mid-1990s. **Tourism** has continued to expand and export-oriented horticulture in Almería and Huelva has developed apace. The problem is that, distant from the major EU centers of population, the territory has found it difficult to attract direct inward investment, build a dynamic skills base, and modernize its service and manufacturing sectors. *See also* AGRICULTURE; ALBERTI, RAFAEL; ARCHITECTURE; GARCÍA LORCA, FEDERICO; MOORS.

ANGUITA GONZÁLEZ, JULIO (1941–). Born in the Andalusian town of Fuengirola, Julio Anguita became the leading figure in the

Partido Comunista de España (PCE) during the 1990s. A charismatic and didactic speaker, Anguita first came to prominence as the mayor of Córdoba between 1979 and 1986. He was elected PCE general secretary in February 1988 and in 1992 also took over the leadership of the leftist electoral coalition **Izquierda Unida** (IU). Under his leadership the PCE slowly began to regain the standing it had enjoyed in the late 1970s. However, sectors of the left were strongly critical of his decision, following the demise of Communism in Eastern Europe, not to follow the example of the Italian Communists to dissolve the Partito Comunista Italiano (Italian Communist Party) and reconstitute it under a social-democratic banner. This led to a direct confrontation with the "Renovators" within the party, captained by Nicolás Sartorius (1938–), who formed a group called Nueva Izquierda (New Left), in the run-up to the 1993 general elections.

He was also criticized for his hard-line opposition to the governing **Partido Socialista Obrero Español** (PSOE), which led him to work with **José María Aznar** to undermine the position of the prime minister, **Felipe González**. In the 1993 and 1996 general elections, IU improved its standing, receiving 10.5 percent of the votes in 1996. However, there was a sense that because Anguita had failed to outline any clear alternative strategy, his coalition had not benefited from the crisis in the PSOE as much as it could have. Between 1996 and 1998, divisions emerged over whether to work with the PSOE now that it was in opposition. Dissidents, led by Cristina Almeida (1945–) and Diego López Garrido (1947–), turned Nueva Izquierda into a party. It integrated into IU but pushed for it to work with the PSOE. Meanwhile, the Catalan left-wing coalition, **Iniciativa per Catalunya-Verds**, also expressed its displeasure at Anguita's policies. Both these groups were expelled by Anguita in 1997. However, it was ill health rather than political opposition that would finally derail his political career. He suffered a heart attack in the run-up to the 1993 elections and was unable to participate in the final stages of the campaign. It seemed that he had made a full recovery, but in 1998, following a further heart attack, he handed over the reins of the PCE to Francisco Frutos (1939–), and, in December 1999, suffering from continuing heart problems, also ensured Frutos was chosen as IU candidate for president in the forthcoming general elections.

ANNUAL, DISASTER OF. The battle of Annual (so named because of the **Moroccan** village around which it was fought) was the greatest disaster to befall the Spanish **military** in the 20th century. The origins of the disaster were to be found in the plan of the high commissioner of the Spanish Protectorate, General **Dámaso Berenguer**, to create a land link between the Spanish garrison towns of Ceuta and Melilla. As part of this plan, from February 1921 the military commander of Melilla, General Manuel Fernández Silvestre (1871–1921), attempted rapidly to advance his forces from Melilla to the Bay of Alhucemas. But, having overextended his lines, on 22 July Silvestre suffered a devastating counterattack at the hands of the Riff tribesmen led by Abd al-Krim al-Khatabi (1882–1963). The Spanish troops were routed and fell back on Melilla in chaos. In all, 9,000 soldiers were killed and the territorial gains of a decade lost. Indeed, if the tribesmen had attacked, Melilla itself would have fallen.

Most of the losses were recouped in the following year. Nevertheless, in left-wing and liberal circles the cry went up for responsibilities, and in its aftermath the new Partido Conservador coalition government, led by **Antonio Maura**, appointed General José Picasso to head an investigation into the technical and military aspects of the defeat. In April 1922, the Supreme Council of War and the Navy was charged with apportioning blame. This produced anger among *africanistas*—apparently shared by King **Alfonso XIII**—that while the military was being put on trial, little was being done to look into responsibilities in political circles. Furthermore, there was anger among the colonial troops that, under pressure from public opinion, governments were reluctant to put into practice the aggressive "forward police" they favored in Morocco. Hence, pro-*africanista* generals began conspiring with General **Miguel Primo de Rivera** in the summer of 1923 and the colonial officers gave their support to the latter's coup d'etat in September.

APERTURISTAS. *Aperturistas* (those who seek an opening) was the name given to elements within the **Franco regime** that, from the 1950s and especially 1960s, saw the need for political reform. There were two main reforming currents. The first reforming current was made up of members of the **Movimiento Nacional**, most notably a number of men who had worked within the regime's student union, the **Sindicato Español Universitario**. Within their ranks were to be found **Manuel Fraga, José Solís,** and Rodolfo Martín Villa (1934–). Their power base was located in the apparatus of the regime, and they hoped that by making the Movimiento Nacional more responsive to public opinion, they would both strengthen the regime and consolidate their position within it. The second reforming current comprised young men close to the **Asociación Católica Nacional de Propagandistas,** who had contacts with the ecclesiastical hierarchy and the worlds of industry and finance. Within these latter groups, there were growing criticisms of Francoism. From the late 1960s, the **Catholic Church**'s higher echelons largely broke with the regime, while big business also became increasingly exasperated by what it saw as the regime's inability to protect it from the demands of labor and get Spain into the **European Economic Community**. In these circumstances, by the early 1970s many of these young lay Catholics, influenced by **Christian-democratic** precepts, went further than the Movimiento *aperturistas* and began to think in terms of a far-ranging overhaul of the regime. In 1973, they founded a group called **Tácito.** As popular protest continued to grow during 1974–1975, members of Tácito came to realize that political democratization would be needed in order to avoid a dangerous crisis, which might lead to political and social polarization. It was on this basis that they began to negotiate with the opposition a controlled dismantling of the structures of Francoism leading to a **transition to democracy.**

ARAB WORLD. *See* COLONIES; DECOLONIZATION; FOREIGN POLICY; ISLAM AND SPAIN; MOORS; MOROCCO.

ARAGÓN, CROWN OF. *See* CROWN OF ARAGÓN.

ARANA Y GOIRI, SABINO DE (1865–1903). Sabino de Arana is regarded as the founding father of Basque nationalism. Not only did he organize the major party of Basque nationalism, the **Partido Nacionalista Vasco** (PNV), in 1895, he also played a key role in creating the myths and symbols that were thereafter to sustain Basque nationalism, including the invention of the name **Euskadi**, the nationalist term for the **Basque Country,** and the design of the nationalist **flag,** which he called the Ikuriña.

He probably first became interested in nationalism while living in **Barcelona** between 1882 and 1887. But his nationalist doctrine was rather different from that emerging in **Catalonia**. Arana came from a **Carlist** family and remained highly clerical. Moreover, his nationalism had clear racist elements, stressing the superiority of the Basques over "Spaniards." Like other anti-state nationalists, Arana looked back to a mythical golden age in which the Basques had lived in harmony. This was, he maintained, threatened for the first time in the ninth century when the Dominion of Vizcaya (Senorío de Vizcaya) and the **Crown of Castile** united. According to Arana the Basques still valiantly defended their independence—indeed, his most widely read work, *Cuatro patrias glorias* (*Four Glories of the Fatherland*), eulogized four mythical battles fought to retain Basque freedoms—but they were slowly sapped by intermarriage with Castilians. Basque freedom was then totally lost when the Basques' ancient privileges, the *fueros*, were undermined by Spain in 1839. Arana was, therefore, a convinced separatist, and he was only to waver in his demand for an independent Basque homeland in the final two years of his life under pressure from a more moderate group of Basque nationalists, known as the *euskalerríacos*. When he died in 1903, the PNV was still a small organization, but he was quickly deified in the Basque nationalist canon, and his ideas were to reverberate throughout the subsequent history of Basque nationalism.

ARANDA EZGUERRA, VICENTE (1926–). The filmmaker Vicente Aranda has come to prominence since the mid-1970s because of his success in adapting a number of major Spanish novels to the screen. An underlying theme of his films is the struggle for political, personal, and sexual freedom against the stifling values of **Catholic** conservatism and authoritarianism. In many of these films, he has drawn inspiration from antiestablishment, iconoclastic lifestyles and traditions in his native **Barcelona**. This can be seen, for example, in his first major success, *Cambio de sexo* (*Change of Sex*, 1976), a docudrama about transsexuals; in his adaptation of the critique of early Francoism, Luis Martín Santos's *Tiempo de silencio* (*A Time of Silence*, 1986); and in his sympathetic portrayal of female anarchist fighters during the **Spanish Civil War** in *Libertarias* (*Libertarians*,

1996). In 1992, he won the Goya Prize for best director and best film for *Amantes* (*Lovers*, 1991).

ARANJUEZ UPRISING/MOTÍN DE ARANJUEZ. This is the name given to a popular uprising against King **Carlos IV**'s unpopular favorite, **Manuel de Godoy** (and, by implication against the king himself), at the palace of Aranjuez near Madrid on 17–18 March 1808. It was orchestrated by the king's son, Fernando (the future **Fernando VII**), to whom the king was forced to abdicate. Its political content was reactionary; Fernando not only wished to seize power, he also aimed to halt the pro-**Enlightenment** policies pursued by Godoy.

ARAQUISTÁIN QUEVEDO, LUIS (1886–1959). Araquistáin was one of a number of intellectuals who joined the **Partido Socialista Obrero Español** (PSOE) after it signed the *conjunción* with the **republicans** in 1910. Araquistáin was not a convinced Marxist but a democrat who believed that, given the weakness of republicanism the PSOE was the only force that could economically and politically modernize the country. Yet once in the party he became radicalized. With the proclamation of the **Second Republic** he was made a subsecretary in **Francisco Largo Caballero**'s Ministry of Labor, and thereafter he became strongly identified with Largo Caballero's increasingly revolutionary discourse. Between 1934 and 1936, from his position as director of the mouthpieces of the PSOE left *Claridad* and *Leviatán*, his role became very much that of justifying Largo Caballero's actions in theoretical terms. With the onset of the **Spanish Civil War**, he became ambassador in Paris, but the fall of Largo Caballero in May 1937 provoked his own eclipse. The experience of the civil war also served to cool his revolutionary ardor, and in exile in the 1940s and 1950s he became a virulently anti-Communist liberal socialist.

ARBITRISTAS. This was the term used to describe a group of writers who, during the 17th century, commented on the ills of Spain, most notably its perceived "decline" from the late 15th century. Remedies varied, but there was a strong emphasis on the banning of foreign manufactures and on the reform of the tax system in order to take pressure off the more productive sectors of Spanish society. The *arbitristas* also evinced a strong hostility toward the Spanish empire in Europe, because of the heavy cost of defending it. The **count-duke of Olivares** tried to implement some of their ideas. Moreover, their emphasis on state action to improve the country's economic performance was taken up in the mercantilist policies pursued during the 18th century, most notably during the reign of **Carlos III**.

ARCHITECTURE. The historical roots of Spanish architecture are very eclectic. In **Andalusia** (under **Moorish** rule for up to seven centuries, depending on the area), Moorish influence can be seen in the so-called *mudéjar* style. Neo-*mudéjar* then made its appearance in the late 19th century and was popular in much of Spain. In **Catalonia**, the greatest architecture prior to the modern era dates from the Gothic period, in which the **Crown of Aragón** built a Mediterranean empire, while in **Castile**, architecture flowered during the Renaissance, when the **Crown of Castile** was at the heart of the Spanish **Habsburg** Empire. In the late 19th century, Catalonia was once again to rise to the forefront of Spanish architecture on the back of the *modernista* movement. *Modernisme*, which was inspired by European art-nouveau, drew on the territory's Gothic past and also flirted with neo-*mudéjar*. Its greatest exponent was **Antoni Gaudí**. In Spain as a whole, the 1920s were to see an interest in new modernist tendencies, but the **Franco regime**, in line with its traditional cultural policies, imposed a neoimperial style, which borrowed heavily from European Fascism. New European trends were, however, visible from the 1960s. From the **transition to democracy**, the new political elite and local authorities put urban renewal at the heart of their project to create a new modern Spain. This has over the last 20 years converted Spain into one of the most dynamic architectural centers in the world. In **Barcelona**, a key figure was Oriol Bohigas (1925–), who worked in tandem with the city council and played a lead role in the architectural renewal of the city in the run-up to the 1992 Olympics. Furthermore, major international figures, such as Norman Foster and Arata Isozaki, were given commissions. The 1980s also saw the emergence in **Valencia** of **Santiago Calatrava**, an architect who quickly achieved an international reputation. From the 1990s, Spanish cities also became increasingly aware of the importance of architecture in attracting **tourism**. The most impressive result is the titanium-clad Guggenheim

Art Gallery, designed by Frank O. Gehry, in Bilbao (and which draws inspiration from **Pablo Picasso**'s cubist art).

ARENAS BOCANEGRA, JAVIER (1957–). Javier Arenas is the most important figure within the **Partido Popular** (PP) in **Andalusia**. He was born in Seville and studied law at the local university. He built up his power base as a member of the **Unión del Centro Democrático** (UCD) in Seville local and Andalusian regional politics, reaching the position of head of the UCD youth wing. After the UCD imploded, he joined the PP and in 1989 became a PP parliamentary deputy for Seville. In **José María Aznar**'s 1996–2004 governments, he was appreciated for his greater ability to reach compromises and negotiate than some ministers, thereby giving the party a more centrist image. He was minister of labor in Aznar's first government. Then, in 1999, he took over as party secretary general, a post he held until 2003. In the July 2002 reshuffle, he also became the minister of public administration. In 2003, when **Mariano Rajoy** took over the party leadership, he was made government vice president (*ministro de la presidencia*). Following the PP defeat in the March 2004 general elections, he has focused on Andalusian politics and was the PP's candidate for the presidency in the 2008 regional elections. The PP substantially improved its position with respect to the 2004 elections, but the **Partido Socialista Obrero Español** was victorious.

ARIAS NAVARRO, CARLOS (1908–1989). Arias Navarro came to prominence during the death throes of the **Franco regime**, presiding over the last Francoist ministries from January 1974 to December 1975, and the first ministry of King **Juan Carlos I** between January and July 1976. He grew up in a lower-middle-class **Madrid** family, studied law, and entered the civil service in 1929. A convinced right-winger, during the **Spanish Civil War** he was briefly imprisoned by the Republican forces in Málaga. He was released when the **Nationalists** took the city, whereupon he was named military prosecutor and orchestrated the violent repression that followed (for which he became known in leftist circles as the "Butcher of Málaga").

During the Franco regime he maintained his reputation as a renowned hard-liner, his most notorious post being that of director general of security between 1957 and 1965. He first entered government as minister of the interior in **Luis Carrero Blanco**'s first government in June 1973. This was the result of a personal instruction by General **Francisco Franco** who, in response to the growing tide of opposition, wanted a sure pair of hands to deal with subversion. With the assassination of Carrero Blanco by **ETA** in December 1973, he became the new prime minister, after, it appears, Franco was convinced by diehards in his household that only a man like Arias Navarro could guarantee the survival of the regime. It was, therefore, a mark of the gravity of the crisis that Arias Navarro felt the need to offer some reform in order to mollify the moderate opposition and, most importantly, bring critics from within the regime onboard. Hence, he appointed some relatively liberal figures to his first ministry, including the reforming **Catholic** Pío Cabanillas (1923–1991), who was made minister of information and tourism.

A speech given by Arias Navarro on 12 February appeared to herald an "opening" (*apertura*) by the regime. The project of political associations within the **Movimiento Nacional**, first championed by **José Solís**, was disinterred, the election rather than appointment of mayors was proposed, the number of **Cortes** deputies not simply appointed was to be increased, and the **Organización Sindical Española** was to be given greater bargaining power. After this speech, there was talk of a reforming "spirit of 12 February." However, maneuvers by Francoist right-wingers, known from this year as the **Bunker**, or *ultras*, were to ensure that all these projects were to run into the sand. Within the **military**, the counteroffensive led to the replacement of the reforming chief of staff, General Manuel Diez Alegría, by a hard-liner, General Carlos Fernández Vallespín. The government's image was further compromised when the Bunker persuaded Arias Navarro to take action after the bishop of Bilbao, Antonio Añoveros (1909–1987), had on 24 February authorized four homilies calling for the respect of the rights of the Basques and other national minorities. Its standing took a further blow on 1 March when Franco refused to commute the death sentences passed by a military court on two anarchists, Salvador Puig Antich (1948–1974) and Pole Heinz Chez, accused of murdering a police officer while resisting arrest. At the same time, *ultras* launched a press campaign against reformers within the administration. Of most impact was the broadside by **José Antonio Girón** in the pages of the Movimiento daily *Arriba* (the so-called *Gironazo*). All this was played out against the background of ever-increasing worker, student, and nationalist protest. The final straw came when in October, convinced by his entourage that Pío Cabanillas was responsible for the wave of pornography that was supposedly invading Spain, Franco demanded he be sacked. A number of reformers then resigned in solidarity. This was an unheard-of step, and it was indicative of the weakening of the regime.

The project for the establishment of political associations continued, but it was now under the wing of the *ultra* minister secretary general of the Movimiento, José Utrera Molina (1926–). As a result, when it was approved by the Cortes in January 1975, it was so restrictive as to be virtually meaningless. Arias Navarro finally took some action against the *ultras*, sacking the director of the Movimiento press and the daily *Arriba*, after the paper had ignored the anniversary of his 12 February speech. And on 4 March he did put a somewhat more reform-oriented cabinet together. In particular, Utrera Molina was replaced by the known *aperturista* Fernando Herrero Tejedor (1920–1975). But Arias Navarro and the new government's aim was still to reform rather than dismantle the Franco regime. A more far-reaching transformation would not be contemplated until the death of Franco on 20 November 1975. It was once **Juan Carlos** came to power that the **transition to democracy** really began. King Juan Carlos I, who had already indicated his reforming intentions, at first moved cautiously and reappointed Arias Navarro, but he was quickly to prove himself incapable of presiding over major reform, and so, after being declared an "unmitigated disaster" by Juan Carlos, he was asked to resign in June.

ARMY. *See* MILITARY.

ARRESE Y MAGRA, JOSÉ LUIS DE (1905–1986). José Luis de Arrese reached prominence as minister secretary general of the **Franco regime**'s single party, the **Falange Española Tradicionalista y de las Juntas de Ofensiva Nacional Sindicalista** (FET y de las JONS), during the 1940s and 1950s.

He was related by marriage to **José Antonio Primo de Rivera**'s mother and joined the **Falange Española** during the **Second Republic**. With the outbreak of the **Spanish Civil War**, he initially opposed the Falange's subordination to the Francoist state and in April 1937 was briefly jailed as an "old-shirt" rebel for backing maneuvers against General **Francisco Franco**, led by the Falange's leader Manuel Hedilla (1902–1970). Once released, however, he showed himself eager to cooperate with the regime, was made provincial chief of the Málaga branch of the FET y de las JONS, and began to write on Falangist social policy. After the crisis of May 1941, in which the Falangist daily, *Arriba*, criticized the appointment of Colonel Valentín Galarza (1882–1951) as minister of the interior, Arrese was appointed secretary general of the single party by Franco. Franco knew that Arrese's old-shirt credentials and radical rhetoric would be pleasing to Falangist veterans, while at the same time Arrese would be loyal to his person and could be relied on to domesticate the Falange and ensure its subordination. Moreover, unlike **Ramón Serrano Suñer**, Franco had no fear that he would try to build a personal power base. In this respect, Arrese did a good job. Nevertheless, with the defeat of the Axis, Arrese was compromised by his Fascist past and pro-German beliefs. Hence, when in 1945 the regime felt it necessary to foreground its **Catholic** image, Arrese lost his post (which was to remain vacant for three years), even though he remained on friendly terms with Franco.

Nevertheless, once the regime had been stabilized, Franco felt strong enough briefly to bring Arrese back in February 1956, following student and worker protest. Indeed, in order to counterbalance rising pro-**monarchist** agitation, he was given the go-ahead by Franco to redefine the role of the single party. His plan would have given the FET y de las JONS a far more powerful role within the state apparatus. This was, however, to prove the party's swan song. The plan was undermined by Church and **military** resistance, and Arrese was moved to the minor post of minister of housing in the new cabinet reshuffle of 22 February 1957. He retained the position for three years but resigned in March 1960 after complaining that the Ministry of Finance was blocking his house-building program. He subsequently retired from public life.

ARZALLUS ANTIA, XABIER (1932–). Arzallus was the key figure of the **Partido Nacionalista Vasco** (PNV) during the 1980s and 1990s. He was born in the town of Azcoitia (Guipúzcoa) into a **Carlist** family. This very much conditioned his early life. He joined the Jesuits at the age of 10 and remained in the order until 1967. During this time, he completed an arts degree at the University of Salamanca and a PhD in Germany. However, in 1967 he renounced his vows and moved into nationalist politics, affiliating with the PNV. By the time of the **transition to democracy**, he had become a leading figure within the party. He was on its more moderate wing, through he strongly defended the restoration of the Basque *fueros*, with the result that he was critical of the **Constitution of 1978**, which he did not believe had gone far enough. He was a deputy in the Spanish parliament between 1977 and 1979 and was elected president of the PNV in 1979. Arzallus remained president through to 1984 and again held the post between 1986 and 2003.

The early years were marked by a confrontation between Arzallus (and his supporters) and the PNV president of the Basque autonomous government (*lehendakari*), Carlos Garaikoetxea (1938–), with the latter taking a more radical line than Arzallus and rejecting collaboration with the **Partido Socialista Obrero Español** (PSOE) in the Basque autonomous parliament. Garaikoetxea broke with the PNV in 1986 and set up his own party, **Eusko Alkartasuna**. Between 1982 and 1996, Arzallus favored working with the ruling PSOE and, subsequently, after the Partido Popular (PP)'s electoral victory in this latter year, gave the green light to an agreement with the party, allowing **José María Aznar** to form his first government. However, faced with an erosion of the Basque nationalist vote during the 1990s and the assumption by the PP of an aggressive Spanish nationalist discourse, from 1998 he shifted his stance in order to unite the Basque nationalist camp. This involved what could be termed the adoption of a defensive radical discourse and strategy. He sanctioned an accord with **ETA**'s political wing, **Herri Batasuna**, aimed at bringing ETA violence to an end while emphasizing the **Basque Country**'s right to independence. This new stance culminated in the "Plan Ibarretxe" (named after the PNV *lehendakari* Juan José Ibarretxe [1957–]), which, if implemented, would give the Basque parliament powers to call a referendum on the territory's future political status. Arzallus's radical language earned him the enmity of the Spanish nationalist camp, and in his last years as president he was the subject of bitter, often personal, attacks by the right-wing press. Nevertheless, he is a straight-talking charismatic figure, widely revered in Basque PNV circles. He has recently unambiguously declared himself a separatist.

ASOCIACION CATÓLICA NACIONAL DE PROPAGANDISTAS (ACNP)/NATIONAL CATHOLIC ASSOCIATION OF PROPAGANDISTS. The ACNP was an elite lay Catholic association founded in 1909 in order to defend and disseminate Catholic values among the upper classes and, at the same time, win over the lower orders. Under the leadership of Angel Herrera Oria (1886–1968), the association promoted its views though the daily paper *El Debate* (along with a host of regional papers), organized summer schools and lecture tours, and played a key role in the propagation of the Catholic agrarian associations in central and northern Spain through the foundation of the **Confederación Nacional Católica Agraria**. Its ultimate aim was a more authoritarian, confessional, Catholic state. It therefore welcomed the coming of the **Primo de Rivera dictatorship** and played a key role in institutionalizing the regime and molding its ideology. In order to furnish the regime with a political base, in the autumn of 1923 it began to set up provincial associations called Uniones Patrióticas (Patriotic Unions), which the regime's military directory then turned into its single party. This ensured that in subsequent years the regime's ideology would be **corporatist-**Catholic.

Less congenial was the coming of the **Second Republic**. From the outset, the ACNP worked hard to set up a mass Catholic party. It was the major force behind the creation of the **Confederación Española de Derechas Autónomas** in 1933, threw its weight behind the **Nationalist** forces during the **Spanish Civil War**, and played a key role in the elaboration of **National Catholicism** during the **Franco regime**. However, from the 1950s, like the **Catholic Church** as a whole, it began to lose its unity of purpose as some members of the organization began to call for reform and liberalization. A key figure in the first stages of this process was **Joaquín Ruiz-Giménez**, who, after being sacked as minister of education in 1956, organized a **Christian-democratic** opposition to the regime. Subsequently, members of the reforming **Tácito** group, founded in 1973, who were associated with the ACNP, began calling for a total democratic overhaul of Francoist institutions.

ASOCIACIÓN DE VÍCTIMAS DEL TERRORISMO (AVT)/ ASSOCIATION OF TERRORIST VICTIMS. This was an association formed in 1981 by people who had been affected by the **terrorist** activities of **ETA** and **GRAPO**. It has come into prominence since the late 1990s, as ETA's post-1992 strategy of targeting local politicians produced growing discontent in **Basque** and Spanish society. A key moment in this respect was the murder of the **Partido Popular** (PP) councilor Miguel Ángel Blanco in July 1997. After the electoral victory of the **Partido Socialista Obrero Español** (PSOE) in the March 2004 general elections, under the presidency of Felipe Alcaraz, it was very much identified with the policies of the opposition PP. Hence, it demanded that there should be no discussions with ETA and **Herri Batasuna** and that ETA prisoners should serve their full prison terms. Following contacts between the government and ETA in 2005, in 2006 it mobilized against government policies, holding a number of major demonstrations. These were marked by an aggressive antigovernmental rhetoric (which included accusations that **José Luis Rodríguez Zapatero** was in ETA's pocket) and strident Spanish nationalism. At present, it has about 6,000 members. However, most of those affected by the March 2004 **Madrid train bombings** affiliated with an alternative association, Asociación 11-M Afectados del Terrorism, under the presidency of the left-wing sympathizer Pilar Manjón. This association was very critical of the PP's decision to back the **Iraq war** and of the PP's attempts to claim that ETA was involved in the Madrid attacks. On the contrary, the AVT backed PP claims that the government was hiding the truth and that ETA had some kind of role in the bombings.

ASTURIAN REVOLUTION. *See* OCTOBER 1934 REVOLUTION.

AUTARKY. The word *autarky* is commonly used to refer to the policy pursued by the **Franco regime** between 1939 and 1959. Autarky was the outcome of the clerico-Fascist discourse of early Francoism, which affirmed that Spain should rediscover greatness from within rather than look to destructive foreign influences. Inspiration should above all be sought in the values of the Spain of the **Catholic Monarchs**, which had been insidiously undermined by the foreign **Enlightenment**, liberal, and socialist ideas that had penetrated Spain since the 18th century.

Autarky had both economic and cultural facets. The policy of economic autarky was formally initiated on 5 June 1939. As far as possible, imports were substituted for home-produced goods, and incentives were given to manufacturers to set up new factories in areas designated of national interest. These **industries** were then forced, where possible, to use domestic raw materials and capital goods. In order to implement this program, a state holding company, the **Instituto Nacional de Industria**—modeled on Benito Mussolini's Istituto per la Ricostruzione Industriale—was set up in 1941 to stimulate heavy industry, electricity supply, shipbuilding, and the automobile industry. At the same time, the peseta was grossly overvalued and a system of export and import licenses and exchange controls established. This put a brake on imports and made it virtually impossible for many sectors of the **economy** to export. Preference was at least rhetorically given to **agriculture**, and the Castilian peasantry was eulogized as the incarnation of Spanish values. Yet, in reality, the peasants had to hand over wheat to the state at low fixed rates, while landlords were able to operate through the black market.

Economic autarky soon showed its limitations. The attempt to limit imports caused shortages and led to bottlenecks. Moreover, the lack of fertilizers and agricultural machinery meant that agricultural production did not recover its prewar levels during the 1940s, leading to serious food shortages. Rationing and the complex range of licenses and incentives also led to massive **corruption** within the state apparatus and the appearance of a burgeoning black market. In urban Spain, the working class, deprived of independent unions, suffered greatly, seeing its real wages reduced to 50 percent of prewar levels, and this in turn greatly reduced the market for manufactures.

Cultural autarky manifested itself in both restrictions on foreign books and newspapers and on travel and cultural exchange with western Europe. It was reinforced by the ideological discourse, mentioned previously, which cast suspicion on foreigners and foreign culture and denigrated liberal-democratic systems of governance. However, the failings of economic autarky, along with the evident economic success of economic liberalization in much of western Europe, led to the relaxation of autarkic controls in the 1950s. The shift was further stimulated by growing ties with the United States, which, because of the Cold War, moved closer to the staunchly anticommunist Franco regime. Economic autarky was finally abandoned with the 1959 **Stabilization Plan**. The promotion of foreign **tourism** and short-term migration of Spanish workers in the 1960s subsequently signaled the relaxation of cultural autarky. *See also* ECONOMIC POLICY; TARIFF POLICY.

AUTONOMOUS COMMUNITIES. *See* STATE OF THE AUTONOMIES.

AVUI. *Avui* is **Catalonia**'s leading daily newspaper published in **Catalan**. It first came out in 1976 and has since adopted a strongly **Catalanist** stance, supporting campaigns for both the "normalization" of the **Catalan language** (i.e., generalized usage in the public sphere, schools, and administration) and for greater autonomy for the territory. However, because it has been closely associated with the conservative Catalanist coalition **Convergència i Unió** (indeed, it receives funding from the Catalan autonomous government, the **Generalitat**), and because its general coverage of international affairs, culture, and society has not been that strong, it has not built up a very large circulation. In 2007, it sold a little over 28,000 copies a day.

AZAÑA DÍAZ, MANUEL (1880–1940). Manuel Azaña was the leading light in liberal-**republican** politics in early 20th-century Spain. He was born into a **liberal** family in Alcalá de Henares on 10 January 1880, and soon showed himself to be an extremely able student, studying law at the University of Zaragoza. In the second decade of the century, he turned to journalism and politics. In 1913, he was made secretary of the Madrid Athenaeum (Ateneo), where he developed his oratorical skills, and joined **Melquíades Álvarez**'s Partido Reformista. He strongly supported the Allies during **World War I**, sending back reports from the front in 1916. From 1918, he also edited the prestigious journal *España* with **José Ortega y Gasset**.

During these years, then, Azaña was a reformer but by no means a radical, believing, like many liberal intellectuals of the time, that **education** and culture were the keys to the country's modernization. The **Primo de Rivera dictatorship** had a radicalizing effect. In 1925, he declared himself a republican and formed his own party, Acción Republicana (Republican Action). He played a leading role in the conspiracy against **Alfonso XIII**, which culminated in the **San Sebastián Pact** of August 1930. In the republican/**Partido Socialista Obrero Español** (PSOE) government, set up in April 1931, he became minister of war, a post confirmed after the June 1931 general elections. Azaña's most important task during 1931 was to put in place the government's **military** reforms, aimed at creating a more efficient, nonpolitical army. He was also closely involved in the government's anticlerical legislation, uttering the (in)famous phrase in parliament in December 1931 that "Spain is no longer **Catholic**." When **Niceto Alcalá Zamora** resigned as prime minister in October 1931 over the issue of Church reform, Azaña took his place. Over the next year and a half, he would be concerned that the reform program should be put into effect in an orderly fashion. This led to clashes with the far left and particularly with the **anarchists**. In one especially unfortunate incident in January 1933, during an attempted anarchist uprising against the Republic, some peasants were massacred in the Andalusian town of **Casas Viejas**. This led to a campaign against the government and Azaña in particular in the right-wing **press**.

Following the left's defeat in the November 1933 elections, Azaña's star was for a time eclipsed as the leader of the PSOE left **Francisco Largo Caballero** held center stage with his talk of proletarian revolution. Following the **October 1934 revolution** Azaña, despite not having participated, was nevertheless jailed for over a month. Once released, he again quickly returned to the fore. The fact that the road to revolution had led to a dead end meant that the need to rebuild the 1931–1933 alliance between the PSOE and the republican parties was once again on the agenda. Azaña quickly took the lead. From April 1934, he managed to unite the various left republican groupings into a new party, called Izquierda Republicana (Republican Left), under his leadership. He then entered negotiations with **Indalecio Prieto**, the leader of the moderate wing of the PSOE. At the same time, he held a number of open-air meetings at which he outlined his program. They were massively attended, showing the groundswell of support for unity. Prieto wished to re-form the 1931–1933 coalition, but the main obstacle was the left Socialists under Largo Caballero. This was not resolved until December 1935, when it was decided that a **Popular Front** coalition would be formed to fight the next election, but if it won the elections, the government would be limited to republicans.

This made it possible for Azaña once again to become prime minister in February 1936. The following months would not, however, be happy ones. The relatively weak republican government was caught in the middle of an increasingly polarized social confrontation. This was made worse in May, when Azaña was elevated to the post of president. This was part of a maneuver to bring Prieto into the government as prime minister, but the move was blocked by Largo Caballero, leaving the post of prime minister to be filled by the ineffective Santiago Casares Quiroga (1894–1950). As president, Azaña was never again to play a central role in Spanish politics. During the **Spanish Civil War**, he was troubled by the social revolution in the Republican zone and became increasingly uneasy at the growing role of the **Partido Comunista de España** in Republican politics. From 1937, he was also pessimistic at the Republic's chances of survival. This finally led him to resign on 5 February 1939, because he felt it was useless to make further sacrifices. He died in poverty in exile in Bordeaux the following year.

AZCÁRATE MENÉNDEZ, GUMERSINDO DE (1840–1917). Azcárate was one of the leading exponents of **Krausism** in late 19th- and early 20th-century Spain. He was from an intellectual background—he studied law at the Universities of Oviedo and Madrid before gaining a chair at the University of Madrid in 1873. During the **Democratic Sexennium**, he was affiliated to the **Partido Progresista**, but, with the **Cánovas Restoration**, he moved into the **republican** camp. From his position on the "governmental" wing of the republican movement, Azcárate defended both the need to extend democratic liberties and to institute social reforms. He was to hold a number of important posts. After being expelled from his university chair, he played a key role in setting up the **Institución**

Libre de Enseñanza, and, from 1903, he presided over the **Instituto de Reformas Sociales**. In 1913, he accepted **Melquíades Álvarez**'s strategy of reforming the Restoration regime from within rather than looking to overthrow it from outside, and joined the Partido Reformista.

AZNAR LÓPEZ, JOSÉ MARÍA (1953–). Aznar governed Spain between 1996 and 2004, handing over power to **Mariano Rajoy** shortly before the March 2004 elections. He was born into a conservative, well-to-do Madrid family; like many of his class, he was sent to the well-known private Catholic school El Pilar and then went on to study law at the Complutense University of Madrid. On completing his studies in 1975, he became a tax inspector in Logroño, but soon became interested in politics. Both his grandfather and father were Francoists, and during the **transition to democracy**, Aznar considered himself a Fascist **Falangist** (a supporter of the "authentic" Falangists, who throughout the regime had demanded a "real" Fascist revolution—the so-called *revolución pendiente*). However, on joining the rightist coalition led by **Manuel Fraga Ibarne**, **Alianza Popular** (AP), in 1979, he began to shift his stance. He proved hardworking, tenacious, and efficient and progressed rapidly through the party apparatus. He was elected to parliament for the district of Ávila in 1982 and became a member of the AP's national executive committee and directing committee. In June 1987, he led AP to victory in the elections to the autonomous community of Castile-León, making him the only young party activist to hold a position of considerable responsibility. This was to catch the eye of Fraga.

This occurred in a context in which AP's inability to seriously challenge the **Partido Socialista Obrero Español** (PSOE) government was producing a growing crisis in the party. Aznar was a member of a group of younger party members who argued that AP needed both to be more centralized and present a more centrist image. Given the ineffective leadership of Antonio Hernández Mancha (1951–), Fraga supported this stance and, from 1988, pushed strongly for Aznar to take over the reins of the party. As a result, in the party's ninth congress, held in January 1989—at which AP changed its name to **Partido Popular** (PP)—Aznar became vice president and the party's presidential candidate for the October 1989 general elections.

In the party's 10th congress in March–April 1990, he then became president, and in February 1993 was again chosen to lead the party into the next general election.

Aznar was not a charismatic figure, and he was also prone to adopt a cold and strident tone. However, under his strong leadership the party underwent a generational renewal, became more unified and toned down some of its more right-wing policies. As a result, Aznar would build up an unassailable position as party leader. The PP also took the opportunity afforded by the weakening of the PSOE government — particularly the **corruption** scandals in which it was immersed — to vociferously deny its fitness to govern. This combination of factors turned it into a serious alternative. Finally, the party won the March 1996 general elections, though it lacked an overall majority. In the wake of Thatcherism, Aznar believed that neoliberalism provided the key to Spain's economic modernization, and, once in power, emphasized the need to balance the budget and introduce tax cuts, and accelerated the Socialists' timid program of **privatizations**. At the same time, he wanted give Spain a higher profile on the world stage and maintained that a more Atlanticist stance was the key to such recognition.

During his first government, between 1996 and 2000, he needed the support in parliament of **Basque** and **Catalan** nationalists. This moderated Aznar's policies and tone, but after the party won an overall majority in 2000, he took a more aggressive and confrontational stance, tending to demonize adversaries. He also adopted a regal and distant air and was quick to dismiss criticism. This could be seen in a number of areas. His government's attempt to impose labor and university reforms led to one-day strikes, and its decision to upgrade the importance of religious education in schools produced a bitter polemic. Aznar was also concerned that the claims of Catalan and, in particular, Basque nationalists were endangering Spanish unity, and from 1998 onward savagely attacked the **Partido Nacionalista Vasco** for, in his view, giving succor to **ETA terrorism** (ETA, it should be noted, had come close to assassinating him in Madrid in April 1995). He combined this stance with an unabashed attempt to reassert Spanish identity and portrayed himself as the defender of Spanish unity. And he was also not afraid to take his Atlanticism to its ultimate consequences and give vociferous backing to the U.S.-led invasion of **Iraq**. This engendered widespread opposition in

Spain, manifested in massive antiwar demonstrations. Many on the left responded that Aznar's claims to "centrism" were a sham, which served as a cover for his assertive neoconservatism.

As a result, Aznar has become a very controversial figure. He was much admired by more conservative sectors of the electorate, who saw him as unafraid to champion Spanish interests and carry through reforms that would benefit the country in the teeth of fierce opposition (and here the comparison with Margaret Thatcher again raises its head). On the left, however, he was increasingly viewed as a hardline right-winger, who by mobilizing Spanish nationalism and allying Spain with the neoconservative "war on terror" was playing a dangerous game. The combined result of these factors was an increasingly polarized political climate, especially from 2000.

At the beginning of his second legislature he announced that he would not present himself as presidential candidate in the next elections. His power within the party was indicated by the fact that in 2003, he was able to handpick his successor, **Mariano Rajoy**, who was then ratified in a party congress. Subsequently, Aznar has taken up a number of lucrative consultancies with U.S. companies (most notably Centaurus Capital and J. E. Roberts), and in June 2006 was given a seat on the board of Rupert Murdoch's News International. Nevertheless, he still remains influential within the PP.

AZORÍN. *See* MARTÍNEZ RUIZ, JOSÉ.

– B –

BANDERA ROJA/RED BANNER. This far-left-wing organization, formed in 1968, provided the main opposition to the **Partido Comunista de España** (PCE)-**Partit Socialista Unificat de Catalunya** (PSUC) within the labor confederation **Comisiones Obreras** (CC. OO) in **Catalonia** during the early 1970s. Bandera Roja criticized the Catalan Communists' "reformism," thereby taking on the mantle of previous leftist organizations that had fought for socialist revolution. It had a significant working-class base among young men in the Baix Llobregat valley near **Barcelona**. In 1970, it was renamed Organización Comunista (Communist Organization), but in 1973 the more moderate wing, led by Jordi Sole Tura (1930–), broke away to form Bandera Roja de Cataluña (Catalan Red Banner). Sole Tura and many of his supporters were later to integrate into the PSUC.

BANKING. Spain's industrialization process was accompanied, from the late 19th century, by the establishment of a powerful financial oligarchy (centered above all in **Madrid** and Bilbao), which had a major stake in the country's large-scale **industry** (most notably **iron and steel** and shipbuilding in the **Basque Country**). Under the **Franco regime**, the country's major banks enjoyed official protection, ensuring both high profits and poor service. This encouraged the growth of mutual savings banks (*cajas de ahorros*), which were originally founded by the **Church** or local authorities. Two in particular, La Caixa and La Caja de Madrid, have expanded rapidly in recent years, setting up branches throughout Spain. At the same time, the commercial banks' close connection with industry persisted (with the six major banks controlling over 40 percent of the largest private industrial companies in Spain in the 1970s). This combination of state protection and close connections with industry did at least ensure that when the banking system was liberalized after **Francisco Franco**'s death, several commercial banks had the financial muscle to become significant international players. A process of mergers, set in train from the late 1980s, has led to the emergence of two major Spanish banks, Banco de Bilbao Vizcaya Argentaria (BBVA) and Banco Santander Central Hispano (BSCH). These two banks bought into the newly **privatized** Spanish industries in the 1990s and also invested heavily in **Latin America**, both in local banks and in major businesses (often themselves in the process of privatization). Subsequently, they have also sought to establish a presence in Europe, China, and India. The BSCH acquired the British building societies Abbey National and Alliance and Leicester in 2005 and 2008 respectively, while in 2006 BBVA bought into the Chinese bank CITIC. In 2000, in terms of market capitalization, BBVA and BSCH were Europe's eighth and sixth largest banks respectively. *See also* CONDE, MARIO.

BARCELONA. Barcelona, the capital of **Catalonia**, is situated on the northeast coast of Spain. It occupies a plain flanked by the Tibidabo and Montjuïc mountains and by the Llobregat and Besòs Rivers. In 2007, there were 1,595,110 people living in Barcelona proper and 3,150,380 in the greater metropolitan area.

Although **Madrid** is the capital of Spain, over the past two centuries Barcelona has been the most industrially and culturally dynamic Spanish city. It was the only Spanish city significantly to industrialize from the early 19th century, when **cotton textiles** were mechanized and a factory-based system of manufacture was established. Growth was relatively sluggish during much of the 19th and 20th centuries, but from the 1960s a new wave of industrial development transformed the greater metropolitan area of Barcelona, with large chemical, metal, and automobile plants making their presence felt.

The genesis of an industrial society meant that in the 19th century the physiognomy of the Catalan capital was rapidly transformed. In the early 19th-century city, life was centered on the medieval Gothic Quarter, but from the second half of the century, new urban space opened up, with a concomitant recasting of social and geographical relations. The wealthy middle classes moved into the rectilinear Eixample (Extension), designed by Ildefons Cerdà (1815–1876), which stretched up from the outer limit of the old town (the Plaça Catalunya) to the neighboring town of Gràcia (integrated into Barcelona in 1904). Henceforth, the richer one was, the nearer one lived to the Passeig de Gràcia. Workers, many migrants from the surrounding countryside and further afield, moved into proletarian districts on the periphery (Sants, Sant Martí de Provençals, Sant Andreu de Palomar, Poble Nou). From the 1960s, however, these districts themselves became increasingly gentrified and working-class habitats were pushed out to "satellite towns" like Bellvitge and Cornellà.

The middle classes felt that they had little to learn from courtly Madrid society and instead looked to Paris for fashion and social mores. From the mid-19th century, a new bourgeois cultural milieu grew up, centered on the opera, theater, and café. From the 1890s, proximity to the Western centers of cultural production also fostered a dynamic cultural climate, exemplified by the *modernista* architecture of **Antoni Gaudí** (who designed the emblematic Sagrada Família or Church of the Holy Family) and Lluís Domènech i Montaner (1850–1923), and by the painting of **Pablo Picasso**, and later, **Salvador Dalí** and **Joan Miró**.

But industrial society also brought social conflict. The **Unión General de Trabajadores** was first set up in Barcelona in 1888 (though the Socialists found it difficult to recruit in the city before the **Spanish Civil War**). Barcelona was also a center of **republicanism** from the 1860s and the stomping ground of the virulently anticlerical followers of **Alejandro Lerroux** in the first decade of the 20th century. It became, most significantly, the headquarters of Spanish **anarchism** and the birthplace of the anarcho-syndicalist **Confederación Nacional del Trabajo** in 1910. As a result, during the first third of the century, the city was the focus of sustained, often violent, worker protests and strikes. This was to culminate during the civil war, when much of the city's industry was collectivized. The **transition to democracy** in the 1970s was also to witness a revival of strikes and protest, but without the violence associated with the early part of the century.

In addition, Barcelona was the focus of the Catalan nationalist or **Catalanist** movement, which became such a central element of Spanish political life in the 20th century. This growth had much to do with the feeling in middle-class Barcelona circles that the city's expansion was being held back by inefficient administration from Madrid. And the existence of a separate **Catalan language** and a different economic and cultural milieu allowed this discontent to be expressed in nationalist terms. The key moments in the rise of Catalanism were the foundation of the conservative regionalist/nationalist party the **Lliga Regionalista** in 1901 and the more radical **Esquerra Republicana de Catalunya** in 1931. The Catalanist challenge brought a violent reaction in right-wing Spanish circles, with claims that the unity of the Spanish nation was in jeopardy, and, consequently, the right-wing authoritarian dictatorships of General **Miguel Primo de Rivera** and General **Francisco Franco** attempted to stamp out Catalan(ist) culture and the Catalan language. Most liberal and leftist Spaniards have, on the other hand, been more understanding, with the result that during the **Second Republic** and again after the **transition to democracy**, it proved possible to negotiate home rule, giving Catalonia its own autonomous government—the **Generalitat**—whose headquarters is to be found in the Plaça Sant Jaume in Barcelona.

Since the return of democracy, Barcelona has prospered. It suffers from relatively high levels of petty crime (much of it drug-related), but under the intelligent direction of the Barcelona mayors, Narcís Serra (1943–) and, especially, **Pascual Maragall**, the city has been greatly improved. Much of the Gothic Quarter has been pedestrianized and squares rehabilitated. The 1992 Olympic Games in particular were used to modernize the city's road infrastructure and to open up the city to the sea. This involved the reconstruction of the old working-class district of Poble Nou, and a total reform of the port, with the building of a great new walkway and beaches along the city's sea frontage. This has been accompanied by a cultural revival, especially in the fields of theater—with such groups as Teatre Lliure, Els Comediants, and the **Fora dels Bous**—and design. The result is that Barcelona is now rightly regarded as a key attraction for tourists and one of Europe's central cultural destinations.

BARCELONA FC. Fútbol Club Barcelona was founded by a Swiss, Hans Kamper (usually referred to by his Catalanized name, Joan Gamper), in 1899. However, it was transformed into "més que un club" (more than a club) during the **Primo de Rivera dictatorship** in the 1920s, when it became identified with **Catalanist** resistance to the dictator's Spanish nationalist policies. The club's symbolic status was heightened during the **Franco regime**, which, particularly during the 1940s, fiercely repressed the leftist and Catalanist opposition and the **Catalan language** (with the exception of Church publications). At the same time, the regime tried to downgrade what were now widely seen as manifestations of Catalan identity to a marginal regional-folkloric status. Support for FC Barcelona therefore became a way of surreptitiously expressing opposition. It is also in this period that the bitter rivalry with **Real Madrid** developed, the latter widely viewed in **Catalonia** as the regime's team. As a manifestation of this opposition, in the 1960s FC Barcelona democratized its organizational structure and is now owned by its 110,000 members (*socis*). Over the years, it has also expanded its remit to cover other sports, most notably basketball and handball. *See also* BARCELONA.

BARDEM MUÑOZ, JUAN ANTONIO (1922–2002). Along with **Luis Berlanga** and **Luis Buñuel** (who, however, hailed from the 1930s surrealist generation), Bardem was the best-known Spanish director of the Francoist era. He made his mark with social comedies that satirized both the political regime and Spanish society, most notably *Bienvenido Mr Marshall* (*Welcome Mr Marshall*, 1952), which was codirected with Luis Berlanga. Subsequently, he produced darker and subtler critiques, with *Muerte de un ciclista* (*Death of a Cyclist*, 1955) and *Calle mayor* (*Main Street*, 1956) receiving international critical acclaim at the Cannes and Venice film festivals respectively. At the same time, Bardem became a member of the clandestine **Partido Communista de España** and spent time in prison. In post-Franco Spain, he maintained a critical-realist perspective in such works as *El Puente* (*The Long Weekend*, 1977) and the television film *Lorca, muerte de un poeta* (*Lorca: The Death of a Poet*, 1988). *See also* CINEMA.

BAROJA Y NESS, PÍO (1872–1956). Baroja formed part of the outstanding group of writers who made up the "**Generation of 1898.**" He was born in San Sebastián, but spent most of his life in **Madrid**. In the 1890s, he sympathized with **anarchism**, but he was first and foremost an individualist and was strongly influenced by the ideas of Friedrich Nietzsche (1844–1900) and Arthur Schopenhauer (1788–1860). This was reflected in his novelistic work, the central theme of which was the individual at war with himself and the world around him. His best-known work is *El árbol de la ciencia* (*Tree of Knowledge*, 1911).

BARRIONUEVO PEÑA, JOSÉ (1942–). Barrionuevo was an effective, no-nonsense home secretary in **Felipe González**'s governments between 1982 and 1998, and he was also minister of transport between 1988 and 1992. However, his standing was undermined when it emerged that he had played a leading role in the dirty war against **ETA** carried out by the **terrorist** group **GAL** between 1983 and 1988. In 1995, he lost his parliamentary immunity and in 1998 he was tried and found guilty of the kidnapping of Segundo Marey (who had been mistaken for a leading ETA activist). He only spent three months in prison and was given a partial pardon by the **Partido Popular** government of **José María Aznar** in December of that year. However, his sentence was confirmed by the Constitutional Tribunal in 2001 and he was imprisoned for three years.

BASQUE COUNTRY. The Spanish Basque Country is situated in the north of Spain, with the Bay of Biscay on its northern frontier and the Pyrenees on its eastern flank. It stretches inland about 150 kilometers, taking in the eastern end of the Cantabrian cordillera (the Basque mountains) and pushing on toward the Ebro plain. It comprises the provinces (or, in Basque nationalist terms, historical territories) of Álava, Vizcaya, and Guipúzcoa. In 2007, these three provinces had a **population** of 2,141,860 and since 1980, they have formed an autonomous community. Three smaller Basque provinces are also to be found in France (known as Iparralde in the Basque language), and these, together with the neighboring region of **Navarre**, which forms a separate autonomous community, are considered by Basque nationalists as an integral part of Basque territory. In referring to the autonomous community, it is now common to use the term **Euskadi**, first devised by the founder of Basque nationalism, **Sabino de Arana**, while radical Basque nationalists refer to their proposed pan-Basque area as **Euskal Herria**.

During most of the 19th century, the Basque Country was largely agricultural. Much of the land was owned by a relatively prosperous smallholding peasantry, who ensured that it was not subdivided by passing it on, through a system of primogeniture, to the eldest son. The Basque provinces had, since the early Middle Ages, formed part of the **Crown of Castile**, but, unlike the rest of the territory, they were largely self-governing, enjoying local privileges known as *fueros*. During the **War of Succession** in the early 18th century, privileges enjoyed in the **Crown of Aragón** were abolished by the new Bourbon king **Felipe V**, but the *fueros* were retained in the Basque provinces and in the Kingdom of Navarre. The peasantry also had its own **Basque language**, a pre-Roman tongue that was in no way related to **Castilian**, Spain's official language from the 18th century. The territory was a bulwark of the **Catholic Church**. Among the peasantry and in small provincial towns the percentage of priests in the local population was high and Church attendance by the whole family the norm.

During the early 19th century, these peasant and small-town communities were to come into direct conflict with the Spanish state. This was the result of the latter's attempt to centralize administration and abolish the *fueros*, its attack on the Church, and its policy of disentailment or *desamortización*, which, in the peasants' eyes, put land on the market that was rightfully theirs. In response, the Basque peasants, led by their local parish priests, flocked to the cause of **Carlism**. Only slowly, as the Church was partially integrated into the liberal regime from mid-century, did support for Carlism wane.

The entire social and economic structure of the Basque Country was shaken between the 1870s and 1900s when Vizcaya underwent a rapid industrial revolution. The basis of this revolution was the export of red hematite ore, largely to Great Britain, and the reinvestment of a large part of the profits in the construction of an indigenous **iron and steel industry**, followed by the diversification of capital into other sectors including, crucially, shipping and **banking**. This resulted in new social tensions and conflicts. Migrant workers from other Spanish regions flooded into the Basque Country, and from the 1890s began affiliating with the **Partido Socialista Obrero Español** (PSOE)-**Unión General de Trabajadores (UGT)**. This produced a virulent reaction in **Traditionalist** Basque circles. Under the leadership of **Sabino de Arana**, the nationalist **Partido Nacionalista Vasco** (PNV) was founded in 1895. Its program was the repatriation of the "foreign" workers, who were seen as endangering Basque traditions and customs, along with the call for a theocratic, independent Basque homeland. Arana even invented a new **flag** (the Ikuriña), christened the Basque language with the name of Euskera, and named the Basque territory "Euskadi."

Carlism's anticentralist vision made it relatively easy for ethnic Basques to make the transition to nationalism. Moreover, the identification of many priests with Basque particularisms meant that part of the Basque Church would in the future sympathize with nationalist aims. By the first decade of the century, as a result, Basque society was divided four ways. Many migrant workers were integrated in the PSOE-UGT, while the peasantry tended to maintain its allegiance to Carlism. The lower middle classes in Bilbao and other towns in Vizcaya began to rally behind the PNV. Large-scale industrialists, on the other hand, were highly dependent on the state and so put their weight behind the **Cánovas Restoration**. In the 1880s, they founded the **Liga Vizcaína de Productores** (Vizcayan League of Producers) to pressure the state into giving their **industries** greater **tariff** protection and state contacts, while at the same time integrating into the Spanish social elite. This pattern, in some respects, persisted until the 1930s. By this time, the PSOE-UGT had consolidated itself as the principal representative of the working class (though many ethnic Basque workers were members of the trade union Solidaridad de Obreros Vascos [Basque Workers' Trade Union], which was close to the PNV). The PNV integrated wide sectors of the ethnically Basque population, and big business remained largely linked to the "Spanish" right.

During these years the PNV found itself in a difficult position. It was a confessional party that rejected the **Second Republic**'s Church reforms, but at the same time it opposed the Spanish right's centralizing tendencies. Finally, during the **Spanish Civil War**, it came down on the side of the Republic, and in recognition the Basque Country was granted an autonomy statute in October 1936. This decision resulted in a fierce repression when the Francoist forces took Euskadi in the summer of 1937. The historic Basque town of Guernika was destroyed by German planes as part of the offensive and war casualties included 16 Basque nationalist priests assassinated by the Francoist rebels. Once it had defeated the Republic, the **Franco regime** tried to obliterate all traces of a separate Basque identity. In the official media, the Basque Country was referred to as the region of Vascongadas and its autochthonous language was forced underground.

From the 1960s, in the context of the "Spanish economic miracle," the territory was to experience further social disruption with a new, massive expansion of heavy industry in Vizcaya, and to a lesser extent in Guipúzcoa and Álava. The social tensions that resulted produced two largely separate opposition movements to Francoism. In the first place, workers launched a series of strikes for improved working conditions and free trade unions. Second, in the late 1960s, a group of young radicals who had broken away from the PNV to form **ETA** began a campaign of **terrorist** attacks on the **police** and **military**. In the early 1970s, political opposition to Francoism escalated throughout urban Spain, but nowhere was protest as intense and widespread as in the Basque Country. While Basque workers paralyzed whole towns and industries, a campaign was launched in favor of Basque language and culture, and ETA terrorist activity stepped up. The violent reaction of the authorities had by 1975 created an almost prerevolutionary climate. This would ensure that ETA emerged from the **transition to democracy** with a significant popular base. This was confirmed when its political front, **Herri Batasuna** (HB), was founded in 1978 and proceeded to obtain nearly 20 percent of the Basque vote at election time.

Nevertheless, the PSOE and PNV once again emerged as the largest parties in the area in the first democratic elections of 1978. This reflected the Socialists' strength in the working-class migrant community and the fact that most Basque nationalists were still socially conservative. The PNV had in the second half of the Franco regime also somewhat modernized its image, taking a **Christian-democratic** stance, and placing greater emphasis on language and culture, rather than race, as defining elements of Basque culture. The **Unión del Centro Democrático** government tried to calm the agitated Basque waters by granting a relatively generous autonomy statute (the Guernika Statute), which, as in the case of **Catalonia** and **Galicia**, made the local language co-official. However, the violence of the last years of the Franco regime would ensure that independence for the Basque Country retained quite a wide popular appeal (even among supporters of the PNV, which tacitly accepted the goal of autonomy rather than independence). Hence, ETA and HB were only slowly and partially marginalized from political life. A key moment in this respect was the 1988 Ajurea Enea Pact, which was signed by all the major Basque parties with the exception of HB, and which committed them to rejecting violence, working within the Guernika Statute, and working toward the reincorporation into civil life of ETA terrorists who rejected violence.

After its victory in the first Basque elections in 1980, the PNV (which governed in coalition with the Socialists from 1985 through to 1998) tried to reinvigorate the Basque language and local cultural traditions through Basque schools and **television**. However, it faced a more uphill struggle than its nationalist counterparts in Catalonia, in part because of the large number of migrants who spoke no Basque (only 21 percent of the population could speak Basque in 1984) and the extreme difficulty of learning the language.

The PNV also faced difficulty in generalizing nationalist sentiment. At their high point in the Basque elections in 1986, nationalist parties gained 68 percent of the vote, but this figure was to decline in the 1990s. One important reason may well have been the shift in ETA strategy after the capture of its leadership in Bidart in 1992. A new generation of ETA terrorists, thrown onto the defensive, resorted to sponsoring street riots (the Kale Barroka) and assassinating **Partido Popular** (PP) and PSOE local politicians and public figures in order to pressure the authorities. This probably eroded overall support for Basque nationalism. An organization first founded in 1981, the **Asociación de Víctimas del Terrorismo** (AVT), became much more vociferous, and from 1996, ETA assassinations were followed by big anti-ETA demonstrations in Basque towns and cities and in other parts of Spain. Then, following the assassination of the PNV local councilor from Ermua, Miguel Ángel Blanco, in July 1997, a number of left-leaning but anti-Basque nationalist intellectuals responded by forming an organization called the Foro de Ermua, many of whose members then joined the more overtly political platform, **Basta Ya**. In addition, Basque nationalism was put under further pressure because 20 years of democracy, accompanied by strong economic development from the mid-1880s, had produced a more confident Spanish political elite and a resurgent Spanish nationalist discourse. This became apparent when the PP came to power in 1996. It quickly showed itself keen to promote a stronger sense of Spanish identity, and, while it respected the **State of the Autonomies**, it rejected any permissive modifications.

Between 1997 and 1998, the PNV reacted to these developments by adopting what might be termed a defensive radicalism, attempting to end ETA terrorism and unite the nationalist political forces to a greater degree. In order to do this, it radicalized its discourse, demanding the reform of the Guernika Statute and claiming the right of the Basque Country to independence. At the same time it negotiated with HB an ETA cease-fire. The culmination of this approach was the 12 September 1998 Declaration of Lizarra (or Estela Pact) and the 16 September ETA cease-fire. With no signs of political concessions by the PP government, ETA broke its cease-fire the following November. Nevertheless, the PNV continued in the same vein, with the PNV *lehendakari* (president of the Basque parliament), Juan José Ibarretxe (1957–), putting forward his "Plan Ibarretxe" in September 2002. It reaffirmed the unity of all the Basque provinces (including Navarre and Iparralde) and proposed that the Basque parliament should have the right to call a referendum on the question of Basque independence and that the Basque Country should become a "free associated state" (*estado libre asociado*).

All this would have to be approved by the Spanish parliament. Nevertheless, the stance taken by the PNV provoked an increasingly virulent confrontation with the PP. Divisions were played out in the Spanish media, especially because both Catalanists and Galician nationalists also began calling for a reform of their statutes. Firebrand Spanish nationalist journalists, like Federico Jiménez Losantos (1951–), denounced Basque nationalism for endangering the unity of Spain and supposedly giving succor to ETA. Such fears were also voiced by non-Basque nationalist Basque commentators like the prestigious academic Jon Juaristi (1951–).

Once again, therefore, the "national question" was at the center of Spanish political life, and, unlike the situation during the transition to democracy, there seemed little appetite to reach a compromise. From the early 1990s, PP support in the Basque Country had grown rapidly and in the May 2001 Basque elections it hoped to inflict a historic defeat of the PNV and enter the Basque government. Its candidate for the presidency was the leading Basque politician **Jaime Mayor Oreja**, who had stepped down from his post as home secretary to present his candidacy. This offensive produced an intense and bitter campaign and a defensive reaction by much of the Basque nationalist community (including many radicals who normally backed HB), who voted for the nationalist coalition slate of PNV-**Eusko Alkartasuna** (EA). As a result, the PNV was able to hold on to power, forming a coalition government with EA and the small left-wing party Ezquer Batua Berdeak (which formed part of the Spanish political federation, **Izquierda Unida**). Nevertheless, Basque nationalist parties achieved only 52.4 percent of the vote—less than in any previous elections to the Basque parliament since the transition—while the major non-Basque nationalist statewide parties, the PP and Partido Socialista de Euskadi (PSE)-PSOE, attained 40.7 percent of the vote.

During 2002–2003, the PP then contemplated taking legal action against the PNV. It quickly appealed to the Constitutional Tribunal to declare the "Plan Ibarretxe" unconstitutional and introduced new legislation allowing for the imprisonment of anyone organizing an illegal referendum. Furthermore, the public prosecutor's office (*fiscalía*) brought an action against the PNV president of the Basque parliament, Juan María Atutxa (1941–), for not enforcing Spanish legislation and illegalizing Socialista Abertzaleak (as HB temporarily called itself). During 2003, Jaime Mayor Oreja also insinuated that the Basque autonomy statute could be suspended. This would have led to a grave social and political conflict of unforeseeable consequences.

However, the climate changed in the aftermath of the Socialist victory in the March 2004 general elections. The new prime minister, **José Luis Rodríguez Zapatero**, was more understanding of demands for the reform of the State of the Autonomies, though he rejected the Plan Ibarretxe, both because the PNV had not reached a consensus in the Basque Country, and, more importantly, because it questioned Spanish unity. The Basque branch of the PSOE, the PSE-PSOE, was also now favorably disposed toward Basque nationalism. The general secretary of the Basque Socialists between 1998 and 2001, Nicolás Redondo Terreros (the son of **Nicolás Redondo Urbieta**), had belonged to the more anti-Basque nationalist wing of the party and had taken a hard anti-PNV line, but this led to fears that the party was being eclipsed by the PP. Hence, he was forced to stand down at the end of 2001 and was replaced in March 2002 by Francisco Javier "Patxi" López (1959–), who was more inclined to enter into a dialogue. From this date, the president of the Basque PSOE, Jesús Eguiguren (1954–), held informal discussions with the leader of HB, Arnaldo Otegi (1958–), on ways of bringing ETA violence to a peaceful end. They had agreed that the key was to separate negotiations regarding the dissolution of ETA from political discussions on the future of the Basque Country.

Rodríguez Zapatero saw this as a possible way to bring ETA terrorism to an end once and for all. In March 2004, ETA accepted the proposal and in June 2005 secret discussions were held between ETA and government representatives in Geneva. An accord was finally reached the following month and ratified in December, leading ETA to declare a "permanent" cease-fire on 22 March 2006. However, it soon ran into similar problems as its predecessors. It had been agreed that the Basque parties would meet to discuss changes to the Basque statute, but by August ETA was unhappy that no political progress had been made and relaunched the Kale Barroka. Responding to this pressure, in November HB called for the rapid establishment of a joint Basque-Navarre legislative body. This, however, was rejected by both the PSE-PSOE and the PNV. The PSOE affirmed that the first thing HB had to do was unequivocally renounce violence. With respect to the PNV, it was represented in the negotiations by its new, more moderate president, Josu Jon Imaz (1963–), who stressed that all violence had to cease before an accord could be reached and that any accommodation would have to be accepted by all the major political forces in the Basque Country and Navarre.

In a meeting between ETA and government representatives in mid-December 2006, the former then once again put its political demands on the table regarding Navarre and Basque independence. On 30 December, it then effectively reneged on the cease-fire, bombing Madrid Barajas airport and, in the process, killing two Colombian migrant workers. The big problem once again proved to be that ETA was not willing to renounce violence without political concessions, and HB could not help deliver a compromise acceptable to both the PNV and the PSE-PSOE. After ETA confirmed that it had broken the cease-fire in June 2007, the government launched an all-out offensive. It also made clear that it was willing to negotiate modifications to the Basque autonomy state, but continued to reject the Plan Ibarretxe. *See also* ARCHITECTURE; UNAMUNO Y JUGO, MIGUEL DE.

BASQUE LANGUAGE. The Basque language grew up on both sides of the northern Pyrenees, in what are now the three French Basque departments, in the three provinces that make up the Spanish **Basque Country** (Guipúzcoa, Vizcaya, and Álava), and in the separate Spanish autonomous community of **Navarre**. At present it is regularly spoken by about 630,000 of these territories' three million inhabitants (a little over 20 percent of the population).

It is the only non-Indo-European language spoken in western Europe. Its origins are in dispute but—given the historical isolation and weak Romanization of the Basque territories—the most likely explanation is that its roots lie in the languages spoken prior to the Roman invasion of Iberia. Until the late 19th century, the Spanish Basque Country was largely rural, and this, together with the mountainous landscape, meant that the language had divided into a number of tongues that were, to a large extent, mutually unintelligible. Then, when Vizcaya began to industrialize in the late 19th century, the widely held view that Basque was a language of the backward peasantry, heavy migration from other parts of Spain, the fact that Basque was so different from **Castilian**, and the wide range of Basque dialects meant that Castilian became the dominant language in the rapidly expanded urban centers (especially Bilbao). Usage of Basque was bolstered by the growth of the Basque nationalist party, the **Partido Nacionalista Vasco** (PNV), from the 1890s, but the problems outlined above still put a break on its development. Subsequently, under the Spanish nationalist **Franco regime**, it faced heavy repression. Nevertheless, from the 1970s, with the **transition to democracy**, serious efforts have been made to revive the language. A standardized tongue (*batúa*) was adopted by the new Royal Academy of the Language, and, from 1980, the PNV-dominated autonomous governments have given strong financial support to the teaching of Basque.

BASTA YA/ENOUGH. This political platform has its origins in the Foro de Ermua, an association founded by a number of intellectuals in the **Basque Country** in July 1997, following the assassination by **ETA** of the **Partido Popular** (PP) local councilor Miguel Ángel Blanco. Its leading figures are the novelist and philosopher Fernando Savater (1947–) and Rosa Díez (1952–), the latter, until recently, increasingly isolated on the anti-Basque nationalist wing of the Basque **Partido Socialista Obrero Español** (the Partido Socialista de Euskadi [PSE]-PSOE). Basta Ya maintained that it could not be classified as either right- or left-wing, and defined itself as an antinationalist association that defended the Spanish constitution and the Basque Statute of Autonomy and that opposed negotiations with ETA under any circumstances. Its evolution has been marked by its hostility toward the "peripheral nationalisms" (above all the Basque, Catalan, and Galician nationalist parties), and opposition to further transfers of power to the autonomous communities. During 2005–2006, it was highly critical of the PSOE government for its decision to meet with ETA representatives and try to achieve a mediated solution to the Basque conflict. From the "peripheral nationalist" and PSOE camps, there have been criticisms that behind the nonnationalist facade lies a Spanish nationalist political agenda, as shown by the support it has received from the right-wing Spanish **press**, most notably *El Mundo*.

In June 2007, its leaders announced that they wished to set up a new political party to take on both the PSOE and PP in the March 2008 elections, and in August Rosa Díez (1952–) resigned from the PSE-PSOE in order to help build the new organization. It was formed in September under the name **Unión de Progreso y Democracia**. However, it failed in its attempt to link up with a similar movement operating above all in **Catalonia, Ciudadanos de Cataluña,** which had received strong backing from the Basta Ya leadership. Its key objective is to reform Spain's electoral law in order to reduce the weight of the "peripheral nationalisms" in Spanish political life.

BAYONNE CONSTITUTION. The Napoleonic Bayonne Constitution was in effect in occupied Spain between 1809 and 1813. On 23 May 1808, **Cortes** were convened to discuss the new constitution. However, participation was limited to collaborators (the so-called *afrancesados*), the "Three Estates" of French tradition (nobles, clergy, and the Third Estate) met separately, and a number of ecclesiastics, nobles, and others were simply handpicked. The Assembly of Notables met in the French town of Bayonne on 15 June. They presented a draft constitution to Napoleon Bonaparte along the lines of similar constitutions promulgated in the central and southern European French protectorates, which was promulgated on 6 July 1808.

The Bayonne Constitution combined authoritarian political structures with a partial liberalization of economy and society. Legislative initiative rested with the king, and bills were simply discussed (but could not be amended) by the various state organs—the State Council, Senate, and Cortes. The State Council and Senate were to be chosen by the king, and the franchise for elections to the Cortes was highly restrictive. At the same time, the size of entailed estates was limited and legal privileges abolished. As in other areas under French jurisdiction, the Napoleonic Code was also imposed. *See also* WAR OF INDEPENDENCE.

BERENGUER FUSTÉ, DÁMASO, COUNT OF XAUEN (1878–1953). Berenguer was one of the leading figures within the **military** and in Spanish political life between 1918 and 1931. An *africanista*, he had risen rapidly through the ranks in **Morocco**, achieving the rank of general in 1909, and was appointed minister of war in November

1918 and high commissioner for the Spanish Protectorate of Morocco in August 1919. As high commissioner, Berenguer devised an ambitious plan to pacify the Protectorate, which was to end ignominiously in July 1921, when the forces led by the military commander of Melilla recklessly advanced on the Bay of Alhucemas and were cut down by Moroccan tribesmen. A commission was then set up to look into what came to be known as the disaster of **Annual**, and as a result of its findings Berenguer was forced to resign and abandon active service. Following General **Miguel Primo de Rivera**'s coup, however, he was first pardoned and then given the position of head of the royal household. Further promotion was to follow after the resignation of Primo de Rivera in January 1930, when he was named head of government by King **Alfonso XIII**. For a year, Berenguer's so-called Dictablanda (mild dictatorship) would try to engineer a return to constitutional monarchy, but with the experience of the **Cánovas Restoration** discredited, it was to be an impossible task. He was finally replaced by Admiral Juan Bautista Aznar (1860–1933) on 17 February 1931, remaining in the cabinet as minister of war. After the left's victory in the municipal elections of 12 April, he made little attempt to defend the monarchy, but was, nevertheless, arrested by the new Republican authorities on 17 April for his involvement in the Annual disaster and role in the execution of the Republican martyrs Fermín Galán (1899–1930) and Ángel García Hernández (1900–1930), on 14 December 1930. He was found not guilty by the Republican Supreme Tribunal in 1935, but the trial of military figures such as Berenguer did much to fuel military resentment toward the new regime.

BERLANGA MARTÍ, LUIS GARCÍA (1923–). An early graduate of the National Film School, Berlanga gained an international reputation for his works of biting comic satire, critical of the Spanish social moors and of the **Franco regime**. He made his name with *Bienvenido Mr Marshall* (*Welcome Mr Marshall*, 1952), which he codirected with **Juan Antonio Bardem**, and followed it up with the harder-hitting works (developed in collaboration with the scriptwriter and novelist, Rafael Azcona [1926–]) *Plácido* (1962) and *El verdugo* (*The Executioner*, 1963). Lighter in tone was his successful post-Francoist social comedy *Escopeta nacional* (*National Rifle*, 1978). His 1985 metaphoric comedy reflecting on the **Spanish Civil War**,

La vaquilla (*The Little Bull*), also proved a great success. Subsequently, he won the Goya prize for best film and director for his 1994 film *Todos a la cárcel* (*Everyone off to Jail*). *See also* CINEMA.

BESTEIRO FERNÁNDEZ, JULIÁN (1870–1940). Besteiro was the most eminent of a group of intellectuals who affiliated with the **Partido Socialista Obrero Español** (PSOE) during the second decade of the 20th century. He was born in **Madrid**, studied arts at university, and went on to become a philosophy professor. From the turn of the century, he also became involved in **republican** politics, joining the **Unión Republicana** and later the **Partido Republicano Radical**. Nevertheless, after a trip to Germany between 1909 and 1911 he was converted to Marxism and joined the PSOE on his return. He enjoyed the patronage of **Pablo Iglesias** and rose rapidly through the Socialist ranks. He was elected to the executive of the **Unión General de Trabajadores** (UGT) in July 1914 and became vice president on the PSOE executive committee in October 1915. He resigned his post with the executive in April 1920 to concentrate on lobbying union support against the attempt to get the party to join the Third International, but once the so-called *terceristas* had been defeated, he was named vice president of both the PSOE and UGT.

Despite his middle-class origins, Besteiro built his power base within the UGT. His ideology was well suited for this role. He adopted an extremely passive reading of Marxism, arguing that in Spain it was the task of the bourgeoisie (whom he equated with the republicans) to carry through its democratic revolution. The Socialists, he maintained, should meanwhile build up their position within the polity and strengthen their unions in preparation for the day it would be their turn to take over and construct socialism. This allowed the UGT to go about its business of expanding its working-class base and conquering positions of power without much reference to the political climate. Significantly, Besteiro took no action to defend parliamentary rule (albeit in the bastardized form of the **Cánovas Restoration**) in 1923, and then supported tacit collaboration with the **Primo de Rivera dictatorship**. By the late 1920s, Besteiro's fortunes were riding high. In 1928, he was elected president of both party and union.

However, it was an illusion to think that the PSOE-UGT could avoid taking an active role on the Spanish political scene. As the

Primo de Rivera dictatorship weakened, the opportunity arose to ally with the republicans in order to bring about democratic reform. Besteiro argued that this was not the job of the Socialists, but he was defeated by his erstwhile colleague, the UGT's real strongman, **Francisco Largo Caballero**, who realized that the Socialists' concourse would be needed to bring about a parliamentary democracy and that within such a democracy the party and unions' influence would be enormously enhanced. Once the **Second Republic** had been proclaimed, Besteiro opposed collaboration with the republicans in government, but at the same time recommended that the UGT unions pursue traditionally moderate union practice. This again led him to clash swords with Largo Caballero, who from 1933 began increasingly to radicalize his discourse. In January 1934, Besteiro was again defeated and forced to resign the UGT presidency. Thereafter he became a somewhat marginal figure. During the **Spanish Civil War**, he looked for a compromise with the **Nationalist** forces and backed the **Casado coup** in February 1939. He was, nevertheless, jailed by the Francoists, dying in prison in 1940.

BIENIO NEGRO/BLACK BIENNIUM. The phrase is used in left-wing circles to refer to the period of right-wing rule during the **Second Republic** between the elections of November 1933 and February 1936. *See also* CONFEDERACIÓN ESPAÑOLA DE DERECHAS AUTÓNOMAS; PARTIDO REPUBLICANO RADICAL.

BIENIO REFORMISTA/REFORMING BIENNIUM. This term is often used to describe the opening phase of the **Second Republic** between the elections of June 1931 and November 1933, when a coalition made up of various republican parties and the **Partido Socialista Obrero Español** tried to reform and democratize Spain's political institutions and social structure. *See also* AZAÑA DÍAZ, MANUEL.

BLACK HAND. *See* MANO NEGRA.

BLOC OBRER I CAMPEROL (BOC)/WORKERS AND PEAS-ANTS' BLOC. The BOC was a dissident, anti-Stalinist, communist party founded in **Catalonia** in December 1930 under the leadership of Joaquín Maurín (1896–1973). It grew out of a group of syndicalists working within the Catalan **Confederación Nacional del Trabajo** (CNT), who, between 1919 and 1921, became increasingly influenced by Marxist ideas. During the **Second Republic**, it remained a largely Catalan political force. Within this ambit, the party overshadowed the Catalan branch of the **Partido Comunista de España** and—though at a considerable distance—provided the main alternative to the **anarchist** insurrectionists who had taken control of the CNT. The BOC laid particular emphasis on the need to build a federal socialist state that would be respectful of the **Catalan language** and Catalan culture. As a first step, in 1931 it argued that an interclass coalition was needed in order to carry through a democratic revolution, but by 1933 it maintained that the time was now ripe for socialist revolution. It was behind the initiative to form the **Alianzas Obreras** in 1933—committees linking all the various working-class organizations together—and led the general strike in Catalonia during the **October 1934 revolution**. In September 1935, it fused with the small Trotskyist party led by Andreu Nin (1892–1937), Izquierda Comunista de España (Spanish Communist Left), to form the **Partido Obrero de Unificación Marxista.**

BLOQUE DE IZQUIERDAS. *See* LEFT BLOC.

BLOQUE NACIONALISTA GALEGO (BNG)/GALICIAN NATIONALIST BLOC. The BNG is a left-wing **Galician** nationalist coalition, whose key achievement has been both to unite most of the Galician nationalist vote and turn Galician nationalism into a serious political force.

It was first set up in September 1982, but in its first years it had little strength. Its leader, the charismatic economist and prolific political writer Xosé Manuel Bieras (1936–), was elected to the Galician autonomous parliament as the formation's sole representative in 1985. Over the next seven years it was able to consolidate its position, uniting most of the left-wing Galician nationalist groupings under its wing, and in the 1993 elections to the autonomous parliament gained 13 (out of 75) deputies. However, its greatest triumphs came in 1996–1997, when it had two deputies elected to the Spanish parliament in the general elections and, in the following year, 18 deputies elected to the autonomous Galician parliament. This latter result represented 28.7 percent of the vote and made the BNG the second largest group in the parliament behind the **Partido Popular** (PP). On the one hand, it benefited from the loss of prestige of the **Partido Socialista Obrero Español** (PSOE) during its last, scandal-ridden years in power. In addition, the perceived power and influence of the **Catalan** and **Basque** nationalist organizations **Convergència i Unió** and the **Partido Nacionalista Vasco** (PNV) (which, between 1993 and 2000, had been able to attain concessions from both the PSOE and PP in exchange for parliamentary support) encouraged some voters to switch across to the BNG. It subsequently built a working relationship with the Galician Socialist party, the Partido Socialista Galego-PSOE, making it possible for it to take over the running of five of Galicia's seven largest cities in coalition with the Socialists after the 2000 municipal elections.

However, both the PP's overall majority in the 2000 general elections and the recovery of the PSOE, under **José Luis Rodríguez Zapatero**, in the same year led to a drift of voters away from the BNG. This coincided with a generational renewal in the leadership of the coalition, with Anxo Quintana (1959–) taking over from Bieras as the coalition's national spokesperson and candidate for president of the Galician government (the Xunta) in 2001. In the context of the Spanish nationalist offensive by the PP government and the fierce polemics in the **press** over its demand that sovereignty be vested in the Basque people and the PNV's declared aim that the Basque Country be a separate (though federated) state, this generation shift was accompanied by a radicalization in the coalition's discourse, with Quintana making similar demands to those of the PNV's leading figures, **Xabier Arzallus** and Juan José Ibarretxe (1957–). Yet this decline in support and radicalization has coincided with the BNG's first taste of real power. In the 19 June 2005 elections to the autonomous parliament, it got just 13 deputies elected (18.7 percent of the vote), but because the PP lost its overall majority, it was able to form a coalition government with the PSG-PSOE. As a result, Anxo Quintana became the vice president of the Galician Xunta. *See also* TABLE 10.

BLUE DIVISION. The Blue Division was a Spanish infantry regiment that fought on the Russian front between 1941 and 1943. It was formed on the instigation of **Ramón Serrano Suñer** after the German invasion of the Soviet Union in June 1941. This had produced a great wave of emotion in **Falangist** circles, and was seen by the **Franco regime** both as a way of showing that the country was participating in the struggle against Communism without actually entering **World War II** and as a means of occupying Falangists disenchanted with the realities of the political situation in Spain. Recruitment was voluntary, though the **military** authorities ensured it would be firmly under their control. One of the most pro-Fascist generals, **Agustín Muñoz Grandes**, was put in change of the Blue Division, but it was not a party militia and was incorporated into the German army. In all, 18,692 troops left for the Russian front between June and July. The division was stationed north of Novgorod on the Volkhov River between August 1941 and August 1942 and on the Leningrad front under a new commander, General Emilio Esteban-Infantes (1892–1966), from September 1942. Under Allied pressure, the division finally withdrew between October and December 1943, though a small number of troops were organized into a Spanish legion and remained until February 1944, when they were ordered out by Adolf Hitler. In all, about 47,000 troops served on the Russian front, with casualties numbering almost 4,000.

BOLSHEVIK TRIENNIUM/TRIENIO BOLCHEVIQUE. The term is used to refer to the massive upsurge of peasant protest that rolled across southern Spain, and especially **Andalusia**, between 1918 and 1921. At its root were the miserable conditions in which the land-hungry peasantry lived, exacerbated by rapid inflation during **World War I**. The peasants were stimulated to take action by the mobilization of workers in urban Spain and by news of the Bolshevik Revolution, which acted as a powerful symbol of emancipation (hence the name "Bolshevik Triennium," coined by the period's principal chronicler, Juan Díaz del Moral [1870–1948]). The movement took off in the summer of 1918, with strikes for improved wages, the abolition of piece rates, and the recognition of the unions. Although the authorities at first adopted a rather conciliatory tone, from the end of the year they began to intervene more decisively on the side of the landowners. The movement centered on the Córdoba plain, where in the spring of 1919 groups of peasants began to occupy parts of the great estates. In this area, the government reacted to a general strike in May 1919 by declaring martial law and closing down local union headquarters. From this time, the movement began to decline in strength. There was some reorganization in the autumn, but from the end of 1919 the authorities pursued the labor unions with renewed vigor and again closed down union headquarters.

BONO SALOBRE, JOSÉ (1950–). José Bono has been one of the best-liked, charismatic figures in the **Partido Socialista Obrero Español** (PSOE) since the 1980s. He was born in the town of Salobre (Albacete) into a **Catholic, Francoist** family and studied law and economics at the private Catholic University of Deusto. However, he was radicalized by the anti-Francoist struggle and began working for the PSOE as a lawyer in 1970. He then went on to establish his position as a leading figure within the party as president of the autonomous government of Castilla-La Mancha between 1983 and 2004. As a result, he became one of the party's regional "barons," who, from the 1990s, exercised a powerful influence over party policy. In July 2000, following the resignation of **Joaquín Almunia**, at the PSOE's 35th congress he challenged for the party leadership. He had the tacit backing on the established leadership but—partly for this reason—in a context in which a thorough overhaul of the party's personnel and policies was needed, he appeared too closely associated with its past. As it was, he was beaten by **José Luis Rodríguez Zapatero** by just nine votes.

In Rodríguez Zapatero's first government, formed after the party's 14 March 2004 electoral victory, he became minister of defense. He played an important role. He was on the right of the party and his Spanish nationalist rhetoric and conservative morality (he is regular churchgoer) served to weaken accusations from the opposition **Partido Popular** that by allowing the reform of the **State of the Autonomies** and by sponsoring cultural liberal initiatives such as gay marriage, the government was jeopardizing Spanish unity and undermining Catholic values. However, he unexpectedly resigned on 7 April 2006, stating that he wished to spend more time with his family, and then turned down Rodríguez Zapatero's request that he be the PSOE candidate for mayor of Madrid. The media speculated that the real reason behind Bono's resignation was his opposition to discussions with **ETA** and to the reform of the **Catalan** autonomy statute.

BORBÓN Y BATTENBERG, JUAN DE. *See* JUAN DE BORBÓN Y BATTENBERG.

BORBÓN Y BORBÓN-PARMA, CARLOS MARÍA ISIDORO BENITO DE. See CARLOS MARÍA ISIDORO BENITO DE BORBÓN Y BORBÓN-PARMA.

BORBÓN Y DAMPIERRE, ALFONSO DE. *See* BUNKER.

BORRELL FONTELLES, JOSEP (1947–). Borrell was the prime ministerial candidate of the **Partido Socialista Obrero Español** (PSOE) between 1998 and 1999. A Catalan from a poor Castilian-speaking migrant family, he was a talented student, taking a degree in aeronautical engineering. He rose quickly through the ranks of the Catalan Socialist party, the **Partit dels Socialistes de Catalunya-Partido Socialista Obrero Español**, in the 1970s and was elected to parliament in 1979. He held posts in secondary ranks of government in the 1980s and in 1991 became the minister of transport, public works, and environment. However, he was regarded as on the left of the party and he was not personally close to **Felipe González**. When the PSOE's general secretary, **Joaquín Almunia**, decided that there should be internal primary elections to decide who should be the party's contender for prime minister in the next elections (which Almunia himself expected to win), Borrell put his name forward and, unexpectedly, came out on top at the party's April 1998 congress. Borrell had in his favor that he was distant from the old party leadership, was much more charismatic than Almunia, and was further to the left. He was therefore popular with those who wanted to see a thorough overhaul of party structures and a more forceful and radical opposition to the **Partido Popular** government. However, Almunia stayed on as general secretary and Borrell faced hostility within the party hierarchy. At the same time he faced rumors, which he denied, that he was gay. He resigned in May 1999, ostensibly because two collaborators of his in the Ministry of Finance were involved in fraudulently doctoring tax payments by a number of Catalan companies in return for kickbacks. He has remade his political career in the **European Union**, and between July 2004 and January 2007 was president of the European Parliament.

BOURBON DYNASTY. The Bourbons have been the ruling dynasty in Spain for most of the period since 1700, when they displaced the **Habsburgs**. This was the result of the last Habsburg king, **Carlos II**, dying childless and agreeing to the succession of Philippe of Anjou, the grandson of King Louis XIV of France. He was crowned **Felipe V** in Madrid in 1700. His disputed claim to the throne was based on the fact that his grandmother, María Teresa, was the daughter of **Felipe IV** of Spain (She had been known in France as Queen Marie Thérèse d'Austriche). And to consolidate his position, he had to fight the **War of Succession** against the backers of the rival Habsburg claimant to the throne, Archduke Charles of Austria.

On two occasions since then the Bourbon monarchy has been threatened. The first followed the so-called **Glorious Revolution** of September 1868, when Queen **Isabel II** was forced into exile. The Bourbon monarchy was, however, restored under **Alfonso XII** at the end of 1874. The second was during the **Second Republic** and **Franco regime** between 1931 and 1975. King **Alfonso XIII** was forced into exile in April 1931 after the proclamation of the Republic. When General **Francisco Franco** came to power in 1939, he proclaimed himself regent for life and promised that a monarchy would be "installed" upon his death. But the regime did not recognize the Bourbon heir, Juan Carlos, as Franco's successor until 1969. This opened the way to a new constitutional monarchy under **Juan Carlos I** after Franco's death in 1975.

BOYER SALVADOR, MIGUEL (1939–). Miguel Boyer was born into a **republican** family in San Juan de Luz in 1939. During his student days in the 1950s, he became involved in clandestine anti-Francoist politics, joining the Madrid branch of the **Partido Socialista Obrero Español** (PSOE) in 1960. When **Felipe González** arrived in Madrid as first secretary in 1974, he stayed in Boyer's house, and in the late 1970s Boyer was to be his most faithful supporter within the generally hostile Madrid PSOE. At the same time, he pursued a high-flying career as an economist, working as subdirector in the **Instituto Nacional de Industria** under **Francisco Fernández Ordóñez**. Boyer was a convinced social democrat on the right of the party. His economic prescriptions ignored, he was briefly to leave the party to join Fernández Ordóñez's Partido Social Demócrata (Social Democratic Party) during 1977. However, after 1979, with Felipe González and **Alfonso Guerra** in control of the party and trying to present a moderate governmental image, he returned to the fold and after the PSOE's victory in the 1982 general elections, he was made economics minister.

Boyer's policies were quickly to spark polemic. He pursued quite an orthodox monetary policy, looking to keep down wage costs in order to bear down on inflation, while rebuilding the profitability of Spanish **industry**. In 1983, he took the seemingly daring step of nationalizing the holding company RUMASA, whose massive debts threatened to send Spain's whole financial system into crisis. But he then used public funds to refloat the companies and sell them off to the private sector. These policies led to charges from the PSOE left that Boyer was favoring business elites. The charges were strengthened when, in 1985, news broke of his romance with Isabel Preysler (1951–), the former wife of Spanish pop star Julio Iglesias (1943–) and current wife of the Marquis of Griñón. He went on to marry Preysler in 1988. It was claimed that Boyer had become one of the Marbella jet set of "beautiful people" and had abandoned any ethical tie with the **Pablista** Socialist tradition. Boyer's increasing power also led to disquiet within the Socialist apparatus. It seems that Boyer's attempt to take full control of government **economic policy** in 1985 was effectively blocked by the vice president, Alfonso Guerra, leading him to resign. Since leaving government he has pursued a successful career in business and banking. In 1996, he also resigned from the PSOE and openly favored a **Partido Popular** victory in the elections.

BULLFIGHTING. Bullfighting is the second most popular sport in Spain after football. Its heartlands are in southern and central Spain, though bullfights (*corridas*) are popular in most parts of the country. During the 19th century, the European Romantic movement identified bullfighting as a key component of Spanish cultural identity (along with **flamenco**), and this ascription was adopted by Spaniards themselves (with the sport baptized *La Fiesta Nacional*

[National Festivity]). In the 20th century, leading bullfighters became—like film and, later, rock stars—popular idols, whose often grisly deaths led to great outpourings of grief. From the 1970s, the sport became enmeshed in the world of the sensationalist media (especially the so-called *revistas del corazón*), with bullfighters' romantic trysts frequently appearing in the pages of the likes of *¡Hola!* The first major example was Francisco Rivera, "Paquirri" (1948–1984), who married one of Spain's best-known singers, Isabel Pantoja (1956–), before being gored to death by a bull in 1984. This has no doubt been the key factor in the resurgence of bullfighting's popularity (though more traditional *aficcionados* view these developments with disdain). Animals rights activists have, up until now, made relatively little impact, except in the **Canary Islands** and **Catalonia**, areas in which rival nationalist discourses have labeled the bullfight a "Spanish" import, not in tune with their own cultural traditions. In the Canary Islands, bullfighting has been banned, while in Catalonia there is a strong movement (with considerable support in the **Generalitat**) against the sport.

BUNKER. The name "Bunker" (or *ultras*) was used from the early 1970s to refer to those die-hard Francoists who fought against any reform of the system. An *ultra* right, tacitly supported by the president of the government, **Luis Carrero Blanco**, first emerged around 1970–1971 when the **Franco regime** showed its first signs of entering into crisis, with calls for fundamental reform increasingly widespread. The organizational forums for the far right were the group known as Fuerza Nueva (New Force), led by Blas Piñar (1918–) of the **Movimiento National** Council, and "action squads" such as the Guerrilleros de Cristo Rey (Guerrillas of Christ the King). During 1973, the growing presence of the *ultras* could be detected in the shrill right-wing tone of demonstrations organized by the regime during the Burgos trial of **ETA**'s leading figures, at which support was expressed for **Francisco Franco** personally rather than his ministers, and shouts were heard against liberal bishops. Over the next two years, *ultra* gangs attacked left-wingers and daubed slogans on walls. The latter included right-wing anticlerical offerings such as "Justice for red bishops," and "Tarancón to the firing squad (*Tarancón al paredón*)."

Within the regime's apparatus, the Bunker was strong in the **military**, sections of the Movimiento Nacional establishment, and among members of Franco's family circle, who had the dictator's ear (the *camarilla*, as they were often called). These included the *caudillo*'s wife, Doña Carmen (1902–1987), and his son-in-law, Cristóbal Martínez Bordiu, the Marquis de Villaverde (1922–1998). Also influential within the Francoist household was the die-hard **Falangist José Antonio Girón**. Afraid of the heir **Juan Carlos**'s liberalizing tendencies, they tried to promote the claims of his far-rightist cousin, Alfonso de Borbón y Dampierre (1936–), especially after he married Franco's eldest granddaughter, María del Carmen Martínez Bordiu, in March 1972. These plots finally came to nothing. However, as the crisis of the regime intensified from 1973, the *camarilla* were instrumental in using Franco to block change. After the new president, **Carlos Arias Navarro**, had, on 12 February 1974, announced his intention of carrying out a number of limited reforms, the Bunker moved into action to scuttle any such plans. The *ultra* attack was led by José Antonio Girón outside the government and was backed by the minister general secretary of the Movimiento Nacional, José Utrera Molina (1926–), while Franco's family sought to convince him that his achievements were in peril. It was as a result of a dossier on pornography in Spain, prepared by *ultras* close to Franco, that he demanded the resignation of the reforming minister of information, Pío Cabanillas (1923–1991), in September 1974. This quashed any possibility of serious reform while Franco was alive. After his death, moreover, the *ultras* hoped to use an army uprising to reestablish a right-wing authoritarian regime. During Franco's funeral, cries were to be heard of "Power to the army!" The first elections of June 1977 demonstrated that there was little support for a return to dictatorship. Nevertheless, disgruntled civilian and military *ultras* immediately began plotting against the new democratic authorities. Matters would come to a head with the attempted coup—the **Tejerazo**—of February 1981. But its failure would herald the definitive marginalization of the far right from Spain's political life.

BUÑUEL PORTOLÉS, LUIS (1900–1983). Spain's best-known filmmaker during the 1960s and 1970s, Buñuel was above all influenced by the surrealist movement of the 1920s. While based in the famous

Madrid Residencia de Estudiantes, he met **Federico García Lorca** and **Salvador Dalí,** and after moving to Paris, where he worked under the French film director Jean Epstein, in collaboration with Dalí he made his first film, *Un chien andalou* (*An Andalusian Dog,* 1929), quickly followed by his *L'âge d'or* (*The Golden Age,* 1930). From the onset of the **Franco regime,** Buñuel went into exile in France, the United States, and Mexico, and his films became more overtly political, in particular satirizing the **Catholic Church** and the staid, conservative social moors of bourgeois Spanish society, while championing anti-authoritarian individualism. His best known films were *Viridiana* (1961), *El ángel exterminador* (*The Exterminating Angel,* 1962), *Tristana* (1970), and *El discreto encanto de la burgesía* (*The Discreet Charm of the Bourgeoisie,* 1972). To demonstrate greater openness, the Franco regime chose *Viridiana* as the Spanish entry in the Cannes Film Festival. It won the Palme d'Or, but, after criticism from the Vatican, was banned in Spain itself.

BUSINESS ASSOCIATIONS. *See* CONFEDERACIÓN ESPAÑOLA DE ORGANIZACIONES EMPRESARIALES; FOMENT DEL TREBALL NACIONAL; LIGA VIZCAÍNA DE PRODUCTORES; SINDICATOS LIBRES; TERRORISM.

– C –

CACIQUE. The word *cacique* was originally used to refer to the chiefs of indigenous tribes under Spanish rule in America. However, by the 18th century, it was also being used to describe influential figures in Spanish local life. In small-town Spain, the *cacique* or *caciques* were typically the local landowners and their representatives, the large tenant farmers (*arrendatarios*), and usurers (often also a major landowner), and they were, most likely, closely associated with the parish priest, judge, lawyer, and doctor. Because of their wealth and power over others, the *caciques* held great sway among the local population. In the north, where social relations were often close, respect and deference were key factors. In the south, where during the 19th century social conflict became increasingly bitter, the sheer economic muscle of the large landowners could be enough to cow the local peasantry.

These *caciques* came to use this influence to political advantage, either ensuring their election or that of political acquaintances to parliament. During the **Cánovas Restoration** in particular, a close relationship was established between local *caciques* and the **Madrid**-based political elite, whereby the *caciques* would deliver the candidate of their party's choice, often in return for favors. These favors were sometimes personal and could consist of posts in local government, which *caciques* were able to use to further enhance their interests and offer perks to their supporters ("for my enemies the law, for my friends a favor," as the saying went). Sometimes the *cacique* might also be able to demonstrate his power and contacts with central government by getting a railway station, new road, etc., for his local area. Hence, the whole Restoration regime came to be known as based on *caciquismo*.

CACIQUISMO. *Caciquismo* was the word used to describe the system whereby, between 1875 and 1923, during the **Cánovas Restoration**, governments were able to secure the election of candidates of their choice through their influence over local elites known as *caciques*.

    Caciques had been enormously influential before the Restoration regime. From the early 19th century, they had used their economic power and social prestige not only to dominate the affairs of the locality but also to get either themselves or their political allies elected to parliament. As a result, a close relationship was established between the **Madrid**-based political establishment and the local *caciques*. During the 19th century, the Spanish state was too weak and inefficient to establish bureaucratic, administrative control over the localities. Instead, to a large degree, it was left to the local elites to ensure the operation of local and provincial government, backed up if need be by the **Civil Guard** and the **military**. Madrid-based politicians could put pressure on the local men to ensure the candidate of the government's choice was elected. This could be seen, for example, in the elections of 1872, when the minister of the interior used contacts at local level to combat the threat of **republican** candidates. *Caciques*, of course, would only fight for a candidate they believed would broadly guarantee their interests, but could nevertheless hope to receive favors from the provincial civil governor and minister of the interior in return for cooperation.

Nevertheless, it was during the Cánovas Restoration, as noted, that *caciquismo* really came into its own. One of the essential features of the regime was that the two official parties, the **Partido Conservador** (PC) and **Partido Liberal (PL)**, would alternate in power, and contacts with the *caciques* were used to ensure the system's operation. The system had several stages. In the first place, the monarch (or regent) would choose a new head of government and hand over to him the decree for the dissolution of parliament. There then followed a complex process of negotiations whereby a majority for the incoming government was ensured, while the official opposition party was given a creditable representation (and a few leading figures within the nonregime parties would usually also be allowed into parliament). Negotiations with the local and regional *caciques* took place via the provincial civil governor. These *caciques* tended to line up behind either the PC or PL, though this often had more to do with convenience than ideology. Sometimes particularly powerful *caciques* would have themselves or their representatives continuously elected. Often, however, they would have to stand aside if the new government deemed it necessary. After this process of negotiations was complete, the so-called *encasillado* was drawn up, that is, a list of the government's preference for each seat in the country. Then, on election day, it was the *caciques'* responsibility to ensure that the preferred candidates were elected. Hence the election was "made" before it actually took place, with the result that the actual functioning of the system had little to do with the formal **constitution**.

The system worked smoothly until 1890, when universal male suffrage was reinstated. Thereafter, though the *caciques* were still largely able to control rural areas (though coercion was sometimes necessary in the south), in the large urban centers the governments had increasing difficulty getting their candidates elected. This was particularly so with the mobilization of public opinion that followed Spain's defeat in the **Spanish-American War** of 1898. Yet as the PL and PC weakened and split into several factions, post-1914 rural *caciques* were also able to assert greater independence. After the fall of the Restoration regime in 1923, the *caciquista* system per se would never again function. Nevertheless, in rural Spain at a local level during the **Second Republic**, local notables continued to exercise a considerable degree of influence over the population.

CÁDIZ CORTES. *See* CORTES OF CÁDIZ.

CALATRAVA VALLS, SANTIAGO (1951–). Perhaps Spain's internationally best-known architect, Calatrava studied architecture in the University of Valencia and then completed a doctorate in civil engineering in Zurich. His training as an engineer has allowed him to focus on large projects such as bridges and stations. Like his predecessor, **Antoni Gaudí**, he shows great interest in organic forms, though in his case the emphasis is on underlying structure. This is evident in his greatest work, *La ciutat de les arts i de les ciències* (*The City of Arts and Sciences*) in **Valencia.**

CALVO SOTELO, JOSÉ (1893–1936). José Calvo Sotelo was the major representative of the far right during the **Second Republic**. He was born in Tuy near Pontevedra and went on to study law at the University of Madrid. He entered politics by the hand of **Antonio Maura** and became a leading light within the majority right-wing current of the **Maurista** movement. Like many others within this milieu, from 1919 in particular he began to question parliamentary liberalism and look to more authoritarian, **corporatist** solutions to the country's political crisis. Under General **Miguel Primo de Rivera**, he was rapidly promoted, holding the office of minister of finance from 1925 to 1930. With the dictator's demise, he became the key figure among the **Alfonsoist monarchists**. These were ultraconservatives, often members of the social elite, who financed right-wingers planning the violent overthrow of the Second Republic. While **José María Gil-Robles** and his **Confederación Española de Derechas Autónomas** (CEDA) coalition seemed to be enjoying success in their more gradualist approach aimed at transforming the Republic through the ballot box, Calvo Sotelo remained in the shade. However, with the **Popular Front** victory in the elections of February 1936, the CEDA was eclipsed and he came to the fore. He was not, however, to see his dream of a **Catholic**, corporatist regime realized. In revenge for the murder by a Fascist gang of a Republican police officer, on 13 July 1936 a rogue group of Assault Guards took him from his flat and assassinated him. Their action had monumental consequences. The planned army coup against the Republic was already under way, but the most prestigious right-wing general in the army, **Francisco**

Franco, now definitively confirmed his participation and the date was set for 18 July.

CAMACHO ABAD, MARCELINO (1918–). Marcelino Camacho was the leading figure behind the labor confederation, **Comisiones Obreras** (CC.OO), between 1967 and 1987. He was born to working-class parents in Osma de Rasa in the province of Soria on 21 January 1918. He joined the **Partido Comunista de España** (PCE) in 1934, and fought on the **Republican** side during the **Spanish Civil War**. He was arrested at the end of the war, but was able to escape to French **Morocco** after being released conditionally in 1941. He returned to Spain in 1957 after an amnesty, and after finding employment in Perkins Hispania in **Madrid**, he quickly became involved in trade union work. In consonance with the PCE's policy of operating within the official state union, the **Organización Sindical Española**, he became a union official, while also playing a leading role in organizing CC.OO. By the time of his arrest on 1 May 1967 as a result of a government crackdown, he was considered the movement's leading official. He was to spend most of the time between this date and the death of General **Francisco Franco** in November 1975 behind bars, but following his release he was once again to play a key role in both CC.OO and the PCE. He became CC.OO's general secretary, a member of the PCE's Central Committee, and Communist parliamentary deputy for Madrid between 1977 and 1981. He was one of those who pressured the party's general secretary, **Santiago Carrillo**, to step down after the 1982 elections. During the 1980s, he was a bitter critic of the governing **Partido Socialista Obrero Español**'s economic policies. He retired as general secretary of CC.OO in November 1987 to make way for the young, dynamic figure of Antonio Gutiérrez (1951–). In recognition of his achievements, Camacho was elected to the honorary post of president. However, he stood down in 1995 in protest at what he saw as the rightward drift of the union and its decision to distance itself from the PCE.

CAMBÓ I BATLLE, FRANCESC (1876–1947). Cambó was the major Catalan and **Catalanist** politician of the years 1901–1923. He was born into a middle-class family in a rural setting in Verges (Girona) and from his student days became involved in Catalanist politics.

He supported the more moderate "possibilist" sector of **Catalanism**, led by **Enric Prat de la Riba**, participating in the foundation of the **Lliga Regionalista** in 1901. From the outset, he proved himself a dynamic and quick-minded political figure, and rapidly established himself as the party's parliamentary spokesman. He was on the more conservative wing of the party. This could be seen in his vision of Catalan industrial interests as in the vanguard of Spanish modernity and in his gradualist strategy of negotiation, and cooperation when necessary, with Spanish political elites. Hence, it was a speech given by Cambó in the presence of the King **Alfonso XIII**, on 7 April 1904, which led the more leftist and hard-line nationalists to leave the party. Later, between 1907 and 1909, he established cordial relations with **Antonio Maura**'s Conservative administration and backed (with amendments) his bill to reform and decentralize local administration. Cambó and Maura were thereafter to work together on more than one occasion until the latter's death in 1925.

The industrial boom that followed the outbreak of **World War I** brought prosperity and a sense of greater power in **Catalonia**. Cambó, with the support of Prat de la Riba, responded by launching the "For a Great Catalonia and Spain" campaign, whose aim was to link up with regionalist and nationalist groupings and manufacturing interests in other parts of Spain, in order to reform the political system. During 1916 and 1917, he toured the **Basque Country**, Asturias, **Galicia**, and **Valencia**, arguing that with Catalonia and other industrialized areas at the helm, Spain could become a rejuvenated modern state, one which could once more play an important role on the world stage, while also granting political autonomy to those territories that so desired. In the summer of 1917 the growing crisis of the **Cánovas Restoration**, following the intervention of the **Juntas de Defensa**, led him to radicalize his stance and call an assembly of parliamentarians, which tried to force Alfonso XIII and the government to accept a reformed **constitution**.

However, the failure of this approach, combined with growing working-class agitation, led him to draw back. Now, following the death of Prat de la Riba, in total control of Lliga policy, he returned to his strategy of trying to work with the Restoration parties. Under his direction, the Lliga participated in the coalition government headed by **Manuel García Prieto** (1859–1938) in 1917–18, while Cambó was personally to hold important positions in two governments headed by Maura in 1918 and 1921–1922. Yet his achievements were limited. His strategy of both backing Catalan nationalist demands and working with the Restoration parties led to strong criticism in many quarters. In a parliamentary debate in December 1918, he was accused by the **Partido Liberal** centralist **Niceto Alcalá Zamora** of trying to play the role of Simón Bolívar in Catalonia and Otto von Bismarck in Madrid, and in more radical Catalanist circles it was claimed that he had sold out. Most damaging for the Lliga's future was the party's failure immediately to condemn the military coup by General **Miguel Primo de Rivera** in 1923. This followed three years of intense working-class agitation in Barcelona, during which Cambó backed business and conservative middle-class demands that order had to be restored above all else.

During the **Primo de Rivera dictatorship** Cambó tried to reestablish his liberal credentials. In March 1931, following the dictator's fall, he created the Centro Constitucional (Constitutional Center), a coalition of the Lliga and other conservative groupings, whose aim was to create a Spanish-wide regionalist party, operating in the context of a liberal-constitutional monarchy. However, he had by this time lost most of his credibility in the Catalanist camp and his coalition could do nothing to prevent an overwhelming electoral victory by **republicans** in urban Spain and Catalonia in the 12 April municipal elections. With the proclamation of the **Second Republic**, Cambó reorganized the Lliga under the name **Lliga Catalana**. He supported the autonomy statute for Catalonia but was much vexed by growing labor agitation and the rise of the working-class left. When the **Spanish Civil War** broke out, Cambó was abroad. He did not approve of the **Nationalists**, but given the threat of social revolution saw them as the least bad alternative, and so he gave financial support to the Burgos government under General **Francisco Franco**.

CAMPOAMOR RODRÍGUEZ, CLARA (1888–1972). Clara Campoamor was the leading figure in the Spanish **feminist** movement during the 1920s and 1930s. She was born into a lower-class **Madrid** family. From a young age, she began writing for the **press** (including *El Sol*) and went on to study law at the University of Madrid between 1924 and 1926. At the same time, she formed part of the most important **women**'s feminist organization, the Asociación Nacional de Mujeres de España (National Association of Spanish Women). In her writings and speeches she focused her attention, above all, on women's inferior legal status. With the proclamation of the **Second Republic**, she affiliated with the **Partido Republicano Radical** (PRR). The decision of the provisional government to allow women to stand for parliament in May 1931 allowed her to become one of the first two women deputies to be elected in the June 1931 general elections (the other was Victoria Kent [1898–1967]). They were joined by Margarita Nelken (1894–1968) at the end of the year.

Given its democratic foundations, the Republic was disposed to give women equal rights, though there were serious misgivings over whether women should immediately be given the vote. Campoamor was on parliament's constitutional commission and played a significant role in ensuring that women's equal legal status was fully enshrined in the **Constitution of 1931**. In the parliamentary debate on the vote in October 1931, she strongly defended the immediate concession of the suffrage to women. This contrasted with the position of the other two female deputies, who maintained that a period of education would first be needed. Otherwise, because of their conservative education, women were likely to hand power over to the right. Campoamor won the day, but she was strongly criticized in left-wing circles when the November 1933 elections did, indeed, produce a right-wing majority (though the division of the left was a much more important factor than the supposed conservative inclinations of Spanish women). The PRR played a leading role in government between 1933 and 1936 and Campoamor left the party after the violent suppression of the **October 1934 revolution** in Asturias. During the **Spanish Civil War**, she left Spain for Switzerland. She tried to return in the 1940s and 1950s, but this was blocked by the **Franco regime** because she had been affiliated with the masonry.

CANALEJAS Y MÉNDEZ, JOSÉ (1854–1912). Canalejas was the major reforming figure in the **Partido Liberal** (PL) after the death of **Práxedes Mateo Sagasta** in 1903. He was by training an academic and journalist. A disciple of **Emilio Castelar**, he joined the **Partido Demócrata** in the 1860s. But he was never a radical, and after the establishment of the **Cánovas Restoration** he joined Sagasta's PL.

During the late 19th and early 20th centuries, he led a semi-dissident **regenerationist** current within the party, but as the Restoration regime became increasingly discredited, from the turn of the century his reforming ideas came into favor and he moved onto center stage. Canalejas realized that in order to survive, the regime would need to widen its base, and so when he came to power in March 1910, he tried to attract the moderate left. He was in favor of social reform and believed the power of the **Catholic Church** should be curtailed.

Yet in office his achievements were limited. He was able to abolish the hated *consumos* (taxes on basic consumer goods) and the modified **military service** (the *quinta*), ensuring that the sons of the well-to-do (who had been able to buy themselves out) would have to undertake a (relatively short) period of military training. In this respect, he went at least some way in meeting two of the key demands of Spanish **republicanism**. However, his anticlerical program was very timid. He did not contemplate a separation of Church and state, and his Associations Law (known as the Ley de Candado, or Padlock Law), which aimed to put a stop to the growth of the religious orders, was never implemented. Moreover, he proved unable to push his proposed social legislation through the **Cortes** (a nine-hour day in the mining industry, a 62-hour working week in **textiles**, the prohibition of female night work), while his harsh reaction to strikes, which he believed threatened the state, also alienated working-class sympathy. In September 1911, he outlawed the **Confederación Nacional del Trabajo** after an attempted general strike, and in 1912, during a nationwide **railway** strike, he called up all the strikers who were reservists and put them under military discipline. His life was tragically cut short when he was assassinated by an **anarchist** gunman in November 1912 while still in office.

CANARY ISLANDS. The Canary Islands are an archipelago of seven volcanic islands located off the northwest coast of Africa. In 2007, their **population** was 2,025,951. The **Crown of Castile** began colonizing the islands in the early 15th century, but faced stiff resistance from the native Guanche inhabitants. It was only from the 1490s, when they became a key stopover to the New World, that they were definitively incorporated into Spain. **Agricultural** produce and wine became the islands main exports, with bananas a key cash crop from the early 20th century. However, since the 1960s, **tourism** has become the islands' major industry. At present around 10 million tourists visit each year. The islands became an autonomous region in 1982. Since then, the local conservative, regionalist-nationalist party **Coalición Canaria** has become an important political player. In early 2008, the president of the autonomous community was Paulino Rivera, the leader of Coalición Canaria.

CÁNOVAS DEL CASTILLO, ANTONIO (1828–1897). Antonio Cánovas del Castillo was one of the most talented politicians in the second half of the 19th century, managing to combine his political work with the writing of novels and historical studies. He was also the most influential, being the principal architect of the regime usually referred to as the **Cánovas Restoration**. He was born in Málaga, and like many ambitious young men of his day, he went on to study law at the University of Madrid. It was while in **Madrid** that Cánovas was attracted to conservative politics, joining the editorial staff of *La Patria* in 1849. In 1854, he became the personal archivist of General **Leopoldo O'Donnell**, and over the next 13 years he identified closely with the **Unión Liberal**, founded by O'Donnell in that year. He therefore became a staunchly conservative liberal, though in the 1860s he criticized what he saw as the reactionary excesses of the **Partido Moderado**.

After the **Glorious Revolution** of 1868, and with the death of O'Donnell in the previous year, he became the leader of the small minority of liberal-conservative deputies in the constituent **Cortes** elected in 1869. Cánovas rejected both universal male suffrage and the freedom of worship proclaimed in the new **Constitution of 1869**, and quickly began to work for the restoration of the **Bourbon** monarchy. With the abdication of **Isabel II** in favor of her son Alfonso in June 1870, his supporters became known as **Alfonsoist monarchists**. Given the instability of the political situation and the escalating social unrest, Cánovas gained strong support among the country's social elites, conservative middle classes, and many in the **military**. His chance finally came in late 1873 with the virtual disintegration of the **First Republic**.

Cánovas would have preferred the restoration to have been a peaceful process in order to preserve a legalistic continuity. As it was, the return of the monarchy was brought about by a military *pronunciamiento* led by General Arsensio Martínez Campos (1831–1900) on 29 December 1874. Cánovas immediately set about structuring the new regime. His aim was to stabilize Spanish political life, preventing the army from meddling in politics, and ensuring that the country's social elites and upper-middle classes would in the future be able to exercise political power untroubled by popular protest. The mechanisms would be *caciquismo* and the *turno pacífico*. This corresponded with Cánovas's conservative and pessimistic vision of Spain's place in the world. He felt that in order to maintain Spain's international standing, it needed to adopt the facade of parliamentary democracy, but never trusted the (to use his own words) "miserable and begging masses." At the same time, convinced that since the 17th century the "Latin races" had been in decadence, his foreign policy was prudent but tilted toward Germany.

On his own terms, until the **Spanish-American War** of 1898, Cánovas's settlement proved largely a success. Spain went through a quarter of a century of relative social peace and enjoyed considerable economic growth. The price was, however, high. The regime's *caciquista* foundations proved a barrier to the democratization of political life. Moreover, the Spanish lower orders were marginalized from the regime rather than integrated, and, particularly when Cánovas's **Partido Conservador** was in power, labor and peasant discontent was dealt with harshly. Indeed, Cánovas himself would be a victim of the bitter underlying social tensions. He was assassinated while in office by the Italian **anarchist** Michele Angiolillo on 8 August 1897 in revenge for the executions that followed the **Montjuïc Trial**.

CÁNOVAS RESTORATION. The political regime of the period 1875–1923 is usually referred to as the Cánovas Restoration after its architect, **Antonio Cánovas del Castillo**. The regime was ushered in by the *pronunciamiento* of General Arsensio Martínez Campos (1831–1900) against the **First Republic** on 29 December 1874. The young king, **Alfonso XII**, then made his triumphal entry into **Madrid** on 14 January 1875.

Cánovas del Castillo quickly took over the reins of power. The aim of Cánovas and his supporters was to overcome the instability of the previous 40 years, healing the bitter divisions within the ruling liberal parties, which had both encouraged the **military** to intervene and conjured the specter of radical social and political change. The new settlement was put into place in a number of phases. In the first place, in order to restore social control, the left-wing opposition was suppressed and the **labor movement** was forced underground. Then, at the end of 1875, a new constitution was drafted. With the aim of maintaining a semblance of legality and continuity, universal male suffrage was maintained for the 31 December elections, which would serve to ratify the new constitution. They were, however, manipulated, and the law of 28 December 1878 limited the number of voters to under 5 percent of the population. The **Constitution of 1876** was very much in the conservative liberal tradition of the **Partido Moderado**, although there were certain more progressive elements. In particular, though **Catholicism** was to be the country's official religion, private worship of other religions was permitted.

This concession was part of Cánovas's plan to unite the country's political and social elites behind a new constitutional settlement, bringing onboard more radical liberal-monarchists (former members of the **Partido Progresista**, **Partido Radical**, and Partido Constitutionalista), who had been appalled by the political passions and social ferment unleashed during the **Democratic Sexennium**. Cánovas, therefore, formed a **Partido Conservador (PC)**, but, at the same time, encouraged the organization of an opposition **Partido Liberal (PL)**. The challenge was taken up by the former Partido Constitucionalista leader **Práxedes Mateo Sagasta**.

The facade was, therefore, that of British parliamentary democracy, but the reality would be very different. Through the 1885 Pardo Pact, the PC and PL agreed that in order to ensure stability they would alternate in power (the so-called *turno pacífico*). Governments would not, in consequence, be the outcome of free and fair elections, but the seats would be carved up between the major parties (with, for the sake of appearances, a few seats for the opposition) before the election took place. This required the operation of a system subsequently referred to as *caciquismo*. Civil governors in each province, under instructions from the minister of the interior, would enter into negotiations with the local bigwigs (or *caciques*), using their influence to get the government's choice of candidate elected in return for government favors. The whole system was able to operate quite well until 1898. Even after the reintroduction of universal male suffrage in 1890, *caciques* were able to ensure that in rural Spain the government's choice of candidate was delivered. It was only in urban areas that opposition **republican** parties could, on occasion, hope to gain a seat against the government's wishes.

From 1898, however, with the growing mobilization of the masses, the regime began to weaken. The trigger was Spain's defeat in the **Spanish-American War** of 1898 and the loss of its **colonies** in America and the Pacific. The psychological impact in Spain was huge. The defeat confirmed that Spain, once a great imperial power, was now in military and economic terms a second-rate nation. This led to much soul-searching among intellectuals and writers—the **Generation of 1898**—as to the reasons behind Spain's apparent inability to adapt to the modern world. There was also a burst of publications on the reasons behind Spain's malaise. The most commonly cited cause was the corrupt and inefficient nature of the country's political system, and the cry therefore went up for political reform, or to use the phrase fashionable at the time, regeneration. The **regenerationists** gained a sympathetic ear from Catalan businessmen, shocked at the loss of major export markets, and from manufacturers, retailers, and the professional middle classes in general, bitter at the extra taxes they had to pay to finance the war. In the climate of political effervescence that followed the defeat, and with a stunned government relaxing its repression of the opposition, republicans and the labor left were also able to revive their fortunes, and in **Catalonia** a new mass party, the conservative **Lliga Regionalista**, was founded.

These events coincided with the rise to prominence of a new generation of PC and PL leaders. Cánovas was assassinated in 1897 and Sagasta died in 1903, and over the next decade figures such as **Antonio Maura**, **Segismundo Moret**, and **José Canalejas** came to the fore. Afraid of the rising tide of discontent, the more farsighted members of the "official parties" realized that reform was necessary. However, they wished to channel the process rather than be swept away by it. Thus they called for "**revolution from above**": orderly reform from within the regime rather than "revolution from below." Its major element was the recognition that the regime could no longer function simply through the operation of *caciquismo*, and that it would have to broaden its public appeal. "Revolution from above" came under a PC and PL guise. However, between 1901 and 1914, neither party was able substantially to reform the regime. The state began to operate more effectively, at last the **education** system began to improve significantly, and social legislation was introduced (but often not enforced). However, *caciques* continued to be used in order to ensure electoral victories, the power of the **Catholic Church** remained virtually unchallenged, and the military remained a law unto itself.

To make matters worse, with the deaths of Cánovas and Sagasta, the "official parties" became increasingly fragmented. Growing divisions were in part a reflection of the fact that they were not modern mass parties but parties of oligarchs who followed particular leaders, and with the deaths of their undisputed champions several possible poles of attraction emerged. Moreover, as the official parties dipped their toes into the cold waters of mass politics, they became divided over substantive political issues. These factors would, by 1913, lead to a crisis of the *turno*. First the PL became divided between Segismundo Moret and Eugenio Montero Ríos (1832–1914), with Moret trying to attract the more moderate republicans. Matters further deteriorated when, between 1907 and 1909, the PC prime minister, Antonio Maura, took a hard line against left-wing agitation, culminating in a severe repression of anticlerical disturbances in **Barcelona** known as the **Tragic Week**. The PL, under the figure of Moret, circumstantially allied with the republicans against Maura's policies, and after the Tragic Week supported a campaign for his removal. This finally culminated when King **Alfonso XIII**, afraid that international protest against the repression of the Tragic Week might endanger the monarchy, accepted an offer of resignation by Maura. Maura never forgave the PL and refused in the future to have anything to do with them. Hence, after a period of Liberal rule, in October 1913, when the king wished the Conservatives to return to power, he called on Maura's rival, **Eduardo Dato**, with the result being that the PC split into two factions.

The economic and social tensions unleashed during and after **World War I** further weakened the regime. Rapid industrial development, accompanied by spiraling inflation, strengthened the urban middle classes and led to an unprecedented unionization of the working class. Furthermore, by the summer of 1917, the first

Russian Revolution and the increasing likelihood that the Allies would win the war encouraged agitation for democratic change. The Catalan **Lliga Regionalista**, along with the **Partido Socialista Obrero Español** (PSOE), **anarchists**, and republicans, took the opportunity to challenge the regime during the so-called **crisis of 1917**. The revolt failed in part because of divisions within the reform camp, in part because the military remained loyal to the regime. This would not, however, save the Restoration regime. Over the following three years, social conflict continued to escalate. With the onset of economic depression after the end of the European war, industrialists looked desperately to undermine the labor unions and cut costs. At the same time, the elites' fears were heightened by the Bolshevik Revolution and the tide of social revolt that was sweeping across central Europe. The PC and PL found it difficult to respond effectively, forming a series of short-lived governments or coalitions whose policies vacillated widely from conciliation to repression of the labor movement. For Spain's social elites this, increasingly, was not good enough. Business and the conservative middle classes, in particular, began to push for a more authoritarian political system. This attitude was seconded by the conservative press and the military, which saw the Restoration politicians as too weak and ineffectual to impose order. The right was encouraged to take such views by events in Europe, where by 1922 authoritarian rulers were gaining ground. Most importantly, during 1923, the Barcelona captain general, **Miguel Primo de Rivera**, came to see himself as the guardian of conservative interests against the revolutionary threat. At the same time, discontent in the military—at its rawest in the Barcelona garrison—was further inflamed by the radicalization of the **Catalanist** movement.

From July 1921, a further destabilizing factor became the bloody defeat of the Spanish army at **Annual**. In liberal and left-wing circles, the cry went up for those responsible to be brought to justice, and the new coalition government, under Antonio Maura, responded by setting up the Picasso Commission to investigate the military aspects of the debacle. This angered the colonial *africanista* army, who felt that it was being made a scapegoat. *Africanistas* were further alienated by the Restoration governments' reluctance to pursue an aggressive "forward policy" in **Morocco**, by debates in parliament in which the incompetence of the Morocco campaign was discussed. Hence, by the summer of 1923, much of the army was united in its determination to bury the regime. Primo de Rivera took the lead and linked up with pro-*africanista* generals based in Madrid. King Alfonso XIII also gave his tacit support. By this time, the Restoration parties had gone some way to reconstructing the *turno* (albeit without any undisputed leaders, now based on the various groupings within the main parties). The PL coalition government had also introduced a number of significant political reforms. Yet the regime's *caciquista* foundation meant that it had little popular support, with the result that no one came to its aid when Primo de Rivera launched his coup attempt on 13 September 1923. *See also* TABLES 7 AND 8.

CANTONALIST REVOLT. The term refers to a series of rebellions launched by the so-called intransigent **republicans** against the government of the **First Republic** from July 1873. The revolt began in the city of Cartagena and then spread to other towns and cities through **Andalusia** and the Mediterranean littoral.

The leaders of the revolt believed that the Republic should be built from below and that the pace of reform was too slow. They were supported by the urban lower classes and sectors of the rural peasantry, who felt that the regime should do more to offer improved working conditions, cheaper food, and land. In some areas, the revolt was backed by members of the pro-**anarchist Federación Regional Española**, and, in general, took on elements of a social revolution. To combat the rebellion, the regime shifted to the right. **Francesc Pi i Margall** was forced to resign the presidency and was replaced by **Nicolás Salmerón**, who used the **military** to crush it. Most of the "cantons" were defeated during August, though Cartagena held out until 11 January 1874.

CARLISM. During the 19th and early 20th centuries, Carlism represented an antimodernist protest movement of rural and small-town Catholic Spain against economic modernization and cultural change. Its aim was to establish an idealized rendition of the "traditional" pre-**Bourbon** composite monarchy represented by the **Catholic Monarchs**. Its major rallying cry was the need for conformity to Catholic values in all walks of life.

The movement was at its height between 1833 and 1876, but survived as a significant force down to the 1930s. At a political level, it emerged after a quarrel between King **Fernando VII** and his brother, **Carlos María Isidoro Benito de Borbón y Borbón-Parma**, over the succession. While Fernando favored his daughter, Isabel, Carlos argued that the 1713 Salic Law prohibited a female succession and claimed the throne for himself. On Fernando's death in 1833, hostilities erupted between the liberal backers of Isabel and Don Carlos's sympathizers (hence the name Carlist).

More importantly, Carlism represented a social revolt by those sectors of society who felt threatened by **liberal** reforms. It was backed by the **Catholic Church**, whose vast wealth and power the liberals sought to diminish. It was attractive to the conservative northern peasantry, who were under strong Church influence, felt threatened by liberal tax reforms, and, from the 1830s, protested at the loss of rights over the land as a consequence of the liberal *desamortización*. And it also gained support among increasingly marginal urban groups, such as independent artisans, who were challenged by the development of capitalist relations of production. All these elements resisted the centralizing tendencies of the liberal state. In the **Basque Country**, people mobilized under the banner of the reestablishment of the region's historic liberties or *fueros*.

The Church had already captained peasant resistance to the "godless" French invader in the 1790s and during the **War of Independence**, and in the late 1820s it led a new peasant revolt (La Guerra dels Malcontents, or War of the Discontented), which affected much of **Catalonia**. It was, however, with Carlos's claim to the Spanish throne in 1833 that resistance to liberalism spread throughout much of northern Spain. The First Carlist War of 1833–1840 was the most serious attempt launched by the Carlists to seize power, but they finally succumbed because of their inability to rally support in urban areas. The **Vergara Pact** of 1839 virtually brought the war to an end, and by integrating much of the Carlist officer corps into the official army, it weakened the Carlist cause. There was a small uprising in Catalonia between 1846 and 1847 (the Second Carlist War), but it was easily put down. The Carlists' position was further weakened by the beginnings of a reconciliation between the conservative wing of liberalism (represented by the **Partido Moderado**) and the Church establishment, consummated by a new concordat with the Vatican in 1851. With the **Glorious Revolution** of 1868 and the coming to power of more radical liberal administrations, the Carlists again took up arms, but the establishment of the more conservative **Cánovas Restoration** regime in 1875 once again undercut Carlist support. The new authorities made an all-out effort to subdue the Carlist revolt. The superior military power of the Alfonsoist generals was finally to bear results, with the Third Carlist War officially brought to an end with the Proclamation of Somorrostro of 1876. Carlism was never again by itself to prove a threat to the liberal state.

In the mid-19th century, Carlism continued to enjoy widespread sympathy within the clergy and among much of the clerical laity. This broad base received the name of **Traditionalism** and included a number of intellectuals, most notably **Juan Donoso Cortés** and Jaume Balmes (1810–1848). However, after the establishment of the Cánovas Restoration, in particular, divisions grew. Increasing numbers of antiliberal Catholics recognized the need to reach an accommodation with the new regime and, under **Alejandro Pidal**, integrated into the **Partido Conservador** in 1884. They were backed by the Catholic hierarchy. Traditionalists were also rent by growing splits. Hard-line insurrectionists formed their own separate **Integrist** movement in the 1880s. Further divisions emerged in the early 20th century, when the new Carlist pretender, Jaime de Borbón y Borbón-Parma (1870–1931), took a less overt antiliberal line, leading the leading Carlist theoretician, **Juan Vázquez de Mella**, to form his own Partido Tradicionalista (Traditionalist Party) in 1919.

The anticlerical policies of left-wing governments during the **Second Republic** produced a revival of Carlism, which was able to expand outside its remaining stronghold of **Navarre**. By 1934, Carlists were drilling and collecting arms, and, in the same year, the **Alfonsoist monarchist** Antonio Goicoechea (1876–1953) set up a meeting between Carlist leaders and Benito Mussolini in Rome to ask for support. In the first months of the **Spanish Civil War**, recruitment into the Carlist militia, the Requeté, took off. This was, however, to prove the Carlists' swan song, for in April 1937 they were forcibly fused by General **Francisco Franco** with the **Falange Española** into a single party, the **Falange Española Tradicionalista y de**

las Juntas de Ofensive Nacional Sindicalista. Many high-ranking Carlists became reconciled to the **Franco Regime**, which, they could argue, at least served to preserve traditional Catholic values. On the death of Franco, a small group, under the Carlist pretender Carlos Hugo (1930–), adopted a populist, "socialist" Carlism, but they were totally marginalized during the **transition to democracy**.

CARLOS I (1500–1558). Carlos I was the first **Habsburg** ruler of Spain. His coronation was the result of the dynastic match between the daughter of the **Catholic Monarchs**, Juana, and Archduke Philip of Austria and Burgundy, the son of the Holy Roman Emperor, Maximilian I of Habsburg. Its aim was to build an alliance against France, the **Crown of Aragón**'s chief political enemy. Juana became the heir to the throne after the death of **Isabel I** in 1504, but was mentally incapacitated and unfit to govern. Hence, following the death of Fernando II of Aragón in 1516, her son was proclaimed Carlos I, king of Aragón and Castile. On his coming of age in 1515, he had already inherited the ancestral Habsburg lands in the Low Countries and Franche Compté. In 1519, following the death of his grandfather, Maximilian I, he was then crowned Charles V, Holy Roman Emperor, taking charge of the Habsburgs' Germanic possessions. This meant that Spain suddenly became a key component (especially because of its new American possessions) of Europe's major empire.

Carlos had been brought up in a Dutch court and at first spoke no **Castilian**. On his arrival in Spain in 1518, he also proceeded to ask the Castilian **Cortes** for taxes and place his Flemish courtiers in key positions. This provoked the **Comuneros' revolt** in 1519. Its defeat in 1521–1522 ensured that the Castilian Cortes would play no significant role in government and weakened its ability to oppose his demands for taxes in order to conduct military operations on the European continent. Nevertheless, it made the king more circumspect. In the future, he would be careful to promote Castilian officials, would learn the language, and made clear that the **Crown of Castile** was the rock upon which his empire was built. However, because of his position he spent much of his time outside Castile and never established a permanent capital.

During his rule, Carlos I's major aim was to maintain the Habsburgs' hegemonic position in Europe. At the same time, he viewed himself as the principal defender of Christendom against the "infidel" Ottoman Empire, and hence took the lead in fending off its expansion. In part, this represented a continuation of the Catholic Monarchs' policy of containing France and preventing Ottoman penetration into the western Mediterranean, but Carlos also drew Spain into the broader European theater of war. Thus, the Habsburg Empire became embroiled in a series of wars with France between the 1520s and 1540s (gaining possession of the Duchy of Milan in the process). From the 1540s, the monarchy also took up arms to defend the empire's unity against the revolt of the Protestant German provinces, finally having to accept the equality of the Catholic and Protestant faiths in the 1555 Peace of Augsberg. Faced with the struggle against Protestantism, in the late 1540s the aging king became convinced of the need to block the spread of "heresy" in his dominions at all cost, thereby strengthening the position of the **Spanish Inquisition**. The overall consequences of this constant warfare were severe budget deficits and heavy borrowing, which placed a heavy burden on the Crown of Castile above all. Infirm with gout and depressed by the failure of his German campaign, and in order to ensure a smooth succession, in 1556 he had a residence built alongside the monastery at Yuste (Cáceres)—where he lived for the final two years of this life—and abdicated in the name of his son, who was crowned **Felipe II**.

CARLOS II (1661–1700). Carlos II was the only legitimate heir of **Felipe IV** to survive. An invalid at birth, he remained both chronically ill and was, at best, slow-witted. His father died in 1665 when he was only four years old, so his mother, Queen Mariana of Austria (1634–1696), held the position of regent and governed alongside a five-man committee though to 1675. This led to bitter infighting at court in a context in which, despite having divested itself of the United Provinces and reached a long-lasting peace with France, the **monarchy** continued to face constant financial crises. These were exacerbated because of its continued possession of the Franche Compté and several Italian states. Concern for French expansion meant that it remained involved in armed conflict on the European mainland. In what was a blessing in disguise, it lost the Franche Compté in 1668 following war with France.

The increasing certainty that Carlos II would produce no issue also led to division over his successor. France supported the claims of the descendants of Felipe IV's daughter, María Teresa, who had married King Louis XIV of France in 1660. This position was backed by a powerful faction at court who felt that—providing the two monarchies remained separate—it would be better to have France as a friend rather than an enemy. Queen Mariana, on the other hand, pressed the claim of the German **Habsburgs**. Carlos II was persuaded to accept a French **Bourbon** succession in the person of Philippe of Anjou, the grandson of Louis XIV, shortly before his death in November 1700, given that the alternative, it increasingly seemed likely, was the breakup of his empire. Philippe of Anjou was crowned **Felipe V** at the end of the month. This arrangement was, however, rejected by England, Holland, and the German Habsburgs, leading to the **War of Succession**.

CARLOS III (1716–1788). Carlos III, the stepbrother of **Fernando VI**, was crowned king in 1759. He is the figure most identified with the policy of enlightened despotism pursued by the country's 18th-century **Bourbon** monarchs. Strongly influenced by moderate **Enlightenment** thinkers, who stressed the link between the diffusion of scientific thought, state-interventionist economic policies (mercantilism), and economic growth, he promoted reforming ministers like the José Moñino, the Count of Floridablanca (1728–1808), and Pedro Rodríguez, Count of Campomanes (1723–1802). These ministers put into effect a series of policies that had an overall positive effect on the Spanish **economy**. They opened up trade between the **colonies** and all Spanish ports in the 1760s and 1770s, thereby making possible the economic takeoff of Catalan **industry**. They also improved the Spanish **transport** system and made efforts to curb the import of manufactures into Spain and ensure that the colonial export trade favored Spanish manufactures. They pursued **educational** reforms, introducing mathematics, medicine, and law of nature and nations into the university system. Less successfully, they introduced reforms that aimed to curb the power of local oligarchs, with the intention of creating a more prosperous peasantry. Carlos III's efforts to develop the Spanish economy were aided by the fact that he to a large extent managed to stay out of European conflict (though his close links with France did lead to war with Great Britain between 1761 and 1763). In addition, he continued the policy of subordinating the **Catholic Church** to the state, ruthlessly expelling the Jesuit order from Spain in 1766 because of its opposition. *See also* AGRICULTURE; CARLOS IV.

CARLOS IV (1748–1819). King Carlos IV was the second son of **Carlos III**. He became heir when the king's elder son, Felipe, who was mentally retarded, was forced to abdicate. Nevertheless, he was a weak monarch, prone to leave policy in the hands of powerful figures in the court. He came to the throne in 1788, though at first most of the work of government was actually carried out by his father's advisor, José Moñino, the Count of Floridablanca (1728–1808). Carlos was shocked by the **French Revolution** of 1789, and his attempt to save the life of his cousin, King Louis XVI, provoked war with France in 1793. By this time, the court favorite, **Manuel de Godoy**, had concentrated power in his hands. Through much reviled as the secret lover of the queen, María Luisa de Parma (1751–1819), Godoy was not lacking in talent. He made every effort to bring the war with France to an end. More controversially, he then allied with France in 1796, bringing Spain into conflict with Great Britain. This policy would lead to the destruction of much of the Spanish navy at the Battle of **Trafalgar** in 1805. In the elaboration of policy, Carlos IV seems to have been little more than by bystander. From 1800, Godoy became all-powerful, provoking divisions at court, with the king's son, Fernando, fearful lest Godoy should attempt to usurp the monarchy. These divisions finally led to the **Aranjuez uprising** in March 1808, the culmination of a plot by Fernando to have both Carlos IV and Godoy deposed, and have himself crowned **Fernando VII**. The intrigue surrounding the Spanish throne also allowed Napoleon Bonaparte, whose troops had been allowed to pass through Spain, supposedly to pursue the **Portuguese**, to intervene directly in Spanish politics. He called Carlos and Fernando VII to France, where he forced them both to renounce the throne and pronounced his own brother Joseph José I, king of Spain. The former king was to die in exile in Rome in 1819. *See also* WAR OF INDEPENDENCE.

CARLOS MARÍA ISIDORO BENITO DE BORBÓN Y BORBÓN-PARMA (1788–1855). Carlos María was the younger brother of **Fernando VII**. It was under his leadership that the Spanish absolutists were to rise up against the establishment of a **liberal** economy and society from 1833 (hence the name **Carlists**). Like his brother, Carlos was to be deeply affected by the French revolutionary wars and the attempted liberal uprisings in Spain. By the 1820s, he was identified with the most intransigent sectors at court. He opposed an amnesty for the liberals after the reestablishment of absolutist rule in 1823, and during the **Ominous Decade** became involved in antiliberal intrigues at court. He opposed the designation of Fernando VII's daughter, Isabel (the future **Isabel II**), as his successor in 1830, arguing that the 1713 Salic Law prohibited a female succession. On his brother's death, he claimed the crown, declaring himself Carlos V of Spain, and from 1834 personally led the Carlists' attempt to seize the reins of power during the First Carlist War. The Peace of **Vergara** of 1839, however, cut short his ambitions. In 1845, he abdicated in favor of his son, Carlos Luis de Borbón y de Braganza (1818–1861), taking up residence in Trieste. See also FERNANDO RESTORATIONS; FRENCH REVOLUTION.

CAROD ROVIRA, JOSEP LLUÍS. *See* ESQUERRA REPUBLICANA DE CATALUNYA.

CARRERO BLANCO, LUIS (1903–1973). Carrero Blanco was, after General **Francisco Franco**, the most important figure within the **Franco regime**. He was born in Santona, in the province of Santander, on 4 March 1903. He joined the Naval School in 1918, and thereafter specialized in submarine warfare. During the **Spanish Civil War**, after escaping **Madrid** he fought with the **Nationalist** navy in the north.

Carrero Blanco had first met Franco during the **Moroccan** campaigns of the 1920s, and they renewed their acquaintance in 1933, when they coincided in the Balearic Islands. His views were very close to those of Franco. He was a **Catholic** monarchist who maintained strong militaristic and hierarchical values. This and his reputation as an efficient administrator gained him Franco's confidence. After the end of the civil war, in May 1941, he became subsecretary to Franco's presidency and, therefore, an intermediary between Franco and the political elites. This was the start of Carrero Blanco's meteoric rise within the regime. In 1945, he was made second vice president of the **Cortes**, his post of subsecretary was upgraded to cabinet status in 1950, and he replaced **Agustín Muñoz Grandes** as vice president of the cabinet in July 1968.

As a result, Carrero Blanco accumulated vast patronage in his hands. Like Franco, he was to a degree a pragmatist who was willing to accept reform as long as the regime's fundamentals remained intact. In the early years, like many in the **military**, he felt distaste for the single party, the **Falange Española y de las Juntas de Ofensiva Nacionalista Sindicalista**, and was instrumental in undermining the position of **Ramón Serrano Suñer**. His essential aim was to build an authoritarian regime based on what he saw as the rule of law. During the 1950s, he recognized the need for economic reform and, indeed, was of key importance in the rise of the **Opus Dei** technocrats to positions in government in 1957. Nevertheless, he always opposed a significant political opening (*apertura*), and instead led a current within the regime that favored the designation of the **Bourbon** heir, **Juan Carlos**, as Franco's successor in order to perpetuate the regime after Franco's death (so-called *continuismo*). Franco's decision to take this step in July 1969 was, therefore, seen as a triumph for Carrero Blanco against the so-called **Regentialists**, who wanted a nonmonarchist successor. Carrero Blanco's *continuismo* brought him into conflict with *aperturistas* (reformers) within the regime, such as **Manuel Fraga**. He always had the advantage that in the last instance he had Franco's ear. This was demonstrated during 1969 when, following the **Matesa scandal**, with Franco's health failing, he virtually controlled the cabinet reshuffle that followed and had the three major reformers, Manuel Fraga, **José Solís**, and **Fernando María Castiella**, removed from government. Carrero Blanco's prominence was further confirmed in June 1973 when Franco, too weak to play an active role in politics, relinquished his post as prime minister to him.

Under Carrero Blanco there was little chance of serious reform. This was reflected in the stagnation of projects for political associations and reform of the vertical union, the **Organización Sindical Española**. Carrero Blanco's spectacular murder by **ETA** activists in Madrid on 20 December 1973—his chauffeur-driven car was blown onto rooftops by a massive bomb planted under the road—therefore removed one of the most serious obstacles to change.

CARRILLO SOLARES, SANTIAGO (1915–). Santiago Carrillo was the general secretary of the **Partido Comunista de España** (PCE) between 1960 and 1982 and a key figure in the **transition to democracy**. He was born in Gijón on 18 January 1915 into a working-class family that sympathized with the **Partido Socialista Obrero Español** (PSOE). In 1913, when he began working, he joined the youth movement of the PSOE, and in 1934 became the PSOE youth's general secretary. Carrillo moved into the orbit of the PCE and was one of the architects of the unification between the Socialist and Communist youth in 1936, resulting in the formation of the Juventud Socialista Unificada (Unified Socialist Youth, JSU). Under Carrillo's leadership, the JSU soon came under Communist control. Carrillo actually joined the PCE in November 1936. During the **Spanish Civil War**, he became a member of the Defense Junta that ran **Madrid** after the evacuation of the Republican government of **Francisco Largo Caballero** in November 1936. It was during this period that he was accused by right-wingers of ordering the execution of a number of **Nationalist** prisoners at Paracuellos de Jarama.

Following the war, Carrillo was based in Moscow, where, for a brief time, he worked as secretary of the Communist Youth International. At the end of **World War II**, he moved to Prague, the headquarters of the PCE in exile. Carrillo was at this time a convinced Stalinist. At one stage he went so far as to denounce his own father for forming part of the **Casado** National Defense Council at the end of the civil war, leading to great bitterness in the PSOE camp. By the early 1950s, however, he had become increasingly uneasy about Stalinist dogma, and along with other younger Communists began to argue that the party needed to throw off its sectarian, Stalinist past, and forge a broad, interclass alliance in order to overthrow the **Franco regime**.

The death of Joseph Stalin in 1953, followed by Nikita Khrushchev's denunciation of Stalin at the 20th congress of the Communist Party of the Soviet Union (CPSU) in 1956, opened the door to change. Carrillo was from this year the de facto leading figure within the party, and at the party's sixth congress in 1960 became its general secretary. Under Carrillo, the PCE slowly liberalized its policies. At first he remained strongly aligned with the CPSU, but relations chilled with the overthrow of Khrushchev in 1964 and then the invasion of Czechoslovakia in 1968. In order to broaden the PCE's appeal, Carrillo began to forge closer ties with the Italian Communist Party (PCI) and adopted the latter's strategy of Eurocommunism. This committed the PCE to a liberal model of socialist democracy. The strategy was confirmed in Carrillo's major theoretical work, *Eurocomunismo y el estado* (*Eurocommunism and the State*, 1977), and in the party's ninth congress, held in April 1978, which endorsed Eurocommunism and dropped the aim of implementing the dictatorship of the proletariat.

However, Carrillo remained strongly marked by his Stalinist past and he maintained an iron grip on the party apparatus. This generated resentment among younger Communists active in Spain, who in the late 1970s began to call for a democratization of party structures. Carrillo was never prepared to countenance this, with the result that in the early 1980s, a large number of these so-called renovators were expelled and the PCE split three ways. The result could be seen in the October 1982 general elections, when the Communists received barely 4 percent of the vote.

As a result, Carrillo was forced to resign as general secretary and was replaced by Asturian miner Gerardo Iglesias (1945–). Under Iglesias, the PCE began to open up to non-Communist leftist forces, leading to the celebration of an extraordinary conference that called for leftist convergence in March 1985. This strategy was opposed by Carrillo and his supporters, who instead pushed for a reunification of Spanish Communism. In response, the party executive demoted Carrillo to the rank of an ordinary party member. An outright split could not now be avoided. Carrillo left the PCE and formed his own coalition, the Mesa para la Unidad de los Comunistas (Round Table for Communist Unity), at the heart of which was a new party, the PCE-Marxista Revolucionario, later renamed the Partido de los Trabajadores Españoles (Workers' Party—PTE). In the June 1986 general elections, Carrillo's coalition tried to emphasize its Communist roots as against the PCE-dominated coalition, **Izquierda Unida**, which, it argued, was little more than a "mini-PSOE." Results were, however, disappointing, with the coalition gaining no seats in parliament.

Yet by the late 1980s, Carrillo's stance had radically changed. In the context of the collapse of Communism in eastern Europe, he now ironically began to argue that the Communist road was at an end and urged Spanish leftists to seek a "common home" within the PSOE. The result was that though Carrillo bowed out of active politics, the PTE joined the Socialists en masse at the end of 1990.

CASADO COUP. The Casado coup at the end of the **Spanish Civil War** represented an attempt by anti-Communists within the Republican camp to eliminate the **Partido Comunista de España** and reach a negotiated settlement with General **Francisco Franco**. It was launched in **Madrid** on 4 March by the commander of the Republican Army of the Center, Colonel Segismundo Casado (1893–1968), together with prominent figure within the **Partido Socialista Obrero Español Julián Besteiro** and disillusioned **anarchists**, who formed a National Defense Junta. Several days of fighting followed in Madrid, with the Communists finally going down to defeat. Franco, however, would hear nothing of negotiations, and after he entered the Spanish capital virtually unopposed on 27 March, Communists and non-Communists were to share the same fate.

CASAS DEL PUEBLO/HOUSES OF THE PEOPLE. Casas del Pueblo were, by the 1930s, associated with the **Partido Socialista Obrero Español-Unión General de Trabajadores**. They were workers' centers that provided not only space for the trade unions, but also operated cooperatives, and provided mutual benefits, schooling, entertainment, and other services, thereby making up for the deficiencies of state social provision and tying workers to the organization. The first Casa del Pueblo (minus the trade unions) was, however, opened in **Barcelona** by **Alejandro Lerroux** in August 1907, and a large number of **republican** centers in **Catalonia** and **Valencia** undertook similar functions on a smaller scale. The first Socialist Casa del Pueblo was opened in Madrid on 26 November 1908. *See also* LABOR MOVEMENT.

CASAS VIEJAS MASSACRE. Casas Viejas is a small town in the Cádiz province known for an infamous incident that occurred there in January 1933. By 1932, the majority wing of anarcho-syndicalist

Confederación Nacional del Trabajo had broken with the **Second Republic** and was trying to organize a series of uprisings to overthrow it. One such attempt was made in January 1933. Support was patchy but in Casas Viejas, the peasants took control of the town and proclaimed libertarian communism. The response of the authorities was ruthless. The new Republican force of Assault Guards laid siege to the village, killing about 20 peasants. This had a psychologically negative impact on the **republican-Partido Socialista Obrero Español** coalition government. On the left, it led to disillusionment, while it allowed the right to open an opportunistic campaign against the prime minister, **Manuel Azaña**.

CASTELAR Y RIPOLL, EMILIO (1832–1899). Castelar was one of Spain's leading late 19th-century journalists and politicians. He was born into a **liberal** family in Cádiz and from an early age became involved in democratic and **republican** politics. He was, however, always a believer in the free market and—with his attention fixed on France—argued that a republican regime was compatible with order. Hence, during the **First Republic**, he became the leader of the republican right, and when he came to power on 17 September 1873, as a consequence of the **Cantonalist revolt**, he moved against the rebels without compunction. This, however, led to the alienation of many republicans and to the promotion of monarchist **army** officers to positions of seniority. The way was, therefore, laid open to the restoration of the **Bourbon** monarchy following the coup by General Manuel Pavia (1827–1895) in January 1874. With the establishment of the **Cánovas Restoration**, Castelar broke totally with the **federalist**-republican tradition, and founded his own Partido Republicano Posibilista (Republican Possibilist Party). His party pushed for an extension of civil liberties but proved willing to work within the bounds of the Restoration regime. Finally, after the major reforms carried out by the **Partido Liberal** between 1885 and 1890, in 1893 Castelar agreed to integrate into it.

CASTELLANO CARDALLIAGUET, PABLO (1934–). Pablo Castellano was one of the leading "renovators" within the **Madrid** section of the **Partido Socialista Obrero Español** (PSOE) in the 1960s. After the ousting of the **Rodolfo Llopis**'s exiled leadership in

1972, he was poised to take over, but his position was weakened by divisions within the Madrid party branch and criticism of his "social democratic" views by the party's Seville branch. At the October 1974 Suresnes congress, Madrid was marginalized and the leadership largely carved up between Seville and Bilbao. Castellano was elected to the party's national executive, but resigned soon afterward. He was to reemerge in 1979 as a key figure among those leftists who opposed the party's turn to the right under **Felipe González**. Castellano criticized the party's electoralism, the weight of the apparatus, and the stifling of internal democracy. In this year, along with other leftists, he formed Izquierda Socialista (Socialist Left), which operated as a "current" within the PSOE. However, the group was always handicapped by fear of expulsion and the requirement for all Socialists to defend party congress decisions. He was, finally, forced out in 1987 and formed part of the small left-socialist **Partido de Acción Socialista** (PASOC). He was during the 1990s to play an important role in the construction of the left-wing coalition **Izquierda Unida**, but grew increasingly unhappy with the policies pursued by its leader, **Julio Anguita**.

CASTIELLA Y MAIZ, FERNANDO MARÍA (1907–1976). Fernando María Castiella was **Francisco Franco**'s foreign minister between February 1957 and October 1969. He was born into an upper-class family in Bilbao on 9 December 1907, and went on to study law at the University of Madrid. He was from an early age drawn to **Catholic** politics, joining the **Asociación Católica Nacional de Propagandistas** and writing for *El Debate*, the mouthpiece of the **Confederación Española de Derechas Autónomas**, during the **Second Republic**.

As the regime played up its Catholic image from 1945, he moved into prominence. Between 1941 and 1942, he had fought in the **Blue Division**, but once he had been made foreign minister he formed part of a group of high-ranking Catholics who discreetly sought reform. His time as foreign minister was marked by an attempt to follow a foreign policy to a degree independent from the United States by consolidating relations with the Third World. Once the Vatican began to move in a more liberal direction from the early 1960s, he also entered into negotiations in order to try to stabilize relations. This earned him the ire of Franco's right-hand man, **Luis Carrero Blanco**, who saw him as one of a group of dangerous liberals (*aperturistas*) who were calling the fundamentals of the regime into question. Carrero Blanco, therefore, took advantage of the **Matesa scandal** to have him dismissed along with **Manuel Fraga** and **Ruiz Solís** in October 1969. *See also* FOREIGN POLICY.

CASTILE. The kingdom (*reino*) of Castile ("Castilla" in the **Castilian language**) emerged in the eighth century in the north of the actual province of Burgos. It was in this area that Castilian developed during the 11th century. During the Middle Ages, it was integrated into the **Crown of Castile**, but from the 16th century, the area corresponding to the central Spanish *meseta* (plateau) became differentiated, with the south known as New Castile (Castilla La Nueva) and most of the north (which included the city of **Madrid** and the Atlantic coastal areas which presently comprise the autonomous communities of Cantabria and La Rioja) called Old Castile. León, which was in the far north of the *meseta* and also formed part of the Crown of Castile, was recognized as a separate region. These regions would not, however, have any administrative functions. When the new administrative map of Spain, corresponding to the **State of the Autonomies**, was drawn up in 1978, Madrid became a separate autonomous community, the area corresponding to New Castile became Castilla-La Mancha, and most of the territory comprising Old Castile (except the Atlantic coast), along with León, became Castilla y León.

From the early 20th century, figures as diverse as **Miguel Unamuno** and General **Francisco Franco** have seen Castile (and especially the Castilian peasantry) as the bedrock of Spanish identity, but there is, at the same time, a strong sense of regional belonging. In left-wing circles, from the mid-nineteenth century the people of Castile were associated with the defense of local and national liberties. This could be seen, it was argued, in such events as the **Comuneros' revolt** in the 16th century and the Madrid rising against the forces of the troops of Napoleon Bonaparte on 2 May 1808. On the right, on the other hand, ideologues have looked back to the central role medieval Castile played in forging Spanish unity and building an empire in the Americas. Hence they have seen Castile as the core of Spain's Catholic-imperial heritage.

CASTILE, CROWN OF. *See* CROWN OF CASTILE.

CASTILIAN LANGUAGE. Throughout most of Spain's history, the country's major language (and the language that most people outside Spain refer to as "Spanish") was known as Castilian (*castellano*). This made sense because it was, in fact, one of the four major languages spoken in the country (the others being **Basque, Catalan,** and **Galician**). It grew out of Latin in the 11th century in the area in the north of the actual province of Burgos, and was subsequently exported to the south with the "**Reconquest**." It was also codified very early. Antonio de Nebrija's 1492 Castilian grammar was the first of any European language.

During the following two centuries, its importance grew for two reasons. First, by the reign of the **Catholic Monarchs** it was the dominant language of the **Crown of Castile**, the major partner in the 1479 **Union of the Crowns**. Hence, it became the language of the Spanish court and of the central administration. Second, the colonization of America was a Castilian enterprise, with the result that it became the language of Spain's vast colonial administration and of the new American ruling class. Moreover, during the 17th century it also established itself as the major vehicle of elite literary culture in both the Crown of Castile and the **Crown of Aragón**. Subsequently, in the early 18th century, Spain's first **Bourbon** king, **Felipe V**, abolished the privileges (*fueros*) enjoyed in the Crown of Aragón. This meant that Castilian was now the single language used throughout the Spanish administration. The language's status as Spain's official language was reflected in the foundation, in 1713, of the Real Academia Española (Spanish Royal Academy), whose role was to standardize the language and produce a standard dictionary and grammar.

Until the early 20th century, the language was still referred to as Castilian. However, in the context of the process of nation building, outside **Catalonia**, in elite political and cultural circles, it was increasingly called "Spanish." This was a process boosted by Spain's two periods of dictatorship, under **Miguel Primo de Rivera** and **Francisco Franco**, when the name "Spanish" was used to emphasize that it was the country's official language (while the country's other languages were merely regional tongues with no official status). This change in status was reflected in the decision by Real

Academia Española, in 1929, to change the name of its dictionary from *Diccionario de la lengua castellana* to *Diccionario de la lengua española*. After the death of Franco, the **Constitution of 1978** recognized Spain's linguistic plurality (with a degree of purposeful ambiguity), stating that "Castilian is the official Spanish language of the state." However, in central and southern Spain, the general public almost invariably calls the language "Spanish." This contrasts with the **Basque Country**, Catalonia, and **Galicia**, where people normally refer to the Castilian language.

CASTRO Y MURGUÍA, ROSALÍA DE (1837–1885). Rosalía de Castro was one of Spain's foremost 19th-century poets. She was born in Santiago de Compostela and lived in **Galicia** until moving to **Madrid** at the age of 19. There she married the journalist, historian, and future Galician nationalist politician Manuel Martínez Murguía (1833–1923). Castro herself wrote part of her *oeuvre* in the **Galician language**, hence contributing the resurgence of Galician literary culture—the so-called Ruxurdimento. Her first great collection of poems, *Cantares Gallegos* (*Galician Songs*), published in 1863, was a defense of Galician folklore and customs and an ode to the Galician countryside.

CATALAN LANGUAGE. Catalan (*català*) is spoken in **Catalonia**, **Valencia** (where it is known as **Valencian** [*valencià*]), the Balearic Islands, a strip of land within Aragón (La Franja), several municipalities in Murcia, the country of Andorra (of which it is the official language), the French territory of Roussillon, and the city of L'Alguer on the island of Sardinia. Within Spain, it is regularly spoken by around seven million people. It is one of the Romance languages that developed out of Latin following the fall of the Roman Empire, with its major contours established by the 10th century. Its prestige was bolstered because it was the principal language of the **Crown of Aragón**, which during the Middle Ages established a powerful Mediterranean empire. Its status slowly declined after the unification of Spain under the **Catholic Monarchs** in 1479, with **Castilian** (or "Spanish") establishing itself as the language of the Spanish court and, increasingly, of elite culture. However, both Catalonia and Valencia retained their own separate parliament (**Cortes**) and internal administration, in which Catalan remained the official language.

This was only to change when **Felipe V**'s Nueva Planta decrees of 1707–1716 swept away Catalan and Valencian institutions (or *fueros*). Catalan then lost all official status, though it continued to be spoken widely by the local population. This remained the case in the early 20th century, most notably because, given the poor **education** system, the Spanish state failed to extend the use of Castilian to nonnative speaking areas very effectively. In the mid-19th century, the new Romantic movement, the **Renaixença**, tried to reestablish Catalan as a literary language in both Catalonia and Valencia. However, at the end of the century the paths taken by the language in Catalonia and Valencia began to diverge. In Catalonia, it was given a great boost in the 1900s when it was adopted by the Catalan nationalist or **Catalanist** movement as a major signifier of Catalan national identity. Henceforth, this increasingly powerful Catalanist movement would demand home rule. Furthermore, in 1914 Catalonia's first decentralized administrative body, the **Mancomunitat**, standardized the language by adopting the orthographic and grammatical norms that had been devised by the philologist Pompeu Fabra (1868–1948). Pro-Catalanist identity was strengthened by the Spanish nationalist dictatorships of generals **Miguel Primo de Rivera** and **Francisco Franco**. During the **Franco regime**, demands for home rule and for the co-official status of the Catalan language became entwined with calls for democratization of the country's political structures. For this reason, even parties and unions like the **Partit Socialista Unificat de Catalunya** and **Comisiones Obreras**, a large part of whose members came from Castilian-speaking southern Spain, integrated into the Catalanist consensus.

With the democratization of Spain following Franco's death in 1975 and the organization of the **State of the Autonomies**, Catalanists were able to put their program into effect. Catalan became the principal language of the autonomous government, called the **Generalitat**, and of the Catalan parliament. The Catalan nationalist party, **Convergència i Unió**, also promoted the "normalization" of Catalan usage. Most important in this respect has been the elevation of Catalan to the principal language in the territory's state **education** system. The existence of a strong nationalist movement has meant that Catalan has remained the dominant language of the indigenous middle classes, which, in turn, has resulted in migrant families from outside Catalonia identifying the language with social advancement. This has led Spanish nationalists to claim that the Castilian language is now under threat in Catalonia. This is a view held, above all, by the **Partido Popular**, and, within Catalonia, by a new party called **Ciudadanos de Cataluña**. However, helped by large-scale migration, first from southern Spain, and then, from the 1990s, from North Africa and South America, Castilian remains widely spoken in the larger towns and cities. Its widespread usage has been further reinforced by the fact that it is the language of the central state and most of the media. Indeed, Catalan nationalists still see their language as on the defensive. Around 95 percent of Catalans understand the language, but a study by the Generalitat carried out in 2003 indicated that it was the "usual language" of just over 50 percent of the inhabitants of Catalonia. *See also* FLAGS OF SPAIN.

CATALAN SOLIDARITY. *See* SOLIDARITAT CATALANA.

CATALANISM. Catalanism was an ideology developed by **Valentí Almirall**, who, in the 1880s, demanded political autonomy for **Catalonia** and a predominant role for the **Catalan language** within the territory. It has often been seen as synonymous with Catalan nationalism, but the term was in fact rather ambiguous, allowing both Catalan nationalists (who claimed Catalonia was a totally separate nation) and regionalists (who wanted Catalan autonomy, but saw themselves as both Spaniards and Catalans) to work within the same parties. This was the case of the **Lliga Regionalista**, the major Catalanist party of the early 20th century. Recently, members of the Catalan Socialist party, the **Partit dels Socialistes de Catalunya-Partido Socialista Obrero Español**, have argued that they are Catalanists but not Catalan nationalists. They associate nationalism with an aggressive imperialistic political stance, but maintain that they are simply in favor of Catalan home rule. *See also* FLAGS OF SPAIN.

CATALONIA. Catalonia is to be found in the north of Spain, on the eastern Mediterranean coast. It is delineated by the Pyrenees to the north, stretches just beyond the River Ebro to the south, and reaches past the River Segre to the west. The territory is very mountainous. Apart from the Pyrenees, the coastal plane is separated from the interior by the Catalan Mountain Range (*cordillera catalana*). The territory is made up of four provinces (though Catalan nationalists would regard the province as an artificial imposition of centralizing Spanish governments): **Barcelona**, Girona, Lleida, and Tarragona. In 2007, the population of Catalonia was 7,210,508, of which 5,332,513 lived in the province of Barcelona. Catalonia has its own separate **Catalan language**, dialects of which are also spoken, above all, in **Valencia**, the Balearic Islands, Andorra, and the French territory of Roussillon.

In the early Middle Ages, Catalonia formed part of the **Crown of Aragón**, which established a prosperous commercial empire in the Mediterranean. However, in the 15th century, its component parts were seriously weakened by epidemics and by fierce social and political conflict. Hence, it was the junior partner in the dynastic union with the **Crown of Castile** in 1479. Over the next two centuries, Catalonia formed part of a composite monarchy in which it retained its own parliament (**Cortes**), which had the power to grant taxes and which continued to use the Catalan language. However, the lack of contribution from Catalonia in particular, and the Crown of Aragón in general, to the maintenance of the Spanish **Habsburg** Empire led to tensions. In 1640, the growing financial and military demands of the **count-duke of Olivares** provoked a rebellion in Catalonia, which lasted for 12 years. Matters came to a head after **Felipe V**, the grandson of King Louis XIV of France, came to the throne in 1700. Significant sectors of Catalan society supported the rival pretender to the throne, the Habsburg Charles of Austria, and the territory became the focus of opposition to the **Bourbon** succession. In response, after the fall of Barcelona in September 1714, the territory's institutions were swept away and the Catalan language lost all official status.

Over the past 100 years, **Catalanist** demands for home rule and a powerful and sometimes highly radicalized **labor movement** have meant that the territory has frequently been the center of the attentions of central government. The precocious growth of labor unions was the result of Catalonia's early industrialization, based, above all, on the expansion of the **cotton textile industry**. From the 1870s through to the 1930s, **anarchists** or anarcho-syndicalists played a key role in the organization of labor federations, which were founded in Barcelona and which subsequently spread to other parts of Spain.

The most notable example was the **Confederación Nacional del Trabajo** (CNT), which was set up in 1910. Labor grew particularly rapidly in the boom conditions that followed the declaration of **World War I** in 1914. As the economic climate deteriorated, from 1919 violent social conflict spread onto the streets of Barcelona. And in the 1930s, important sections of labor would remain wedded to the CNT, which collectivized much of Catalan industry during the **Spanish Civil War**.

The transformation of Catalan nationalism (or regionalism) into a mass movement can be traced back to the late 19th century. The 19th century saw Catalan social elites abandoning the native Catalan tongue for **Castilian**, Spain's official language. However, from the 1830s, groups of writers and poets tried to revive the language and exalt Catalan traditions. This movement, known as the **Renaixença**, reached its peak in the 1880s. In this same decade, **Valentí Almirall** drew up a specifically Catalanist program of action. It was not, however, until Spain's defeat in the **Spanish-American War** of 1898 that Catalanism really took off, with the foundation of the **Lliga Regionalista** in 1901. The "disaster" had led to the loss of important markets for Catalan industry in Cuba and Puerto Rico, and in its aftermath the central government put up taxes on industry and commerce in order to try to deal with the ballooning budget deficit. This crystallized a widespread belief that inefficient **Madrid**-based governments were ruining Catalonia and that only representatives of specifically Catalan parties would defend Catalonia's interests. It seems that it was the survival of a separate language and customs that allowed the frustrations experienced to be expressed in specifically nationalist terms. Furthermore, the sense of Catalan modernity in comparison with the rest of Spain was reinforced by the appearance of the **architectural** and artistic **modernista** movement, epitomized in the figures of **Antoni Gaudí** and the young **Pablo Picasso**. Catalonia's emergence as a major European center of the arts would subsequently be reinforced by the emergence of **Salvador Dalí** and **Joan Miró**.

Catalanism was, at the same time, reinforced by the support it received from sectors of the Catalan **Catholic Church**. Over the next 30 years, the right-wing Lliga and also various left-of-center **republican** parties pushed for Catalan autonomy. The Lliga would retain hegemony until the years 1919–1923, but its compromises with the central government would lead it to become discredited and overtaken by more radical options. During the **Second Republic**, the most powerful Catalanist party would be the left-wing **Esquerra Republicana de Catalunya** (ERC). A degree of administrative decentralization was achieved with the setting up of the **Mancomunitat** in 1914, but it was not until 1932, during the Second Republic, that home rule was granted.

Catalan nationalism and labor organization were, in the late 19th and early 20th centuries, viewed with suspicion if not hostility by central government, much of the Church hierarchy, and the **military**. The military in particular was violently opposed to Catalan nationalism and wedded to the principles of hierarchy and order. It is no surprise then that between 1923 and 1931 the **Primo de Rivera dictatorship** drove the CNT, Catalan nationalists, and the Catalan language underground. More brutal was the **Franco regime**, which assumed the reins of power in 1939. Under Franco, independent unions were banned, home rule abolished, and, at least in the 1940s, the Catalan language virtually prohibited.

From the 1950s, Spain rapidly industrialized and Catalonia underwent massive economic and social change. In Barcelona and surrounding towns, large new chemical and metal plants sprang up and a great flood of migrants from southern Spain arrived in search of work. This led to the belief in many circles that the Catalan language was all but dead. The prognosis was to be proved wrong, for from the 1960s both working-class and Catalanist opposition revived and achieved a high degree of cooperation. Working-class protest was channeled through the dissident working-class branches of **Acción Católica**, the **Juventud Obrera Católica** and **Hermandad Obrera de Acción Católica**, and through **Comisiones Obreras** and the Communist **Partit Socialista Unificat de Catalunya** (PSUC). Catalanist dissent was more middle-class and based on the Catalan wing of the Catholic Church and student and cultural associations. It was given a popular edge by the **Nova Cançó** protest song movement that emerged in the late 1950s. But because Catalan nationalism was based more on culture than ethnic origin, it was not hard for migrant workers, Catalan leftists, and Catalanists to ally in the demand for political freedoms, trade union rights, and an autonomy statute. The key moment was the formation in 1971 of a wide opposition front called the Assemblea de Catalunya (Catalan Assembly). And between this date and 1975, Catalonia was the center of a wave of large strikes and demonstrations by the opposition forces.

Once Franco had died and regime reformers acquiesced to a **transition to democracy**, it was obvious Catalonia would have to be granted a new autonomy statute that would make Castilian and Catalan co-official languages. The Spanish prime minister, **Adolfo Suárez**, agreed provisionally to restore the **Generalitat** in 1978. Then, following the approval of the **State of the Autonomies** in the same year, the first elections to the Generalitat were held in 1980. During the following two decades, what might be called a Catalanist consensus operated in the territory. The key political forces, the left-wing **Partit dels Socialistes de Catalunya-Partido Socialista Obrero Español** (PSC-PSOE) and PSUC, and the center-right nationalist coalition **Convergència i Unió** (CiU), all backed home rule and official status for the Catalan language. At the same time, given its anti-Catalanist stance, the Spanish right-wing coalition, **Alianza Popular**, and its successor, the **Partido Popular**, failed to achieve the same levels of support as in most of Spain. This consensus meant that there was little room for extremism. A **terrorist** group called Terra Lliure (Free Land), which aimed for total Catalan independence, emerged, but it remained extremely small and was never able to launch a serious campaign of violence. Since 1979, the federalist-Catalanist PSC-PSOE has won all the general elections, while the CiU coalition was the most voted force in elections to the autonomous parliament between 1980 and 1996 (and its leader, **Jordi Pujol**, was president of the Generalitat from 1980 to 2003). Since the elections to the autonomous parliament of November 2003, government has passed into the hands of a coalition of left-wing parties (the PSC-PSOE, ERC, and the left-green party **Iniciativa per Catalunya-Verds**), but it has followed a similar pro-Catalanist policy to that of its CiU predecessors. The presidents of the Generalitat have been the PSC-PSOE leaders **Pascual Maragall** (2003–2006) and José Montilla (2006–2008).

The Generalitat has, since 1980, tried to strengthen the Catalan language through **television**, publishing and education. Most controversially, in 1993, the Catalan parliament approved a decree making Catalan rather Castilian the main instrument of instruction within the primary and secondary **education** system. At present Barcelona is a bilingual city, while in small-town and rural Catalonia Catalan is the dominant language. However, in the 1990s, growing dissatisfaction with the Catalan autonomy statute emerged, especially because of what were seen as its financial limitations. This has helped spur the revival of the more radical nationalist party, ERC. By 2003, reform of the Catalan statute was supported by all the main Catalan parties with the exception of the PP. Hence, a proposed new statute was approved by 90 percent of the Catalan parliament in September 2005. Parts of the statute were opposed by the PSOE government (particularly the financial aspects and the declaration that Catalonia was a nation). This led to tense negotiations between November 2005 and January 2006. A compromise was finally reached, allowing the statute to be approved in a referendum on 18 June 2006. The push to Catalanize Catalan society provoked a reaction in some liberal antinationalist Catalan circles and to concerns in sectors of the migrant community. This led to the appearance of a new anti-Catalan nationalist party, **Ciudadanos de Cataluña**. The opposition PP also launched a campaign against the new autonomy statute and appealed to the Constitutional Tribunal to annul several of its articles. This was accompanied by an anti-Catalanist campaign in sectors of the right-wing press and media (especially *El Mundo*, **COPE**, and *Libertad Digital*). As a result, in the March 2008 general elections, there was a good deal of tactical voting, with considerable numbers of Catalans switching to the PSC-PSOE in order to keep the PP out of government. The result was a massive PSC-PSOE victory in Catalonia (with 25 seats as against seven for the PP). This was a key factor in the PP's defeat.

CATHOLIC CHURCH. In medieval Spain, crown, Church, and nobility were the three great powers of the land. Ideologically, the Church played a key unifying role, giving a sense of mission to the "**Reconquest**" of Spain from the **Moors** and to the conquest of America. In an increasingly intolerant religious climate, from the late 15th century the **Catholic Monarchs**, also gave it the task—through the **Spanish Inquisition**—of maintaining religious orthodoxy in the face of the supposed threat posed by **Jews** and Moors. In the 16th century, with the **Crown of Castile** at the center of Europe's major empire, the Church then became a key component in the Catholic **Counter-Reformation** against the new Protestant "heresy." This merged into a broader struggle to raise the standard of the clergy and to put pressure on the population to ensure that it adhered to Catholic morality.

The Church also built up extensive landholdings. By the late 16th century, it was estimated that it owned about one-sixth of the land in the country. Furthermore, it had jurisdiction over large tracts of land that it did not own (so-called *señoríos eclesiásticos*), on which it was able to raise revenue from the local peasantry. However, from the reign of the Catholic Monarchs it was, in fact, increasingly subordinated to the state, above all through the crown's imposition on the pope of its choice of prelates. This right was accepted by the pope in 1523, and the monarch's dominant position was subsequently justified by the doctrine of regalism. Moreover, though the Church did not pay direct taxes, by surrendering part of its income from tithes (the *tercios reales*), sale of indulgencies (the *cruzada*), and the monarchs' mastership of the great military orders (which enjoyed ecclesiastical status), an increasingly large proportion of its income—estimated at around a half by the late 16th century—went to the state. The Spanish Inquisition itself was under the direct control of the monarchy.

During the weak rule of **Carlos II** in the late 17th century, the Church regained some autonomy, but the dominant position of the state was confirmed in the 18th century by the new **Bourbon** dynasty. From the 1700s, in part over this question, divisions were to open up within the Church. Spain's rulers, especially **Carlos III**, championed the introduction of moderate **Enlightenment** ideas into Spain, maintaining that scientific and economic progress went hand in hand. Such a position was supported by a small but influential group within the Church known as the Regalists or Jansenists. However, major sectors of the Church (the *ultramontanos* as they were increasingly called), their scholastic teachings under threat, feared that these ideas would undermine religious belief and threaten crown and altar. Rather than pander to "foreign ideas," they argued, Spain should look for inspiration in her glorious Catholic past. The Jesuits were particularly vociferous in this respect, leading to their expulsion from Spain in 1764.

The **French Revolution**, they believed, showed how right they were. In France, as a result, the clergy became servants of the state, their privileges were abolished, and Church land was nationalized and sold on the open market. Their Spanish brethren were to learn of its consequences firsthand, when many French clergy refused to abide by the 1891 French Constitution and were then forced to flee to Spain to avoid persecution. They were welcomed with open arms, and the stories they told hardened attitudes against the French. Ideological opposition turned to action when in 1793 France declared war on Spain, and French troops advanced into northern Catalonia. The local clergy were often at the forefront of a bitter guerrilla war against the French forces. The figure of the militant clergyman, virulently antiliberal and wedded to the old order, was thereby born. He was to be of crucial importance in the **Carlist** wars that raged through Spain over the next half century.

With the retreat of the invading army in the following year, the position of the Catholic Church seemed relatively secure. This was shattered in 1808 with the invasion of the Napoleonic army and the coronation of Napoleon's brother Joseph as King **José I** of Spain. Between 1810 and 1812, Spanish political opposition to the French invader was led by **liberals**. The constitution approved by the **Cortes of Cádiz** did not contemplate a separation of Church and state. Spanish liberals were Catholics, though they believed that the power and privileges of the Church had to be curtailed and that it should be subordinated to the state. However, most of the clergy remained fearful of liberalism, which they saw as inimical to the teachings of God and, therefore, as apostasy. Not surprisingly, then, with the return to Spain of **Fernando VII** in 1814, the Church strongly supported the reestablishment of absolutist rule. It was also instrumental in mobilizing support against the liberals during the **Constitutional Triennium** of 1820–1823, and greeted the new absolutist restoration of 1823 with great joy. The watershed for the Church finally came in the late 1820s when Fernando VII realized the need to compromise with the liberals. His appointment of his wife as regent shortly before his death in 1833 opened the door to a controlled transition to a liberal economy and society. Most of the clergy reacted by moving into opposition and supporting the claims of Fernando's absolutist brother, **Carlos María Isidoro Benito de Borbón y Borbón-Parma**, to the throne.

Over the next seven years, the clergy strongly supported the violent struggle waged by the so-called Carlists to destroy liberalism and reimpose absolutist rule. In response, the liberals imposed an ecclesiastical settlement harsher than that contemplated by their predecessors. The property of both the religious orders and the secular clergy was nationalized and sold off, and most of the male religious orders suppressed. The economic base of the Church's power was, therefore, cut away. This meant that with the defeat of the Carlists in 1839, the Church had to try to reach a compromise with the triumphant liberals. This was possible because the dominant rightwing strand of liberalism, embodied in the **Partido Moderado**, was not anticlerical. On the contrary, *moderados* believed that once the Church accepted its new position in society, through its teachings it could play an important role in ensuring social peace and stability. Negotiations between the Church and *moderados* culminated in the concordat of 1851, which confirmed Catholicism as the country's official religion, while the state also assumed the obligation to pay the salaries of the lay clergy and allowed a limited reestablishment of the clerical orders. In return, the Vatican accepted the sale of Church land carried out over the previous 30 years.

Apart from the parenthesis of the years 1868–1873, the concordat formed the basis of Church-state relations until 1931. It also made possible a tacit alliance between the Church hierarchy and the most conservative liberals. Most clergy remained suspicious of all manifestations of liberalism, but a *modus vivendi* with right-wing liberals had the advantage of affording them state support. However, the Church's identification with the right and its employment of a discourse that anathematized religious and other freedoms and extolled the inevitability of social inequality earned it the opposition of the left and much of the urban populace. This was brought to the fore with the anti-Church disturbances that broke out during the **Democratic Sexennium** of 1868–1874. With the rise to power of more radical liberal parties after the **Glorious Revolution** of 1868, the Church once more saw itself as under threat. The new **Constitution of 1869** did not dissolve the official ties between Church and state, though it permitted freedom of worship for the first time in Spanish history. However, the Republican constitution of 1873 (which did not, finally, come into force) sanctioned a break between Church and state. Most clergy in northern Spain reacted by throwing their weight behind the rekindled Carlist rebellion, but much of the

Church hierarchy was not adverse to a restoration of the Bourbon monarchy to safeguard its position.

Under the **Cánovas Restoration** of 1875, the understanding between the Church hierarchy and conservative liberals was strengthened. The new **Constitution of 1876** reestablished the ties between Church and state, though in order to bring less conservative liberals onboard, Article 11 allowed for the worship of other religions in private. Though this angered the clergy, the hierarchy was willing to compromise. This was encouraged by Pope Leo XIII, who called for the Church to work with Europe's liberal regimes. The key figure in this respect was **Alejandro Pidal**, who, with the backing of much of the Church establishment, integrated his Unión Católica (Catholic Union) into the **Partido Conservador** in 1884. Most of the lower clergy, however, continued to sympathize with Carlism and **Traditionalism**, many backed the extreme **Integrist** movement set up by Cándido Nocedal (1821–1885) and his son, Ramón Nocedal (1846–1907). Yet the hierarchy's conciliation with the Restoration regime was a banner of convenience, and the Church still hankered after a totally confessional state. This would remain the case until well into the 20th century, with **Christian-democrat** ideas making little progress. This was manifest in the work of the major Catholic thinker of the time, **Marcelino Menéndez y Pelayo**.

Between 1875 and 1914, the Church was able to raise its profile in Spanish society considerably. Lay associations were founded, most importantly the broadly-based **Acción Católica** (AC) and the more elitist **Asociación Católica Nacional de Propagandistas** (ACNP), aimed at winning the hearts and minds of social elites and the masses. At the same time, the number of religious orders grew rapidly and spearheaded the Church's policy, begun at mid-century, of reestablishing its social standing by educating the sons and daughters of the well-to-do. In this it was very successful. By 1900, in many areas there were more private Catholic schools, run by the orders, than state schools. It also managed to link important sectors of the peasantry to the cause with the organization of agrarian syndicates, which from 1917 were integrated into the **Confederación Nacional Católica Agraria**.

It enjoyed less success in urban working-class circles, mainly because the **Catholic unions** it established, under the influence of the ultraconservative **Second Marquis of Comillas**, emphasized class harmony over the fight to improve working conditions. Indeed, among the urban working and lower-middle classes, antagonism toward the Church intensified from the turn of the century, during the "clerical" **Francisco Silvela** and **Antonio Maura** administrations. Nowhere was this opposition greater than in **Barcelona**, where in July 1909 there were serious anticlerical riots, baptized with the name of the **Tragic Week**. After 1900, the **Partido Liberal** also showed itself willing to try to limit the power of the Church in order to gain some popular recognition. Most important was the so-called Ley del Candado (Padlock Law) passed in December 1910 by the **José Canalejas** administration, which aimed—unsuccessfully—to limit the growth of the orders.

Growing social turbulence after 1914 made the Church fearful that it would, in a revolutionary conjuncture, be the object of popular vengeance. It was with relief, therefore, that most of the hierarchy greeted **Miguel Primo de Rivera**'s coup d'etat in September 1923. The **Primo de Rivera dictatorship** was strongly influenced by the antiliberal Catholic-corporatist ideas that were expressed by figures like **José Calvo Sotelo** in the ACNP and on the right of the **Maurista** movement, and responded to clerical demands by establishing censorship and enforcing Catholic morals in public. The proclamation of the **Second Republic** in April 1931, therefore, came as a great shock to the Church. The new Republican authorities were strongly anticlerical, abolishing state payment of clergy's wages and forbidding members of the orders from teaching. Meanwhile, the new **Constitution of 1931** separated Church and state. This only served to confirm in the clergy's eyes the evils of liberalism and democracy. In order to combat the Republican administrations, Catholics realized that they had to mobilize in opposition. This was the background to the formation of the first mass Catholic party in Spain, the **Confederación Española de Derechas Autónomas**.

Catholics were the natural allies of the **Nationalists** during the **Spanish Civil War**. Support was cemented by a wide-ranging persecution of clergy in the Republican zone, particularly in **anarchist**-dominated areas. Overall, over 6,000 priests and members of the religious orders were assassinated. The Nationalists came to see the war as in large measure a crusade of Catholic Christian civilization against the atheistic, Bolshevik hordes. The Nationalist side and, subsequently, the **Franco regime**, drew on the imagery of the "**Reconquest**" of the peninsula from the Moors, and looked back fondly to the 15th- and 16th-century imperial triumphs of the Catholic Monarchs. It was this traditional Catholic Spain that, the Nationalist propagandists affirmed, had to be recaptured. This backing was reciprocated by almost all the Church hierarchy. Hence, on 29 December 1936, the primate and archbishop of Toledo, Cardinal **Isidro Gomá**, and the leader of the Nationalist forces, **Francisco Franco**, signed a six-point agreement whereby Franco promised the Church full freedom in all its activities. **Education** was put totally in the hands of the Church, though it had to accept Franco's right to appoint bishops. In return, on 1 July 1937, a collective letter by the hierarchy of the Church was published supporting the regime, with only two dissident prelates refusing to sign. As in the case of the Primo de Rivera dictatorship, only in **Catalonia** and the **Basque County**, where sectors of the Catholic middle-class supported autonomy, was there much dissent.

The political importance of the Church further increased from 1943, with the declining fortunes of the Axis powers and the regime's consequent desire to play down the importance of the fascistic single party, the **Falange Española Tradicionalista y de las Juntas de Ofensiva Nacional Sindicalista**. This phase of Francoism, which came to be known as **National Catholicism**, would last at least until the late 1950s. Franco's awareness of the need to raise the profile of the Church to gain Western sympathy (or at least minimize condemnation) was reflected in the appointment of a leading figure within AC and the ACNP, **Alberto Martín Artajo**, to the post of foreign secretary in 1945. It was a position he was to retain for 14 years. At the same time, in order to advance the regime's reconciliation with the West, Franco wished to establish a new concordat with Rome. It was finally signed in 1953, and, together with the military pacts with the United States in the same year and Spain's admittance to the United Nations in 1955, it signified the end of the regime's postwar isolation.

The consolidation of the Franco regime saw an attempt to impose traditionalist Catholic orthodoxy in all walks of public and private life. On the surface, this seemed to be a success, yet by the 1950s voices of discontent at the Church's total identification with the

Franco regime were to be heard. Divisions first emerged within AC. Specialized branches of the association aimed at recruiting among workers, the **Juventud Obrera Católica** (JOC) and **Hermandad Obrera de Acción Católica** (HOAC), were set up in the 1940s. These associations showed a concern for problems facing the youth and workers and developed an interest in social issues. Many workers were, especially from the 1950s, to join these movements because they provided a vehicle for them to voice their demands with less fear of persecution than they faced if they joined the clandestine opposition. Hence, by the early 1960s, these branches had about 110,000 members, and they played a significant role in the development of the semi-clandestine workers' labor organization, **Comisiones Obreras** (CC.OO). Indeed, the growing links between Catholicism and the workers' movement led, in the 1960s, to the emergence of "worker priests," who opened their churches to clandestine labor meetings. Most radical of all was the **Frente de Liberación Popular** (FLP), which preached a revolutionary, egalitarian Christianity. These changes were also marked by a shift in the stance of some leading Christian intellectuals, such as **Pedro Laín Entralgo** and José Luis López Aranguren (1909–1996), who by the 1950s had come to reject the sectarianism of the Spanish Church and stressed the need for dialogue between different faiths and cultural traditions.

This growing dissent needs to be viewed in the context of the stabilization of liberal democracies in western Europe and the accelerating cultural change to which the Church had to respond. Yet during the 1950s, such perspectives were rejected by the old hierarchy. Moreover, the decade was to see the rise of a new lay right-wing grouping within the Church, the **Opus Dei**. The *Opus Deistas* were Francoists, but were at the same time economic liberals. They had powerful friends within the administration and were able to mold the regime's **economic policy** from the late 1950s. Nonetheless, the following decade was to see growing calls from within the Church for a loosening of the ties with the state. Such demands were encouraged by the appointment, in 1958, of a new, more liberal pope, John XXIII, who, in 1962, convened the Second Vatican Council (1962–1965). The conclusions of the council fell like a bombshell on the Spanish Church. They expressed concern for human rights and social justice, and emphasized the need for dialogue. This accelerated the movement for reform, which was again particularly strong in Catalonia and the Basque Country. Between 1965 and 1968, Francoists still predominated within the hierarchy, and AC silenced the HOAC and JOC by taking away their autonomy, thereby driving many reformers away from the Church. But when, in February 1969, Franco was forced to appoint the reformer Vicente Enrique y Tarancón (1907–1994), primate of Spain, in order to maintain cordial relations with the Vatican, the pace of change accelerated rapidly. In 1966, the Conferencia Episcopal Española (Spanish Episcopal Conference—CEE) was established, implementing the Vatican Council's decision to give national hierarchies a more collegiate structure, and it was through this body that reform was pushed through.

Between this date and 1973, under Vatican pressure, the CEE appointed a large number of more liberal bishops. By the early 1970s, reforming clergy were in the ascendant. Hence, in September 1971, a priests' and bishops' conference, rejecting the role the Church had played over the last 40 years, called for a "reconciliation" of Spaniards divided by the civil war. Then, in January 1973, the CEE set out the view of the majority of bishops in a document entitled "The Church and the Political Community." The CEE defended the Church's independence from the state, calling for an end of the head of state's right to appoint bishops and demanding respect for political pluralism. From that date, the Church was increasingly alienated from the Francoist authorities. This produced great anger and charges of ingratitude among the Francoist elite, but the action the state could take was limited. Indeed, the clergy's privileges had been enhanced by the 1953 concordat. Eventually, a special prison was set up to cater to dissidents in the town of Zamora.

The Church's embracing of political pluralism made the **transition to democracy** far easier and meant politics in the mid-1970s would be much less polarized than in the mid-1930s. Under democracy, the institutional relationship between Church and state has changed. In 1976, King **Juan Carlos I** renounced the head of state's privilege of appointing bishops, though the question of the separation of Church and state was fudged in the **Constitution of 1978**. In order to avoid Church discontent, subsequent governments have continued to pay clergy's salaries. From 1988, the mechanism employed has been to allow taxpayers to pay 0.52 percent of income tax either to the Church or to charity (raised to 0.7 percent by the Socialist administration in 2005). In general elections, practicing Catholics have tended to vote for the right, but they have largely voted for the center-right rather than the far-right. Nevertheless, a considerable degree of pluralism has been visible. Already in the first democratic elections, held in June 1977, 10 percent of the Catholic vote went to the **Partido Socialista Obrero Español** (PSOE), and as its program became more moderate in the 1980s, so the percentage of its members who were practicing Catholics increased. Politically, the Church has been associated with conservative cultural causes. Hence, in 1983, it was at the forefront of a campaign against the PSOE government's proposed abortion law. At the same time, it has campaigned for the preservation of traditional family values and against sexual permissiveness. It has been able to get its views over more effectively than would otherwise have been the case by operating its own radio station, **COPE**.

Since the demise of Franco, the Church has had to cope with the secularization of society. In 2002, while 80.8 percent of Spaniards declared themselves Catholics, only 18.5 percent went to church every Sunday and 46 percent never went to church at all. However, it still retains an important influence over the middle class through its control over much of Spain's large private education sector. After the **Partido Popular** (PP) came to power in the mid-1990s, in line with the evolution of the Spanish right, it adopted a more strident tone in defense of conservative Catholic moral values. This attitude intensified after the victory of the PSOE in the March 2004 elections, with the Church, backed by the PP, launching campaigns against government legislation making divorce quicker, legalizing homosexual weddings, and against its education law, which introduced a new citizenship course that would involve discussion of same-sex parenting and would allow state schoolchildren to opt out of religious education. At the same time, it also reopened debate on the 1985 abortion law. Under such figures as the archbishop of Toledo and primate of Spain Antonio Cañizares (1945–) and the archbishop of Madrid Antonio María Rouco Varela (1936–), the Church adopted a "neotraditionalist" ideology, once again claiming the right of moral tutelage over society.

The government, with its vice president, **María Teresa Fernández de la Vega**, at the forefront, tried to compromise by improving Church finance, watering down its educational reform, and holding back on legislation in its electoral program legalizing euthanasia and making abortion easier. This had little effect. After a big concentration in Madrid in "defense of the Christian family" on 30 December 2007, in which the government was overtly attacked, the PSOE's federal executive hit back, defending cultural pluralism and accusing the Church of political interference. On 31 January 2008, the permanent commission of the CEE went further, tacitly calling on voters to support the conservative right and vote against the PSOE. The Socialist leadership reacted angrily, especially because the Church's communiqué criticized the government for having established contacts with **ETA**. The fact that on 4 March 2008 Rouco Varela was elected president of the CEE indicates that relations between the Church and the new PSOE executive will remain tense.

CATHOLIC MONARCHS. The title of Catholic Monarchs (*Los Reyes Católicos*) was conferred on the king and queen of Spain, Fernando II of Aragón (1452–1516) and Isabel I of Castile (1451–1504), by Pope Alexander VI in 1494 as an expression of gratitude following the capitulation of the **Moorish** Kingdom of Granada.

Their rule, between 1479 and 1504/1516, has often been seen by **Catholic** historians as a glorious period during which the foundations for Spain's rise to the status of a great world power were laid. When they were married in 1469, Fernando was heir to the throne of the **Crown of Aragón** and Isabel the disputed heir to the throne of the **Crown of Castile**. Isabel was proclaimed queen of Castile in 1474, and, over the next two years, with the help of Aragonese forces, defeated her pro-Portuguese opponents in civil war. Fernando then succeeded his father as king of the Crown of Aragón in 1479. This opened the way to the integration of the Crowns of Aragón and Castile into a single monarchy, with geographical boundaries similar to those of Spain today. Nevertheless, it was a dynastic match (under which Fernando and Isabel retained their separate dynastic titles and maintained equal power) and did not signify the abolition of the two crowns. (Indeed, they were almost to go their separate ways once more, after the death of Isabel I in 1504.) At this time, the term "Spain" had no political meaning. It simply referred to the various peoples of the Iberian Peninsula. As a result, although the Crown of Castile was militarily and economically much stronger, the Crown of Aragón would retain its own separate institutions.

Nevertheless, after the dynastic match, with the resources of both kingdoms behind them, the monarchs were able to pursue their goals of strengthening their own power within their kingdoms and the international status of the Crowns of Castile and Aragón in Europe, and of imposing the Christian faith on their dominions, much more effectively than would otherwise have been the case. It proved a good partnership. Isabel was pious and honest and inspired loyalty and respect, while Fernando was a wily political operator. Within the Crowns of Aragón and Castile, they reestablished order after the civil wars of the previous century and began to build a more effective state machine: the political power of the aristocracy was checked, the administration and judiciary developed, and efforts made to moralize the Church.

At the same time, Fernando, who directed military and foreign policy, launched a 10-year siege of Granada, the last Moorish kingdom in the Peninsula (greatly helped by financial support from the Papacy). It fell at the beginning of 1492. Later in the year, Christopher Columbus, who had been commissioned by the Catholic Monarchs to find a new route to Asia (*Las Indias*) via the Atlantic, arrived in the Caribbean, thereby "discovering" America. The full importance of this event would become clear in the subsequent decade as Castile began to build its **colonial** empire on the American continent. More pressing problems for Fernando were the need to secure the Crown of Aragón's eastern border from the ever-present French threat and fend off the growing influence of the Ottoman Empire in the western Mediterranean. This he was, to a large extent, able to do with a combination of Castilian troops and intelligent international alliances. He secured French acquiescence to the definitive incorporation of Roussillon and the Cerdagne into the Crown of Aragón in 1493; captured the Kingdom of Naples in 1504, thereby thwarting French plans to control Italy and securing the Crown of Aragón's trade routes; and integrated part of the Kingdom of **Navarre** into the Crown of Castile in 1515.

However, the Catholic Monarchs' attempts to secure religious unity brought zealotry. In this case, it was Isabel who took the lead. In

1478, with papal blessing, they established the **Spanish Inquisition** in order to ensure that **Jews** who had converted to Christianity were really practising the Christian faith, and in 1492 all nonconverted Jews were expelled from the country. Moreover, from the late 1490s, in the Crown of Castile, Moors were forced to convert to Christianity. A situation was created in which "new Christians" were viewed with suspicion and became second-class citizens. This would be at the root of the "pure blood" (*limpieza de sangre*) movement, which began to make its presence felt in the 1480s, through which positions in the leading professions, public institutions, and the Church were reserved for old Christian families.

CATHOLIC UNIONS. Catholic unions were set up in Spain between the late 1880s and the 1930s in order to try to wean workers away from **anarchism** and socialism. However, most of these unions were under the control of the hierarchy of the **Catholic Church** and **Acción Católica**. In 1894, a Consejo Nacional de Corporaciones Católico-Obreras (National Council of Catholic Worker Corporations) was set up under the presidency of a shipping magnate, the **Second Marquis of Comillas**. In 1919, the council was renamed the Confederación Nacional de Sindicatos Obreros Católicos (National Confederation of Catholic Workers' Syndicates). These were highly conservative bodies, under strong employer influence, that laid stress on the moral redemption of workers rather than the defense of their economic interests. In these circumstances, they made little impact in working-class circles and could offer no effective opposition to either the anarchist **Confederación Nacional del Trabajo** (CNT) or the Marxist **Unión General de Trabajadores** (UGT). Only where Catholic unions were formed outside of the control of the hierarchy could they be more effective in channeling working-class demands and attain greater success. This was the case of the so-called **Sindicatos Libres** and of the trade union wing of the **Partido Nacionalista Vasco**, Solidaridad de Obreros Vascos (Basque Workers' Solidarity). *See also* LABOR MOVEMENT.

CAUDILLO. *Caudillo* was a **Castilian** word for military leader in medieval Spain. It was adopted by **Francisco Franco** during the **Spanish Civil War** as an equivalent to the German term Führer and the Italian Duce and in order to posit a link between his exploits and those of Spain's heroic warriors—preeminently El Cid Campeador (1044–1099)—during the "**Reconquest**" of Spain from the **Moors**. *See also* FRANCO REGIME.

CELA TRULOCK, CAMILO JOSÉ, MARQUIS OF IRIA FLAVIA (1925–2002).

Cela was one of the most important literary figures in 20th-century Spain, winning the Nobel Prize for Literature in 1989. He earned a reputation for quality writing in a diverse range of styles, in which the human condition took center stage. This could be seen in such works as *La familia de Pascual Duarte* (*The Family of Pascual Duarte*, 1942) and *Mrs Caldwell habla con su hijo* (*Mrs Caldwell Talks to Her Son*, 1953). Though he came from a conservative background, and at first sympathized with the **Franco regime**, he was also critical of its empty rhetoric and false morality. This came through in his bleak portrayal of postwar **Madrid**, *La colmena* (*The Hive*, 1951). In his latter years (rather like Kingsley Amis in Great Britain), he very much became the old curmudgeon of the Spanish literary scene, writing frequent columns in the press marked by his sarcastic criticisms of Spanish society.

CENTRE NACIONALISTA REPUBLICÀ (CNR)/NATIONALIST REPUBLICAN CENTER.

The CNR was a **republican**, **Catalan** nationalist party, formed in **Barcelona** in December 1906. Its founders had split from the **Lliga Regionalista** in April 1904, either because they considered it too conservative or insufficiently nationalist. From the beginning, the party was divided into two wings. Most influential were a group of center-left liberals, the best known of whom were Jaume Carner (1867–1934), Ildefons Sunyol (1866–1913), and, when he joined the party in 1909, Pere Coromines (1870–1939). Second, there were a group of young radical journalists who wrote for the party's daily, *El Poble Català*, including Gabriel Alomar (1873–1941), Antoni Rovira i Virgili (1882–1949), Claudi Ametlla (1883–1966), and Josep Pous i Pages (1873–1952). Under the leadership of Carner and Coromines, though attaining significant lower middle class support in Barcelona, the CNR was never seriously to challenge the Lliga for its upper middle class clientele nor able to gain a wide working-class base. In April 1910, it integrated into a new, broader-based party, the **Unió Federal Nacionalista Republicà**.

CENTRO DEMOCRÁTICO Y SOCIAL (CDS)/DEMOCRATIC AND SOCIAL CENTER. *See* SUÁREZ GONZÁLEZ, ADOLFO.

CERVANTES Y SAAVENDRA, MIGUEL DE (1547–1616). Cervantes was one of the greatest writers in early modern Europe, with his two-volume work, *Don Quijote de la Mancha* (1605 and 1615), widely regarded as the first modern novel. He was born into a noble family of moderate means in Alcalá de Henares. The first 33 years of his life were marked by a series of adventures on which he was to draw in his later work. He volunteered for military service and was wounded in the battle of **Lepanto** in 1571. Subsequently, in 1575, while returning home his ship was captured by Turkish pirates; he was ransomed and held as a captive for five years. On release in 1580, he settled in **Madrid**, took to writing, and earned a modest income as a tax farmer. On two occasions, in 1597 and 1602, he was briefly imprisoned because he could not pay off his debts. He started off writing plays before turning to prose fiction. But significant success eluded him until the publication of the first volume of *Don Quijote*. Parody and comic satire were his stock in trade, balanced by humanity and pathos. It was this combination that was behind the novel's phenomenal popularity.

CEUTA. *See* COLONIES.

CHRISTIAN DEMOCRACY. Christian democracy developed in Europe from the late 19th century. It represented an attempt to reconcile the **Catholic Church** with **liberalism** and to give the Church a more active role in the development by the state of programs of social reform. The strength of conservative, antiliberal sentiment in the Spanish Church meant that Christian-democratic ideals made headway slowly. The first unambiguously Christian-democratic politician was **Ángel Ossorio y Gallardo**, who, inspired by the Italian Partito Popolare, formed his own **Partido Social Popular** in 1922. However, most of the secular Catholic right supported General **Miguel Primo de Rivera**'s **corporatist** dictatorship in the 1920s. In the charged political atmosphere of 1930s, Spain, the Catholic Right, and Church hierarchy lined up behind the **Nationalist** rebellion against the **Second Republic**. From the 1950s, more reforming elements, above all linked to the lay Catholic associations **Acción Católica** and the **Asociación Católica Nacional de Propagandistas**, again raised the banner of Christian democracy. From the 1960s, **José María Gil-Robles** and **Joaquín Ruiz-Giménez** set up their own (more conservative and left-wing) Christian-democrat organizations and would fight the first elections after the death of General **Francisco Franco** in June 1977 under the banner of a Christian-Democrat Federation.

In the early 1970s, a group of younger reforming figures from elite Franco regime families formed a separate group called **Tácito**. However, as the **transition to democracy** got under way, rather than try to form a specifically confessional Christian-democratic party, they integrated into **Adolfo Suárez**'s **Unión del Centro Democrático** (UCD). Given the Church's support for the **Franco regime**, until the late 1970s they, no doubt correctly, felt that it made more electoral sense to join broader parties of the center and right rather than go it alone. The UCD went on to win the 1977 elections while the Christian-Democrat Federation gained no seats in parliament. Within the UCD, most Christian-democrats operated as a conservative current within the party, which grew increasingly disaffected with Suárez's leadership, most especially when he pushed a divorce law through parliament despite their opposition. When the UCD broke up, most of these figures joined **Alianza Popular**. And when the AP was refounded under the name of **Partido Popular** (PP) in 1990, it joined the Christian Democratic International. Other parties that declare themselves Christian-democratic are the **Basque** nationalist party, the **Partido Nacionalista Vasco**, and the **Catalan** regionalist/ nationalist party Unión Democràtica de Catalunya (Catalan Democratic Union), which forms part of the coalition **Convergència i Unió**.

CIERVA Y PEÑAFIEL, JUAN DE LA (1872–1936). Juan de la Cierva, a hard-line **Conservative** politician, played an important role in government during the latter period of the **Cánovas Restoration**. He was born in Mula in the province of Mucia and he built up his power base in Murcian local politics, establishing control over the *caciquista* networks in the region. He was first elected as a **Partido Conservador** (PC) deputy for Murcia in 1896. He was subsequently to become **Antonio Maura**'s right hand. He established close contact with Maura in 1905 and was his minister of the interior between 1907 and 1909. From this position, he "made" the April 1907 election, ensuring a PC victory (thereby calling into question Maura's reforming intentions). His authoritarian instincts were shown in the aftermath of the **Tragic Week**, when (with the approval of Maura) he orchestrated a wide-ranging repression, precipitating the government's fall in October. When the party divided at the end of 1913 he formed his own small faction, which was close to the **Mauristas**.

During the **crisis of 1917** he became closely linked to the military **Juntas de Defensa**, both defending their interests and using them as a springboard to strengthen his own position. In the November 1917 coalition government, he came in as minister of war and forced through legislation favorable to the Juntas. It was the divisions produced by his stance that, in good measure, brought the government down in March 1918.

From 1919, Cierva became a key representative of the right of the PC, who put the need to deal with the left-wing revolutionary threat above all other considerations. In Maura's April–June 1919 government, despite being minister of finance, he played a leading role in the repression of the Catalan **Confederación Nacional del Trabajo** (CNT) and was also active in the (largely unsuccessful) efforts to "make" the 1 June elections in favor of the Maurista and Ciervista candidates. With respect to his links with the **military**, a shrewd operator, he turned on the Juntas as their position weakened during 1921–1922. He was minister of war in Maura's August 1921–March 1922 coalition government and he played a key role in their illegalization. After the fall of this coalition, he would constantly criticize the PC government of **José Sánchez Guerra** and **Partido Liberal** coalition of **Manuel García Prieto** for their supposed lack of resolution in the face of subversion. Hence, he helped prepare the atmosphere that made the September 1923 coup by General **Miguel Primo de Rivera** possible. He withdrew from active politics during the dictatorship, but was involved in the attempt to resurrect the Restoration regime under Admiral Juan Bautista Aznar (1860–1933) at the beginning of 1931. He was one of the few important figures who tried to convince King **Alfonso XIII** to resist the coming of the **Second Republic** by all means in April of that year.

CINEMA. Cinema became an increasingly popular medium in Spain after 1914. Under the **Franco regime**, the industry was nationalized and heavily censored. The most interesting work was undertaken by directors like **Juan Antonio Bardem, Luis García Belanga, Carlos Saura,** and (from exile) **Luis Buñuel,** who, from the 1960s, satirized and criticized the regime's patriarchal, conservative, **Catholic** values. The overt sexuality and playful surrealism of Buñuel's films turned him into an international star, while Saura's portrayal of **gypsy** and flamenco culture also proved popular. In the 1980s, under the director general of cinematography, **Pilar Miró,** considerable sums were pumped into the Spanish film industry, though much of the output proved worthy rather than exciting. **Pedro Almodóvar,** a child of the *movida madrileña,* was however, to provide a new direction. His iconoclastic style was able to reach out to a wide national and international audience. In his slipstream, from the 1990s, other directors have aimed at international fame. Most successful has been Alejandro Amenábar (1972–), whose film *Mar Adentro (Sea Inside,* 2004) won the 2005 Academy Award for best foreign language film. Since the 1950s, Spain has also developed a strong acting tradition. The path was opened by Fernando Rey (1917–1944) and, subsequently, **Victoria Abril.** Spain now has a crop of internationally renowned actors including Antonio Banderas (1960–), Penélope Cruz (1974–), and Javier Bardem (1969–). Bardem won the 2008 Academy Award for best actor in a supporting role for his portrayal of a mass murderer in *No Country for Old Men* (2007).

CIUDADANOS DE CATALUÑA. This organization was founded by a number of Catalan intellectuals on 21 June 2005. Its most charismatic figure was and is the theater director and actor Albert Boadella (1943–). This initiative took place in the context of the growth of **Basta Ya** in the **Basque Country** and negotiations over the reform of **Catalonia**'s autonomy statute. Its key concern has been what it sees as the attempt by Catalan nationalists to impose the **Catalan language** and its rendition of Catalan culture on Catalonia. In contrast, it defends the bilingual nature of the territory and stresses its affinity with the rest of Spain. It has also denied that it can any way be classified as right wing, stating that it recruits from throughout the political spectrum. Catalan nationalists have hit back, accusing it of being a Spanish nationalist front and of having links with the right-wing Spanish media. On 7–8 August 2006, it became a political party, Ciutadanos de Cataluña-Partido de Ciudadania. It then did surprisingly well in the 1 December elections to the Catalan autonomous parliament, gaining 3 percent of the votes and three parliamentary seats. Subsequently, in its June 2007 congress, it declared itself to be a party of the center left. It has tried to recruit in other parts of Spain, but has been weakened by internal divisions. During the autumn of 2007, there were negotiations with **Basta Ya**, which formed a new political party to fight the March 2008 elections called **Unión de Progreso y Democracia**. However, its president, Albert Rivera (1979–), was opposed and no agreement could be reached. It performed poorly in these elections, obtaining only 0.7 percent of the vote.

CIVIL GUARD/GUARDIA CIVIL. From its creation in 1844 through to the 1970s, the burden of maintaining public order in Spain fell, to a large extent, on the shoulders of the Civil Guard. From the beginning, it was given the task of policing the countryside and smaller towns. It was set up as a civilian **police** force but was thereafter militarized, and in 1878 became an integral part of the Spanish **military**. This has been seen by historians as one of the major manifestations of the Spanish liberal state's inability to establish an effective civil administration. The Civil Guard was also isolated from the local population. From the force's inception, recruits never served in their own region, and members of the service were housed in barracks, often with their own food stores and school. This reflected the emphasis that the conservative-liberal political elite placed on the repression of dissent rather than the integration of the lower classes into the polity.

The Civil Guard also tended to establish close ties with local elites, who sometimes went so far as to pay for the construction of its accommodation. Not surprisingly, therefore, the institution tended to line up behind the political right. This could be seen during the July 1936 military rebellion when, outside the larger cities, the Civil Guard largely supported the **Nationalists**. During the early years of the **Franco regime**, the institution was employed as a counterinsurgency force to fight against the Republican guerrillas or *maquis*. At the same time, it was also given the task of policing Spain's frontiers and responsibility for traffic control over the country's main roads. Since the **transition to democracy**, it has shared policing duties with the National Police (Cuerpo Nacional de Policía). This has led to some overlap, ambiguities, and calls for reform. In addition, its links to the military have also been questioned, though, as yet, it has not been placed under civilian control. In recent years, it has also played a central role in the fight against **ETA terrorism**, drug trafficking, and illegal **immigration**.

CIVIL SERVICE. *See* PUBLIC ADMINISTRATION.

CIVIL WAR. *See* CARLISM; SPANISH CIVIL WAR.

COAL MINING. Coal **mining** in Spain has centered on the Asturian coal field. The first important mining enterprises were formed in the 1830s. Until the 1850s, however, the industry stagnated because of lack of demand. An opportunity for further growth was provided by the foundation of iron and steel and machine construction firms in Mieres and La Felguera from the end of the decade. But from the late 1880s, the focus of the **iron and steel industry** shifted to Vizcaya, and the Vizcaya steel industry became largely dependent on coal imports from Great Britain. This once again left Asturias out on a limb. The coal was of poor quality and could not compete with the price of British coal on arrival in Spain. This situation was only to improve in the 1890s when new **tariffs** were placed on foreign imports, a new **railway** line was opened linking the main line from Gijón to León, and the peseta was devalued.

Spanish neutrality during **World War I** provided a short-lived bonanza for the industry, but from the 1920s the old problems—aggravated by the growing difficulty of mining the Spanish seams and the opening of a large number of marginal pits—returned, leading to increasingly embittered social conflict. The authorities reacted by raising tariffs further in 1921 and, from 1926, by forcing Spanish **industry** to consume a proportion of Spanish coal. However, coal mining remained in crisis during the depressed economic climate of the 1930s. This produced a radicalization of the Asturian coal miners, who played a key role in the **October 1934 revolution**. State support was intensified during the **autarkic** phase of the **Franco regime**, with the result that productivity remained low, while the industry also had difficulty meeting Spanish demand. The liberalization of the late 1950s, therefore, led to a serious crisis. The state tried to stimulate productivity and rationalize production but, afraid of the social unrest a drastic restructuring would bring and pressured by powerful industrial interests who faced serious losses, it ended up nationalizing the sector with the foundation of HUNOSA in 1967. The state has from the **transition to democracy** tried to restructure mining, but has at the same time accepted heavy losses in order to contain the social costs.

COALICIÓN CANARIA/CANARY ISLANDS' COALITION. This is a conservative-regionalist party that operates in the **Canary Islands**. It was originally a coalition of parties, formed in 1993, and since 1995 it has been in charge of the islands' regional government (and its candidate has been president), in alliance with either the local **Partido Socialista Obrero Español** or **Partido Popular**. In the context of serious internal tensions, it became a single party in 2005. The present president (2008) of the regional government, Paulino Rivero (1952–), is the leader of the party, which has two deputies in the Spanish parliament.

COLD WAR. *See* FOREIGN POLICY; FRANCO REGIME; NORTH ATLANTIC TREATY ORGANIZATION; OPUS DEI.

COLONIES. Spain built an empire in the Americas (*Las Indias* or New World, as it was normally referred to) following the continent's "discovery" by Christopher Columbus in 1492. The empire took shape between the 1500s and 1540s, largely on the ruins of the old Aztec and Inca empires. By the 17th century, it stretched from California in the North to Chile in the south. From the early 1490s, the **Canary Islands** became a key stopover on the way to Spain's newly acquired American possessions and were also definitively incorporated into the mainland.

During this period, in the context of constant warfare with the Ottoman Empire and raids on Spanish territory by Barbary pirates, Spain also established a number of outposts along the North African coast. These included Melilla in 1497, to which the enclave of Ceuta was added in 1640. The latter had been conquered by the Portuguese in 1415, but remained in Spanish hands after the Portuguese broke away from the Spanish **Habsburg** Empire in this year. In addition, Spain occupied the **Philippines** in 1563, and from the end of the century established a link between the Philippines and Mexico.

At first, the conquest of America was an enterprise solely undertaken by the **Crown of Castile**. Commerce was funneled through the port of Seville (later Cádiz), the territory was governed by Castilian law, and the right to emigrate to America was largely limited to Castilians until 1596. It quickly attained great economic importance, both because it provided a market for Spanish food and manufactures, and because Spain imported great quantities of gold and, above all, silver. However, during the 16th and 17th centuries, much of the silver was used to fight the Habsburgs' continental wars, while within Spain itself it caused inflation, helping to make Spanish **agricultural** production and manufactures uncompetitive.

During the 18th century, discontent began to surface among local American elites (*criollos*), due to the new **Bourbon** monarchs' determination to centralize power, collect taxes more efficiently, and use the country as a captive market for Spanish goods. The upheavals at the end of the century then showed that Spain was no longer strong enough to hold on to its colonial possessions, while the North American and **French Revolutions** provided the example and the nationalist ideology necessary for the Americans to wage a struggle for independence. Spain's ability to retain her colonies was undermined by a series of events that occurred from the 1790s. In 1796, because of the Spanish-French alliance, British ships blocked the port of Cádiz, making it impossible to maintain the colonial trade. Furthermore, in the 1805 battle of **Trafalgar**, the Spanish navy was badly damaged. Finally, in 1808, Napoleon Bonaparte invaded the peninsula and tried to impose French dominance. The 1812 **Cortes of Cádiz** constitution attempted to maintain the colonial relationship, but Spain faced a series of separatist insurrections. By the reign of

Fernando VII, the country was too weak to reconquer the American possessions, with the result that by 1833 the Spanish colonial empire was reduced to its African enclaves, **Cuba** and Puerto Rico in America, and the Philippines, Guam, the Mariana and Caroline Islands, and Palau in the Pacific.

During the rest of the 19th century, Spain tried to extend its colonial empire into Africa. It occupied part of Guinea in 1844, the areas around Río de Oro (West Africa) in 1860, and Río Muni, south of **Morocco**, in 1877. In 1847, Spain also created the post of captain general of North Africa. Defeat in the **Spanish-American War** of 1898 then led to the loss of all Spain's colonial possessions in the Caribbean and Asia. This was a tremendously traumatic experience for the Spanish public, who watched Spain give up its last valuable colonies while the industrially powerful European states rapidly expanded their empires. It resulted in growing opposition to the political system and a powerful movement for reform known as **regenerationism**.

Henceforth, the military and colonial interests were to intensify efforts to carve out an empire in Morocco. In 1904, France agreed to leave the northern zone of Morocco in Spanish hands, but the poor arid land Spain controlled was to bring far more pain than glory. There were disturbances against the colonial war, which pitted the Spanish *africanista* army against the Berber tribesmen. The most dramatic of these culminated in the events known as the **Tragic Week** in **Barcelona** in 1909. Ironically, the final **decolonization** of Morocco was to be presided over by the *africanista* general **Francisco Franco**, who had built his reputation on the struggle to extend Spanish power in the region. Spain's only colonies in North Africa are now the garrison towns of Ceuta and Melilla. The former has a large Spanish population, while the latter includes an important number of Arabic speakers, who in recent years have demanded educational rights and official recognition of their religion. Ceuta's position close to the Spanish coast has also made it a magnet for illegal immigrants, leading to the construction of an eight-and-a-half-mile perimeter fence. Morocco claims that both towns form part of its territory, while Spain counters that when they were colonized the country of Morocco did not exist.

COMILLAS, SECOND MARQUIS OF (CLAUDIO LÓPEZ BRU)

(1853–1925). López Bru was the son of a great Cantabrian shipping magnate, Antonio López (1817–1884), who established himself in **Barcelona** in the mid-1850s. From his father he inherited both his title (which made him a grandee) and companies, including the Hispano-Colonial Bank, Transatlantic Shipping Company, and the Philippine Tobacco Company. From the late 19th century, in association with **Catalan** business interests—most notably Eusebi Güell y Bacigalupi (1846–1918), who married his daughter—he further developed trade with the colonies and built up the family's interest in **railways**, investing in the Compañía del Norte (Northern Company) and in the largest **coal mine** in Asturias, Hullera Española (Spanish Coal). After the loss of the last American **colonies** in 1898, he moved into **Morocco** with the foundation of the Sociedad Hispano Africana (Hispano-African Society), which invested in the Riff mines.

Politically, Comillas maintained strong links with the most conservative-**Catholic** wing of the **Partido Conservador**, headed by **Alejandro Pidal**. At the same time, he played a key role within the Catholic lay association **Acción Católica**, occupying its presidency from 1894 until his death in 1925. Given Comillas's business interests, his major sphere of action was the **Catholic unions**, which were designed to ward off the left-wing threat. He was behind the setting up of a Consejo Nacional de Corporaciones Católico-Obreras (National Council of Catholic-Worker Corporations) in 1896, and strongly backed the Jesuit priest Gabriel Palau, who in 1907 founded the Catholic lay association Acción Social Popular (Popular Social Action) in Barcelona, which organized so-called Uniones Profesionales (Professional Unions) in the city. He also sponsored Catholic company unions in the Compañía del Norte and in Hullera Española. The problem with these organizations was that they saw the workers' salvation as coming through moral redemption rather than through improvements in working conditions. They therefore never operated as proper trade unions and hence were never in a position to seriously challenge leftist labor confederations, such as the **Unión General de Trabajadores** (UGT) and **Confederación Nacional del Trabajo** (CNT).

Comillas's high profile in trying to block the advance of the leftist labor unions, along with his great wealth and key role in the defense of conservative Catholic values and Catholic workers' associations, made him very much the *bête noire* of the Catalan working-class left, which viewed him as the epitome of the "Vaticanist" plutocracy that, it claimed, was running the country. *See also* LABOR MOVEMENT.

COMISIONES OBRERAS (CC.OO)/WORKERS' COMMISSIONS. CC.OO was an independent movement of organized labor that grew up under the **Franco regime** in the 1960s. Its origins were to be found in the 1958 Law of Collective Agreements, which allowed factory-level bargaining between workers' committees and employers within the framework of the compulsory state union, the **Organización Sindical Española** (OSE). Workers were allowed to elect their own representatives, and many chose not the official OSE candidates but independents and leftist sympathizers. At the same time, when collective bargaining broke down, workers began organizing outside the structures of the OSE. From 1964, these efforts took on a more permanent form. Members and sympathizers of CC.OO combined work within the OSE with the organization of semi-clandestine, local, industry-wide committees and area commissions. These commissions then developed growing contacts between each other, and in 1967 a national leadership emerged.

Between 1962 and 1966, as a consequence of the regime's policy of *apertura* (opening), designed to promote a positive image to the outside world, CC.OO was able to operate relatively freely and had considerable success in both channeling worker discontent (though by no means all labor protest took place within the bounds of CC.OO) and colonizing the lower echelons of the OSE. By the beginning of 1966, it had 25 provincial committees and regional committees in **Catalonia**, the **Basque Country**, **Navarre**, Asturias, **Andalusia**, Center, Levant, **Galicia**, and Aragón. But, for this very reason, it was increasingly seen as a threat by the regime, leading, from the end of 1966, to a crackdown. On 16 February 1967, it was declared illegal by the Supreme Tribunal and large numbers of independent and opposition officials were sacked, including the organization's leading figures, the most important of whom was **Marcelino Camacho**. The leadership had to move underground. In addition, a wage freeze was declared in November, undermining its negotiating role. Yet, with the massive upsurge in labor protest from 1969, CC.OO was rapidly to revive. From that date, it cleverly combined economic demands with political calls for the legalization of free trade unions. These were demands to which workers could relate, and which, at the same time, called the regime into question. Between 1973 and 1976, labor agitation further escalated, with the frequent declaration of "area general strikes," which brought out the entire working population of clusters of towns or whole cities. These strikes often began as economic disputes but were aggravated by police repression and/or the sacking or arrest of union delegates. By this time the industrial relations system was breaking down, with CC.OO forming the spearhead of a broad opposition movement.

At first CC.OO had been a very pluralistic movement, but the range of ideological and political options had narrowed by the end of the 1960s. Both the Marxist **Unión General de Trabajadores** (UGT) and the **anarchist Confederación Nacional del Trabajo** (CNT) refused to have anything to do with the OSE because they believed that to participate in the union elections would only serve to shore up the regime, and so they became marginalized from CC.OO in particular and labor opposition to the Franco regime in general. The **Partido Comunista de España** (PCE) and its **Catalan** counterpart, the **Partit Socialista Unificat de Catalunya** (PSUC), on the other hand, were enthusiastic, and soon became the backbone of CC.OO. Moreover, in the early years, progressive Catholics affiliated with **Acción Católica**'s worker branches, the **Hermandad Obrera de Acción Católica** (HOAC) and **Juventud Obrera Católica**, playing a key role. They were joined by the independent labor federations, the Catholic **Unión Sindical Obrera** (USO) and the Catalan dissident socialist Aliança Sindical Obrera (Workers' Union Alliance—ASO), and by various far-left organizations. Indeed, in the early and mid-1960s many CC.OO clandestine meetings were held in locals owned by the **Catholic Church**. However, the move by the Church hierarchy to undermine the workers' Catholic associations undermined the influence of the progressive Catholics and left the PCE and PSUC to a large extent in control of policy.

These parties pursued a strategy of open protest combined with the formation of semi-clandestine committees. The PCE and PSUC hoped to use CC.OO as a battering ram against the Francoist state, eventually organizing a general strike, supported by a broad range of opposition forces, which would bring down the regime and make possible a **transition to democracy**. In the early 1970s, this goal seemed in sight. Strikes escalated, while the regime shied away from alienating western European opinion through heavy repression. The 1975 union elections were a great success for coalition slates of CC.OO and independent anti-Francoist candidates. By this time, some parts of the OSE apparatus were under virtual CC.OO control.

Nevertheless, it never proved possible to organize a nationwide political strike. Instead, between 1976 and 1977, regime reformers, along with the PCE and **Partido Socialista Obrero Español** (PSOE), negotiated a controlled transition to democracy. As a result, CC.OO was faced with a number of new challenges. At first it had hoped to form the nucleus of a single Spanish union, but given the determination of the rejuvenated PSOE to resurrect its sister union, the UGT, it had to accept that this would not be possible. Between 1976 and 1977, CC.OO became a legal independent labor confederation. In 1978, buoyed by the intense labor protest of previous years, it claimed to have two million members (the **labor movement** as a whole had over four million members, more than 70 percent of the labor force). But between 1978 and 1980, it found itself in increasing difficulties. First, the years after 1973 witnessed a gathering economic crisis, which began to bite at the end of the decade. Second, there was a degree of disenchantment at the burdens workers were expected to bear during the transition. Most notably, in October 1977, in order to consolidate the new democracy by tackling the economic crisis, CC.OO was pressured by the PCE into accepting the **Moncloa Pacts**, which stipulated a cut in workers' real living standards in exchange for promised improvements in social benefits. Finally, CC.OO was finding to its cost that it was easier to organize strikes than it was to build a union.

These problems led to a weakening of the labor movement from 1980. By the mid-1980s, CC.OO's membership had fallen to a little over 500,000. In order to keep control of labor costs, the governments of the **Unión del Centro Democrático** (UCD) and PSOE tried to reach a series of pacts between union and management over wages, working conditions, and social security. The UGT was at first eager to participate. CC.OO was, however, more wary and quickly gained a reputation as the more militant of the two labor confederations. Many CC.OO activists felt that labor had borne the cost of the transition. This opposition hardened in 1985, when the Spanish economy began to recover. In this year, CC.OO held a partially successful one-day strike against the government's program to restructure Spanish **industry**. The following years also saw discontent grow within the UGT. As a result, at the beginning of 1988, CC.OO and the UGT agreed on a common bargaining stance with government. When no agreement could be reached, they called a one-day general strike on 14 December. The strike was a great success, with over seven million workers staying at home. This encouraged the unions to maintain their critical stance and consult frequently over policy. In May 1992, a new day of action was called to protest against the cut in unemployment coverage and on 27 January 1994, the unions once again called a one-day general strike to show their disagreement with the government's policy of extending the legality of temporary contracts. Marcelino Camacho remained as general secretary of CC.OO from the union's legalization in 1977 until his retirement in 1987, and under his leadership the union remained closely identified with the PCE.

However, the new general secretary, Antonio Gutiérrez (1951–), subsequently took a far more independent position and, during the 1990s, became increasingly critical of what he perceived as the extremism of the PCE's general secretary, **Julio Anguita**. After the 1996 elections, in which the PSOE lost power, Gutiérrez was if anything closer to the Socialists. The union proved willing to negotiate with the new **Partido Popular** (PP) administration, and held tripartite negotiations with the government and employers' association, the **Confederación Española de Organizaciones Empresariales** (CEOE). In these discussions, CC.OO (along with the UGT) successfully softened the impact of the government's neoliberal policies on its working-class base. However, after winning an overall majority in March 2000, the PP took a harder line, and new legislation in June 2002 (the so-called *decretazo*, because it was imposed without prior negotiations) made it much easier to fire workers and reduced unemployment benefits. Hence, it was met by a one-day strike, supported by both CC.OO and the UGT. In subsequent negotiations, the government backed down. Antonio Gutiérrez stepped down as general secretary in April 2001 and was replaced by José María Fidalgo (1948–), who has maintained the latter's independent stance. Fidalgo was subsequently reelected in April 2004.

COMPANYS I JOVER, LLUÍS (1883–1940). Lluís Companys was one of the most significant figures on the Catalan political stage in the early 20th century, combining **republicanism**, **Catalanism**, and social reformism. He was born into a prosperous rural family in Nace de Tarrós in the province of Tarragona, moved to study in **Barcelona**, and from his teens became involved in republican politics. In the first years of the 20th century, he formed part of the **Unión Republicana**, and was, between 1912 and 1914, involved in the attempt by **Melquíades Álvarez** to develop his Partido Reformista in Catalonia. With the outbreak of **World War I** and the growth in social conflict that followed, he moved further to the left, developed contacts with syndicalist leaders such as **Salvador Seguí**, and helped found a new party, the Partit Republicà Català (Catalan Republican Party), in April 1917. His aim was to give Catalanism a working-class base. His political activism led to his imprisonment in Mahón Castle during 1920. It was reflected in his collaboration in the newspaper *La Lucha* and in his legal defense of the labor movement. In 1921, he also played a leading role in the foundation of the peasants' association Unió de **Rabassaires** (Rabassaires' Union).

With the fall of the **Primo de Rivera dictatorship**, he participated in the foundation of **Esquerra Republicana de Catalunya** and went on to play a leading role in the Catalan parliament. After the death of **Francesc Macià**, he was elected president of the **Generalitat** in January 1934. Immediately he was faced with the hostility of the right, who had won the November 1933 general elections. The right managed to get the Tribunal of Constitutional Guarantees to declare unconstitutional a law passed by the Generalitat in June 1934 to allow the *rabassaires* to buy the land they rented. Later in the year, fearful of the growing power of the **Confederación Española de Derechas Autónomas**, Companys supported the **October 1934 revolution**. The revolt in Catalonia was, however, easily put down by the **military**, and Companys found himself sentenced to 30 years' imprisonment. He was released after the **Popular Front** victory in February 1936, and once again became president of the

Generalitat. With the outbreak of the **Spanish Civil War** he retained his position. He supported the policy pursued by the republicans and **Partido Comunista de España-Partit Socialista Unificat de Catalunya** of reconstituting state power, but tried as far as possible to reconcile the anarcho-syndicalist **Confederación Nacional del Trabajo**. With the fall of Catalonia, he fled to France, but was picked up by the German military and returned to the forces of General **Francisco Franco**. He was shot by a firing squad on 15 October 1940.

COMUNEROS' REVOLT. This was a rebellion led by the Castilian towns against what were seen as abuses of royal power between May 1520 and February 1522. It was sparked by the succession to the Spanish throne of the **Habsburg** dynasty in 1516 in the figure of King **Carlos I**. The king could not speak the **Castilian language** and, moreover, began his reign by asking the Castilian **Cortes** for subsidies and by appointing his Flemish advisors to key posts. It was precipitated in the aftermath of a meeting of the Cortes in March 1520 in Santiago de Compostela, after which the king hurriedly left the country. It was led by the Castilian town councils represented at the Cortes. At first it had widespread support, including many nobles and members of the **Catholic Church**, but it began to spread to the countryside and take on aspects of a social revolution (with revolts against seigniorial dues), leading wealthy landed aristocrats to abandon it and side with the king. The Comuneros were decisively beaten in the battle of Villalar on 23 April 1521, though they struggled on until early 1522. In the future, Carlos I would be careful to take the views of the Cortes into account and appoint Castilian nobles to positions of influence. However, the Comuneros' defeat meant that the Castilian Cortes would not play any role in decision making and made it easier for the monarchy to raise taxes for its imperial wars. Since the 19th century, the revolt has been eulogized in some left-wing and Spanish nationalist discourses as a struggle both to maintain political liberties and throw off foreign rule.

CONCORDAT. *See* CATHOLIC CHURCH; FRANCO REGIME; MARTÍN ARTAJO, ALBERTO; NARVÁEZ, RAMÓN MARÍA; PARTIDO MODERADO.

CONDE, MARIO (1948–). Mario Conde was the archetypal representative of the new generation of business people who came to prominence during the economic boom of the late 1980s, when Spain was
gripped by a fever of ostentatious consumption, and who fell from
grace in the wake of economic crisis in the first half of the 1990s.
He was born in the Galician town of Tuy into a conservative middle-
class family. From 1965 to 1971, he studied law at the Jesuit University of Deusto in Bilbao. He soon showed himself to be academically extremely able, achieving the top mark in the entrance exam to
the post of state attorney in 1973. He moved into the private sector
in 1977 after having met the high-flying industrialist Juan Abelló
(1941–). Under Abelló's wing he got onto the board of his company,
Laboratories Abelló, and then moved on to take control of another
pharmaceutical company, Antibiotics S.A. Conde and Abelló were
able to make an enormous profit through the sale of this company to
the Italian multinational Montedison in 1986, and this allowed them
to move into finance. They bought into the **banking** group Banesto,
of which Conde was soon to become president. In the euphoric
economic climate of the late 1980s, Conde quickly embarked on a
program of accelerated expansion, as part of which in May 1988 he
negotiated a fusion with the Banco Central (Central Bank).

Yet from this date Conde's success story began to turn sour. He
was never able to take control of the new group, leading Banesto and
Banco Central to split in 1991. At the same time, Banesto became
weighed down by growing debts, in large measure because the economic climate was deteriorating, but also, it quickly transpired, because Conde himself was siphoning off funds at the cost of the bank's
shareholders. The vice president of the **Partido Socialista Obrero
Español** (PSOE) government, **Narcís Serra**, launched an investigation into Conde's activities. This led the Bank of Spain to intervene
in December 1993 and remove Conde and his fellow directors from
the board. At the same time, the state attorney (*fiscal*) charged Conde
with embezzlement. Incredibly, Conde reacted by trying to blackmail
the government. He made contact with Juan Alberto Perote, who had
been number two in the Centro Superior de Información de la Defensa (CESID) between 1983 and 1991. When Perote retired, he had
smuggled out a large number of compromising documents, a number
of which demonstrated that the CESID had been involved in illegal

phone tapings and also implicated the government in the dirty war being waged by the **GAL** against **ETA**. Conde wanted the government to drop the charges and pay him compensation in return for the documents remaining secret. However, the story broke in May–June 1995, when first *El País* (which was close to the PSOE) revealed the links between Conde and Perote and then *El Mundo* (close to the opposition **Partido Popular**) published extracts of the secret documents. Both Serra and the minister of defense, Julián García Vargas (1945–), had to resign, and Perote was put behind bars. Conde was finally sentenced to 10 years imprisonment in March 2000 (increased to 20 years, following his appeal, in July 2002).

CONFEDERACIÓN ESPAÑOLA DE DERECHAS AUTÓNO-MAS (CEDA)/SPANISH CONFEDERATION OF AUTONO-MOUS RIGHT-WING GROUPS. The CEDA was the major right-wing force during the **Second Republic**. It was a coalition, founded in February 1933 under the leadership of **José María Gil-Robles**, at the heart of which was the **Catholic** agrarian party **Acción Popular**. From the start, the CEDA aimed to work within the Republic in order to reform it from within. In order to do this, it could not declare itself unambiguously anti-Republican and so maintained it was "accidentalist." The crux of accidentalism, it asserted, was that it was the policies of a regime, rather than its actual form, that were crucial. Yet, given the CEDA's total opposition to the major Republican reforms and the **monarchist** sympathies of many of its members, it could not but be seen as de facto opposed to the Republic. The CEDA was, during 1933, able to take advantage of opposition to government reforms in conservative and Catholic circles in order to increase its strength. In the November 1933 elections, it also benefited from divisions in the leftist camp and the disillusionment of many workers and peasants with the government's performance. It emerged as the largest formation in the new parliament, with 115 seats, but was unable to form a government as the president of the Republic, **Niceto Alcalá Zamora**, doubted the organization's democratic credentials.

The major worry for the left was, in effect, not only that the CEDA was committed to destroying the reforming legislation of the **Bienio Reformista**, but that the coalition's commitment to democracy was very much open to doubt. Like members of many other rightist parties on the European continent in the 1930s, most *cedistas* believed that liberal democracies led to chaos and anarchy, and that what was needed was a more authoritarian, **corporatist** form of government. Hence, though it cannot be considered as Fascist, the CEDA daily newspaper, *El Debate*, praised Benito Mussolini's Italy and Adolf Hitler's Germany, while its youth movement, Juventud de Acción Popular (Popular Action Youth, JAP), displayed many of the trappings of a Fascist movement, holding large military-style rallies and calling for all power to their leader.

Alcalá Zamora called on **Alejandro Lerroux's Partido Republicano Radical** (PRR) to form a government, but it was dependent on CEDA support. As a result, agrarian legislation passed by the previous republican-Partido Socialista Obrero Español government was allowed to lapse and an offensive was launched against the Socialist land workers' union, the **Federación Nacional de Trabajadores de la Tierra**. From the summer of 1934, the CEDA began to press for cabinet posts. This they finally achieved on 5 October, when three of its members entered the government. Following the **October 1934 revolution**, the CEDA called for an exemplary repression (including the execution of leftists involved). The PRR would not agree to such extreme measures, but during 1935 it was forced to largely follow the policy line the CEDA dictated. In April, the CEDA managed to increase its government ministers to five, including **José María Gil-Robles**, who became minister of war. The coalition's dream of total power was, however, soon to be shattered. After the PRR was undermined by a series of scandals, Alcalá Zamora called new elections rather than entrusting power to the CEDA. After the **Popular Front** victory, much of the Spanish right abandoned the CEDA's gradualist approach and opted for violent methods. The CEDA was, therefore, rapidly eclipsed by more extremist, insurrectionary groups, such as the **Falange Española, Carlists**, and **Alfonsoist monarchists**.

CONFEDERACIÓN ESPAÑOLA DE ORGANIZACIONES EMPRESARIALES (CEOE)/SPANISH CONFEDERATION OF EMPLOYERS' ORGANIZATIONS. The CEOE, which was set up in 1977, brought most employers' organizations under its umbrella over the next three years. Thus, by 1982, there were over 100 bodies confederated, representing 1.3 million firms, which employed 70 percent of the country's workers. By the mid-1990s, it had increased its power further, with firms affiliated now representing 90 percent of the workforce. During the **transition to democracy**, the CEOE accepted collective negotiations with the unions, but was unhappy with the **economic policy** pursued by the governing **Unión del Centro Democrático** (UCD), which it saw as too social-democratic and interventionist. From 1980, under the leadership of Carles Ferrer Salat (1931–1998), it helped to undermine the UCD by strongly backing **Alianza Popular**, while also making every effort to block the rise of the **Partido Socialista Obrero Español** (PSOE). This strategy backfired in 1982 with the PSOE election victory. However, the new government proved willing to listen to the CEOE's economic and financial demands, and the team who ran **economic policy** (under **Miguel Boyer**) largely agreed with the CEOE's assertion that Spain's rigid labor market had to be made more "flexible" in order to reduce labor costs. This led to an escalating confrontation between the government and labor unions. Nevertheless, the CEOE continued to back Alianza Popular/**Partido Popular** (PP) at election time. After the PP's victory in the 1996 elections, the CEOE supported its attempts to further liberalize the **labor market**, but also continued to participate in tripartite negotiations involving government and the main labor unions. José María Cuevas (1935–) was its leader between 1984 and 2007. In April of 2007, he was replaced by Gerardo Díaz Ferrán (1942–), the president of the Madrid employers' association, the Confederación Empresarial de Madrid (Madrid Employers' Confederation—CEIM).

CONFEDERACIÓN NACIONAL CATÓLICA AGRARIA (CNCA)/NATIONAL CATHOLIC AGRARIAN FEDERATION. From the first decade of the 20th century, in reaction to the first socialist incursions into the peasant heartlands of northern and central Spain, the **Catholic Church**, along with local landowners, began to finance the formation of agrarian syndicates to aid the local peasantry. In 1906, a coordinating body, the Secretariado Nacional Católico Agrario (National Catholic Agrarian Secretariat), was set up, which in 1917 was renamed the CNCA. It was integrated within the Catholic lay association **Acción Católica** and developed close links with the **Asociación Católica Nacional de Propagandistas**.

Both landlords and priests played a key role in the association. These conservative groups were able to mobilize and integrate the peasantry effectively because the smallholding peasants and tenant farmers, dominant in these areas, could be helped without this posing any threat to property relations (most notably it did not require land redistribution). In practical terms, the confederation served to keep the peasants out of the clutches of moneylenders by providing them with credit facilities, machinery, seeds and warehousing, and technical expertise. Politically it also had the effect of cementing the peasantry to the Church and the Spanish right. This would be seen in the **Second Republic** when small-town central Spain provided the reservoir of political support for the rightist coalition, the **Confederación Española de Derechas Autónomas**, and in the **Spanish Civil War**, when the peasantry provided the bulk of the foot soldiers for the **Nationalist** army.

CONFEDERACIÓN NACIONAL DEL TRABAJO (CNT)/ NATIONAL LABOR CONFEDERATION. The **anarchist**-syndicalist labor confederation, the CNT, was to play a major role in Spanish social and political life between 1917 and 1939. Its founding congress was organized by the Catalan labor confederation **Solidaridad Obrera** in **Barcelona** in September 1910. From this early date, the organization's main centers of support were already apparent. Its heart was industrial **Catalonia**, but it also recruited widely in **Andalusia**, **Valencia**, and Aragón. Its first phase of life was, however, to be short-lived. It was illegalized following its second congress in September 1911, when it tried to organize a general strike against the war in **Morocco**. The Catalan CNT was not to reorganize until the end of 1915, and other regions did not begin to affiliate in great numbers until 1918.

However, growth over the next two years was prodigious. At its national congress, held in **Madrid** in December 1919, it was to claim 550,000 members, with another 200,000 more workers close to the organization. It was to play a significant role in the **crisis of 1917**, supporting the failed attempt to overthrow the **Cánovas Restoration** through a general strike. During the years 1917 to 1923, it would then be at the forefront of working-class agitation. It was more radical than the **Unión General del Trabajo** (UGT), frequently resorting to strikes and mobilizing workers at the street level, and was not beyond resorting to assassinations in order to intimidate employers into making concessions. A good example of this was the Catalan La Canadenca strike, which began in an electricity generating plant, Riegos y Fuerzas del Ebro, in early February 1919 and lasted for over a month. The CNT's radicalism was also on show in other areas. Most notably, Andalusia was to see a massive wave of peasant unrest between 1919 and 1921, which became known as the **Bolshevik Triennium**.

This is not to say that there were no ideological and political divisions within the CNT. Between 1910 and 1913, the Barcelona leadership had been in the hands of a group of radical anarchist-syndicalists, headed by José Negre, who were virulently "antipolitical" and attempted to call revolutionary general strikes at every possible opportunity. However, there were more moderate men in the organization—generally referred to as syndicalists—who laid more stress on the need to build up the unions and not undertake rash action that would put it in jeopardy. They took control of the skeletal Catalan organization in September 1913 and over the next four years, they were able to consolidate their position within the CNT. They were headed by **Salvador Seguí** and their number included such figures as Josep Viadiu (1890–?), Joan Peiró (1887–1942), and Simó Piera (1892–?). Moreover, Seguí was also largely supported by the somewhat more hard-line figure of Angel Pestaña (1886–1936). These men were not as cautious as their UGT counterparts, but they argued that the CNT unions had to organize effectively in order to combat their employers. Hence, at the Catalan CNT's Sants congress, held from 28 June–1 July 1918, they introduced local industrial federations, known as Sindicatos Unicos (Single Unions), to strengthen labor's bargaining power. Moreover, they were not as fiercely "antipolitical" as the radical anarchist-syndicalists and did not take an all-or-nothing attitude to the revolution, believing that workers would benefit from a republican state in which civil liberties were guaranteed. For this reason, during the crisis of 1917, Seguí and his followers largely backed the attempt to overthrow the Cánovas Restoration and put in its place a more democratic regime.

However, the standing of Salvador Seguí was seriously challenged between 1920 and 1923. This has to be understood within the context of an employer offensive against the CNT unions during these years. The offensive was backed up by the Barcelona **military** and police, who launched a dirty war against the CNT, paying gunmen from the **Sindicatos Libres** to gun down the confederation's trade union leadership. This included Salvador Seguí himself, who was murdered in March 1923. These circumstances facilitated the appearance of a generation of young CNT extremists who, like their predecessors, supported violent, revolutionary general strikes but also argued that an audacious group of revolutionaries could spark the revolution. The groups' members, whose leading figure was **Buenaventura Durruti**, came to be known as anarcho-communists.

Within the CNT, divisions between the syndicalists and anarcho-communists deepened during the 1930s. In 1929–1930, the syndicalists, now led by the glassworkers' leader, Joan Peiró (the secretary general of the Barcelona-based National Committee), collaborated with **Partido Socialista Obrera Español** (PSOE) and **republicans** in order to bring about the fall of the **Primo de Rivera dictatorship**, and then welcomed the proclamation of the **Second Republic**. During the regime, many of these syndicalists began to edge away from their anarchist principles. They did not actively prevent workers from voting and, in some cases, joined **Esquerra Republicana de Catalunya** or the **Partit Socialista Unificat de Catalunya** (PSUC). For his part, Angel Pestaña founded a small Partido Sindicalista (Syndicalist Party) in 1934. Moreover, the syndicalists also began working within the arbitration boards set up by the minister of labor, **Francisco Largo Caballero**, and accepted the intervention of **Generalitat** representatives in industrial disputes.

However, they were opposed by the insurrectionaries, who saw themselves as the guardians of anarchist orthodoxy. In 1927, many of them had set up a tight-knit conspiratorial organization, the Federación Anarquista Ibérica (Anarchist Iberian Federation—FAI), aimed at controlling the CNT. And in Catalonia, between 1931 and 1933, they took advantage of a strike wave and consequent clashes with the Republic's security forces to impose their dominance. At the height of this wave, between 1932 and 1933, the CNT claimed one million members. The FAI activists argued that there was no difference between the Republic and previous bourgeois regimes, and therefore also launched a series of insurrections aimed at establishing libertarian communism. The Republican government reacted harshly. This served partly to disorganize the CNT but also reinforced FAI criticisms of the Republic and led to working-class disillusionment. One of the worst episodes, the massacre of a group of anarchist peasants by the Republican Assault Guard in the Andalusian town of **Casas Viejas** in January 1933, weakened the government.

These divisions resulted in a split within the CNT. In 1932, the syndicalists left to form their own group, known as the **Treintistas**. From 1933, factional rivalry, together with a worsening economic depression, saw the beginnings of CNT decline. By May 1936, even including the newly reintegrated Treintistas, membership had fallen to 550,000. The reaffiliation of the Treintistas was made possible because during 1936, in the face of the rightist threat, the CNT had taken a more realistic position, tacitly accepting that their base should vote left in the **Popular Front** elections of February and then draw closer to the UGT. Nevertheless, part of the Treintista trade union base joined the PSUC.

The **Spanish Civil War** was to demand new doses of realism. The first days of the war saw a great burst of enthusiasm and a collectivist revolution spearheaded by the CNT and left-wing PSOE-UGT activists. Yet in the following months, the CNT had to face up to the need to reconstitute state power and impose discipline in order to defeat the **Nationalist** enemy. The lead was taken in September by the Popular Front government, which, under Francisco Largo Caballero, began to roll back the social revolution. Anarchist leaders finally had to come to terms with the fact that they had either to participate in government in order to have some influence on the decision-making process or be on the end of resolutions over which they had no control. In these circumstances, they reluctantly decided to join the Catalan Generalitat on 26 September and the national government on 4 November. This produced considerable discontent within the rank and file. These tensions were to explode during the **May Events** in Barcelona, when anarchists and members of the **Partido Obrero de Unificación Marxista** fought on the streets of Barcelona against the PSUC and the Republican police. After these events, a new government, headed by **Juan Negrín** without anarchist participation, rolled back the social revolution faster than before, undermining local and regional organs of worker power (most spectacularly the **Consejo de Aragón**), militarizing the militia, and imposing central control on industry. This led to widespread disillusionment in anarchist circles.

Under the **Franco regime**, the CNT tried to maintain a union presence, particularly in Barcelona, but was met by blanket government repression. Moreover, its refusal, on ideological grounds, to work within the **Organización Sindical Española**, meant that in urban Spain during the 1950s and 1960s it was rapidly displaced by **Comisiones Obreras**. In exile, divisions remained between "collaborationists" (i.e., those willing to work with leftist political parties) and "purists." An outright split occurred in October 1945 when two CNT members entered the Republican government in exile. Henceforth, two CNTs operated, one "political," the other "antipolitical." These divisions, and the inability of the CNT to cope with life under Francoism, meant that the organization emerged greatly weakened during the **transition to democracy**. Thereafter, the CNT proved unable to adapt in a world in which electoral politics were hardly questioned and government encouraged tripartite negotiations between itself, unions, and employers. The year 1975 saw a brief unification between the two sectors, but from 1979 they again split. The main CNT union confederation emerged as a small organization, which, in line with its libertarian values, refused to participate in state-sponsored bargaining machinery or receive any state subsidies. *See also* LABOR MOVEMENT.

CONJUNCIÓN/ALLIANCE. This was name given to a pact signed between the **Partido Socialista Obrero Español** (PSOE) and the various **republican** parties in October 1910. Its short-term aim was to bring down the **Partido Conservador** prime minister **Antonio Maura**, who was responsible for the repression of the **Tragic Week**, while its longer-term goal was to overthrow the **Cánovas Restoration**. The *conjunción* signified the end of the years of Socialist isolationism from all "bourgeois" forces. It worked well in areas like **Madrid** and Bilbao, where both Socialists and republicans were strong and gave the PSOE a far higher profile in national politics. However, there were criticisms of the *conjunción* in Socialist ranks, first manifested at the PSOE's ninth congress, held in October 1912. This took two forms. On the one hand, left-wingers, like **Manuel Núñez de Arenas**, argued that the republicans were so weak and divided that the pact had little purpose. On the other, union activists, like Facundo Perezagua (1860–1935), maintained that they should concentrate more on trade union affairs. This opposition intensified with the radicalizing effect of the impact of **World War I** and then the Bolshevik Revolution in Spain. The radicals were finally able to engineer a break with the republicans at the beginning of 1920. Similar divisions would again occur during the **Second Republic**.

CONSEJO DE ARAGÓN/COUNCIL OF ARAGÓN. This was a coordinating body set up by the **Confederación Nacional del Trabajo** (CNT) at the beginning of the **Spanish Civil War** in order to ensure the collectivization of peasant land in Aragón. It was supported by the landless peasantry but met considerable resistance from peasant smallholders, and the **anarchists** were not above using force to impose their objectives. With the government of **Juan Negrín** trying to establish central state power, it was abolished on 11 August 1937 and broken up by the troops of the pro-Communist military commander Enrique Líster (1907–1995). Many of its leading figures were subsequently arrested and land on some of the collectives under its control was returned to the former peasant owners.

CONSERVATIVES. *See* PARTIDO CONSERVADOR.

CONSTITUTION OF 1812. *See* CORTES OF CÁDIZ.

CONSTITUTION OF 1837. The Constitution of 1837 was largely drawn up by **liberals** linked to the **Partido Progresista**. It represented an attempt to reconcile the more conservative **Partido Moderado** by producing a text that had elements of both the 1812 Constitution, drawn up by the **Cortes of Cádiz**, and the **Royal Statute** of 1834. In comparison to the 1812 Constitution, the sovereign was given more power, and an Upper House or Senate was added to increase the weight of conservative interests. As in the Cádiz constitution, ministers were to be named by the crown. Both **Cortes** and sovereign could introduce legislation, but the crown now had an absolute veto. The crown had, moreover, a large measure of influence in the choosing of representatives to the Upper House. **Catholicism** also remained the country's official and only religion. The accompanying law of 20 July

1837 did liberalize suffrage somewhat, but in elections held between 1837 and 1843, still only between 3.9 percent and 4.3 percent of the population voted.

CONSTITUTION OF 1845. The elaboration of this constitution by the **Partido Moderado** signified a rejection of the attempt by the **Partido Progresista** to reach a compromise acceptable to the whole liberal family through the **Constitution of 1837**. As a result, over the next 30 years, each major change in the balance of political power would lead to the drawing up of a new constitution. Compared to the Constitution of 1837, the power of the crown was enhanced and a largely noble Upper House or Senate was created, the members of which were chosen by the monarch. Political freedoms were also reduced and the independence of the judiciary limited. The accompanying legislation, moreover, restricted the electorate to less than 1 percent of the population. The *moderados* were largely to dominate Spanish politics until 1868 and the conservative **Cánovas Restoration** of 1875 used the 1845 Constitution as a major inspiration. It therefore became the key expression of the ideals of the dominant conservative trend within 19th-century Spanish liberalism.

CONSTITUTION OF 1869. The Constitution of 1869, whose promulgation followed the **Glorious Revolution** of 1868, was the first largely democratic constitution in Spanish history. For the first time, elections to the **Cortes** were to be held under universal male suffrage. The people's civil liberties were laid out in great detail and included for the first time the rights of meeting and association. The state would continue to support the **Catholic Church**, but the private worship of other religions was tolerated (this was to be the spark that ignited the Third **Carlist** War). The constitution was monarchic but power was to reside in the Cortes. This was to be made up of two houses, a Lower House (Congreso) to which election was direct, and an Upper House (Senado), to which election was indirect. The more conservative Senate was, therefore, envisaged as putting a brake on the Lower House. Finally, as in previous constitutions, a division of powers was proclaimed, but on this occasion concrete measures were announced to guarantee the independence of the judiciary.

CONSTITUTION OF 1876. The Constitution of 1876 largely saw a return to the conservative-liberal tradition embodied in the **Constitution of 1845,** though in order to bring onboard former members of the **Partido Progresista** and **Unión Liberal,** aspects of the **Constitution of 1869** were also incorporated. Power was once again shared by the monarch and **Cortes,** though the monarch was reserved an extremely powerful position. Both the monarch and parliament could sanction and promulgate laws. The monarch named and replaced ministers and called, suspended, and dissolved parliament. Parliament was to be divided into two houses. Suffrage to the Lower House was to be direct but subject to property restrictions, though the exact extent was left to a future law (this was to be modified in 1890 with the introduction of universal male suffrage). The Upper House was extremely elitist, with representation limited to those named by the king and elected by the major corporations and the wealthy propertied classes. Many of the rights enshrined in the Constitution of 1869 were again included, though they were to be regulated by future laws. Moreover, these rights could be suspended in times of emergency by the government (a recourse to which Restoration governments would turn with regularity). Catholicism was once again to be the state religion, and the **Catholic Church** was to be maintained by the state, though as a sop to more radical liberals the private worship of other religions was permitted.

CONSTITUTION OF 1931. This was the first Republican constitution put into effect in Spanish history. The constitution was also the most democratic that had yet been promulgated. The classic liberal civil liberties were enshrined, but **women** were also given the right to vote for the first time, and, reflecting the influence of the **Partido Socialista Obrero Español** in its elaboration, areas in which social legislation could be legislated were detailed and the right of private property was made dependent on the public good. This made possible nationalization by the state as long as the owner was indemnified. Church and state were separated, and in the controversial Articles 26 and 27, the wealth of the Church was strictly controlled and the religious orders' involvement in **education** was prohibited. With respect to the legislature, the **Cortes** were unicameral and given a high degree of power. Moreover, to guard against governmental abuse, common during the **Cánovas Restoration**, the suspension of constitutional guarantees was tightly regulated. The figure of the president was also created. He chose the prime minister and government, but they were answerable to the Cortes. The president could also dissolve the Cortes on two occasions during his six years in office, though after the second dissolution the Cortes could examine the president's motives, and if the action was considered unjustified could force his resignation (this was actually to happen in May 1936). Guarantees were also introduced to ensure the independence of the judiciary. In order to deal with nationalist agitation, regions could also draw up their own autonomy statutes, which then had to be approved by the Cortes. A Tribunal of Constitutional Guarantees was created to oversee the legality of new laws. Finally, the constitution could be reformed, though this would require the calling of elections to a new constituent Cortes.

CONSTITUTION OF 1978. The new post-**Francoist** constitution, approved in a referendum on 6 December 1978, returned parliamentary democracy to Spain after almost 40 years of dictatorial rule. Unlike previous constitutions, it had the advantage of being largely consensual, the result of negotiations between the various democratic parties between June 1977 and May 1978. Finally, the only major democratic party not to vote in favor was the **Partido Nacionalista Vasco** (because it did not explicitly recognize the **Basque Country**'s historic rights, the *fueros*). Half of the **Alianza Popular**'s deputies took a similar step (because they felt that the use of the term "nationalities" endangered national unity). Under the constitution, Spain became a constitutional monarchy. This represented a necessary compromise, given the need to maintain a semblance of legality when dismantling the structures of Francoism, and was a recognition of the role King **Juan Carlos I** had played in bringing about democratization. The king's powers were theoretically limited. As head of state, he appointed the prime minister, but only after consultation with the party leaders and subject to a vote of confidence by the **Cortes**. However, given the power of the **military**, his position as its commander-in-chief was, in the years after its promulgation, in reality crucial. The state had no official religion, though the "role of the **Catholic Church**" was recognized. Again, this formula served to defuse unwanted antagonism. As in the **Constitution of 1931**, the principle of autonomy for the "nationalities and regions" was accepted, but on this occasion the whole structure of the state was to be decentralized, with the formation of the **State of the Autonomies** (Estado de las Autonomías).

The parliament or Cortes is bicameral. The Lower House (the Congreso) is made up of 350 deputies who represent 52 constituencies and who are elected through the d'Hont method of proportional representation. Of the 256 senators, 204 are directly elected by a limited vote system at provisional level, while 48 are indirectly elected by the autonomous communities. Because of the small constituencies, the Spanish system is one of the least proportional in Europe and favors both large Spanish-wide parties and smaller regionalist-nationalist parties concentrated in particular areas. This system was adopted in order to avoid instability. The Senate can make amendments but has no veto power, and hence is rather weak. In the constitution it is referred to as a "Regional House" (*cámara territorial*), but has yet to be fully constituted as such.

CONSTITUIONS. *See* BAYONNE CONSTITUTION; CONSTITUTION OF 1837; CONSTITUTION OF 1845; CONSTITUTION OF 1869; CONSTITUTION OF 1876; CONSTITUTION OF 1931; CONSTITUTION OF 1978; CORTES OF CÁDIZ; ROYAL STATUTE.

CONSTITUTIONAL TRIENNIUM/TRIENIO CONSTITUCIONAL. The term refers to the period of **liberal** rule between January 1820 and April 1823. It was ushered in by a *pronunciamiento* by General Rafael de Riego (1785–1823) in Cádiz, backed by troops who were being sent out to fight in the **colonial** wars in America. The troops were not able to take Cádiz, and at first it seemed as if the *pronunciamiento* would fail. However, there then followed proliberal uprisings in a number of Spanish cities. These events, together with the unreliability of the **Madrid** garrison, finally convinced **Fernando VII** that he should accept the 1812 Constitution approved by the **Cortes of Cádiz**. Immediately after, a liberal Consultative Junta was appointed to advise the king, legislation approved by the Cádiz Cortes was once again enacted, and the Cortes summoned to continue its work. As a result, Church and common land was put up for sale and the *mayorazgos* abolished. Moreover, in order to reduce the power of the **Catholic Church**, the number of monasteries was drastically reduced and those remaining were prohibited from acquiring new property. This was accompanied by measures designed to integrate the national market and stimulate economic development. For example, the import of grain was prohibited until prices reached a certain level at home, and measures were taken to encourage the transport of national grain from the Atlantic to the Mediterranean. These measures, it was hoped, would be to break the closed, nonmonetary economy of central Spain and open it to Spanish manufactures.

As in the past, moderate liberals wished to integrate the nobility into the new order. Again, therefore, the pretensions of the peasantry were ignored, and new fiscal burdens were imposed on the countryside. Despite this, throughout rural Spain, opposition to the regime, led by the local clergy, enjoyed the support of most of the nobility. At the same time, Fernando VII busily plotted against the regime. As a result, the regime's writ only ran to the towns. Yet even here a nascent left-wing antigovernment party, known as the *exaltados*, was emerging. The level of discontent soon called the regime into question. In northern Spain, absolutist bands took to the hills and harassed government forces, and in Madrid there were pitched battles between the **National Militia**, which enjoyed strong popular support, and the Royalist Battalions. Finally, absolutism was restored in April 1823 after the coalition of absolutist European powers, the Holy Alliance, sent a French army into Spain to overthrow the regime (the so-called Hundred Thousand Sons of Saint Louis [Cien Mil Hijos de San Luis]). The authorities hoped for a repeat of the guerrilla war that had greeted the French during the **War of Independence**, but with the countryside alienated, it was not to be. Indeed, many clergy now greeted the French as their liberators. *See also* CARLISM; FERNANDO RESTORATIONS.

CONTINUISTAS. This word is used to describe those members of the Francoist establishment who, in the 1960s, though they were economic liberalizers, were opposed to significant political reform. They were identified with the **Opus Dei** technocrats and their leading figure was the number two in the **Franco regime**, **Luis Carrero Blanco**. As the regime entered into crisis in the early 1970s, they were increasingly referred to as *inmovilistas*, the term indicating that they were opposed to significant change.

CONVERGÈNCIA DEMOCRÀTICA DE CATALUNYA/CATALAN DEMOCRATIC CONVERGENCE. *See* CONVERGÈNCIA I UNIÓ; PUJOL I SOLEY, JORDI.

CONVERGÈNCIA I UNIÓ (CiU)/CONVERGENCE AND UNION. CiU is a center-right Catalan nationalist coalition. Under the leadership of **Jordi Pujol**, it was the key force in the political life of **Catalonia** between 1980 and 2003. It was formed in the summer of 1978, representing a pact between two parties, the centrist, populist Convergència Democràtica de Catalunya (Catalan Democratic Convergence) headed by Pujol and the **Christian-democrat** Unió Democràtica de Catalunya (Catalan Democratic Union). In the 1979 general elections, it won nine seats, but the big surprise came in the 1980 elections to the Catalan autonomous parliament, in which it gained 43 seats and almost 28 percent of the votes, making it the biggest political force. Its general secretary Jordi Pujol became president of the Catalan government, the **Generalitat**, an institution that CiU largely controlled until 2003. CiU was able effectively to subordinate the smaller leftist nationalist party **Esquerra Republicana de Catalunya** (ERC) during the 1980s, while the **Partit dels Socialites de Catalunya-Partido Socialista Obrero Español** (PSC-PSOE) was weakened because it was seen by many voters as too close to the ruling PSOE government. From this time, Pujol was effectively able to portray himself as champion of Catalan national identity and a tenacious yet diplomatic and crafty negotiator with "Madrid" governments. Between 1984 and 1991, CiU gained over 45 percent of the votes in the Catalan autonomous elections and totally dominated Catalan politics.

During the 1990s, CiU increased its influence in the Spanish political arena because Spanish governments needed its votes in the parliament, though Pujol, unlike his lieutenant, **Miquel Roca i Junyent**, preferred to offer support in return for specific concessions rather than actually entering government itself, which he believed would lose the coalition credibility. Following the June 1993 general election, in which the PSOE lost its overall majority in the **Cortes**, it was dependent on CiU in order to remain in power. It received CiU support in return for further Catalan autonomy and for accepting CiU additions to the budget. Likewise, when the **Partido Popular** (PP) won the election in 1996, it failed to achieve an overall majority and had to sign a pact with CiU. Pujol was able, above all, to negotiate greater financial autonomy for the Generalitat while also pursuing policies aimed at the "normalization" (i.e., generalized usage) of the **Catalan language**. Of key importance here was legislation approved between 1993 and 1999 that made Catalan the main language within Catalan state schools. Under Pujol's dynamic leadership, CiU was also to forge a strong international identity. Pujol himself played a leading role in the construction of the so-called "Europe of the Regions" within the **European Union** and also traveled abroad frequently in order to strengthen commercial and cultural ties. This has been backed by the establishment of a large number of cultural and trade offices throughout the world and the promotion of the teaching of the Catalan language in foreign universities through the Ramon Llull program.

However, post-1996 CiU faced the problem that the PP was gaining conservative votes at its expense and that the PSC-PSOE and ERC were becoming more serious rivals for Catalanist votes. In response, CiU took a more decidedly nationalist stance, arguing that Spain should adopt a more confederal model of government. In July 1998, it signed the Declaration of Barcelona with the **Partido Nacionalista Vasco** and **Bloque Nacionalista Galego**, which called for the redefinition of Spain as a plurinational country. It had lost its overall majority in the 1995 Catalan elections, though it was still able to govern comfortably. Matters worsened in the 1999 elections when it was backed by only 37.7 percent of the electorate and gained less votes (though more seats) than the PSC-PSOE (now headed by the charismatic figure of **Pascual Maragall**), and subsequently had to rely on PP votes to remain in power. Furthermore, after the PP had achieved an overall majority in the Spanish general elections of 2000 it lost all influence on central government.

After the 1999 elections, Pujol announced that he would not stand again and began grooming Artur Mas (1955–) as his successor. Mas took over as secretary general of Convergència Democrática de Catalunya in 2000, became Pujol's *conseller en cap* (first minister) in 2001, and, in the same year, replaced Pujol as the president of CiU and its candidate for the presidency of the Generalitat. This led to tensions with CiU's more conservative coalition partner, Unió Democràtica de Catalunya, whose leader, Josep A. Duran i Lleida (1952–), hoped to succeed Pujol. In order to placate Duran i Lleida, he was elected to the newly created position of CiU general secretary in 2001. Then, after tough negotiations, in December of the same year it was agreed that CiU would operate as a closer-knit federation, rather than a coalition.

In Mas's first outing as presidential candidate for the Generalitat in November 2003, CiU performed badly. It only attained 31.2 percent of the vote and got fewer votes (though, again, more seats) than the PSC-PSOE. In the aftermath of the elections, for the first time since 1980, CiU lost the presidency of the Generalitat, with the leftist parties (PSC-PSOE, ERC, and the post-Communist **Iniciativa per Catalunya**-Verds) forming a coalition government. However, Mas has performed well in opposition. The new president of the Generalitat, Pascual Maragall, took up the call for reform of the Catalan Statute, and when the PSOE came to power, following its victory in the March 2004 elections, negotiations began. However, CiU was not a spectator. Because of the importance of CiU votes (especially as ERC refused to consider modifications to the statute proposed by the government) in the Madrid parliament, Mas was able to play a key role in these negotiations, reaching an agreement with the prime minister, **José Luis Rodríguez Zapatero**, in January 2006. In the November 2006 elections to the autonomous parliament, CiU was rewarded when it was once again the most voted party. However, the left reformed its tripartite pact, leaving Mas in opposition once more.

While Mas has focused on the Catalan scene, Duran i Lleida has become CiU's principal representative in **Madrid**. He was made leader of CiU's parliamentary group in Madrid after the March 2004 elections, and in tough negotiations in September 2007 (before which the possibility of CiU breaking up was aired) it was agreed he would lead the list of CiU candidates for **Barcelona** in the forthcoming March general 2008 elections. Like Miquel Roca, he favors entering government if the conditions are right, rather than giving conditioned support from the sidelines. In these elections, the PSOE failed to gain an overall majority, while CiU, with 11 seats, is the third largest party in parliament. This means that the government will have, on occasion, to turn to CiU in order to get its legislative program through parliament. However, it seems that it will negotiate specific measures with CiU rather than offer it a cabinet post. *See also* TABLE 10.

CONVERSO JEWS. *See* JEWS.

COORDINACIÓN DEMOCRÁTICA/DEMOCRATIC COORDI- NATION. *See* JUNTA DEMOCRÁTICA.

COPE (CADENA DE ONDAS POPULARES ESPAÑOLAS)/ POPULAR SPANISH AIRWAVES' NETWORK. This is a private radio station in which the **Catholic Church** has a key stake. It was originally founded under the **Franco regime**, and during the 1970s and 1980s had little impact. The situation was transformed in 1993, when the **PRISA** media group took over the radio station Antena 3 and a number of radio presenters and journalists, including José María García (1944–), Antonio Herrero (1955–1988), Luis Herrero, and Federico Jiménez Losantos (1951–), moved across to COPE. The latter three championed a new right-wing, populist political line, a key component of which was the defense of Spanish national identity and a full-blooded critique of the "peripheral nationalisms" and of language policy in **Catalonia**. It played an important role (along with *El Mundo*) in airing and publicizing a number of **corruption** scandals involving the ruling **Partido Socialista Obrero Español** (PSOE) in the 1990s. Since the PSOE returned to power in 2004, it has once again led attacks on the party for its **education** policy, its decision to negotiate with **ETA** and **Herri Batasuna**, and its reform of the Catalan autonomy statute. It has also been at the forefront of claims that ETA was involved in the **Madrid train bombings** and that there has been a cover-up involving the security services. It is Spain's second most popular radio station behind **SER**. In 2007, the most popular program was Jiménez Losantos's "La Mañana."

CORPORATISM. Corporatism has two very different meanings. On the one hand, it can refer to democratic corporatism, in which the state plays an active role in society, and on the other, it refers to reactionary right-wing corporatism, which defends an authoritarian alternative to liberalism and democracy.

The first meaning encompasses the tripartite negotiations between the government, the employers' association, and unions following the **transition to democracy** (sometimes referred to as neocorporatist). The most important such negotiations resulted in the **Moncloa Pacts** in October 1977. Subsequently, under both the **Partido Socialista Obrero Español** (PSOE) and **Partido Popular** (PP) governments, tripartite negotiations have been held to deal with such matters as employment legislation, workers' rights, and wage increases.

Right-wing corporatist ideas, on the other hand, at first grew up in the 19th century within the **Catholic Church**. Most members of the Church rejected liberalism, which they saw as undermining the position of the Christian doctrine and unleashing revolutionary forces that questioned the social order. They tended to hark back to the supposedly harmonious institutions of pre-**Bourbon** medieval Spain as their model. A central tenet was that rather than governments being based on election by individual suffrage (which led to a negative atomization of society), the country's venerable corporations should play a leading role in political life. Particularly important in this respect was the **Carlist Juan Vázquez de Mella**, who, at the beginning of the 20th century, produced a detailed blueprint of his proposed Catholic-corporatist state and society. Corporatist ideas were then taken up in broader right-wing circles, especially after 1914, as a reaction against mass politicization in urban Spain and the growth of left-wing politics. Catholicism remained central to this new generation's ideas, though they no longer rejected industrialization and laid emphasis on the need to build a strong state in order to control and channel popular unrest. These ideas could be discerned in the **Maurista** movement in the second decade of the century and in the **Asociación Católica Nacional de Propagandistas** under Angel Herrera (1886–1968), and fed into the ideology of the **Confederación Española de Derechas Autónomas** and the **Alfonsoist monarchist** movement during the **Second Republic**. Much corporatist thought was also compatible with the ideology of the overtly Fascist **Falange Española**, set up during these years. Finally, antiliberalism found sympathy in **military** circles, where there was a belief that corrupt and weak politicians were at the root of Spain's decline, combined with a strong attachment to the virtues of order and discipline. The first regime to propound corporatist values was the **Primo de Rivera dictatorship** of 1923–1930. It was followed by the **Franco regime**, particularly during its **autarkic** phase in the 1940s. However, economic liberalization in the late 1950s was followed by political liberalization in the 1970s. This signaled the decline of corporatist doctrines within the right and their replacement by a neoliberal set of values. *See also* CORTES.

CORRUPTION. Corruption has a long history within Spanish public life. In the 16th century, **Felipe II** began selling offices in order to help pay off the public debt and this practice was continued by subsequent **Habsburg** monarchs. This helped consolidate a class of rich and powerful figures (who would become known as *caciques*) who had control over local politics. In the 19th century, the Spanish liberal state, rather than building an impartial bureaucratic machine, reached a symbiosis with the *caciques*. *Caciquismo* reached its apotheosis during the **Cánovas Restoration**, when the two official parties rotated in power on the basis of pacts with the *caciques*. Even **republican** political parties were drawn into a spoils system, with leading figures taking advantage of the power and influence they obtained to enrich themselves and their friends. This was most notably the case of **Alejandro Lerroux's Partido Republicano Radical**. With the rise of **regenerationist** political currents from the turn of the 20th century, criticism of *caciquismo* grew. The most notable figure in this respect was **Joaquín Costa**. In the 1930s, the **Second Republic** cut back on the power of the *caciques*, and made a serious effort to clean up local politics. However, during the early years of the **Franco regime**, under the economic system of **autarky**, corruption spread throughout the state machine. From the late 1950s, with the end of autarky and the rise of a new breed of technocratic ministers linked to the **Opus Dei**, matters improved somewhat. However, the 1969 **Matesa scandal** revealed that figures close to the Opus Dei had also become involved in illicit activities.

The hopes that the new democratic political system, forged between 1976 and 1978, would put an end to corruption have been disappointed. This can seen at both a national and local level. In the early 1990s, a whole series of scandals relating to corruption in high places came to light, some directly implicating the ruling **Partido Socialista Obrero Español** (PSOE). The first major scandal involved the use of official PSOE premises for private purposes by the brother of the deputy prime minister, **Alfonso Guerra**. This finally forced Guerra's resignation in January 1991. Then, in June, the PSOE's treasurer, Carlos Navarro, was forced to resign following allegations of illegal donations to the party. In January 1992, this was followed by the resignation of the minister of health and consumer affairs, Julián García, who was accused of being involved in fraudulent land purchases while head of RENFE, the state-owned **railway** company. Even more serious, at the end of 1992, news broke that the judiciary was investigating illegal funding of the party through a holding company called **Filesa**, after a police raid on the PSOE's offices in Madrid. In April 1994, the former head of the **Civil Guard**, **Luis Roldán**, who had been a PSOE official and was a government appointee, absconded in the face of allegations of massive corruption involving the adjudication of building contracts for Civil Guard barracks. This forced the resignation of the minister of the interior, Antoni Asunción (1951–). The following month, the former governor of the Bank of Spain, Mariano Rubio (1913–1998), was arrested for insider trading. Then, at the end of the year the ex-president of the banking group Banesto, **Mario Conde**, was arrested on charges of corruption.

One problem in this respect has been the lack of investigative journalism. Spain's most prestigious daily, *El País*, was close to the government and played no part in unearthing corrupt practices. The lead was taken by *El Mundo*, which was close to the opposition **Partido Popular** (PP). This was a welcome departure, but its unwillingness to build on this tradition of investigative journalism between 1996 and 2004, under a PP government, indicates that its previous diligence was, in part at least, politically motivated. At the same time, state **television** has remained under a high degree of government control and, since the late 1980s, private companies have preferred to invest in cheap, sensationalist programming rather than serious politics. It is to be hoped that the decision of the PSOE government, under **José Luis Rodríguez Zapatero**, that the director of state television should be elected by parliament rather than chosen by the prime minister will lead to it developing a more critical stance toward the authorities.

Post-1996 PP governments were careful to be seen as honest and trustworthy, though the **Gescartera scandal** indicated that there were nepotistic practices among officials linked to the Ministry of Economics. However, in recent years, the continued problem of corruption at local level has come to the fore. This is closely linked to Spain's construction boom and has centered on the reclassification of terrain by the local authorities in order for it to be built on (thereby vastly increasing its value). A whole series of cases of urban corruption came to light in 2006. Most seriously, leading figures within the Marbella town hall were arrested and a technical commission brought in to run the town until the next local elections. The PP has been the party most affected, but there have also been cases of corruption involving local PSOE councilors. The PSOE government plans to bring in a new "land law" that, it claims, will clamp down on corrupt practices linked to land reclassification. At the end of 2007, functionaries in the Madrid local council were found to be demanding illegal commissions in return for granting licenses allowing new commercial premises to open. Several arrests have been made.

CORTES. Cortes is the **Castilian** word for parliament. In the various Christian realms of Spain, Cortes developed during the 12th century. They typically consisted of three estates: the Church, nobles, and towns' representatives (though Aragón had a fourth estate made up of the lesser nobility). The towns' representatives came to be the key body, given that the Cortes were called by the **monarch** above all to raise funds, and nobles and the Church paid no direct taxes. In the **Crown of Aragón**, the Cortes ("Corts" in **Catalonia** and **Valencia**) were particularly strong because they were charged with maintaining the existing laws (*fueros*), with the monarch unable to legislate or raise revenue without their approval. On the other hand, in the **Crown of Castile** the king had the right to make laws. This became particularly important when first, the Crown of Castile and Crown of Aragón were united in 1479, and then, in 1516, they were incorporated into the **Habsburg Empire**. Spain's Habsburg rulers found in far easier to raise revenue for their European wars from the Castilian Cortes (especially after the defeat of the **Comuneros' revolt** in 1522) than their Aragonese counterparts. For this reason, in the 17th century, the king's advisor, the **count-duke of Olivares**, tried to weaken the Catalan Corts, provoking the Catalan revolt of 1640. The privileges enjoyed by the Crown of Aragón were finally swept away by the new **Bourbon** monarch, **Felipe V**, during and after the **War of Succession** in the early 18th century. As part of this policy, the territories Cortes were abolished. Henceforth, they were invited to send their own representatives to the Castilian Cortes, with the result that a unified Spanish Cortes operated for the first time. However, Felipe V had at the same time instituted a system of absolutist rule so that their function was merely ceremonial.

The **French Revolution** totally transformed the political landscape. In its aftermath, **liberal** ideas spread through urban Spain and demands were made for the operation of a single unified Cortes based on male suffrage (though most liberals still believed in the need for a property franchise). Such ideas came to fruition between 1810 and 1813 in the **Cortes of Cádiz**. Absolutist rule was, however, reimposed by **Fernando VII** in this latter year and only in 1834, with the **Royal Statute**, would there be a timid liberal opening. Throughout the rest of the century, liberal Cortes functioned, though it was only between 1868 and 1874 and after 1890 that universal male suffrage (at least theoretically) operated.

The early 20th century was then to see growing criticism of liberalism on the Spanish right inspired by Catholic-**corporatist** ideas. This reached its apogée under the **Franco regime**, during which an antidemocratic Cortes was established. The regime saw the liberal tradition as anti-Spanish, and an attempt was made to link the new Cortes to what was seen as the glorious tradition of the Castilian Cortes of the **Catholic Monarchs** and **Felipe II**. Plans by the Franco regime to set up a new corporative Cortes were first announced on 17 July 1942 and the first session held on 17 March 1943. In the early 1960s, as opposition to the regime grew, minor reforms were undertaken to make the Cortes seem somewhat more representative. Yet after the death of Franco, it became clear that such tinkering with the system was insufficient. From July 1976, the new president, **Adolfo Suárez**, showed himself committed to a democratic overhaul of the system. In order to get the army in line, he had to respect established legality and in effect convince the Francoist Cortes to vote themselves out of existence. This they did in mid-November. Elections were then held to a new liberal Cortes in June 1977, and a new liberal-democratic constitution came into effect in December 1978. The **Constitution of 1978** decentralized the Spanish political system, dividing the country up into a number of autonomous communities, each with their own parliament. It should, however, be noted that the title of Cortes was reserved for the national parliament.

During the Franco regime the flame of a democratic Cortes was kept alive by the Republican Cortes in exile, which first met on 10 January 1945, and formed a government in exile under José Giral (1879–1962). But with the shift of opposition to the interior from the 1950s, it became increasingly irrelevant. *See also* CONSTITUTION OF 1837; CONSTITUTION OF 1845; CONSTITUTION OF 1869; CONSTITUTION OF 1876; CONSTITUTION OF 1931.

CORTES OF CÁDIZ. The Cortes of Cádiz, which was called by the "patriot" forces struggling against the occupying Napoleonic armies, produced (with the partial exception of the Napoleonic **Bayonne Constitution**) the first **liberal** constitution in Spanish history. The Cortes first met on the island of León, across the bay from the city of Cádiz, on 24 September 1810, under the protection of the British fleet. The ideology of those who opposed Bonaparte was mixed. However, two factors ensured that the liberals—a name first used at the Cortes—would be in a majority. First, the mercantile cities of the Spanish littoral found it easier to send deputies to Cádiz. Second, people resident in the city itself—a bustling commercial port—substituted for those who either could not attend or arrived late.

On 9 December, a commission was elected to draw up the constitution. The draft was then discussed between August 1811 and March 1812. The final document was in many ways reminiscent of the "bourgeois" French constitution of 1791. In political terms, it established a constitutional monarchy with a single parliament (**Cortes**) and a restricted franchise. Legislative power resided with the king and the Cortes. The judiciary was to be independent. At the same time, noble privileges were swept away. The constitution recognized civil liberties, freedom of the press, and equality before the law. Finally, the formation of a new armed force to defend the constitution, the **National Militia**, was anticipated. The legislative work of the Cortes also prepared the ground for the replacement of feudal property relations by a free market in land and property. Church property was secularized and the **Spanish Inquisition** abolished. Moreover, indirect taxes were replaced by a new wealth tax. Nevertheless, the men of 1812 were moderate constitutionalists, who had no sympathy for the French Jacobin experiment of 1793. Thus they ensured that there would be no widespread redistribution of property, turning the old *señoríos territoriales* (entailed estates) into private property. In addition, they maintained **Catholicism** as the country's sole religion, and ensured religious matters would be the one area in which freedom of speech remained restricted.

The work of the Cádiz Cortes was of great importance, with the 1812 Constitution remaining the program of "progressive" liberal politicians for the next half century. Yet its authors had little time to put their measures into effect. The deputies held their last session on 14 September 1813. A new Cortes met 12 days later, but due primarily to ecclesiastical influence in the election process, they were far more conservative. Six months later, after having been released from French custody, **Ferdinand VII** brought the constitutional experiment to an end and reestablished absolutism. *See also* FERNANDO RESTORATIONS; FRENCH REVOLUTION.

COSTA MARTÍNEZ, JOAQUÍN (1846–1911). Costa was the outstanding figure of the **regenerationist** current that emerged in late 19th-century Spain. He was a self-made man who was born into a peasant family in Huesca and who through determination and privations studied law at the University of Madrid. He then went on to become a prolific critic of Spain's political elites. Costa's critique centered on the **corruption** of Spanish political life and its oligarchic system of government. Reflecting his rural roots, one of the major remedies Costa proposed to Spain's backwardness was a new system of irrigation and public works. Politically, however, he was never a radical. His hopes for the regeneration of Spain lay in what he referred to as the "neutral classes," what today we would define as the middle classes, or more specifically, rural middle classes. But these were never going to be a force sufficiently powerful or politically aware to transform Spain. For this reason, his attempt, from 1898, to mobilize a political opposition based on the country's chambers of agriculture and his alliance with Basilio Paraíso (1849–1930) in the **Unión Nacional** was to run into the sand. Because of his disgust with Spanish parliamentary liberalism, Costa suggested that an "iron surgeon" may be necessary to reform Spain. He maintained that he only saw this as a temporary measure and did not advocate the abolition of parliament. Nevertheless, his arguments were later to be used by **Miguel Primo de Rivera** as a justification for dictatorship. His key work was *Oligarquía y caciquismo como forma actual de gobierno de España y modo de cambiarla* (*Oligarchy and Caciquismo as the Present Form of Government in Spain and the Way to Change This*, 1901).

COTTON TEXTILE INDUSTRY. From the late 18th century, the cotton textile **industry** emerged as the "leading sector" in Spain's industrial development. The industry was centered on **Catalonia**, which, between 1861 and 1913, absorbed over 90 percent of Spain's imports of raw cotton. The origins of the industry's rapid growth can be traced to the 1780s, with the introduction of the English spinning jenny. From the 1800s, the beginnings of a system of factory-based production could be discerned on the weaving side of the industry. Growth was, however, totally dislocated by the Napoleonic Wars of 1808–1814. Much of Catalan territory was invaded, thereby disrupting production and opening the way for contraband. Moreover, a large part of the industry's production had been destined for the South American market. This was largely lost with the revolt of the American creoles against Spanish rule. The postwar years saw a slow reconstruction of the industry. From the 1830s, this growth quickened in pace, reaching its height between 1833 and 1885. This development was based on the expansion of the country's internal market as a result of urban growth and the increase in agricultural production that followed the *desamortización*.

The process, however, stalled in the mid-1880s. This followed the invasion of the Spanish home market by cheap American and Russian grains, throwing Spanish **agriculture** into crisis and thereby provoking a reduction of demand for textiles among the rural **population**. The government responded by raising **tariff** barriers. Textile manufacturers also looked to the remaining colonial markets—**Cuba**, the **Philippines**, and Puerto Rico—to absorb surplus production. This served to temporarily alleviate the problem, but with the loss of the **colonies** in the 1898 Treaty of Paris, the industry again had to deal with the problem of surplus production.

Until 1914, the industry grew slowly. It was protected by high tariff barriers, but because it was in large measure dependent on the demands of a poor peasantry and urban populace, it could not match the rate of growth of equivalent industries in the more advanced Western states. The industry was to benefit greatly from Spain's neutrality during **World War I**, exporting intensively to the warring nations, but in the 1920s and 1930s, it again found it difficult to compete with the major international companies. The early years of the **Franco regime** were disastrous because of restrictions on the import of cotton. Then, from the 1950s, the industry suffered from increasing competition from the developing world and the growing use of new artificial fibers. Spain's entry into the **European Union** in 1986 further worsened the situation. However, since the 1990s, a small but profitable textile industry has survived, focused on the high end of the market.

COUNCIL OF ARAGÓN. *See* CONSEJO DE ARAGÓN.

COUNTER-REFORMATION. This term refers to the reaction within the Catholic world against the rise of Protestantism from the 1540s. Under an aging **Carlos I** and then his son **Felipe II**, the Spanish **Habsburg monarchy** was at the heart of this reaction. It comprised two main elements: first, the persecution of "heresy" through the **Spanish Inquisition**; second, the attempt to reform the **Catholic Church** in order for it to more effectively impose Catholic morality on the population. The main thrust of this reform was to better educate the clergy, banish semi-pagan practices, and pressurize the population to conform to Catholic principles in areas such as the blasphemy and marital fidelity.

COUP ATTEMPTS. *See* MILITARY; PRONUNCIAMIENTO; TEJERAZO.

CRISIS OF 1917. The crisis of 1917 can be seen as a failed attempt by the representatives of the more reforming sectors of Spanish society to democratize the **Cánovas Restoration**. In social terms, the urban middle and working classes were to the fore. The major organizations were the **republicans**, the working-class left, and, in **Catalonia**, the **Catalanist Lliga Regionalista**. Two elements had helped strengthen the reformers in the previous three years: first, the economic boom in the country, which increased the weight of urban Spain, above all manufacturing interests and the organized working class; second, the impetus toward the democratization of European society provided by both the first Russian Revolution of February 1917 and by the growing likelihood of an Allied victory in **World War I**. Reformers were further encouraged by growing divisions within the Restoration parties from 1913.

The crisis was sparked by the formation of **Juntas de Defensa** by army officers during 1916. This led both the Lliga Regionalista and the Spanish left to hope that the **military** might help them undertake an offensive against the regime. Thereafter, a number of overlapping initiatives were launched. First, representatives of the major labor confederations, the **Confederación Nacional del Trabajo** (CNT) and **Unión General de Trabajadores** (UGT), met in March 1917 and agreed at some future date to call an indefinite general strike in order to force "fundamental changes in the system." Then, in June, the **Partido Socialista Obrero Español** (PSOE) linked up with republicans and the **Partido Reformista**, agreeing to work for the establishment of a provisional government that would pave the way for general elections and a constituent parliament or **Cortes**. The implication was that the unions would act as a battering ram to bring down the Restoration regime, leaving the way open for the formation of a left-wing provisional government. Finally, the Lliga Regionalista devised a less revolutionary plan, which it hoped would also bring more conservative reformers onboard. With the Cortes closed, the Lliga's leader, **Francesc Cambó**, called an assembly of parliamentary deputies, which demanded an independent government prepare elections to a constituent Cortes. He hoped to get the backing both of reforming members of the **Partido Conservador**, under **Antonio Maura**, and the Juntas de Defensa, thereby piling unbearable pressure on King **Alfonso XIII** and the government to capitulate. The prime minister, **Eduardo Dato**, declared the meeting subversive, but allowed it to go ahead on 19 July. Republican and PSOE deputies now backed the Lliga's initiative and attended. However, both Maura and the Juntas refused to give their support, with the result that it did not have sufficient power to force the authorities into submission.

The question was, therefore, what next? With considerable trepidation the PSOE-UGT had begun preparations for a general strike with the CNT. The assembly road blocked, they once again considered the strike route. The hope was that if the army stood aside the government would have to give way. Unfortunately, it was called precipitously on 13 August before preparations were complete. It was supported by the CNT and followed throughout much of urban Spain. The military, however, showed no qualms about putting it down. In part, the strike's defeat was the result of divisions within the reform camp. The Lliga was afraid of being outflanked on the left and so distanced itself. Furthermore, rural Spain had not yet been mobilized by the labor unions and remained quiet throughout. Most importantly though, the army showed it still supported the established order.

Two months later it did, however, seem that substantial reform might be on the table. The Juntas, smarting at the role Dato had put them in, forced his government to resign. The assembly met again on 30 October and Cambó was asked to participate in a coalition government. He demanded as his price that the interior minister allow free elections to take place. This, he argued, meant that the program of the assembly movement was effectively being implemented. The problem was that in the run-up to the February 1918 elections, other ministers were involved in electoral manipulation and in rural areas *caciquista* networks remained strong. Hence, in the elections, the reforming candidates did not obtain enough seats to introduce any substantial constitutional reforms.

CROWN OF ARAGÓN. The Crown of Aragón was a confederation of states, presided over by a single monarch, whose origin lay in the union between the County of **Barcelona** and Aragón in 1137. Subsequently, the lands of Mallorca (1230), Ibiza (1235), **Valencia** (1232–1245), and Menorca (1287) were "reconquered" from the **Moors** and incorporated into the crown. During the late 13th and 14th centuries, it established a powerful seaborne, commercial empire, its possessions including the islands of Sardinia and Sicily from 1409. However, in the 15th century, it was seriously weakened by epidemics and fierce social and political conflict, as indicated by the fact that at the end of the century the territory's **population** did not exceed one million inhabitants. In 1411, moreover, the Castilian Trastámara dynasty acceded to the throne (through the so-called Casp Compromise), laying the basis of the unification of the Crowns of Aragón and Castile in 1479. Its territorial fortunes matched that of its rulers. Under the **Catholic Monarchs**, in 1483 Roussillon and Cerdagne were definitively incorporated into its dominions, and in 1504, in collaboration with the **Crown of Castile**, it took control of the Kingdom of Naples. However, with France in the ascendancy through the 1659 Treaty of the Pyrenees, it lost Roussillon and part of the Cerdagne to its neighbor.

The Crown of Castile was easily the most powerful component in the 1479 match, and over the next century it would consolidate its central role in the forging of an empire. However, the Catholic Monarchs and, subsequently, the **Habsburg** dynasty, did not rule over a united country, but a confederation of dominions. This was reflected in the fact that they did not hold one title, but maintained separate titles for each of their crowns and kingdoms. As a result, the Crown of Aragón was, for over two centuries, to maintain its own institutions and a high degree of independence. The Catholic Monarchs established a Council of Aragón at their side to help them govern, and with both monarchs largely based in Castile they remained in contact through viceroys. But the Crown of Aragón's three kingdoms retained their own parliament (**Cortes**) and representatives of these three parliaments would occasionally hold a general Cortes in the presence of the monarch (though they met separately). Because of these territories' strong feudal tradition of mutual obligations, a contractual monarchy had evolved, in which the consent of the Cortes was needed to enact laws and raise finance. The Crown of Aragón also retained its own laws (*fueros*), administration, currency, system of tax collection, and customs barriers.

This provoked tensions with the monarchy. Under **Felipe II** a constitutional crisis was provoked when the king's former favorite, Antonio Pérez (1569–1611), sought refuge in Aragón. It was resolved in the king's favor when he sent in the army, had the kingdom's chief law officer executed, and ensured that in future he could be removed by the king. The Crown of Aragón's ability to block the granting of royal taxes also caused growing annoyance, especially as the Habsburgs became embroiled in a whole series of European wars. This came to a head between the 1620s and 1640s, when King **Felipe IV**'s favorite, the **count-duke of Olivares**, tried (unsuccessfully) to pursue a more centralizing policy. Such a policy was finally adopted after the **Bourbons** took over the Spanish throne in 1700 in the figure of **Felipe V**. During and after the **War of Succession**, the component parts of the Crown of Aragón lost all their privileges and its Cortes's representatives were asked to join the Cortes of Castile (which, however, had become simply a decorative body). This, Felipe V maintained, was because it had been guilty of betrayal, as it had supported the rival pretender to the throne. However, **Catalonia**, Aragón, and Valencia had in reality been divided in their allegiance. It seems that Felipe V in any case wanted to impose a more centralizing model closer to that practiced by the French monarchy. At the end of the war Spain also lost all its Italian possessions. Subsequently, in 1746, the country was divided into provinces.

CROWN OF CASTILE. The Crown of Castile (which comprised the northern Atlantic coast, central and southern Spain) established itself as the largest and most powerful state in the Iberian Peninsula during the 15th century, at the end of which it possessed around five million of its seven million inhabitants. Its manufacturing base was weak, but it had built up a prosperous pastoral economy based on sheep farming and the export of wool. It had also acquired a formidable **military** reputation during the so-called "**Reconquest**" of Spain from the **Moors**. Hence, it would be the dominant partner in the new composite monarchy established after unification with the **Crown of Aragón** under the **Catholic Monarchs** in 1479. This was especially clear from 1561, when **Felipe II** located the court and state administration in **Madrid**, and positions of power and influence became dominated by Castilian aristocrats. It could also be seen in Castile's leading role in the conquest of an empire in America and in the establishment of **Castilian** as the language of the court and of the major state councils.

Not that this benefited the majority of the population. The Castilian **Cortes** was weaker than those of the Crown of Aragón. This weakness was further accentuated with the defeat of the **Comuneros' revolt** of 1520–1522, following which the Cortes could only petition the monarch and could be more effectively pressurized than its Aragonese counterparts into granting taxes (*servicios*). As a result, Castile's population—especially the peasantry and urban artisans and manufacturers—had to foot much of the bill for the continuous European wars of the Spanish **Habsburg monarchy** between the 1520s and 1650s. This exacerbated the territory's relative poverty, contributing to the lack of gains in **agricultural** productivity and its inability to modernize its manufacturing base. After the **War of Succession**, the new **Bourbon** monarch, **Felipe V**, turned the Cortes of the Crown of Castile into a Spanish-wide body, while however emptying it of all remaining powers.

CUBA. Cuba was first conquered by Spanish forces in 1511 and by the late 19th century it had become easily Spain's most significant **colonial** possession. Its place within the Spanish trading system was that of a captive market, particularly for Castilian flour and grain producers and Catalan **cotton textile** industrialists. This was ensured through extremely high **tariffs** on foreign, and especially North American, producers. At the same time, however, Cuban produce, and particularly sugar, found its entry into the Spanish market blocked, with the result that it had to export most of its produce to the United States (where, in retaliation for the duties on imports into Cuba, it faced heavy tariffs). Through its surplus trade with Cuba, Spain was able to make up its large commercial deficit with other parts of the world. Not for nothing was Cuba known in Spain as "the richest colony in the world."

This led to growing discontent among the indigenous creole (*criollo*) population, local inhabitants born and bred in Cuba but of Spanish ancestry. Many were further alienated by the lack of political freedom and the fact that men who retained close links with Spain (the so-called *peninsulares*) dominated politics on the island. Following a three-year recession, poor landowners rose up against Spanish rule in the east of the island (*Oriente*) in 1868. The so-called Ten Years' War was to cost both Spain and the indigenous Cubans dear. In all, over 100,000 Spanish troops were to die, and the Spanish government would spend around 365 million pesos. However, the rebellion failed to gain the support of many rich landowners based in the west (*Occidente*), who were afraid that it would encourage a slave rebellion and put their social status in jeopardy. Nevertheless, it was only after the fall of the agitated **First Republic** and the end of the Third Carlist War that the Spanish state was able to put all its resources into quelling the uprising. The war was finally brought to an end through the Zanjón Peace of February 1878.

Some concessions were made to the Cubans but they were not given any notable measure of autonomy. In 1892, the **Partido Liberal** overseas minister, **Antonio Maura**, drew up plans for an autonomy statute for the colony. It was, however, defeated by the die-hard colonial interests in the Spanish parliament, the **Cortes**, in 1895. As a result, the creoles despaired of any significant concessions being made, and hence poorer landowners again initiated a new insurrection on the island, which began in February 1895. On this occasion, moreover, they gained the backing of many former slaves (slavery had been abolished in 1885), who came to see the revolt as a social revolution to improve their status and working conditions. The war was again to drain the resources of the treasury, and the youth of Spain's lower classes (the rich could buy their way out of **military service**) once again paid a heavy price: another 100,000 soldiers died in three years, most not in combat but through disease. From January 1896 to October 1897, Spain tried ruthlessly to crush the revolt through any means possible. General Valeriano Weyler (1838–1930) practiced a scorched-earth policy and herded the civilian population into concentration camps (the so-called Política de Reconcentración). It was all to no avail. A new Partido Liberal government took a softer line from October 1896, having Weyler replaced and giving the island a measure of autonomy, but it was too late. With the sinking of the American warship *Maine* in the Cuban port of La Havana in February 1898, a campaign was launched in the United States in favor of military intervention. It culminated in the **Spanish-American War** of May–July 1898. The campaign was to be short-lived, and in the **Treaty of Paris**, signed on 10 December, Spain had no choice but to renounce Cuba, Puerto Rico, and the **Philippines**.

CU-CUT! INCIDENT. *Cu-Cut!* was a satirical weekly produced by the Catalanist **Lliga Regionalista**. On 25 November 1905, it published a cartoon that lampooned the **military** by suggesting that any victory in Spain could only be a civilian affair. This led army officers to wreck the offices of *Cu-Cut!* along with those of the regionalist daily, *La Veu de Catalunya*. The army's actions signaled its growing intervention in Spanish politics and triggered a new alignment of political forces in **Catalonia**. The prime minister, Eugenio Montero Ríos (1832–1914), was quick to capitulate to army demands that there should be no repetition. Hence, on 30 November, constitutional guarantees were suspended in the province of **Barcelona**. This was followed by the government's resignation and its replacement by a new **Partido Liberal** administration presided over by Montero Ríos's rival, **Segismundo Moret**. The government, under pressure from King **Alfonso XIII** and the military, then passed the so-called Jurisdictions Law, which subjected future criticisms of the army to military jurisdiction. It was as a reaction to this attack on freedom of speech and in order that constitutional guarantees might be reestablished that on the initiative of **Francesc Cambó** and **Nicolás Salmerón**, the leaders of the Lliga and the **Unión Republicana**, a series of political parties and groups in Catalonia formed an alliance, transformed on 15 January 1906 into an electoral coalition known as **Solidaritat Catalana**.

– D –

DALÍ I DOMÈNECH, SALVADOR (1904–1989). Dalí was the outstanding Spanish surrealist painter of the 20th century. He was born in the **Catalan** town of Figueres and went on to study at the National School of Fine Arts and the Royal Academy of San Fernando in **Madrid**. During this time, he made friends with both **Luis Buñuel** and **Federico García Lorca**, and quickly gained a reputation as an iconoclast with a talent for self-publicizing. His rise to fame came from 1928 when he moved to Paris and collaborated with Buñuel in the making of two films, *Un chien andulou* (*An Andalusian Dog*, 1929) and *L'âge d'or* (*The Golden Age*, 1931). At the same time, he began to produce his monumentally successful surrealist, dream-sequence paintings. Much of his success was based on his ability to marry a sophisticated and detailed painting technique (apparently modeled on 17th-century Dutch painter Johannes Vermeer) with deformed, plastic images and scenes supposedly drawn from the world of dreams (though some surrealists called this into question). He remained abroad during much of the **Second Republic** and **Spanish Civil War**, even though he declared himself an ardent Republican. With the victory of the **Nationalists**, he moved to the United States, where he became something of a celebrity, combining painting with commercial assignments and even collaborating with Alfred Hitchcock in the dream sequences of *Spellbound* (1945). From the 1950s, however, he was to spend more time in his native Figueres and his painting took on a more religious and historic content, while he was to a degree reconciled with the **Franco regime**.

DATO IRADIER, EDUARDO (1856–1921). Eduardo Dato was, along with **Antonio Maura**, a key figure in the **Partido Conservador** (PC) during the second half of the **Cánovas Restoration**. He was born in La Coruña, but moved to **Madrid** as a young lawyer, entering the PC. He quickly became known for his interest in social legislation, which he saw as necessary in order to bind labor to the polity. After his appointment to **Francisco Silvela**'s government in 1900, he introduced Spain's first social laws (with the exception of legislation approved in 1873, which was never enforced) and set up the **Instituto de Reformas Sociales**. During the 1910s, on the other hand, in the face of growing political opposition, he became the most formidable opponent of constitutional renewal, setting his stall against any democratic reform that would undermine the regime's central feature, the *turno pacífico* between its two "official" parties.

After the PC's previous leader, Antonio Maura, had called the system's central tenets into question, quarrelling with King **Alfonso XIII** and refusing to cooperate with the **Partido Liberal**, in October 1913, Dato was called on to govern by the king and two years later took over the leadership of his party. Henceforth, he would be in charge of its majority wing (the so-called *idóneos*), while his rival headed a smaller faction of **Mauristas**. Despite the difficulties, he thereafter tried to maintain the *turno*. The king dissolved parliament, allowing Dato to gain a relative majority in the April 1914 general elections, although the different minority groupings in the **Cortes** would finally force him out.

Growing political and social unrest would endanger the regime during the so-called **crisis of 1917**. The king again turned to Dato on 11 June and over the following two months, he saw two interconnected attempts at major reform. The first was launched by the **Lliga Regionalista**, which organized an assembly of opposition parliamentarians in **Barcelona** who demanded free elections and democratizing reforms to the constitution. The following month the working-class left called a general strike for the same demand. Dato, however, held firm. The Lliga did not count on a wide enough support base and Dato used the **military** to put the general strike down. This was, however, also to be at the root of his downfall. The powerful officers' unions, the **Juntas de Defensa**, smarting at the unpopular role they had played, forced him out in October. Hence, he was unable to fulfill his ambition of calling elections to consolidate his position in power.

He would, however, get one further opportunity. Faced with growing labor unrest, from early 1919, the king and military favored more conservative options. After the *idóneos* thwarted an attempt by Maura to retake the reins of the party in the spring, the king once again turned to them. In the summer of 1919, Dato's close ally, Joaquín Sánchez de Toca (1852–1942), took power, but his position was undermined by fierce social conflict in Barcelona. A second opportunity came in May 1920, when Dato took over the premiership. The *turno* no longer operated effectively, but in new elections in December 1920, he was at least able to ensure that his followers formed the largest block in parliament. Like Sánchez de Toca, his position was weakened by social conflict in Barcelona. Unlike Maura, who favored a hard line against syndicalist agitation, Dato's wing of the party had taken a more moderate stance and tried to integrate the **Catalan** branch of the **Confederación Nacional del Trabajo** (CNT) into a state-sponsored arbitration board. However, this brought down on his head fierce criticism from conservative (especially business) and military circles, who accused the *idóneos* of weakness in the face of **terrorism** and subversion. Dato reacted by tacking rightward, naming tough barracks-room general Severiano Martínez Anido (1862–1938) civil governor of Barcelona in November 1920. Martínez Anido then launched an all-out assault on the Catalan CNT. Dato was to pay the ultimate price. In revenge, a CNT hit squad was sent out from Barcelona and gunned him down on 8 March 1921.

DECOLONIZATION. The **Franco regime** abandoned most of its territories in North Africa after 1950. This was a necessary concomitant of a **foreign policy** that tried to attract the Arab states. Nevertheless, in order to soothe **military** sensibilities, General **Francisco Franco** was careful not to go too fast. In 1956, Spain left the Spanish zone in **Morocco**, though retaining the garrison towns of Ceuta and Melilla, in which there was a large Spanish population. Ifni and Cabo Juno were then ceded to Morocco in 1958. Later, in 1968, Spain withdrew from her possessions in Equatorial Guinea (Río Muni and the islands of Fernando Po). Spain still retained the western Sahara, and this led to tensions with Morocco. At the end of Franco's life, Rabat began to push with renewed vigor for the territory to be handed over. Apparently when Franco, already a sick man, learned that King Hassan II of Morocco was planning a "green march" of civilians into the Spanish Sahara in October 1975, he suffered a heart attack. Just before Franco's death on 14 November, an agreement was signed with Morocco and Mauritania handing over control, and on 26 February 1976, the Spanish forces withdrew. *See also* COLONIES.

DEFENSE JUNTAS. *See* JUNTAS DE DEFENSA.

DEMOCRACY. *See* DEMOCRATIC SEXENNIUM; SECOND REPUBLIC; TRANSITION TO DEMOCRACY.

DEMOCRATIC SEXENNIUM/SEXENIO DEMOCRÁTICO. The term Democratic Sexennium refers to the period between the **Glorious Revolution** of 1868 and the restoration of the **Bourbon** monarchy through the *pronunciamiento* of General Arsensio Martínez Campos (1831–1900) in December 1874.

It was a period during which democratic rights were extended to the adult male population for the first time, but also a time of great political instability and social ferment. The provisional government, formed after the Glorious Revolution under the presidency of General **Francisco Serrano**, was not made up of radicals, but the events of

1868 had resulted in a great political mobilization of the urban lower classes and southern peasantry. Moreover, the decree of 9 November 1868 established universal male suffrage for the first time. The overall result was a rapid growth in political activity and trade unionism. The first point was demonstrated in the January 1869 elections, when the newly founded **Partido Republicano Federalista** managed to gain a sizeable block of seats in the **Cortes**. The second became clear in June 1870, when the **Federación Regional Española** (FRE), a national **labor** confederation under **anarchist** influence, was founded in **Barcelona**.

The monarchical-democratic plotters were, nevertheless, able to win the elections of 1869 with an ample majority. This allowed them to put in place the first largely democratic **constitution** in Spain's history. As part of the constitutional settlement, they also began to look for a new monarch, and finally settled upon a member of the notoriously **liberal** Italian royal family, Luis Amadeo de Saboya, who was crowned **Amadeo I** on 2 January 1872. However, over the following two years, as problems accumulated, the new regime became increasingly unstable. In the first place, the liberal elements within the constitution were taken as a cue by the **Carlists** in northern Spain to rise up against the authorities. Moreover, in October 1868, a revolt broke out in **Cuba**. The expenditure and manpower needed for the Carlist and Cuban wars then made it difficult for the authorities to implement popular policies, such as the abolition of the *consumos* (indirect taxes on basic consumer goods) and the *quintas* (obligatory **military service** for all except the rich, who could buy their way out).

At the same time, between 1869 and 1871, popular agitation continued to grow, with an escalation in strikes and attempts by the peasants of the south to occupy land. Both the FRE and the **republicans** soon showed their hostility to the new authorities, the left republicans launching a number of insurrections. This instability caused the governing coalition to divide into the more conservative Partido Constitucionalista, led by **Práxedes Mateo Sagasta**, who wished to pursue a vigorous policy of law and order, and the **Partido Radical,** captained by Manuel Ruiz Zorrilla (1833–1895). Furthermore, as a result of social and political agitation the social elites and conservative middle classes began to fear for their property and clamored for a return of the Bourbon dynasty. This was reflected in the boycott to which Amadeo was subjected by elite **Madrid** society. Finally, isolated and tired of infighting within the governing coalition, he abdicated on 11 February 1873.

At such short notice, the authorities had no alternative candidate and so almost by default a republic was proclaimed. The **First Republic** was to be marked by several twists and turns. The first government, elected in May, produced a draft of a new **federalist** constitution and planned social and economic reform. However, it was seriously weakened by splits over policies, with the more moderate groups championing ordered reform from above and the intransigents, as the more radical republican sectors were called, mobilizing popular support to speed up the pace of change. This division culminated in the **Cantonalist revolt** of July 1873, an attempt by left-wing republicans to take matters into their own hands and proclaim popular reforms from below. This chaotic situation gave the right the opportunity to strike back. Not only were republicans now fighting among themselves, there was in middle-class circles a widespread demand for a return to order and stability. This included many former members of the **Partido Progresista** and liberal army officers. It was in response to these pressures that on 3 January 1874 General Manuel Pavia (1827–1895) used a detachment of **Civil Guards** to violently dissolve the **Cortes**, thereby paving the way for more authoritarian rule. For several months General Serrano tried to consolidate a "republic of order," but Spanish elites and the respectable middle classes still saw the Bourbons as their best long-term guarantee of stability. Since the beginning of the Sexenio, conservative politician **Antonio Cánovas del Castillo** had been plotting to place the queen's son Alfonso (soon to be **Alfonso XII**) on the throne. The opportunity was finally provided when General Arsensio Martínez Campos (1831–1900) pronounced against Serrano on 29 December 1874. It quickly became clear that Serrano had very little support, and his only option was to flee into exile. Consequently, Alfonso made a triumphal entry into Madrid on 14 January 1875. The **Cánovas Restoration** was about to begin.

DEMOCRATIC TRANSITION. *See* TRANSITION TO DEMOCRACY.

DEMOGRAPHY. *See* IMMIGRATION; POPULATION.

DESAMORTIZACIÓN/DISENTAILMENT. The word *desamortización* is used to describe the process by which, between 1836 and 1856, aristocratic privileges were swept away and the preconditions laid for the growth of capitalist relations of production on the land. The **liberals** who carried out the *desamortización* looked for inspiration to the measures undertaken by the **French revolutionaries** in the early 1790s. The key laws were approved by **Juan Álvarez Mendizábal** between 1836 and 1837. In the first place, between February and March 1836, property held in mortmain (*manos muertas*) by the religious orders was put up for sale on the open market. Then in 1837, *mayorazgos* (entails) were removed from noble land and noble dues (*senoríos jurisdiccionales*) were abolished. This was followed up in 1841 with the sale of land held by the diocesan clergy. The disentailment process slowed between 1843 and 1850, when the more conservative liberals in the **Partido Moderado** came to power. However, with their ousting by the **Partido Progresista**, through the Madoz Law of 1 May 1855, remaining land held by the **Catholic Church**, along with common land that belonged to the municipalities, was put up for sale. The new law was briefly suspended from the end of 1856, but reintroduced in 1858, remaining in force until 1895.

The *desamortización* created an open market for land, but it did not lead to a more even distribution of landholding. At root, behind the *desamortización* was a tacit compromise between the old nobility and untitled men of wealth and property. The nobility was to lose its ancient privileges, but was to retain (or even enhance) its property. It was the men of wealth, irrespective of rank, who were to benefit from the sales. They had the cash in hand, and, in addition, could also use much depreciated government bonds to purchase land at bargain prices. Nobles also benefited from the confusion between *senoríos territoriales* (land that was their property) and *senoríos jurisdiccionales* (land over which they had merely the right to claim certain dues from the peasantry), and were often able to use their influence over local courts to get the latter also declared their own. The losers were the Church and the peasantry. In many areas, the latter lacked the resources to buy land for sale, were deprived of land they believed was theirs, and lost grazing and other traditional rights. These grievances were in large measure to be behind peasant support for **Carlism** in northern Spain, and **republicanism** and later **anarchism** in the south.

DISASTER OF 1898. *See* SPANISH-AMERICAN WAR.

DISENTAILMENT. *See* DESAMORTIZACIÓN.

DON JUAN. *See* JUAN DE BORBÓN Y BATTENBERG.

DONOSO CORTÉS, JUAN (1809–1853). Donoso Cortés was the most extreme **Traditionalist** intellectual of the mid-19th century. He began his political career as an important figure in the conservative-liberal camp, but while in France in the 1840s, he linked up with reactionary **Catholic** circles. He maintained that Christian civilization was threatened by destruction at the hands of the forces of liberalism and socialism. Its only option was to strike back violently. In the short-term, he believed, the solution was a stop-gap **military** dictatorship. This would then give way to a "traditional" (pre-**Bourbon**) Catholic monarchy. His best-known works were *Discurso sobre la dictadura* (*A Treatise on Dictatorship*, 1848) and *Ensayo sobre catolicismo, liberalismo y socialismo* (*An Essay on Catholicism, Liberalism and Socialism*, 1851).

DURAN I LLEIDA, JOSEP A. *See* CONVERGÈNCIA I UNIÓ.

DURRUTI DUMANGE, BUENAVENTURA (1898–1936). Durruti was the most charismatic figure within the radical faction of the **Confederación Nacional del Trabajo** (CNT) in the 1930s. He was born in León on 14 July 1898. During 1915–1917, while working on the **railways**, he became a hot-headed union activist and, in 1917, made contact with **anarchist** circles in Gijón. After fleeing to France to avoid **military service**, he acted as a courier between Spanish and French anarchist groups. On his return in 1920, he then formed part of a team of anarchist gunmen based in San Sebastián. This should be seen in a context in which, since 1916, elements within the CNT had set up "action groups," which targeted employers, foremen, and "yellow" workers in order to strengthen the organization. Along with several colleagues, he then moved to Zaragoza in early 1921, where, along with a daring holdup, he became involved in attempts to form a federation of anarchist groups.

He moved to **Barcelona** in 1922 with several other anarchist gunmen in order to help in the fight against the de facto **military** dictatorship that operated in the city, and in October helped set up a group called Los Solidarios (The Common Cause). This was the most important of a number of groups that the Barcelona CNT was setting up to strike back at the employers and authorities and to organize an anarchist insurrection. Los Solidarios was behind a number of spectacular robberies and, after the assassination of **Salvador Seguí** in March 1923, divided up into three hit squads to exact revenge. Durruti formed part of the group that unsuccessfully tried to hunt down the **Carlist** pretender to the throne, Jaime de Borbón y Borbón-Parma (1870–1931), in France, but the other groups gunned down the former civil governor of Bilbao and the **Traditionalist** cardinal of Zaragoza, José Soldevila Romero. This produced an enormous outcry in conservative circles.

During the **Primo de Rivera dictatorship**, Durruti did not join the anarchist-coordinating group, the Federación Anarquista Ibérica (Anarchist Iberian Federation—FAI), set up in 1927, but was sympathetic toward its general aim of exercising tutelage to ensure the ideological purity of the CNT and, when the time was right, spark off the anarchist revolution. With the arrival of the **Second Republic**, he formed another action group known as Nosotros (Us) and played a leading role in the CNT insurrections launched between 1931 and 1933. Their defeat and the decline of the CNT between 1933 and 1936 indicated the need for more prudence. In February 1936, he even urged workers to vote for the **Popular Front**. With the onset of the **Spanish Civil War**, he played an active role in organizing the proanarchist militias on the Aragonese front. He then transferred to the **Madrid** front, where he was killed by a single shot on 20 November 1936. This led to speculation in anarchist circles that he was assassinated by the **Partido Comunista de España** (PCE). There is, however, no proof of this assertion.

– E –

ECONOMIC POLICY. Government economic policy during the 19th and 20th centuries can be divided into three very broad phases. The first, between the liberal revolution of the 1830s and the 1891 tariffs, saw government pursuing relatively open liberal economic policies. Powerful lobbies such as the Castilian wheat producers and Catalan **cotton textile** industrialists were placated with **tariff** protection, but duties on other imports remained low; foreign financial and industrial interests, most notably **railway** and **mining** companies, were encouraged to invest in Spain. From the second half of the 1880s, however, Spanish economic policy became increasingly nationalistic. In 1891 and again in 1906, tariffs on foreign imports were raised. Then, under the **Partido Conservador** politician **Antonio Maura**, during the first decade of the 20th century, the state began to use state contracts to favor indigenous **industry**. This policy of state intervention was extended by the **Primo de Rivera dictatorship** during the 1920s (when Spanish tariffs became the highest in the world). At the same time, an ambitious program of irrigation schemes and public works programs was devised to improve the country's inadequate infrastructure and stimulate Spanish industry. State intervention reached its apogée during the **autarky** phase of the **Franco regime** in the 1940s and early 1950s, when the state sector was enlarged and all manner of controls were imposed on economic activity.

The policy was only reversed after its evident failure in the late 1950s. Henceforth, under the technocratic guidance of General **Francisco Franco's Opus Dei** ministers, the regime was to liberalize and open the country up to foreign goods and capital while intervening in the **economy** through indicative planning. As part of this strategy, the regime attempted, unsuccessfully, to join the **European Economic Community** (EEC). The liberalization of the Spanish economy was pursued more vigorously by the governments of the **Partido Socialista Obrero Español** (PSOE) and **Partido Popular** (PP) after the death of Franco. Spain finally came into line with the rest of western Europe after becoming a member of the EEC in 1986. In subsequent years, the PSOE administration viewed further European integration as in Spain's interests, entering the Exchange Rate Mechanism

(ERM) of the European Monetary System (EMS) in June 1989 and subsequently joining the euro zone.

In terms of monetary and fiscal policy, Spain was slow to react to the recession produced by the oil price rise of 1973. Weak governments, whose attention was focused on the political climate, were little disposed to take the unpalatable measures the situation demanded. Hence, the price of oil was subsidized, inflation was allowed to rise, and the balance of payments was allowed to lurch into deficit. Serious action was only taken after the democratic elections of 1977. Between 1978 and 1985, both the **Unión del Centro Democrático** (UCD) and the PSOE reacted to the economic recession and inflationary pressures provoked by the oil price rises of 1973 and 1979 by trying to limit the growth in money supply, hold down wage increases, and restore the profitability of Spanish industry. Furthermore, governments also sought to reduce Spain's dependence on oil imports and encourage industrial restructuring into high-growth areas. Hence, in 1979 the UCD government of **Adolfo Suárez** approved a program to boost Spain's nuclear industry.

At the same time, both the UCD and PSOE recognized the need to build a **welfare state** in order to underpin the post-Francoist democratic consensus. Throughout the 19th and 20th centuries, Spanish economic policy had been hindered by the state's narrow tax base. Through to the 1960s, as a result of government's fear of antagonizing social elites, taxes were to a large extent indirect (a large part leveled on staple consumer goods), while vigorous measures were not taken to stamp out fraud and fiscal evasion. Under Franco, the proportion of indirect taxes in total income actually increased significantly and **corruption** in the state became an accepted perk of the job. In order to break with this heritage, the UCD made the key decision (with the support of the left-wing opposition) to introduce a tax on earnings (the Impuesto sobre la Renta de Personas Físicas— IRPF), while making efforts to reduce tax fraud. This has allowed the structure of government income and expenditure to approximate to a greater degree those of the rest of western Europe.

When the PSOE came to power in 1982, a key factor in dictating economic policy was the need to make the Spanish economy more competitive in preparation for entry into the EEC and then the need to put Spain on track to meet the EEC's convergence criteria in order to join a future single currency. In part, its policy was interventionist, with large sums of money put into a "reconversion plan" to restructure Spanish heavy industry (important sectors of which were in state hands) and remove surplus capacity. But under the economics ministers **Miguel Boyer** and Carlos Solchaga (1944–), a more neoliberal approach was taken to reform the **labor market** in order to make the factors of production more mobile, with the introduction of more "flexible" employment contracts, along with temporary and part-time contracts to make it easier for companies to hire and fire and reduce costs of redundancy. This led to serious conflict with the trade unions, including a well-supported one-day general strike in 1988. The need to make Spanish industry more competitive also meant that the economics' team supported the **privatization** of potentially profitable state-owned firms in the 1990s and took measures to help public sector firms grow and invest prior to sale. Eclectic elements could also be seen in the government's program of social spending. As noted, it wished to build a welfare state and hence raised taxes. Yet it also needed to keep down budget deficits (especially after joining the ERM in 1989 and signing up to Mastricht in 1991). Luckily, increasingly large transfers of **European Union** (EU) funds—aimed in part to make Spain's compliance with the convergence criteria easier—helped make up for tight government finances.

In order to win the 1996 general election, the PP had to confirm that it supported the welfare state. Nevertheless, it took a more decidedly neoliberal line that its predecessors. This could be seen in the fruition with which it held down government spending—freezing public sector pay and cutting back on public investment. It also greatly speeded up the PSOE's privatization program, leading to the emergence of a number of major private companies. The reelection of the PSOE in 2004 has not broken this basic consensus on economic policy, though, as is to be expected, post-2004 PSOE governments have placed more emphasis on developing the welfare state. *See also* AGRICULTURE; TRADE.

ECONOMY. In the 1500s, Spain's position as the center of the **Habsburg** Empire and its vast **colonial** possessions in America hid the fact that its economy was relatively weak in comparison with that of the other major European powers. This weakness centered on low **agricultural** productivity, a small manufacturing base, and inadequate financial markets (with Antwerp and Geneva being Europe's major financial centers). The result was that Spain largely exported semi-elaborated and agriculture-based products (like wool, wine, and raw silk) and imported manufactures. Indeed, its relative position worsened during the 16th century as high inflation, caused to a significant degree by the import of silver bullion from America, made Spanish produce expensive and uncompetitive. As a result, not only did Spain increasingly become an entrepôt through which foreign manufactures were reexported to America, but foreign merchants, based in Seville and Cádiz, also came to control much of the colonial trade.

From the late 17th century, there was some recovery, which was further aided by the fact that Spain divested itself of its European possessions and the constant warfare their defense entailed in 1713, following the **War of Succession**. The mercantilist policies pursued by the new **Bourbon** dynasty in the 18th century further stimulated economic development. Most notably, under **Carlos III** the port of Cádiz lost its monopoly over the colonial trade. This made possible **Catalonia**'s economic takeoff toward the end of the century, based, above all, on the growth of **cotton textiles**. In the 1860s, a modern **coal mining industry** began to develop in Asturias, and from the 1890s, **iron and steel** formed the basis of the industrial takeoff in the province of Vizcaya in the **Basque Country**. From the 1850s, the construction of the **railways** also helped to create an internal market. Yet in 1900, about 70 percent of the active population still worked on the land. Spain's major exports remained minerals and agricultural produce, and in return it continued to import manufactures.

Between 1900 and 1936, the Spanish economy expanded at a rather more rapid pace. **World War I** provided a great opportunity. Spanish **industry** was able to substitute goods previously exported by the warring nations in the home market and conquer new foreign markets. **Energy** (in particular the coal and hydroelectric industries), steel and metal, chemicals, textiles, shipping, and **banking** benefited most. Nevertheless, the value of production increased far more than its volume and the concentration on exports led to shortages at home, producing high inflation and consequent severe social tensions. When, moreover, the participants in the war began to recover between 1921 and 1923, many of the previous gains were again lost, throwing Spain into recession.

During the **Primo de Rivera dictatorship**, Spain benefited from the generally buoyant economic conjuncture. The regime aimed to stimulate growth through a program of infrastructural development, which above all favored heavy industry. This was, however, put into reverse by the government of **Dámaso Berenguer** in 1930 in order to cut the escalating budget deficit. From this year, Spain also began to feel the impact of the world economic recession. Nevertheless, the limited importance of foreign trade in the Spanish economy meant that it was cushioned from its most serious effects. Minerals and fruit exports suffered, along with the capital goods industries, though good harvests and rising wages consequent upon the greater strength of the **labor movement** favored consumer-based industries in the early 1930s.

The first years of the **Franco regime** saw the imposition of **autarky**. In part, this was a result of necessity. During **World War II**, the balance of payments worsened as invisibles (emigrant remittances and capital imports) were drastically reduced, and exports suffered because of the substitution of heavy metals (lead, copper) for light. But autarky was in any case the regime's chosen instrument of **economic policy** making. The result was that the poor Spanish economy was further isolated from world markets. Agricultural productivity declined due to a lack of fertilizers, and a drastic fall in real wages following the illegalization of trade unions further reduced internal demand. Moreover, shortages, large government deficits, and lack of competition were soon to lead to growing inflationary pressures. The result was that national income did not recover prewar levels until 1951, and because of **population** growth, per capita income fell to even lower levels.

The timid lifting of some autarkic controls in the 1950s, combined with American aid, allowed an important expansion of industry and improvements in agricultural productivity, but the economy remained dogged by high inflation. This was only corrected with the 1959 **Stabilization Plan**, which marked a fuller integration into the Western economic order. This made it possible for Spain to benefit from the Western economic boom of the 1960s. The result was a transformation of Spain's economic structure. The 1960s have often been referred to as the decade in which Spain really industrialized. Its gross domestic product grew at an average of 7.4 percent, the highest of any Western country, and, between 1960 and 1975, per capita gross domestic product rose from 57 percent to 79 percent of the **European Economic Community** (EEC) average. There were three key factors behind this industrialization process: **tourism**, remittances, and foreign investment. The number of foreign tourists visiting Spain grew from three million in 1958 to 34 million in the early 1970s. At the same time, from the late 1950s, underemployed laborers and peasants were encouraged to work abroad and provided valuable foreign currency in the shape of remittances. Foreign investment finally also brought much-needed capital and technical know-how into the country. This influx of foreign currency allowed Spain to run up an enormous balance of trade deficit in order to pay for the energy, raw materials, and capital goods needed to industrialize. The regime, moreover, could also rely on loans from the United States. These totaled $420.4 million between 1962 and 1968. Only Japan received more. Furthermore, Spain's industrial growth also prompted agriculture to modernize. And as a result of the increases in agricultural productivity, together with new opportunities in urban Spain and abroad, between 1960 and 1972, five million peasants abandoned the land.

The 1970s, in contrast, were to bring recession. The first Arab oil price hike hit the West in 1973 and it was followed by a further increase in oil prices in 1979. Spain was particularly badly affected because much of the economic growth of the 1960s was in the area of energy-intensive heavy industry. Spanish governments were slow to react to these pressures. Political concerns were to the fore and they were loath to take the unpopular, belt-tightening measures necessary. Hence, the decade was to see spiraling inflation and the budget deficit running out of control. It was only after the victory of the **Unión del Centro Democrático** (UCD) in the June 1977 elections, and, especially, that of the **Partido Socialista Obrero Español** (PSOE) in 1982, that governments began to put together more effective economic policies. Between 1975 and 1986, Spanish per capita gross domestic product slipped back from 79 percent to 70 percent of the EEC average.

The Spanish economy took off again following integration into the EEC in 1986. In common with other western European countries, it faced a recession in the early 1990s, but growth has again been high from 1994. Underlying this growth was the fall in oil prices, but it was also stimulated by a boom in foreign direct investment in Spain (now directed, above all, to the **service sector**), and a growth in trade, especially with the **European Union** (EU). Furthermore, from 1994, in particular, EU structural and cohesion funds started to make a big impact, especially in the area of infrastructural investment. Finally, the tourist industry has continued to expand and from the mid-1990s, the country has experienced a construction boom. This has been accompanied by the acceleration of structural changes in the economy already visible from the mid-1970s: the relative importance of agriculture has continued to decline, industry (including construction) has also fallen back somewhat, while the service sector has raced ahead (with each sector representing 5.6, 29.5, and 62 percent of the active population respectively in 2004). During this period, much of state industry has also been **privatized**, the country has joined the single European single currency (the euro), and several significant international Spanish companies have emerged as major international players, above all in banking, telecommunications, the petrochemical industry, and energy production. Moreover, from the 1990s, these companies have been behind a growth of Spanish foreign investment, most notably in **Latin America**, and, since 2000, increasingly in Europe. As a result, Spain has closed the gap with other EU countries, reaching 87 percent of the EU's per capita average in 2001. Economic growth was rapid in 2006 and 2007 (3.9 percent and 3.8 percent respectively), but, as in most of the West, the second half of 2007 saw a rapid deceleration. The housing market stalled, unemployment began to rise, and, stimulated above all by higher oil prices, inflation picked up (reaching a yearly average of 4.3 percent in December, its highest level since 1995).

Overall, since the 1950s, Spain has to a significant degree caught up with the major Western economic centers and is now the world's eighth-largest economy. Nevertheless, there are weaknesses, most notably the big regional imbalances (with per capita gross domestic product above the EU average in Catalonia, **Madrid**, and the Balearic Islands, but well below in **Andalusia** and Extremadura), the country's reliance on foreign investment, the relatively small size of many Spanish companies (which conduct relatively little research and development), the low-skilled nature of much employment, and the overreliance in recent years on a boom in construction. In 2001, Spain allocated a little less than 1 percent of its gross domestic product to research and development, less than half the EU average. Nevertheless, this is an area the **Partido Popular** and PSOE governments have worked on in recent years. *See also* LABOR MARKET; TABLES 2 AND 3.

EDUCATION. In the 19th and early 20th centuries, education in Spain was notoriously poor. The 1857 Moyano Law established the principle of state responsibility for education, but financial responsibility was given to local authorities and parents had to pay fees. Strapped for cash, these authorities never built enough schools and the state never tried to enforce compulsory attendance. Poor facilities, dilapidated buildings, and extremely low wages for teachers only compounded the situation. Families of the poor in particular suffered. Parents were reluctant to pay school fees and in any case often needed their children to work in order to supplement family income. Increasingly, from the 1890s, the middle classes turned to the religious orders of the **Catholic Church** to educate their sons and daughters. Hence by 1931, while one and a half million children were educated in the state sector, probably over 400,000 were taught by the religious orders. This elicited opposition in liberal and left-wing circles. Liberal intellectuals, in general, linked to the **republican** movement, pushed for the laicization of state education, and promoted alternatives to the Catholic-dominated private schools. The most notorious initiative in this respect was the **Institución Libre de Enseñanza**. At the same time, the left tried to supplement workers' education. Republicans and the **Partido Socialista Obrero Español** (PSOE) opened **Casas del Pueblo** and the **anarchists** set up their own institutions, the most famous of which was **Francisco Ferrer**'s **Escuela Moderna**.

The overall result of the deficient state system was extremely high illiteracy rates. In 1910, 50 percent of the population over the age of 10 was illiterate. The situation only began to improve slowly after the turn of the century, when defeat in the **Spanish-American War** produced a strong movement in favor of "Europeanization." The Ministry of Public Instruction was created in 1900. From the following year, teachers' salaries were paid by the central administration and another decree in 1902 gave the state the right to inspect both private and state schools. Nevertheless, in 1931, 30 percent of the population was still illiterate and 50 percent of children did not attend school. The growing influence of the Church over education also produced grave political tensions, as the left and many liberals saw the orders' teachings as reactionary and inimical to the country's cultural and political modernization. The first skirmishes between Church and state over this issue took place in the first decade of the 20th century when **Partido Liberal** governments attempted to reduce the weight of Catholicism and the orders in education. They had already made universities nonconfessional in 1881; in 1913, they allowed children whose parents did not consider themselves Catholics to be exempted from religious classes in state secondary schools (though this did not affect many children). This was combined with a rather unsuccessful attempt to halt the continued growth of the religious orders. These moves provoked a vociferous campaign of resistance in Church circles. Of far greater consequence, however, was the determined effort by the **Second Republic** to laicize Spanish education. Among the articles of the **Constitution of 1931** aimed at reducing the power of the Church in civil society figured the prohibition of the religious orders from teaching. This was combined with an ambitious program of school building, which, however, was handicapped by lack of finance and by the dearth of trained secular teachers.

The **Franco regime** gave the Church the preeminent role in education it had always sought. State schools came under Catholic tutelage, while the maintenance of a large private sector run by the religious orders to educate the wealthy was ensured. At the same time, within the university system, liberal and left-wing lecturers either fled or were purged and predominantly replaced by those loyal to the Church.

This ideological control, along with a continued lack of funding, ensured that the education system was to remain intellectually impoverished and antiquated until the liberalization of the Spanish **economy** in the 1960s. It was then that technocrats within the regime pushed for an overhaul of education to produce the human capital necessary to allow Spain to compete in world markets. The university system, in consequence, expanded massively, with higher education for the first time no longer the preserve of the children of the wealthy. At a primary and secondary level, drastic reform was also forthcoming. In 1967, education was made free and compulsory for children between 6 and 14, while the 1970 General Education Law made the state responsible for public instruction, but, for the first time, provided state subsidies for private religious schools. However, to the regime's consternation, the rapid expansion of the universities, at a time of political effervescence, led to escalating student protest. Indeed, its loss of control of the universities was one of the factors that led to its downfall in the mid-1970s.

Since 1975, the university sector has continued to grow at a rapid rate. In the 1980s, governments of the PSOE for the first time provided scholarships for students of poorer families, and by 2002, 1.4 million students received such subsidies. However, the overcrowding and underfunding of the university system is still a problem. After 2000, the **Partido Popular** (PP) government tried to shake up the system, introducing national tribunals to select lecturers, in order to deal with the practice of endogamous recruitment, and made rectors more democratically accountable. But the fact that these measures were imposed with little dialogue produced bitter opposition, including a one-day strike.

With respect to secondary education, the most important reform introduced by the PSOE was the Fundamental Law of the Right of Education (Ley Orgánica de Derecho a la Educación—LODE) approved in 1984. The law retained the option of government funding for private schools, but stipulated that schools that wished to obtain such funding (so-called *colegios concertados*) had to provide low-cost education for children of families that desired a private religious education but could not afford the full fees, and introduced an element of democracy into these schools' internal workings. Nevertheless, it ensured a large private sector would remain strong. Subsequently, in 1990, the Law to Order the Educational System (Ley de Ordenación General del Sistema Educativo—LOGSE) restructured the curriculum, provided an alternative to religious education in state schools, and raised the leaving age from 14 to 16. From the late 1990s, the administration of primary and secondary education was passed into the hands of the autonomous communities, but the central government retained considerable influence over the curriculum.

After 1996, the new PP government was keen to reform the education system in several ways. First, it was concerned that in the autonomous communities in which "peripheral nationalists" were in control, Spanish national identity was being ignored, and it tried to introduce measures to counteract this. A first attempt to regulate the humanities curriculum (especially the teaching of history) was thrown out by parliament. However, conflict over the curriculum in the autonomous communities and the number of hours of **Castilian**-Spanish that should be taught in **Catalonia** continued after **José María Aznar** won his second term in March 2000. Second, after 2000, the PP government tried to give Catholic education a more central role in the curriculum. State-school students could no longer opt out of religious education; they had to choose between religious classes by teachers chosen by the Church or classes about religion by state teachers. Third, it wished to make the system more elitist. Hence, the 2002 Ley de Calidad introduced a separate vocational route for weaker students from the age of 12, and streamed students according to ability. The left opposed all these reforms, making the question of education more polarized than at any time since the 1930s. Not surprisingly, since the PSOE's electoral victory in 2004, it has began dismantling the PP's reform program. But quite apart from these political disputes, the Spanish education system remains in relative terms underfunded. In 1998, such funding represented 5.3 percent of gross domestic product as compared to the European Union average of 5.8 percent. In 2007, the PISA Report caused a stir in political circles and the media, placing the attainment of Spanish children 36th out of a list of 56 countries. *See also* ESCUELA NUEVA; EXTENSION UNIVERSITARIA; KRAUSISM; RATIONALIST EDUCATION.

EGIN. This daily newspaper was founded in 1977 by radical Basque nationalists after a public subscription, and over the next two decades *Egín* (the Basque word for "action") adopted a stance tacitly (and occasionally not so tacitly) favorable to **ETA**. During this time, it built up an important readership of over 60,000, centered on the **Basque Country** and northern **Navarre**. In 1998, it was closed down by investigative magistrate **Baltasar Garzón**, but was soon replaced by a new radical Basque daily titled *Gara*. *See also* PRESS.

EL DEBATE. *El Debate* was the major **Catholic** daily newspaper published between 1910 and 1936. From the outset, it was closely linked to the elite Catholic lay association, the **Asociación Católica Nacional de Propagandistas**, with its leading activist, Ángel Herrera Oría (1886–1968), the paper's director between 1911 and 1933. During the second decade of the century, it called for the formation of a Catholic front to see off the left-wing threat and for this reason sympathized with the **Partido Social Popular** (PSP) between 1922 and 1923. However, unlike the more progressive wing of the PSP, but like most political figures close to the Church, it supported the **Primo de Rivera dictatorship.** In 1933, the paper played an important role in the formation of the **Confederación Española de Derechas Autónomas** (CEDA) and would henceforth remain closely tied to the party. It had to close after the **Nationalist** uprising of July 1936; in 1939, was not authorized to reopen by the **Franco regime** (which preferred the Francoist-Catholic daily *Ya*).

EL GRECO (DOMÉNICOS THEOTOKÓPOULOS, 1541–1614). El Greco was the most influential painter in 16th-century Spain. He was born in Crete and served his apprenticeship in Venice under Titian (Tiziano Vecellio), before moving on to Rome. He then settled in **Madrid** in 1570 and worked on San Lorenzo del Escorial from 1580. However, his style was not to **Felipe II**'s taste, and he was based in Toledo from 1585. It was here that he really made his mark. His use of dramatic contrasts of light and dark, the intensely spiritual elongated figures, and themes of tragedy and religious ecstasy resonated with the mysticism present in Spanish **Counter-Reformation** religious thought and imagery.

EL MUNDO. Founded in 1989, *El Mundo* now rivals *El País* as Spain's major heavyweight newspaper. Under the editorship of Pedro J. Ramírez (1952–), from its inception it was politically close to the opposition party, the **Partido Popular** (PP), and played a key role in undermining the **Partido Socialista Obrero Español** (PSOE) governments of the early to mid-1990s through its revelations of **corruption** scandals and of the administration's connections with the anti-**ETA** terrorist group, the **GAL**. The appearance of serious investigative journalism in Spain was a welcome sight, though its rather less dogged pursuit of the PP government between 1996 and 2004 (most notably apparent in its reaction to the **Gescartera scandal**) was indicative of the political conditionings of its previous stance. Since the return of the PSOE to power in 2004 it has once again played a key role in attempting to destabilize the government, fiercely criticizing contacts with ETA and attempting to establish a Basque terrorist connection to the 11 March 2004 **Madrid train bombings** (as the PP claimed at the time). It even claimed that the bombings were a plot to undermine the PP government, in which the security services were implicated. During the 1990s, it benefited from *El País*'s reputation as the paper of the establishment and was an important component in the rise of a new, assertive, nationalist right in Spain, which saw itself as in tune with the shift, in the West, to a more neoliberal economic agenda and an interventionist neoconservative political stance. In 2007, it sold an average of 337,000 papers daily, making it the second most widely read (non-free) newsaper behind *El País*.

EL PAÍS. Founded by the **PRISA Group** in 1976 and modeled loosely on *Le Monde*, *El País* rapidly became Spain's leading heavyweight newspaper. Between 1976 and 1979, it gained great popularity in more liberal middle-class circles given its support for a peaceful **transition to democracy**. At the same time, it was technically well produced and well informed, and developed an unrivalled international section. In politics and economics, it took a moderate center-left stance, strongly supporting **Felipe González**'s efforts to lead the **Partido Socialista Obrero Español** (PSOE) in a social-democratic direction and thereafter playing a significant role in the Socialist election victory of 1982. Subsequently, however, it suffered because it was rather too close to the Socialist administration. Moreover, it never really developed investigative journalism. These twin failings came back to bite in the early 1990s when its new rival, *El Mundo*, took the lead in revealing Socialist **corruption** scandals and the links between the Socialist administration and the anti-**ETA** terrorist group, the **GAL**. Nevertheless, its circulation rose once again in the aftermath of the **Partido Popular** (PP) victory in the 1996 elections, and, post-2001, its opposition to the neoconservative interventionism of the U.S. administration of George W. Bush was popular in Spain. In the highly charged political climate that followed the PSOE victory in the March 2004 general elections, it was once again close to the ruling party. Most notably, it strongly defended the position taken by the government that there was no connection between ETA and the **Madrid train bombings**. In 2007, it had the highest circulation of any (non-free) daily in Spain, with an average of 426,000 readers.

EL SOL. *El Sol* was a prestigious **Madrid**-based daily that appeared between 1917 and 1939. The key figure behind the publication for most of this time was **José Ortega y Gasset**. Between 1917 and 1923, in particular, it attracted an unrivaled list of contributors (including **Ramón J. Sender** and **Ramiro Maeztu**). Under Ortega y Gasset, it took a prodemocratic reform stance, but was wary of social radicalism. However, as an elite publication it never acquired a large readership.

EMPIRE. *See* COLONIES; DECOLONIZATION.

EMPLOYMENT. *See* LABOR MARKET.

ENERGY. During the 19th century, Spain was hampered by the dearth of a high-quality supply of coal. **Coal mining** was developed in Asturias, but it was low grade and seams were often difficult to mine. For this reason, in the second half of the 19th century, the country became to a large extent dependent on imported British coal, while important sectors of Spanish **industry** (most notably Catalan **cotton textiles**) turned to water power. The growth of Spanish protective **tariffs** from the 1890s stimulated the expansion of the Asturian coal mining industry, but this was at the cost of keeping production costs high. The growing use of electricity, especially after 1914, therefore gave a great boost to the **economy** and stimulated the rise of an important hydroelectric industry. However, during the economic boom of the 1960s, Spain became increasingly dependent on imported oil, with the result that the country was badly hit by the oil price hikes of 1973 and 1979. Moreover, since the 1980s, it has also become increasingly dependent on imported gas. It has tried to diversify since the 1970s, building eight nuclear power stations, and has in recent years made efforts to develop wind and solar power. In 1999–2000, oil accounted for 65.1 percent of Spain's energy requirements, gas 13 percent, and electricity 19 percent (of which 13 percent was produced by nuclear power stations). Over 20 percent of Spain's total energy production came from renewables.

ENLIGHTENMENT. Enlightenment ideas began to make an impact in Spain from the early 18th century, above all in the areas of scientific thought and political economy. They were stimulated by Spain's **Bourbon** monarchs, most notably **Carlos III**, and were received with interest by cultured Spaniards, concerned at the country's perceived decline from the 15th century and backwardness in comparison with France and Great Britain. Such ideas were spread in a number of ways: first through the appearance and growth, for the first time, of the **press** network; second, through the formation of learned institutions, above all the *sociedades de amigos del país* (Societies of Friends of the Country); third, through the reform of the universities, with the introduction of courses in medicine, mathematics, and law of nature and nations; and finally, through the works of individuals. Most important in this respect in the early 18th century was the Benedictine monk, Benito Jerónimo Feijoo (1676–1764), who published his *Teatro crítico universal* from the 1720s. Subsequently, under Carlos III, the major Enlightenment reformers José Moñina, the Count of Floridablanca (1728–1808), and Pedro Rodríguez, the Count of Campomanes (1728–1808), came to play a central role in government, and pushed on with a program of mercantilist reforms.

However, this support was not extended to the French *philosophes*, whose radical social critiques were banned by the **Spanish Inquisition**. Important sectors of the **Catholic Church** were, indeed, suspicious of Enlightenment thought *tout court*, which they saw as questioning religious dogma and established political and social institutions. They were given added impetus by the **French Revolution**, which, they argued, vindicated their concerns. Between 1789 and 1808, King **Carlos IV** in general tried to maintain a moderate pro-Enlightenment course, but between 1814 and 1833 his son, **Fernando VII**, attempted unsuccessfully to institutionalize an anti-Enlightenment absolutist regime.

ENRIQUE Y TARANCÓN, VICENTE. *See* CATHOLIC CHURCH; OPUS DEI.

ENTAIL. *See* MAYORAZGOS.

ESCRIBÁ DE BALAGUER, JOSÉ MARÍA. *See* OPUS DEI.

ESCUELA MODERNA/MODERN SCHOOL. The Escuela Moderna was set up by the Catalan **anarchist Francisco Ferrer** in central **Barcelona** in 1901. Although its stated aim was to provide open "**rationalist education**" in opposition to the conservative **Catholic** schools, in reality the focus was on antireligious, anarchist, and radical **liberal** doctrine. The school did not educate the children of the working class. Fees were set at 15 pesetas a month, too high for working-class parents. Instead, it was to operate as an elite training ground for anarchist cadres. Workers, Ferrer argued, would benefit when these students became professors and from the cheap pedagogic material the school published, which would be used in other institutions in which workers would be taught. However, with the support of left-wing **republicans** (Ferrer had close contacts with **Alejandro Lerroux**), a network of such schools was established in the Barcelona suburbs and other Catalan towns and these did cater to the working and lower-middle classes. At the movement's high point in 1906, there were 49 schools in **Catalonia** teaching over 1,000 students. The original Escuela Moderna briefly became fashionable among the liberal and republican middle classes. Talks were well attended, and it established a publishing house. However, it was closed in May 1906 when an employee of Ferrer's publishing house, Mateo Morral (1880–1906), tried to assassinate the king, **Alfonso XIII**, and his bride. It was never to reopen. Thereafter the republicans withdrew their support and the movement collapsed.

ESCUELA NUEVA/NEW SCHOOL. The Escuela Nueva was the brainchild of **Manuel Núñez de Arenas**. It was conceived of as "having the mixed character of a popular university and socialist school," which would attract workers to socialism through its educational and cultural activities. It was set up in 1910 within the Madrid **Casa del Pueblo** of the **Partido Socialista Obrero Español** (PSOE), and over the next two years it organized short and technical courses and cultural evenings. In 1912, it also staged a series of talks on the history of socialism. Not all the speakers, however, were members of the PSOE, and the unorthodox nature of some of them (particularly one given by **José Ortega y Gasset**), led to criticisms of the school in the party hierarchy.

At first, the Escuela Nueva took a largely reformist stance, modeling itself on the British Fabian Society. During **World War I**, most of its members supported the Allies. However, the Bolshevik Revolution and subsequent revolutionary wave that swept postwar Europe proved a radicalizing experience. Hence, by 1919, many of its members, with Núñez de Arenas at the fore, backed affiliation with the Third International and then supported the Communist split with the PSOE and the formation of the **Partido Comunista de España** (PCE). With the forced exile of Núñez de Arenas following the **military** coup by General **Miguel Primo de Rivera** in September 1923, it went into decline.

ESPARTERO ÁLVAREZ DE TORO, BALDOMERO, COUNT OF LUCHANA, DUKE OF VICTORY, PRINCE OF VERGARA (1793–1879). Espartero was one of the major soldier-politicians of mid-19th-century Spain. He was born in Granatula (Ciudad Real) in modest circumstances. Like many, he joined the army during the **War of Independence**, where he was exposed to the new **liberal** currents. Rising quickly through the ranks, he became head of the Army of the North in 1836 during the First Carlist War. His forces defeated the **Carlists** at the key battle of Luchana in July, then three years later he signed a favorable peace treaty, the **Vergara Pact**, with the Carlist general, Rafael Maroto (1783–1847), for which he was given the title of Duke of Victory.

This gave Espartero enormous prestige in liberal circles. As a result, during the late 1830s he was drawn into the dispute between the **Partido Moderado** and **Partido Progresista**. The queen regent, **María Cristina of Naples**, who favored the *moderados*, tried to gain his support by making him president of the cabinet in September 1839. Espartero, however, refused to back *moderado* designs to replace the **Constitution of 1837** and centralize local government. The *progresistas*' cause was, during this month, strengthened by a number of uprisings in urban centers, followed by the formation of radical liberal local committees or *juntas*. As a result, María Cristina was forced into exile in October 1839, and in the following March the new **Cortes** elected Espartero regent. The **Espartero regency** was to last for a little over two years. During this time, political liberties were widened somewhat, but the *progresistas* were not helped by divisions within their own camp. Espartero was accused by his detractors of using high-handed methods and of favoring personal friends. He was forced out of office and into exile by a combined *moderado* coup and new uprisings in urban Spain, and during the so-called **Moderate Decade** of 1844 to 1854 remained marginalized from power. He was, however, recalled to head the government during the **Progressive Biennium** of 1854 to 1856. Again, the Cortes widened civil liberties and also drew up a new more open **constitution** (which was never to be implemented), but in July 1856, the Partido Moderado and its allies were once again to force Espartero from power. On this occasion, he was allowed to retire to Logroño, and was never again actively to engage in politics. In 1871, he was granted the title of Prince of Vergara by King **Amadeo I**.

ESPARTERO REGENCY. The name Espartero regency refers to the period between March 1841 and July 1843, during which the soldier-politician **Baldomero Espartero** took on the role of regent until the coming of age of Isabel, the daughter of **Fernando VII**. The regency was to see some widening of political liberties. This was to allow the first trade unions to form in **Barcelona**, the most powerful of which was the textile workers' Protección Mutua de Tejedores de Algodón (Cotton Weavers Mutual Benefits Association). However, Espartero's assumption of the regency caused splits within the **Partido Progresista** camp. In urban centers, these were exacerbated because it was felt the *progresistas* were not carrying through the reforms they had promised. November 1842 saw an insurrection in Barcelona supported by the first **republican** nuclei, leading to the bombing of the city from the **military** base on the mountain of Montjuïc. Officers attached to the **Partido Moderado** also conspired to overthrow the regime. An attempted *moderado pronuncimiento* in September 1841 failed, but in May 1843 the Espartero regime faced a new double challenge. On the one hand, the urban radicals were able to launch new insurrections, but on the other, the *moderados* launched another military revolt. After the defeat of his forces in battle at Torrejón de Ardóz on 22–23 July, Espartero was forced into exile. Thereafter, the *moderados* were able to control the situation, especially after the election of right-wing military commander Luis González Brabo (1811–1871) as prime minister on 1 December. The **Moderate Decade** had begun.

ESQUERRA REPUBLICANA DE CATALUNYA (ERC)/ CATALAN REPUBLICAN LEFT. ERC was to be the hegemonic party in **Catalonia** during the **Second Republic** and, since 2000, has once again come to play a significant role in Catalan political life. It was founded in a conference held between 19–21 March 1931 by three groups; the hard-line Catalan nationalist party, Estat Català, led by **Francesc Macià**; a group of liberal Catalanist intellectuals who had founded the newspaper *L'Opinió*; and members of the Partit Català Republicà (Catalan Republican Party), made up of leftist, socially reforming Catalanists, captained by **Lluís Companys** and Marcelino Domingo (1864–1939).

Under the impact of the **Primo de Rivera dictatorship**, the 1920s had seen a radicalization of **Catalanism** and growth in **republican** sentiment in Catalonia. ERC was able to reap the rewards of this swing. Its component parts had supported the pact of **San Sebastián** in return for Spanish republicans and the **Partido Socialista Obrero Español** (PSOE) accepting an autonomy statute for Catalonia. To the surprise of many, ERC went on to win the 12 April municipal elections throughout urban Catalonia, with Macià then declaring a Federal Catalan Republic two days later. Nevertheless, the party agreed to negotiate its demands within the framework of the forthcoming constituent **Cortes**. At the same time, as a demonstration of good faith, the new central authorities allowed the establishment of an autonomous government with minimal powers called the **Generalitat**. From the time the statute of Catalan autonomy was approved by the Spanish government in September 1932 until the **October 1934 revolution**, the Generalitat was to be dominated by ERC.

There were several strands to its policy. In the first place, it promoted the **Catalan language** and Catalan(ist) culture. Second, it supported socially reforming measures such as the Llei de Contractes de Conreu (Law of Cultivation Contracts) of 1934, which allowed the peasant vine growers of Catalonia (the *rabassaires*) to buy the land that they rented from the owners. Nevertheless, there were tensions in the party between the more hard-line nationalists, headed by Josep Dencas (1900–1966) after the death of Macià in January 1934, and socially reforming liberal nationalists under **Lluís Companys**. The intransigent nationalists were violently anti-**anarchist**, and, partly because of this, ERC quickly came into conflict with the Catalan **Confederación Nacional del Trabajo** (CNT), and was prepared to use strong-arm tactics to undermine it. The Generalitat favored more moderate parties and unions, most notably the **Treintistas** and later the **Partit Socialista Unificat de Catalunya** (PSUC), which were closer to the Catalanist camp.

After the victory of the right in the November 1933 elections, relations between the central and Catalan governments became increasingly strained. In June 1934, the Spanish government managed to get the ERC's contracts law declared unconstitutional. Then, in October 1934, Lluís Companys seconded the PSOE-led revolutionary general strike. Without CNT support, the revolt was easily put down. In its aftermath, leading ERC leaders were either jailed or forced into exile and the autonomy statute was suspended. At the same time, because of the revolt's failure, the Dencas tendency, which most enthusiastically backed armed resistance, was seriously weakened.

Following the victory of the **Popular Front** (Front d'Esquerres [Left Front] in Catalonia), ERC again took over the running of the Generalitat. With the declaration of the **Spanish Civil War**, authority in Catalonia at first fell into the hands of the CNT and revolutionary left. Companys, however, remained as president of the Generalitat, and, with the help of the PSUC, was slowly able to reassert state power. Like their Spanish counterparts, the Catalan republicans and Communists wished to rebuild the state, but they were, at the same time, opposed to the concentration of power in the hands of the central Republican government. This was to prove increasingly difficult to prevent in the aftermath of the 1937 **May Events**. Once the war had been lost, ERC continued to function in exile and also maintained a Generalitat government in exile. From 1954, the president was Josep Tarradellas (1899–1988).

The party was reformed in 1976 under the presidency of Heribert Barrera (1917–), and in the 1977 elections it represented a more leftist and nationalist alternative to **Jordi Pujol**'s Convergència Democràtica de Catalunya (Democratic Convergence for Catalonia).

It was in the following years a minor force on the Catalan political scene. In the aftermath of the 1980 election, it backed Jordi Pujol's bid to become president of the Generalitat, with the result that Heribert Barrera was elected president of the Catalan parliament. This support was renewed from 1984, when ERC entered the autonomous government. However, this meant that it failed to provide any clear alternative to Pujol, leading to a decline in support (from 8.9 percent in the 1980 autonomous elections to 4.1 percent in 1988) and growing discontent in the party's ranks. During this period, part of the separatist cultural association La Crida joined the party, along with the left-wing radical nationalist party Entesa de Nacionalistes d'Esquerra (Understanding of Left-Wing Nationalists). These elements would then spearhead renewal, with the separatist nationalist and former leader of the Crida, Angel Colom (1951–), taking over as general secretary in the party's 1988 congress. In the early 1990s, the party grew in strength on the back of the radical nationalist vote, but it was shaken by political infighting in the middle of the decade. Colom was challenged by a section of the party that believed it was too focused on the issue of independence and that it should take a somewhat more pragmatic stance and also put more emphasis on social reform. The latter took control following the November 1996 elections to the National Council, which saw Josep Lluís Carod Rovira (1952–) elected general secretary.

Subsequently, ERC was to profit from the decision of **Convergència i Unió** (CiU) to ally with the **Partido Popular** (PP) central government after the November 1999 elections in order to remain in power in Catalonia. In the 2003 elections to the Catalan parliament, it received over 16 percent of the vote and consolidated its position as Catalonia's third largest party, and in the March 2004 general elections, its parliamentary representation jumped from one to eight deputies. After the 2003 Catalan elections, it entered into negotiations with the Catalan Socialists, the **Partit dels Socialistes de Catalunya-Partido Socialista Obrero Español** (PSC-PSOE), and the red-green party **Iniciativa per Catalunya-Verds** and formed a new tripartite government (the *tripartit*). Carod Rovira became **Pascual Maragall**'s chief minister (*conseller en cap*). However, in January 2004, it was plunged into crisis after the PP government leaked information obtained by the security services that Carod Rovira had held a clandestine meeting with **ETA** representatives in France, at which a possible ETA cease-fire in Catalonia was discussed. Carod Rovira was, as a result, forced by Maragall to resign.

ERC remained in the Catalan government but new tensions were to emerge after the PSOE won the March 2004 elections. Unlike the PP, the PSOE favored a reform of the **State of the Autonomies**, which it saw as leading to a further federalization of Spain. Prime minister **José Luis Rodríguez Zapatero** viewed the new Catalan statute as a possible model. However, after it was approved in the Catalan parliament in September 2005 there were serious reservations on the part of the government with respect to its content. Finally, the PSC-PSOE, PSOE, and CiU reached a compromise deal, but ERC refused to support the new statute and recommended that the citizens vote against it in the 18 June 2006 referendum. The party was particularly upset at the fact that recognition that Catalonia was a nation was excluded from the main text. Maragall then dismissed the ERC ministers and called new elections. The result was not that different from those in 2003, and, surprisingly at first sight, a new left-wing coalition government (*tripartit*) was formed, and ERC once again rejoined the Generalitat, under Maragall's Socialist successor, José Montilla (1955–). ERC maintains that it is still a separatist party, with Carod Rovira stating that a referendum on independence should be held some time in the future. However, radicals within ERC have become increasingly critical of his leadership, accusing him of becoming enmeshed in government and losing sight of the party's goals. ERC performed poorly in the March 2008 general elections as large numbers of left-of-center Catalan voters switched to the PSC-PSOE in order to keep the PP out of government (with great success). This has put additional pressure on Carod-Rovira. *See also* TABLE 10.

ESTADO DE LAS AUTONOMIES. *See* STATE OF THE AUTONOMIES.

ESTAT CATALÀ. *See* ESQUERRA REPUBLICANA DE CATALUNYA; MACIÀ I LLUSÀ, FRANCESC.

ESTATUTO REAL. *See* ROYAL STATUTE.

ETA (EUSKADI TA ASKATASUNA)/BASQUE HOMELAND AND FREEDOM. ETA is a leftist, intransigently nationalist, **terrorist** movement that operates in the **Basque Country**. It first came to prominence in December 1973 when one of its commandos assassinated the prime minister, **Luis Carrero Blanco**, and it has since that date waged an armed campaign for the independence of the Basque Country, which it defines as encompassing those territories that at present comprise the Basque autonomous community, along with **Navarre** (Nafarroa) and the three French Basque provinces (Iparralde).

The movement was first formed in July 1959 by a group of youngsters dissatisfied at the passivity of the historic party of Basque nationalism, the **Partido Nacionalista Vasco** (PNV) in the face of political and linguistic repression by the **Franco regime**. At first there was little difference between the ideology of the new group and that of the PNV, but the PNV's traditionalist, ruralist beliefs seemed out of step with a society that was rapidly industrializing and hence attracting large numbers of "Spanish" migrants. This formed the background to the emergence of a number of often-contradictory currents in ETA in the 1960s. First, criticisms of the PNV's inactivity led to support for the armed struggle. Second, impatience at the PNV's willingness to compromise Basque independence and accept autonomy provoked the emergence of a harder-line nationalism, which would only be satisfied by total independence. Finally, the escalation of labor unrest from 1962 encouraged a more responsive attitude to non-Basque migrant labor, the working-class struggle, and socialism.

All of these elements coexisted within ETA. The growth of labor agitation in the West during the 1960s, the expansion of Marxist literature, and the explosion of anticolonial struggles in the Third World propitiated the radicalization of nationalist Basque youth. The rebellions in **Cuba**, Vietnam, and Algeria, in particular, seemed to offer a synthesis between the various elements of ETA ideology by fusing nationalism and socialism. The guerrilla struggle was adopted at ETA's third assembly in April–May 1964, and to it was added the action-repression theory, which posited that an attack by ETA on the institutions of the state would provoke indiscriminate repression and thereby consolidate the movement's support.

ETA was only strong enough to begin the armed struggle in 1967 with a series of bank robberies and bombings. Its most audacious act was the assassination of the head of the San Sebastián Brigada Social (political police), Melitón Manzanas (1921–1968), on 2 August 1968. The regime responded by declaring a state of emergency in the Basque Country and launching a crackdown. In this respect, the action-repression cycle seemed to operate. The movement's members were highly regarded as patriotic Basques and received support from broad sections of the population, while hatred of the regime drew large numbers of young Basques into the organization. ETA followed this action up with a bombing and shooting campaign, but in the following months the **police** were able to arrest its leading figures and therefore leave it without a central organization.

While ETA's notoriety grew, serious tensions developed within the organization. As industrialization progressed during the 1960s and working-class protest became more pronounced, some members of ETA became uneasy with a theory that equated the Basque Country with the Third World. They came to see the working class as the prime mover for change and, therefore, laid growing stress on trade union work. But they were denounced as *españolistas* (pro-Spaniards) in more traditional-minded ETA circles, and it was these people who were more in touch with the small-town, ethnically Basque, nationalist constituency. These denunciations led to the expulsion of the "communist" ETA leadership, based in the Basque Country (the "interior leadership"), in 1966, and to withdrawal by the so-called Red Cells or ETA-Berri in August 1970 (who went on to found the **Movimiento Comunista de España**). Yet even then ETA remained split between the "Third Worldists" (who came to be known as ETA-VI because their leadership was confirmed at the movement's sixth assembly, held in 1970), and the *milis* or ETA-V (who refused to accept the validity of the sixth assembly), who laid more emphasis on the defense of the **Basque language** and culture.

The early 1970s saw ETA grow further in prestige. A central event was the Burgos trial, which began on 3 December 1970. This was a mass public trial of the *etarra* leadership captured in late 1969. The regime took this step calculating that ETA's violent methods and revolutionary goals would lead to public revulsion. However, ETA was able to mount a massive campaign that gained widespread backing among all sections of the Basque population. The regime sentenced six of the accused to death but Franco, faced with mass internal and international protest, finally commuted the sentences. Over the next year, ETA remained quiet. Its leadership, ETA-VI, was moving away from the armed struggle and trying to build up a following within the **labor movement**. This led them to team up with the Trotskyist Liga Comunista Revolucionaria (Revolutionary Communist League) in 1972. ETA-V, however, still championed the armed struggle, and was effectively able to move into the void and take over the organization. From 1971, it carried out a new campaign of bombings and robberies, and on 20 December 1973, successfully executed ETA's most spectacular action, the assassination of Luis Carrero Blanco.

When the **transition to democracy** got under way after the death of General **Francisco Franco** in November 1975, most politicians outside the Basque Country hoped that ETA would renounce violence. It was not to be. Part of the problem was that while from 1976 there were reforming noises from Madrid, on the ground repression remained harsh. Moreover, once **Adolfo Suárez** came to power, fearing the reaction of the **military**, he was slow to grant ETA prisoners amnesty, thereby giving rise to massive protest demonstrations, often brutally broken up by the security forces. The result was to maintain support in the Basque Country for radical nationalist aspirations. Meanwhile, ETA was to split again during 1974. The organization had been divided into a number of fronts. Guerrilla or terrorist attacks were carried out by the military front, and during the year there were criticisms by the other fronts at the lack of control over its activities. Divisions came to the fore after the indiscriminate bombing of the Rolando Café in **Madrid** on 13 September. This led a majority of ETA members to form ETA Político-Militar (or ETA-PM), which, through not rejecting the use of force, laid more stress on mass action and the political arena. The military front, on the other hand, became known as ETA-Militar (or ETA-M) and centered its activities on the armed struggle.

ETA-PM was over the next four years to move slowly away from violence. Some of its members were committed socialists, and, like their leftist predecessors in the organization, they came to defend the need to link up with other left-wing groups. ETA-PM formed a political front during 1977 called Euskadiko Iraultzaraka Alderia (Party of the Basque Revolution—EIA), which participated in the June elections, leading the coalition **Euskadiko Esquerra**. It did relatively well, and this further drew the sector of ETA-PM most identified with EIA away from military action.

Hard-line nationalists, however, regrouped under the banner of ET-M, and in April 1978, formed their own political front—the coalition **Herri Batasuna** (HB). ETA-M argued that nothing had changed since the death of Franco. The Francoist torturers were still free and the Basque Country was still an oppressed nation. Under the new constitution it was more difficult for the security forces to act with impunity, thus allowing ETA-M to relaunch its terrorist campaign with unparalleled ferocity. HB also showed a great capacity for mobilization, and it was only after the approval of the Basque autonomy statute in October 1979 by referendum in the Basque Country that support for ETA-M began slowly to decline.

When the **Partido Socialista Obrero Español** (PSOE) came to power in 1982, its strategy to deal with ETA was varied. It was prepared to negotiate terms for the end of the violence. Negotiations were held in Algeria between 1986 and 1989, though they eventually came to nothing. The main sticking point was that while the PSOE was willing to discuss issues like the early release of ETA prisoners and an amnesty for wanted *etarras*, ETA demanded political concessions, most notably the recognition of the Basque Country's right to independence and the incorporation of Navarre. At the same time, the government aimed to demoralize the organization by dispersing its prisoners throughout Spain and offered reductions in their sentences if they renounced ETA. It also sought to isolate ETA and HB politically. Its greatest success came in 1988, when all the parliamentary parties in the Basque Country, with the exception of HB, signed the Pact of Ajuria Enea, totally rejecting the use of violence. This was accompanied by the replacement of the hated **Civil Guard** in the Basque Country by an autonomous police force, the Ertzaintza. Throughout this time, the security forces kept up the pressure on ETA. Their greatest success came in 1992, when the ETA leadership was captured in Bidart in southern France.

Far murkier was the operation, between 1983 and 1988, of an anti-ETA terrorist group called the **GAL** in the French Basque Country.

Many ETA activists lived in France, and were subject to a campaign of assassinations by the GAL. Its aim was to spread fear in the ranks of ETA and end French tolerance for members of ETA operating on French soil. This seemed to succeed, with the French adopting a more active role in cooperating with the Spanish authorities from 1986. However, it soon became clear that elements within Spanish state and the PSOE government were involved. Indeed, the minister of the interior between 1982 and 1988, **José Barrionuevo**, was imprisoned in 1998 for his role in the GAL. The combined results of these strategies were to seriously weaken ETA. It has been estimated that the organization had 300 armed activists in 1982 but only a dozen by 1993. Furthermore, among those imprisoned were its most experienced figures. In the mid-1990s, this would lead to a change in strategy, with more precise military-style operations directed against the army and security forces replaced by attempts to implicate broader sectors of the Basque population and put greater pressure on the political elite to make concessions by creating a situation that was intolerable. First, in 1995 youngsters close to ETA were instructed to launch the so-called Kale Barroka, which consisted of mass acts of vandalism and violent protests that frequently culminated in attacks on the security forces (including the Ertzaintza, which was accused of collaborating with the Spanish state). Second, rather than just focusing on the military and police, threats and attacks were now aimed at representatives of "Spanish" parties (above all members of the PSOE and **Partido Popular** [PP]), and other public figures seen as hostile to radical Basque nationalism. As part of this new strategy, ETA attempted unsuccessfully to assassinate the future Spanish prime minister **José María Aznar** in Madrid in April 1995. Local Basque PP and PSOE councilors proved a particularly easy target and focusing on them had the additional advantage that protecting them through bodyguards was expensive. This led to growing popular opposition to ETA. Thus, the assassination of the Basque Socialist politician Fernando Múgica and the Autonomous University of Madrid professor Francisco Tomás y Valiente in February 1996 led to a mass demonstration of 850,000 in Madrid.

When the PP came to power in the spring of 1996 it broadened the government offensive against ETA, placing greater emphasis on neutralizing those individuals and groups that gave ETA support. ETA, for its part, continued to target politicians, assassinating the PP local councilor from the Basque town of Ermua, Miguel Ángel Blanco, on 12 July 1997. He had been captured two days before, and the government was given an ultimatum of 48 hours to relocate ETA prisoners to the Basque Country. This assassination produced mass protests throughout Spain, with about six million people taking to the streets. The public reaction was referred to as the "Spirit of Ermua."

This very much put ETA on the defensive. Furthermore, the government and judicial offensive against ETA and its milieus (*entorno*) continued unabated, with the HB leadership imprisoned at the end of 1997 (although the Constitutional Tribunal would annul this sentence in July 1999), and the radical Basque nationalist daily, *Egin*, forced to close in the spring of 1998. However, the increasingly radical political stance taken by the PNV gave ETA a way out. From the spring of 1998, the PNV showed itself willing to push for the recognition of Basque independence in return for an end to ETA violence. The culmination of negotiations between the PNV and HB (of which ETA was kept informed) was the Pact of Lizarra (or Declaration of Estella) on 12 September 1998. ETA declared a cease-fire four days later. It was willing, it seemed, to abandon violence in return for moves toward an independent Basque Country. The problem was that while the PP government wished to encourage ETA down this route (through releasing a number of ETA prisoners and relocating others closer to the Basque Country, and, apparently, postponing police operations), it was totally opposed to making political concessions. Just one meeting between government and ETA representatives was held in Switzerland in May 1999, but nothing came of it.

Given that the leadership of ETA would not wind up the organization without some sort of political negotiation, it broke the truce on 28 November 1999. It then became clear that ETA had used the relative respite of the previous year to reorganize and integrate younger figures involved in the Kale Barroka. It killed a Civil Guard lieutenant colonel in Madrid on 23 January 2000 and 20 more assassinations followed during the year. The most high profile of these assassinations once again led to mass demonstrations. It was estimated that over one million people took to the streets of Madrid after the shooting of the Basque PSOE politician Fernando Buesa on 22 January, and 900,000 protested in **Barcelona** on 23 November after the former PSOE minister Ernest Lluch was assassinated in the city. After achieving an overall majority in the 2000 elections, the PP government was determined to end ETA purely through police measures and would follow this policy quite effectively over the next three years. In 2002, ETA "only" murdered five people, the lowest number over the past 20 years. In the international climate created in the aftermath of the September 11, 2001, attacks on the Twin Towers the government was also able to move more effectively against HB, with parliament voting for its illegalization in August 2002.

Government policy was, however, to change in the aftermath of the PSOE's victory in the March 2004 general elections. The PSOE believed that the **State of the Autonomies** needed reform and hoped this might provide the basis for a settlement. It was helpful that ETA had not carried out any assassinations since early 2003. Moreover, since 2002 there had been contacts between the Basque branch of the Socialist party (the Partido Socialista de Euskadi [PSE]-PSOE) and HB on ways of reaching a settlement. Stress was laid on the fact that negotiations over the end of violence and on the political status of the Basque Country should be differentiated. This suited the government, which was willing to discuss the release of some ETA prisons and the relocation of the rest closer to the Basque Country, but could not be seen as making political concessions to ETA. ETA agreed to this in August 2004 and negotiations were held in Geneva during June and July 2005 and in Oslo in December of the same year. Veteran ETA leader Josu Ternera (1950–) was the organization's key representative. It was agreed that ETA would announce a "permanent cease-fire," followed by a declaration by the prime minister accepting a dialogue with ETA once it was clear all violence had ceased. Both would affirm that the future status of Euskadi would be discussed in negotiations between the Basque parties. ETA declared the cease-fire on 22 March 2006 and **José Luis Rodríguez Zapatero** made the government's declaration to parliament on 29 July.

However, problems were quickly to surface. By August, ETA was frustrated that little progress had been made on the political front and reignited the Kale Barroka. In a final meeting with government representatives in mid-December, Ternera was replaced by two younger activists, who stressed that rapid progress needed to be made regarding the incorporation of Navarre into the Basque autonomous community and the Basque Country's right to independence. On 30 December, it then planted a bomb in Barajas airport, killing two Colombian migrants. It argued that it did not wish to break the cease-fire and that it was a warning. However, the government could no longer maintain any dialogue. During 2007–2008, it redoubled efforts to bring ETA to its knees through the actions of the police and judiciary. An important breakthrough came in July 2007 when the French police discovered the whereabouts of the leadership of ETA's logistics apparatus, making three arrests and confiscating a large amount of material. ETA hit back on 7 March 2008, two days before the general elections, murdering the former Socialist local councilor Isaias Carrasco. In protest, the various parties agreed to cancel the final meetings of the election campaign. The key problem is that in return for an end to the armed struggle, ETA is still determined to force major concessions on the integration of Navarre and the right to self-determination. The government, however, will only accept a settlement based on negotiations encompassing all the actors on the Basque and Navarre political stage.

EUROPEAN ECONOMIC COMMUNITY (EEC), EUROPEAN COMMUNITY (EC), EUROPEAN UNION (EU). During the 1960s, despite anti-Western rhetoric, entry into the EEC became one of the major priorities of the **Franco regime**'s **foreign policy**. It officially applied to join in 1962. The member states rapidly confirmed Spain would not be eligible for membership until its political system was democratized. Nevertheless, a preferential **trade** agreement (known as the Luxembourg Accord), signed on 29 July 1970, did grant Spain a substantial reduction in its external tariff in return for a modest cut in duties on industrial goods and agricultural products imported into Spain from the EEC. However, as repression intensified to counteract growing popular protest in the early 1970s, relations cooled, leading the EEC to condemn the regime without palliatives.

With the fall of the Franco regime, the political elite redoubled efforts to join. Integration into Europe was viewed by more liberal and democratic sectors as of key importance in order to economically and culturally modernize Spain and ensure against any future authoritarian inversion. The reaction of the EEC was now more favorable but there were commercial problems. In particular, Spanish Mediterranean **agriculture** would have a big impact on French and Italian producers. The French farmers from the Midi were especially opposed to Spanish entry. In response, in June 1980, the French president, Valery Giscard d'Estaing, called for a freeze on negotiations until a way was found of ensuring that Spanish entry would not harm French farming interests. In the following years, negotiations for entry into the EEC became entangled with discussions over Spain's entry into the **North Atlantic Treaty Organization**. Spain joined NATO in 1981 in part, it seems, on the understanding that the United States and other European countries would put pressure on France to modify its position. Whether for this reason or not, the French began to take a softer line in 1983. In October 1983, the EEC agreed to a new marketing and price support system to protect the Mediterranean's agricultural production from low-cost Spanish competition in an enlarged European Community. Then, in June 1984, the dispute between Great Britain and France over budgetary contributions was solved. Serious negotiations began thereafter, with the French attitude now far more positive. They were concluded in March 1985 and the treaty of accession was signed on 12 June.

Spain formally joined on 1 January 1986, after which there was a transitional phase of seven years. Membership was beneficial in a number of respects. The removal of investment controls and free access to EEC/EU markets brought a boom in foreign direct investment that helped modernize the Spanish **economy** and gave a large boost to Spanish exports. As a relatively poor country, Spain also benefited greatly from EEC–EU structural funds, particularly after they were doubled in 1992, and from a new cohesion fund established in 1994. Between 1994 and 2006, Spain got 22.3 percent of EU structural and cohesion funds, more than any other country. Such funds were directed primarily at **transport** infrastructure and **telecommunications** between 1988 and 1993, and, subsequently, more effort has been put into encouraging research and development. Spanish agriculture also benefited increasingly from CAP subsidies (receiving 14.7 percent of such EU subsidies by 2001), though **industry** was hit by intensified competition (both from the EU and the developing world).

The result of Spain's integration into the EU single currency, the euro, has also, probably, been favorable (though there is scope for debate). The pro-Europeanism of the Spanish political elite meant that the country would fully back moves in this direction. Spain joined the Exchange Rate Mechanism (ERM), which limited fluctuations between individual currencies, in June 1989; signed the Maastricht Treaty, committing her to meet the EU's convergence criteria, in February 1992; signed the 1996 Growth and Stability Pact, which limited the budget deficit to under 3 percent of gross domestic product; and was a founding member of European Monetary Union (EMU) in January 1999. The peseta was than replaced by the euro on 1 January 2002. In order to meet these convergence criteria, Spanish governments had to keep a tight grip on the budget and maintain relatively high interest rates (though strict controls of government spending were partly compensated for by the transfer of EU funds, and the government did devalue the currency in 1992 and 1993). The removal of exchange rate costs has led to substantial savings, but at the cost of surrendering the setting of interest rates to the EU. And since 2000, there have been complaints that the switch has led to rising prices in the **service sector** (particularly in bars and restaurants), and that, because of the German economic recession, interest rates have been set too low for the Spanish economy, fueling the runaway housing boom.

On the issue of monetary union, both **Partido Socialista Obrero Español** (PSOE) (1982–1996) and **Partido Popular** (PP) (1996–2004) governments pursued the same course. In other areas, there have been both similarities and differences. Under **Felipe González**, the PSOE strongly backed the creation of a "social Europe" and during the 1989 Spanish presidency championed the Charter of Fundamental Workers' Rights. The PSOE also tried to deepen economic and social ties between the EU and Arab countries on the southern rim of the Mediterranean. In this respect, it held a major conference in **Barcelona** in November 1995, which inaugurated the Euro-Mediterranean Partnership, the goal of which was, above all, to establish a free-trade zone and greater cooperation in security matters. These objectives have run into difficulties, but it is envisaged that a free-trade area will operate from 2010. During this period, Spain also tried to strengthen ties between the EU and **Latin America**, leading to the EU-Mercosur agreement.

Between 1996 and 2004, under **José María Aznar**'s PP governments, more emphasis was laid on protecting national interests and making the EU states more competitive internationally. This was combined with a more pro-American Atlanticist foreign policy. Aznar annoyed the German chancellor, Gerhard Schröder, by holding out for the maintenance of Spanish structural funds, despite the fact that Spain was now considerably richer (moving from 74 percent of average per capita EU gross domestic product in 1988 to 81.4 percent in 1998), and that the EU was going to expand eastward and integrate poorer former Soviet-bloc countries in 2004. In January 2003, a compromise was reached, with the agreement that there would be a transitional period through to 2113, during which Spain's subsidies would be cut and redirected to the new central and eastern European members. In line with his pro-Atlanticist foreign policy, Aznar supported the U.S.-led invasion of **Iraq** in March 2003, exacerbating tensions with France and Germany. However, since the PSOE victory in the March 2004 general elections, Spain has once again taken a more prointegrationist stance. The Spanish prime minister **José Luis Rodríguez Zapatero** established close ties with the "Franco-German axis" of Gerhard Schröder and Jacques Chirac. However, the assumption of power by Angela Merkel in Germany in November 2005 and Nicolas Sarkozy in France in May 2007 led to the dissolution of what many saw as an anti–George W. Bush front.

EUSKADI. This is the **Basque language** name, devised by the founder of Basque nationalism **Sabino de Arana**, to refer to the Basque nation. It was accepted by statewide parties operating in the **Basque Country** in the aftermath of the **transition to democracy**, but used solely in relation to the Basque autonomous community. For this reason, radical Basque nationalists have, since the 1990s, adopted the old Basque name, Euskal Herria, when describing what they see as the linguistic and cultural Basque nation, which includes not only the Basque autonomous community, but also **Navarre** and the French Basque provinces.

EUSKADIKO ESQUERRA (EE)/BASQUE LEFT. EE was at first a coalition formed in the run-up to the June 1977 elections by the political wing of **ETA-PM**, Euskadiko Iraultzaraka Alderdia (Party of the Basque Revolution), along with the far-leftist **Movimiento Comunista de España**. Over the next four years, the component parts of EE came to reject ETA violence and tried to combine Basque nationalism and work within the **labor movement**. This strategy was given a boost in 1982, when it fused with the majority wing of the Basque branch of the **Partido Comunista de España** (PCE) to form a new party, which was still called EE. During the 1980s, EE moved in a social-democratic direction. It still saw itself as inside the nationalist camp, but it became extremely hostile to the fundamentalist nationalism of ETA's political wing, **Herri Batasuna** (HB), arguing the need to work within the bounds of the 1980 autonomy statute and accept that all Basques (not just Basque nationalists) formed part of the Basque community. It was never a large party, receiving only about 10 percent of the Basque vote. Nevertheless, because of the fragmented nature of nationalist politics, it was able to play an important role in the formation of a broad anti-HB front from 1988. Over the next three years, the majority "socialist wing" grew steadily closer to the Basque branch of the **Partido Socialista Obrero Español**, and finally integrated into it in the spring of 1993. Dissident "nationalists" tried to maintain an independent party, which they now called Euzkal Esquerra, but it went into rapid decline.

EUSKALERRÍACOS. *See* PARTIDO NACIONALISTA VASCO.

EUSKAL HERRIA. This is the name that, from the early 1990s, radical Basque nationalists have used to refer to what they see as the culturally and linguistically unified Basque space, made up of the Basque autonomous community, **Navarre**, and the three Basque French provinces. This entails a rejection of the term **Euskadi** (which refers only to the Basque autonomous community), because they see it as legitimizing the division of the Basque territories. Their ultimate aim is the unification of these areas in an independent greater **Basque Country**.

EUSKO ALKARTASUNA (EA)/BASQUE SOLIDARITY. EA is a Basque nationalist party, which was formed in 1986 after a split within the **Partido Nacionalista Vasco** (PNV). Under the former *lehendakari* (prime minister) of the Basque parliament, Carlos Garaikoetxea (1938–), the party has adopted a more left-wing and hard-line nationalist stance than the PNV, declaring itself social democratic and separatist while at the same time rejecting ETA **terrorism**. It began strongly, capturing about 16 percent of the vote in the 1986 Basque elections, but was never able to replace the PNV as the major Basque nationalist party. Furthermore, since 1998, when the PNV began to take a more radical line, differences between the two parties have become blurred. Faced with the growing strength of non-Basque nationalist parties from the early 1990s, it has also begun to ally with the PNV at election time and, from 1998, has participated in PNV-dominated coalition governments. It failed to get any seats in the March 2008 general elections, seriously calling its future into question. *See also* TABLE 10.

EXALTADOS/EXALTED ONES. The name refers to the radical **liberal** tendency that emerged during the **Constitutional Triennium** of 1821–1823 in opposition to conservative-liberal tendency that favored reconciliation with the old order. The *exaltados* were strongly anticlerical and called for wide suffrage and the extension of civil liberties. Their social base was the lesser bourgeoisie, artisans, shopkeepers, workers, and intellectuals—in general, town dwellers who felt excluded from the proposed new settlement. They congregated in "patriotic societies" founded on the French model. They were able to win the 1822 general elections, but their victory was to be short-lived. In April 1823, the liberal regime was swept away by an invading French army at the behest of the reactionary European Holy Alliance. *See also* PARTIDO PROGRESISTA.

EXTENSION UNIVERSITARIA. This was an institution set up by a number of reforming professors from the University of Oviedo to educate the local working classes between 1900 and 1909. Given the prestige of the professors—Rafael Altamira (1866–1951), Adolfo González Posada (1860–1944), Álvarez Buylla, and the great novelist **Leopoldo Alas "Clarín"**—and the novelty of their efforts, the Extension has attained an important symbolic status in the history of Spanish **education** and social reform.

– F –

FALANGE ESPAÑOLA/SPANISH FALANGE. The Falange Española was created by **José Antonio Primo de Rivera** in October 1933. The party was strongly influenced by European Fascism and was therefore rabidly nationalist and anti-Marxist, though the more **Traditionalist** elements in Primo de Rivera's ideology could be seen in the party's **Catholicism** (Falangists, in his words, should be "half monk, half soldier").

Nevertheless, in line with totalitarian Fascist thinking, the party believed that the Church should be subordinate to the state. In February 1934, in order to increase support, it joined with a more openly Fascist organization led by Ramiro Ledesma Ramos (1905–1936), the Juntas de Ofensiva Nacional Sindicalista (Juntas of the National Syndicalist Offensive—JONS) to form the Falange Española y de las JONS (but still usually referred to as the Falange). The new party proclaimed its intention to wage a violent struggle to install a new authoritarian "national-syndicalist" state. Primo de Rivera was soon able to take over control of the new organization. He was named national chief in October 1934 and Ledesma Ramos was forced out the following January. Under Primo de Rivera, the Falange claimed to be a new movement neither of the right nor the left, but despite his disquiet that following a coup the party would be subordinated to the **military**, he consistently supported conspiracies by sections of the officer corps to overthrow the Republic. Between 1934 and February 1936, with its cult of youth, its modernizing veneer, and its violent rhetoric, it appealed to middle- and upper-class youth dissatisfied with the stultifying conservatism of their parents but fearful of social revolution. However, while social elites still felt they could halt Republican reforms through legal channels, the **Confederación Española de Derechas Autónomas** (CEDA) remained the main party on the right and the Falange remained a small, peripheral force. Following the **Popular Front** victory in the February 1936 elections, the party was illegalized and its leaders arrested. Despite this setback, the realization that reforms could now only be thwarted through force led Falangist support to grow rapidly, the most spectacular coup being represented by the defection of the CEDA youth movement, the Juventud de Acción Popular (Popular Action Youth), en masse to the Falangist cause.

In the months before the outbreak of the **Spanish Civil War**, Falangist youth played a significant part in undermining the Republic by engaging leftists in street fighting, thereby fueling the right's claim that action was needed to restore law and order. Once war had broken out, Falangists rushed to aid the **Nationalist** cause. As the only party (apart from the **Carlists** in **Navarre**) who could galvanize popular enthusiasm for the war effort, the Falange grew apace. It put its **press** and propaganda network to the service of the rebellion and began rapidly to build its organization. Yet as Primo de Rivera had feared, the Falange was soon subordinated to the new military authorities. On 18 April 1937, the head of state, General **Francisco Franco**, in order to institutionalize his regime, announced his decision to fuse the Falange and the Carlists into a new organization, the **Falange Española Tradicionalista y de las Juntas de Ofensiva Nacional Sindicalista** (FET y de las JONS).

FALANGE ESPAÑOLA TRADICIONALISTA Y DE LAS JUNTAS DE OFENSIVA NACIONAL SINDICALISTA (FET Y DE LAS JONS)/TRADITIONALIST SPANISH FALANGE AND THE JUNTAS OF THE NATIONAL SYNDICALIST OFFENSIVE. When **Francisco Franco** fused the **Carlists** and **Falange Española** in April 1937, he was above all concerned to unify the **Nationalists'** war effort and ensure that the various organizations were subordinate to his person. The FET y de las JONS was to be the only legal party in the new Spain. At first Franco met with some opposition. With **José Antonio Primo de Rivera** held behind enemy lines, in September 1936 Manuel Hedilla (1902–1970) took over temporary leadership of the party. Hedilla rejected the terms of the new merger but few followed him, for while the Falange might not have achieved its ideal of a totalitarian Fascist state, it could expect to exercise considerable power within the **Franco regime**. The Falange was the dominant partner within the FET y de las JONS (and, indeed, it remained common to refer to the new organization as the Falange); its ideological preeminence was demonstrated by the fact that 26 of the 27 points in its program (the first of these points, which stated the so-called New State would be run by the Falange, was excluded) were officially adopted as the goals of the new regime. Moreover, through a whole series of bodies, it reached into almost every aspect of daily life. It set up the corporatist "vertical" trade union, the **Organización Sindical Española** (OSE), which replaced the old employers' and workers' unions; controlled the universities through the **Sindicato Español Universitario** (SEU); indoctrinated youth through the compulsory Youth Front; mobilized large numbers of **women** through its women's front, the **Sección Feminina**; and staffed a vast press and propaganda network. Finally, all members of the state administration had to join the FET y de las JONS, its Fascist-style salute was adopted by the regime, and Franco himself seemed to take on many of the trappings of a Fascist leader.

During 1939–1941, the position of FET y de las JONS was enormously strengthened by the Axis's seemingly dominant position in **World War II**. Its status was boosted in July 1939 when Franco's brother-in-law, **Ramón Serrano Suñer**, became president of its executive committee, the Junta Política. Serrano Suñer soon showed himself to be strongly pro-Nazi. In order to widen his own power base, he sought to strengthen the position of the single party within the regime. This was reflected in the establishment of a Falangist Center for Political Studies and in the approval of new laws laying the foundations of the OSE and SEU. Furthermore, in the summer of 1940, the Junta Política began to prepare the draft of a proposed Law of State Organization, which would give it a key role in decision making. This provoked a great deal of **military** opposition, leading Franco to shelve the project. Finally, on 1 May 1941, with Serrano Suñer's approval, the FET y de las JONS's press was freed from censorship, creating an independent fascistic press network. Franco, however, began to worry that Serrano Suñer was concentrating too much power in his hands, with the result that in a cabinet reshuffle in May 1941, Franco moved to ensure that the single party was firmly subordinate to the state, and in September 1942, Serrano Suñer was ousted, with Franco taking over the presidency of the FET y de las JONS. From this date, the growing likelihood that the Axis would lose the war led Franco to downplay the Fascist components of the regime. The pace of "de-Falangization" quickened from 1945, when the Fascist salute was dropped, and after the approval of the Fundamental Principles of the Regime in 1958 the single party was renamed the **Movimiento Nacional**.

During the early years of the regime, the failure to establish a full-blown Fascist state in Spain led to sporadic conspiracies from within the single party's ranks. In 1940, a group of veteran Falangists (or "old shirts," as they were known) sought to replace Franco with a man totally identified with their cause. They asked the military officer most closely identified with their ideals, **Juan Yagüe**, for aid. He refused, but for his troubles was still sacked as air force minister by Franco. These were, however, only a very small minority and had no chance of success. Most veteran Falangists were co-opted into the regime and became dependent on its survival for their own advancement. Best known of this new generation of loyal Falangist bureaucrats were **José Luis de Arrese** and **José Antonio Girón**, minister general secretary of the FET y de las JONS and minister of labor respectively from May 1941.

During the late 1940s and early 1950s, the single party largely became a bureaucratic machine, with little capacity to mobilize the Spanish population. Franco nevertheless was never willing to contemplate its dismantling because it provided a source of cadres and because he knew that most of its activists would remain loyal. Indeed, once the regime had secured a degree of Western recognition, the party made something of a comeback. In 1948, a new secretary general was appointed (the post had been vacant for three years). Then, in 1953, despite the opposition of some cabinet members, Franco gave the go-ahead for the celebration of the FET y de las JONS's first (and only) national congress. He presided over the act and then gave a speech at a massive rally held at the Chamartín sports stadium. Finally, faced with growing worker and student protest in 1956, Franco briefly seemed prepared to give the party a greater role in government policy. José Luis de Arrese was charged with producing a blueprint designed to redefine the role of the party. His proposed plan would have given it a far more powerful role within the state. These plans were, however, scotched by army and Church opposition and proved the prelude to its further downgrading. During the 1950s, Spain's mounting economic crisis had demonstrated the shortcomings of the regime's **autarkic economic policy**, with which the FET y de las JONS was strongly identified. Franco was finally persuaded by his right-hand man, **Luis Carrero Blanco**, that the regime's stability could only be assured through a significant liberalization of economic policy. This was strongly opposed by hard-line Falangists, such as Arrese and Girón. Their defeat was reflected in their replacement in the cabinet reshuffle of February 1957 and in the rise of the **Opus Dei** technocrats. This was followed in 1958 by the change of name and replacement of the Falange's 26 points by a **Catholic**-traditionalist set of goals.

During the 1960s, a number of divisions opened up within the Movimiento. Old-style Falangists like Girón lamented the passing of the postwar system of autarky. But a new generation of reforming Falangists also emerged, the best known of whom were **Manuel Fraga** and **José Solís**. They realized that the Movimiento was becoming a lifeless hulk, and believed that the only way it could be revitalized (and hence the Movimiento's position within the regime shored up) was through making it more responsive to the membership. Thus, after being appointed minister general secretary of the FET y de las JONS in 1957, José Solís sought to give worker representatives greater influence in collective bargaining within the OSE, and hoped to open the Movimiento up by allowing the formation of associations and the contrast of opinions. Franco, however, blocked any such reforms in the belief that they might end up undermining the essentials of his regime.

By the early 1970s, then, the Movimiento was heading nowhere. Its original fascistic ideology had been totally diluted and it was divided between die-hard Francoists (who came to be known as the **Bunker**), bureaucrats who would flow with the prevailing political tide, and reformers who were increasingly aware that they would have to undertake a major overhaul of the Francoist regime if their power and privileges were not to be swept away by the leftist opposition. Once the **transition to democracy** got under way, the Movimiento was quickly dismantled and abolished on 7 April 1977. Nevertheless, many party bureaucrats retained their posts within the administration and many reforming (and opportunistic) figures within the single party were able to continue their political career in the new democratic system, in either the **Unión del Centro Democrático** or **Alianza Popular**.

FALCÓN O'NEILL, LIDIA (1935–). Lidia Falcón was the most influential figure in the radical **feminist** movement that emerged in

1970s Spain. In her writings, most notably *Mujer y sociedad* (*Woman and Society*, 1969) and *La razón feminista* (*Feminist Reason*, 1980–1982), she tried to synthesize Marxism and the women's liberation movement. She was at the same time a leading political activist (who was arrested by the **Franco regime** in the early 1970s because of her suspected links to **ETA**) and founded the country's first feminist party, the Partido Feminista, in 1979, along with the feminist magazines *Vindicación feminista* and *poder y libertad*.

FALLA MATHEU, MANUEL DE (1876–1946). Manuel de Falla is probably the leading Spanish composer of the 20th century. He was born in Cádiz. His first burst of creative activity came during a stay in Paris between 1907 and 1914, where he wrote his best-known work, *Noches en un jardín español* (*Nights in a Spanish Garden*). From 1922, he lived in Granada, where he wrote his harpsichord concerto. He left Spain for Buenos Aires at the end of the **Spanish Civil War** and died in Argentina.

FARMING. *See* AGRICULTURE.

FASCISM. *See* FALANGE ESPAÑOLA; FALANGE ESPAÑOLA TRADICIONALISTA Y DE LAS JUNTAS DE OFENSIVA NACIONAL SINDICALISTA; FRANCO REGIME; PRIMO DE RIVERA Y SAÉNZ DE HEREDIA, JOSÉ ANTONIO.

FEDERACIÓN ANARQUISTA IBÉRICA (FAI)/ANARCHIST IBERIAN FEDERATION. *See* ANARCHISM; CONFEDERACIÓN NACIONAL DEL TRABAJO; DURRUTI DUMANGE, BUENAVENTURA.

FEDERACIÓN DE TRABAJADORES DE LA REGIÓN ESPAÑOLA (FTRE)/FEDERATION OF WORKERS OF THE SPANISH REGION. This confederation, set up in 1881, was a continuation of the **anarchist**-inspired **Federación Regional Española** (FRE). Behind this organization were a series of anarchist Catalan labor leaders, who called a congress of Spanish workers in September 1881 in **Barcelona**. It was at this congress that the new confederation was born. Over the next two years the organization grew rapidly. At its second congress, held in Seville in September 1882, it had about 60,000 members. This was roughly equivalent to the FRE at its high point in 1873. However, **Andalusia** was now the strongest region, with 66 percent of its members, followed by **Catalonia** with 23 percent. This reflected both the spread of labor organization in Andalusia between 1881 and 1882, and the fact that the Catalan **labor movement** had, from the late 1870s, become divided between an anarchist wing and a more moderate "reformist" wing, linked to the **cotton textile** labor federation, the **Tres Clases de Vapor.**

Between 1881 and 1888, nevertheless, the confederation's leadership was located in Barcelona. Under figures like Rafael Farga Pellicer (1844–1890) and Francisco Tomás (1850–1903), it tried to combine revolutionary ideology with the defense of open trade union organization. This brought it into conflict with many Andalusian anarchists who advocated reprisals (crop burning, attacks on landowners) and who believed that the revolution would be the work of secret anarchist groups, who would spark off an insurrection. These differences were probably the result of the very different social structures in Andalusia and Barcelona. In the rural south, it was more difficult for labor unions to function and individual **terrorist** acts were often the only means of protest. Dissidents from the provinces of Seville, Cádiz, and Córdoba formed a group called Los Desheredados (The Disinherited) in January 1883. It was disowned by the Barcelona leadership, but conspiratorial activity in the south was used as an excuse by the government, which had become increasingly worried at the extension of labor protest, to undermine the FTRE.

In 1883, the local authorities in the province of Cádiz claimed to have discovered a secret society known as the **Mano Negra** (Black Hand), whose aim was to assassinate local landowners. The existence of the Mano Negra is disputed. What is clear is that its supposed discovery was used to carry out a wide-ranging repression of labor organization in Andalusia. In Catalonia, moreover, as the economic climate deteriorated from 1884, employers struck back against the FTRE. The Catalan leadership responded by trying to limit the number of strikes in order to preserve the organization. This led to criticisms by a younger generation of anarchists, led by figures like Leopoldo Bonafulla (pseudonym of Joan Baptista Esteve) and Federico Urales (pseudonym of Joan Montseny [1864–1942]), that the organization was too moderate and bureaucratic. They argued that in line with anarchist postulates it should be operated as a loose coordinating body and that workers should be encouraged to mobilize against the bourgeoisie. In the context of the FTRE's disintegration in the late 1880s, these men were to gain the upper hand. The FTRE was finally wound up in 1888 and was replaced by a Pacto de Unión y Solidaridad (Pact of Union and Solidarity) as an umbrella organization for the unions and an Organización Anarquista de la Región Española (Organization of the Spanish Region), whose mission it was to coordinate the anarchist groups. Yet, in the violent, repressive climate of the 1890s, it would prove impossible to relaunch anarchist labor organization in any part of Spain.

FEDERACIÓN NACIONAL DE TRABAJADORES DE LA TIERRA (FNTT)/NATIONAL LAND WORKERS' FEDERATION. The FNTT was the peasant branch of the **Unión General de Trabajadores** (UGT) during the **Second Republic**. From the start, its main centers of support were among the land-hungry peasants and laborers of **Andalusia** and Extremadura. It was founded in April 1930 and grew rapidly after the proclamation of the Republic, reaching the figure of 392,953 members, 38 percent of the UGT's overall membership, in 1932. The federation thus came to exercise a strong influence on the policies pursued by the **Partido Socialista Obrero Español** (PSOE). Its first president was Lucio Martínez Gil (1883–1957), who formed part of the moderate **Julián Besteiro** wing of the PSOE-UGT. During 1931 and 1932, the federation's leadership supported the attempt by the PSOE-**republican** coalition government to improve working conditions for the peasantry and, particularly, the introduction of the **Agrarian Reform Law**. However, at the grassroots level, there developed an increasing frustration at the power of the local landed oligarchy to block reform and at the slow deliberations of the Spanish parliament. Frustration with the shortcomings of "bourgeois democracy" was also reflected at national level by the increasingly radical rhetoric of **Francisco Largo Caballero** and the PSOE left. This radicalization continued after the right came to power following the November 1933 elections. Within the FNTT, this could be seen in the replacement of Gil by the *caballerista* Ricardo Zabala (?–1940) in January 1934. This took place in the context of an offensive against the FNTT by local landowners, aimed at rolling back the gains peasants had made since 1931. The FNTT called a general strike in protest in June 1934, but the full rigors of state power were used to ensure it was defeated and greatly weakened. As a result, the southern peasantry played no role in the **October 1934 revolution**. However, the federation quickly reorganized following the **Popular Front** victory of February 1936. At the same time, some peasants began to take over the landed estates, particularly in Extremadura, without any government resistance.

During the **Spanish Civil War**, the FNTT was, as much as the **anarchist Confederación Nacional del Trabajo** (CNT), a driving force behind the collectivizations in rural areas controlled by the Republic. However, it was to encounter opposition, first by Largo Caballero and then by **Juan Negrín**, who wished to centralize state power and preserve as far as possible the Republican status quo. The federation was suppressed by the **Franco regime**. It was to reorganize again in the 1970s, but given Spain's massively changed social structure, it was never to have anything like the impact it had had in the 1930s.

FEDERACIÓN POPULAR DEMÓCRATA/POPULAR DEMOCRATIC FEDERATION. *See* GIL-ROBLES Y QUIÑONES, JOSÉ MARÍA.

FEDERACIÓN REGIONAL ESPAÑOLA (FRE)/SPANISH REGIONAL FEDERATION. The FRE was the first labor organization with a clearly socialist ideology to operate in Spain. It was able to function in the context of the relatively liberal climate in Spain after the **Glorious Revolution** of 1868 and at its founding congress took the decision to join the International Working Men's Association (IWMA) founded by Karl Marx in London in 1864. Unlike most of the branches of the IWMA, the FRE adopted the **anarchist** teachings of Marx's rival within the organization, Mikhail Bakunin. The reason was, in the first instance, that the Spaniards had gotten to know of the IWMA at the end of 1868 through an emissary of Bakunin, Giuseppe Fanelli. Subsequently groups of workers from **Catalonia** established contact with Bakunin, and when the local **Barcelona** unions called a congress to form a national labor confederation to be held in the city in June 1870, they were in a strong position to set the agenda. The FRE remained weak during much of 1870 and 1871, but from the end of this latter year it began to grow quite rapidly and had about 60,000 members in 1873. Catalonia was its main center of support, followed at some distance by **Andalusia**, **Valencia**, and **Castile**. Most of the FRE's leading figures regarded themselves as anarchist revolutionaries, but disagreements soon developed over the tactics to pursue. In Catalonia, union leaders involved in the day-to-day realities of labor organization maintained that the revolution would be brought about through a general strike, but pushed this into the future, arguing that the working class was not yet strong enough. However, other anarchist leaders, particularly outside Catalonia, believed that capitalism could immediately be overthrown through an insurrection. Insurrectionaries dominated the FRE's leadership, located in the Valencian town of Alcoy during 1873, and put this theory into practice in July when they backed the **Cantonalist revolt** against the **First Republic**. The Catalan unions, however, refused to follow suit, and, indeed, supported the Republic in its struggle against the **Carlists** in northern Spain.

After the Alcoy revolt had been put down, the FRE's leadership moved to **Madrid**. The new team responded to harassment by the authorities with hints that individual acts of terror might be necessary in order to combat the bourgeoisie. This nihilist current was greatly strengthened by the blanket repression that followed the coup by General Manuel Pavia (1827–1895) on 3 January 1874. Over the next six years, the FRE was only able to hold a series of secret district (*comarcal*) congresses in which nihilist theses, calling for **terrorist** acts by secret anarchist groups, were expounded. This, however, never convinced the majority of Catalans, who were in favor of more open trade union activity. In February 1881, led by Farga Pellicer, they were finally able to retake control of the organization and called a new union congress for September. Luckily this coincided with the coming to power of the **Partido Liberal**, which, at first at least, proved far more tolerant of union organization. When the congress was held, a new confederation was born, the **Federación de Trabajadores de la Región Española**. *See also* LABOR MOVEMENT.

FEDERACIÓN REGIONAL ESPAÑOLA DE SOCIEDADES DE RESISTENCIA (FRESR)/SPANISH REGIONAL TRADE UNION FEDERATION. This was a pro-**anarchist** labor confederation that operated in Spain between 1900 and 1907. Its first congress was held in Madrid in October 1900, with anarchist Federico Urales (1864–1942) claiming that 52,000 workers were represented. However, the confederation played little active role within the **labor movement**. In line with anarchist postulates at the time, the members only paid voluntary dues, and the leadership (the "regional office"), therefore, retained only a very limited contact with affiliated unions.

FEDERALISM. Federalism has been a strong current in Spanish political life since the mid-19th century. It first manifested itself in the opposition by more radical **liberals** to the centralizing measures of the Spanish liberal state. It drew on Spain's "pactist" history, as represented by the autonomy of the **Crown of Aragón** and the **Basque** provinces under the **Catholic Monarchs** and during the **Habsburg** dynasty. Federalism became fused with republicanism in the 1860s. The federal republicans, with their stress on local liberties, were particularly concerned with the need to build democratic local government as a bulwark against authoritarian central government. They were particularly strong in **Catalonia**, where they were captained by **Francesc Pi i Margall**. The federal republicans founded the **Partido Republicano Federalista** immediately after the **Glorious Revolution** in October 1868. This party was to play a key role in Spanish political life during the **Democratic Sexennium**, but was undermined by political divisions between moderate reformers and radical "intransigents." From the 1880s, federal republicanism lost further support as its base fragmented, with the rise of the working-class left, **Catalanists**, and Spanish nationalist republicans. The latter were represented above all by the figures of **Nicolás Salmerón** and **Alejandro Lerroux**, who maintained that the demand for regional decentralization was compatible with a more belligerent Spanish nationalist discourse. Pi i Margall set up a new **Partido Republicano Federal Democrático** in 1880, but it was much weaker than its predecessor. Nevertheless, the demand for the federalization of the Spanish state has remained an important current in Spanish political discourse. It has resurfaced in recent years on the Catalan left, where it is voiced by **Pascual Maragall** and the **Partit dels Socialistes de Catalunya-Partido Socialista Obrero Español** (PSE-PSOE), and by the eco-left party **Iniciativa per Catalunya-Verds.**

FELIPE II (1527–1598). Felipe II was the most imposing **Habsburg** king of Spain. He had already acted as regent, on occasion, since 1543, and so had experience of government. He proved hardworking and meticulous. This combined with his reluctance to leave decisions in the hands of others meant that an inordinate amount of paperwork passed across his desk. He was also austere and appeared rather distant to those outside his inner circle.

The accession of Felipe II of the throne in 1556 signified a Castilian reorientation of the empire. He had been brought up in **Castile** and **Castilian** was his first language. His father, **Carlos I**, had agreed that the Germanic Habsburg Empire should be ruled by his brother, Ferdinand, thereby increasing the weight of Spain (above all the **Crown of Castile**) within the monarchy. This was especially so given the growing importance of silver bullion from the Americas in sustaining its finances. Indeed, one of the new king's first moves was to establish **Madrid** as the court's capital in 1561. He would henceforth rule his dominions from Madrid or from the imposing summer residence he had built nearby, the monastery palace of San Lorenzo del Escorial (along with the palaces in Aranjuez and Valsaín). Castilians would also come to dominate the court and administration, leading to disquiet in his other kingdoms. Correspondingly, he was troubled by the level of independence enjoyed by the **Crown of Aragón**. This led to tension. In 1591, following an incident with one of his former favorites, Antonio Pérez (1569–1611), who sought refuge in Zaragoza, he sent in the army to quell unrest and reduced the power of the Kingdom of Aragón (one of the three component parts of the Crown of Aragón), making its chief law officer, the justiciar, removable by the king.

Felipe II had a strong sense of his divine right to rule and was convinced that it was his and Spain's destiny to defend the **Catholic** faith. Hence, under his rule, Spain became the heart of the anti-Protestant **Counter-Reformation**; he was involved in an almost constant succession of conflicts to bolster his empire and defeat "heresy." From 1556, he was engaged in a defensive battle to defeat rebellion in his Dutch possessions while also captaining efforts to contain the expansion of the Ottoman Empire. It was above all because of his fear of Protestantism and Islam that he pursued the policy initiated by his father of allowing the **Spanish Inquisition** to grow in strength. Furthermore, he also favored putting pressure on Spain's **Moorish** (*morisco*) population to ensure that they sincerely converted to Christianity. This led to a major rebellion in the Alpujarras in 1567. Subsequently, he backed the *moriscos*' expulsion from Spain, though the policy was not actually carried out until after his death.

In the 1570s, however, the situation stabilized. The *morisco* rebellion had been quelled by 1570 and in the following year Spanish forces played a decisive role in the defeat of the Ottoman Empire in the battle of **Lepanto**. With respect to the Low Countries, through the 1579 Treaty of Arras, he was able to reconcile the southern Walloon Estates, though the northern Dutch provinces remained in revolt (and enjoyed de facto independence). The incorporation of **Portugal** into his empire in 1580 and growing supplies of silver from his American colonies then encouraged him to take a more aggressive stance. Most importantly, after England had opened hostilities in 1585, he dispatched the **Spanish Armada** to invade the country in 1588. Its defeat was the bitterest blow he had suffered. Like Carlos I, he faced the problem that his imperial ambitions outstretched his financial resources, leading him both to raise taxes in the Crown of Castile in the 1590s and declare the state bankrupt on several occasions (1557, 1576, and 1596). He was succeeded by his son, **Felipe III**.

FELIPE III (1578–1621). Felipe III came to power in 1598 in extremely inauspicious circumstances. He inherited both the rebellion in the United Provinces and war with England in a context of extreme financial weakness. This was worsened by a long-term recession that had hit the Castilian **economy** in the 1580s, with epidemics leading to **population** decline. Hence his recourse to debasing the coinage in 1599 and 1617 and declaring the crown bankrupt in 1607.

Unlike his father, **Felipe II**, he liked to delegate responsibility and fell under the influence of his court favorite (*valido*), Francisco Gómez de Sandoval y Rojas, the duke of Lerma (1552–1625). Nevertheless, the **foreign policy** pursued during his reign was not unintelligent. Unable to subdue England and the United Provinces, he agreed to peace with the former in 1604 and to a 12-year-truce with the latter in 1609. The problem was that as the Dutch still demanded outright independence, the truce only postponed the problem. And he was not able to stay out European warfare for long; in 1628 he was drawn into a confrontation on the side of the German **Habsburgs** against Bohemian rebels supported by the Dutch. With respect to internal affairs, in 1609 he made the ill-judged decision to expel the **Moors** (*moriscos*) from Spain, worsening the economic crisis and putting an end to the country's history of ethnic diversity. Overall, the whole problem of how to defend a large, heterogeneous empire with insufficient resources while faced by a number of hostile powers was passed on to this son, **Felipe IV**.

FELIPE IV (1605–1665). Felipe IV was only 16 years of age when he came to power in 1621. From the first he was strongly influenced by the Andalusian courtier, Gaspar de Guzmán (referred to as the **count-duke of Olivares** from 1625). Under his reign the accumulated problems of trying to defend the empire with both insufficient resources and a lack of unity of purpose finally exploded. Like his father, **Felipe III**, he faced a constant struggle to raise sufficient funds and was dogged by periodic financial crises. The count-duke's solution was to forge a more united and efficient Spain and aggressively defend the Spanish **Habsburg** possessions. He resumed war against the de facto independent United Provinces in 1624, but made little headway and faced harassment by English and French forces. Finally, an increasingly powerful France declared war into 1635, forcing the empire onto the back foot. The count-duke's whole project fell apart in 1640 with revolts in **Catalonia** and **Portugal**, leading Felipe IV to confine him to his estates in 1643.

Henceforth, under the stewardship of the count-duke's nephew, Luis de Haro, the monarchy to a large degree accepted its diminished place in the world. Felipe tried to maintain peninsular unity and after a long struggle—with Catalan rebels backed by France—he managed to retake **Barcelona** in 1552 and reincorporate the province into the empire (being careful to respect its *fueros* or privileges). However, the Portuguese rebellion remained unsubdued, with Portuguese forces inflicting several painful defeats on the Spanish army. In 1648, through the Treaty of Munster, Felipe IV accepted the independence of the United Provinces. However, during the 1550s he remained under pressure from England, France, and Portugal, forcing him to reach an unfavorable peace with France in 1559. Through the Treaty of the Pyrenees, the **Crown of Aragón** lost Roussillon and part of the Cerdagne to France, and in the following year Felipe IV's daughter, the Infanta María Teresa, married King Louis XIV of France. It was a recognition of the Spanish Habsburg Empire's declining power. The marriage of María Teresa would also have unforeseen consequences, leading to a **Bourbon** succession to the Spanish throne in 1700.

FELIPE V (1683–1746). Felipe V was Spain's first **Bourbon** monarch. He was the grandson of King Louis XIV of France and the Spanish Infanta María Teresa, who had married in 1560. At the time, **Felipe IV** had stipulated that their heirs could not accede to the throne. However, the childless **Carlos II** agreed to Felipe V's coronation in 1699, faced with the alternative of the breakup of the Spanish **Habsburg** Empire. Though crowned king in the following year, Felipe V faced the rival claim of Archduke Charles of Austria, backed by the English and Dutch, and the German Habsburgs. The result was the **War of Succession**. Felipe V emerged victorious in 1713, but had to renounce all Spanish possessions on mainland Europe. This proved a blessing in disguise, allowing the country to focus on internal reconstruction.

Under his rule, Spanish administration would undergo a profound transformation. He put an end to the composite monarchy of the Habsburgs and introduced a more centralized, absolutist system of government much closer to the French model. This entailed the abolition of the *fueros* of the component parts of the **Crown of Aragón** and the integration of representatives of these territories into the **Cortes** of the old **Crown of Castile**. Only the **Basque** provinces and **Navarre** retained their local liberties, because they had largely supported the king in the War of Succession. At the same time, the Cortes was emptied of the limited powers it still possessed, and became little more than a ceremonial body. Subsequently, custom barriers between the distinct parts of Spain were (with the exception of the Basque provinces and Navarre) abolished and a new tax system introduced, through which the tax burden was distributed more evenly across the Spanish state. Rule was also centralized on **Madrid**, with the abolition of the Council of Aragón, and, following the French example, the creation of five ministers (*secretarios de estado*) to oversee the various branches of the administration, along with the introduction of a system of local administrators (*intendentes*) in the former *fuero* territories.

FEMINISM. Movements in favor of **women**'s rights were slow to develop in early 20th-century Spain. The working-class left (most notably the **anarchists**) rejected conservative claims that women were intellectually inferior to men and should have no role in the public sphere. And a number of important female figures emerged within this tradition, most notably the anarchist **Federica Montseny** and the Communist **Dolores Ibárruri** ("La Pasionaria"). However, these movements did not generally reject the idea that women above all occupied the private family sphere, while men should play a dominant role in the world of work. Hence, they did not undertake a systematic critique of patriarchal assumptions. Indeed, they criticized continental feminist movements because, in their opinion, they subordinated the class struggle to women's rights.

In **liberal** circles a middle-class feminist movement began to emerge in the second decade of the century. The key figure in this respect was **Clara Campoamor**, who championed both the legal equality of women and their right to the suffrage. A nationwide association, the Asociación Nacional de Mujeres Españolas (National Association of Spanish Women), was founded in 1918 under the presidency of Benita Asas Manterola (1873–1966). The dominant ideology within the organization was liberal conservative, and for this reason it rejected divorce. However, it did support female suffrage, equal pay, and a woman's right to enter the liberal professions. Other organizations were set up in particular parts of Spain. The **Madrid**-based Cruzada de Mujeres Españolas (Crusade of Spanish Women) was responsible for the first demonstration in Spain in favor of female suffrage in May 1921. On the **Catholic** right, women's organizations had until that date centered their attention on the "moralization" of working-class women, above all through inculcating attendance of mass and teaching parenting skills. However, some Catholic circles also began to discuss the issue of female suffrage. This was the case of Acción Católica de la Mujer (Female Catholic

Action), founded in 1919 by the archbishop of Toledo, Cardinal Victoriano Guisasola y Menéndez (1852–1920). The proclamation of the **Second Republic** in April 1931 resulted in a profound change in women's social status. Given the regime's democratic foundations, it was favorably inclined to equal legal status. Nevertheless, Clara Campoamar, one of Spain's first three female deputies, played a significant role in ensuring that there were no limitations placed on this principle in the **Constitution of 1931** and in making sure women were immediately conceded the right to the vote. The largely left-wing, anticlerical **Cortes** also had no problem in approving civil marriage and a divorce law in 1932. Meanwhile, the principle of coeducation was enshrined in the state **education** sector.

This was thrown into reverse by the **Franco regime**, which tried to reimpose "traditional" Catholic values on the population. The **Constitution of 1978** once again affirmed women's legal equality. In the increasingly radicalized climate of the 1970s, a militant feminist movement, which married the struggle for women's rights and for socialism, also raised its head. The standard-bearer was **Lidia Falcón**, who launched her own Partido Feminista (Feminist Party) in 1979. In **Catalonia**, 1976 was to see the formation of an Associació Catalana de la Dona (Catalan Women's Association). However, from 1979, it fragmented between the radical left-wing feminists and feminists focused more specifically on issues relating to women's rights.

In the wider political sphere, after the demise of the Franco regime, demands relating to women tended to be integrated within the broader campaign by the anti-Francoist opposition for a **transition to democracy**. This meant that large number of women who considered themselves feminists operated within the major left-wing parties. These parties integrated feminist demands such as the right to contraception, abortion, and a divorce law into their programs. At first the **Partido Comunista de España** and **Partit Socialista Unificat de Catalunya** took the lead. In 1965, a very active Movimiento Democrático de Mujeres (Women's Democratic Movement) was set up, which was close to the Communists. Then, when the **Partido Socialista Obrero Español** (PSOE) came to power in 1982, it founded an **Instituto de La Mujer**, which played a key role in trying to ensure that the theoretical equality of women, enshrined in the constitution, was put into practice. Nevertheless, the PSOE wished to compromise with the political right and, most especially, with the still powerful **Catholic Church**, and for this reason did not go as far as its feminist supporters would have wished in some areas. Most notably, the 1985 abortion law decriminalized abortion only when the woman's life was in danger, she had been raped, or the fetus was badly deformed.

There was criticism of these "institutionalized feminists" from more radical socialist and "difference" feminists. They were accused, in some circles, of having sold out on the women's movement and reaching excessive compromises with government. However, the radical feminist movement itself remained fragmented in the 1980s and 1990s, limiting its appeal. Overall, the "institutional feminism" model adopted in Spain since the transition to democracy, backed above all by the PSOE, has achieved considerable success in combating the social and cultural inequalities facing women. Feminist demands in areas such as equality in the world of work, an active presence of women in the political system, and liberal divorce laws, have been embraced, especially by a younger generation of urban professional women. Yet, many of these women tend to distance themselves from "feminism" because of its association with the radical political activism of the transition and "unfeminine" behavior.

FERNÁNDEZ DE LA VEGA SANZ, MARÍA TERESA (1949–). Fernández de la Vega shot to fame in April 2004 when she became the first female vice president as well as the government's spokesperson. She was born in **Valencia**, but studied law in the Madrid Complutense and went on to do a PhD at the University of Barcelona. While in **Barcelona**, she affiliated with the **Partit Socialista Unificat de Catalunya** (PSUC), but in 1979 joined the **Partido Socialista Obrero Español** (PSOE).

During the **transition to democracy**, she formed part of the left-wing grouping Justicia Democrática Hoy-Jueces por la Democracia (Democratic Justice Today-Judges for Democracy). In the 1980s and early 1990s, she then held a number of political positions within the Ministry of Justice, culminating in 1994 in her appointment as secretary of state for justice. At the same time, she became a magistrate in

1979 and in 1994 was elected by the Senate onto the Consejo General del Poder Judicial (General Council of the Judiciary). She was elected as a PSOE parliamentary deputy for the first time in 1996 and became secretary general of the Socialist group in parliament. Her rise to the first rank in politics would come by the hand of **José Luis Rodríguez Zapatero** after the March 2004 elections. An overt **feminist**, she has proved a popular and effective vice president. She communicated the government's message without stridency, projecting a favorable image in comparison with the harsher tone of many of the **Partido Popular**'s leading parliamentary figures. She also played a leading role in efforts to improve relations between the government and **Catholic Church**, in this case with little effect.

FERNÁNDEZ-MIRANDA Y HEVIA, TORCUATO (1915–1980). Fernández-Miranda was born into a conservative **Catholic** family in Oviedo on 10 November 1915. His Catholic upbringing would be the most important factor in his future intellectual formation. He studied law at the University of Oviedo before fighting on the **Nationalist** side during the **Spanish Civil War**. After the war, he rose rapidly through the bureaucratic apparatus of the **Franco regime**. He became professor of constitutional law at the University of Oviedo in 1946 and was named rector of the university in 1951 (which also automatically made him a member [*procurador*] of the **Cortes**). From 1954 to 1969, he was to hold a number of key posts in the educational establishment. In the early 1960s, moreover, he became Prince **Juan Carlos**'s personal tutor and in 1969, became minister general secretary of the **Movimiento Nacional**. Further promotion came in the summer of 1973. When **Luis Carrero Blanco** was made prime minister, he became his deputy, and when Carrero Blanco was assassinated in December he was thrust into the limelight when he temporarily took over the post of prime minister. However, his rise through the ranks of government was seemingly brought to an abrupt halt when, to his great disappointment, **Carlos Arias Navarro** was chosen as the new prime minister in January 1974.

Up to this date, Fernández Miranda had shown himself to be a firm Francoist. However, in the final twist in his political career, after the death of General **Francisco Franco** he was named by King Juan Carlos as president of the Cortes and president of the Council of the Realm. From this position, he was to work with the king in dismantling the structures of Francoism and setting Spain on course for the establishment of a constitutional monarchy. First, he was able to use his influence to make sure that the Council of the Realm would select the king's favorite, **Adolfo Suárez**, as prime minister in June. He then led the Francoist Cortes down the path of its own self-destruction in the second half of 1976. He was later to claim to have been the mastermind behind the **transition to democracy**. This was certainly a gross exaggeration. As a man closely identified with the institutions of Francoism, he had the skills necessary to put into effect fundamental reforms that would, nevertheless, not break with the outward trappings of Francoist legality, and was useful in conferring the transition with legitimacy and in convincing regime bureaucrats that they should not rock the boat. But he was the executor rather than the initiator of reform. He was, moreover, never a convinced democrat. The reasons for his brusque about-face are not, therefore, altogether clear. Opaque at the best of times, he never explained his motives. The most probable answer is that, called upon by Juan Carlos (and perhaps piqued at having been dropped by Franco), he felt it was his duty to do the king's bidding. His work complete, he resigned his posts on 30 May 1977.

FERNÁNDEZ ORDÓÑEZ, FRANCISCO (1930–1992). Fernández Ordóñez was one of the most respected figures in the Spanish political scene of the 1970s and 1980s, and the only leading politician to begin his professional life as a Francoist bureaucrat and end up in the **Partido Socialista Obrero Español** (PSOE). He was born in **Madrid** and after studying law in the 1950s became a high-flying career civil servant. By the 1970s, he had gained a reputation as an *aperturista* and resigned his post as president of the state holding company, the **Instituto Nacional de Industria**, in **Carlos Arias Navarro**'s government, after the dismissal of the reforming minister of information, Pío Cabanillas (1923–1991), in October 1974. During the **transition to democracy**, he declared himself a social democrat and in 1977 formed the Partido Social Demócrata (Social Democratic Party), which, after a brief existence, integrated into the **Unión del Centro Democrático** (UCD). Under **Adolfo Suárez**, he served in government first as treasury minister (where he reformed Spain's tax system by introducing a tax on earnings), and then, from 1980, as justice minister. On the left of the UCD, he was strongly criticized by the coalition's **Christian-democratic** right. This reached a crescendo in 1980, when he steered a divorce bill through parliament with PSOE votes.

As the UCD fell apart, he broke away in 1981 to form the small Partido de Acción Demócrata (Party of Democratic Action), which later in the year joined the PSOE. After the PSOE's electoral triumph of October 1982, he found himself much in demand because of his knowledge of the Spanish administration and finances. He was first made president of the state-dominated Banco Exterior de España and then, in 1985, when **Felipe González** needed a more pro-Atlanticist figure than Fernando Morán (1926–) to oversee the referendum on continued membership of the **North Atlantic Treaty Organization** (NATO), he became foreign minister. Fernández Ordóñez always appeared the epitome of reasonableness, combining backing for social reform with strong support for liberal economic and democratic political values.

FERNANDO VII (1784–1833). The future king of Spain was born on 13 October 1784, the eldest son of **Carlos IV**. As a youngster at court, the young prince developed a burning hatred of **Manuel de Godoy**, leading statesman of the day and reputed lover of the queen. It was, in fact, a letter from Fernando to Napoleon Bonaparte in 1807 asking him to intervene against Godoy that gave Napoleon the excuse to invade Spain at the end of the year. Through the **Aranjuez uprising** of 17–18 March 1808, Fernando was then able to force the dismissal of Godoy and the abdication of Carlos IV, allowing him to accede to the throne. His first period of rule, was, however, to be short-lived. On April 10, the French commander of Madrid, Marshall Joachim Murat, convinced Fernando to leave for France, where Napoleon forced him to abdicate in favor of Napoleon's brother Joseph (**José I**). Fernando remained under house arrest until the defeat of the Napoleonic forces in 1814, when he was again proclaimed king. Greeted as "the chosen one" (*el deseado*) by the clergy and landed elites, for most of his reign Fernando VII was associated with the doomed attempt to turn back the clock of history and preserve absolutist rule. Only in the late 1820s did he realize the need for a reconciliation with Spain's moderate **liberals**. *See also* FERNANDO RESTORATIONS.

FERNANDO RESTORATIONS (1814–1823, 1823–1833). This is the name given to the two periods during which King **Fernando VII** tried to banish **liberalism** from Spanish shores and reestablish the pre-1808 absolutist regime. The moment was propitious. After the defeat of Napoleon Bonaparte in 1814, Europe's absolutist states formed the Holy Alliance, designed to keep revolution at bay. Nevertheless, the attempt was finally to end in failure, leading Fernando VII to compromise with the more conservative liberals shortly before his death in 1833. At the root of this failure was the bankruptcy of the Spanish exchequer. In the aftermath of the **War of Independence**, the Spanish treasury was impoverished. Matters were made worse by the revolt of the American **colonies**, which led to the drying up of silver bullion imports and the disruption of export markets.

Yet at the same time, money was needed to maintain a standing army against any future revolutionary threat, and to try to reconquer the colonies. The problem for Fernando VII was that under an old regime economy and society, such funds would not be forthcoming. Both the **Catholic Church** and nobility maintained their feudal privileges, while the operation of *mayorazgos* (entailment)—which prevented the sale of land on the open market—and the guild system in industry were hardly likely to promote the economic development that might in the future lead to a growth in state revenue. In 1817, there was a timid attempt to impose a tax on wealth in rural Spain, but it was undermined by poor administration and the opposition of local notables. These problems gave the liberals a chance to strike back, and, after the success of the January 1820 *pronunciamiento* by General Rafael de Riego (1775–1823), they were able to force Fernando VII to accept the Cádiz Constitution of 1812. Hence began the so-called **Constitutional Triennium** of 1820–1823, which was cut short by the invasion of French troops under the orders of the reactionary Holy Alliance in order to restore absolutist rule. Not for the last time, foreign intervention had a decisive impact on the course of Spanish history. There followed a brutal persecution of the liberals, thousands of whom were forced into exile. Fernando VII tried to return to the old order, but was again faced with insuperable budgetary problems. This finally led him to realize that he needed to reach an understanding with conservative liberals—the so-called **Partido Moderado**—thereby paving the way for a reconciliation between landed and urban, noble and nonnoble elites. Shortly before his death, in 1832, the king proceeded to name his wife, **María Cristina of Naples**, who had close liberal contacts, regent until the coming of age of his daughter Isabel (the future **Isabel II**). Many of the clergy, however, were appalled by this turn of events and supported the claim to the throne of Fernando's reactionary brother, **Carlos María Isidoro Benito de Borbón y Borbón-Parma**. These supporters of Carlos were to be known as the **Carlists**, and they continued the crusade in defense of the old order.

FERRER Y GUARDIA, FRANCISCO (1849–1909). Ferrer was the key figure in the **anarchist** educational movement in the 1900s. An anticlerical **republican**, he was forced into exile in Paris in 1886 after the abortive attempted coup by General Manuel Villacampa. During his stay in Paris, he took onboard anarchist ideas and developed a strong interest in **"rationalist" education**. When in 1900 he inherited 1,300,000 francs from an elderly spinster, he was able to put his ideas into practice, establishing the **Escuela Moderna** in **Barcelona**. Ferrer's ideology, however, remained eclectic. While supporting **education**, he also advocated revolutionary syndicalism. Hence, between 1901 and 1903, he edited a weekly newspaper called *La Huelga General*, in which he maintained the need for a bloody, revolutionary general strike to overthrow capitalism. At the same time, he maintained contacts with the leftist republican movement, captained by **Alejandro Lerroux**, believing that a political revolution might trigger social revolution. He seems to have been involved in the planning of the assassination attempt on **Alfonso XIII** and his bride in 1906 by Mateo Morral (1880–1906), an employee of the Escuela Moderna's publishing house. He was arrested but his complicity was never proven and he was acquitted by the jury at his trial. The Barcelona Escuela Moderna was, nevertheless, closed. Thereafter, Ferrer funded the new syndicalist trade union **Solidaridad Obrera** when it was set up in 1907 and continued to support anarchist educational initiatives. After the **Tragic Week**, he was accused of being the "commander in chief" of the rebellion. There was absolutely no basis for this claim, but he was, nonetheless, condemned to death by a military tribunal. There followed an international campaign for clemency, but it was all to no avail. Ferrer was executed on 4 September 1909. The international storm would, however, force the resignation of the government of **Antonio Maura** in the following month.

FET Y DE LAS JONS. *See* FALANGE ESPAÑOLA TRADICIONALISTA Y DE LAS JUNTAS DE OFENSIVA NACIONAL SINDICALISTA.

FIFTH REGIMENT. The Fifth Regiment was set up by the **Partido Comunista de España** (PCE) in the first months of the **Spanish Civil War.** Unlike the revolutionary militias that had sprung up in the Republican zone, it laid great emphasis on professionalism, discipline, and authority. This, the PCE maintained, was the only way in which the **Nationalist** forces could be defeated, and fitted in with the party's broader claim that it was necessary to rebuild state power. Because of its seeming efficiency, many army officers joined the PCE and collaborated in the organization of the Fifth Regiment. At the same time, it benefited from the preferential distribution of Soviet arms. In September, it was incorporated into the **Popular Army.**

FILESA. The Filesa scandal hit the government of the **Partido Socialista Obrero Español** (PSOE) at the end of 1992, when the judge Merino Barbiero ordered a search of the party's offices in Madrid. It was subsequently revealed that the Filesa holding company, which had been administered by senior PSOE officials, including the former party treasurer Carlos Navarro, had been used to secure illegal funding for the party. Between 1989 and 1991, illicit contributions to party funds totaling 1,000 million pesetas had been made through Filesa by both public and private corporations in return for fictitious consultancy work. In 1995, 35 people, including a number of PSOE officials, were brought to trial. Eight persons were finally found guilty by the Supreme Court in October 1997 and six were jailed (including two Socialist politicians). It was the first major **corruption** scandal to hit the party. This and subsequent revelations involving nepotism and the embezzlement of public funds were seriously to undermine the party's credibility between 1992 and 1996.

FIRST REPUBLIC. The First Republic was proclaimed on 11 February 1873 after the abdication of **King Amadeo I**. It was not brought about through a pro-Republican revolution but was voted in by parliament, with the support of the monarchist **Partido Radical** for lack of a suitable royal candidate. At first, moreover, the regime was ruled by a coalition of the Partido Radical and the **Partido Republicano Federalista**. It was only after two attempted coups, in which leading Radical figures were involved, that the federal republicans took control. They held elections to a constituent **Cortes** in May and after their victory declared a federal republic on 8 June. On the same day, the leading federalist theoretician, **Francesc Pi i Margall**, took over as president. The **Cortes** then drew up and began to discuss a new federal constitution (though there would never be time for it to be promulgated) and the new government set about a thoroughgoing reform of the country's economic and social structures. Social legislation and agrarian reform were planned, along with a system of arbitration committees to settle industrial disputes. However, the new administration was beset by a whole host of problems. With the proclamation of the Republic, the Third **Carlist** War escalated, while in **Cuba** the insurrectionaries continued to struggle for independence. Furthermore, the organized **labor movement**—which before 1870 had been strongly attached to the republicans—was now led by **anarchists**, and so did not fully support the government. And as strikes and political agitation mounted during 1873, social tensions deepened, leading social elites and the more conservative middle classes—including many who had originally supported the **Glorious Revolution** of 1868—to look to the restoration of law and order under the **Bourbon monarchy**.

The republicans were also greatly weakened by divisions within their own camp. More conservative "unitarian republicans" such as **Nicolás Salmerón** and **Emilio Castelar** wished to maintain a significant degree of central control. "Benevolent" federal republicans, like Pi i Margall, sought a federalist decentralization of the state, but wanted it to be carried out in an orderly fashion. Finally, the leftist "intransigents" pushed for the masses to take matters into their own hands and construct the federal Republic from below. These tensions came to a head in July when, disillusioned with the slow pace of reform, the intransigents rose up in the south and Mediterranean to form their own revolutionary local administrations.

The so-called **Cantonalist revolt** seriously weakened the Republic. Pi i Margall, unable to control the situation, was forced from office and replaced by more right-wing administrations, first under Nicolás Salmerón from 18 July, and then under Emilio Castelar from 7 September. Both used military force to crush the cantons, and Castelar suspended the Cortes in order to forestall opposition. As a result, not only had they turned against a part of their own base, but they had also empowered a number of generals, who were already conspiring against the Republic. Matters came to a head when the parliament was reconvened on 2 February 1874. On the following day, Castelar fell and it seemed a new federal republican government would come to power. To forestall such a possibility, on the same day General Manuel Pavia (1827–1895) used local **Civil Guard** units to violently dissolve the Cortes, thereby paving the way for more authoritarian rule. The Republic limped on for several months under the heavy-handed rule of General Francisco Serrano, but a further *pronunciamiento* by General Martínez Campos (1831–1900) on 29 December ensured the restoration of the Bourbon monarchy.

FLAGS OF SPAIN. The Spanish national flag—comprising three horizontal strips, the two outer strips red and the inner strip yellow—originated in a competition in 1785 to design a flag for the Spanish fleet. In 1843, it was then adopted as the national flag. Over the years, the coat of arms has changed on several occasions. The present design was adopted in 1981. Because the flag became associated with the **Bourbon** monarchy, after the overthrow of the **First Republic**, **republicans** began searching for alternatives. They increasingly adopted the tricolor (with red, yellow, and indigo bands), which became the national flag during the **Second Republic**. These colors had previously been used by the popular **National Militia**.

The flags flown by the various autonomous communities generally have their origin in the "peripheral **nationalist**" movements that developed from the late 19th century. Many **Catalanists** adopted the flag of the **Crown of Aragón**, the four horizontal stripes on a yellow background (the *senyera*). It became the official flag of the Catalan autonomous government during the Second Republic and was immediately readopted after the death of General **Francisco Franco**. It was also taken up, with variants, by the autonomous communities of **Valencia**, Aragón, and the Balearic Islands. There is also a separatist Catalan flag (often on display at **Barcelona FC** football matches), which comprises the *senyera* with a blue hoist triangle that has a star in it. It was designed in 1904 by Catalan nationalists who were inspired by the new **Cuban** flag. It was adopted by Estat Català in 1918 and, in 1930, by **Esquerra Republicana de Catalunya**.

The father of Basque nationalism, **Sabino Arana**, was behind the unusual design for the **Basque** flag (the *Ikurriña*), which was inspired by the Unión Jack. Similarly, the green and white **Andalusian** flag was adopted by the Blas Infante's nationalist movement in 1918, based on what they saw as the principal colors of the **Moorish** Al-Ándalus kingdom. On the other hand, the Galician flag (a blue diagonal stripe on a white background) was originally the maritime flag of the city of A Coruña. It was taken by immigrants traveling to **Latin America** to be the flag of **Galicia**.

FOMENT DEL TREBALL NACIONAL (FTN)/DEVELOPMENT OF NATIONAL LABOR. The FTN was set up in 1889 to defend the interests of the Catalan industrial bourgeoisie. Its policy was to staunchly support economic protectionism for Catalan **industry**, and it played a significant role in the establishment of higher **tariffs** in 1891 and again in 1906. It also championed schemes such as a duty-free port (*puerto franco*) for **Barcelona** and the concession of tax collecting powers for **Catalonia** (the *concierto económico*). Politically, from the turn of the century it was close to the **Lliga Regionalista**. Its mouthpiece, *El Trabajo Nacional*, also quickly established itself as the principal economics journal in the country. With the rise of labor agitation and the anarchist-inspired **Confederación Nacional del Trabajo**, from 1917 it moved in an authoritarian direction, supporting the coup by General **Miguel Primo de Rivera** in September 1923 and the **Nationalists** during the **Spanish Civil War**. With the Nationalist victory it was integrated into the **Organización Sindical Española** (OSE), but maintained its own patrimony. This allowed it to play a key role in the reorganization of Spanish industrial interests during the **transition to democracy**. It participated in the foundation of a new countrywide confederation of industrialists in 1977, the **Confederación Española de Organizaciones Empresariales**, and was thereafter to be one of its most dynamic component parts.

FOOTBALL. *See* BARCELONA FC; REAL MADRID FC.

FOREIGN POLICY. During the reign of the **Catholic Monarchs** at the end of the 15th century, key elements of Spanish foreign policy were the need to check French power and curtail the expansion of the Ottoman Empire in the Mediterranean. These were adopted by Spain's **Habsburg** rulers during the 16th and 17th centuries, but a central new element also became the attempt to maintain the European Habsburg Empire intact. The combined result of these factors was continued Spanish involvement in warfare in northern and central Europe. In the 18th century, the new **Bourbon** rulers laid more emphasis on the need for peace and stability in order to promote economic growth, but, following the **French Revolution**, the country became embroiled in the wars between France and Great Britain, losing much of its fleet at **Trafalgar** in 1805. Subsequently, during the second half of the 19th century, believing Spain was too weak to intervene forcefully in European politics, governments pursued a policy of neutrality.

This was only to change in the 1930s and 1940s, during which the ideologies of liberalism, Communism, and right-wing authoritarianism and Fascism battled for supremacy on the European stage. During **World War II**, General **Francisco Franco** was tempted to enter on the side of the Axis, but, with little encouragement from Adolf Hitler and increasingly fearful of an Allied victory, he finally sat on the sidelines. This did not stop the **Franco regime** from being isolated by the West after the war, as it was seen as a relic of Europe's Fascist past. Over the next four decades, the regime adopted an anti-Western rhetoric. This was in consonance with its right-wing Spanish **nationalist** outlook. It viewed the United States and Britain as aggressive imperialist states that had undermined Spain's position as a world power (in the latter case, this sentiment was exacerbated by British possession of **Gibraltar**), and it also rejected what it saw as the decadent principles of liberalism and democracy (which it, above all, associated with France). Nevertheless, rather contradictorily, given its economic weakness and diplomatic isolation, the regime had to seek reintegration in the Western fold. This was above all symbolized by the military bases agreement with the United States in 1953, through which in exchange for nuclear bases on Spanish soil, the latter provided Spain with loans and made possible its entry into the United Nations and the Western economic organizations. At the same time, in 1962 the regime formally applied to join the **European Economic Community** (EEC). Because Spain was not a democracy this approach was rebuffed, though in 1970 it was given favored nation status.

Following the **transition to democracy**, between 1975 and 1978 Spanish governments tried fully to integrate into the Western sphere. Spain above all pursued entry into the EEC, which was finally achieved in 1986. The government of the **Unión del Centro Democrático** had also taken Spain into the **North Atlantic Treaty Organization** (NATO) in 1981. This elicited significant opposition (given the United States' tacit support for the Franco regime), but, after the ruling **Partido Socialista Obrero Español** (PSOE) was won around to the benefits, membership was ratified in a referendum in 1985 (with the rider that Spain would not form part of NATO's military structure). Between 1986 and 1996, PSOE governments were close to the "Franco-German axis," supported the policy of further European integration, and were enthusiastically in favor of a single European Union (EU) currency. This position was backed by the majority of the population, who identified western Europe with democracy and prosperity. This attitude was reinforced because Spain profited handsomely from European structural funds. At the same time, **Felipe González** championed the social-democratic vision of a "social Europe" and attempted to develop closer ties between the EU and the Arab states on the southern rim of the Mediterranean. Finally, the PSOE followed the traditional policy of forging cultural and economic ties with **Latin America**, setting up the Ibero-American Community of Nations in 1991 (which included **Portugal** and Brazil). The members have since held periodic summits.

As Spain grew wealthier and more confident in the 1990s, its foreign policy also became more interventionist. This was manifested during the breakup of **Yugoslavia** between 1992 and 1996, when the government agreed to the deployment of Spanish troops in Bosnia under both United Nations (UN) and NATO mandates, and when, during 1995, Spanish planes were involved in the bombing of Serbia.

Interventionism grew under the new **Partido Popular** (PP) governments between 1996 and 2004, in keeping with Prime Minister **José María Aznar**'s vision of a resurgent Spain playing a larger role on the world stage. Under these governments, more emphasis was laid on national interests over European integration and on the need for liberal economic reforms in order to make the EU more competitive in world markets. Furthermore, the new government also adopted a decidedly more Atlanticist foreign policy. Hence, the Spanish **military** participated in NATO operations against Serbia during 1999, and Aznar strongly backed the American-led invasions of **Afghanistan** and **Iraq**. This latter stance broke the political consensus that had existed in Spain since the transition, which emphasized the centrality of the UN in the elaboration of foreign policy, the need for EU unity in matters of security and foreign policy, and the necessity to maintain good relations with the Arab world. In the aftermath of the American intervention, the EU split into two camps, with Spain receiving the support of the British government of Tony Blair and the Italian government of Silvio Berlusconi. The war was hugely unpopular in Spain and Aznar's stance played a significant role in the PP's defeat in the March 2004 general elections.

Following the PSOE's victory in these general elections, **José Luis Rodríguez Zapatero** reverted to Socialist policy of the 1990s. He affirmed that it was his aim to "return Spain to the heart of Europe." Most dramatically, he abandoned Aznar's Atlanticist stance and ordered an immediate withdrawal of Spanish forces from Iraq (though perhaps in part to compensate for this he ratified an increase in troop numbers in Afghanistan). Tensions between Madrid and Washington were also exacerbated by the new government's more conciliatory position toward **Cuba** and by its decision, in 2005, to proceed with a large arms deal involving the sale of transport planes and patrol boats to Hugo Chávez's Venezuela (with the United States refusing to give an export license for the exports of components manufactured in the United States). In addition, Rodríguez Zapatero reasserted the 1990s Socialist policy of seeking collaboration with the North African Arab states, calling for an "alliance of civilizations" against fundamentalist

terrorism. However, the PSOE government maintained the country's higher international profile. Following the Lebanon war, in the summer of 2006, Spain agreed to send in peacekeeping troops under the auspices of the UN. The election of the conservative and more pro-American figures of Angela Merkel as German chancellor in November 2005 and Nicolas Sarkozy as French president in May 2007 has left Rodríguez Zapatero more isolated within the EU than when he first came to power. Spain opposed the decision by the United States and the other major EU states to recognize the independence of Kosovo in February 2008 (one suspects because of Spain's own "national problem"). Nevertheless, Spain has agreed that it should become a "European protectorate" and will maintain its military presence. *See also* FOREIGN TRADE.

FOREIGN TRADE. In the 19th and early 20th centuries, compared to its European neighbors, Spain had a relatively closed economy. The uneven nature of Spain's economic development and the fact that much of its **industry** found it difficult to compete with that of the major Western powers also meant that it exported few manufactures while, especially from the 1890s onward, high **tariffs** were put in place in order to limit foreign competition. This pattern only began to change during **World War I**, when Spanish manufacturers were able to introduce their products into markets vacated by the warring powers, but these markets were to a large extent lost after the war. Despite heavy tariff protection, Spanish manufacturers also found it difficult to compete with foreign imports in some more high-tech areas such as machine building. The overall trading relationship was, as a result, one in which Spain imported manufactures and exported primary products, most notably minerals and **agricultural** produce. The trade deficit was in part made up for by foreign direct investment by **mining** companies in Spanish mineral resources.

The Spanish economy became even more closed during the 1940s, when the **Franco regime** adopted the policy of **autarky**. Matters were dramatically to change with the economic liberalization of the 1950s. After the 1959 **Stabilization Plan** in particular, foreign companies from the United States and western Europe began to invest, especially in Spanish heavy industry, transport equipment, and motor vehicles. At the same time, inward capital flows, revenue from **tourism**, remittances from Spaniards working abroad, and loans from the international banking system made it possible for Spain to import the capital goods needed to stimulate economic development. In the 1960s, these factors, combined with export subsidies, would, at last, lead to a rapid growth in the export of manufactures, further stimulated by the 1970 Luxemburg Accord with the **European Economic Community** (EEC). On the other hand, the oil price hikes of the 1970s produced the problem of recurrent balance of payments deficits.

Spain's trading relations entered a new phase after the country joined the EEC in 1986, leading Spain to become further integrated into the European market. By 2000, the **European Union** (EU) would account for 70.6 percent of the total value of Spanish exports and 63.1 percent of the total value of imports. Direct investment—now also dominated by EU countries—grew apace, and was now to a greater extent directed at more technological advanced sectors of the economy. This, along with the Spanish devaluation of the peseta in the early 1990s and some rationalization of Spanish companies, further boosted Spanish manufacturing exports (along with exports of horticultural produce). At the same time, however, the dismantling of trade barriers and growing consumer spending meant that the country failed in increasing manufactured imports, thereby perpetuating the problem of balance of payments deficits. Spain's major exporters were largely Spanish subsidiaries of foreign companies, with automobile manufacturers of particular importance. In the 1990s, with the **privatization** and liberalization of the public sector (most notably petrochemicals, power generation, and public utilities) and the **banking** system, Spain also began for the first time to produce a number of major homegrown companies that invested abroad—especially in **Latin American** markets—to a significant degree. Since 2000, these firms have also begun investing more heavily in western Europe. Overall, the foreign trade contribution to gross domestic product has grown from an average of 18 percent between 1970 and 1979 to 43 percent in 1997.

FORO DE ERMUA. *See* BASQUE COUNTRY; BASTA YA.

FRAGA IBARNE, MANUEL (1922–). Manuel Fraga was one of the key figures in Spanish politics in the second half of the 20th century.

During the second half of the **Franco regime**, he was probably the leading *aperturista*, seeking to save the essentials of Francoism through partial liberalization. Then, after the regime's demise, he captained a group of former Francoists who tried to build a new right-wing coalition that, it was hoped, would sustain them in power.

Fraga was born in the Galician province of Lugo on 23 November 1922. He soon showed himself academically extremely able, obtaining the post of professor of law at the University of **Valencia** at the age of 26. At the same time, he rose rapidly through the ranks of the regime's single party, the **Falange Española Tradicionalista y de las Juntas de Ofensiva Nacional Sindicalista** (FET y de las JONS, or **Movimiento Nacional**, as it was referred to from May 1958). During the 1950s, he worked in the Ministry of Education under **Joaquín Ruiz-Giménez** until the latter's fall from grace in 1956. In 1957, **José Solís** then appointed him national associations' delegate, an important position. It was, therefore, no surprise when in the July 1962 cabinet reshuffle he became the new minister of information and tourism. This appointment reflected the regime's willingness to permit a degree of cultural liberalization. Fraga had already established a reputation on the liberal wing of the Movimiento, and in the 1960s he became closely identified with the easing of social and cultural controls and with attempts to reform the Movimiento through the formation of political associations within its boundaries. His most long-lasting reform was the **press** law of 1966, which removed prior censorship. This earned Fraga the hostility of *continuistas* within the regime, and particularly of General Franco's right-hand man, **Luis Carrero Blanco**, who took advantage of the **Matesa scandal** to have Fraga and other reformers removed from government in December 1969.

Fraga was not to return to government until after the death of Franco in November 1975. He was appointed as minister of the interior in the new government of **Carlos Arias Navarro** of December that year. This was meant to give the administration a new reforming image. Over the next few months Fraga continued work on the associations' project, but his reputation was sullied by his energetic efforts to maintain order in the face of growing protest (particularly as a result of the death of five workers at the hands of the police in Vitoria in March). Finally, when King **Juan Carlos I** decided in July that the pace of reform needed to be speeded up, he passed over Fraga and chose a younger man to take over from Arias Navarro, **Adolfo Suárez**. Fraga was apparently hurt by this decision and refused to serve in the new Suárez administration. But it was probably a wise move on the part of the king, for Fraga was too strongly identified with Francoism to be able to push through a swift **transition to democracy**.

Once it became clear that the structures of Francoism were being dismantled and that democratic elections were to be held in 1977, in September 1976, Fraga, along with a number of leading former Francoists outside the Suárez government, formed a coalition known as **Alianza Popular** (AP). Fraga apparently hoped that the coalition would be able to win the forthcoming elections. He was to be sorely disappointed. Suárez's own alliance, the **Unión del Centro Democrático** (UCD), triumphed, while AP trailed in fourth position with only 8 percent of the vote. The main problem was that, unlike the UCD, AP had not cast off its Francoist aura. Matters were not helped by the image of Fraga himself, for while no one doubted his ability, he was seen as authoritarian and irascible, and while he argued that AP was a neoliberal party forged in the image of the western European right, his identification with clerical and family values fitted ill with the growing secularization and cultural liberalization of Spanish society. Fraga attracted strong personal loyalty, but this was circumscribed to people on the right of the political spectrum who often harbored a certain nostalgia for the Franco years. The attitude of electors who considered themselves on the left and in the center was, on the contrary, hostile.

For this reason, although AP was able to take advantage of the crisis of the UCD to become the country's second largest party from October 1982, under Fraga's leadership it could not seriously challenge the new government of the **Partido Socialista Obrero Español** (PSOE). This finally forced Fraga's resignation in December 1986. He remained within the party but returned to his native **Galicia**, where he worked to rejuvenate the regional party, which in 1987 had lost the presidency of the Galician autonomous parliament or Xunta. In 1989, he briefly returned to the presidency of the PP and oversaw the rise of **José María Aznar**, but he was to subsequently make a highly successful return to the Galician political stage: in 1989, the PP won an overall majority in the elections to the Xunta, and Fraga was subsequently elected president. This victory was repeated in the 1993, 1997, and 2001 autonomous elections. In order to ward off the threat of conservative Galician **nationalism**, under Fraga's leadership the Galician **Partido Popular** (AP's successor party) has become much more open to the Galician language and receptive toward manifestations of Galician cultural traditions. At the same time, it has obtained a high degree of autonomy vis-à-vis the national party. However, the tide began to turn in 2003 when the PP lost its overall majority and its political rivals formed a coalition government. Fraga finally stepped down as leader of the Galician PP in January 2006, taking a seat in the Senate.

FRANCO BAHAMONDE, FRANCISCO (1892–1975). Francisco Franco was made head of the **Nationalist** side in the **Spanish Civil War**, and then, following the Nationalists' victory in March 1939, became dictator of Spain until his death on 20 November 1975. He was born into a military family in the **Galician** town of El Ferrol on 4 December 1892. He grew up very close to his mother, Pilar, a woman of traditional **Catholic** views, and entered the Toledo Infantry Academy at the age of 14. Franco's early career was not a great success. He graduated 215th out of a class of 312. However, he finally got a posting in the Moroccan army in 1912 (the only means of rapid promotion in the Spanish army), and from that date his rise through the ranks was meteoric.

In **Morocco**, Franco showed himself to be both hardworking and courageous in combat. After being seriously wounded in June 1916, he became the country's youngest commanding officer. Between 1917 and 1920, he was put in charge an infantry regiment in Oviedo. It was there that he met his future wife, Carmen Polo y Martínez Valdés (1902–1987), who belonged to a conventional upper-middle-class Asturian family. But he was then once again sent to Morocco to help organize the **Legión Española**; he became its commander in 1923. He played an important part in the Army of Africa's victory over the Riff tribesmen and in recompense, he was made Europe's youngest serving general. These years were to be of great formative impact for Franco. It was here that he imbibed the values of order, hierarchy, and discipline. It was also in the Moroccan campaigns that he came face to face with the savagery of warfare. For Franco, as for other officers, this debased the value of human life and made him believe that all conflicts could be solved through the extermination of the enemy. This helps explain why, during the Spanish Civil War and first years of the **Franco regime**, the Nationalists would use brutal repression and terror to intimidate the opposition. It was also, it seems, in his dealings with local chiefs that Franco learned the skill—so useful in later life—of playing people off against each other.

Franco married in 1923 and, during a stay in **Madrid** between 1925 and 1927, began to mix in upper-class society. Like most officers of his generation he was intensely patriotic. After being made a gentleman in waiting to the crown (*gentilhombre de la cámara de la Corona*) on the occasion of his wedding in 1923, he identified closely with the monarchy and also sympathized with the **Primo de Rivera dictatorship**. He was rewarded by being appointed the first director of the General Military Academy in Zaragoza in 1928. Not surprisingly, given his background, Franco initially viewed the proclamation of the **Second Republic** with alarm, though he was prudent enough not to become involved in any military conspiracies. During the so-called **Bienio Reformista**, he was kept away from Madrid, but following the victory of the right in the November 1933 elections he took center stage. In October 1934, he was made a technical assistant at the Ministry of War, from where he coordinated the repression of the **October 1934 revolution** in Asturias. Then, in 1935, the new minister of war, **José María Gil-Robles**, made him chief of the General Staff (jefe del Estado Mayor del Ejército).

After the **Popular Front** victory, the new republican government moved leading military figures suspected of being hostile to the Republic out of sensitive posts. Franco was made commander of the garrison on the Canary Islands. It was from this time that the military began seriously to conspire. Franco again adopted a cautious stance. It was agreed that he should take command of the elite Moroccan troops, but he did not definitively join the conspiracy until the assassination of the leader of the rightist opposition, **José Calvo Sotelo**, on 13 July. However, once the attempted coup had become a civil war, he was in a strong position to lead the right-wing or Nationalist forces. He commanded the finest troops, was the best known military figure outside the country, and outranked the organizer of the conspiracy, **Emilio Mola**. During August and September 1936, influential friends strongly pushed his case. These included the high-ranking generals Alfredo Kindelán (1879–1962) and Luis Orgaz (1881–1946), along with the field commander of the southern army, Colonel **Juan Yagüe**. Moreover, in a war situation many military figures believed that a single commander was needed. Franco became a member of the military command of the Burgos National Defense Junta, set up by Mola, on 3 August. Then, in a meeting held near Salamanca on 21 September, the Defense Junta agreed that Franco should be made commander in chief (comandante en jefe militar) or Generalísimo. Franco and his entourage were, however, still dissatisfied, and managed to get a new meeting called for 28 September, at which Franco became the head of government (and in press releases was immediately referred to as head of state). His preferred title soon became that of Caudillo, a classic **Castilian** term for leader that dated from the Middle Ages.

Franco was to remain in power until his death on 20 November 1975. His political ideology was never very sophisticated. He had a number of *idées fixes*, chief among which were his hatred of liberalism, freemasonry, and communism and his support for the military values of discipline and hierarchy. In his Manichean worldview, the eternal, traditionalist, Catholic Spain was engaged in a life-and-death struggle against its liberal and Bolshevik enemies both at home and abroad. Nevertheless, within these parameters Franco was politically flexible in order to remain in power. He admired the Fascist regimes of Germany and Italy, hoped they would win **World War II**, and was, during 1940, disposed to go to war on their side if the conditions were right. Nevertheless, despite his distaste for the liberal democracies, once the war had turned against the Axis, during 1943–1944 he adopted a more neutral stance in order to forestall Spain's isolation in the postwar world. Later, with the onset of the Cold War, he played up the regime's anticommunist rhetoric and emphasized its Catholic values in order to try to get Spain readmitted into the Western fold. Franco was also to prove a shrewd judge of character, and was adept at playing off individuals and groups in order to safeguard his own position. Typically, until 1965, his cabinets were balancing acts in which all the various regime "families" (the Catholic Church, the

Falange Española Tradicionalista y de la Juntas de Ofensiva Nacional Sindicalista, and the military) were included. During the 1940s and early 1950s, Franco remained at the center of government. As time passed, however, he took more of a back seat, relying in particular on his most trusted political collaborator, **Luis Carrero Blanco**, to keep him informed. He also became more isolated from the outside world, and restricted his contacts to relatives and a small group of family friends, who only told him what he wanted to hear. He read very little, dedicating himself wholeheartedly to his great passions of hunting and fishing, though hunting trips could also be important political occasions. Nevertheless, all important government decisions had to pass through the Caudillo, and invariably he set his face against major reform. Franco was reluctant to accept the economic liberalization plan of the later 1950s, but was finally convinced of its need by Carrero Blanco and by the minister of finance, Mariano Rubio (1913–1998). Later, in the 1960s, he worried that **Manuel Fraga's press** reforms had gone too far, and ensured that hard-liners were appointed to the Ministry of the Interior. Right up to his death in 1975 he still hoped that his system of government would be preserved under his successor, **Juan Carlos**. Hence, during 1974, under the influence of his reactionary family entourage, he was to ensure that the relatively liberal minister of information, Pío Cabanillas (1923–1991), was dismissed and he blocked any significant political reform within the boundaries of the regime. In any case, by this time, the level of internal opposition and the international context meant that only a full democratization of political life could ensure political stability. As a result, within a year of his death, the regime he had built had totally unraveled.

FRANCO REGIME. The Franco regime lasted from 1939 to 1975. As the name suggests, it was a personal dictatorship of General **Francisco Franco**. The regime grew out of the institutions put in place by the **Nationalists** during the **Spanish Civil War** of 1936–1939. The Nationalist camp was composed of several socioeconomic and political forces. At a social level, it was supported by social elites, much of the middle class, and the conservative Catholic peasantry of northern and central Spain. Institutionally, it received the backing of much of the **military**, the **Catholic Church**, and the various right-wing political parties, the most influential of which were the **Alfonsoist monarchists** of Renovación Española (Spanish Renovation), **Falange Española**, and the **Carlists**. All these groups would benefit from the Nationalist victory, and, indeed, in order to maintain personal loyalty, Franco had no qualms in allowing his supporters to enrich themselves through access to the institutions of the state. In this sense, the Francoist period saw an intensification of the traditional role of the Spanish state as a fount for favor and patronage. The groups that supported Franco did not see eye to eye on all matters. Nevertheless, they had several key elements in common. First, they were antiliberal and wished to put in place **corporatist** governmental structures. Second, they were all (with the partial exception of some radical Falangists) strongly Catholic. This was reflected in Nationalist imagery, which sought inspiration for a revival of Spain's national fortunes in the "**Reconquest**" of Spain from the **Moors** from the 10th through to the 15th centuries and in the imperial expansion that followed in the 16th century. Third, they shared an exclusivist, visceral, Spanish **nationalist** ideology. Their image of Spain was strongly based on the **Castilian** ("Spanish") language and Castilian-**Andalusian** identity, and they were, as a result, determined to centralize government from **Madrid** and stamp out the **Catalan** and **Basque** languages.

The regime slowly took institutional shape between 1938 and 1945. On 28 January 1938, Franco's personal dictatorship was confirmed. Two days later, he appointed his first cabinet. Throughout the regime, it was this body that would take the key decisions. Franco used his power of appointment within the cabinet to balance and play off what were soon to be known as the regime's various "families" (the most important being the military, Church, and Falange). At the same time, Franco and his advisors believed that they needed a mass base for the regime in order to mobilize and regiment opinion. The only parties that could fulfill this task in the Nationalist zone were the Falange Española and the Carlists. At the suggestion of Franco's chief advisor, **Ramón Serrano Suñer**, on 17 April 1937, Franco decreed their amalgamation under his leadership. Henceforth the **Falange Española Tradicionalista y de las Juntas de Ofensiva Nacional Sindicalista** (FET y de las JONS)—often still referred to as Falange—would be the only legal party under the regime. In the early years in particular, it played a key role in the Francoist state, administering the regime's **autarkic** economic policies, and, through the "vertical union" the **Organización Sindical Española** (OSE), the women's organization **Sección Feminina**, the Frente de Juventud (Youth Front), and the **Sindicato Español Universitario** (SEU), reaching into most aspects of people's lives.

After the outbreak of **World War II**, Franco was close to the Axis powers and in the summer of 1940 came close to entering the war on their side. Only from the autumn of 1942, as the war shifted in the Allies' favor, did the regime start to distance itself. Given the major role of the single party and the links between the regime to the Axis, the years 1939–1942 have often been referred to as representing the "fascistic" or "semi-Fascist" phase of Francoism. During these years, Franco himself took on many of the trappings of a Fascist dictator, his face appeared on numerous giant billboards, and he was ecstatically received at rallies to the cry of *"Caudillo, Caudillo!"* Nevertheless, unlike the cases of Germany and Italy, Franco was not the historic leader of the country's Fascist party. Rather, he was a military man and his attachment to Fascist ideals would be both superficial and subject to modification. Furthermore, Franco always had to balance the demands of the FET y de las JONS against those of the other regime "families." Many army leaders were upper-class authoritarian conservatives, who despised the populist demagoguery of the FET y de las JONS. And neither the army nor Church wished to see interference by the single party in their spheres of influence. This should not, however, detract from the fact that the Franco regime was a brutal right-wing dictatorship, which imposed itself on Spain through a reign of terror. Heavy repression continued well into the 1940s, with up to 100,000 Republican sympathizers executed between 1939 and 1945.

Franco faced probably the most serious challenge to his rule during 1943. As the power of the Axis declined, powerful promonarchist generals like Alfredo Kindelán (1879–1962) and Antonio Aranda (1888–1979), backed up by much of the social elite (believing that Franco was too compromised because of his support for Germany), pushed for his replacement by the **Bourbon** heir to the throne, **Juan de Borbón y Battenberg** and for the FET y de las JONS to be dismantled. Franco was able to ride out the storm. Nevertheless, in order to placate the Allies and still disquiet within the regime, the role of the single party was played down and the regime's Catholic credentials emphasized. This was reflected in the appointment of the leading Catholic member of the **Asociación Católica Nacional de Propagandistas**, **Alberto Martín Artajo**, as foreign minister in 1945, a post he was to occupy for 12 years.

From 1945, the regime was dubbed **National Catholic** and the FET y de la JONS was referred to as the **Movimiento Nacional** from May 1958 in order to hide its semi-Fascist origins. Moreover, to draw the fire of Western criticism and allay the fears of promonarchists within the regime, between 1945 and 1947 Franco gave the regime a constitutional facade. A Francoist parliament or **Cortes** had operated since 1942, but suffrage was corporative and it was in reality subordinate to Franco's person. The Fuero de los Españoles, a bill of rights, was proclaimed on 17 July 1945. It was meant to guarantee many of the civil rights enjoyed by the citizens of liberal-democratic societies, but political parties remained illegal and political dissidents were still tried and sentenced by the army. The following year, the Law of National Referendum, which allowed for new legislation to be ratified by referendum, was approved by the Cortes. It was followed by the Law of Succession in 1947. It proclaimed the regime to be a monarchy, but Franco appointed himself as regent, with the power to decide when and how the future monarch would be installed. At the same time, a Regency Council and Council of the Realm were created, to oversee the transition to a monarchy in the case of the death or incapacitation of Franco and assist the head of state during the period of transition respectively. The Law of Succession, Constitutive Law of the Cortes, and the Fuero de los Españoles were declared Spain's "fundamental laws," along with the 1939 Labor Charter, which had announced the regime's intention to set up a single "vertical union," the OSE. In the following years, Franco would claim that Spain was an "organic democracy," in which it was the major corporate interests within Spanish society, rather than the selfish individual, which determined the direction of policy.

The fact that Franco had never been immersed in Fascist culture probably meant that he found it easier to act in a flexible manner, reshaping the regime as the circumstances required. Nevertheless, though the FET y de las JONS was downplayed, for Franco there was never any question of its disappearance. He knew that with the annihilation of the more "authentic" Fascist regimes, Falangists were dependent for their power and privileges on the survival of Francoism and that they would provide a bulwark against any attempts at his replacement. Until the 1960s, the essential components of the regime were, therefore, the Falangist bureaucracy, which was entrenched within the administration; the Catholic Church, which monopolized **education** and was fully integrated into the regime's political structures; and the army, whose essential function was to guard over the regime it had done so much to create.

Despite Franco's overtures to the West, in 1945 the regime found itself isolated from the international community, being excluded from the United Nations (UN) and all Western economic and political institutions. This isolation, however, soon began to weaken. The key to Spain's changing international status was the onset of the Cold War. As a result, the United States began to look with increasing sympathy upon a country whose regime maintained a virulently anticommunist rhetoric and whose territory was of vital strategic importance. The upshot was that in return for the acceptance of American military bases on Spanish soil, Spain was to a large extent readmitted into the Western camp. The key landmarks along this road were the military pacts with the United States in 1953 and admittance into the United Nations in 1955. Moreover, the Law of Succession and the increasing unlikelihood of an Allied intervention allowed Franco to a large extent to neutralize discontent of monarchists close to the regime. A key moment in this respect was the meeting between Franco and Juan de Borbón on 25 August 1948. Here, it was agreed that the pretender's son, **Juan Carlos**, should be educated in Spain. The unspoken understanding was that as long as Juan Carlos adhered to the principles of the regime, he could expect to take over from Franco. Thereafter, those monarchists who were loyal to Franco were given positions of influence, while the regime felt strong enough to treat those who remained discontented with kid gloves, allowing them to operate as a semi-tolerated opposition from the 1950s.

By the mid-1950s, the international position of the regime was stronger than at any time since victory in the civil war. Internally, however, the picture was less rosy. The policy of autarky had proved a complete disaster. The 1940s were known as the "hunger years," with bread-line wages and heavy unemployment generating severe under-lying social tensions. Most dramatically, in **Barcelona** in March 1951, the rising cost of public transport sparked off a boycott of the tram network. There followed strikes in Vizcaya and **Navarre** that spring. The shock of this unrest together, it seems, with pressure from the United States for Spain to open up to world markets, produced a slow easing of autarkic controls. Following a cabinet reshuffle on 18 July 1951, somewhat more liberal figures were appointed to the economics and finance ministries. Furthermore, in what seemed a sop to Western opinion, the moderate Catholic, **Joaquín Ruiz-Giménez**, was appointed minister of education. This seemed to presage a loosening of controls in the political field. American aid, together with growing integration into world markets, allowed improvements in agricultural productivity and rapid industrial growth. Yet Spain found itself caught between two schools. A powerful Falangist lobby wished to maintain the essentials of the social and political system intact and campaigned vigorously against further change. Serious inflationary pressures resulting from the lack of competition in **industry**, coupled with heavy government and balance of payments deficits, an uncontrolled credit boom, followed. More farsighted elements within the regime saw that only further economic liberalization could ensure economic prosperity. They included reformers like **Manuel Fraga**. More important in the short run was a lay association within the Church called **Opus Dei**, which was closely associated with business interests. Its members were fiercely anticommunist, but combined support for authoritarian political structures with a belief in free(er) market capitalism. At the height of the Cold War this made them attractive to U.S. administrations. Within the Francoist elite they also had powerful friends. Most significantly, they enjoyed the sympathy of Franco's right-hand man, **Luis Carrero Blanco**.

The pressure to reform was intensified by both growing social unrest and economic crisis. The spring of 1956 saw a wave of strikes in the Basque Country and Catalonia, combined with growing student protest. Franco, alarmed, decided to crack down. In a cabinet reshuffle, Joaquín Ruiz-Giménez was sacked, along with a number of reformers in junior posts within government. This indicated that Franco had no desire for serious political reform. At first, it seems, he wanted to turn the clock back and give the single party a greater role in state policy. This, however, came up against strong Church and army opposition. Finally he was convinced by Carrero Blanco that further economic reform was unavoidable. The result was the key cabinet reshuffle of February 1957. Franco wanted to make sure a tight rein was maintained on public order. Hence, General Camilo Alonso Vega (1889–1971), a renowned hard-liner who had commanded the **Civil Guard** in the counterinsurgency war against the *maquis* in the 1940s, was named minister of the interior. However, the appointments to the economic and finance ministries reflected the clear aim of liberalizing **economic policy**. The year 1957 saw something approaching a total Opus Dei takeover of the regime's economic policy. Though not yet given a cabinet post, **Laureano López Rodó** would emerge as the most influential Opus technocrat. Closer ties were developed with the international financial community. Meanwhile, the FET y de las JONS was further downgraded. In the reshuffle, the Falangist veteran **José Antonio Girón** was replaced as minister of labor after 12 years in the post, and, in 1958, the party was renamed the Movimiento Nacional and its 26 points were substituted by a Catholic-traditionalist set of goals.

Opus Dei policy was at first somewhat confused. Franco was suspicious of all forms of liberalism and suspected that liberalization in the economic sphere would lead to cultural and political liberalization. However, the deteriorating economic situation—most dramatically illustrated by the fact that Spain was running out of foreign currency—convinced the economics and finance ministers that drastic reform was necessary. Furthermore, the immediate success of the **European Economic Community** (EEC), formed during 1958, pointed the way to the benefits of further economic integration. Under pressure, Franco finally relented, making possible the famous **Stabilization Plan** of July 1959, which aimed notably to liberalize the Spanish **economy**. This was accompanied by the 1958 Law of Collective Agreements, which allowed workers to elect plant-level representatives to negotiate working conditions and wages within the parameters of the OSE. In line with the new administration's liberalizing policies, the goal was that wages should to a greater extent be determined by demand and supply rather than government decree. At the same time, it was hoped, bargaining would become fragmented, and that worker discontent would be aimed at the individual enterprise rather than the state.

The lifting of autarkic controls in the context of a generalized Western economic boom made possible Spain's rapid industrialization in the 1960s. Foreign companies began to invest heavily in Spain. Industrial growth was further stimulated by the massive influx of tourists and an outflow of underemployed peasants in search of employ in the prosperous West. **Tourism** income, the remittances of emigrants to their families, foreign investment, and further American loans allowed the government to run up an enormous balance of trade deficit to pay for the energy, raw materials, and capital goods Spain needed to industrialize. The result was that the face of the country was transformed in a decade. Gross domestic product grew at 7.4 percent per annum, faster than any other industrialized country with the exception of Japan. The country's industrial base both broadened and strengthened. Madrid, in particular, became a major industrial and financial center. The industrialization process also had profound consequences for Spanish **agriculture**. In the early years, the regime's rhetoric had held up the Castilian peasantry as the embodiment of Spanish virtues, but in the 1960s, with the dash for growth, this was all abandoned. Instead, peasants were encouraged to emigrate to the cities and abroad and large-scale mechanized agriculture was championed.

Rapid industrialization also had wide-ranging social consequences. In the first place, it was not accompanied by serious government planning. From the 1950s, shanty towns sprang up on the outskirts of the large conurbations. They were increasingly replaced by (often poorly constructed) blocks of flats in the 1960s, but they lacked basic facilities such as proper paving and adequate sewerage. This was paralleled by the uncontrolled building of hotels and other tourist facilities in many coastal areas, seriously damaging the environment. The root of the problem was the lack of democratic controls on the country's economic elite and the country's small, regressive tax base, which, combined with massive fraud, ensured that the state lacked the resources to significantly expand social provisions and provide adequate urban infrastructure.

Economic growth also had important cultural and political implications. While the country's conservative peasant heartlands emptied of **population**, more secular urban areas expanded rapidly. And growing contacts with the West and its consumerist, individualistic values further undermined Francoism's conservative Catholic code of ethics. Changing values were evident within the "new middle classes," urban managerial and professional groups, who quickly became enmeshed in Western styles of life and who therefore rejected the puritanical cultural norms of the Church hierarchy. Cultural renewal was most notable in the rapidly expanding university system, where Western music and freer social and sexual norms invaded the campuses.

The more foresighted members of the regime realized that these changes were irreversible and so devised new strategies of containment. During the 1960s, the purist *camisa vieja* (old shirt) Falangists were further marginalized, with Opus Dei technocrats and university-trained civil servants coming to dominate the rapidly expanding state administration. Leading *opus deístas* now argued that economic prosperity would lead to the depoliticization of society. This was reflected in a recasting of the regime's rhetoric in the 1960s. Rather than emphasizing its role as the guardian of eternal Spanish values, propaganda now depicted the regime's policies as economically efficient and tailored to provide for growth and prosperity, while avoiding the strife and division inherent in liberal democracies. This image was incompatible with the heavy, repressive atmosphere of the 1940s and 1950s. In the 1960s, therefore, the authorities slowly expanded the boundaries of the acceptable. The most important piece of legislation in this respect was the 1966 Press Law, pushed through by the reforming minister of information and tourism, Manuel Fraga. This removed prior **press** censorship, though an editor could still be fined or even imprisoned if he published material damaging to the state, religion, or accepted social norms. Although far from free, the press would, as a result, be able to expand rapidly in subsequent years. However, direct political criticism of the regime was not permitted and political activism was still dealt with extremely harshly. The overall message was that if one did not become involved in opposition politics (a foolish undertaking since the government's economic experts knew best), one could be assured economic well-being and a large measure of cultural freedom. The message struck a chord among many within the middle class, who became absorbed within the private sphere and sympathized little with those who pushed for a (possibly destabilizing) political transformation.

Yet the new equilibrium was always an unstable one. During the 1960s, as the atmosphere became less repressive, opposition mounted. In industry, an increasingly self-confident working class was unafraid to strike for improved wages and working conditions, and, from the late 1960s, for free trade unions and the end to all state repression. In the universities, student politics became dominated by various Marxist currents and protest escalated. In Catalonia and the Basque Country, demands for respect for the regional languages and cultural and political autonomy resurfaced. Indeed, the radicalization of the nationalist struggle in the Basque Country led to the foundation of the separatist group **ETA**, which from the late 1960s launched a **terrorist** campaign. Just as damaging, within the Church hierarchy voices were raised in favor of political reform. Finally, it was not at all clear that economic growth could be maintained within the confines of Francoism. Spain had already applied to join the EEC in 1962 but was turned down, and it was made clear that it could not expect to join until its political system was brought into line with those of the member states.

This led to divisions within the ranks of the Francoist elite. Many technocrats, led by Carrero Blanco, did not see the need for significant political reform. Instead, they wanted to dismantle the single party and move toward what they saw as a modern, efficient, authoritarian system, crowned—once Franco had died—by the installation of Juan Carlos as monarch. These men became known as *continuistas*. They were opposed by a group of reformers or *aperturistas*, who believed that if the regime were to survive, political change would be needed. The key figures, Manuel Fraga, **José Solís**, and **Fernando María Castiella**, aimed to revamp the regime through such schemes as political associations within the Movimiento Nacional in order to conserve its essential features.

However, proposed *aperturista* reforms fizzled out. The problem was that the *continuistas* had Franco's ear. Franco was not willing to dismantle the *Movimiento Nacional* as Carrero Blanco wished, but he agreed that the situation was getting out of control. Carrero Blanco's position was further reinforced in July 1968 when he was named to the newly created post of deputy prime minister. He was to use his position to strike a devastating blow against the reformers in the following year, taking advantage of the **Matesa scandal** to have Fraga, Solís, and Castiella removed from office. The decision to officially designate Juan Carlos as Franco's successor in 1969 was also seen as a victory for the Carrero Blanco camp. At the same time, the late 1960s saw something of a political reaction to combat what was viewed as the unacceptably high level of opposition. Between 1967 and 1968, the authorities moved hard against the newly created independent labor organization **Comisiones Obreras** (CC.OO), the Church hierarchy moved against dissidents in its ranks, and in the Basque Country, a crackdown followed the assassination of the head of the Guipúzcoa Political Police (Brigada Social) by ETA activists. Furthermore, a new decree reversed the move made five years earlier to reduce the jurisdiction of military courts over political offenders.

By 1970, the regime had, therefore, set itself against further reform. This was, over the next three years, to prove an untenable stance. The period between 1969 and 1973 was to see a further sustained escalation of labor agitation. Protest movements for political autonomy in Catalonia and the Basque Country also gathered pace. In Catalonia in 1971, both working- and middle-class opposition came together in the Assemblea de Catalunya (Catalan Assembly). The crisis of Church-state relations also continued to deepen. Franco had been pressured by the liberal-minded Pope John XXIII into appointing reforming bishops, with the result that after 1969 most of the Church hierarchy advocated profound political reform. The press, meanwhile, was growing emboldened. By the early 1970s, magazines like *Cambio 16* posed an increasingly overt challenge to the regime.

Faced with this sustained pressure, the regime was pushed into a corner. In order to cow the protestors, a massive repressive onslaught would have been necessary, but this would have earned the regime international pariah status and undermined its claim to be a guarantor of prosperity and stability. Instead, it engaged in a holding operation; while it did not unleash a campaign of state terror, the police responded brutally in the face of worker and student demonstrations and torture continued to be regularly used against opponents. This situation convinced a growing number of younger reformers within the administration that in order to guard against a revolutionary conjuncture, far-reaching political reforms were needed. Importantly, they were in touch with the heir apparent, Juan Carlos, who was discreetly establishing himself as a reform-minded figure.

Yet within the regime what were to become known as the *inmovilistas* remained in a powerful position. Of key importance in this respect was Franco's wife, Carmen Polo, and a close group of friends and family. The army also remained almost totally loyal to the regime and it was supported by much of the *Movimiento Nacional* bureaucracy, afraid what their future might be under a democracy. In addition, the first signs of real crisis also saw the emergence of a far right tacitly supported by Carrero Blanco.

It was this constellation of forces that was responsible for the contradictory policies pursued by the regime from 1973 until the death of Franco in November 1975. Carrero Blanco was assassinated by the Basque separatist group ETA on 20 December 1973. This, it seemed, might open the way to a more reforming government in the future. The option was strongly backed by a new Catholic grouping of young professionals from well-connected families known as **Tácito**. Franco reacted by appointing **Carlos Arias Navarro** as the new president on 3 January 1974. This seemed an inauspicious start. Arias Navarro was a well-known hard-liner who had been director general of security between 1957 and 1965. It was, therefore, a reflection of the pressure he was under that his first government included several relatively liberal figures. In addition, in a speech on 12 February he seemed to offer significant reforms.

The aim was still to maintain the essentials of Francoism by offering limited concessions, but it was too much for diehards within the regime, who opposed any opening. These elements, who were known by 1974 as the **Bunker** or *ultras*, had Franco's ear, and in the following months they were to launch a counteroffensive that was to derail the whole reform process. The final blow came in October 1974, when Franco forced the resignation of the minister of information, Pío Cabanillas (1923–1991), and large numbers of reformers resigned from all levels of government in solidarity. The reformers now realized that serious reform of the regime was impossible and that in order to avoid a bloody confrontation, a full-blown democratization of political life would be necessary. This was reflected in the proliferation of meetings between reformers and leading figures within the opposition in the following months and in the setting up of semi-clandestine centrist political parties—the Partido Demócrata (Democratic Party), led by Joaquín Garrigues Walker (1933–1980);

Izquierda Social Demócrata (Social Democratic Left), formed by **Francisco Fernández Ordóñez**; and Unión Social Demócrata Española (Spanish Social Democratic Union), under the leadership of **Dionisio Ridruejo.**

The final year of the regime saw little serious attempt at renewal. An associations law was finally ratified by the Cortes in January 1974, but it was enormously restrictive. Indeed, in its death throes in the second half of the year, faced by massive protest, the regime reverted to further repression. Franco, however, was by this time weak and frail. He fell seriously ill on 13 October and, though he was kept alive on a life support machine for over a month, he finally died on 20 November 1975. Juan Carlos was crowned king and head of state two days later. The opportunity for serious reform had now arrived. *See also* CORRUPTION; FOREIGN POLICY; LABOR MOVEMENT.

FRENCH REVOLUTION. The French Revolution broke out shortly after the accession to the throne of **Carlos IV.** It had an enormous impact on Spain. Within broad sectors of the **Catholic Church,** there was already hostility toward **Enlightenment** ideas, which were viewed as undermining religious teachings and threatening political and social stability. The results of the revolution were seen as vindicating this stance. Hostility grew after the French National Assembly declared that all ecclesiastics had to take an oath accepting the civil constitution. Subsequently, many fled to Spain, spreading stories of the horrors of the revolution. When France declared war on Spain in January 1793 and invaded **Catalonia**, the clergy then mobilized the peasantry in a guerrilla campaign for religion and country against the godless French.

On the other hand, many ministers and cultured Spaniards wanted to maintain the moderate Enlightenment policies of **Carlos III.** Carlos IV oscillated between the reactionary Catholic and pro-Enlightenment camps. However, under his favorite, **Manuel de Godoy,** from 1792 he largely pursued a reforming course. After reaching peace with France in 1795, his policy was to try to maintain royal absolutism intact while protecting the economic reforms of the pro-Enlightenment ministers. This was undermined by the March 1808 **Aranjuez uprising** (*motín de Aranjuez*), a reactionary putsch which forced Carlos IV to abdicate and hand over the reins of power to his son, who was crowned **Fernando VII**. However, almost immediately, both Carlos and Fernando were forced to abdicate in favor of Napoleon Bonaparte's brother (who became **José I**). Some pro-Enlightenment Spaniards—who became known as *afrancesados*—supported the French monarchy, because they saw it as the only chance of an ordered social and political modernization. Many would have to go into exile when the French forces withdrew in 1813. At the same time, from the 1800s revolutionary ideas became to make headway among Spain's city-dwelling middle classes. Though radical Jacobinism failed to take root, support for representative government and laissez-faire economic policies spread. This became clear during the **War of Independence**, when the **Cortes of Cádiz** established a constitutional monarchy between 1811 and 1812. The defeat of Napoleon's occupation therefore left the country divided between liberals and absolutists.

FRENTE DE LIBERACIÓN POPULAR (FLP)/POPULAR LIBERATION FRONT. The FLP (often referred to as Felipe) was the most radical of the clandestine leftist organizations linked to **Catholic** circles to emerge in the late 1950s. It was particularly strong among radicalized students and played an important role in disseminating European Marxist literature. The ideology of its members was a mix of Christian socialism, anti-Stalinist revolutionary Marxism, and Castroism. Hence, it stressed the need for the renewal and liberalization of the Communist movement. It developed contacts with reformers and radicals in the **Partido Comunista de España** (PCE) and other Marxist parties, to which many of its leading figures were to migrate in the late 1960s. In Catalonia, it was federated with the **Front Obrer de Catalunya** (FOC), and its backers included the poet and novelist Manuel Vázquez Montalbán (1939–2003) and **Miquel Roca i Junyent**. It was wound up in 1969.

FRENTE REVOLUCIONARIO ANTIFASCISTA Y PATRIOTA (FRAP)/ANTIFASCIST AND PATRIOTIC REVOLUTIONARY FRONT. This organization was set up by activists in the far-leftist Partido Comunista de España (Marxista-Leninista) (Marxist Leninist Spanish Communist Party) during 1973. In a climate in which the **Franco regime** was entering into terminal crisis, like **ETA**

it advocated revolutionary action rather than negotiations. It quickly turned to armed struggle, shooting dead three policemen during 1975. In retaliation, the regime executed three FRAP activists (along with two members of ETA) on 21 September. This led to widespread national and international protests. Following the regime's demise, it was wound up in 1978. *See also* LABOR MOVEMENT.

FRONT OBRER DE CATALUNYA (FOC)/CATALAN WORKERS' FRONT. The FOC was formed during 1961–1962 by groups of progressive Catholics, socialists, and dissident communists. On a national level, it federated with the **Frente de Liberación Popular** (FLP). During the 1960s, the FOC's ideology was a mixture of Castroism and Christian socialism. It had a strong student and intellectual following and also developed a small working-class base. It operated within **Comisiones Obreras** (CC.OO) and in the late 1960s formed part of a leftist opposition to the dominant **Partido Comunista de España-Partit Socialista Unificat de Catalunya** policy of combining industrial agitation with building a broad interclass alliance for democratic change. The FOC, on the other hand, argued that the "exploited classes" should be subordinated to a revolutionary class party in the struggle for socialism, and wished to replace CC.OO's industrial federations, which were seen as excessively corporatist, with area bodies. In the hothouse atmosphere of radical politics, the organization was to disintegrate under the weight of political infighting and polemic between 1969 and 1970. *See also* LABOR MOVEMENT.

FUEROS. These are the laws and privileges that were enjoyed in several parts of the Iberian Peninsula during the medieval and early modern period. In the **Crown of Aragón** (Aragón, **Catalonia**, **Valencia**, and the Balearic Islands), the Kingdom of **Navarre**, and Kingdom of **Portugal** they were guaranteed by the local **Cortes**. In the **Crown of Castile**, the Cortes was weaker and so most of its territories enjoyed no such privileges. The exception was the **Basque** provinces, whose *fueros*—which gave the Basques fiscal and commercial privileges— were guaranteed by an elected body in each of the Basque provinces (the Juntas Generales). The *fueros* enjoyed by the Crown of Aragón were swept away in the early 18th century following the **War of**

Succession. Given that they had supported **Felipe V,** the **Bourbon** pretender to the throne, the Basque and Navarre territories were allowed to keep their privileges. However, the Basque *fueros* were subsequently abolished by centralizing liberal governments in two stages, in 1833 and 1876. This provoked strong opposition, which was organized by both the **Carlists** and, after 1876, by the so-called *fuerista* movement. This helped created a sense of Basque identity, making possible the emergence of a **nationalist** movement in the 1890s under **Sabino de Arana.** From the 1880s, **Catalanists** also saw their movement as leading Catalonia's struggle to recover the self-government and liberties taken away by Felipe V.

FUERZA NUEVA/NEW FORCE. *See* BUNKER.

FUSIONIST PARTY. *See* PARTIDO LIBERAL.

– G –

GAL (GRUPOS ANTI-TERRORISTAS DE LIBERACIÓN)/ANTI-TERRORIST LIBERATION GROUPS. The GAL was an illegal mercenary force, backed by the Spanish state, which carried out attacks on members of **ETA** in France between 1983 and 1987. In all, 27 people were killed, 10 of whom had no links to ETA. The driving force behind its formation was members of the security apparatus in place since the **Franco regime,** but it was given support by elements in the governing **Partido Socialista Obrero Español** (PSOE) government. It aim was both to demoralize ETA and also to force France to take a tougher stance against members of ETA operating from the French Basque provinces.

In this latter objective it had considerable success. However, the investigation launched by the investigative magistrate **Baltasar Garzón** led to the conviction of two police officers, José Amedo and Michel Domínguez, in 1991. In 1994, these men began to talk, and their revelations found their way into the opposition newspaper, *El Mundo.* Further information was provided by a former member of the intelligence agency, the Centro Superior de Información de la Defensa (Higher Defense Intelligence Center—CESID), Juan Alberto Perote, in the following year. Perote was, at the time, working for the banker **Mario Conde**, who was using papers Perote had illegally removed to blackmail the government into dropping charges of embezzlement leveled against him. The revelations led to the establishment of a committee of enquiry by the Senate despite opposition from the PSOE and **Convergència i Unió** in October. Those most clearly implicated were former interior minister **José Barrionuevo**, former secretary of state for security Rafael Vera (1945–), former civil governor of the Vizcaya Julián Sacristóbal, former civil governor of Guipúzcoa Julen Elgorríaga, and former secretary general of the Basque Socialists Ricardo García Damborenea (1940–), along with members of the Civil Guard and security services, most notably Civil Guard general Enrique Rodríguez Galindo. Damborenea also implicated the Spanish prime minister, **Felipe González**, but this was denied by González and there was insufficient evidence to prosecute. Of some importance for the prosecution, again led by Baltasar Garzón, was that it was able to force the authorities to release the documentation previously seized by Perote ("the CESID papers"). In July 1998, Barrionuevo, Vera, Sacristóbal, and Damborenea, among others, were condemned for their roles in the kidnapping of Segundo Marey, an innocent bystander mistaken for a ETA activist (leading to a demonstration outside the gates of Guadalajara prison by a number of leading Socialists), and in April 2000, Rodríguez Galindo and Julen Elgorríaga were imprisoned for being behind the kidnapping and murder of two ETA activists, José Antonio Lasa and José Ignacio Zabala. Barrionuevo and Vera were given a partial pardon by the government of **José María Aznar** in December 1998.

GALAXIA OPERATION/OPERACION GALAXIA. The Galaxia Operation (so called because it was planned in the Galaxia Bar) was a plot by a number of pro-Francoist *ultras* within the **military** to overthrow the new democratic regime in 1978. The idea was to kidnap the cabinet while it met in the Moncloa palace and install a military government. The plot was only foiled when the government was belatedly informed by its intelligence services. Typically, for this period, the whole episode was played down and the plotters were given only light sentences. *See also* BUNKER; TEJERAZO; TEJERO MOLINA, ANTONIO.

GALICIA. Galicia is a largely agrarian region situated in northwest Spain. It has three provinces, Lugo, La Coruña, and Pontevedra, and in 2007 had an estimated **population** of 2,772,533. During the 19th and early 20th centuries, the region was one of the poorest in Spain. Agricultural development was hampered by landholding structures. Tiny plots, known as **minifundia**, dominated the landscape, making it impossible to produce a surplus of the market, and resulting, until the late 19th century, in periodic subsistence crises. For example, the result of the loss of the potato harvest in 1853–1854 was famine, which was followed by massive emigration to **Latin America**.

Because of the lack of a significant industrial base and large urban centers, an educated middle class and an industrial working class were slow to develop and political awareness remained low. As a result, in the late 19th century, it was ideal territory for the *caciques* of the **Cánovas Restoration**, and the monarchist parties dominated the political landscape. For these reasons, despite the continued general usage of the **Galician language**, nationalist sentiment did not take off in the same way as in **Catalonia** and the **Basque Country**. A theory of Galician nationhood was developed by Manuel Murguía (1833–1923) in the mid-19th century. In his *Historia de Galicia*, published in 1865, he argued that the Galicians formed a Celtic race of Aryan descent, both different from and superior to their Spanish oppressors, who were of Semitic stock. The late 19th and early 20th centuries then saw a proliferation of nationalist and regionalist associations and newspapers. There was also a cultural revival known as the Rexurdimento, led by literary figures such as **Rosalía de Castro**. Yet the nationalists were not to achieve a significant electoral base.

This situation only changed significantly during the **Second Republic**. In La Coruña in 1929, a leftist Galician regionalist party, the Organización Republicana Gallega Autónoma (Autonomous Republican Galician Organization—ORGA), was founded. It signed the **San Sebastián Pact** and was then to integrate into **Manuel Azaña**'s Izquierda Republicana. Two other small nationalist parties were set up soon after, the Partido Republicano Nacionalista (Nationalist Republican Party) in Orense and the Grupo Autonomista (Autonomist Group) in Vigo. For the first time, in the June 1931 elections these regionalist/nationalist parties obtained seats in parliament (two for

ORGA and one for each of the other two groups). This relative success encouraged them to join together to form the Partido Galeguista (Galeguista Party) in December 1931. During the **Second Republic**, conflict with landowning elites and the example of the Catalan autonomy statute maintained the intense political climate. In 1936, the question of Galician autonomy was widely debated, allowing the Partido Galeguista to mobilize considerable support, and in a plebiscite on 26 June 1936, the Galicians voted for home rule. Unfortunately, the **Spanish Civil War** was to break out less than a month later and Galicia quickly fell to the **Nationalist** forces. There followed a wideranging repression of leftists and regionalists.

As in Catalonia and the Basque Country, with the **transition to democracy** nationalist sentiment reemerged. Yet, the dominant conservative political tradition was quick to reassert itself. This occurred within a context in which much of Galician society remained demobilized, with powerful rural landowners still influential. Hence, the **Unión del Centro Democrático** won the elections in 1977 and 1979, and **Alianza Popular** (AP) was victorious in 1982. From the first regional elections of October 1981 through to 2005, AP-**Partido Popular** (PP) dominated the autonomous parliament, and the former Francoist minister **Manuel Fraga** was president between 1989 and 2005. Nevertheless, in order to ward off the threat of Galician nationalism, during this time Fraga took a more regionalist stance than the Spanish PP, showing respect for the Galician language and cultural traditions.

From the 1970s, Galician nationalism very much became the preserve of the left. In 1964, the Unión do Pobo Galego (Union of the Galician People—UPG) was born. However, its combination of Marxism-Leninism and Third Worldist anticolonialism only gained it minority electoral support. As noted previously, from the transition to democracy the center-right was able to dominate the political stage. Indeed, the major alternative did not come from the nationalist left but from the **Partido Socialista Obrero Español** (PSOE). This situation was to change significantly in the 1980s. Of key importance was the functioning of a Galician autonomous parliament and government (the Xunta) from 1981, following a referendum in the previous year. The operation of the Xunta encouraged people to see problems in Galician terms. At the same time, during the 1980s Galician society modernized significantly and the citizenry became more politically active. The result could be seen in the 1985 elections to the autonomous parliament when, for the first time, a center-right Galician regionalist/nationalist political force, the Coalición Galega (Galician Coalition), broke into the political arena, gaining 11 seats, while Galician regionalist/ nationalist parties obtained 23 percent of the vote (up from 13 percent in 1981). These events provoked a significant realignment of the political spectrum. AP won the elections but did not achieve an overall majority, and in order to shore up its position in subsequent years, it would adopt a regionalist stance. This allowed it to incorporate the more conservative wing of Galician regionalism/nationalism.

On the left there was also considerable jockeying for position. Within the leftist nationalist camp the situation was highly complex, with a large number of competing parties. One major trend was, however, visible. During the 1980s, the leftist nationalist parties became increasingly social-democratic and tried to broaden their support base within the urban middle classes and professional strata. Given its more solid organizational structure, the UPG was to play a lead role in the creation of a new coalition, the **Bloque Nacionalista Galego** (BNG), in 1982. At first it was only a small force, but in the mid-1990s, with the Catalan and Basque nationalist parties able to exert strong pressure over Spanish governments and the PSOE discredited by a number of **corruption** scandals, it was able, briefly, to emerge as the second most voted party in the autonomous elections. It has since slipped back to third place, but in June 2005, after the PP lost its overall majority in the autonomous elections, it formed a coalition government with the Galician branch of the PSOE (the Partido Socialista Galego [PSG]-PSOE).

GALICIAN LANGUAGE. Like **Castilian** and **Catalan**, Galician is a Romance language that grew out of Latin after the fall of the Roman Empire. At first, Portuguese and Galician (Galaico-portuguese) developed as a unitary language in the northwest corner of the Iberian Peninsula, in what had been the Roman province of Gallaecia (within which is to be found modern-day **Galicia**). It was then taken south into modern **Portugal** in the wake of the latter territory's "**Reconquest**" from the Moors. Between the 11th and 15th centuries, Portugal and Galicia were in separate kingdoms, causing differences to appear within the language. They were further to diverge with the definitive separation of Portugal from Spain in 1640, though they are still to a large extent mutually intelligible. Galician has in particular been heavily influenced by Castilian (the dominant language in the **Crown of Castile**, into which Galicia was incorporated in 1088, and, of course, modern Spain), but it also retains more archaic elements not found in modern Portuguese.

Because Galicia was a poor rural area and because the Spanish state **education** system was underfunded, in the early 20th century Galician remained the language of the vast majority of the population. However, as no strong middle-class nationalist movement developed in the territory, it did not gain the social prestige of Catalan. Rather, until recently it has been seen as the language of the poor peasantry, while Castilian was viewed as the language of social advancement, politics, culture, and the administration. This began to change when the Galician autonomous government, the Xunta, was set up in 1981. Nevertheless, it did not receive the same degree of political support as Catalan or, indeed, Basque. Only since the integration of the nationalist party **Bloque Nacionalista Galego** into the Xunta in 2005 has the Galician language received forceful backing. Despite these handicaps, 90 percent of the territories' 2.8 million inhabitants (over 2.5 million people) speak Galician.

GARCÍA LORCA, FEDERICO (1898–1936). Probably the best-known Spanish poet and playwright of the 20th century, García Lorca was born into a wealthy middle-class family in Granada. His work is renowned for its fusion of **Andalusian** folklore with the recurrent themes of love, death, and sexuality. A defining moment in his life was his stay in the Residencia de Estudiantes (Students' Residence) in **Madrid** from 1919, where he met both **Salvador Dalí** and the future film director **Luis Buñuel** and absorbed the avant-garde trends of the time. His collection of poems *Romancero gitano* (*Gypsy Romances*, 1928) brought him national fame, and after a trip to the United States, he returned to Spain to write a series of spectacularly successful plays, including *Bodas de sangre* (*Blood Wedding*, 1933) and *La casa de Bernarda Alba* (*The House of Bernarda Alba*, 1936). He also participated in the **Second Republic**'s idealistic attempts to disseminate high culture throughout Spain, setting up the traveling theater company *La barraca* (*The Cabin*). Well known for his libertarian views and latent homosexuality, he was executed by the Francoist forces after they had taken Granada at the outset of the **Spanish Civil War.**

GARCÍA PRIETO, MANUEL, MARQUIS OF ALHUCEMAS

(1859–1938). García Prieto was, along with the **Count of Romanones**, the leading figure within the **Partido Liberal** (PL) between 1913 and 1923. He was the son-in-law of the leading Partido Liberal politician Eugenio Montero Ríos (1832–1914), allowing him to build up a powerful *caciquista* power base in his native Astorga (Asturias). He was first elected to parliament for the town in 1888. Until 1917, he had been in Romanones's shadow, but his big chance came in April of that year, when King **Alfonso XIII** forced the latter to resign as prime minister because he had adopted what the king, **military**, and much of the social elite regarded as a too strongly pro-Allied **foreign policy.** García Prieto was regarded by the king as rather weak and pliable, and his support for strict neutrality found favor. His first government was, however, cut short in June by the revolt of the **Juntas de Defensa.** As the **Cánovas Restoration** entered total crisis over the following months, he presided over a government of national unity between October 1917 and March 1918. But over the next five years, he found new purpose in the attempt (along with the leaders of the **Partido Conservador, Eduardo Dato** and, subsequently, **José Sánchez Guerra**) to reconstruct the *turno pacífico* (albeit accepting that he now had to put together cabinets made up of figures belonging to the various factions of the party). As the leader of a PL coalition, from December 1922 he was given the power to dissolve parliament by the king, thus allowing him to "make" the elections and ensure a majority in parliament. Nevertheless, he was mindful of the fact that governments now needed at least some credibility.

As a result of the July 1921 military disaster of **Annual**, the **Partido Socialista Obrero Español** (PSOE), along with the **republicans**, campaigned vigorously for those responsible to be tried and for a withdrawal from **Morocco**. García Prieto responded to this pressure by pursuing a reforming program. He had in the past tried to attract the moderate republican left and offered a post in government to a member of **Melquíades Álvarez**'s Partido Reformista (Reformist

Party). He also developed a conciliatory policy with respect to social conflict, negotiating with the **anarchist**-syndicalist **Confederación Nacional del Trabajo** in Barcelona. This, however, gained him the animosity of Catalan business and important sections of the **military**. In addition, *africanistas* were unhappy at his reluctance to pursue an aggressive policy in the colonial war in Morocco and at the pursuit of military responsibilities for Annual. Crucially, the king sympathized with these complaints and was also increasingly disillusioned with parliamentary government. The result was that on 13 September, General **Miguel Primo de Rivera** launched a military coup with the king's tacit support. García Prieto put up little resistance. After the dictator's fall in January 1930, he was involved in the unsuccessful attempt to resurrect the Restoration regime. See also WORLD WAR I.

GARRIGUES WALKER, JOAQUÍN. See FRANCO REGIME; UNIÓN DEL CENTRO DEMOCRÁTICO.

GARZÓN REAL, BALTAZAR (1955–). Baltazar Garzón has become, since the early 1990s, the most famous and prestigious investigative magistrate in Spain. His reputation was first earned through his dogged determination to track down those responsible for the organization of the anti-**ETA** terrorist group, the **GAL**. In addition, he has prosecuted both dangerous drug cartels and, from the late 1990s, groups linked to ETA itself. He shot to international fame in 1998 when he demanded the extradition of the former Chilean dictator General Augusto Pinochet from Great Britain to Spain.

This is all a long way from his modest beginnings. He was born in the town of Torres in the southern province of Jaca, the son of an agricultural worker. Through hard work and determination, he was able to study law at the University of Seville between 1974 and 1979 and went on to join the judiciary. He then worked his way up the profession until being appointed a judge at Central Court Number Five in Madrid. It was from this date that Garzón began to investigate the GAL, which had carried out several murders and kidnappings in the French **Basque** provinces between 1983 and 1987. From the start, evidence came to light that implicated elements within the security services, via the payment of mercenaries through the Ministry of the Interior's secret funds. Garzón's inquiries led to conflict with the minister of the interior, **José Barrionuevo**, who refused to release information and instructed the police called to testify to do likewise. Nevertheless, evidence accumulated by Garzón finally led to the imprisonment of the police officers José Amedo and Michel Domínguez in 1991.

In 1990, Garzón was also behind the prosecution of an infamous **Galician** drug-smuggling ring in "Operation Nécora." Garzón's stubbornness in pursuit of the GAL was to lead to criticism within the governing **Partido Socialista Obrero Español** (PSOE). Yet, faced by **corruption** charges and waning popularity, in the run-up to the June 1993 elections the prime minister, **Felipe González**, offered him the chance of running second in the Socialist list in **Madrid** as an independent and a post in the new government. Garzón responded positively, seeing the opportunity to overhaul the judiciary and clean up Spanish politics. He was made head of the government's antidrug plan, but resigned in May 1994, stating that he was disillusioned by the lack of support from González (though others claimed that it was because he had not received a cabinet post). After returning to the judiciary, he once again began to investigate the GAL. His investigations were given a fillip from the end of 1994, when Amedo and Domínguez began to talk and implicated both higher-ranking officers in the police and the former minister of the interior, José Barrionuevo. Furthermore, in 1995, new information came to light in the shape of documentation stolen by a former member of the security services, Juan Alberto Perote, which was aired in the press. Between 1998 and 2000, Garzón secured the conviction of a number of high-ranking officials, including Barrionuevo (who was quickly given a partial amnesty).

At this time, Garzón was also acting on behalf of the families of a number of Spanish citizens who had disappeared after the Chilean coup of 1973. Warrants had already been issued for the arrest of Augusto Pinochet. Therefore, when he visited Great Britain at the end of 1998, Garzón issued instructions for his arrest pending extradition to Spain. This was made possible by the international convention against torture, which had come into effect in 1997. However, the British home secretary, Jack Straw, decided to send Pinochet back to Chile on compassionate grounds, based on his having suffered a number of minor strokes, in January 2000. Garzón has since 1996 also played a leading role in the offensive against Basque radical nationalists with links to ETA, closing down the newspaper *Egin* in 1998 and issuing the order suspending the activities of **Herri Batasuna** (HB) in the autumn of 2002. He took similar action against the Partido Comunista de las Tierras Vascas (Communist Party of the Basque Countries) and Acción Nacionalista Vasca (Basque Nationalist Action), parties closely allied to HB, in the run-up to the March 2008 elections.

GAUDÍ I CORNET, ANTONI (1852–1926). Gaudí is the most original Spanish **architect** of the late 19th and early 20th centuries and the foremost exponent of Catalan *modernista* architecture. Born in Reus, he qualified as an architect in 1878. At the outset, he was strongly influenced by neogothic architecture to which he rapidly incorporated European Art Nouveau styles, reaching a highly innovative synthesis of Catalan craft traditions and modern building techniques. Most notably, through the use of painstaking iron work, ceramics, and undulating stone, he greatly emphasized the organic component in Art Nouveau. Politically, he was a staunch **Catholic** and rejected what he saw as the individualism and centralizing tendencies inherent in the new **liberal** order. His defense of tradition and religion helped secure him the patronage of Eusebi Güell y Bacigalupi (1846–1918), a man at the very pinnacle of **Barcelona** elite society (the "good families"). Early in his career, in the mid-1880s, Güell had commissioned him to design his town house in central Barcelona, the Palau Güell, in which neogothic influence was particularly pronounced. He then went on to commission the chapel crypt for his new company work town, the Colònia Güell, outside Barcelona , and the garden city of what he envisaged would be a new residential development for the Barcelona well-to-do (Parc Güell).

An increasingly prestigious figure, between 1905 and 1907 Gaudí then received two major commissions for houses on Barcelona's most exclusive street, the Passaig de Gràcia. The result was what are regarded by many as his two finest works, Casa Battló (an already existing house, which he remodeled) and, above all, Casa Milà (usually referred to as La Pedrera). It was also his religious connections that got Gaudí the commission to build the great church, the Temple Expiatori de la Sagrada Família, which he worked on tirelessly from 1908 until his death. Indeed, these Catholic-conservative links meant that Gaudí's work was looked on with great suspicion by the left, with the archive of the Sagrada Família destroyed by **anarchists** during the **Spanish Civil War.**

GENERALÍSIMO/GENERALISSIMO. This term, meaning supreme commander of the armed forces, was conferred on General **Francisco Franco** in a meeting of the military's high command on 21 September 1936. During the Franco years, "Generalísimo Franco" was to be the name of thousands of streets and squares throughout Spain. In the years following his death, they were removed from all but some ultraconservative areas in central Spain. *See also* FRANCO REGIME.

GENERALITAT. The term Generalitat originated in the 14th century. It was the name given to the permanent assemblies of the **Cortes** in **Catalonia** and in the Kingdom of **Valencia**. These assemblies ensured political continuity between sessions, collected taxes, and were charged with upholding the rights and privileges of the territories. For this reason, when, in 1931, an autonomous government was set up in Catalonia, it called itself the Generalitat to emphasize continuity with Catalonia's independent past, and the recuperation of liberties deemed to have been destroyed by **Castilian** centralization. Similarly, after the fall of the **Franco regime**, in the late 1970s both the new Catalan and Valencian autonomous governments called themselves the Generalitat.

GENERATION OF 1898. The "generation of 1898" was a group of writers who were based in **Madrid** in the late 1890s, lived through the **Spanish-American War** (the "Disaster of 1898"), and, partly as a result, developed a virulent critique of the Spanish state and its institutions. The main figures within the group were **Miguel Unamuno, José Martínez Ruiz** ("Azorín"), **Pío Baroja, Antonio Machado, Ramiro de Maeztu,** and—with reservations—**Ramón María del Valle Inclán.** They all coincided in seeing "Spain as a problem," and launched into a devastating attack on what they saw as the country's corrupt institutions and backward dominant ideology. Solutions in common to Spain's predicament are, however, more difficult to discern. They were influenced by the positivist and Nietzschean ideas which were in vogue in Europe at this time, and a pronounced individualistic streak can be perceived in their writings. But from the first years of the century they were quickly to grow apart.

GERMANÓFILOS. This was the name given to those sectors of society and political groupings who sympathized with the Germans during **World War I**. Conservative Spain, above all, identified with the German cause. Hence, the Germans enjoyed almost total support among the Church hierarchy and the **Catholic** far right, and had strong backing within the **military**, the **Partido Conservador**, and among the country's social elites.

GESCARTERA SCANDAL. The Gescartera affair broke in mid-2001, doing some damage to the credibility of the **Partido Popular** (PP) government. Gescartera, an investment firm which managed portfolios for clients, collapsed, leaving 15 billion pesetas worth of debts (with a number of public bodies, including the Ministry of Defense and the **Civil Guard**, losing money). An investigation was then launched into whether money had been siphoned off. Several directors of Gescartera had previously worked for the financial regulatory body, the Comisión Nacional del Mercado de Valores (National Stock Market Commission—CNMV), and accusations were made that the previous vice president of the CNMV, PP deputy Luis Ramallo (who subsequently set up his own notary's office, one of whose principal clients was Gescartera), had blocked the investigation and accepted gifts from Gescartera's owner, Antonio Camacho, and that the president of the CNMV, Pilar Valiente, had given the business her support. The secretary of the treasury, Enrique Giménez Reyna, whose sister had presided over Gescartera (and who, along with Camacho, was subsequently imprisoned), was forced to resign, along with the CNMV president. Given that prominent figures within the CNMV were close to minister of the economy **Rodrigo Rato**, his position was also weakened.

GIBRALTAR. The Rock of Gibraltar, located on the southernmost tip of the Spanish mainland, became a British colony through the 1713 Treaty of Utrecht. Over the next two and a half centuries, given its key strategic position at the mouth of the Mediterranean, its retention became a priority for the British. However, it also became a serious source of tension with Spanish governments, which almost immediately began to demand its return. Pressure for the return of Gibraltar grew with the rise of **nationalist** feeling in Spain after 1914. During **World War II**, Nazi Germany had planned to launch an assault on the Rock with the aid of Francoist troops, but with Spain finally not entering the war, the plan had to be dropped. During the **Franco regime**, Gibraltar remained a continuing source of dispute with Great Britain. Spain had some success in getting the United Nations (UN) on its side over this question. In 1963, the UN urged bilateral negotiations to restore Spanish sovereignty. With no progress, in 1967 and 1968 UN resolutions condemned Britain's position, and in December 1968 the UN demanded a termination of "the colonial situation in Gibraltar not later than 1969." When Britain failed to comply, Franco proceeded to cut Gibraltar off from the mainland.

The border with Spain was reopened in 1982, but attempts to find a long-term solution have proved difficult. Negotiations were held between the Spanish and British foreign ministers, **Josep Piqué** and Jack Straw, in the spring of 2002, when a power-sharing agreement was reached. However, Britain insisted that the accord needed Gibraltarian approval. It was then torpedoed by Gibraltarian first minister Daniel Caruana, who called a referendum in November, in which the deal was overwhelmingly rejected. Britain subsequently called off discussions. After the **Partido Socialista Obrero Español** (PSOE) came to power in 2004, the new government agreed to restart negotiations, in which the Gibraltarian government would be involved, and recognized, for the first time, that a solution could not be found without the consensus of the Gibraltarian people.

GIL-ROBLES Y QUIÑONES, JOSÉ MARÍA (1898–1980). José María Gil-Robles was the leading figure on the Spanish right during the **Second Republic**. He was born in Salamanca and went on to study law at university. He came from a staunchly **Catholic** background and from an early age became involved in right-wing politics. During the **Primo de Rivera dictatorship**, he collaborated with **José Calvo Sotelo** in the elaboration of the regime's Municipal Statute. With the coming of the Republic, he played the leading role in the mobilization of the Catholic right against the regime's Church and social reforms. He became leader of **Acción Nacional** in July 1931 and of the **Confederación Española de Derechas Autónomas** (CEDA) when it was founded in March 1933. Gil-Robles believed that the right's best chance of success was not to become involved in an attempted coup but to win power through the ballot box (though he was not above consulting, on occasion, with reactionary army officers as to whether a coup was feasible). However, he was strongly influenced by Catholic **corporatist** ideology and so his ultimate goal was an authoritarian monarchy.

After the CEDA became the largest party in the **Cortes** in November 1933, Gil-Robles's efforts were aimed at pushing for the president of the Republic to accept an all-CEDA government. He achieved a first success on 5 October 1934, when three members of the CEDA entered the government of **Alejandro Lerroux**. He reacted to the **October 1934 revolution** by on the one hand, calling for an exemplary repression and on the other, consulting with rightist army generals on the advisability of taking more drastic action. He was advised that the **military** was in no position to act. In any case, in May 1935 it seemed gradualist tactics were paying dividends, with five members of the CEDA appointed to posts in the cabinet, including Gil-Robles himself, who was made minister of war. While at the War Ministry, Gil-Robles somewhat improved the efficiency of the army, but, more importantly, promoted notoriously conservative generals to high commands. Following the discrediting of the **Partido Republicano Radical** after a number of **corruption** scandals in the summer and autumn of 1935, he was convinced the time had now come for him to lead the country. However, the president of the Republic, **Niceto Alcalá Zamora**, rather than trusting him with government, called new elections.

The victory of the leftist **Popular Front** at these elections led the Spanish right to abandon the gradualist road. In the following months, therefore, the figure of Gil-Robles was eclipsed by the more extreme **José Calvo Sotelo**, and the CEDA quickly lost support. Once the military uprising took place, from his base in **Portugal** Gil-Robles strongly campaigned for the **Nationalists**. **Francisco Franco**'s usurpation of dictatorial powers, however, led to his disillusionment with the regime. From the end of the war, he formed part of the advisory staff of the monarchist pretender, **Juan de Borbón y Battenberg**, and promoted a reconciliation with the more moderate opposition forces with the aim of establishing a constitutional monarchy. From the early 1950s, he also tried to build a **Christian-democrat** opposition. He was exiled from Spain after participating in a meeting of opposition figures in Munich in 1962. During the **transition to democracy**, he attempted to forge a powerful Christian-democratic movement, setting up the Federación Popular Democrática (Popular Democratic Federation) in 1975 and standing for parliament in the 1977 elections as part of a Federación Demócrata Cristiana (Christian Democrat Federation). The attempt, however, proved a failure. Gil-Robles had little financial and human support, with conservative elites backing the **Unión del Centro Democrático** and **Alianza Popular**.

GIRÓN DE VELASCO, JOSÉ ANTONIO (1911–1995). José Antonio Girón was a Falangist "old shirt," who had been a founding member of the Juntas de Ofensiva Nacional Sindicalista (Juntas of the National Syndicalist Offensive) in 1932, which then fused with **Falange Española** in 1934. He served in the Falange militia as the territorial head of Castile (*jefe territorial de Castilla*) during the **Spanish Civil War**, before taking up a series of important posts within the **Falange Española Tradicionalista y de las Juntas de Ofensiva Nacional Sindicalista** (FET y de las JONS) at the beginning of the **Franco regime**. In May 1941, he was brought into General **Francisco Franco**'s cabinet as minister of labor on the advice of **Ramón Serrano Suñer**. This was a post he was to hold for 16 years and during this time he developed a populist rhetoric that, at least verbally, aimed to give a social dimension to the regime's policy. This made him the longest-serving minister of the Franco regime, with the exception of **Luis Carrero Blanco**. Like **José Luis de Arrese**, Girón was useful to Franco in that he was trusted by the Falangist old guard, and yet was personally loyal. During his time in power, he became identified with the group of largely Falangist ministers, who defended the **autarkic** socioeconomic model that had been put in place in the 1940s. For this reason, along with Arrese, he was finally replaced in the February 1957 cabinet reshuffle, which saw **Opus Dei** technocrats take over the economics ministries.

Girón nevertheless remained a powerful figure behind the scenes, with close contacts in Franco's own household. Because of his background and position as the president of the administrative committee of the hard right-wing Falangist daily *El Alcázar*, he was the most influential figure in the so-called **Bunker**, which stifled any chance of serious reform. He ensured that in **Carlos Arias Navarro**'s first government of January 1974, a reliable *ultra*, José Utrera Molina (1926–), was appointed minister general secretary of the **Movimiento Nacional** (as the FET y de las JONS was called from May 1958). And, on 28 April, in the Movimiento Nacional daily *Arriba*, he launched a bitter attack on regime reformers (the so-called *Gironazo*). After the death of Franco, he quickly faded from the political stage, turning his attention to building up a property empire centered in the town of Fuengirola (province of Málaga).

GLORIOUS REVOLUTION/REVOLUCIÓN GLORIOSA. The Glorious Revolution of September 1868 was the culmination of a plot by members of the **Partido Progresista**, **Partido Demócrata**, and **Unión Liberal** against Queen **Isabel II** and the ruling **Partido Moderado**. The moment was propitious, for the country had been suffering from a serious economic downturn since 1864, and the *moderados*' reactionary policies were alienating large sections of society. On 18 September, Admiral Juan Bautista Topete (1821–1885) led a *pronunciamiento* in the bay of Cádiz and immediately received wide-ranging **military** support. The leading conspirators, generals **Juan Prim** and **Francisco Serrano**, then took control of events, publishing a manifesto entitled "España con honra" ("Spain with Honor"). In urban areas, popular support was overwhelming, and after a short battle for control of **Madrid**, the plotters were able to take over the reins of government.

The leaders of the rebellion wished to force the abdication of Isabel II, who they saw as irrevocably tied to the *moderados*, and introduce a more democratic constitution. However, they were by no means radicals, seeking to reestablish order and stability after a swift transfer of power. Yet the hopes of the urban populace had been kindled as never before. Revolutionary committees or *juntas* were set up throughout urban Spain, and in Madrid a democratic militia, the Voluntarios de la Libertad (Volunteers for Liberty), was formed. It was this popular mobilization that was, during the **Democratic Sexennium** of 1868–1874, to take Spain into uncharted territory.

GODOY Y ÁLVAREZ DE FARIA, MANUEL DE, PRINCE OF PEACE (1767–1851). Godoy was the leading Spanish courtier of the reign of **Carlos IV.** Born in Extremadura to a minor aristocratic family, he pursued a **military** career and was to catch the eye of the future Carlos IV and his wife, María Luisa (whose lover he was reputed to be), after he joined the royal bodyguard. When Carlos became king in 1788, Godoy's stock rose rapidly, and after being made secretary of state in 1792, he to a large degree ran the country's affairs. Godoy attempted to continue the **Enlightenment** policies of **Carlos III** while remaining on friendly terms with the **French revolutionary** governments. From 1800, he effectively acted as prime minister, overseeing all aspects of government policy. In 1797, he married María Teresa de Borbón, a cousin of Carlos IV. This led to his being seen as a threat by the king's son Fernando (the future **Fernando VII**), who began to conspire against him. Godoy was finally undone in 1808 when he allowed Napoleon Bonaparte (1769–1821) to cross Spain, supposedly to intervene in **Portugal.** Fernando used his unpopularity to orchestrate a palace coup at **Aranjuez** on 17–18 March 1808. Not only was Godoy made to step down, Carlos IV also abdicated in his son's name. Shortly after, both Carlos IV and Fernando VII were forced to relinquish the crown to the brother of Napoleon, who was crowned **José I.**

GOICOECHEA COSCULLUELA, ANTONIO. *See* CARLISM; MAURISTAS.

GOLPISMO. Until the **transition to democracy**, the term used to refer to **military** interventions in Spanish political life was *pronunciamiento.* However, plots hatched in military circles to thwart democratization between 1975 and 1982 were referred to as *golpismo* (from *golpe de estado*, taken from the French *coup d'etat*). *See also* BUNKER; GALAXIA OPERATION; TEJERAZO; TEJERO MOLINA, ANTONIO.

GOMÁ Y TOMÁS, ISIDRO (1869–1940). As archbishop of Toledo and head of the **Catholic Church** (primate) in Spain during the **Spanish Civil War**, Isidro Gomá was to staunchly defend the **Nationalist** uprising and Francoist cause. He was born in La Riba

(Tarragona) in August 1869, rose rapidly through the ranks of the Church, was appointed to the see of Toledo by Pope Pius XI in April 1933, and was named a cardinal by the Vatican's Cardinal Consistory in December 1935. Gomá's promotion reflected the pope's vehement opposition to the Church reforms being carried out by the **Second Republic**. Gomá was a hard-line theologian, suspicious of **liberalism**, and was a wholehearted defender of the confessionality of the Spanish state. Once the civil war had broken out, from his position as primate and his new post as unofficial (*oficioso*) representative of the Vatican to the Franco government, he established a close relationship with General **Francisco Franco**, justifying the uprising as a religious crusade against godless communism. His most important service to the regime was his key role in the elaboration of a collective letter of the Spanish episcopal hierarchy, "To the Bishops of the Whole World," published on 1 July 1937, which supported the rebellion and defended the regime from accusations of Fascism. Nevertheless, Gomá was himself, in some respects, anxious at the Fascist direction the regime appeared to be taking. He was critical of the key role of the single party, the **Falange Española Tradicionalista y de las Juntas de Ofensiva Nacional Sindicalista**, in the regime, and, in particular, of its monopoly of the media and of the university education. This led him, in August 1939, to issue the pastoral *Lecciones de la guerra y deberes de la paz* (*Lessons of War and Duties of Peace*), which attacked the exaltation of the powers of the state and called for national reconciliation, and was, as a result, suppressed by the Francoist media. These tensions did not, however, mean that the working relationship between the Church and Francoist state had been seriously disturbed at the time of his death in August 1940.

GONZÁLEZ MÁRQUEZ, FELIPE (1942–). Felipe González was prime minister of Spain between 1982 and 1996. He was born in Seville in 1942 and studied law at the University of Seville from 1959. He became active in anti-Francoist student politics in the 1960s. At first he was in the orbit of progressive **Catholic** associations, but in 1966 he joined the **Partido Socialista Obrero Español** (PSOE), and he went on to help found a legal practice that specialized in labor law. At the same time, along with such figures as his great friend **Alfonso Guerra** and Luis Yañez (1943–), he helped build up the PSOE branch in Seville. By the early 1970s, this branch was at the forefront of a movement by younger Socialists to take control of the PSOE out of the hands of the exiled executive headed by **Rodolfo Llopis** in Toulouse and return it to Spain. González, who was elected executive secretary of the Seville provincial branch in 1970, quickly showed himself to be both a charismatic and forceful orator. He played an important role in the August 1970 and August 1972 party congresses, which culminated in a split between the "exterior" and "interior" wings of the party, and subsequently became a member of the anti-Llopis, PSOE-Renovación Executive Commission and a strong candidate for party leader. The opportunity was provided at the party's 1974 Suresnes congress, when the strongman of **Basque** Socialism, **Nicolás Redondo**, stood aside and supported his candidature.

In the following years, Felipe's boyish good looks and relaxed manner proved perfectly suited to the era of **television** politics. As the decade progressed, therefore, the party increasingly became identified with his person. At the same time, with the aid of his lieutenant Alfonso Guerra, he was able to impose his authority on the party. The decisive moment came in 1979, when the apparatus's control over the branches was significantly tightened. Henceforth, the executive would be able to ensure pliant party congresses. Felipe González's ideology was, in the early 1970s, radical and Third Worldist. The aim of his party was, he assured his audiences, to achieve a democratic, socialist Spain, independent of the two major power blocs. However, the new party was never dependent on organized **labor**, and this allowed González to rework his ideology as circumstances dictated. He always showed a keen eye for the strategy needed to attain power, and by the late 1970s, on the advice of European Socialists (particularly Willy Brandt, with whom he had established a very close relationship) and professionals within the party's own ranks (of particular importance here was a group of **Madrid**-based Catholic Socialists, who, when they joined the party in 1976, formed a group known as Convergència Socialista [Socialist Convergence]), he adopted a social-democratic program. The PSOE's task was now to consolidate democracy, modernize the country, and extend social welfare (to carry out the task the bourgeoisie had proved unable to undertake, as he stated in 1982, echoing arguments put forward by Indalecio Prieto in the early 20th century), before, at some future date, moving on to socialism. This socialist vision was, however, abandoned once he attained power in the 1982 elections. To use González's most famous phrase, what mattered was not the color of the cat, but whether it could catch mice, and the implication was that it was the capitalist cat that was the most effective hunter. González and the PSOE remained in power through to 1996. Throughout this time, he remained the party's key figure. His charisma and perceived honesty meant that he maintained the trust of wide sections of the electorate. Yet more than a decade of uninterrupted power took its toll. His support for the government's liberal economics team earned him the enmity of the president of the **Unión General de Trabajadores** (UGT), Nicolás Redondo, and led to a growing split with the followers of Alfonso Guerra. Hence, by the mid-1990s, he presided over a deeply divided party. Furthermore, a son of the transition, he found it more difficult to connect with a new generation of youngsters, either alienated by heavy unemployment or seduced by the consumer boom of the late 1980s. Significantly, in the June 1993 elections the Socialists' most loyal age group was made up of those between 35 and 45 years old.

As problems deepened, González tended to become more detached and isolated in the Moncloa palace. In particular, he was slow to deal with the **corruption** scandals that engulfed the party from 1991. Moreover, after revelations of state and government collusion with the anti-**ETA** terrorist group, the **GAL**, in 1995, the former leader of the Basque Socialists, Ricardo García Domborenea, stated that González was kept abreast of events, and the investigating magistrate, **Baltazar Garzón**, suggested that he was implicated. In large measure because of the deterioration of the PSOE's image, in the June 1993 elections the party lost its overall majority and in 1996 the **Partido Popular** (PP) took power. At the PSOE's 34th congress in June 1997, González then announced his decision to step down as general secretary. However, he has retained the affection of significant sectors of the transition generation. Within the PSOE he has also remained an influential figure.

GOYA Y LUCIENTES, FRANCISCO DE (1746–1828). The greatest early 19th-century Spanish painter, Goya began his professional life in an orthodox manner. He tried to enter the Royal Academy in

Madrid and, after failing, visited Italy between 1770 and 1771. After his return, his artistic career blossomed. He made his name through his designs at the royal tapestry works at Santa Barbara and rose to become a court painter for **Carlos IV** in 1789. His portraits of the royal family hanging in the Prado Gallery in Madrid are renowned for their depiction of a court in decadence and decline. More remarkable are Goya's later prints and paintings. Goya was brought up in the **Enlightenment** tradition, and for this reason he was to support the rule of Napoleon Bonaparte's brother, **José I**, between 1808 and 1813. Yet he was also well aware of the limits of human rationalism and of the demons that lurked in the human psyche. This was reflected in his prints *Los caprichos* (*The Caprices*) and *Los desastres de la guerra* (*The Disasters of War*), which graphically depicted the horrors of the **War of Independence**, and in his Black Paintings, in which humanity is portrayed as at the mercy of dark forces it cannot control. Goya has, as a result, been seen as a precursor of impressionist art (particularly in his painting of the 3 May 1808 executions in Madrid) and of psychological and surrealist painting.

GOYTISOLO GAY, JUAN (1931–). Perhaps Spain's most highly regarded living author, Juan Goytisolo hailed from a middle-class **republican Basque** family that lived in **Barcelona**. His opposition to the **Franco regime's Catholic**, Castilian-centralist narrative of history has strongly influenced his work and also led him into exile in Paris from 1954. Simultaneously, personal freedom from all forms of oppression (be it political or familial) pervades his writing. In his early years, he was a communist, but he subsequently became particularly interested in the country's links with **Islam** and in the importance of Islamic identity in the construction of Spain, and from the mid-1960s he spent part of the year in **Morocco** (and since 1997 has been based in Marrakech). This had led him to identify with North African culture in comparison what he sees as the staid consumerism of the West. At the same time, his own homosexuality became an increasingly important element in his *oeuvre*. The political and sexual themes came together in his best-known novel *Reivindicación del Conde Don Julián* (*Count Julian*, 1971). And the attack on Western consumerism is an important element in his subsequent works, *Juan sin tierra* (*John the Landless*, 1975) and *Makbara* (1980). He is, finally, a passionate defender of the Palestinian cause and ferocious critic of the United States' policy in the Middle East. His two brothers, José Agustín Goytisolo (1928–1999) and Luis Goytisolo (1935–), are also important literary figures.

GRAPO (GRUPOS REVOLUCIONARIOS ANTIFASCISTAS PRIMERO DE OCTUBRE)/REVOLUTIONARY ANTIFASCIST GROUPS FIRST OF OCTOBER. This small **terrorist** group first surfaced in 1975 as the armed wing of the far-left Partido Comunista de España (Reconstruido) (Reconstructed Communist Party of Spain). It achieved notoriety with the kidnapping of the president of the Francoist Council of State, Antonio María de Oriol (1913–1996), in December 1976. During the **transition to democracy**, it carried out a series of terrorist outrages at particularly delicate times for the new institutions, leading to the suspicion that it was infiltrated by the far right. Its last kidnapping was carried out in 1995. Its leadership was detained in 2000, but it was still able to carry out the occasional armed robbery. In June 2007, following a number of arrests, the government announced that it had, finally, totally dismantled the organization.

GRUPOS ANTI-TERRORISTAS DE LIBERACIÓN. *See* GAL.

GRUPOS REVOLUCIONARIOS ANTIFASCISTAS PRIMERO DE OCTUBRE. *See* GRAPO.

GUARDIA CIVIL. *See* CIVIL GUARD.

GUERNICA, BOMBING OF. See BASQUE COUNTRY; PICASSO, PABLO RUIZ.

GUERRA GONZÁLEZ, ALFONSO (1940–). Alfonso Guerra was **Felipe González**'s right-hand man in the governments of the **Partido Socialista Obrero Español** (PSOE) between 1982 and 1987, and he is still an influential figure in the Spanish Socialist movement. He was born into a large working-class family in Seville, was academically very able, and studied humanities at the local university. He quickly became active in student politics, joining the PSOE's Socialist Youth in 1960 and the party itself in 1964. From the mid-1960s, he teamed up with Felipe González and played a key role in defeating the exiled **Rodolfo Llopis** leadership in August 1972 and ensuring that the party's executive commission (soon to be recognized as the legitimate leadership by the Socialist International) returned to Spain. He became a member of the "interior" party executive in 1970, and at the 1974 Suresnes congress, in which Felipe González was elected first secretary, he was made editor of the party's mouthpiece *El Socialista* and press and information secretary. Then, at the PSOE's 26th congress in 1976, he became organizational secretary, and finally, after the Socialists' 1982 election victory, vice president.

From the second half of the 1970s, González and Guerra formed a strong team, with Felipe González's more governmental tone offset by Guerra's radical rhetoric and acerbic, sarcastic attacks on the opposition. At the same time, Guerra took increasing control of the PSOE apparatus, ensuring, from 1979, compliant congresses that would rubber-stamp the leadership's programs. The relationship remained solid in the early 1980s, but was then to come under strain because of divisions over economic and social policy. While González tended to listen more to his neoliberal economics advisors, Guerra laid greater emphasis on the party's socialist tradition. The first crisis erupted in 1985, when Guerra blocked **Miguel Boyer**'s plans to take overall control of **economic policy**, thereby forcing his resignation from government. In the late 1980s, Guerra was rocked on his heels by a **corruption** scandal involving his brother Juan, which eventually forced his resignation as vice president in January 1991. However, he remained the PSOE's organizational secretary and had accumulated a great deal of power within the party apparatus. Over the following two years, the division between *filipistas* (or "renovators") and *guerristas* deepened, provoking a personal estrangement between the two men. This led to outright criticisms by Guerra of what he saw as the government's excessively liberal policies. Divisions were patched up in time for the 1993 general election, but emerged again once the government was back in power. The election of the neoliberal Carlos Solchaga (1944–) as spokesman of the Socialists' parliamentary group in the aftermath of these elections indicated a decline in Guerra's influence. This was confirmed during the celebration of the PSOE's 33rd congress in March 1994, when the *guerristas* were totally defeated by the "renovators."

GUTIÉRREZ DÍAZ, ANTONI (1929–2006). Gutiérrez Díaz, "El Guti," was the leading figure in **Catalan** Communist politics during the 1970s and early 1980s. He was born in the coastal town of Premià de Mar to southern Spanish migrants. He studied medicine at university and after graduating in 1953, practiced as a pediatrician. He joined the **Partit Socialista Unificat de Catalunya** (PSUC) in 1959 and began working to organize the health workers, spending the years 1962–1965 in prison. A convinced Eurocommunist, Gutiérrez was affable and charismatic, and in the late 1960s emerged as the party's number two behind Gregorio López Raimundo (1914–). He played a key role in the establishment of the Assemblea de Catalunya in 1971, and after the death of **Francisco Franco** emerged as the PSUC's best-known figure. He took over as general secretary in 1977, but after the relatively poor showing in the 1979 general elections, he was removed by the party's pro-Soviet wing in 1981. He made a comeback in the following year, resulting in a split within the party. Its showing in the elections of October 1982 was disastrous, but in retrospect he can be seen as laying the basis for the party's evolution in an eco-socialist direction. He stepped down as general secretary in 1986, but became a member of the European parliament in 1987 and between 1994 and 1999 was vice president of the European parliament. He retired from active politics in 1999.

GUTIÉRREZ MELLADO, MANUEL (1912–1995). General Manuel Gutiérrez Mellado played a key role in the **transition to democracy**. During the **Spanish Civil War**, he had fought on the **Nationalist** side, and he then worked his way up the **military** hierarchy, reaching the position of brigadier general in 1975. By this time, he was a known liberal and he was given the post of chief of the general staff by King **Juan Carlos I** in June 1976 with the brief to subordinate the army to civilian government. Then, after the resignation of *ultra* general Santiago de Díaz y Mendívil (1910–1994) in September, in reaction to the legalization of the trade unions, he also took on the post of minister of defense. The job was not an easy one. Much of the military was wedded to Francoist values and suspicious of change. Gutiérrez Mellado's strategy to tame the army was a dual one. On the one hand, he promoted more liberal generals to positions of responsibility; on the other, he streamlined the military's command structure and replaced the three ministers of the armed forces by a single Ministry of Defense under his person. However, he faced the constant abuse of *ultra* generals and the **Bunker** press, and had to contend with growing rumors of a planned coup. Finally, to take him out of the firing line he was replaced as defense minister by Agustín Rodríguez Sahagún (1932–1991) in April 1979 and promoted to the post of vice president.

The fact that a civilian had been given the job of defense minister for the first time since the **Second Republic** was of symbolic significance, but Sahagún proved powerless to halt military conspiracies. The end result would be the **Tejerazo** of February 1981, with Gutiérrez Mellado bravely standing up to the instigators of the attempted coup when they burst into parliament. Gutiérrez Mellado's measures, therefore, only slowly weakened the power of the *ultras* within the military. Nevertheless, the plotters were increasingly isolated and his reforms paved the way for the definitive depoliticization of the army and its subordination to civilian rule following the victory of the **Partido Socialista Obrero Español** (PSOE) in the October 1982 general elections.

GYPSIES. Gypsies first appeared in western Europe toward the end of the 15th century. From the first, their nomadic lifestyle provoked discrimination. Flamenco (or *cante jondo*) developed among the gypsy communities of southern **Andalusia** in the early 18th century. Discrimination intensified during the 18th century under pro-**Enlightenment** ministers, who pursued mercantilist policies aimed at reinforcing the Spanish economy. This engendered a new emphasis on work and sobriety at odds with the gypsies' way of life. Laws were passed outlawing the gypsies' cultural practices (language, dress, dances) and forcing them to adopt a fixed abode and trade. In 1783, a royal decree stated that those who disobeyed would be branded and executed if they reoffended. Enforcement was, however, very uneven, and in the early and mid-19th century, the gypsies were reinvented in Romantic western European literature as one of the chief components of Spanish exoticism. Hence, staple themes of Spanish painters working for the European market would be gypsy dancers and singers, along with bullfighters and *manolas*. In this way, flamenco became branded in the European consciousness as a key cultural identity marker of Spanishness.

– H –

HABSBURGS. The Habsburgs were the Spanish ruling dynasty between 1516 and 1700. The accession of **Carlos I** to the thrones of the **Crown of Aragón** and **Crown of Castile** in 1516 meant that these territories were incorporated into the Habsburg's European empire. Under his son, **Felipe II**, the **Crown of Castile** emerged as the core of the monarchy. His successors **Felipe III, Felipe IV,** and **Carlos II** would face increasing difficulties holding onto its mainland European possessions. The latter died without issue in 1700, provoking the **War of Succession** and a **Bourbon** accession to the Spanish throne.

HERMANDAD OBRERA DE ACCIÓN CATÓLICA (HOAC)/ WORKERS' BROTHERHOOD OF CATHOLIC ACTION. The HOAC was a working-class organization set up by the **Catholic Church.** It grew up in the 1940s and was recognized as a specialized branch of **Acción Católica** in 1946. Unlike the passive **Catholic unions** of the late 19th and early 20th centuries, under the impact of the liberalizing influence of western European Catholicism it began from the 1950s—along with its youth equivalent, the **Juventud Obrera Católica** (JOC)—to play an active role in defending workers' interests. As a result, it was to be a significant element in the clandestine labor confederation **Comisiones Obreras** (CC.OO) and gained working-class support in urban areas. It was, however, undermined by the Catholic hierarchy, fearful of its radicalism, in the late 1960s. *See also* LABOR MOVEMENT.

HERRI BATASUNA (HB)/PEOPLE'S UNITY. Herri Batasuna is a coalition of radical Basque nationalists who call for an independent **Basque Country**, and who have historically been identified with the armed struggle of **ETA.** It was founded in April 1978 and in the highly charged political atmosphere of the day, marked by ETA assassinations and police reprisals, it showed itself able to mobilize large numbers of predominantly young, radical nationalists behind its demand for the withdrawal of the security forces, total amnesty for political prisoners and eventual secession of the Basque Country from Spain. This was reflected its ability to win close to 20 percent of the Basque vote in elections to the Spanish and autonomous Basque parliaments. After the approval of the Basque autonomy statute—which was rejected by HB—that support began to wane somewhat. From the mid-1980s, the climate in the Basque Country became increasingly hostile to violence. This could be seen in the decision by the "democratic" Basque nationalist parties, the **Partido Nacionalista Vasco** (PNV), **Eusko Alkartasuna**, and **Euskadiko Esquerra**, to sign up to the Ajuria Enea pact in 1988. This pact firmly rejected **terrorism** and committed the parties to work within the limits of the Basque autonomy statute. Nevertheless, a radical urban subculture had been created that still served to mobilize sectors of Basque urban youth behind separatism. It was particularly successful among more disadvantaged small-town youth, subject to significant levels of unemployment. In the 1980s, campaigns against the dispersal of ETA prisoners outside the Basque Country and suspicion (which soon proved well-founded) that the authorities were behind the dirty war against ETA conducted by the **GAL** provided rallying points. When in 1995 ETA launched the Kale Barroka—street-level disturbances and riots—to pressurize the authorities, disaffected youth began to play a higher profile in the independence movement. HB continued to effectively operate as the political front of ETA and was unwilling to censure any of its assassinations.

After the **Partido Popular** (PP) came to power in March 1996, it was determined to take more severe action against ETA's support base. Within the judiciary, it found in the leading magistrate, **Baltasar Garzón**, an enthusiastic supporter of this policy. During 1996, the HB leadership was prosecuted for giving over one of its electoral slots to ETA during the 1996 general elections, and at the end of 1997 the HB leaders were found guilty and given seven years in prison. This sentence was subsequently annulled by the Constitutional Tribunal, but both the government and judiciary kept up the pressure, forcing the radical Basque nationalist daily, *Egin*, to close in early 1998.

At the same time, within HB there was considerable disquiet that ETA's terrorist campaign was going nowhere and costing Basque nationalism support. A new, more flexible leadership took over, under Arnaldo Otegi (1958–), at the beginning of 1998, and proved willing to negotiate with the PNV (in consultation with ETA) a possible cessation of ETA violence in return for the PNV captaining a more radical nationalist platform, whose demands would include the renegotiation of the Basque autonomy statute and the right to self-determination. This culminated in the signing of the Declaration of Lizarra on 12 September 1998, quickly followed by an ETA cease-fire. In the October elections in the Basque Country under the name of Eusko Merritarrok (For the Basque People—EM), it was recompensed by an increase in its share of the vote to over 17 percent, and in December it supported the investiture of the PNV's candidate, **Juan José Ibarretxe**, as president (*lehendakari*) of the Basque parliament.

The PNV and EH continued to work together within the Basque parliament during 1999 and in May signed an electoral pact. However, all understanding was brusquely brought to a close when ETA declared an end to its cease-fire in November. HB-EH's continued links with ETA were indicated in the following January, when it refused to condemn ETA's assassination of a Civil Guard lieutenant colonel. This led the PNV to break with EH, after which, in April, the radical nationalists abandoned the Basque parliament. The PNV was left in a minority and forced to call elections for May 2001. In these elections, afraid of a "Spanish" takeover of the Basque parliament, the Basque nationalist electorate rallied round a coalition made up of the PNV and the other mainstream Basque nationalist party, Eusko Alkartasuna, and abandoned EH in droves, leaving it with only 10 percent of the vote. It was clear that a radical nationalist alternative would perform better if ETA violence could be brought to an end.

The PP government, which from 2000 had an overall majority in parliament, now sought to move decisively against HB-EH. In the post-9/11 international climate, it managed to get HB included in both the **European Union**'s (EU) and United States' list of terrorist organizations. It also, with the backing of the PSOE, approved Ley Orgánica de Partidos (Fundamental Parties Law) in the summer of 2002, making possible the illegalization of parties with links to terrorist organizations. In August, the Spanish parliament then specifically voted in favor of the illegalization of HB-EH and its activities were then suspended by the investigative magistrate, Baltazar Garzón. Subsequent judicial action meant that it was not able to participate in either the 2004 general elections or the April 2005 Basque elections, though in the latter case it got round this in part by putting its weight behind a newly founded Partido Communista de la Tierras Vascas (Communist Party of the Basque Territories—PCTV), which came from nowhere to claim 12 percent of the vote.

Because of electoral weakness, growing police pressure, and the sense that "the armed struggle" was a dead end, HB still sought a negotiated way out of ETA terrorism. From the spring of 2002, Otegi had held informal discussions with the president of the Basque branch of the **Partido Socialista Obrero Español** (the Partido Socialista de Euskadi[PSE]-PSOE), Jesús Eguiguren (1954–). They agreed that of key importance in any future negotiations would be to separate discussions regarding the end of ETA terrorism with discussions on the future political status of the Basque Country. The opportunity for more serious negotiations came when the PSOE won the March 2004 general elections. The prime minister, **José Luis Rodríguez Zapatero**, supported reform of the **State of the Autonomies** (though would not countenance the right to self-determination), and so the twin-track approach appeared to offer a way out. ETA agreed to this strategy and declared a cease-fire on 22 March 2006. HB was angered that it still faced harassment by the police and when political negotiations were held in the autumn, they quickly got bogged down. HB refused to subscribe to the Ley Orgánica de Partidos (which would have meant in effect condemning ETA) until the negotiating process was complete, with the result that it remained illegal and contacts had to be maintained in secret. Under pressure from ETA, which wanted to see political advance, it demanded that a joint Basque Country-**Navarre** legislative body be set up within two years. This was rejected by both the PSE-PSOE and the PNV (which, after its "Plan Ibarretxe" had run into the sand, was taking a more cautious approach). On 30 December, ETA then effectively broke the cease-fire, bombing Madrid Barajas airport. HB refused to condemn the attack and blamed the government for not making any political concessions. Since then, it has found itself very isolated. In June 2007, Otegi began a 15-month prison sentence for "justifying terrorism." To get around its illegalization, it has, since 2006, established links with another radical Basque nationalist party, Acción Nacionalista Vasca (Basque Nationalist Action—ANV). However, the PSOE has put its weight behind the illegalization of both it and the PCTV. As a first step, both parties were suspended by Baltasar Garzón in February 2008, preventing them from participating in the March 2008 general elections. *See also* TABLE 10.

HUNGER YEARS. *See* AUTARKY; FRANCO REGIME.

– I –

IBARRETXE MAKUARTU, JUAN JOSÉ (1957–). Ibarretxe has been the **Partido Nacionalista Vasco** (PNV) president (*lehendakari*) of the Basque parliament from December 1998. His period in office has been marked by the party's decision during 1997–1998 to adopt a more radical strategy than previously. The key initiative in this respect has been the "Plan Ibarretxe," which he presented to the Basque parliament in September 2002, and which proposed the **Basque Country** should become a Free Associated State (Estado Libre Asociado) with the right to independence. In part at least, this plan was aimed at achieving greater unity within the Basque nationalist camp against what was seen as the growing threat of statist Spanish parties (especially the governing **Partido Popular** [PP]) and enticing **ETA** away from violence.

Hence, with ETA observing a cease-fire, during 1999 Ibarretxe worked with ETA's political front, Euskal Herritarrok/**Herri Batasuna** (HB) in the Basque parliament. For this he was subject to fierce criticism from the PP government, leading to increasingly bitter political divisions, both in the Basque Country and in Spain as a whole. He was enormously disappointed when ETA broke the cease-fire in November 1999 and suspended all contact with HB when it failed to condemn ETA's first assassination in January 2000. His "Plan Ibarretxe" then led to an increasingly radical confrontation with the PP and with more Spanish nationalist sectors of the **press**. When the **Partido Socialista Obrero Español** came to power after the March 2004 elections, the climate became more conciliatory. The new prime minister, **José Luis Rodríguez Zapatero**, refused to countenance Ibarretxe's proposals, but he allowed them to be debated in the Spanish parliament in February 2005, where they were defeated. Ibarretxe then called elections to the Basque parliament in what was effectively a referendum on his plan, but the PNV-**Eusko Alkartasuna** coalition lost four seats. This was a big blow. The whole issue was put on the back burner while the government held negotiations with ETA-HB between 2005 and 2006, but Ibarretxe has since revived his plan. This has led divisions to emerge between the more radical wing of the PNV represented by Ibarretxe (and supported by the charismatic former president of the PNV, **Xabier Arzallus**), and moderates captained by the PNV president, Josu Jon Imaz (1963–). Imaz's withdrawal from active politics at the end of 2007 has confirmed the victory of the more radical nationalists.

IBÁRRURI GÓMEZ, DOLORES (1895–1989). Dolores Ibárruri, "La Pasionaria," was probably the most charismatic figure on the working-class left during the 1930s. She became famous above all for her impassioned speeches in defense of the **Second Republic** during the **Spanish Civil War**: hers was the famous rallying cry *no pasarán* ("They shall not pass").

She was born in the **Basque** town of Gallarta into a poor **mining** family. In 1915, she married the miner and political activist Julián Ruiz and became involved in union work. She had begun teacher training, but had to give up her studies to help support the family. Nevertheless, she quickly showed a talent for both journalism and speech making, and began writing for the miners' mouthpiece, *El Minero Vizcaíno* (using the pseudonym "La Pasionaria" from 1918). She joined the newly formed **Partido Comunista de España** (PCE) in 1920 and focused on promoting the involvement of **women** in party politics, and in 1923 she backed the formation of Agrupaciones de Mujeres Antifacistas (Groupings of Antifascist Women) within the party. During the 1920s, she held positions in the regional party, then made the jump to national politics when she was elected onto the PCE's central committee in 1930. In the February 1936 elections, she became a deputy for Asturias. During the war, she played a key role in maintaining morale on the Republican side through her speeches. In line with the PCE's policies, she adopted a patriotic discourse, in which she compared the Republic's struggle against foreign Fascist powers to the **War of Independence** against the Napoleonic invasion between 1808 and 1813.

At the end of the war, she set up her home in Moscow, becoming PCE general secretary in May 1942. At first she was an orthodox Stalinist, but after the death of Joseph Stalin in 1953, she gave her support to a group of "renovators" within the PCE, led by **Santiago Carrillo**, who wanted to operate more autonomously from Moscow. After Carrillo became secretary general in 1960, as party president she took a more back-seat role. She returned to Spain after the death of General **Francisco Franco** and once again became a deputy for Asturias between 1977 and 1979, but by this time she was very much a symbolic figure. *See also* LABOR MOVEMENT.

IGLESIAS POSSE, PABLO (1850–1925). Pablo Iglesias was the leading figure in both the **Partido Socialista Obrero Español** (PSOE) and **Unión General de Trabajadores** (UGT) from their foundation in the late 19th century through to his death in 1925. He was born in El Ferrol in **Galicia** on 17 October 1850. Facing extreme poverty, he emigrated to **Madrid** at an early age with his mother and brother. As his mother could not support him, he was forced to live in a children's home and it was here that he first learned the compositors' trade. Once employed, he quickly came into contact with internationalist ideas, joining the **Federación Regional Española** (FRE) in 1871. It was from this time that Iglesias began to show the tenacity and organizational capabilities for which he later became renowned. He joined the breakaway Marxist group that formed the Nueva Federación Española (New Spanish Federation) in 1872 and that was subsequently to construct the PSOE. He became president of the Madrid printers' union, El Arte de Imprimir (Art of Composition) in May 1874 (the heart of the Marxist wing of the **labor movement** in the early years), and when the PSOE was founded in 1879, he immediately became its leading activist. This was confirmed in 1888 when he was formally elected president of the National Committee. Eleven years later, when the UGT was moved to Madrid from **Barcelona**, he also became its president.

Iglesias, therefore, concentrated a great deal of power in his hands. He was an austere figure, incorruptible and honest, though somewhat inflexible. Under his leadership, the party very much developed on the Second International model, combining revolutionary rhetoric with moderate "reformist" practice. For Iglesias, the need to guard the party and union organization he had done so much to build became of paramount importance. He was, as a result, fearful of any acts which might put it in jeopardy. Hence, he was skeptical of the general strike called during the **crisis of 1917**, and between 1919 and 1923 he opposed the pro-Bolshevik *terceristas'* more radical practice. He was seriously ill from the second decade of the century, and devolved increasing power into the hands of his protégés, **Julián Besteiro** and **Francisco Largo Caballero**.

IMAZ SAN MIGUEL, JOSU JON. *See* BASQUE COUNTRY; PARTIDO NACIONALISTA VASCO.

IMMIGRATION. Between the 1840s and 1960s, as a relatively poor country Spain had been a provider of labor for **Latin America** and, later, the major European economic powers. This changed as the **economy** strengthened from the mid-1980s, with the level of immigration accelerating rapidly from the late 1990s. In the mid-1990s, there were about 500,000 legal immigrants in Spain, but this figure grew to 1.1 million in 2001 and almost 1.9 million in 2006. In addition, in this latter year it was estimated that there were nearly two million illegal immigrants in the country. The latest figures for 2007 indicate that there are at least 4.5 million immigrants and the figure might be as high as 4.8 million (9.4 percent of the population). Close on 1 million are wealthier Europeans (with 269,000 British the largest contingent) who have bought housing, especially on the Mediterranean coast, but the majority comprise young men and **women** in search of work. The greatest number come from Latin America, which accounts for around 1,800,000 immigrants, with Colombians (372,000) and Equadorians (299,000) making up the largest groups. In addition, there are around 540,000 Moroccans and 531,000 Bulgarians and Rumanians. Many work on the black market, which has been estimated as comprising around 25 percent of gross domestic product.

All the data point to the positive effect immigration has had on Spanish economic development, with immigrants taking jobs (above all on the land and in domestic service) that Spaniards do not wish to perform. Nevertheless, the unprecedented wave of immigration into what had previously been quite a culturally homogeneous country has produced tensions. There have been accusations of immigrants undercutting local workers' wages. Furthermore, some underemployed young immigrants have become involved in petty crime and drug dealing (a trend encouraged by the inefficiency of the police and judiciary in dealing with them). Fear of crime has in recent years become a major concern among Spanish citizens, which some blame, above all, on young immigrants. This has led to several riots and, in the worst incident in the town of El Ejida province in Almería in 2000, attacks on short-term Moroccan laborers. In recent years, the sense of immigration running out of control has been exacerbated by the great numbers of illegal immigrants who have undertaken the hazardous journey from the North African coast to the **Canary Islands** in small boats. Almost 30,000 would-be immigrants tried to enter Spain by this method in 2006.

Such concerns prompted the Partido Popular (PP) government to try to take action in 2000 by cracking down on the employment of illegal immigrant workers, removing benefits from such immigrants, and initiating their repatriation. Nevertheless, in recognition of the importance of immigrants for the Spanish economy, this was accompanied by measures to allow illegal immigrants in work to legalize their situation. The PP (followed by the **Partido Socialista Obrero Español** [PSOE] from 2004) also favored immigration from Latin America over immigration from North Africa, because it deemed Latin American immigrants as culturally closer and easier to assimilate. New measures cracking down on illegal immigrants were taken between 2001 and 2003, but they had little impact. PSOE governments have, from 2004, adopted a more positive approach, making it easier to obtain temporary work permits and legalizing large numbers of illegal immigrants. In 2005, the government declared an "amnesty" for 700,000 illegal immigrants, allowing them to obtain temporary residence permits. This led the PP to launch an offensive during the March 2008 election campaign, demanding that immigrants sign a pledge to integrate into Spanish culture and promising legislation that would allow for the expulsion of immigrants without work. In a context in which the economic slowdown was causing unemployment to rise rapidly, this gained the sympathy of significant sections of the population (though it proved insufficient for the PP to actually win the elections). In February 2008, it was estimated that there were 400,000 unemployed foreigners in Spain.

INDUSTRY. The medieval and early modern Spanish **economy** was marked by a weak manufacturing base, with semi-elaborated and agriculture-based products the main exports and large-scale imports of manufactures. Inflation in the 16th century, followed by pestilence and a demographic crisis in the 1680s, worsened matters. There was a large-scale woolen textile industry in New **Castile**, but it above all produced a cheap, low-quality product for the general market. During the 18th century, the situation improved. Most notably, from the 1760s, a modern **cotton textile industry** grew up in **Catalonia** based on the reexport of profits from the **colonial** trade. However, in the 19th century, industrial development was geographically localized. From the 1860s in Asturias, **coal mining** developed on a large scale, while Vizcaya in the late 19th century saw an industrial takeoff based on the reinvestment of profits from the export of iron ore, making possible the development of a modern **iron and steel industry**. In other urban centers, production tended to remain artisanal, with large amounts of capital tied up in construction and in a whole host of consumer-based trades. Overall, the small internal market, the result of the backwardness of Spanish **agriculture**, limited industrial expansion and capital concentration. Matters were worsened because Asturian coal was of poor quality, leading to high energy costs. In western European terms, therefore, Spanish industry tended to be small-scale and suffered from low levels of productivity.

From the late 19th century, Spanish companies successfully pressured successive governments into ever-higher restrictions on imported goods. This was hardly likely to produce a dynamic, innovative, industrial sector. Nevertheless, **World War I** provided a much-needed boost to Spanish industry, which was able to take advantage of the country's neutrality by filling the gap left by the warring powers in the home market and also stepping in and taking over foreign markets. Moreover, this occurred in a context in which the rapid growth of the Spanish hydroelectric industry reduced dependence on expensive coal. These factors afforded a bonanza to all of Spain's major industries. At the same time, the need to substitute foreign imports encouraged some industrial diversification. In Catalonia, there was a move into electrical goods, engineering, and the metal industry, and in cities such as **Barcelona**, Cáceres, and Huelva, heavy chemical plants opened. Growth was most spectacular in Vizcaya, where the **banking** system was greatly strengthened and the iron and steel, shipping, and hydroelectric industries all grew apace.

However, the end of hostilities was to bring an economic slump between 1920 and 1922. The depression, moreover, made clear the fact that in many sectors of the economy, industrialists had not taken advantage of the exceptional circumstances to update plants and machinery. This was the case in the Catalan cotton textile industry, which would now have to fall back on the inadequate home market. It was also the case in Asturias, where in wartime conditions many marginal mines were opened, and where the general poor quality of the coal and growing geological problems kept up costs.

Nevertheless, during the 1920s, Spanish industry benefited from a buoyant international economic climate and, in particular, from the nationalistic economic policies of the **Primo de Rivera dictatorship**, which aimed to use state intervention to stimulate economic growth. From 1926, a large public works program was begun, benefiting the steel, metal, cement, construction, coal, and hydroelectric industries. Yet, when in 1930 the massive budget deficits caused the new regime of General **Dámaso Berenguer** to call a drastic halt to public expenditure, heavy industry was immediately driven into a new slump. The Great Depression of the 1930s limited economic expansion during the **Second Republic**, and, though Spain's industrial infrastructure suffered relatively limited damage during the **Spanish Civil War**, the disastrous policy of **autarky**, pursued by the **Franco regime** during the 1940s, combined with the economic boycott imposed by the United Nations, produced a large contraction in the **economy**. As a result, industrial production did not rise above the peak prewar year of 1929 until 1950. During this period, the state also took a significant role in trying to direct industrial investment though a public holding company, the **Instituto Nacional de Industria** (INI).

Henceforth, the pace of industrial expansion was to quicken enormously. The regime slowly began to liberalize the economy, received large amounts of aid from the United States, and started to attract foreign investment. Particularly important was the 1959 **Stabilization Plan**, which laid the foundation for greater economic liberalization. The result was unprecedented rates of growth, with industry and construction's contribution to Spain's gross domestic product growing from 29.3 percent in 1958 to 39.7 percent in 1974. For the first time, great enterprises employing over 1,000 workers, usually based on foreign capital, were superimposed on the sea of small Spanish firms. Growth rates were highest in the chemical, metal, automobile, and transport industries, in which foreign investors could take advantage of relatively low labor and land costs. One important consequence was that Spain acquired a competitive automobile industry. In this context, the geography of Spanish industry also spread out from its traditional centers of Catalonia and the **Basque Country** to **Madrid**, Seville, Zaragoza, Vitoria, Pamplona, and other locations.

However, Spain was hit very hard by the oil price hikes of 1973–1974 and 1979–1980 because most of the growth of the previous period was based on energy-intensive heavy industry. In addition, Spain faced intensifying competition from developing countries. Hence, between 1974 and 1985 the steel, cement, chemical, and metal industries were decimated and over one million jobs were shed in the manufacturing sector. From 1982, the **Partido Socialista Obrero Español** (PSOE) governments tried to encourage labor and capital to move into higher growth sectors of the economy through "reconversion plans," which aimed to restructure the finances of loss-making companies and provide financial support for industrial diversification in those areas most seriously affected by the recession. The impact of the recession was cushioned and some companies were refloated, but at a heavy cost to Spanish taxpayers. It was also during this period that neoliberals within the Socialist administration convinced **Felipe González** of the benefits of reforms to the **labor market**, which would make it easier for companies to hire and fire workers, and of the **privatization** of profitable or potentially profitable companies.

The corner was to a significant degree turned after 1986, when the rapid fall in the price of crude oil was accompanied by Spain's entry into the **European Economic Community** (EEC). This provided new opportunities for foreign investors, and direct investment in the Spanish economy grew from 177 million pesetas in 1985 to 640 million pesetas in 1990. The automobile industry continued to grow in importance (by 1999 Spain was the third largest producer in the European Union [EU] and the sixth largest in the world, and the fourth largest car exporter in the world), and there was now also greater investment in high-tech areas like electronics, aerospace equipment, and computers. This investment then helped boost Spanish exports. During this period, through mergers and consolidations, Spanish business became more competitive. Moreover, nationalized companies were encouraged to build and diversify prior to privatization, under the new conservative **Partido Popular** (PP) government in the second half of the 1990s, and this encouraged the emergence of a number of major Spanish businesses, which invested heavily in **Latin America** and have recently turned their attention to Europe. In the manufacturing sector, the most important is the petrochemical giant **Repsol**, followed by the power-generating company Iberdrola (which, in 2006, bought the British company Scottish Power). However, at the same time, the country's manufacturing base faced intensifying competition from producers in the EU and developing world. For example, there was a large contraction in the size of the workforce engaged in clothing and textiles, which only stabilized in the mid-1990s when what remained of these industries specialized in the high-quality end of the market.

Spain was badly hit by the global recession of the early 1990s, but growth thereafter resumed. However, since the 1990s, competition from eastern Europe and the developing world began to bite harder. This could be seen in the automobile industry, which declined by 12.7 percent between 2004 and 2005 (while production in the Czech Republic grew by 35.4 percent during the same period). In recent years, the economy has also become overdependent on a housebuilding boom, stimulated by rapid **immigration**, both by Westerners buying second homes in or retiring to the Mediterranean coast and by migrants from the developing world in search of work. The rapid slowdown in the construction industry during the second half of 2007 augurs a period of retrenchment. Overall, as in other western European countries, the importance of industry within the economy overall has declined (representing 30 percent of gross domestic product in 2004). There is a high-tech end in which foreign capital is heavily represented, while the 1990s saw the emergence of some internationally competitive Spanish companies. But there remain a great number of small-scale concerns which invest little in research and development. *See also* FOREIGN TRADE; TABLES 2 AND 3.

INFANTE PÉREZ DE VARGAS, BLAS. *See* ANDALUSIA.

INICIATIVA PER CATALUNYA-VERDS (IC-VERDS)/ INITIATIVE FOR CATALONIA-GREENS. This is a left-wing **Catalan** party, which has its origin in a coalition of parties, known as Iniciativa per Catalunya, formed in 1986. At the heart of IC was the Communist **Partit Socialista Unificat de Catalunya** (PSUC). From the early 1980s, the PSUC had been seeking to move away from its orthodox Communist origins and ally with new social movements, and the coalition provided the vehicle. In 1993, IU linked up with the ecological organization Confederació Ecològica de Catalunya (Catalan Ecological Confederation) to form the coalition Iniciativa per Catalunya-Verds. At first it worked within the Spanish left-wing coalition, **Izquierda Unida**, but in 1997, divisions with the general secretary of the **Partido Comunista de España** (PCE) and coordinator of Izquierda Unida, **Julio Anguita**, led the IC to break away. Anguita was accused by IC of taking a sectarian, blindly anti-government line. In 2002, the decision was taken to turn the coalition into a single party. It has had only a modest presence on the Catalan political stage, but it shot to prominence in November 2003 when its leader, Joan Saura (1950–), formed part of a coalition of leftist forces, under **Pascual Maragall**, which took over the running of the Catalan autonomous government, the **Generalitat**. The coalition government was reformed after the 1 November 2006 elections to the autonomous government, with Saura maintaining his post in the government.

INMOVILISTAS. This is the name which is often used to refer to those members of the **Franco regime** who in the early and mid-1970s refused to contemplate major reform. *See also* BUNKER.

INQUISITION. *See* SPANISH INQUISITION.

INSTITUCIÓN LIBRE DE ENSEÑANZA (ILE)/FREE EDUCATIONAL INSTITUTE. The ILE was founded in 1876 in **Madrid** by

liberal university professors after the publication of the Orovio decree, which prohibited any teaching that did not conform to **Catholic** doctrine. The ILE was strongly influenced by **Krausism**, emphasizing scientific enquiry and freedom of speech, and tried to develop a more egalitarian relationship between staff and students. In 1881, when the Orovio decree was annulled and the professors were once again able to take up their chairs, the ILE began to specialize in primary and secondary education, where it adopted "**rationalist**" teaching methods. In 1907, it also set up the Junta para la Ampliacion de Estudios (Commission for Educational Development), which gave about 50 grants a year for students to study abroad. In the same year, it set up a training college, and in 1911 was behind the construction of a student residence (the famous Residencia de los Estudiantes, in which **Luis Buñuel**, **Salvador Dalí**, and **Federico García Lorca** were to meet). The ILE remained small, but its importance lay in the fact that it had been the rallying point of high-powered intellectuals opposed to Spain's arch-conservative Catholic tradition. Former members of the ILE, like its founder Francisco Giner de los Ríos (1839–1915), Fernando de los Ríos (1879–1949), and **Gumersindo de Azcárate**, were thereafter involved in numerous initiatives to modernize Spanish state and society. They developed close contacts with **republicans** and with the **Partido Socialista Obrero Español** (PSOE) and were to play a key role in drawing up the educational reforms of the **Second Republic**. "Institutionalists" also pushed for social reform and the extension of collective bargaining, and were therefore closely involved in initiatives like the **Instituto de Reformas Sociales**.

INSTITUTO DE LA MUJER. This organization was created by the **Partido Socialista Obrero Español** (PSOE) government in 1983 to ensure that the equality of **women** in society, enshrined in the Constitution of 1978, was put into practice. In addition, when Spain joined the **European Economic Community** (EEC) in 1986, it became responsible for making Spanish law compatible with EEC law in matters relating to women. It was modeled on the French Ministry of Women's Rights and located in the Ministry of Culture. Under its first general secretary, Carlota Bustelo, a number of feminists close to the PSOE were brought onboard. In 1988, it moved across to the newly created Ministry of Social Affairs, allowing it a greater impact on policy. It produced two major reports in 1990 and 1993 on priorities and ways of achieving them. These included measures needed to achieve equality at school and in the workplace, and to provide women with financial support and health care rights. These recommendations then fed into the PSOE's legislative program, though by no means all the Institute's recommendations were accepted. At the same time, it also funded studies in a wide range of areas affecting women. From 1988, it decentralized its activities, promoting the establishment of women's offices within the autonomous and larger municipal governments. These then produced equality of opportunity plans under the guidance of the institute. It has sometimes been criticized for being long on recommendations and short on action. Nevertheless, it has played an important role in promoting its equality agenda through all levels of the state administration and also in raising levels of awareness among women.

INSTITUTO DE REFORMAS SOCIALES (IRS)/INSTITUTE FOR SOCIAL REFORMS. The Instituto's foundation, by royal decree on 23 April 1903, was the result of the growing realization in government circles that social reform was needed in order to try to integrate the working classes into the polity. The IRS's task was to prepare social legislation, study social conditions, and produce social statistics. In this respect, it carried out a vital function. However, it soon found that to legislate was one thing and to put this legislation into practice was another. From the outset, it faced hostility in employer circles, among local elites, and within sectors of organized **labor** (especially the **anarchist**-syndicalists, who in 1910 founded the **Confederación Nacional del Trabajo** [CNT]). Hence, the underfunded body of factory inspectors, set up in 1906, often found it extremely difficult to enforce the observance of legislation on female and child work (which became law in 1901), and later legislation limiting female night work and working hours. It was finally wound up by the **Primo de Rivera dictatorship** in 1924. *See also* AZCÁRATE MENÉNDEZ, GUMDERSINDO DE; KRAUSISM.

INSTITUTO NACIONAL DE INDUSTRIA (INI)/NATIONAL INSTITUTE OF INDUSTRY. The INI was a holding company created in September 1941 under the leadership of General **Fran-**

cisco **Franco**'s boyhood friend, the **military** engineer Juan Antonio Suanzes (1891–1977), as one of the key instruments of the **Franco regime**'s policy of **autarky**. Its aim was to promote Spanish industrial development, especially in what were considered the key areas of **iron and steel**, **coal**, electricity generation, **transport**, shipbuilding, oil refinery, and car making. Industries under its control, whether nationalized or partly owned by private capital, were the privileged recipients of easy credit and export and import certificates. However, it was both inefficient and overbureaucratized, and often undertook projects for reasons of national prestige. With the economic liberalization of the late 1950s, its role was downgraded, while the new **Opus Dei** technocrats made it somewhat more efficient. From the 1960s, more profitable companies were privatized, but it was charged with trying to develop economic sectors deemed of national importance that were not competitive on the international field. This included some industries with a future (such as the petrochemical and automobile industries) and also chronic loss makers which had to be nationalized (such as the coal industry giant HUNOSA).

The post-1973 economic recession, combined with the fear among policy makers that simply to allow companies to fold would produce serious social disturbances, meant that this latter role was expanded over the next decade, and it played an important role in supporting the iron and steel, shipbuilding, and textile industries. But from 1982, the governing **Partido Socialista Obrero Español** (PSOE) took a harder line, instructing it to shut down loss-making companies considered of no strategic importance (while giving financial support to workers who lost their jobs), or sell them on to multinationals that could turn them around (the buyout of the car maker SEAT by Volkswagen was the prime example of this policy). At the same time, through its "reconversion plan," the PSOE hoped to reduce the losses of key industries that were either nationalized or in which the INI played an important role (especially iron and steel, mining, and shipbuilding). In 1995 (together with a spin-off, the INH, a holding company involved in the areas of petroleum and natural gas), it was replaced by two new bodies: the Sociedad Estatal de Participaciones Industriales (SEPI), which was meant to restructure enterprises which could then be sold off to the private sector; and the Agencia Industrial del Estado (AIE), which grouped together loss-making concerns. Through a determined policy of **privatizations**, the new **Partido Popular** (PP) government would reduce very substantially the size of the state industrial sector in subsequent years.

INTEGRISM. Integrism was a movement launched by the hardest-line **Traditionalist** Catholics in the late 19th century. The key figures were Cándido Nocedal and his son, Ramón. From 1874, Cándido edited the daily newspaper, *El Siglo Futuro*, which was very popular among the lower clergy and within the Jesuit order. Then, in 1889, Ramón founded the Partido Integrista Español (Spanish Integrist Party). They were above all inspired by the writings of **Juan Donoso Cortés**, for whom Christian civilization would defeat the forces of liberalism and socialism in a bloody confrontation. However, they faced the opposition to the **Catholic Church** hierarchy, which, from 1878, backed the stance of the new pope, Leo XIII, who called for the Church to work with Europe's liberal regimes. In addition, the pope's 1902 encyclical, *Dum multa*, emphasized the need for both Catholic unity and subordination to the Church hierarchy. The key figure in this respect was **Alejandro Pidal**, whose Unión Católica (Catholic Union) integrated into the **Partido Conservador** in 1884. In 1905, leading Jesuits broke with the Integrists, arguing that it was necessary to vote for the least bad political alternative operating within the bounds of the regime (the Partido Conservador under **Antonio Maura**).

INTERNATIONAL BRIGADES. The International Brigades were composed of foreign volunteers who fought on the Republican side during the **Spanish Civil War**. Though not all of them were Communists, they were almost entirely recruited through the Comintern's national Communist parties from the summer of 1936. Most of the men who came to fight were working-class leftists fired by the need to halt the advance of Fascism across Europe. The first volunteers arrived at the end of September and were sent to train in Albacete. However, the first serious military action they faced was in **Madrid** in November. The first brigades marched into the city on 8 November, just as the Republicans were gearing up to defend the city from the expected **Nationalist** onslaught. Their presence was a significant morale-booster and they were to play an important part in the fight to stave off the Francoist advance over the following weeks. From the start, they were incorporated into the disciplined **Popular Army**, set up by the **Partido Comunista de España** (PCE), forming five brigades. Overall, it is estimated that about 60,000 volunteers were integrated into the brigades. They were in most evidence in the winter and spring of 1937, when they were usually to be found in the thick of battle. Thereafter, the number of casualties grew faster than replacement by volunteers and their military importance began to decline. On 21 September 1938, the prime minister, **Juan Negrín**, took the decision to withdraw them in the vain hope that the German and Italian forces supporting the **Nationalists** might take a similar step.

INTERNATIONAL WORKING MEN'S ASSOCIATION. *See* FEDERACIÓN REGIONAL ESPAÑOLA.

INVINCIBLE ARMADA. *See* SPANISH ARMADA.

IPARRALDE. This is the Basque name for the French Basque provinces. Basque nationalists, including both the **Partido Nacionalista Vasco** and **Herri Batasuna-ETA**, argue that the **Basque Country** (**Euskadi** or **Euskal Herria** in Basque) is made up of Vizcaya, Guipúzcoa, Álava, **Navarre**, and the thee French Basque provinces, and that they should be united as a single entity (which should be either totally independent or federated with France and Spain).

IRAQ WAR. The **Partido Popular** (PP) government of **José María Aznar** gave strong backing to the U.S.-led invasion of Iraq in March 2003. This was in line with both the government's Atlanticist **foreign policy** and with Aznar's desire for Spain to play a larger role in world affairs. Spain was at the time a temporary member of the United Nations Security Council and took an uncompromising stance. In addition, Aznar was the main initiator of a letter signed by eight European leaders who defended U.S. policy on 29 January, and met up with George W. Bush and Tony Blair in the U.S. military base of Terzeira in the Azores on 16 March, just before the invasion. Spain did not participate in the ground offensive, but subsequently sent 1,500 troops, mainly to the Shiite area of Diwaniya in central Iraq. This ensured that Spanish troops would not face any significant insurgency, but in the worst incident, the country lost seven secret agents in an ambush.

Aznar presented the invasion as part of the global war on terror and drew parallels with the struggle against **ETA** in Spain. However, it was hugely unpopular in Spain itself, with around three million Spaniards taking to the streets between March and April. This opposition was supported by the **Partido Socialista Obrero Español** (PSOE), which in particular criticized the fact that no debate had taken place in parliament on the sending of troops. On the back of this protest movement, the PSOE overtook the PP in the polls for the first time. It was subsequently to be an important factor in the PP's defeat in the March 2004 general elections, though polling data suggests it would not have had such an impact if the **Madrid train bombing** of 11 March, carried out by Islamic extremists inspired by **al-Qaeda**, had not concentrated voters' minds on the vulnerable position in which the government's foreign policy had left Spain. Aznar's support for the invasion also broke the consensus on foreign policy that had existed in Spain since the **transition to democracy**, which emphasized the central role of the United Nations in the development of international law, the need for a **European Union** (EU) consensus in foreign and security policy, and the advisability of maintaining good relations with the Arab world. The EU split into two camps, with Aznar backed by Tony Blair and Silvio Berlusconi. Spanish policy in Iraq was to change dramatically following the PSOE's victory in the March 2004 elections, with **José Luis Rodríguez Zapatero** making the decision to immediately withdraw Spanish troops on 14 April. The withdrawal was completed by 21 May.

IRON AND STEEL INDUSTRY. Until the 1870s, the growth of the iron and steel **industry** in Spain was slow. **Andalusia** was the dominant region, but charcoal was still the main fuel and costs were high. At the same time, stimulated by government policy, the country imported great quantities of rolled iron and machinery. The situation only began to change in the late 1880s. Over the previous 20 years, **Basque** mine owners had been heavily involved in the extraction of iron ore from the Vizcayan mines and its sale to Great Britain, and they were able to reinvest their profits in the creation of an autochthonous iron and steel industry. They enjoyed considerable cost advantages: high-quality British coal could be transported back to Vizcaya on the return journey of the iron ore shipments. The industry was further aided by the **nationalist** policies pursued by Spanish governments from the 1890s. **Tariffs** on imported iron and steel were increased in 1891 and again in 1906. Furthermore, new duties were put on imported railway stock in 1886, and subsidies were given to the shipbuilding industry in 1887 and 1908. This combination of factors allowed the industry to prosper. It was in these years that firms such as Altos Hornos y Fábrica de Hierro y Acero de Bilbao (1882) and La Vizcaya (1882) were founded. In 1902, together with La Iberia, they founded by far the largest steel complex in the region, Sociedad Anónima Altos Hornos de Vizcaya. It was on the back of this development that in the early 20th century Vizcaya became the most prosperous region in Spain.

Spanish neutrality during **World War I** was to benefit the industry greatly, and, after a short depression in the early 1920s, it was able to take advantage of the **Primo de Rivera dictatorship**'s ambitious public works program. This was, however, put into reverse in 1930 by the new government of **Dámaso Berenguer** in order to tackle the enormous budget deficit. The industry languished during the **Second Republic** under the effects of the Great Depression. During the early years of the **Franco regime**, its fortunes took a further dip when Spain was cut off from international markets by the policy of **autarky**. As a result, it could not import essential inputs such as coal and ferromanganese and it quickly became technologically obsolescent. With the liberalization of the late 1950s, aided by the input of multinational capital, the industry again expanded rapidly. Steel, metal, and automobile plants sprang up in many of Spain's new industrial centers during these years. Yet from the early 1970s, the industry was severely hit by the economic crisis and by growing competition from Japan and the developing world. From the early 1980s, the government of the **Partido Socialista Obrero Español** developed a "reconversion plan" that aimed to transfer labor and capital out of the old heavy industries—with the steel industry top of the list—into more dynamic sectors of the **economy**.

ISABEL I OF CASTILE. *See* CATHOLIC MONARCHS.

ISABEL II (1830–1904). Isabel was the daughter of **Fernando VII** and **María Cristina of Naples**. She was crowned queen in 1833, after the death of Fernando, but María Cristina exercised power as regent until Isabel was declared of age in October 1843. She would rule until forced into exile by the **Glorious Revolution** on 29 September 1868. Like her mother, María Cristina, she would only support the most conservative of **liberals** who made up the **Partido Moderado**. This helped ensure that most of her reign was dominated by law-and-order governments, which dealt with the threat of subversion harshly, retained a tight rein on the **press**, and maintained highly restrictive property qualifications for voting. It would also lead the *moderados'* liberal opponents, the **Partido Progresista**, to seek to overthrow her regime by force. This they were finally to achieve through the **Glorious Revolution**. Thereafter, Isabel lived in exile in France, abdicating in favor of her son, Alfonso (later **Alfonso XII**) in 1870. Despite Isabel's marriage to her cousin, Francisco de Asís, the Duke of Cádiz (1822–1902), in 1846, like her mother she engaged in a seemingly endless round of amorous affairs, both bringing the **Bourbon** dynasty into disrepute and giving **republican** propagandists ammunition.

ISLAM AND SPAIN. Moorish invaders entered the Iberian Peninsula in 711 and in under a century were to take over most of the territory. What has then often been referred to as a Christian "**Reconquest**" of the Muslim lands (Ál-Ándalus) began in earnest in the 10th century, with the last bastion of Islamic rule, in Granada, falling in 1492. Subsequently, the new Christian authorities demanded that the Moorish population convert to Christianity and adopt Christian dress. This was enforced with increasing severity during the 16th century. Finally, 1611 saw a wholesale expulsion of the Moors.

Until the 20th century, the links between Spain and the Islamic world were more evident in areas such as Arabic influence on **architectural** design, town planning, the **Castilian language**, and in the major Islamic monuments that were left standing (above all the Alhambra in Granada and the converted mosque that became the Cathedral of Córdoba), rather than any cultural affinity. Despite this, in the 19th century, European Romantics and, later, social Darwinists (in a positive and negative light respectively) drew parallels between Spanish and Islamic culture and values. Then, toward the end of the century, in the wake the rise of anti-Spanish "peripheral nationalisms" (most notably in **Catalonia** and the **Basque Country**), a small Andalusian regionalist-nationalist movement grew up, which emphasized links between Islam and southern Spain, idealized the Ál-Ándalus, and rebaptized the Reonquest as a brutal conquest. Important in this respect were a group of ethnologists and folklorists led by Antonio Machado y Núñez, professor of natural history at the University of Seville. This strand in Andalusian political and cultural thought has been present throughout the 20th century and briefly came to the fore in the aftermath of the brutal, centralizing dictatorship of General **Francisco Franco** during the **transition to democracy**—as witnessed by the rapid but ephemeral growth of the Partido Socialista de Andalucía (Andalusian Socialist Party). It can also be seen in the interest taken by some writers and novelists—most notably **Juan Goytisolo**—in ethnic and cultural ties between Spain and North Africa. At the same time, rapid **immigration** from the 1990s has led to the establishment of an important **Moroccan** population. This has produced some disquiet in Spain, particularly in the context of the U.S.-led "war on terror." The **Madrid train bombings** of 11 March 2004 greatly increased fears regarding the impact of this Muslim population, especially as radical Islamic groups, inspired by **al-Qaeda**, have called for Spain's reintegration into the Islamic fold. This must, however, be balanced by the key role North African labor now plays in the Spanish **economy**.

IZQUIERDA REPUBLICANA. *See* AZAÑA DÍAZ, MANUEL.

IZQUIERDA UNIDA (IU)/UNITED LEFT. Izquierda Unida, a coalition of forces to the left of the **Partido Socialista Obrero Español** (PSOE), was formed in April 1986. The key force behind the coalition was the remnants of the **Partido Comunista de España** (PCE), led by Gerardo Iglesias (1945–), and its most important allies were the pro-Soviet Partido Comunista de los Pueblos de España (Communist Party of the Peoples of Spain), the Federación Progresista (Progressive Federation, captained by Ramón Tamames), and the small dissident socialist party, the **Partido de Acción Socialista** (PASOC). The alliance had to all intents and purposes been formed to coordinate the campaign in favor of Spain's withdrawal from the North Atlantic Treaty Organization (NATO) in the lead up to the referendum on continued membership in 1986. About 11 million Spaniards voted for withdrawal, but IU found it difficult to translate this discontent into votes. The coalition's showing in the 22 June 1986 general elections was something of a disappointment. It received 4.6 percent of the vote (only 0.5 percent better than the PCE's disastrous showing in the October 1982 elections). On the left, **Santiago Carrillo**'s Mesa para la Unidad de los Comunistas (Round Table for Communist Unity) was an irritant, and it was never able to integrate the leftist Basque party, **Euskadiko Esquerra** (EE). More important, most Spaniards still did not see it as a serious alternative to the PSOE.

The situation improved during 1987–1988, as the trade union opposition (supported by IU) to the PSOE's **economic policies** grew. Between 1989 and 1991, however, it was seriously hit by the fallout from the collapse of the Eastern bloc and the fall of the Communist Party of the Soviet Union (CPSU). Critical voices within the coalition argued that this marked the end of the historical road for Communist parties and that either the IU should become a political party or there should be an attempt at rapprochement with the PSOE. This was firmly resisted by **Julio Anguita**, general secretary of the PCE from 1988 and IU general coordinator from 1991, but at the cost of serious splits within the coalition. This was an important factor behind IU's inability to fully exploit disillusionment with the PSOE in the June 1993 and 1996 elections (with 10.5 percent of the total vote in the latter).

Divisions remained after 1996. Dissidents led by Diego López Garrido (1947–) and Cristina Almeida (1945–) formed a separate party, Izquierda Nueva (New Left), and argued that IU should try to work with the PSOE opposition. They briefly joined the coalition but were expelled in 1997 (after which Izquierda Nueva joined the PSOE). The Catalan left-wing alliance, **Iniciativa per Catalunya-Verds**, also left for similar reasons. Anguita was forced to retire from active politics in December 1999, after which Francisco Frutos (1939–)—who had already taken over as general secretary of the PCE in December 1998—became IU general coordinator and candidate for prime minister in the 2000 general elections. The problem was that Frutos had spent most his life in the PCE apparatus, lacked charisma, and was not well known among the general public. In these elections, despite the previous anti-Socialist stance of Julio Anguita,

Frutos accepted the offer of the PSOE leader, **Joaquín Almunia**, of an electoral pact (which, after negotiations, finally only covered the Senate). The decision was taken on tactical grounds, but was little understood by much of IU's electorate. The elections proved a disaster, with IU reduced to only 5.5 percent of the vote.

It was under these circumstances that in IU's October 2000 federal assembly **Gaspar Llamazares** narrowly defeated Frutos for the post of general coordinator. He quickly proved a far more convincing figure, working hard to open the coalition to new social movements, and entering into dialogue with the Socialist opposition. Under his leadership, IU played a leading role in galvanizing opposition to the **Iraq war** in 2003, significantly upping his profile. It has also linked up with Iniciativa per Catalunya-Verds once more and its regional federations (which enjoy a great deal of autonomy) have allied with local green and nationalist parties. However, when it came to the March 2004 elections, it suffered because of tactical voting for the PSOE in order to oust the ruling right-wing **Partido Popular** (PP) government, and only received 5 percent of the vote. At present, it is very divided between the supporters of Llamazares, on the one hand, and orthodox Communists, on the other. Llamazares saw off the challenge to his position by so-called PCE *críticos* in the meeting of IU's federal presidency on 18 December 2007. IU once again performed very poorly in the March 2008 elections, again suffering from tactical voting as many of its sympathizers, fearing a PP victory, voted in favor of the PSOE. This led Llamazares to declare that he would not be putting his name forward for reelection at the next federal assembly.

– J –

JACA UPRISING. *See* SAN SEBASTIÁN PACT.

JEWS. Many medieval Spanish towns had a significant Jewish population, with the largest centers in **Barcelona**, Burgos, Girona, Seville, Toledo, **Valencia**, and Zaragoza. Jews in the larger nuclei lived in their own neighborhoods (*juderías*, *aljamas*, or *calls*), under their own systems of authority (though, until the late 15th century, even in these areas there remained considerable overlap with the Christian population). The Jewish communities stood out both culturally and economically. They excelled as scholars and physicians. Moreover, a significant number of Jews had accumulated considerable wealth through commerce, money lending, and tax gathering, and had a notable presence in the various medieval parliaments (**Cortes**). This generated envy within sectors of the Christian community, with the result that, in a context of growing religious intolerance during the 14th century, Jews were subject to hostile propaganda and were, on occasion, on the receiving end of riots. In the worst incident, in 1391, Jews were massacred in Barcelona, Toledo, and Valencia. At the same time, a movement excluding Jews from many professions and public posts gained strength and efforts were made to segregate the Jewish and Christian populations. Most notably, from 1480 the **Catholic Monarchs** ordered the establishment of *juderías* in all towns in which Jews lived and local officials isolated them from the surrounding Christian town (going so far as to force the Jews to wear special insignia when they left their quarter).

In response, many Jews converted to Christianity. However, whether real or motivated by malice, suspicion was expressed as to whether they continued secretly to practice the Jewish faith. In response, in 1478, Isabel I of Castile was convinced by leading figures within the **Catholic Church** of the need to ask the pope for permission to set up a Tribunal del Santo Oficio (more generally known as the **Spanish Inquisition**) to look into the religious practices of the so-called *converso* Jews (or "New Christians"). It began to function in both the **Crown of Aragón** and **Crown of Castile** in 1480. The practice of allowing anonymous denunciations meant that *converso* Jews lived in constant fear of arrest. Furthermore, growing pressure was placed on practicing Jews to convert. In 1492, to rid Spain of the people who were seen as supporting the *conversos* in their heresies, those who refused to take this step were expelled. About 50,000 permanently emigrated while 80,000 made the decision to convert. In addition, around 250,000 Jews who had already converted remained. Nevertheless, they continued to face prejudice, especially as the "pure blood" (*limpieza de sangre*) movement—by which only men from old Christian families were eligible for posts in public professions and the Church—which originated in the 1480s, gained strength from the 1550s. Furthermore, "pure blood" also became a requirement in order to be granted noble status by the crown. The Spanish Inquisition was not abolished until 1834 and legislation favoring "Old Christians" was not totally repealed until 1854. Nevertheless, under the **Enlightened** 18th-century **Bourbon** rulers, discrimination abated and *converso* families found it easier to fully integrate into Christian Spanish society. Small Jewish communities settled in Spain during the 19th century. The number of Jews in Spain is currently estimated to number around 12,000.

JOSÉ I, JOSEPH BONAPARTE (1768–1844). The elder brother of Napoleon Bonaparte, Joseph was proclaimed king of Spain on Napoleon's instructions on 6 June 1808, shortly before the Napoleonic **Bayonne Constitution** was approved by a pliant **Cortes**. He had some support in Spain among elements within the elite, intellectuals, and administrators (the so-called *afrancesados*), who saw him as providing the opportunity for an orderly transition to **liberalism**. He remained in power in the occupied territories until the defeat of the Napoleonic armies in 1813.

JUAN CARLOS I (1938–). Juan Carlos was proclaimed king and head of state by the Francoist **Cortes** on 22 November 1975 following the death of General **Francisco Franco**, and since the introduction of a democratic **constitution** in 1978, he has reigned as a constitutional monarch. He was born in Rome in 1938, the grandson of **Alfonso XIII** and son of **Juan de Borbón y Battenberg** (Don Juan). When Alfonso XIII abdicated in favor of Don Juan in 1941, Juan Carlos became, according to **Bourbon** monarchists, next in line to the throne after his father. Franco, however, though having monarchist sympathies, was determined that there should be no monarchist succession until after his incapacitation or death, and that any future monarch should accept the principles of his regime. Don Juan, therefore, had to accept that he would not reign and that his son would only do so if he were educated in Spain under Franco's watchful eye. In 1948, as a result, Don Juan agreed that Juan Carlos should go to school in **Madrid**, and in 1954 that he should complete his education in the academies of the three military services, the army, navy, and air force. From the early 1960s, Juan Carlos began to be groomed for office, with regime bureaucrat and law professor **Torcuato Fernández-Miranda** put in charge of his education.

Under the influence of **Luis Carrero Blanco**, Franco finally agreed to support the designation of Juan Carlos as his successor in 1969. His designation was presented to the Council of the Realm on 21 July, and one day later it was approved by the **Cortes** by 491 votes to 19. On 23 July, Juan Carlos officially swore "loyalty to his Excellency the chief of state and fidelity to the principles of the **Movimiento Nacional** and the fundamental laws of the kingdom." Nevertheless, by 1970, he had discreetly established himself as a reformer. Indeed, early in the year there was tension with Franco when Juan Carlos told *The New York Times* that the form of government would in future have to be different from that of postwar Spain. The comments were published under the headline "Juan Carlos Wants a Democratic Regime."

There were probably a number of reasons behind Juan Carlos's reforming stance. He was intelligent and was no doubt convinced by *aperturista* arguments that reform was needed in order to guarantee the future of the **monarchy**. In particular, he was on friendly terms with a number of reform-oriented young professionals, who in 1973 formed a group called **Tácito**. Moreover, by the early 1970s, the democratic Western powers, and especially the United States, had come to realize that a controlled opening was necessary in order to forestall a crisis. Juan Carlos first officially visited the United States in June 1971 and then established a close relationship with the American ambassador Robert P. Hill. It seems likely that these contacts encouraged Juan Carlos to back democratic change. The message was, it seems, reinforced by the American president Gerald Ford during a visit to Madrid in May 1975.

Juan Carlos first took over the reins of power in July 1974 when Franco was hospitalized after a bout of phlebitis. Reformers within the regime called for him to be invested with full powers, but the prime minister, **Carlos Arias Navarro**, equivocated, allowing the Francoist **Bunker** to move quickly and encourage Franco to resume power as soon as possible. This he did on 3 September.

Juan Carlos would not get a further chance until Franco's death. On taking office, he was convinced of the need for quite far reaching reform. In order not to upset die-hard Francoists, he had to tread warily. Arias Navarro was, therefore, confirmed as prime minister, but more reforming ministers were brought into other areas of government. Torcuato Fernández-Miranda was made president of the Cortes and Council of the Realm, **Manuel Fraga** became the minister of the interior, José María de Areilza (1909–1998) became foreign minister, and Antonio Garrigues (1904–2004) was chosen as minister of justice. It was under these men that the **transition to democracy** got under way. They were all in the reform camp and were quick to establish contacts with the opposition. However, Arias Navarro was incapable of carrying out fundamental reform, leading Juan Carlos to force his resignation in July. This confirmed that Juan Carlos wanted to push democratization further. He was under pressure because of the intensification of popular protest and also probably further encouraged by the United States. Henry Kissinger had visited Spain in January and Juan Carlos made a triumphal visit to the United States in June shortly before sacking Arias Navarro. Under the new prime minister, **Adolfo Suárez**, Spain would quickly dismantle the **Franco regime** and put in place new democratic structures.

Over the next five years Juan Carlos continued to play an important role behind the scenes in trying to ensure democratic stability. His biggest headache was the Spanish **military**, much of which was wedded to the Francoist past. His greatest test came on the night of 23 February 1981 when he faced an attempted military coup, the so-called **Tejerazo**, which was only foiled by his decisive personal intervention. He was able to keep the majority of the army in line because of his status as king of Spain and commander-in-chief of the armed forces. His actions gained him enormous respect among the Spanish populace. Following the election of the **Partido Socialista Obrero Español** (PSOE) in October 1982 and the stabilization of the country's democratic institutions, he has been able to play a more back-seat role as an ambassador for the new democratic Spain. During most of his reign, there has been a tacit agreement within the media and political elites not to criticize the royal family. This changed in 2007 following the confiscation of the satirical magazine, *El Jueves*, for running a lewd cartoon featuring the king's son, Prince Felipe, and his wife. The **Catholic** right sees Juan Carlos as too liberal (in a debate in the radio station, **COPE**, there was a call for his resignation) and "peripheral nationalists" view him as a symbol of Spanish unity.

He shot to prominence in the Ibero-American summit of November 2007 when, faced with the Venezuelan president Hugo Chávez, who was interrupting the Spanish prime minister **José Luis Rodríguez Zapatero** and referred to the previous Spanish prime minister, **José María Aznar**, as a Fascist (because he had supposedly supported an attempted coup against him), Juan Carlos interjected, "Why don't you shut up?" This actually went down rather well with Spanish public opinion.

On 14 May 1962, Juan Carlos married Princess Sophie of Greece and Denmark. They have two daughters, Elena and Cristina, and a son, Felipe. Felipe, who is married with three children, is the heir to the throne.

JUAN DE BORBÓN Y BATTENBERG (DON JUAN), COUNT OF BARCELONA (1913–1993). Juan de Borbón was the only **Bourbon** heir not actually to rule since the Bourbon dynasty had been established in Spain. Nevertheless, through his negotiations with the **Franco regime** he was able to ensure that his son, **Juan Carlos**, would reign after the death of General **Francisco Franco** in 1975. At first he was third in line to the throne behind his two elder brothers, but the eldest, Alfonso, renounced the throne in 1933 to marry a nonroyal, and the second eldest, Jaime, was forced to renounce the throne because he was deaf and dumb. At the beginning of the **Spanish Civil War**, he tried to enlist as a volunteer in the **Nationalist** army but was turned away. Alfonso XIII abdicated in his favor shortly before his death in 1941. Immediately, Don Juan (as he was often referred to, he also used the family title of Count of Barcelona) asked that the **monarchy** be restored in Spain.

Franco's reaction was ambiguous. On the one hand, he wished to keep onboard promonarchist **military** men, who favored a Bourbon restoration, and he himself had strong monarchist sympathies. But, on the other, he was determined to safeguard his own position. He therefore answered that a monarchy would be the eventual coronation of the regime so long as it adhered to its principles. Don Juan responded by trying to put further pressure on Franco. In the early stages of the war, he had been pro-Nazi, but as the war progressed and moved against the Axis he declared himself a constitutional monarch. Don Juan had powerful supporters in Spain. Conservative social elites still identified with the Bourbon cause and within the army high-ranking generals, such as Alfredo Kindelán (1879–1962) and Antonio Aranda (1888–1979), afraid that Franco's identification with the Axis might lead to an Allied intervention, pushed for a monarchist restoration between 1942 and 1943. Franco, however, held firm, confident that these monarchists would not move against him for fear of destabilizing the political situation.

During 1945–1947, while Allied opposition to the regime was still strong, Don Juan flirted with the democratic opposition, including the proscribed **Partido Socialista Obrero Español** (PSOE), from his headquarters in Estoril in **Portugal** (where he was based from February 1946). In his Lausanne Manifesto of 19 March 1945, he specifically called on Franco to make way for a constitutional monarchy under his rule. However, by 1948, it had become clear that Franco's position was strong and Don Juan realized that he would have to play a longer game. Hence, he began to distance himself from his more democratic pronouncements, meeting Franco on his personal yacht, *Azor*, on 25 August 1948 to discuss the future of the monarchy. The previous March, in order to project a more acceptable image in the West, the Franco regime had approved the Law of Succession, which allowed Franco to "install" (rather than restore) a monarchical successor and he intimated to Don Juan that this would be a Bourbon figure as long as the future king accepted the principles of the regime. Don Juan now retreated and agreed that his son, Juan Carlos, should be educated in Spain. The tacit compromise was therefore reached whereby though Don Juan might never reign, after the incapacitation or death of Franco, either he or his son would be crowned king.

During the 1950s and 1960s, Don Juan still maintained the support of influential figures within the social elite and armed forces. Their pronouncements in his favor annoyed Franco, but he allowed them to act as a semi-tolerated opposition. Don Juan himself never fully accepted the regime, and tried to push Franco to liberalize. Nevertheless, in 1955, he felt he had no choice but to compromise further by accepting that Juan Carlos's education in Spain should be completed at the academies of the three military services. This was then to be followed by studies at the University of Madrid and crowned by experience in the practice of government at the Caudillo's side. This followed a meeting between Franco and Don Juan on the estate of the Conde de Ruiseñada (Don Juan's representative in Spain) in the province of Cáceres on 29 December 1954, at which Don Juan was warned that any attempt to take Juan Carlos out of Spain would be regarded as an abdication of the throne. During the 1960s and early 1970s, Don Juan continued to press his own case to accede to the throne. In 1965, he virtually set up a shadow cabinet under the ex-ambassador to France, José María de Areilza (1909–1988), the Count of Motrico. The decision by Juan Carlos to accept the throne as Franco's successor in July 1969 therefore led to a temporary break between father and son. At a meeting of the PSOE-dominated Plataforma Democrática (Democratic Platform) on 14 June 1975, Don Juan affirmed his commitment to human rights, assured that the monarchy would need to be popularly endorsed, and even reasserted his position as legitimate heir to the throne, thereby calling into question Juan Carlos's succession. Nevertheless, once it became clear that a **transition to democracy** was under way under his son's guidance, he relented, abdicating in favor of Juan Carlos on 14 May 1977 and thereby giving him the historical legitimacy he desired.

JUNTA DEMOCRÁTICA/DEMOCRATIC JUNTA. This was a co-alition of anti-Francoist parties formed under the aegis of the **Partido Comunista de España** (PCE) in June 1974. The **Partido Socialista Obrero Español** (PSOE), however, refused to join, fearful of coming under Communist influence, and in June 1975 it was behind the creation of an alternative forum, the Plataforma Democrática (Democratic Platform). They were to unite in March 1976 with the formation of Coordinación Democrática (Democratic Coordination)—at the time often referred to as the Platajunta. *See also* TRANSITION TO DEMOCRACY.

JUNTAS DE DEFENSA/DEFENSE JUNTAS. The Juntas de Defensa were associations formed by officers below the rank of major, largely based in mainland Spain (and therefore referred to as *peninsulares*), to push for improvements in pay and conditions. These officers were seriously affected by the inflationary spiral which had gripped the country since 1914. Furthermore, they were jealous of the rapid promotions enjoyed by front-line *africanista* officers in **Morocco**, and called for promotion by seniority (the *escala cerrada*) to prevent what they saw as favoritism and political promotions. The final straw was the introduction of aptitude tests during 1916. The technical corps already had their own Juntas and the cavalry and infantry officers followed them. Most important were the infantry officers, who set up a Junta Central in **Barcelona** in the autumn. The infantry *junteros* couched their language in **regenerationist** terms, and thereby enjoyed the sympathy of regionalist and **republican** politicians, who hoped they might be able to spearhead a bloodless revolution. In May 1917, under instructions from King **Alfonso XIII**, the Barcelona leadership was arrested. However, the Barcelona Junta reacted threateningly, buoyed up by the support it received from officers throughout the country. This led both the king and government to capitulate, and was an important factor in the decision of the **Partido Liberal** (PL) government of **Manuel García Prieto** to resign several days later. This set in train the so-called **crisis of 1917**. **Catalanists** and the left were by this time pushing for constitutional reform and hoped for *juntero* support. They were to be sorely disappointed. Despite their rhetoric, most officers were conservatives who believed in order and the sacred unity of Spain, and who could not therefore stomach either left politics or Catalanism. Moreover, the new **Partido Conservador** (PC) government, led by **Eduardo Dato**, introduced significant pay raises. Both these factors explain why the *junteros* refused to support the Assembly movement, launched by the **Lliga Regionalista** in July, and put down a general strike called by the **Partido Socialista Obrero Español** (PSOE) on 9 August.

Over the next five years, the *junteros* continued to play a key role in Spanish political life. Angry at the loss of popular support they had incurred by putting the August general strike down, they forced the Dato government out in October 1917. At the same time, they established close links with the hard-line conservative **Juan de la Cierva** and ensured he entered the cabinet of the subsequent coalition government led by **Manuel García Prieto**. Cierva then forced through a decree that gave the Juntas their demand that promotion be based on seniority and further boosted their wages. However, more intense military operations in Morocco from 1919 led the *africanistas* to gain an upper hand in inter-army politics and this allowed the PC **Sánchez Guerra** government to theoretically outlaw them in November 1922 with the support of the king and senior generals, while limiting promotion by merit. Nevertheless, they continued to play an important role in the shade, actively backing the coup by General **Miguel Primo de Rivera** in 1923. *See also* MILITARY.

JUNTAS DE OFENSIVA NACIONAL SINDICALISTA/JUNTAS OF THE NATIONAL-SYNDICALIST OFFENSIVE. *See* FALANGE ESPAÑOLA.

JURISDICTIONS' LAW. *See* ALFONSO XIII; CU-CUT! INCIDENT; SOLIDARITAT CATALANA.

JUVENTUD DE ACCIÓN POPULAR (JAP)/POPULAR ACTION YOUTH. *See* CONFEDERACIÓN ESPAÑOLA DE DERECHAS AUTÓNOMAS; FALANGE ESPAÑOLA.

JUVENTUD OBRERA CATÓLICA (JOC)/CATHOLIC WORKERS' YOUTH. The JOC was the youth branch of **Acción Católica** during the **Franco regime**. It grew up in the late 1940s and 1950s, and, like its adult equivalent, the **Hermandad Obrera de Acción Católica** (HOAC), it came to play an important role in defending workers' interests and criticizing the support the **Catholic** hierarchy gave to the Franco regime. It was precisely this social and political radicalism which led both it and the HOAC to be dismantled by the Church between 1967 and 1968. *See also* COMISIONES OBRERAS; LABOR MOVEMENT.

– K –

KINGDOM OF CASTILE. *See* CROWN OF CASTILE.

KRAUSISM. The philosophical ideas of Karl Friedrich Krause were imported into Spain from Germany by the Madrid philosophy professor Julián Sanz del Río (1814–1869) in the mid-19th century. Krausism was a rationalist, **liberal** humanist ideology, which laid stress on the power of **education** to change society. It therefore found favor among the liberal, middle-class, intellectual elite, who rejected the dogmatism and intolerance of the Spanish **Catholic Church**. The leading figures in this tradition, men like Francisco Giner de los Ríos (1839–1915), **Nicolás Salmerón**, and **Gumersindo de Azcárate**, emphasized tolerance, respect for ideological and political pluralism, while showing a marked concern for social reform. They were, in general, **republicans**, but they developed links with the more liberal sectors of the **Cánovas Restoration**, were involved in educational initiatives like the **Institución Libre de Enseñanza**, and supported and participated in reform projects such as the **Instituto de Reformas Sociales**, which drew up plans for social legislation aimed at integrating the working classes into the polity. The movement's importance, therefore, outweighed the numerical significance of its adherents. Yet the liberal-republican forces it backed were unable to democratically reform the Cánovas Restoration and failed to prevent the radicalization of Spanish workers, who increasingly turned to Marxist and **anarchist** labor unions.

– L –

LA FURA DELS BAUS. La Fura is a Catalan performance group, which since arranging the opening ceremony in the 1992 **Barcelona** Olympic Games, *Mar Mediterránea* (*Mediterranean Sea*) has shot to international fame. It is renowned for its frenetic, violently charged performances, which combine music and dance and which blur the boundaries between the actors and the audience. Since 2000, it has put on a number of macroshows, like *L'home del mil·leni* (*The Man of the Millennium*) in Barcelona, to celebrate the new millennium, which attract audiences in the tens of thousands along with mass company sponsorship.

LA GRANJA REBELLION/MOTIN DE LA GRANJA. The La Granja rebellion was carried out by the regiment of the Royal Guard based in the town of La Granja on 12 August 1836. It was part of a larger movement by urban **liberals** to ensure the return of the leader of the **Partido Progresista Juan Álvarez Mendizábal** to power. The regent, **María Cristina of Naples**, who was staying at La Granja, was forced to accept the Constitution of 1812 and a new Partido Progresista administration.

LA PASIONARIA. *See* IBÁRRURI GÓMEZ, DOLORES.

LABOR MARKET. In the 19th and early 20th centuries, within a western European context, Spain's **economy** was marked by the rather late and uneven nature of its **industrial** development. Hence, there remained a large agricultural sector. In southern Spain, large numbers of landless laborers worked on great estates, known as *latifundia*, while in much of the north, peasant families worked on much smaller plots of land. Both types of **agriculture** suffered from relatively low productivity and from the mid-19th century, large numbers of rural Spaniards began to emigrate abroad, especially to **Latin America**. The late 19th century also saw growing internal migration to the large industrial centers, especially **Catalonia** (from Aragón and **Valencia**, and later Murcia), and Vizcaya (from **Galicia** and New **Castile**) within the **Basque Country**. However, Spain's highly cyclical internal market also meant that, especially in consumer-based industries like **cotton textiles**, there were frequent slumps leading to high unemployment. Until 1914, this, along with employer hostility and state repression, meant that **trade unions** found it difficult to establish a firm hold.

The labor market became much tighter in the boom conditions that accompanied **World War I**, allowing a rapid growth in the power of the trade unions. A serious slump followed between 1920 and 1922, but heavy public spending on infrastructure during the **Primo de Rivera dictatorship** gave a strong boost to industries like **iron and steel** and construction. Because Spain was a relatively closed economy, the Great Depression hit rather later than in the major industrial economies, but from 1932 unemployment began to rise. However, the much more liberal political climate of the **Second Republic** meant that trade unions were able to strengthen greatly between 1931 and 1933 and again (after the **Bienio Negro**) in 1936.

With respect to the sexual division of labor, through to the 1910s it was very much taboo for **women** in established middle-class families to undertake paid labor (though lower-middle class women would often secretly work from home), but the 1920s and 1930s began to witness the incorporation of younger middle-class women into the growing **service sector**. However, working-class women had little choice but to work in manufacturing when young, given low family income. Once of child-bearing age, they would often retire to the domestic sphere but continue working from home. In peasant families, girls either helped on the land or worked as domestic servants, and peasant women would continue to supplement their husbands' work in the fields throughout their lives.

The disastrous **autarkic economic policies** pursued by the **Franco regime** during the 1940s meant that despite the great loss of human life that occurred during the **Spanish Civil War** and its aftermath, the large numbers of **Republicans** who migrated abroad, and the attempt to force women back into the home, there were high rates of unemployment. This was soaked up during the 1950s and 1960s as the regime liberalized the economy and integrated into the Western economic system. In particular, heavy direct foreign investment in manufacturing made possible the consolidation of a much broader industrial base. As a result, internal migration resumed on a larger scale than ever, with **Madrid**, Catalonia, and Vizcaya the principal destinations. However, the oil prices rises of the 1970s produced an economic slump and led unemployment to rapidly escalate. According to official figures, average unemployment stood at only 1.5 percent between 1965 and 1974, but it averaged 12 percent between 1977 and 1986. Moreover, despite an economic recovery after 1985, unemployment resumed its upward trend from 1991, hitting a high of 24 percent in 1995. It was only during a new phase of rapid economic growth from this latter year that the tide was turned. It began to decline significantly from 1998, and was down to a little under 8 percent in the second semester of 2006, but has risen to over 8 percent at the end of 2007 in the context of a rapid economic slowdown.

The economic boom was accompanied between 1996 and 2005 by a growth in the adult participation rate in employment from 46.9 percent to 63.8 percent (almost exactly the **European Union** [EU] average). High unemployment from the 1970s slowed down the incorporation of women into the labor market. After falling during early Francoism, the number of women in work grew from the 1960s, with female participation rates rising to 38 percent in 1995 and 55 percent by 2007.

Several factors were behind the problem of unemployment from the 1970s. Spain was particularly badly hit because the 1960s boom had been to a significant degree based on energy-intensive heavy industry. Furthermore, as Spain integrated into the **European Economic Community** (EEC) and world markets, both old heavy industry (especially **mining**, steel, and shipbuilding) and much of the small-scale industrial base found it difficult to compete, with firms either going bankrupt or rationalizing production. In either case, job layoffs were the consequence. In addition, neoliberal economists argued that the high cost of firing workers was slowing economic restructuring and stifling the creation of employment. This was a legacy of the Franco regime, when a high level of job security was the compensation workers received for a lack of trade union rights and an underdeveloped **welfare** system. During the period in office of the **Partido Socialista Obrero Español** (PSOE) between 1982 and 1996, the governments' Ministry of Economics, under **Miguel Boyer** and subsequently Carlos Solchaga (1944–), sought to make the labor market more "flexible." Measures were taken to reduce the job security of permanently employed workers and make it easier to employ workers on temporary and part-time contracts. This met with heavy trade union opposition, including a well-supported one-day general strike in 1988.

Employers were, however, quick to take up the opportunity to employ cheap, nonunionized workers, with about one-third of the workforce on such contracts by 1997. This was a problem that affected young people and especially women, with many facing no prospect of progressing from temporary to permanent contracts. Arguably, the government should have put more effort into training programs and improving Spain's underfunded state university sector. Cheap Spanish labor found it increasingly difficult to compete with eastern Europe and the new industrializing countries in the areas of lower and semi-skilled manufacturing. In order to try to correct these problems, in 1997 and 2002 the **Partido Popular** (PP) government made it more difficult for employers to issue temporary contracts, while further reducing job security on permanent posts. This seems to have had little success, with most jobs created after 1996 based on temporary and fixed-term contracts. In 2007, 32 percent of workers were on temporary contracts, with over 60 percent of youngsters between the ages of 15 and 24 on temporary contracts (as against an average of 10 percent of workers on temporary contracts in those countries—including Spain—that belong to the Organization for Economic Co-operation and Development). However, as previously noted, the post-1995 boom has led to falling levels of unemployment. Much new employment has, in particular, been created in the booming service sector. Moreover, when discussing unemployment it is important to note that the official statistics are rather misleading. There is a large black market in Spain that, according to some estimates, makes up between 20 and 25 percent of gross domestic product. In part, this sector comprises low-paid workers who do more than one job (*pluriempleo*), and, in part, workers who are registered as unemployed, or do not receive unemployment benefit, and who are moonlighting. Often they have no choice but to work in the black economy because employers will not offer them legal contracts.

Furthermore, one has to bear in mind that young people in Spain tend to live with their parents until they are in their early thirties and that family structures are still strong, with the result that income from family members in employment (and unemployment benefit) is spread more evenly across the family than is the case in more northern European countries. This means that youngsters and the unemployed are often reluctant to undertake low-paid menial tasks and heavy labor. These factors, together with rapid job creation from the second half of the 1990s, explain why **immigration** from Latin America and **Morocco** has soared, with immigrant workers largely employed in areas (especially in agriculture and domestic service) in which Spaniards no longer wish to work. *See also* LABOR MOVEMENT.

LABOR MOVEMENT. The labor movement has played a key role in the history of modern Spain. During the first 40 years of the 20th century, Spain was racked by often violent conflict between the leftist working-class parties and unions and the right. In the early 1970s, working-class opposition was of fundamental importance in undermining the **Franco regime** and thereby making possible a **transition to democracy**.

The first Spanish unions were founded in **Catalonia**, Spain's only **industrialized** territory, in the 1840s, and in the **latifundia** districts of southern Spain between the 1840s and 1860s, where peasants also showed their discontent at the consequences of the *desamortización* through such acts as crop burning and cattle maiming. It was, however, only in the more democratic climate of the **Democratic Sexennium** that trade unions were able to proselytize with some success. In 1868, a large **cotton textile** workers' federation, the **Tres Clases de Vapor**, was organized in **Barcelona**. June 1870 then saw the foundation of the Spanish branch of the International Working Men's Association, the **Federación Regional Española** (FRE), which was to gain considerable support among Catalan urban workers and to a lesser extent the land-hungry peasantry of the south.

The leadership of the FRE was predominantly **anarchist**. This represented the beginnings of a tradition that was to be maintained through to the 1930s. Throughout this period, anarchists or anarchist-syndicalists were to captain a number of labor federations, which were to recruit large numbers of workers in Catalonia, southern Spain, Aragón, and **Valencia**. The FRE was almost totally destroyed by the onslaught on union organization that followed the **Cánovas Restoration** of 1875. However, new anarchist-syndicalist labor federations rose up to take its place: the **Federación de Trabajadores de la Región Española** (FTRE) in the 1880s, the **Federación Regional Española de Sociedades de Resistencia** (FRESR) in the early years of the 20th century, and from 1910 the **Confederación Nacional del Trabajo** (CNT). However, the Marxist tradition was not to be absent from Spain. The year 1879 was to see the formation of the **Partido Socialista Obrero Español** (PSOE), and in 1888 its trade union ally, the **Unión General de Trabajadores** (UGT), was born. At first the PSOE-UGT's base was to be found in Madrid, but it was soon to put down roots in the industrializing northern regions of Vizcaya and Asturias.

The anarchist-syndicalists and PSOE-UGT were to compete ferociously for working-class patronage. Labor organization remained rather weak until 1914, but the economic boom that followed the onset of **World War I** made it possible for the CNT and PSOE-UGT to grow rapidly in strength from 1917. This stimulated both Socialists and anarchists to ally to try to bring down the Restoration regime and replace it with a more democratic political system. Hence, during the **crisis of 1917**, they joined with **Catalanists** and **republicans** to try to force the Restoration politicians to step aside. This offensive failed in August, when a general strike called by the Socialists with anarchist backing was bloodily put down by the **military**. Yet over the next six years, labor protest continued to escalate and class conflict became increasingly embittered when Spain was hit by an economic downturn during 1920–1922, thereby stimulating industrialists to undertake a counteroffensive against the unions.

The high levels of labor protest were an important reason why the conservative middle classes and elites received news of the September 1923 coup by General **Miguel Primo de Rivera** with relief. Under Primo de Rivera's law-and-order government, the CNT and the small **Partido Comunista de España** (PCE) were suppressed, but the more moderate Socialists were allowed to continue operating in the open and to participate in the industrial tribunals set up to solve labor disputes. This meant that when, in April 1931, the **Second Republic** was proclaimed, the PSOE-UGT was in an excellent position to play a key role in the new regime. During the Second Republic, the labor movement grew rapidly in strength. After several years of falling real wages, unions began to push hard for improvements in working conditions, and as the economic climate deteriorated in 1933, this was to lead to large numbers of bitter and protracted strikes. Workers flooded into the ranks of both the UGT and CNT during these years. Smaller leftist parties and unions such as the dissident-communist **Bloc Obrer i Camperol** (BOC) and the syndicalist **Treintistas** were also founded. Under the leadership of the far-leftist Federación Anarquista Ibérica (Anarchist Inerian Federation), the CNT adopted all-or-nothing tactics and launched a number of insurrections against the Republic. The Socialists, on the other hand, entered a coalition government with the republicans, and attempted to carry through a program of social reforms. Most important was the bid to reform agrarian structures in the southern latifundia belt by redistributing part of the great estates to the peasantry. This reforming wave would, however, break on the determined resistance by landowning elites, with the result that the Socialists' rhetoric became increasingly radicalized, and, after the right's victory in the November 1933 elections, in **October 1934** they launched a general strike and insurrection aimed at toppling the new government.

The insurrection would fail and in the repressive climate of 1935, the labor movement would weaken considerably. A new opportunity was provided by the left's victory in the **Popular Front** elections of February 1936. Five months later, sections of the military rose against the Republic, plunging Spain into a three-year civil war. The attempted coup was to provoke a social revolution over much of Republican Spain. At grassroots level, both the CNT and UGT would collaborate in setting up agrarian and industrial collectives. Yet this social revolution would be rolled back before the final victory of the forces of General **Francisco Franco**. The key to this retreat was the rising power of the PCE and its Catalan sister party, the **Partit Socialista Unificat de Catalunya** (PSUC), consequent upon the Republic's dependence on Soviet arms. On instructions from the Soviet Union, which did not wish to antagonize the democratic Western powers, the PCE argued that the fight against the enemy should take precedence over social revolution, with the result that from 1937 the Communists began returning land and factories to private industry.

The right's victory in March 1939 provoked a dramatic break in the history of the labor movement. Under the Franco regime, independent unions were banned, and both workers and management were required to operate within the confines of the single state union, the **Organización Sindical Española** (OSE). Yet from the 1950s, workers were slowly able to reassert themselves. They did this by using channels for negotiation between unions and management within the OSE itself to elect independent candidates who would truly represent workers' interests and mobilize on their behalf. In the 1960s, the movement became known as **Comisiones Obreras** (CC.OO). CC.OO was a broad-based, loosely articulated movement. Many of its supporters had no political affiliation, though others had links to the Catholic **Hermandad Obrera Católica** (HOAC) and **Juventud Obrera Católica** (JOC), the **Unión Sindical Obrera** (USO), and the PCE-PSUC. By the late 1960s, the Communists were increasingly to dominate CC.OO, and this was to provide the organizational base for the revival of the PCE-PSUC during the transition to democracy in the mid-1970s.

From the early 1970s, labor's offensive against the Franco regime was stepped up. Large-area general strikes were called in protest against repression and in favor of independent unions. In the aftermath of General **Francisco Franco**'s death, unions were again legalized and during 1976–1977, CC.OO grew at a vertiginous rate, while the UGT also rapidly reorganized. It therefore seemed that the labor movement would play a key role in Spain's political future. Indeed, following the electoral victory of the **Unión del Centro Democrático** (UCD) in July 1977, a **corporatist** tripartite system of wage and social policy bargaining was instituted, with unions, management, and government sitting around the same table. The unions' position was reinforced because all workers at shop-floor level were given the right to vote for union delegates in elections even if they were not unionized.

Yet over the next four years the worsening economic climate weakened union power. Both the UGT and CC.OO were also pressured into accepting cuts in real wages to tackle inflation and restore the profitability of Spanish industry. Finally, not even a PSOE victory in the October 1982 elections would ensure the unions a key role in policy making. The Socialists were by this time trying to appeal to a wide interclass audience, and when they came to power, with respect to the **labor market**, they applied rather neoliberal policies. From 1988, this was, on the one hand, to lead to open conflict between the PSOE government and the UGT, and, on the other, to an alliance between the UGT and CC.OO. With the importance of manufacturing in the **economy** declining and the rapid growth of the **service sector**, the profile of the labor unions has declined since the 1990s. The number of workers unionized has fallen from a high point of almost 34 percent in 1980 to under 20 percent from the late 1980s. However, the post-Francoist system of collective bargaining means they continue to play a key role in negotiations between management and the workforce, and in the public sector they are still able to mobilize their members effectively. *See also* TABLES 5 AND 6.

LAÍN ENTRALGO, PEDRO (1908–2001). Laín Entralgo became one of the leading dissident intellectuals in General **Francisco Franco**'s Spain. Born in Teruel, he studied medicine and chemistry at the University of Valencia. After the **Spanish Civil War**, he moved in **Falangist** circles, was made professor of the history of medicine at the University of Madrid in 1940, and cofounded the journal *Escorial*. However, like other fellow educated Falangists, such as **Dionisio Ridruejo** and Antonio Tovar (1911–1985), he became disgusted at the mediocrity of the **Franco regime** and the lack of the most basic civil liberties. This was reflected in his key political work *España como problema* (*Spain as a Problem*), published in 1949.

LANGUAGE. *See* BASQUE LANGUAGE; CASTILIAN LANGUAGE; CATALAN LANGUAGE; GALICIAN LANGUAGE; VALENCIAN LANGUAGE.

LARGO CABALLERO, FRANCISCO (1869–1944). Largo Caballero was a key figure within the **Partido Socialista Obrera Español** (PSOE) and in its sister labor confederation, the **Unión General de Trabajadores** (UGT), between 1910 and 1939. He was born into a poor working-class family in **Madrid**, eventually finding work as a plasterer's apprentice. He joined both the UGT and PSOE in the late 19th century, and as the UGT grew he became one of the prime movers behind the consolidation of a paid bureaucracy within the organization. Hardworking and meticulous, he quickly rose to positions of the highest influence. In 1904, he became a worker representative in the **Instituto de Reformas Sociales**, vice president of the UGT in 1910, and the union's general secretary in 1918. During these years, he adopted an attitude similar to that of his social-democratic colleagues in northern and central Europe. He was jealous of his own position and that of his "team" within the UGT, put the growth of the confederation before any other consideration (hence a lifelong obsession would be to take over the working-class base of the **anarchist**-syndicalist **Confederación Nacional del Trabajo** [CNT]), was opposed to any radicalization of the UGT's union practice, and was wary of revolutionary adventures that might undermine the organization. For all of these reasons, he was totally opposed to the PSOE joining the Communist Third International between 1920 and 1921, and played a key role in mobilizing support within the UGT to ensure that the motion to join was rejected in the PSOE's extraordinary congress, held in April 1921.

However, Spain was not northern Europe, and the need to combat the entrenched forces of conservatism and reaction led the PSOE-UGT, on occasion, to be drawn into revolutionary action. Hence, Largo Caballero was at the forefront of the declaration of general strikes in August 1917, December 1930, and October 1934. Largo Caballero's moderate "reformist" background was, nevertheless, apparent in the typically halfhearted nature of the preparations and the lack of conviction with which they were carried out. This reluctance to be cast in the role of a revolutionary was more generally apparent when Largo Caballero became the spokesman of the PSOE-UGT left during the **Second Republic**. He had entered the **republican**-PSOE coalition government of 1931 as minister of labor. His primary aim was to carve out a powerful position for the UGT within the state apparatus and turn it into the country's only labor confederation. However, the right's ability to block his intended reforms led to widespread worker protest. This in turn encouraged Largo to radicalize his discourse, afraid that he might otherwise lose his working-class base. By 1933, Largo Caballero, referred to mistakenly as the "Spanish Lenin," was talking of the need for proletarian revolution. Yet this radicalism was almost purely rhetorical. This, indeed, was to have extremely grave consequences, for while he frightened the right, little was actually done to work for revolution.

This became clear during 1934. Largo Caballero was at the center of preparations to carry out a revolutionary uprising should members of the **Confederación Española de Derechas Autónomas** (CEDA) enter government. At the same time, he developed contacts with the **Partido Comunista de España** (PCE), and, through the **Alianzas Obreras**, also established links with other parties and unions on the far left. However, when the *caballeristas* launched the **October 1934 revolution**, it was both poorly planned and executed, with its main aim, it seems, to pressurize the president of the Republic, **Niceto Alcalá Zamora**, into not allowing CEDA ministers into government. The failure of October 1934 weakened the position of Largo Caballero. The initiative passed to **Indalecio Prieto** and **Manuel Azaña**, who wished to reorganize the republican-PSOE coalition of 1931–1933. Largo Caballero maintained his revolutionary discourse but in November 1935, with new elections imminent, accepted the formation of the **Popular Front** electoral coalition. Nevertheless, in order to give the coalition more of a working-class feel and to strengthen his position vis-à-vis Prieto, he insisted that it only be an electoral alliance and that other leftist organizations be allowed to participate. He also wanted the PCE to be involved in the forthcoming negotiations over the strategy to be followed, but this was blocked by Prieto and Azaña, leading Largo Caballero to resign from the PSOE executive committee on 16 December 1935.

Henceforth, in the months leading up to the **Spanish Civil War**, the Socialists would be totally divided, with Prieto heading the PSOE and Largo Caballero entrenched within the UGT. These divisions and the personal animosity felt between Largo Caballero and Prieto would very much influence the course of Republican politics during the civil war. In an atmosphere of revolutionary enthusiasm, Largo Caballero accepted the post of prime minister in a new Popular Front government in September 1936. In the following months, his moderate instincts once again came to the fore, and he was to follow PCE and republican advice and roll back the trade union revolution—which was just as much a revolution of the UGT base as of the CNT—and reconstruct state power. Nevertheless, the Communists saw him as an obstacle to their dominance of the Republican state, and the *prietista* Socialists and republicans had not forgiven him for the barriers he had placed in the way of republican-Socialist unity during the Second Republic. Hence, they were all keen to take advantage of the **May events** in **Barcelona** to engineer his downfall. Thereafter, the *prietistas*, supported by the PCE, mounted an assault on the position of the left-Socialists within the PSOE and UGT. Largo Caballero, vilified by the PCE press as an enemy of the working class, played no further role in the war. At its conclusion, he sought exile in France, where he was imprisoned by the Vichy government and finally sent to the Orianenburg concentration camp. He was liberated by Polish troops at the end of the war, but died in Paris on 22 March 1946. *See also* LABOR MOVEMENT.

LARRA Y SÁNCHEZ DE CASTRO, MARIANO JOSÉ DE (1809–1837). Larra was the leading Romantic essayist and literary critic of early 19th-century Spain, celebrated for his mordant wit and use of irony. He was born into an *afrancesado* family and spent his childhood in Bordeaux. His first series of articles appeared in 1828 under the title *El duende satírico del día* (*The Day's Satirical Magic*). Here, as in his later work, he combined literature of manners with literary criticism and social reformism. Throughout his life, his work was to be marked by an ironic critique of Spanish life, seen in, for example, his attack on the indolence of **Madrid** public life, *Vuelva usted mañana* (*Come Back Tomorrow*), and by a belief in the reforming mission of **liberalism**. In true Romantic style, his personal life was convoluted in the extreme and he committed suicide at the age of 28.

LAS INDIAS. Las Indias (the Indies) was the term generally used by Spaniards to refer to America after the continent's "discovery" by Christopher Columbus in 1492. The name reflected the mistaken belief that he had found a new route to the Asian lands of India, China, and Indonesia (baptized as Las Indias by Marco Polo). Nevertheless, until the 20th century Spaniards continued frequently to refer to **Latin America** as Las Indias. Hence the natives were referred to as Indians (*indios*), a name subsequently adopted by English-speaking American colonizers, and men who made their fortune in the Indies before returning home to Spain were called *indianos*.

LATIFUNDIA. During much of Spain's history, in **Andalusia**, Extremadura, and parts of La Mancha the landscape was dominated by great estates known as latifundia. During the "**Reconquest**" of Spain from the **Moors**, vast tracts of land were given over to the monarchs' Christian backers in the **Catholic Church**, nobility, and the military orders. Often the landowners (known as *latifundistas*) were given ownership of the land and in addition were granted rights to administer justice, collect taxes, nominate officials, and raise armies for the king (the so-called *señoríos territoriales* or territorial lordships). Later grants of land, while giving nobles and the Church these same privileges, did not give them outright ownership (*señoríos jurisdiccionales* or jurisdictional lordships). They were further extended during the 16th and 17th centuries as kings sold off crown and Church land in order to bring in much-needed revenue.

These latifundia specialized in the staple crops of wheat, olives, and, to a lesser extent, vines. By the 18th century, they were run by administrators or by wealthy tenant farmers and were worked by a vast army of miserable landless laborers or land-hungry peasants known as *braceros* or *jornaleros*. The disentailment or *desamortización* of the early 19th century only served to strengthen *latifundismo* because lands were auctioned off on the open market to the highest bidder. The latifundia system occasioned Spain enormous economic and social costs. Productivity on the great estates tended to be low and the half-starved *braceros* could not offer a significant market for manufactures. The social climate on these estates also became explosive. The *braceros* demanded the redistribution of land (which they often claimed had been robbed from them during the *desamortización*) and from the mid 19th century they began to join **republican, anarchist,** and Marxist unions. From 1914, the key union confederations became the **Confederación Nacional del Trabajo** and **Unión General de Trabajadores.** Meanwhile, the *latifundistas* attempted to break the back of the peasants' associations and sought authoritarian solutions to defend their property. Indeed, historians have often seen the intractable social conflict in the Spanish south as one of the key causes of the **Spanish Civil War.**

The **Franco regime** very much defended the interests of the *latifundistas*, and so did little to reform landholding structures in the south. Change only came in the 1960s, when under the impact of industrialization, peasants flocked to the cities in search of new opportunities, and landowners mechanized to compensate for rising labor costs. Today, therefore, the large extensions of land remain, but they are highly technologized (and often run by agribusinesses) and employ a relatively small number of laborers. *See also* AGRARIAN REFORM LAW; AGRICULTURE; FEDERACIÓN NACIONAL DE TRABAJADORES DE LA TIERRA; MINIFUNDIA.

LATIN AMERICA. After the "discovery" of America (**Las Indias** or the New World, as Spaniards referred to the region) by Christopher Columbus in 1492, Spain quickly colonized much of the continent. The empire took shape between the 1500s and 1540s, largely on the ruins of the old Aztec and Inca empires. By the 17th century, it stretched from California in the north to Chile in the south.

The independence movements of the late 18th and 19th centuries (on the mainland between the 1790s and 1820s and in **Cuba** between 1895 and 1898) had a major impact on Spanish politics. Great resources were poured into the attempt to maintain the Spanish **colonies** in the early 19th century. The effort to defeat the Cuban insurrectionaries, which culminated in the **Spanish-American War** of 1898, also bankrupted the Spanish exchequer. In the age of nationalism, the loss of Spain's remaining colonies in America and the Pacific also had a profound impact on the Spanish psyche. There were heartfelt laments at Spain's apparent inability to compete in the modern world and vigorous efforts to identity the guilty parties. The number one culprit became the **Cánovas Restoration** regime, because of what were seen as its corrupt, *caciquista* political foundations. The "Desastre" therefore marked the beginning of the end of oligarchic liberal politics in Spain.

Within Spanish politics, elites, and public opinion, the experience of the loss of the American colonies engendered bitterness against the "Anglo-Saxon powers." This was based on the key role that Great Britain and the United States had played in undermining Spanish rule and the fact that they had subsequently replaced Spain as the most influential powers in the region. From this perspective, the humiliating defeat at the hands of the United States in 1898 was the culmination of this assault. In right-wing circles, the idea began to take shape that a rejuvenated Spain might once again hegemonize Spanish-speaking America and take on the Anglo-Saxon powers. Such a perspective was known as Hispanismo. It culminated during the early years of **World War II,** when General **Francisco Franco** and his advisors discussed the possibility of joining the war on the side of Axis. Luckily for Franco, he was to pull back. More benignly, politicians and commentators of all hues maintained the need to retain cultural and economic ties with Spanish-speaking Latin America. Links with the Argentinean government of General Juan Domingo Perón in the late 1940s were vital in securing supplies of much-needed wheat. In general, however, despite the rhetoric, under the **Franco regime** the ties amounted to little more than (typically folkloric) cultural exchanges.

The question of trade and investment in Latin America has grown in importance in recent years. In the 1980s, **Felipe González** worked hard to develop closer ties between the **European Union** (EU) and Latin America, leading to the holding of EU-sponsored Ibero-American summits from 1991. At the same time, Spanish foreign direct investment in Latin America began to grow rapidly in the 1990s. This was based on the emergence of a number of powerful companies in Spain in the areas of **banking** (BBVA and BSCH), **telecommunications** (Telefónica), petrochemicals (**Repsol**), power generation, and public utilities (Iberdrola, Unión Fenosa, Endesa) in the run-up to and aftermath of the **privatizations** of this decade. Furthermore, these years were to witness the emergence of major Spanish **tourism** companies (Sol Meliá, Barceló), which also made major investments in Latin America. This occurred at the same time as the majority of Latin American countries were preparing privatizations in these same areas. By 2000, Latin America accounted for 61 percent of Spanish foreign direct investment, Spain was the largest European investor, and in overall terms was second only to the United States. The number one target of such investment has been Argentina, 10 percent of whose gross domestic product was in the hands of foreign companies in this year. This has led to some resentment and talk of the "new conquistadors." During the Argentinean financial crisis of 2002, the Spanish embassy and the offices of Spanish companies were attacked in Buenos Aires. The big investors were badly hit by this crisis but have since recovered fast.

Spain's rapid economic development has also been accompanied by a reversal of migration flows between Spain and Latin America. During the late 19th and early 20th centuries, large numbers of Spanish **immigrants** left for the American continent (three million between the 1880s and **World War I**). But from the 1990s, increasing numbers of Latin Americans (with Ecuador, Colombia, and Argentina taking the lead) have emigrated to Spain (with the important difference that while most Spaniards set up a new life in Latin America, most Latin Americans are in Spain on temporary contracts). In January 2006, according to official statistics, there were 1.4 million migrants from Latin America living in Spain, but this underestimated the true figure. *See also* FOREIGN TRADE.

LEFT BLOC. This was the name given to a coalition of forces that from the end of 1908 and through 1909 tried to remove **Antonio Maura** from power. It was captained by **Segismundo Moret**, the leader of one of the factions within the **Partido Liberal** (PL), and was supported by part of **Nicolás Salmerón**'s **Unión Republicana** outside **Catalonia** (Moret was known for his trenchant anti-Catalanist views so **Catalanist republicans** stood aloof) and by **Alejandro Lerroux**'s **Partido Republicano Radical**. New life was breathed into the movement as a consequence of the events of the **Tragic Week** in July 1909. However, once Antonio Maura had fallen on 20 October and Moret had been offered the premiership, he opportunistically abandoned his former leftist allies. Maura, for his part, never forgave the PL and would, in future, refuse to work with it. The bloc was important in that for the first time a leading figure within one of the two "official parties" of the **Cánovas Restoration** had allied with outsiders against the other official party, provoking bitter divisions between them. It therefore represented a key phase in the disintegration of the *turno pacífico*, a consequence of the growing role of public opinion in Spanish political life.

LEGIÓN ESPAÑOLA/SPANISH LEGION. The Tercio (or Legión [Española] as it was usually referred to) was a force of volunteers created in August 1920 in imitation of the French Foreign Legion in order to fight in **Morocco**. Under the maniacally brave major José Millán Astray (1879–1954) with **Francisco Franco** second in command, the Legión was forged from a motley crew of convicts and desperados, but after intensive training soon became renowned for both its discipline and savagery. Between June 1924 and February 1926, Franco was its commander and under his orders it performed well in both the retreat from Xauen in late 1924 and the landing in Alhucemas Bay in September 1925. But with Morocco pacified, the Legión was increasingly used to quell domestic protest. Hence it would mercilessly put down the Asturian uprising during the **October 1934 revolution**, and legionnaires would be the shock troops of Franco's Army of Africa during the **Spanish Civil War**.

LEPANTO, BATTLE OF. To ward off the growing threat of the Ottoman Empire in central Europe and the Mediterranean, the papacy put together a coalition, made up of its own forces and those of Venice and the **Habsburg** Empire, known as the Holy League (Liga Santa). They achieved a major victory at the naval battle of Lepanto on 7 October 1571—destroying almost the entire Turkish fleet—thereby decisively weakening Ottoman sea power.

LERROUX GARCÍA, ALEJANDRO (1864–1949). Lerroux was born into a lower-middle-class family in the province of Córdoba. After a brief spell in the **military**, he became involved in **republican** politics after settling in **Madrid** in 1886. His big break came in 1889, when he was made director of the daily mouthpiece of the **Partido Republicano Progresista**, *El País*. Lerroux soon became the leading figure on the far left of Spanish republicanism. He was virulently anticlerical and adopted a direct, aggressive style. In 1897, he left *El País* to found his own paper, *El Progreso*. He was quickly convinced that in order to prosper, republicanism needed to widen its working-class base, and so from the end of the year, his paper launched a campaign for a judicial review of the **Montjuïc Trial**. This gained him a sympathetic audience in leftist and republican circles in **Catalonia**. Realizing that Catalonia would be the center of any antimonarchist uprising, he then transferred to **Barcelona** in 1901.

Once in Barcelona, Lerroux was soon able to build the strongest republican movement in Spain. The reasons were both ideological and organizational. On the one hand, in the early years Lerroux adopted a quasi (or pseudo) **anarchist** stance. He presented himself as the defender of the workers' interests and argued that the republic he proposed would open the gates to social justice. On the other, he founded one of Spain's first modern political parties. Lerroux created a staff of professional electoral supervisors to guard against fraud. At the same time, electors were tied to the party through republican centers, which operated schools, cooperatives, and social welfare services and provided entertainment and a place to meet. Supporters were also mobilized through periodic meetings and excursions.

This allowed Lerroux to dominate Barcelona politics between 1903 and 1907. He had already been elected a deputy in 1901, and from 1903, his organization eclipsed its nearest rival, the Catalanist **Lliga Regionalista**. From 1903, Lerroux's republicans formed part of the **Unión Republicana**, under the leadership of **Nicolás Salmerón**. Tensions, however, soon developed with more moderate republicans of higher social standing who opposed the direction being taken by Barcelona republicanism under Lerroux. These were resolved after the 1905 *Cu-Cut!* incident. Lerroux supported the actions of the military, breaking with the moderate republicans, who backed **Solidaritat Catalana** (SC). He apparently took this action in order not to antagonize army officers, who he felt would have an important role to play in any future republican revolution, and to ensure his undisputed leadership over Barcelona republicanism. In the April 1907 elections, Lerroux launched a fierce anti-**Catalanist** campaign. He was defeated in Barcelona by the SC, but still maintained a strong working-class following, while attracting support from non-Catalan, anti-Catalanist residents.

In order to consolidate his position, in 1908 he formed the **Partido Republicano Radical** (PRR). Lerroux aimed to break out of his Catalan base and turn the PRR into a national party. In order to do this, he felt he had to move to the political center and adopt a more interclass ideology. In 1910, therefore, he took up residence in Madrid. Over the next 10 years, he largely lost his working-class base in Catalonia, but was able to build new centers of support, especially in Madrid, Aragón, and **Valencia**. By the 1920s, Lerroux tried to portray himself as a governmental republican. His chance of power came in 1931 with the fall of the **monarchy**. Many more conservative elements and even landowning elites now turned to Lerroux as the best guarantor of their interests in a Republican context. This was reflected in his policies. Although at first he participated in the republican-**Partido Socialista Obrero Español** (PSOE) coalition government as minister of state, he resigned on 17 December 1931 because of the left republicans' refusal to break their alliance with the PSOE. Thereafter, he drew close to the **Catholic** right. After the rightist victory in the November 1933 elections, he was to govern first with the support of the right-wing **Confederación Española de Derechas Autónomas** (CEDA) coalition and then with CEDA ministers in government. This simply confirmed the abandonment of the ideals of Lerroux's youth. In leftist circles, he was seen as an opportunist who put the attainment of power above all else. One element of Lerroux's practice had not, however, changed. He had always built his power base on patronage and favor. This blew up in his face during 1935, when the PRR was discredited by a number of **corruption** scandals. Lerroux himself lost his seat in the February 1936 elections, and with the start of the **Spanish Civil War** gave his support to the forces of General **Francisco Franco**.

LIBERAL. The word *liberal* originated in Spain. The first usage of the term occurred during the **Cortes of Cádiz**, when it was used to differentiate the anti-Napoleonic supporters of the Constitution of 1812 from the so-called *serviles*, who supported either Napoleonic or absolutist rule. The years between 1813 and 1875 were thereafter to see a long **military** struggle between the supporters of liberal or bourgeois revolution and reactionaries integrated from 1833 within the **Carlist camp**. The **Cánovas Restoration** of 1875 represented a victory of the conservative rendition of liberalism favored by social elites and upper-middle classes. The regime and its ideological underpinnings would, however, be increasingly challenged from the turn of the century—on the left by more radical liberal-democratic groupings (represented above by the **republicans**, Marxists, and anarchists) and on the right by increasingly **nationalistic** and authoritarian elements. The **Second Republic** represented a victory of the more moderate reforming left, represented by the various republican parties and by the **Partido Socialista Obrero Español** (PSOE). Republicans were intent on introducing what they saw as modernizing reforms, aimed at drastically reducing the power of the **Catholic Church** and laying the basis of a liberal-democratic lay state, and Socialists were determined to implement far-reaching social reform. The victory of the right in the **Spanish Civil War** was to lead to the establishment of the antiliberal, **corporatist Franco regime**. Only with the **transition to democracy** in the 1970s has a fully liberal-democratic regime been firmly put in place.

LIBERAL BIENNIUM. *See* PROGRESSIVE BIENNIUM.

LIBERAL MONARCHY. *See* CÁNOVAS RESTORATION.

LIBERAL TRIENNIUM. *See* CONSTITUTIONAL TRIENNIUM.

LIBERTAD DIGITAL. This is an Internet daily that has operated since March 2000 and has achieved a wide circulation. The key figure in its formation and development has been the journalist and radio broadcaster Federico Jiménez Losantos. It defines itself as **liberal**, but the dominant reading of liberalism among the collaborators may be described as neoconservative, given that they generally defend the stance adopted by the hierarchy of the **Catholic Church** (with the Catholic group Intereconomía owning half the shares in the publication). It combines a Spanish **nationalist** outlook with a strong antipathy toward the "peripheral nationalisms." It also tends to be culturally conservative and is very hostile toward the ruling **Partido Socialista Obrero**

Español (PSOE). This means that it is often close to the **Partido Popular** (PP), but it did not support the previous PP government on all occasions. Since the **Madrid train bombings**, it has played a leading role in trying to demonstrate complicity by **ETA** and an attempted cover-up by the security services, and it was vociferously opposed to the PSOE government's attempt to bring a negotiated end to ETA violence. Hence, it wholeheartedly backed the antigovernment demonstrations launched by the **Asociación de Víctimas del Terrorismo**. It has recently also set up its own digital **television** station. In 2007, it has over 7 million hits on its website. *See also* EL MUNDO; PRESS.

LIGA VIZCAÍNA DE PRODUCTORES/VIZCAYAN LEAGUE OF PRODUCERS. The Liga Vizcaína was a powerful pressure group of Vizcayan heavy industry businesses set up in 1894. Over the following two decades, it campaigned successfully in favor of state support for steel exports, state contracts for the **Basque** shipping **industry**, and, most crucially—allied to **Castilian** wheat interests and the **Catalan Foment del Treball Nacional** (FTN)—higher **tariffs** on imports. This campaign was to culminate in the ultraprotectionist **tariff** of 1906. Seventeen years later, Vizcayan industrialists were to be behind the formation of an all-Spanish industrial lobby, the Federación de Industrias Nacionales (Federation of National Industries). These pressure groups would establish close contacts with the Spanish right. Very few major Basque industrialists sympathized (or sympathize) with **Basque nationalism**.

LITERATURE. *See* ALAS URENA, LEOPOLDO ("CLARÍN"); ALBERTI, RAFAEL; BAROJA Y NESS, PÍO; CASTRO Y MURGUÍA, ROSALIA DE; CELA TRULOCK, CAMILO JOSÉ; CERVANTES Y SAAVENDRA, MIGUEL DE; GARCÍA LORCA, FEDERICO; GENERATION OF 1898; GOYTISOLO GAY, JUAN; LARRA Y SÁNCHEZ DE CASTRO, MARIANO DE; MACHADO Y RUIZ, ANTONIO; MAEZTU Y WHITNEY, RAMIRO DE; MARTÍNEZ RUIZ, JOSÉ ("AZORÍN"); MODERNISM; MODERNISME; PÉREZ GALDÓS, BENITO; RENAIXENÇA; SENDER GARCÉS, RAMÓN JOSÉ; UNAMUNO Y JUGO, MIGUEL DE; VALLE INCLÁN, RAMÓN MARÍA DEL.

LLAMAZARES TRIGO, GASPAR (1957–). Gaspar Llamazares has been the general coordinator of the left-wing coalition **Izquierda Unida** (IU) since October 2000. He was born in Logroño, studied medicine, and became a doctor. He joined the **Partido Comunista de España** (PCE) in Asturias in 1981 and made his mark in Asturian regional politics. He narrowly defeated the PCE general secretary Francisco Frutos (1939–) for the post of general coordinator in IU's October 2000 federal assembly, following the coalition's poor showing in that year's general elections. He quickly proved a far more convincing figure than Frutos, working hard to open the coalition to new social movements, articulating environmental concerns, and entering into dialogue with the **Partido Socialista Obrero Español** (PSOE) opposition. Under his leadership, IU played a leading role in galvanizing opposition to the **Iraq war** in 2003, significantly upping his profile. However, when it came to the March 2004 elections, IU suffered because of tactical voting for the PSOE in order to defeat the ruling **Partido Popular** (PP) government, and only received 5 percent of the vote. He is faced by strong opposition from orthodox Communists within the PCE, who wish to oust him as the leader of IU at the next assembly. His position was strengthened in a meeting of IU's federal presidency on 18 December 2007. However, IU again performed poorly at the March 2008 general elections (with, on this occasion, leftists afraid that the PP might again retake power). Llamazares quickly announced that he will not be presenting his name for reelection at the next federal assembly.

LLIGA CATALANA/CATALAN LEAGUE. This was the name adopted by the **Lliga Regionalista** when it reorganized in 1933. The new party supported the Catalan autonomy statute and this set it apart from most of the Spanish right. Moreover, its critique of the **Second Republic** was never to be as intransigent as that of other right-wing groups in Spain. However, its defense of **Catholic** values and of order and property meant that it gravitated to the right of the Catalan political spectrum. Given the divisions and despondency on the Spanish left, with its allies it was able to win the November 1933 general elections in **Catalonia**, with 28 seats as compared to the 26 gained by **Esquerra Republicana de Catalunya** (ERC), which governed the Catalan autonomous government, the **Generalitat**.

Between 1934 and 1936, it generally remained on good terms with the right-wing Spanish governments, and it played a key role in the decision of the Spanish Constitutional Tribunal to annul the ERC's Law of Cultivation Contracts in June 1934, which allowed peasant tenants, including the *rabassaires*, to buy their land. Following the **October 1934 revolution**, some of its most intransigent agrarian supporters left the party to join the Spanish right-wing coalition, the **Confederación Española de Derechas Autónomas** (CEDA). This led the Lliga Catalana to move toward the center. Nevertheless, its collaboration with the Spanish right had already alienated much middle-class Catalan support. Hence, it was beaten in the January 1934 elections to the Catalan autonomous parliament by a leftist coalition led by ERC. In the February 1936 elections, not without tensions it formed part of a right-wing Catalan alliance, the Front d'Ordre Català (Catalan Alliance for Order). It was, however, again decisively defeated by the Catalan left, further strengthening the more moderate elements within the party. In the months that followed, though it was disturbed by the political and social effervescence, it played no role in the preparation of the **military** uprising of July 1936. This did not save its leadership from being persecuted and forced into exile when the **Spanish Civil War** broke out. Some leading figures, like **Francesc Cambó**, reacted to the subsequent social revolution in Catalonia by collaborating with the forces of General **Francisco Franco**.

LLIGA REGIONALISTA/REGIONALIST LEAGUE. With the birth of the Lliga in 1901, **Catalanism** moved from being a cultural movement with limited political impact to becoming a major political force in Catalan, and by extension Spanish, politics. It was set up in the climate of anger and recriminations directed at the political elite of the **Cánovas Restoration**, following the **Spanish-American War** of 1898. At a political level, the Lliga was a fusion of conservative Catalanists who had militated in the Centre Nacionalista Català (Catalan Nationalist Center), the best known of whom was **Enric Prat de la Riba**, and representatives of the Catalan industrial bourgeoisie and propertied classes, angry at the loss of the **Cuban** market. The party was also able to get wider middle-class support in Barcelona, especially after the 1899 protest movement against tax increases, the *tancament de caixes*.

From its foundation, the Lliga sought to achieve both autonomy for Catalonia and a leading role in Spanish political life. In the March 1901 general elections in **Barcelona**, before the formation of the new party had been officially announced, the "four presidents" candidature it promoted proved a success and this provided a springboard for future growth. In 1907, the **Solidaritat Catalana** coalition it captained gained 40 out of 44 seats in Catalonia, thereby ensuring the almost total defeat of the "official parties." Like its main rival in Barcelona, the **Partido Republicano Radical** (PRR) under **Alejandro Lerroux**, the Lliga formed a modern mass party, with thousands of members, its own locals, newspapers, and electoral machine. From the beginning, its outlook was conservative. This was accentuated in 1904, when **republicans** and harder-line nationalists left to form the **Centre Nacionalista Republicà**.

Until 1916, its successes had been modest. In 1913, under pressure from the Lliga, central government had granted a measure of administrative autonomy, the **Mancomunitat**. This gave the party a great deal of credibility and widened its support base. After the outbreak of **World War I**, under the political leadership of **Francesc Cambó** the party then launched a far more ambitious campaign aimed at ensuring a leading role in Spanish politics for the Lliga and the representatives of industrial and manufacturing classes in other regions. As part of this drive, its language became more democratic, as it emphasized the need for free elections in order to break the *caciquista* foundations of the regime. This campaign culminated in the **crisis of 1917**, a failed attempt, led by the Lliga, to force the king and central government to accept a new constituent **Cortes**, which would put in place a decentralized, constitutional monarchy.

However, over the next four years Catalanist protest would be submerged under a wave of social agitation. As a result, the Lliga, fearful of social revolution, softened its antigovernmental stance and opted for the safer policy of pursuing reform from within the boundaries of the Restoration regime. This was symbolized through the Lliga's participation in three Spanish governments between 1917 and 1922. This, however, lost the party credibility at home among the youth, intellectuals, and much of its Catalanist middle-class base. The result was the foundation of a serious rival to the Lliga, **Acció Catalana**, in June 1922. Matters were made worse by the fact that many Lliga politicians sympathized with the General **Miguel Primo de Rivera** coup in 1923 (though quickly distancing themselves once its anti-Catalanist thrust became clear). Moreover, after the fall of Primo de Rivera in 1930, despite the fact that under the impact of dictatorship there had been a radicalization of Catalanist sentiment and that there was now a powerful upsurge in popular enthusiasm for a Republic, **Francesc Cambó** defended the continuance of the **monarchy**. The combined result of these factors was that with the declaration of the **Second Republic** in April 1931 the Lliga would no longer be the dominant Catalanist party in Catalonia. This mantle was now taken over by the explicitly republican **Esquerra Republicana de Catalunya** (ERC). The party was reorganized in 1933 under the name **Lliga Catalana**. *See also* TABLES 7 AND 8.

LLOPIS FERRÁNDIZ, RODOLFO (1895–1984). Rodolfo Llopis is best known as general secretary of the **Partido Socialista Obrero Español** (PSOE) in exile between 1954 and 1972. His first important role was general secretary of the anti-**Juan Negrín** sector of the PSOE in exile in a congress held in Toulouse in September 1944. He was chosen because it was felt that his credentials as a follower of **Francisco Largo Caballero** would serve to hold the majority anti-Communist wing of the party together. Over the next 10 years, he became very much identified with the failed policies of **Indalecio Prieto**, which consisted of entering into negotiations with the monarchists and encouraging Allied intervention in Spain. Nevertheless, when the PSOE decided to transfer its executive outside Spain to Toulouse in July 1954, Llopis became the new general secretary.

His centralization of the party in Toulouse during the next 28 years ensured organizational continuity. However, the Llopis years were also marked by excessive caution and inactivity. Rodolfo Llopis had inherited from Largo Caballero his zeal for the conservation of the organization above all else and an ideological outlook which justified a policy of wait and see (in this case for the inevitable crisis of Francoism). Furthermore, he also came to identify the party with his own person and could not bear to relinquish control. Accordingly, in the early 1970s, he fought tooth and nail attempts by younger elements to return the executive to Spain. And when in 1972 these Socialists bypassed him and held their own congress in July, Llopis split the party by organizing a rival congress in December. Llopis argued that the new party, the **Partido Socialista Obrero Español-Histórico**, was the legitimate heir to the Socialist tradition, but its credentials were rejected by the Socialist International and it generated little enthusiasm within Spain. *See also* FRANCO REGIME; TRANSITION TO DEMOCRACY.

LOAPA (LEY ORGÁNICA DE HARMONIZACIÓN DEL PROCESO AUTONÓMICO/FUNDAMENTAL LAW TO HARMONIZE THE AUTONOMY PROCESS). *See* PARTIT DELS SOCIALISTES DE CATALUNYA; STATE OF THE AUTONOMIES; TEJERAZO.

LÓPEZ RODÓ, LAUREANO (1920–2000). López Rodó was the leading light in the "technocratic revolution" that transformed Spain from the late 1950s. He was born into an upper-class **Barcelona** family on 18 November 1920. He studied law at the University of Barcelona, where he joined the **Opus Dei**, and went on to lecture in law at the University of Madrid. He caught the eye of General **Francisco Franco**'s right-hand man, **Luis Carrero Blanco**, in 1950, and was taken onboard as his chief of staff. López Rodó was soon to prove both hardworking and extremely competent, and from 1957, under Carrero Blanco, he spearheaded moves to streamline government and open the Spanish **economy** to the West, to uncouple the regime from the **Falange Española Tradicionalista y de las Juntas de Ofensiva Nacional Sindicalista** (FET y de las JONS), and to engineer an eventual succession of the pretender's son, **Juan Carlos**. All of these measures were part of a plan to build what Carrero Blanco's supporters saw as a modern authoritarian regime, in which the FET y de las JONS would be transformed into a neutral bureaucracy and decisions would be taken by the professional experts.

At the end of 1956, López Rodó was made head of a technical secretariat within Carrero Blanco's President's Office and charged with preparing the major administrative reforms. The emasculation of the FET y de las JONS and rise of the Opus Dei technocrats in the cabinet reshuffle of February 1957 opened the door to change. A first important law, published on 25 February 1957, announced the creation of a new ministerial department, the Government Presidency, charged with drafting new legislation, the formation of new inter-ministerial committees, and the creation of an Office for Economic Coordination and Planning. This reflected the increasing complexity of government, but also meant that the new class of professionally trained technocrats would be able to concentrate further power in their hands. López Rodó was made head of the Office for Economic Coordination and Planning. This was followed by the abandonment of **autarky** and the liberalization of the regime's **economic policy**, above all following the implementation of the 1959 **Stabilization Plan**. Nevertheless, López Rodó did not wish to go as far as some of his economic advisors and through new **tariffs** established in 1960 ensured that Spanish **industry** retained significant protection.

More overtly political was the Declaration of the Fundamental Principles of the **Movimiento Nacional**, drafted by López Rodó's collaborators and unveiled to the **Cortes** in May 1958, which changed the name of the FET y de las JONS to Movimiento Nacional (National Movement), drawing a veil over its Fascist past and providing an anodyne **Catholic** definition of the regime. López Rodó's power was further increased in January 1962 after the administration had decided to develop a series of economic development plans along French lines. He was made the head of the Commissariat for the Development Plan. Finally, in July 1965, he became a cabinet minister without portfolio. More difficult was to convince Franco that he should put in place the machinery to guarantee the succession of Juan Carlos. A Fundamental State Law (Ley Orgánica del Estado), which established the principle of a monarchist succession, had already been produced by López Rodó in 1957. At first it was blocked by a combination of Franco's reluctance to name a successor lest it weaken his own position and opposition from powerful elements within the Movimiento. Nevertheless, the law, patronized by Carrero Blanco and López Rodó, was finally approved by the **Cortes** in 1966, and Juan Carlos was eventually confirmed as Franco's successor in July 1969.

Yet from this moment, López Rodó's star began to wane. As protest against the regime escalated during 1969–1970, Carrero Blanco took an increasingly hard line, and within regime circles, voices were heard saying that the technocrats were too soft on the opposition. López Rodó remained in government until the death of Carrero

Blanco in 1973, but was then marginalized. During the **transition to democracy**, he formed part of the group of former regime figures that integrated into **Manuel Fraga**'s **Alianza Popular** (AP) coalition at the end of 1976.

LORDSHIPS. *See* SEÑORÍOS.

LORENZO, ANSELMO (1841–1914). By the first decade of the 20th century, Anselmo Lorenzo was known as the "grandfather" of Spanish **anarchism**. He was born in Toledo but at an early age had moved to **Madrid**, where he became a compositor. Like many workers in the 1860s he came under the spell of **republicanism**, but after having met Mikhail Bakunin's Italian emissary Giuseppe Fanelli between 1868 and 1869, he joined his secret International Alliance of Socialist Democracy and helped found the Spanish branch of Marx's International Working Men's Association (IWMA), the **Federación Regional Española** (FRE). Lorenzo met Karl Marx and Frederick Engels when he traveled to London as the FRE's representative to the London Congress of the IWMA in 1871. As divisions between anarchists and Marxists crystallized in Spain over the next two years, Lorenzo tried to conciliate the two sides, leading to his marginalization within the Bakunist-dominated FRE. From 1874, however, he resolutely joined the anarchist current and was elected onto the FRE's executive during between 1874 and 1881, a period during which it had to function clandestinely. Thereafter, he would not figure among the leadership of the various anarchist labor organizations founded in **Catalonia**, but through conferences, articles in the anarchist press, and translations (including works by Élisée Reclus and Pietr Kropotkin), he would play a leading role in disseminating the anarchist ideal in working-class circles. For this he was to be continuously harassed by the **Cánovas Restoration** regime. He was exiled to France during the **Montjuïc trial**, imprisoned after the 1902 general strike, and deported to Alcañiz following the **Tragic Week** in 1909. Lorenzo was what could be referred to as an orthodox anarchist-syndicalist. He approved of anarchists working through the trade unions, but always believed that it was the anarchists' duty to lead them in a revolutionary direction. For this reason, after first supporting **Solidaridad Obrera** (SO) between 1908 and 1909 he became increasingly critical, believing it was taking a moderate "reformist" road. He was, however, more satisfied with the ideology and tactics of the **Confederación Nacional del Trabajo** (CNT) during its first years. *See also* LABOR MOVEMENT.

– M –

MACHADO Y RUIZ, ANTONIO (1875–1939). Machado is one of the great Spanish poets of the 20th century. He was born in Seville in 1873, but in 1885 his family moved to **Madrid**. In the 1890s, he made the acquaintance of the "**Generation of 1898**." Politically, Machado was in his early years a radical **liberal**. He attended the **Institución Libre de Enseñanza**, and was a disciple of Francisco Giner de los Ríos (1839–1915) and **Francesc Pi i Margall**. At first, his poetry showed a strong **Modernist** influence, but from the publication of *Campos de Castilla* (*Castilian Countryside*) in 1912 he evinced great sympathy for the common people and developed a critique of the reactionary forces in Spanish society (it was with Machado that the concept of the "two Spains" was most closely associated). He strongly supported the Republican cause in the 1930s and, as a result, he was forced into exile, dying in Collioure shortly after the end of the **Spanish Civil War**.

MACIÀ I LLUSSÀ, FRANCESC (1859–1933). Francesc Macià came to lead the first separatist movement in Catalan politics in the 1920s, and then, in the early 1930s, became the first president of the Catalan autonomous government, the **Generalitat**. He was born into a merchant family in Vilanova i la Geltrú, and at first followed a **military** career. However, as a result of the 1905 *Cu-Cut!* incident he entered **Catalanist** politics. He integrated into the **Solidaritat Catalana** coalition and was elected to parliament as an independent in 1907. At this time, he was seen as close to the **Lliga Regionalista**, but from 1910 became increasingly radicalized. In 1922, he formed the first separatist movement in Catalan history, Estat Català (Catalan State). During the **Primo de Rivera dictatorship**, he attempted, from exile in France, to build a military movement that would be capable of overthrowing the regime, even visiting the Soviet Union in 1925 in a vain attempt to procure funds. His one attempt to invade Spain in 1926 was easily put down by the Spanish authorities at Prats de Molló.

After the fall of the dictatorship, Macià signed the **San Sebastián Pact** and joined the Catalan Revolutionary Committee. His Estat Català was also one of the components of the new leftist Catalanist party founded in March 1931, **Esquerra Republicana de Catalunya** (ERC). Macià immediately became the most senior figure in the party, and two days after the fall of the **monarchy**, on 14 April 1931, at a mass meeting he declared **Catalonia** to be a separate state within a federal Iberian federation. However, he was convinced by the Spanish provisional government that he should wait for the decision of the constituent **Cortes** and was in the meantime named president of a nominal autonomous government. Macià accepted the Spanish **constitution** approved in December 1931 and the Catalan autonomy statute of September 1932 as stepping stones to further independence. He continued as president of the formally constituted Generalitat until his death on Christmas Day 1933.

MADRID. Madrid became the Spanish capital in 1561, when **Felipe II** made it the permanent location of the Spanish court (except for a brief period between 1601 and 1606 under **Felipe III**, when the court moved to Valladolid and then back again). At the time it was only a small town, but its position in the geographical center of the Iberian Peninsular was seen as having symbolic importance. Henceforth, Madrid was to become the hub of the Spanish administration. By the end of the 18th century, it had a **population** of 160,000. Most of the city was encompassed within the walls built in the 1620s, but it had also begun to spread south across the Manzanares River. In the 19th century, growth quickened. The walls were pulled down, and subsequently to the north the new districts of Salamanca, Argüelles, and Pozuelo were urbanized. In the following decades, Salamanca became the center of a new, bourgeois Madrid, while poorer, working-class areas grew up on the periphery.

By 1900, the population of Madrid had passed the half million mark. Nevertheless, over the previous century, **Barcelona** rather than Madrid had become Spain's major industrial conurbation. This was reflected in the fact that Barcelona overtook Madrid as Spain's largest city in the 1920s. Madrid's growth accelerated during this decade as a result of the ambitious public works programs sponsored by the **Primo de Rivero dictatorship**, but the **Second Republic** was a time of retrenchment.

Politically, during the second half of the 19th century, Madrid became polarized between the conservative, Catholic social elites and upper-middle classes and the **republican** subaltern classes. The **Partido Socialista Obrero Español** (PSOE) was also set up in Madrid in 1879, and from the first decade of the new century rapidly expanded its trade union base. In the 1930s, Madrid became a major focus of social protest, with militant construction workers in the vanguard of strike action. The city quickly became one of the major theaters of the **Spanish Civil War**. During the war, it remained in Republican hands, and had to withstand a frontal assault by the Francoist forces between November and December 1936. The Republicans resisted, and the city did not fall until the war's close in March 1939.

Henceforth, the majority of the city's population had to undergo a decade of poverty and privation, known as the "hunger years." It was only when the **Franco regime** began to liberalize in the 1950s that the situation was to change. The 1960s saw heavy foreign investment in the city. For the first time, heavy industries such as machine buildings and chemicals sprang up, peasants flocked in the tens of thousands to the city in search of new employment opportunities, and foreign multinationals set up their business headquarters. As a result, a new proletarian city was consolidated south of the Manzanares River. Moreover, Madrid was once again confirmed as Spain's largest metropolis.

In the heady days of the **transition to democracy**, this was accompanied by a cultural renaissance, spearheaded by the city's youth, known as the *movida madrileña* (Madrid scene). Its most famous son would be the filmmaker **Pedro Almodóvar**. Yet the threat of economic recession also hung over the city from the early 1970s. This adverse economic climate was only reversed during the frantic economic boom of the second half of the 1980s. From the 1990s, its position as a modern industrial, financial, and administrative center has been consolidated, with a population of 3,132,463 in 2007 (6,081,689 in the entire Madrid Autonomous Community). This has led to a rapid influx of **immigrant** workers, above all from **Latin America** and **Morocco**. Poor planning and the concentration of the population in such a small area also meant that it has been increasingly plagued by traffic congestion and pollution. These years have also witnessed important administrative changes. Following the approval of the **State of the Autonomies**, in February 1988 the province of Madrid became an autonomous community (La Comunidad de Madrid). In subsequent years, as the ruling PSOE government entered into crisis, the city also moved in a conservative direction. The **Partido Popular** politician **Alberto Ruiz-Gallardón** won the elections to the autonomous community in 1994. He had to make way for his arch rival in the party, **Esperanza Aguirre**, in 2003, but was then elected mayor of the city of Madrid.

MADRID TRAIN BOMBINGS. On the morning of 11 March 2004, three days before the general elections, 13 terrorists planted satchel bombs on four trains traveling from Alcalá de Henares to **Madrid**. Ten exploded, causing 191 deaths and leaving over 1,500 injured. The **Partido Popular** (PP) government claimed that **ETA** was to blame. This very much fitted into its offensive against the "**terrorist gang**" (*banda terrorista*). Yet evidence quickly emerged that Islamic extremists, who may well have had links with **al-Qaeda**, were behind the attack. On the first day, a van was found at Alcalá de Henares with traces of explosives, detonators, and a tape with verses from the Koran. Subsequently, the mobile phone and card found in an unexploded satchel bomb led police to the shop owned by a radical Islamist in the Lavapiés district of Madrid. This was bad news for the PP because it shone a light on its unpopular support for the **Iraq war**. The opposition would immediately argue that by irresponsibly following the president of the United States, George W. Bush, it had placed the Spanish population in harm's way. It seems that this was why the government continued to insist that ETA was behind the bombings until the day of the elections (though this is strenuously denied by the PP). This led to a big popular mobilization against the PP between 12 and 13 March under the slogan "Who was it?" It was led by Spain's more politicized youth, with cell phones used to inform people of spontaneous demonstrations outside PP headquarters. Dramatically, on 14 March, the PP lost the elections. Commentators have since noted that the opposition **Partido Socialista Obrero Español**

(PSOE) was already closing the gap on the PP before the bombings. Nevertheless, the bombings clearly had a large impact, bringing the Iraq war to the forefront of people's minds. Some electors changed their voting intentions at the last moment. More importantly, great numbers of younger voters, many of whom would probably have abstained, voted PSOE. Compared to the 2000 elections, turnout jumped almost 10 percent.

Subsequently, on 2 April, an attempt was made to blow up high-speed trains traveling from Madrid to Lleida and Seville, but the explosives failed to detonate. Police were quickly on the trail, and on 3 April they surrounded a flat in Leganés in which seven of the terrorists were holed up. As police burst in they blew themselves up, killing themselves and one special services agent. Almost 80 people were subsequently detained.

After losing the election, the PP was bitter at what it considered was the unfair manner in which it had been ousted and at what it saw as the complicity of the opposition (and it was no doubt the case that some PSOE activists were involved in the post-March 11 mobilization against the government and the demonstrations outside PP headquarters on 13 March, which should have been a "day of reflection"). The Spanish parliament created a commission to look into the bombings and in its hearings, the PP's leading figures insisted that there was complicity between ETA and Islamic terrorists in the bombing and also began to argue that it was a plot to remove them from power. For **José María Aznar**, for example, "if the elections had been on 7 March, then the attack would have taken place on the fourth" (*Anuario El País 2005*, 92). Media outlets close to the PP, most notably the daily **El Mundo** and the Internet newspaper **Libertad Digital**, talked of a conspiracy to remove the PP from power that included elements in the security services. This was one of the elements which contributed to the constant mobilization by the PP of right-wing opinion against the PSOE between 2004 and 2007. There was some confusion in police circles with respect to the explosives used. However, this seems more the result of incompetence rather than any plot. The dynamite came from an Asturian mine and was obtained with the help of an ex-miner, José Emilio Suárez Trashorras (a police informer), who stole it and trafficked it for cocaine via intermediaries. Contact was made by a leading member of the Islamist terrorists, Jamal Ahmidan, a former drug dealer who had been radicalized while in prison in **Morocco**. A four-month trial of the remaining suspects began in July 2007. When the verdicts were read out at the end of October, 21 of the 28 defendants were found guilty of varying degrees of complicity. It was established that while the defendants were inspired by al-Qaeda, there was no actual funding or operational link. The judge, Javier Gómez Bermúdez, also confirmed that there was no evidence of ETA involvement.

MAEZTU I WHITNEY, RAMIRO DE (1875–1936). A prolific essayist of the "**Generation of 1898**," Maeztu was to be remembered as one of the few Spanish intellectuals who supported General **Francisco Franco**'s cause during the **Spanish Civil War**. He was born in Vitoria to a Spanish father and English mother in 1875, and by the 1890s was a regular correspondent in the Bilbao daily, *El Porvenir Vasco*. He met the rest of the Generation of 1898 in the **Madrid** of the late 1890s, establishing his reputation as a major writer with the publication of the regenerationist collection of essays *Hacia otra España* (*Toward another Spain*) in 1901. In the early years of the new century, he identified with the left, but with the experience of the Bolshevik Revolution he was drawn increasingly to antiliberal Spanish **Catholicism**. This led him to support both the **Primo de Rivera dictatorship** in the 1920s and the **Nationalists** at the outbreak of the civil war. He was executed by a Republican firing squad on 29 October 1936.

MANCOMUNITAT. The Mancomunitat was a body constituted in April 1914 that took over many of the functions of **Catalonia**'s four Catalan provincial councils (*diputacions*), thereby, for the first time since the **War of Succession** in the early 18th century, giving the territory a measure of administrative (though not political) autonomy. Pressure for home rule had built up from the turn of the century with the foundation of the **Lliga Regionalista** and the growth of **Catalanism**. The Mancomunitat's origin was to be found in a plan devised by the president of the Barcelona Provincial Council, **Enric Prat de la Riba**, in 1911, and supported by the other three Catalan provincial councils. It was finally accepted by the **Partido Conservador**

administration of **Eduardo Dato** in December 1913. Prat de la Riba was to be its first president. From the outset, it worked in a number of directions. It sought to improve Catalonia's poor economic infrastructure along with its technical and professional education. At the same time, it encouraged the use of the **Catalan language** in the public sphere. Hence, it set up the Institut d'Estudis Catalans (Institute of Catalan Studies), which codified Catalan grammar and orthography. The ultimate goal was to boost Catalonia's economic development and promote a **nationalist** rendition of Catalan culture. Within the modest limits of its budget, it is generally regarded as being a considerable success. Yet it was viewed with suspicion by the centralist Spanish right, and as part of an onslaught against Catalanism, it was abolished by the **Primo de Rivera dictatorship** on 12 March 1925.

MANO NEGRA/BLACK HAND. In December 1882, the police in Jerez de la Frontera claimed to have discovered a secret **anarchist** association called the Mano Negra, dedicated to the assassination of its political enemies. The existence of the organization was never proved, but the repression that followed served to put an end to peasant agitation and strikes in **Andalusia,** which had grown rapidly since 1881, and had turned it into the largest section of the anarchist-led labor confederation, the **Federación de Trabajadores de la Región Española** (FTRE). Three trials were held in the spring and summer of 1883 and resulted—after confessions had been extracted through the use of torture—in seven executions. More important, there were widespread imprisonments of union activists and union locals were closed down. The result was to undermine the FTRE in the south.

MANZANARES MANIFESTO. *See* O'DONNELL, LEOPOLDO; PROGRESSIVE BIENNIUM.

MAQUIS. The word *maquis* was first used to refer to the French guerrillas who fought against the Nazi occupation and the Vichy regime in France during **World War II**. By association, the Spanish guerrillas who fought against the **Franco regime** in the 1940s and early 1950s were also known as *maquis*. Between 1939 and 1945, the guerrilla campaign was very much a defensive affair, fought by Republicans who had been caught behind enemy lines at the end of the war. However, from 1945, the **Partido Comunista de España** (PCE) strongly backed guerrilla activity, believing that it could spark a popular uprising against the regime. The guerrillas were reinforced by experienced fighters who had been at the forefront of the struggle against Adolf Hitler, and the PCE sought to improve coordination and planning. They were able to set up important groups in **Andalusia**, Aragón-Levant, and **Galicia**. Guerrillas linked to the **Partido Socialista Obrero Español** also operated in Asturias (though without the approval of the party leadership) and there was an **anarchist** urban guerrilla group in **Barcelona**.

It soon became clear, however, that the *maquis* could not achieve their goals. The rural population was both war-weary and cowed, while the Franco regime launched a massive anti-insurgency campaign. The *maquis* found some peasant support in Andalusia and Galicia—areas in which peasants had backed the **Second Republic**—but in the center and north of the country the reaction of the rural population was largely hostile. In these adverse conditions, guerrilla activity began to wane from the second half of 1947. In response, after a meeting with Joseph Stalin in October 1948, the PCE and its Catalan counterpart, the **Partit Socialista Unificat de Catalunya** (PSUC), decided to abandon the attempt at a frontal assault on the regime and to try instead to undermine it from within. There followed a planned evacuation of Communist *maquis* to France. Guerrilla activity thereafter tailed off rapidly, and in the 1950s was reduced to isolated attacks on the security forces by leftists still trapped in Spain.

MARAGALL I MIRA, PASCUAL (1940–). Pascual Maragall is the major Catalan Socialist politician of the last 20 years. He was born into a cultured upper-class **Barcelona** family in 1940 (his grandfather was the poet Joan Maragall [1860–1911]), studied law and economics at the University of Barcelona, and then went on to specialize in urban planning, taking courses in both Paris and at the New School of Social Research in New York. During the **Franco regime**, he was strongly involved in clandestine left-wing politics, while also working within the Barcelona local government. It was because of this expertise that in 1979 he was placed second in the list of **Partit dels Socialistes Catalans-Partido Socialista Obrero Español** (PSC-PSOE) candidates for the local government elections. He went on to serve as a local councilor until 1983, when he was elected mayor of Barcelona. He was reelected in both 1987 and 1991, masterminding the organization of the 1992 Olympic Games, which were used as an opportunity to modernize the city's infrastructure, undertake major redevelopment, and construct several kilometers of beachfront.

However, while Maragall was strutting the Barcelona stage, the fortunes of his party were in decline, reaching a nadir in the Catalan autonomous elections of 1995, when it achieved only 25 percent of the vote (its unpopularity heightened by its links to the scandal-ridden PSOE government). Hence, Maragall stepped down as mayor in September 1997 in order to launch a serious challenge to the **Generalitat** president **Jordi Pujol**. He could count on the prestige accumulated during his time as mayor. In addition, he was on the **Catalanist** wing of the party and hoped to attract more middle-class votes. In the 1999 Catalan elections, with 40 percent of the votes his party (along with a civic front he had created in order to Catalanize the Catalan Socialist movement, Ciutadans pel Canvi [Citizens for Change]) secured more votes than **Convergència i Unió** (CiU) but fewer seats, and Pujol was able to remain in power with the support of the Catalan **Partido Popular** (PP). He got his revenge in the November 2003 Catalan elections. The PSC-PSOE's overall vote fell, but in the election's aftermath he formed a coalition government with the separatist **Esquerra Republicana de Catalunya** and the green-left party **Iniciativa per Catalunya-Verds**. He was elected president of the Generalitat by the Catalan parliament in December.

Maragall strongly supported a reform of **Catalonia**'s autonomy statute, which would give the territory greater financial autonomy. In the autumn of 2003, with the exception of the PP, the Catalan parliament voted unanimously for such a reform. The PSOE leader, **José Luis Rodríguez Zapatero**, did not oppose changes to the **State of the Autonomies**, which would take Spain in a more federal direction, and in July 2000 he put Maragall in charge of the party's powerful Federal Committee. In 2003, his proposal that the **constitution** be reformed in order to turn the Senate into a proper "territorial House" was accepted by the party. After the PSOE's victory in the March 2004 elections, Maragall then led the way in trying to enact these changes. However, there was strong opposition within the PSOE to the proposed Catalan statute, which by giving Catalonia wide-ranging tax-raising powers was seen as breaking the financial model of the State of Autonomies (which operated in all of Spain with the exception of the **Basque Country** and **Navarre**). In Spanish PSOE circles, Maragall was criticized for allowing an over-radical statute to be approved by the Catalan parliament, which had put the new government on the defensive and allowed the opposition PP (which launched a campaign against it) to mobilize Spanish **nationalist** opinion. It was only backed by the Rodríguez Zapatero at the end of 2005 after the Catalan Socialists had agreed to significant concessions. This led to a crisis of Maragall's coalition government, with ERC refusing to give the reformed statute their backing. As a result, the PSOE needed the support of CiU to get it through the Spanish parliament.

At the same time, the growing abstention among migrant workers from Barcelona's "red belt" in the 2003 Catalan elections, combined with Maragall's "Blairist" political outlook—seen in his assertion that the party had to move beyond the right-left divide—led to further criticism from the PSC-PSOE's more left-wing elements. In May 2006, faced by the rebellion of ERC, Maragall dismissed the ERC ministers in his government and called new elections. Given the level of opposition he faced within the PSC-PSOE, he decided to step down as the PSC presidential candidate. José Montilla (1955–), who was much closer to the PSOE leadership, took his place.

MARÍA CRISTINA OF NAPLES (1806–1878). María Cristina was the daughter of Francisco I, king of the Two Sicilies. She married **Fernando VII** in 1829, becoming his fourth wife. From the outset, she opposed absolutist designs of the king's brother, **Carlos María Isidoro Benito de Borbón y Borbón-Parma**, strongly favoring an understanding with the more conservative liberals (the **Partido Moderado** or *moderados*, as they were called). With the king moribund, from September 1832 she was appointed regent until the coming of age of their eldest daughter, Isabel (the future **Isabel II**). Under María Cristina's regency, Spain took a decisive step down the road of liberalization of economy and society. However, not only did she face an armed rebellion by the supporters of Don Carlos, the **Carlists**, her refusal to support all but the most conservative liberals led to further instability. In response, General **Baldomero Espartero**, who was linked to the **Partido Progresista**, forced her into exile in 1840. Espartero was himself overthrown in 1843. The new *moderado*-dominated provisional government then declared Isabel II of age, but María Cristina was able to return to Spain and, at least in *progresista* eyes, exercise a nefarious influence over the new queen by supporting the most reactionary elements within the Partido Moderado. The influence of what was seen as the court *camarilla* was only broken in 1868 when, following the **Glorious Revolution**, both the queen and queen mother were forced into exile.

MARTÍN ARTAJO, ALBERTO (1905–?). Alberto Martín Artajo was General **Francisco Franco**'s foreign minister between 1945 and 1957, from which position he presented the world a more acceptable **Catholic** image of the **Franco regime**. Artajo was born in **Madrid** on 2 October 1905. From an early age, he was groomed to become a leading light among the defenders of traditionalist Catholicism in Spain. He studied law at the Jesuit University of Deusto and at the University of Madrid. In 1931, he joined **Acción Católica** and, once the **Second Republic** had been proclaimed, integrated into the **Confederación Española de Derechas Autónomas** (CEDA) and wrote for its daily, *El Debate*. By the **Spanish Civil War**, he had risen to become one of the foremost figures in Acción Católica and in the **Asociación Católica Nacional de Propagandistas** (ACNP), and played a leading part in presenting the conflict as a Catholic crusade against Bolshevism. Moreover, from 1937, he was heavily involved in drawing up the **Franco regime**'s fundamental laws. He was offered the post of minister of foreign affairs by General **Francisco Franco** on 24 July 1945. He was a convinced monarchist. He also believed that the regime was in need of reform, favoring a reduction in the power of the single party, the **Falange Española Tradicionalista y de las Juntas de Ofensiva Nacional Sindicalista** (FET y de las JONS), and a limited degree of liberalization. Nevertheless, he accepted the past after consultations with the primate of Spain, Enrique Pla y Deniel (1876–1968). Franco had, apparently, convinced him that a return to **monarchy** was being contemplated, but was in reality able to use Martín Artajo to gain international Catholic backing for the regime without undertaking any serious reform. Martín Artajo was behind the negotiations with the Vatican that led to the signing of a new concordat in 1953. He was finally replaced by his confidant, **Fernando María de Castiella**, on 25 February 1957, but he was to remain an influential figure in both regime and Church circles.

MARTÍNEZ DE LA ROSA, FRANCISCO DE PAULO (1787–1862). A native of Granada, Martínez de la Rosa became involved in liberal politics during the **War of Independence**. During the **Constitutional Triennium** of 1820 to 1823, he lined up behind the more conservative **liberals** known as **moderados** and was, therefore, seen as an ideal figure to lead the timid liberalization initiated by the queen regent, **María Cristina of Naples**, between 1833 and 1835. He became prime minister in January 1834, and, along with Javier de Burgos (1778–1849), he produced a new constitution, the **Royal Statute** (Estatuto Real), in the same year. However, unwilling to carry out further liberalization and caught between a **Carlist** uprising and urban liberal protest, he was forced from office in the summer of 1836. Though never again regaining such high office, he remained an influential figure within the liberal camp until his death. *See also* PARTIDO MODERADO.

MARTÍNEZ RUIZ, JOSÉ ("AZORÍN") (1873–1967). "Azorín" was a member of the "**Generation of 1898.**" He was born into an upper-middle-class family in Monovar (Alicante), but moved to **Madrid** to make his name in the **press** and literary circles in the 1890s. In his early years, he was influenced by individualist **anarchism**, but after marrying in 1908 moved to the right, became a **Maurista** deputy, and between 1914 and 1919 became a subsecretary in the Ministry of Education. Like **Miguel de Unamuno**, he was concerned with the "essence" of Spain, which he saw as embodied in the Castilian peasantry (an idea incorporated into the ideology of the early **Franco regime**). His best-known literary essays on this theme are *La ruta de Don Quijote* (*Don Quixote's Route*, 1905), and *Castilla* (*Castile*, 1912).

MAS I GAVARRÓ, ARTUR. *See* CONVERGÈNCIA I UNIÓ.

MATESA SCANDAL. The Matesa scandal blew up in August 1969, seriously damaging the credibility of the **Franco regime**. Essentially, it was a scam by which export credits were given to the company Maquinaria Textil del Norte, SA (Matesa) for bogus exports. These dealings were made known by members of the **Movimiento Nacional** in order to damage their **Opus Dei** rivals because two Opus Dei cabinet ministers were involved. They were, as a result, forced to resign, but the vice president, **Luis Carrero Blanco**, was able to use the reshuffle to strengthen the Opus Dei's position within government. The director of Matesa, Vila Reyes, was at first imprisoned, but after threatening to spill the beans on other financial irregularities involving regime figures, he was pardoned.

MAURA Y MONTANER, ANTONIO (1853–1925). Antonio Maura was probably the country's most important political figure during the decline and fall of the **Cánovas Restoration** between 1898 and 1923. He was born in Mallorca into a middle-class family, studied law in **Madrid**, and went on to work in the law firm of the powerful political figure Germán Gamazo (1838–1901), who was closely linked to Castilian wheat-growing interests. It was through Gamazo—soon to be his father-in-law—that he was to enter politics. He quickly established a reputation as a reformer within the **Partido Liberal (PL)**. When made overseas minister in 1892, he drafted a plan for the autonomy of **Cuba** and Puerto Rico. Had it been accepted, it might have saved Spain the travails of the Cuban insurrection and **Spanish-American War** of 1898, but it was defeated in the **Cortes** by the powerful colonial lobby, thereby forcing Maura's resignation.

At the end of the decade, the Gamazo faction broke with the PL and, after the death of Gamazo in 1901, Maura led the group into the **Partido Conservador** (PC) which, under the leadership of **Francisco Silvela**, he saw as more capable of renewing the regime. Maura still maintained his reforming zeal, but from this date it was channeled in a more conservative direction. He adopted Silvela's **regenerationist** discourse, calling for a "**revolution from above**," which would make possible the construction of a new bipolar party system—within the boundaries of the Cánovas Restoration—based on "sound public opinion" (the "neutral mass" or *masas neutras*) rather than *caciquismo*. But for Maura, this public opinion was moderate and conservative in nature, and he therefore saw no contradiction between significant democratization of political life and the maintenance of right-wing policies in areas like relations with the **Catholic Church** and public order. Moreover, reflecting his view that elites should govern, there was a **corporatist** element in his thought. Though he believed in a free vote in the Lower House of parliament, he argued that in other areas (especially local government) this should be balanced by block votes for respectable corporations. Herein were to lie the major contradictions of his time in office.

In the second Silvela government of 1902–1903, he was given the post of minister of the interior, and, unlike his predecessors, during the May 1903 elections he did not use the regime's *caciquista* networks to manipulate the outcome. The growth in the **republican** vote on this occasion hardly endeared Maura to King **Alfonso XIII** and made him draw back on his reform strategy. Following the death of Silvela in 1903, Maura took over the leadership of the PC, exercising power between 1903 and 1904 and between 1907 and 1909. There were several strands to his policy. First, he continued to pursue "revolution from above," though he did not now see this as incompatible with using electoral manipulation. He seems to have believed that the ends justified the means and that he first needed to consolidate his position in power. A key part of his strategy was the decentralization of local government, with the aim of energizing local life and the parliamentary system as a whole. Between 1907 and 1909, he tried, unsuccessfully, to push a reform bill through parliament that would have introduced such changes. Second, he emphasized the need to combine reform with the maintenance of order and favored the illegalization of the revolutionary left. As a result, between 1907 and 1908, he promoted an antiterrorist bill, which endangered the ability of the **anarchist** movement to operate in the open. Third, he was a Spanish **nationalist** who aimed to mobilize support behind the **flag** at home and reassert Spanish power on the world stage. This could be seen in the funding his 1907–1909 government provided for reconstruction of the Spanish fleet (to be built in Spanish shipyards) and his backing for the colonization of **Morocco**. Finally, he aimed to gain the backing of conservative Catholic opinion, establishing close links with the **Alejandro Pidal**, the leader of the Catholic right within the party.

From 1908, the PL, alarmed at Maura's "antiliberalism," circumstantially allied with the republicans in a so-called **Left Bloc**, and, after the Maura government's harsh repression of the **Tragic Week** in July–August 1909, maintained the alliance, orchestrating a "Maura No!" campaign. At the same time, there were protests in foreign capitals at the repression, and particularly at the execution of the anarchist freethinker **Francisco Ferrer**. As a result, fearing for the instability of the monarchy, King Alfonso XIII refused to renew his confidence in Maura in October 1909, forcing him to resign and allowing the PL to take power. Henceforth, Maura saw the PL as unfit to govern and refused to have any dealings with them. This attitude was behind the growing divisions within the PC in the following years. The Conservatives desired to return to power, and after efforts to make Maura change his mind had failed, **Eduardo Dato** accepted office on the party's behalf in October 1913. Maura then resigned as party leader and, while he remained within the party, allowed an independent movement known as Maurismo to operate.

Over the following decade, Maura's policies remained a rather contradictory mix. He continued to champion the "revolution from above" but his conservatism became further accentuated. Hence, he laid great emphasis on the need to fight subversion and allowed a strong antidemocratic New Right current to take root in the **Maurista** movement. Given his prestige, he came back into government between 1918 and 1923, presiding over three ministries (March–November 1918, April–June 1919, and August 1921–March 1922). Yet there was little attempt to renew Spanish political life. The first and third were coalition governments formed in periods of crisis, and the second focused on countering the revolutionary threat posed by the working-class left. Overall, the democratizing impetus promised by the "revolution from above" was stymied by Maura's timidity, his closeness to hard-line conservatives, and his unwillingness to work with the moderate left. He never broke with liberalism, but in September 1923, with the Cánovas Restoration under attack from various fronts, saw a "**military** parenthesis" as inevitable.

MAURISTAS. This term refers to the followers of **Antonio Maura**, who formed a distinct political grouping, known as Maurismo, during 1914. They were encouraged to take such a stance for two reasons. Firstly, from the turn of the century Maura had stressed the need to mobilize right-wing opinion in order to reform the **Cánovas Res-**

toration. Then, in October 1913, he effectively lost the leadership of the **Partido Conservador (PC)**, provoking his most enthusiastic backers to take action. **Ángel Ossorio y Gallardo**, a close personal friend, took the lead, setting up a national leadership in Madrid in June 1914. Local committees and youth organizations were then organized in urban areas. These Mauristas were inspired by Maura's **regenerationist** rhetoric, which was informed by **Catholicism** and Spanish **nationalism**.

From 1917, the movement was to head in two directions. One group under Ossorio y Gallardo, which was particularly influenced by social-Catholicism, broke away to form a separate party, the **Partido Social Popular**, modeled roughly on the Italian Partito Popolare, in June 1922. However, the majority, headed by Antonio Goicoechea (1876–1953), wished to retain the link with Maura. This Mauristas were particularly concerned at the threat of left-wing revolution and were of great importance in the formation of local bourgeois parastate militias (sometent and civic unions) from 1919. From this year, their discourse took on an increasingly antiparliamentary, authoritarian political tone. They also reacted violently to the **Catalanist** agitation of late 1918, radicalizing their Spanish nationalist rhetoric.

Antonio Maura himself was, however, to stay aloof. He still hoped to retake the leadership of the PC and work within the system. The Maurista movement was, in fact, constructed independently, and, while he remained in close contact with its leaders, he seems to have viewed it as no more than a ginger group, which might agitate for his return to power. This contradicted the position of men like Ossorio y Gallardo, who wanted Maura to take on the Restoration parties at the head of the movement. In addition, because of Maura's ambiguous position, old-style *caciques* remained attached to the Maurista movement, viewing it as simply another fraction within the PC and **Partido Liberal**. And as Maura again took leading positions within the regime between 1919 and 1923, it lost dynamism and fragmented.

All Mauristas accepted the September 1923 coup by General **Miguel Primo de Rivera**, which they saw as inevitable, but this is as far as unity went. Maura himself largely retained his liberal ideals and wanted to see a return to civilian rule after a military "parenthesis." This was also the position of part of the Partido Social Popular, under Ossorio y Gallardo. However, the bulk of the Mauristas, like

Antonio Goicoechea, completed their evolution toward an antiliberal, **corporatist** discourse and integrated into the upper echelons of the dictatorship. Subsequently, old Mauristas were to play a significant role in the **Franco regime**. They were instrumental in forging the corporatist alternative to liberal democracy, which was such an important feature of Spanish political life from the 1920s to the death of **Francisco Franco** in 1975.

MAY EVENTS. This expression refers to the civil war within a civil war that pitted various Republican factions against each other in **Barcelona** between 3 and 7 May 1937. The two main groupings were, on the one hand, the **anarchists** and members of the dissident communist **Partido Obrero de Unificación Marxista** (POUM), and, on the other, the Catalan Communist party, the **Partit Socialista Unificat de Catalunya** (PSUC), and the various **republican** parties, most notably **Esquerra Republicana de Catalunya** (ERC). Discontent had been brewing in Barcelona for some time. After the **military** uprising of 17–18 July 1936, the anarchist **Confederación Nacional del Trabajo** (CNT), along with other far leftist groups, had launched a social revolution in **Catalonia** that had led to the decentralization of power to local committees and to the collectivization of much of the region's **industry**. From 1937, however, the Republican government sought to reimpose central control and roll back the revolution. Anarchists had joined the government in November in order to have a say in the decision-making process, but among the rank-and-file there was a great deal of discontent. A particularly radical grouping of anarchists, the Friends of Durruti, was formed in March 1937 to defend the revolution, and by May had between 4,000 and 5,000 members.

Tensions exploded on 3 May when police occupied the lower floors of the Barcelona telephone exchange, which had been held by the CNT since the beginning of the war. This was an important strategic prize because its occupation had allowed the CNT to listen in on government communications. Several days of street fighting ensued. A cease-fire was finally arranged on 7 May, when the city was swamped by Republican Assault Guards. The uprising allowed the Republican government to greatly curtail the power of the CNT in Catalonia and to further increase central control. The **Partido Comunista de España** (PCE)-PSUC, backed by the more moderate "reformist" members of the **Partido Socialista Obrero Español** (PSOE) and by the republicans, also used these events to oust the prime minister, **Francisco Largo Caballero**, from power. They called for the POUM to be illegalized, and when Largo Caballero refused, they provoked a cabinet crisis. In the new cabinet, led by **Juan Negrín**, the PCE was in a significantly stronger position. *See also* SPANISH CIVIL WAR.

MAYOR OREJA, JAIME (1951–). Mayor Oreja has been one of the leading figures in the **Partido Popular** (PP) over the last decade. He was born in San Sebastián and completed a degree in agronomy. His uncle, Marcelino Oreja (1935–), had been an important politician in the **Unión del Centro Democrático** (UCD), and Jaime entered politics under his wing. In 1980, he was elected to the Basque parliament. He subsequently switched to **Alianza Popular** (AP) and by the early 1990s had consolidated his position as the PP's leading politician in the **Basque Country**. At the same time, he became involved in **European Union** (EU) politics, coordinating the PP's campaign in the 1998 European elections.

In **José María Aznar**'s first government in 1996, he was made minister of the interior. His calm and straightforward manner gained him considerable popularity. After the 1996 elections, in which the PP had emerged as the largest party but not achieved an overall majority, he negotiated **Partido Nacionalista Vasco** (PNV) support for an Aznar government, and stated he wanted to work with the PNV in the fight against **ETA**. Subsequently, he launched an offensive against both ETA and those groups that gave it political cover, seriously weakening its offensive capacity. However, when the PNV radicalized its nationalist discourse during 1997 and tried to bring ETA in from the cold in return for an end to **terrorism**, he took an increasingly hard line, accusing the PNV of in reality giving ETA succor. And when ETA declared a truce between 1998 and 1999, he was very skeptical it would lead anywhere.

The problem was that these events led to an increasingly radicalized confrontation between Spanish and Basque **nationalists**. This occurred at a time when the PP vote in the Basque Country had risen greatly and the Basque nationalist vote had been in decline. It led to the belief in PP circles that the party could inflict a historic defeat on

Basque nationalism. The man chosen was Mayor Oreja. He stayed on as minister of the interior after the 2000 general elections, but then stepped down in 2001 in order to put his name forward as PP candidate for president (*lehendakari*) in the Basque elections. It was not to be. The PP vote did further increase, but Basque nationalists flocked to the PNV-**Euskal Alkartasuna** (EA) coalition slate, fearful of a "Spanish" takeover of Basque institutions. Mayor Oreja's star thereafter began to wane somewhat. In 2001, he had been the favorite to succeed Aznar as PP party leader, but in 2003, Aznar picked the more emollient figure of **Mariano Rajoy**. He may have been concerned that Mayor Oreja's intransigence in Basque politics could lose the party votes in the future. The month after the **Partido Socialista Obrero Español** victory in the March 2004 general elections, he was chosen to lead the PP's campaign in the forthcoming European elections.

MAYORAZGOS. *Mayorazgos* were estates that had been entailed by their owners, making it impossible for them to be broken up. This practice became increasingly common during the reign of the **Catholic Monarchs**, when it was encouraged as a way to prevent inheritance disputes between nobles. They were removed in 1837 during the *desamortización*, which created a free market in land.

MEDIA. *See* PRESS; RADIO; TELEVISION.

MELILLA. *See* COLONIES.

MEMORIAL DE GREUGES/PETITION OF COMPLAINTS. *See* ALMIRALL I LLOZER, VALENTÍ

MENÉNDEZ Y PELAYO, MARCELINO (1856–1912). Menéndez y Pelayo was the greatest conservative thinker of late 19th- and early 20th-century Spain. He was strongly supported by the Spanish prime minister, **Antonio Cánovas del Castillo**, who helped him gain a chair in Spanish literature in the University of Madrid in 1878. Menéndez y Pelayo reciprocated this favor, standing as a deputy and senator for the **Partido Conservador** (PC) on several occasions.

Despite his links with the PC, his most polemical works, *La ciencia española* (*Spanish Science*, 1876) and *Historia de los heterodoxos españoles* (*History of Spanish Heterodoxies*, 1880–1882), had an anti-**liberal** component. He defended traditional Catholic values and accused authors who had not adhered to this tradition of being anti-Spaniards. He believed that Spain's greatness had been forged under Catholic hegemony in the 16th and 17th centuries, but that the country had been poisoned by 18th-century **Enlightenment** philosophy and that it had once again to find its true Catholic self. He therefore saw radical liberals and freethinkers as antipatriotic Spaniards who were collaborating in the country's downfall. His ideas were warmly received by the hierarchy of the **Catholic Church**, and, after his death, his legacy was to be taken up by the extreme right. During the **Franco regime**, he was to be showered with tributes and posthumous honors.

MESTA. The Mesta was a powerful sheepowners' guild that was organized in the 13th century. During the spring and summer, it drove vast flocks of sheep from the south of Spain up to Burgos (the main commercial center), where they were shorn. The wool was then exported, largely through Bilbao. Under the **Catholic Monarchs**, it attained a privileged position because of the revenue the export trade afforded the crown. The tide turned against the Mesta in the 1780s under **Carlos III**, when **Enlightenment** ministers, who saw it has holding back the development of **agriculture**, took away land it had used to pasture its flocks. It was wound up in 1836.

MILICIA NACIONAL. *See* NATIONAL MILITIA.

MILITARY. In the Middle Ages, Spanish monarchs recruited soldiers through their noble vassals and through local militias. Moreover, the use of mercenaries was common practice. Until the end of the 15th century, powerful nobles were a law unto themselves, using their armies to fight each other and take on the **monarchy**. However, the **Catholic Monarchs** were then able to check the power of the nobility, used professional commanders more effectively, and took more direct control over military operations. The **Crown of Castile**, in particular, had forged a powerful fighting force during the "**Reconquest**" and both the Catholic Monarchs and their successors were able to employ the Castilian forces successfully in continental Europe. Under the **Habsburgs**, moreover, forces were drawn from the rest of the empire. Yet, under **Felipe II** in the second half of the 16th century, constant budget deficits led to problems paying the troops and in discipline.

The overall result of constant warfare was that the Spanish state became highly militarized. This tradition was maintained during the 19th century by conservative liberals, who largely left law and order in military hands. After the division of Spain into provinces in 1833, the key figure in each province became the captain general, who had the power to declare states of emergency. These states of emergency were frequently used to repress political opposition and maintain the peace. Even the Spanish police force, the **Civil Guard**, was militarized.

In the early 19th century, much of the army was antiabsolutist. This was a consequence of the **War of Independence**, during which a new breed of lower- and middle-class army officers came to the fore. During the first absolutist restoration by **Fernando VII**, between 1814 and 1820, these men saw their chances of promotion blocked and so participated in **liberal** plots to force the Constitution of 1812 on the monarch. It was during these years that the classic method of overthrowing the government of the day became the army coup or *pronunciamiento*. There were several attempted coups between 1814 and 1820. They culminated in the *pronunciamiento* by Major Rafael de Riego (1785–1823) in January 1820, which finally succeeded in making Fernando VII accept the liberal 1812 Constitution.

The definitive replacement of absolutism by a new liberal political order from 1833 did not lead to a reduction of the role of the army in Spanish politics. Divisions soon developed between the more conservative **Partido Moderado** and the more radical **Partido Progresista**, with each faction calling upon the army to propel it to power. The tradition of the *pronunciamiento* was thereby perpetuated, while the figure of the army politician also emerged, with men like **Baldomero Espartero**, **José María Narváez**, and **Juan Prim** dominating political life. At the same time, the regular army was faced with a number of civil wars against the **Carlists** and several **colonial** campaigns, culminating in the **Spanish-American War** of 1898. Manpower was provided by the introduction of **military service** during the early 19th century. The army, therefore, became a key institution in Spanish life. Its representatives were entrenched within the Senate and important decisions could not be made without its approval. It was also enormously costly, accounting for about 20 percent of the state budget. Problems were worsened by the fact that it was a highly inefficient institution, which lacked modern equipment and comprised poorly trained troops and a bloated officer class.

In 1875, by stabilizing the political system, **Antonio Cánovas del Castillo**, the architect of the new Restoration regime, was able to keep the military out of politics for a time. However, this was at the cost of giving it almost complete institutional autonomy and giving generals strong political influence, with the result that all attempts at military reform were effectively blocked. From the turn of the century, important divisions opened up in the army, most notably between front-line cavalry and infantry officers in **Morocco**, the so-called *africanistas* (who traded the danger of active service for rapid promotion), and the *peninsulares*, officers largely based on the mainland who, while assured an easygoing life, had to endure the tedium of inactivity. Nevertheless, the various sections of the officer class also had much in common. In the first place, the Cánovas Restoration saw the army develop into a self-enclosed caste cut off from the rest of society. It was also becoming more conservative, a reflection of the fact that from the 1830s, officers were to an increasing extent recruited from the middle classes and social elites. The dominant military values during these years were order and discipline, combined with a ferocious Spanish **nationalism**, exacerbated by the fact that most officers were drawn from **Castile** and **Andalusia**.

Moreover, following the Spanish-American War, the growing weakness of the Cánovas Restoration again led the army to become more openly interventionist. Within military circles, it became common currency to believe that politicians were weak and corrupt, unable or unwilling to give the military the means to get on with the job, and only too willing to try to blame them when things went wrong. Weakness, they believed, was above all evident in most Restoration governments' supposed inability to deal with left-wing and Catalan nationalist agitation firmly. These attitudes made all too likely a new military coup as the **Cánovas Restoration** entered into crisis from 1914. They were visible in the **Juntas de Defensa** movement in 1917 and were also held by both many senior generals and *africanista* officers. Finally, in September 1923, General **Miguel Primo de Rivera** moved into action, sweeping the politicians aside and establishing his own dictatorship. The **Primo de Rivera dictatorship** did not, however, prove stable. In army circles, there was a great deal of resentment at the dictator's attempt to increase efficiency by reforming the system of advancement by seniority. As a result, when Primo de Rivera fell in January 1930 and then, in April 1931, King **Alfonso XIII** was forced to flee the country, the military temporarily stood aside. Nevertheless, in military circles there was considerable suspicion of the **Second Republic**. This was compounded by **Manuel Azaña**'s attempt to reform the army. A right-wing organization dedicated to the overthrow of the Republic, the **Unión Militar Española**, operated from 1933. It grew rapidly in 1936, and by the summer its supporters numbered one-third of the officer corps. After the **Popular Front** electoral victory of February 1936, a wide-ranging conspiracy was organized by General **Emilio Mola** from his headquarters in Pamplona. When the attempted coup was launched on 17–18 July, by no means the entire military rose up in support. The concept of loyalty to the established order was also an important one, and among military detachments in some urban areas there was considerable sympathy for the Republic. Nevertheless, a majority of middle-ranking officers joined in the revolt.

General **Francisco Franco** very quickly emerged as the key figure on the **Nationalist** side and throughout the **Spanish Civil War** the military was always the final arbitrator of Nationalist politics. Not surprisingly then, the military played a key role within the **Franco regime**. It was infused with the military values of discipline and hierarchy. This was summed up in the doctrine of *caudillaje*, or military command. The military were also the regime's ultimate guarantors. They administered repression and organized the police. Despite the fact that the **Falange Española Tradicionalista y de las Juntas de Ofensiva Nacional Sindicalista** (FET y de las JONS) was the regime's single party, at cabinet level, military generals carried more weight. Salaries remained low but officers enjoyed special privileges, especially through well-stocked commissaries. The officer corps also remained overstaffed, the armed forces were not significantly modernized, and they still took a large part of the budget (41 percent in 1940 and 34 percent in 1945).

The military were not, however, a homogenous force, and there was no universal support for Franco. Many of the older generals were strongly promonarchist, and in the early 1940s there was some fear that Franco's identification with the Axis might lead to Allied intervention. The key figures in this respect were Alfredo Kindelán (1879–1962) and Antonio Aranda (1888–1979). However, Franco was able to rely on the support of younger officers trained during the civil war, who identified with their commander. He could also count on the military's reluctance to rock the boat in case this should let in the forces of the left. And, from 1944, with the upsurge of leftist activity in Spain and in the teeth of the Allies' ostracism, he succeeded in consolidating military support. As older generals retired, the new generation of pro-Francoist officers who totally identified with the regime's ultranationalistic, authoritarian culture came to the fore.

Nevertheless, from the 1940s the political role of the army began to wane. This was reflected in a decline in the number of military cabinet ministers and in state spending on the army, which by 1968 represented about 15 percent of the state budget. The military was given new equipment after the signing of the military basis agreement with the United States in 1953, but it was not state of the art. Furthermore, the relative pay of officers fell, and, from the 1960s, many took part-time jobs. Yet, though there may have been grumbles, for the reasons already outlined the bulk of the armed forces remained staunchly behind Franco. His was a regime they had played a key role in creating and with whose values they could readily identify.

Consequently, the reaction of the military was the most difficult problem with which the politicians behind the **transition to democracy** had to contend. In 1976, **Adolfo Suárez** presented his project for political reform to senior officers. Given that it was supported by King **Juan Carlos I**, the legitimate heir to Franco, they backed it reluctantly as long as it was approved by the **Cortes**. Yet within the armed forces, the Francoist diehards, or **Bunker** as they were often called, had considerable support, and in the years between 1977 and 1981 they were spurred on by the rise in **ETA terrorism** and by the creation of the **State of the Autonomies**, which was seen by many officers as a dire threat to national unity. Hence, there were a series of conspiracies against the new democratic institutions. They began with the 1978 **Galaxia Operation** and culminated in the **Tejerazo** of

February 1981. Only with the failure of the Tejerazo and the coming to power of the **Partido Socialista Obrero Español** (PSOE) in 1982 was the military effectively subordinated to civilian rule. The only serious incident since then involved the captain general of Seville, who affirmed in a speech in the 2005 Easter military parade that if the new Catalan statute violated the constitution, the army would have to intervene. He was subject to house arrest for eight days and then put on the reserve list.

During the 1980s and 1990s, following Spain's integration into the political structure of the North Atlantic Treaty Organization (NATO), the military went through a process of significant modernization. However, there were still too many officers and the continued operation of military service did not produce a well-trained, efficient force. Furthermore, there was increasing resistance within civil society to military service, with the result that it was phased out between 1999 and 2001 and a new professional army was set up. However, poor wages meant that the army faced difficulties recruiting. At the end of 2001, it had recruited 77,000 professional soldiers, 9,000 less than it had planned (and this total had previously been revised downward). In 2002, the government improved the wages of non-commissioned officers (*suboficiales*) and soldiers who had stayed for over two years, and introduced a bonus for soldiers who completed their four-year contract, but problems remained. In 2005, **José Luis Rodríguez Zapatero**'s Socialist administration introduced new legislation, raising the retirement age for professional soldiers from 35 to 45 years and improving pensions. At the same time, wages were increased significantly and the government announced that it would make further modernization of the armed forces a priority.

As Spain has begun to play a more active role on the world stage, the international presence of the Spanish military has also grown. From 1989, it began participating in United Nations peacekeeping missions. In addition, it has participated more actively in NATO missions, especially after the Atlanticist **Partido Popular** government of **José María Aznar** came to power in 1996 and integrated Spain into NATO's military structure. Following the breakup of **Yugoslavia**, Spanish planes participated in the bombing of Serbian troops in 1995 and 1999, and in 1997 it also intervened on the ground under a NATO mandate. From 2001, Spanish troops have also been deployed in **Afghanistan**, formed part of the coalition forces in **Iraq** between 2003 and 2005, and made up an important part of the peacekeeping force sent to Lebanon in September 2006, following the war between Israel and Hezbollah. However, when Rodríguez Zapatero came to power in March 2004, consequent upon his party's opposition to the war in Iraq, he quickly withdrew Spanish forces.

In 2008, the Spanish armed forces had 132,000 personnel (including 79,000 troops, of which 14,000 are women). There were 1,070 Spanish troops stationed in Lebanon, out of a total number of 2,560 troops involved in missions abroad. In 2006, the Ministry of Defense was allocated 7,696 million euros. This represented 2.6 percent of the state budget.

MILITARY BASES AGREEMENT. *See* FRANCO REGIME; MILITARY; NORTH ATLANTIC TREATY ORGANIZATION.

MILITARY JUNTAS. *See* JUNTAS DE DEFENSA.

MILITARY SERVICE. Military service was introduced in the early 19th century. However, it was not compulsory for all the country's male youth, with the middle and upper classes able either to buy their way out or find a substitute. The situation was partly rectified in 1912, though middle-class families could still pay to undertake a shorter period of service (5 to 10 months). This made military service extremely unpopular in lower-class circles, especially because of the high casualty rates in the **colonial** wars of **Cuba** and later, **Morocco**. Around 60,000 Spaniards were killed opposing the Cuban insurrection between 1895 and 1898, and 9,000 soldiers were massacred in one day by Moroccan tribesmen at **Annual** in July 1921. Most dramatically, in 1909, during the so-called **Tragic Week**, the calling up of army reservists to fight in Morocco led to the declaration of a general strike, the erection of barricades, street fighting, and several days of church burning. In addition, as the **military** moved rightward, military service increasingly meant indoctrination in its brand of exalted, authoritarian, Spanish **nationalist** ideology. This was particularly the case during the **Franco regime**, during which, in addition, recruits found themselves subject to brutal treatment at the hands of their superiors (and older recruits) and often acted as unpaid servants at the beck and call of the officer class.

Not surprisingly, then, in the aftermath of the **transition to democracy**, there was great opposition to military service among the country's youth, especially among the better educated in the larger cities. From 1984, it became possible to declare oneself a conscientious objector and undertake "social services" instead. The number of conscientious objectors thereafter rose rapidly, from 11,049 in 1988 to 163,396 in 1999, despite the fact that social service lasted two years and military service only one. At the same time, there was a growing realization in political and military circles that a professional army was needed to fight in technologically sophisticated modern warfare. The move was finally made after the 1996 general elections, when the Catalan coalition **Convergència i Unió** (CiU) insisted the army be professionalized in return for it supporting a minority **Partido Popular** (PP) government. The new law, which envisaged a transitional period lasting from 1999 to 2002 (subsequently reduced to 1999 to 2001), was approved in 1998. From 2001, the Spanish military has been fully professionalized.

MINIFUNDIA. Minifundia were tiny plots of land that predominated in the agrarian system of the northern province of **Galicia** and in parts of Old **Castile** from the Middle Ages. The spread of the minifundia was the result of a leasing arrangement known as the *foro*, whereby land was rented and then sublet to peasant farmers (or *foreros*). The system was economically disastrous, for it locked peasants into a largely subsistence economy and allowed them little capital to invest in technical improvements. State aid and especially large-scale **emigration** to urban Spain from the 1960s improved the situation, though many plots are still too small to be economically viable. *See also* AGRICULTURE; LATIFUNDIA.

MINING. Modern mining industries developed after the laws of 1849 and 1859, which brought all mining deposits into state ownership. In 1868, civil governors were given the power to grant concessions in perpetuity. There followed a mining boom. Over the next 20 years, much of this **industry** fell into foreign hands. Thus, by 1913, foreign interests probably owned about half of Spain's mining enterprises, including many of the country's most lucrative concerns. Only in the Asturian **coal mining** industry and in Vizcayan iron ore mining did Spanish businesses predominate. In part, this reflected the indebtedness of Spanish governments during the 19th century and their consequent subordination to foreign financial interests. In part, it was a consequence of the far greater capital resources of these investors. Foreign ownership was particularly dominant in the branches of lead, copper, and mercury. Foreign mining concerns included the copper pyrites Riotinto deposits, leased to Matherson and Co. of London in alliance with the Deutsche National Bank of Bremen and Rothschild in 1873 and the Almadén mercury deposits, which fell into the hands of the House of Rothschild in 1870. The rapid growth in the exploitation of metals and minerals led to a transformation in the structure of Spanish **foreign trade**. Between 1899 and 1908, they accounted for almost one-third of all Spanish exports.

This situation began to change after 1914. First, from the 1920s, as **economic policy** became more **nationalist**, preference was given to Spanish concerns. This reached its apogee in the **autarkic** years of the **Franco regime** in the early 1940s. As a result, the weight of Spanish businesses within the sector grew rapidly. But in any case, from 1914, Spanish mineral resources were becoming of less interest to foreign investors, and from the 1940s, the sector almost totally lost its former significance within the Spanish **economy**. *See also* IRON AND STEEL INDUSTRY.

MIRÓ I FERRÀ, JOAN (1893–1983). Joan Miró was one of the most popular Catalan painters of the 20th century. In his youth, he was strongly influenced by the colorful *modernista* architecture of **Antoni Gaudí** and Lluís Domènech i Montaner (1850–1923). Then, when he moved to Paris in 1920, he began to develop his own style. He met **Pablo Picasso** at the turn of the century in **Barcelona** and renewed the acquaintance on visiting Paris in 1919. Nevertheless, though influenced by cubism, his work was never fully in the cubist tradition, and, although he signed the 1924 Surrealist Manifesto, he could never really be encompassed within the surrealist movement. Rather, he was one of the pioneers of an abstract art, in which visual impact and emotion are given primacy over meaning. His use of rounded abstract shapes and bright Mediterranean colors gained him an international reputation from the 1940s, and in the following years he was contracted to paint a series of giant murals (Terrace Plaza in Cincinnati, the UNESCO building in Paris, Harvard University, the Congress and Exhibition Palace in **Madrid**). He died in Palma de Mallorca on 25 December 1983.

MIRÓ ROMERO, PILAR (1940–1997). Pilar Miró was one of the most influential figures in Spanish **cinema** in the 1980s and 1990s, combining script writing, producing, and directing, with important posts in the administrations of the **Partido Socialista Obrero Español** (PSOE). She shot to fame in 1979 with her film *El crimen de Cuenca* (*The Crime of Cuenta*), which led to an unsuccessful attempt to prosecute her for slander by the **Civil Guard**. Subsequently, she became well-known for adaptations of literary works, most notably *Werther* (1985) and *El perro del hortelano* (*Dog in the Manger*, 1996). In 1982, the new PSOE government appointed her director general of cinematography, allowing her to significantly increase state financial support for Spanish films. In 1986, she was then put in charge of Spanish state **television**. She was forced to resign amid allegations of impropriety in 1989, but they were subsequently shown to have been ill-founded.

MODERADOS. *See* PARTIDO MODERADO.

MODERATE DECADE. This name is used to refer to the years between 1843 and 1854, during which the **Partido Moderado** was able to consolidate its hold over the Spanish polity.

MODERN SCHOOL. *See* ESCUELA MODERNA.

MODERNISM. This was a literary movement that took off in the Hispanic world in the late 19th century and that reached its zenith between about 1890 and 1914. Its major figure was Ruben Darío (1867–1916) of Nicaragua, who visited Spain between 1892 and 1899, and its foremost Spanish exponents were Manuel Machado (1874–1947), and, in their early years, **Ramón María del Valle Inclán** and **Antonio Machado**. The movement was marked by a rejection of staid bourgeois norms, though the group's poetry and prose tended to represent an escape from the mundane realities of the present world, with an emphasis on exotic themes, a romantic and melancholic undercurrent, and the adoption of an aesthetic style that stressed form over content.

MODERNISME. The so-called *modernista* movement was at its height in **Barcelona** between the 1890s and 1914. It comprised two rather different strands. On the one hand, one can talk of a literary and artistic *modernista* movement made up of such figures as Santiago Rusiñol (1861–1931) and Ramon Casas (1866–1932). On the other hand, there was the **architectural** movement, whose leading lights were **Antoni Gaudí** and Lluís Domènech i Montaner (1850–1923). The artistic *modernistes* drew their inspiration from the antibourgeois individualism of such writers as Henrik Ibsen and from postimpressionist Parisian artistic circles, and paraded their anticonformist "decadent" lifestyle to the consternation of polite middle-class Barcelona society. In this respect, there were parallels with Hispanic **Modernism.** The bohemian Els Quatre Gats café was their stamping ground in their heyday between 1897 and 1903, though commercial success in the 1900s would subsequently lead them in a more conformist direction. In this atmosphere, the young **Pablo Picasso** was introduced into avant-garde artistic circles.

The *modernista* architects, on the other hand, were more directly influenced by the European Art Nouveau movement, which like Romanticism looked back wistfully to the preindustrial world and rejected mass production and functionalism. They took inspiration from **Catalonia**'s Romanesque and Gothic past and craft traditions, while taking full advantage of new building methods. In Catalan *modernisme*, Art Nouveau's interest in organic forms was particularly accentuated, with Gaudí its most accomplished exponent. This emphasis on Catalonia's roots meant that architectural *modernistes* were more conservative than their artistic counterparts, were practicing **Catholics,** and established closer ties with the social elite. Nevertheless, both wings tended to sympathize with **Catalanism,** viewing their cultural production as symptomatic of Catalonia's distinctive spirit and modernity (symbolized by closer ties with avant-garde European artistic movements), in comparison with the much more classical architectural styles and realist artistic tradition still dominant in **Madrid**. *Modernisme* fell out of fashion after 1914 and until the 1970s, was regarded as an eccentric anachronism. Since then, it has enjoyed an enormous revival in popularity. Within Catalonia and outside, it is once again viewed as a major hallmark of Catalan distinctiveness and has played a key role in turning Barcelona into one of Europe's premier city-break **tourist** destinations.

MOLA VIDAL, EMILIO (1887–1937). General Emilio Mola organized the **military** conspiracy against the **Second Republic** in the spring and summer of 1936. He was born in Placetas, **Cuba**, into a military family. As was expected, he was also to tread the military path. He graduated from the Toledo Infantry Academy in 1907, then between 1909 and 1929 rose through the ranks in the *africanista* army of **Morocco**. Like most of his fellow officers, he was a political conservative and showed a great esteem for King **Alfonso XIII**. Between February 1930 and April 1931, he was the director general of security, and after the proclamation of the **Second Republic**, he escorted the king out of Spain. This led to his arrest at the hands of the new Republican authorities on 21 April 1931, and though his case was eventually dropped he was retired from active service and like most *africanista* officers, he came to nurture a deep loathing for the **liberal** authorities. He reacted by writing a series of books criticizing **Manuel Azaña**'s military reforms. However, he was rehabilitated by **Alejandro Lerroux**'s coalition government, which was backed by the right-wing **Confederación Española de Derechas Autónomas** (CEDA), in March 1934; in November 1935, he was named commander in chief of the Spanish army in Morocco. Following the **Popular Front** victory in the February 1936 elections, Mola became convinced that only an army coup could save Spain from the threat of chaos and communism. The republican government reacted by removing most generals suspected of disaffection from sensitive postings, but Mola was unwisely put in charge of the Twelfth Infantry Brigade in the **Carlist** stronghold of Pamplona, where he was able to coordinate the rebellion.

Once the **Spanish Civil War** had begun, Mola took charge of the Northern Army. At first, it seems he only envisaged replacing the government by a military directorate, which would administer a

"Republic of order." In the month following the uprising of 17–18 July, he was seen as a possible rival to General **Francisco Franco**'s aspirations to power. Realizing that Franco was in a stronger position, he supported Franco's nomination for the post of commander in chief of the armed forces (**Generalísimo**) for the duration of the war on 21 September 1936, but had qualms about him becoming head of state seven days later. Mola, it seems, still planned to play a key political role in the new regime, resulting in tension between the two building up over the following year as Franco consolidated his power and began to set up a semi-totalitarian regime under his supreme authority. A clash seemed inevitable, but Mola died in a plane crash en route to visit Franco in Burgos on 3 July 1937. Because of this rivalry, Mola's key role in the uprising would henceforth be downplayed by the Francoist propaganda machine.

MONARCHY. In the last 550 years, Spain has changed dynasties four times and has also undergone two interludes of Republican government. Spain was "unified" in 1479 under the Castilian Trastámara dynasty (to which both of the **Catholic Monarchs** belonged). Then, following the accession to the throne of **Carlos I** in 1516, the **Habsburgs** would be the ruling dynasty for almost 200 years. The dynasty would change hands in 1700, after the childless **Carlos IV** invited Philippe of Anjou, the grandson of King Louis XIV of France, to succeed him. Only after the **War of Succession** would the new king, **Felipe V**, consolidate his position in power. The **Bourbons** have been the ruling dynasty in Spain for most of the period since then, but have had a checkered history and have found themselves challenged and questioned on several occasions. Following the War of Succession, the Bourbon monarchs established absolutist power and promoted a moderate reading of the European **Enlightenment**. Thy key figure in this respect was **Carlos III**.

However, the impact of the **French Revolution** threw the dynasty on the defensive. During most of **Fernando VII**'s reign in the early 19th century, the crown was identified with a defensive anti-**liberal** absolutism. In the late 1820s, Fernando VII began to look for a compromise with the more conservative liberals. This led to a division in the Bourbon family ranks on the death of Fernando VII in 1833, with his brother, **Carlos María Isidoro Benito de Borbón y**

Borbón-Parma, claiming the throne. Carlos supported a continuance of absolutism and his followers—the **Carlists**—would wage a century-long struggle against the liberal state. They were, however, unsuccessful, and over the next 100 years, under the figures of **Isabel II** (Fernando VII's daughter), **Alfonso XII**, and **Alfonso XIII**, the monarchy tended to back more conservative liberals while establishing a close relationship with the Spanish **military**. This meant that to be a left-liberal or a socialist one also had to be an antimonarchist with the result that among Spain's urban populace, democratic rule and the dethronement of the Bourbon dynasty became intertwined. For this reason, when in September 1868 a coalition of liberal forces overthrew the **Partido Moderado** government, Queen Isabel II was forced to flee the country and the search began for a new dynasty. **Amadeo** de Saboya, the son of the king of Italy, Victor Emmanuel II (1820–1878), briefly reigned between 1871 and 1873, but divisions within the ruling coalition led to his abdication in February 1873, followed by the proclamation of a republic (later known as the **First Republic**).

However, the Bourbon monarchy retained the allegiance of Spain's social elites and members of the old political establishment (the so-called **Alfonsoist monarchists**), and the growing chaos into which the new regime was plunged allowed conservative army officers to stage a *pronunciamiento* in favor of Isabel's son, Alfonso. He made a triumphal entry into **Madrid** on 14 January 1875. Between 1876 and 1923, under the **Cánovas Restoration**, the king shared power with parliament. Alfonso XII was very much the model of a constitutional king, but Alfonso XIII, who reigned from 1902, increasingly exercised the considerable authority vested in him by the **Constitution of 1876**. This coincided with a growing crisis of the Restoration regime, which led the king to support a coup by General **Miguel Primo de Rivera** in September 1923. This was to seal his fate. Once the dictator's popularity had waned in the late 1920s, the king could no longer rely on the backing of the old political elites, while the urban lower classes and southern peasantry remained violently antimonarchic. This was the background to the proclamation of the **Second Republic** in 1931. Alfonso XIII, like his grandmother, again had to abandon the country, though he refused to abdicate. However, spiraling social and national tensions led first to the **Spanish Civil War** and then, from 1939, to a personal dictatorship by General **Francisco Franco.**

Franco was a monarchist and had been close to Alfonso XIII. Yet he was mindful of his own power and therefore would only accept a Bourbon succession if it took place after his own death and assimilated the fundamentals of the regime he had built. Alfonso XIII abdicated in favor of his son, Don **Juan de Borbón y Battenberg**, in 1941, and from then the new pretender tried to pressurize Franco into stepping down. Unsuccessful, Don Juan had finally to accept that he would probably not reign, and that only by grooming his son, **Juan Carlos**, for office would the dynasty survive. In 1948, he therefore agreed to Juan Carlos's being educated in Spain. In 1969, when he was named Franco's successor, Juan Carlos then swore to uphold the fundamental principles of the **Movimiento Nacional**. Yet the future king was discreetly establishing contacts with more liberal figures within the regime and as the regime entered into crisis in the early 1970s, he became convinced of the need for democratic change. On assuming power after Franco's death in November 1975, Juan Carlos therefore put his weight behind the effort by regime reformers to dismantle Francoism and put a constitutional monarchy in its place. The Francoist edifice quickly crumbled and a new **constitution** was drawn up during 1978. Yet Francoists remained a powerful force in the military. It was here that, as head of the armed forces, the king's role in the **transition to democracy** was crucial. First, he prevented the generals from blocking democratization and then, in February 1981, he decisively opposed an attempted military coup (the **Tejerazo**). It is because of the positive role played by Juan Carlos in the transition that consensus regarding the monarchy is probably wider now than it has been at any other time over the past 150 years.

MONCLOA PACTS. The signing of the Moncloa Pacts between 25 and 27 October 1977 represented a key moment in the consolidation of the new democratic institutions in Spain. The pacts were signed by the **Unión del Centro Democrático** (UCD) government and the main opposition parties. Their aim was to tackle the economic crisis by keeping wage increases below the level of inflation in return for an extension of the **welfare state** and tax reform. Labor unions did not sign, but the major left-wing parties, the **Partido Socialista Ob-**

rero Español (PSOE) and **Partido Comunista de España** (PCE), tried to ensure that their sister unions, the **Unión General del Trabajadores** (UGT) and **Comisiones Obreras** (CC.OO), would respect the accord. Overall, the pacts seem to have had some impact in bringing down inflation, though the government's tardiness in introducing welfare reforms led to bitterness in left-wing circles. More important, perhaps, the pacts showed that all the democratic parties were united in trying to lay the foundations of the new democratic institutions and tackle the country's economic difficulties.

MONTJUÏC TRIAL. This was the name popularly given to the trial of **anarchist** suspects in the military castle of Montjuïc following the **terrorist** attack on the Corpus procession in **Barcelona** in June 1896. Four hundred suspects were arrested and 87 put on trial by the **military** authorities. Confessions were obtained through the use of torture, with the end result of five executions. There followed, between 1898 and 1899, a massive left-wing campaign for a judicial review of the trial orchestrated from **Madrid** by **Alejandro Lerroux**.

MONTSENY MAÑÉ, FEDERICA (1864–1994). Federica Montseny was one of Spain's leading **anarchist** activists and writers in the early 20th century. Her parents were the anarchist theoreticians Joan Montseny (1864–1942, pseud. Federico Urales) and Teresa Mañé (1865–1939, pseud. Soledad Gustavo). She first made her mark in the 1920s, editing the anarchist theoretical magazine *La Revista Blanca* and writing short stories and novels inspired by anarchist moral themes. Such writing was extremely important in broadening the movement's following. During the **Second Republic**, she then emerged as a talented orator on the more orthodox wing of the anarchist movement. With the outbreak of the **Spanish Civil War**, she joined the central committee of the anarchist syndicalist labor federation, the **Confederación Nacional del Trabajo** (CNT). Despite her anarchist beliefs, she became minister of health and social affairs under the Republican government of **Francisco Largo Caballero** in November 1936. This very much went against anarchist principles, which insisted that all forms of state power were oppressive. However, the reality was that if the anarchists did not participate in government they would be on the receiving end of policies devised by other elements within the

Republican coalition. This appointment also meant she was the first female minister appointed in a western European country. She was forced out of office following the fall of Largo Caballero after the **May events** in Barcelona. After the Republic's defeat, she would spend the **Franco regime** exiled in France. Despite her experience as a minister, she would remain an orthodox "antipolitical" anarchist. In 1945, splits within the anarchist camp would provoke the division of the anarchist confederation, the Movimiento Libertario Español (Spanish Libertarian Movement). Montseny led the "purists" who refused to have dealings with political parties.

MOORS. As Moorish Spain fell to the advancing Christian armies during the "**Reconquest**" between 10th and 15th centuries, a large number of Moors (or *mudéjares*, as the Muslim inhabitants of Christian territories were known) remained in Spain. Most worked the land under Christian landowners, and they were particularly numerous in the areas of Aragón, **Valencia**, and Granada. Following the fall of Granada, the last Moorish stronghold in Spain, in 1492, in the **Crown of Castile** decrees were issued forcing the Moors convert to Christianity (which, in Granada, was accompanied by the mass burning of Arabic books). In the **Crown of Aragón**, they received greater protection, but in the early 1520s in Valencia, during a popular rebellion known as Las Germanías, the Christians turned on the *mudéjares* and forced them to convert en masse. Then, in 1526, **Carlos I** issued several decrees ordering the conversion of all Spain's *mudéjares*.

However, large numbers of *moriscos* (as *mudéjares* who had supposedly converted to Christianity were called) only observed the Christian faith superficially. In the Crown of Aragón in particular, because many worked on seignorial land, it was difficult for the authorities to take action (though the quid pro quo was their harsh working conditions). Tensions were further increased by the intensifying struggle with the Ottoman Empire from the 1530s and by raids by Barbary pirates from the North African coast. It was clear that many Spanish *moriscos* maintained contacts with their North African brethren and claims were made that they were involved in contraband and kidnappings. This fueled fears among the Christian elite that they might operate as a kind of fifth column in the case of an Ottoman attack on Spain. From the 1550s, greater efforts were made to enforce the decrees, which demanded the *moriscos* abandon the Arabic language and their cultural practices, with the **Spanish Inquisition** taking a growing interest into heresy within the *morisco* community. As in the case of the *converso* **Jews**, the rise of the "pure blood" (*limpieza de sangre*) movement—which limited work in prestigious public professions and the Church to men from old Christian families—exacerbated the discrimination to which they were subject.

A crackdown in Granada in 1567 led to an open rebellion in the Alpujarras region, in which there were large numbers of *morisco* silk weavers, which was only put down after two years of heavy fighting. In response, more than 50,000 Granada *moriscos* were dispersed throughout Castile and settlers brought in to replace them. In the aftermath of the rebellion, **Felipe II** provisionally decided to expel the *moriscos* from Spain, though this was not acted upon during his lifetime. Finally, in 1609, despite much controversy, **Felipe III** went ahead. It is estimated that the expulsion affected 300,000 *moriscos* out of the total population of 320,000. The vast majority found their way to North Africa. This had a serious impact on Spanish **agriculture**, most notably in Valencia, and put an end to Spain's multiethnic heritage. *See also* ISLAM AND SPAIN.

MORET Y PREDERGAST, SEGISMUNDO (1838–1913). Segismundo Moret was born in Cádiz, studied law at university, and taught for a time as professor at the University of Madrid. He joined the **Partido Progresista** and after the fall of the **First Republic** integrated into **Práxedes Mateo Sagasta**'s **Partido Liberal** (PL). By the 1890s, he was holding major ministerial posts and he went on to dispute the leadership of the party with Eugenio Monteros Ríos (1832–1914) after the death of Sagasta in 1903. Unlike Sagasta, by the time Moret reached the top of the party he could not rely on the *turno pacífico* to fabricate majorities and, therefore, needed to descend to the level of mass politics. His reaction was contradictory. He was a fierce anti-**Catalanist** and agreed to steer the Jurisdictions Law through parliament in 1906 after the *Cu-Cut!* **incident**. At the same time, however, between 1908 and 1909, he championed the "attraction" of Spanish **republicans** to the PL in order to make the system more representative. Hence, in 1908, he participated in the **Left Bloc** against **Antonio Maura**'s right-wing policies, and championed the

"Maura No!" campaign after the repression of the **Tragic Week** in the fall of 1909. This was an important element in King **Alfonso XIII**'s decision to remove Maura from office in October 1909. His policies were not, however, radical enough to win republicans over to the **monarchist** camp and they damaged the operation of the *turno* because Maura now saw the PL as unfit to govern and refused to work with it. He was called by Alfonso XIII to form a government after Maura's fall from grace, but the king got his revenge for Moret's perceived disloyalty to the regime in February 1910 by refusing to give him a decree to dissolve parliament. As a result, he was forced to resign, and was replaced as prime minister by his new rival, **José Canalejas**.

MORISCO. This was the name given to **Moors** who (at least officially) converted to Christianity during the 16th century.

MOROCCO. The **military** enclaves of Melilla and Ceuta had been in Spanish hands since the 15th and 17th centuries respectively. It was not, however, until the 19th century that Spain showed an interest in further penetrating into North Africa. In 1847, a Captaincy-General of North Africa was created, but Spain had almost no control in the region outside of its two garrison towns. Interest was heightened after the loss of its rich American **colonies** following the **Spanish-American War** of 1898, when Morocco came to be seen by political elites as an alternative avenue of imperial grandeur and by commercial interests as a possible market for Spanish goods and as a source of mineral wealth.

Spain's occupation of northern Morocco needs to be seen in the context of French ambitions in the area. Great Britain did not dissent to the French advance so long as **Gibraltar** was safe, with the result that in the Anglo-French agreement of April 1904, Britain agreed to French occupation of most of Morocco provided that the area across the straights from Gibraltar was in Spanish hands. In October 1904, therefore, France granted the northern zone to Spain, which in 1912 became a protectorate. From 1919, the colonial Army of Africa tried for the first time to conquer all the land encompassed within the protectorate, but it quickly proved difficult to hold down and of limited commercial value. An overambitious advance provoked the military disaster at **Annual** in July 1921 and though the region was finally pacified with French help in 1925, it remained a heavy burden on the exchequer. There was certainly little enthusiasm among much of the Spanish populace. Indeed, protest at the war in Morocco was to precipitate the events of the **Tragic Week** in Barcelona in 1909. With the exception of Ceuta and Melilla, Morocco was finally **decolonized** during the **Franco regime**.

After the **transition to democracy**, Spanish governments made great efforts to maintain cordial relations with Morocco and to develop trade with and investment in Morocco and her neighbors. During the 1990s, the **Partido Socialista Obrero Español** (PSOE) governments also tried to establish closer ties between the **European Union** and Arab countries on the southern Mediterranean rim, which, it was hoped (overoptimistically), would result in the establishment of a free-trade area by 2010. From the 1990s, with the liberalization of the Moroccan economy, Spanish foreign direct investment has grown rapidly in areas such as phosphate mining and **banking**. However, serious tensions surfaced with the **Partido Popular** (PP) government of **José María Aznar** after Morocco broke off its fishing treaty with Spain in 2001. The Spanish government's support for a referendum to decide the status of the Western Sahara then led Morocco to withdraw its ambassador in October. Tensions were greatly heightened on 11 July 2002, when Moroccan troops briefly occupied the uninhabited rocky outcrop of Perejil just off the Moroccan coast, claiming that it should have reverted to Moroccan hands in 1956 when Spain had handed over sovereignty. It was quickly recaptured by Spanish forces without bloodshed and an agreement was then reached, under the auspices of the U.S. secretary of state Colin Powell, whereby both countries agreed that the island should maintain its status as formerly Spanish but unoccupied. Diplomatic contacts were then renewed in December with a meeting between the Moroccan and Spanish foreign ministers, leading King Mohamed VI to allow the Galician fleet to fish in Moroccan waters and to the return to Madrid of the Moroccan ambassador in January 2003. A visit by King **Juan Carlos** to Ceuta and Melilla led to renewed tension at the end of 2007, with Morocco withdrawing its ambassador for consultations. However, after a personal letter from Prime Minister **José Luis Rodríguez Zapatero**, the ambassador returned to Madrid.

MOVEMENT. *See* MOVIMIENTO NACIONAL.

MOVIDA MADRILEÑA. This was the term coined for the dynamic, culturally subversive youth scene, which took off in **Madrid** in the late 1970s and then spread to other Spanish towns and cities. At its heart was a new transgressive lifestyle, which, stylistically, borrowed heavily from punk and encompassed the rock-and-roll litany of abuse of alcohol and drugs, but also embraced a more open sexuality and the championing of gay rights. It was particularly shocking to conservative middle-class opinion as it came so soon after the fall of General **Francisco Franco**'s arch-conservative dictatorship. A whole series of new bands, most notably Alaska y los Pegamoides, Nacha Pop, and Radio Futuro, were born. Alaska, the lead singer in the first group (real name Olvido Gara), became an iconic *movida* figure. In addition, young designers, painters, and filmmakers were attracted to the *movida* scene. Of key importance here was **Pedro Almodóvar**, whose early films reflected and embraced *movida* subculture. Indeed, Alaska starred in his first film, *Pepi, Luci, Bom, y otras chicas del montón* (*Pepi, Luci, Bom, and Other Girls on the Heap*, 1980). The movement died out in the mid-1980s.

MOVIMENT SOCIALISTA DE CATALUNYA/SOCIALIST MOVEMENT OF CATALONIA. This was an independent socialist party that operated in **Catalonia** during the **Franco regime**. It was formed in 1945 largely by dissidents from the **Partido Obrero de Unificación Marxista** (POUM) and the **Partit Socialista Unificat de Catalunya** (PSUC). Its main characteristics were its anti-Stalinism and **Catalanism**. It was soon to eclipse the official Catalan branch of the **Partido Socialista Obrero Español** (PSOE), which was virtually nonexistent, and was able to take over the Catalan branch of the Socialist labor union, the **Unión General de Trabajadores** (UGT). As against the policy pursued by the PSOE, it developed contacts with the PSUC and worked within the official state union, the **Organización Sindical Española** (OSE). In 1962, it teamed up with the Catalan **anarchists** and a small **Catholic**-Catalanist union, Solidaritat d'Obrers Cristians de Catalunya (Solidarity of Catalan Christian Workers—SOCC), to form a union front, the Aliança Sindical Obrera (Workers' Trade Union Alliance—ASO), which integrated into the semi-clandestine union confederation **Comisiones Obreras** (CC. OO). In 1968, it was to divide into two groups, but the various Catalan socialist parties were to reunite with the formation of the **Partit dels Socialistes de Catalunya** (PSC) in 1978.

MOVIMIENTO COMUNISTA DE ESPAÑA (MCE)/SPANISH COMMUNIST MOVEMENT. This far left party was originally formed under the name Movimiento Comunista (Communist Movement) in the **Basque Country** in 1967 by a number of former **ETA** members, who had been known as the Red Cells or ETA-Berri. Federations were then formed in other parts of Spain, leading to the change of name in 1972. During the 1970s, the MCE tried to build up a base in the trade union movement, having some success particularly in Guipúzcoa, where it rivaled **Comisiones Obreras** (CC.OO). It retained from its ETA days a strongly antistate nationalist ideology supporting the right of the various Spanish "nations" to self-determination. In the June 1977 elections, the Basque branch teamed up with the political front of ETA-PM, Euskadiko Iraultzaraka Alderdia (Party of the Basque Revolution), to form the coalition of **Euskadiko Esquerra** (EE). It was very active in the campaign against entry into the North Atlantic Treaty Organization (NATO) in the mid-1980s and enthusiastically backed the general strikes against the **Partido Socialista Obrera Español** (PSOE) government from 1988, but with increasingly few activists, it disintegrated in the early 1990s.

MOVIMIENTO NACIONAL/NATIONAL MOVEMENT. This was the name that was used to refer to the **Franco regime**'s single party, the **Falange Española Tradicionalista y de las Juntas de Ofensiva Nacional Sindicalista** (FET y de las JONS), after the approval of the Fundamental Principles of the Regime in May 1958. The aim was to bury the party's Fascist past and to emphasize that the regime could in no way be regarded as Fascist. *See also* LÓPEZ RODÓ, LAUREANO.

MUDÉJAR. This was the name given to the Muslim inhabitants of territories conquered by the advancing Christian armies during the "**Reconquest.**" *See also* MOORS.

MUÑOZ GRANDES, AGUSTÍN (1896–1970). Muñoz Grandes was best known for his role as commander of the **Blue Division**, which fought on the Russian front between 1941 and 1943, and then for his loyal service to the **Franco regime** until his final retirement in July 1967. Like many **Nationalist** officers, he was an *africanista*. Nevertheless, during the **Second Republic**, he appeared to be a professional military man with no political sympathies. He played a major role in organizing the Republican Assault Guards during 1931–1932, and in July 1936 he refused to join the **military** conspiracy, though he resigned his post in order not to be an obstacle. This led to his arrest by the Republican authorities. He was subsequently found not guilty of subversion by a Republican court in April 1937, allowing him to pass over to the Nationalist side. He was given a divisional command by Franco and soon established a reputation for efficiency. At the same time, he began to profess pro-Falangist sentiments and was rewarded by being made secretary general of the **Falange Española Tradicionalista y de las Juntas de Ofensiva Nacional Sindicalista** (FET y de las JONS) in August 1939. In this way, while the Falangists might consider one of their men to be in charge, Franco could feel the organization was securely under the control of a military figure.

Muñoz Grandes resigned as head of the FET y de las JONS in March 1940. He was strongly pro-German and pressed for Spain's entry into the war on the side of the Axis. During his stint as Blue Division commander, from June 1941 he was cultivated by Adolf Hitler (who awarded him the Iron Cross), who convinced him of the need for a pure Fascist regime at home. At a meeting with Hitler on 12 July 1941, Muñoz Grandes seems to have agreed that on his return to Spain he should become chief of government under a weakened Franco. Franco wished to recall Muñoz Grandes to Spain, but given Hitler's request that he stay on, did not do so until December 1942. Upon finally returning, he was promoted to lieutenant general, but was at first prudently left without an active military posting, though he was made head of Franco's Personal Military Staff (Casa Militar) on 3 March 1943.

Nevertheless, over the next 10 years, Muñoz Grandes's role within the regime was to become more prominent. Like **Juan Yagüe**, he could be relied on to head off promonarchist plots within the military against Franco. And as the Axis's military effort waned, his enthusiasm for entry into the war faded and he became one of Franco's staunchest supporters. Within the army, moreover, he was respected because of his personal honesty and role in the Blue Division. His reward came on 3 March 1945, when he was promoted to the key post of captain general of **Madrid**. Then in July 1951, he was appointed army minister. He was replaced in February 1957, but in July 1962 was given the newly created post of vice president. This meant that he would become regent in the case of Franco's death or incapacitation. In the cabinets of the 1950s and 1960s, he was linked to a group of pro-Falangist **Regentialists**, who defended the FET y de las JONS (**Movimiento Nacional** from May 1958) and wished Franco to be succeeded by a new authoritarian regent rather than a **Bourbon** king. For this reason, he gained the antipathy of Franco's right-hand man, **Luis Carrero Blanco**, who was pushing for a monarchist succession. Dogged by ill health, he was no match for Carrero Blanco, and a combination of illness and opposition by Carrero Blanco were responsible for his losing his post on 22 July 1967.

MUSIC. *See* GYPSIES; MOVIDA MADRILEÑA; NOVA CANÇO.

– N –

NAFARROA BAI. *See* NAVARRE.

NARVÁEZ Y CAMPOS, RAMÓN MARÍA, DUKE OF VALENCIA (1800–1868). Narváez was the leading **Partido Moderado** soldier-politician of the mid-19th century. He was born in Loja in Granada (hence his nickname in left-liberal circles, *el espadón de Loja* [the big sword of Loja]), and established his **military** reputation during the First **Carlist** War. Toward the end of the war, he clashed with General **Baldomero Espartero** and this probably played an important role in inclining him toward the *moderados*. He was to lead the *moderado* military ***pronunciamiento*** against Espartero in 1843, and over the next 25 years he was the major figure on the right of *moderado* politics. His rule was marked by a determination to maintain law and order at all costs, not make any compromises with the

Partido Progresista, and to reconcile liberalism with the **Catholic Church**. Hence, Narváez's administrations were behind the creation of the **Civil Guard** in 1844, the highly restrictive **Constitution of 1845**, and the concordat with the Vatican in 1851. Thereafter, he played the part of the strongman who could be drafted into power in times of crisis. From October 1847, his three-year stint in office saw the establishment of a near-dictatorship, and from July 1866 he again intensified repression of the **liberal** opposition, which was rapidly growing in strength. He was to die in office in April 1868.

NATIONAL CATHOLICISM. This was the name that critics gave to the period during the **Franco regime** when anti-**liberal Catholic** values were emphasized above all else. This phase is usually seen by historians as lasting from 1943–1945 through to the late 1950s. This periodization is, however, a matter of degree. Between 1939 and 1942, the regime's quasi-Fascist single party, the **Falange Española Tradicionalista y de las Juntas de Ofensiva Nacional Sindicalista** (FET y de las JONS) was given greater prominence than was subsequently the case. Nevertheless, from the outset, the Church was totally integrated into the regime's structures. Bishops and archbishops sat in all the major Francoist institutions and were appointed to the corporative **Cortes**. This alliance was demonstrated through frequent open-air Catholic rituals, such as the consecration of statues of the Sacred Heart, Marian pilgrimages, street processions during Holy Week, and the Corpus Christi celebrations, attended by the civil and **military** authorities and the propertied classes. Nevertheless, from 1943, in order to quiet claims that the Franco regime was Fascist, the role of the Church was foregrounded. Censorship passed from the FET y de las JONS to the Ministry of Education. Moreover, from 1945, the Ministries of Foreign Affairs, Education, and Justice were all placed in Catholic hands. At the same time, an attempt was made to impose traditional Catholic values on all walks of Spanish life. However, Church influence was somewhat reduced in 1951 when the Ministry of Information and Tourism took over censorship from the Ministry of Education. National Catholicism then began to break down in the late 1950s, when sections of the Church began slowly to distance themselves from the regime and more liberal cultural trends began to open up Spanish society.

NATIONAL MILITIA/MILICIA NACIONAL. Between 1814 and 1870, the National Militia became synonymous with the more leftist forces of **liberalism** in general and the **Partido Progresista** in particular. It was first set up by the 1812 Constitution, approved by the **Cortes of Cádiz**, which stipulated that a force to defend the constitution should be organized in each province and that it should be open to almost all men over the age of 35. Henceforth, given its popular nature, the National Militia became a bastion of urban radicals. Over the next 50 years, each time the **Partido Moderado** came to power, the militia was dissolved, and each time urban Spain rose up in revolt for political reform, the reinstatement of the militia was a major demand. The militia actually operated during the short periods of *progresista* rule. After the **Glorious Revolution** of 1868, it was transformed into the Milicia de los Ciudadanos (Citizens' Militia), which in 1873 was renamed Voluntarios de la República (Republican Volunteers). It was, not surprisingly, wound up by the authorities at the outset of the **Cánovas Restoration.**

NATIONALISM. Spain stands out in western Europe because of the strength of its anti–central state nationalist and regionalist currents. The strongest peripheral nationalist movements are to be found in **Catalonia** and the **Basque Country**, though a significant nationalist movement also developed in the 1930s in **Galicia**. During the **transition to democracy** in the 1970s, regionalist feelings then extended to other territories, in particular **Andalusia** and the **Canary Islands**.

In part, this proliferation of nationalist and regionalist movements must be seen as a consequence of the weakness of Spanish nationalism itself. The Spanish nationalist tradition is based on the **Castilian**-Andalusian cultural axis and on the **Castilian language** (often outside Spain simply referred to as the Spanish language). During the 19th century, the frequently bankrupt Spanish exchequer did little to extend the **educational** system to the Spanish masses. Hence, the process of socialization in the symbols and traditions of the Spanish nation was imperfect, and the mass of the population in Catalonia, the rural Basque Country, and Galicia continued to speak their own tongues and, to a degree at least, to maintain their own separate identities, even when they had no distinct nationalist sympathies. In addition, the authorities found it difficult to construct the myths and shared identities so necessary to produce a feeling of common purpose. Of key importance here was Spain's defeat in the **Spanish-American War** of 1898, which led to the loss of the remnants of Spain's **colonial** empire in the Americas, followed by a bloody and futile war over the barren territory of northern **Morocco**. Rather than drawing the nation together, this loss produced an outpouring of writings on Spain's failure in the modern world, and the unsuccessful, bloody campaigns led to extreme working-class discontent.

Matters were made worse because the Spanish nation was being created from the economically more underdeveloped center. The peripheral regions of Catalonia and the Basque Country rapidly became Spain's most industrialized areas, and with this wealth came civic pride and resentment at what was seen as inefficient rule from **Madrid**. Given linguistic and cultural differences in these regions, these sentiments could easily take nationalist forms. This was particularly clear in Catalonia, where a powerful middle-class party, the **Lliga Regionalista**, grew rapidly from the turn of the century. In the Basque Country, the industrial elite was more closely tied to the center and was, therefore, more pro-Spanish. However, resentment within the Basque lower-middle classes against large-scale immigration from poorer Spanish areas also gave rise to nationalist sentiments, and after the crisis of 1898, sectors of the more established middle class and some manufacturing interests also rallied to the cause. This discontent found political expression in the **Partido Nacionalista Vasco** (PNV), which was set up in 1895. In Catalonia and the Basque Country over the next 30 years, nationalist parties were able to create broad interclass coalitions. During the **Second Republic**, Catalonia was able to achieve home rule as, briefly, was the Basque Country during the **Spanish Civil War**. Despite also possessing a separate language and maintaining close cultural links with **Portugal**, political nationalism was slower to develop in Galicia. This was a consequence of its economic backwardness, which resulted in it remaining under the domination of monarchic *caciques* until the Second Republic and did not foster the growth of a strong middle class proud of its own cultural inheritance.

The upsurge of peripheral nationalism led to a violent response in Spanish right-wing circles. The Spanish **military** in particular saw it as a dire threat to national unity and was determined that it be eradicated. Hence, the **Primo de Rivera dictatorship** and then the **Franco regime** banned the **Catalan, Basque**, and **Galician languages** and frowned upon any manifestations of cultural distinctiveness. However, dictatorship was not in the long run able to solve Spain's national problem. Indeed, in the Basque Country, Francoism spawned a violent separatist organization known as **ETA**. This became even clearer during the **transition to democracy** in the 1970s. The consequence of Franco's repressive, centralist rule was that in the mid-1970s, Spanish national identity entered into crisis and there was an explosion of non-Spanish regionalist and nationalist sentiment throughout much of the territory. As a result, Spain's political elites realized that it would no longer be enough to give autonomy statutes to Catalonia and the Basque Country alone and in the **Constitution of 1978** decentralized power, dividing Spain into a series of autonomous regions and giving each its own parliament.

This so-called **State of the Autonomies** served to diffuse nationalist sentiment to a large degree, with the result that in the 1980s, only in the traditional nationalist bastions of Catalonia and the Basque Country were nationalist parties to control the autonomous governments. In Catalonia, the Catalanist coalition **Convergència i Unió** governed the **Generalitat**, while in the Basque Country, the PNV once again took on the mantle of the hegemonic party. During these years, it seemed that this new constitutional settlement had produced stability. ETA was the main threat to the status quo, but from the mid-1980s, popular backing for ETA in the Basque Country began to wane, and from the 1990s, the security forces greatly weakened the organization. However, the 1993 decision by the Generalitat to make Catalan the primary teaching medium in schools led to negative response in other parts of Spain. This was utilized by the right-wing opposition party **Partido Popular** (PP) to attack the Spanish prime minister **Felipe González**, who relied on Convergència votes in the Spanish parliament to remain in power.

After the PP victory in 1996, nationalist tensions escalated. The PP articulated a more self-confident and aggressive Spanish nationalist discourse. This was to lead to a particularly dangerous confrontation in the Basque Country where the PNV, feeling itself under threat, radicalized its discourse, trying to engineer a peace deal with ETA and achieve a higher degree of unity among the Basque nationalist forces. Matters were made worse because of the insistence by much of the Catalan political elite that the autonomy statutes needed reform in order to give the autonomous communities greater financial resources. The opposition PSOE sympathized with these demands (behind which, in part, were its Catalan sister party, the **Partit dels Socialistes de Catalunya-Partido Socialista Obrero Español**), and so after its victory in the March 2004 elections made it possible to undertake a wholesale reform of the State of the Autonomies. This, however, produced a Spanish nationalist counteroffensive by the PP, focused on opposition to negotiations with ETA and the new Catalan autonomy statute. The PP showed its ability to mobilize support through demonstrations and petitions, but also frightened moderate sectors of public opinion. In the run-up to the March 2008 general elections, the PP leader, **Mariano Rajoy,** moderated his tone somewhat. However, its poor showing in Catalonia above all was a key factor in its defeat in these elections. *See also* FLAGS OF SPAIN.

NATIONALISTS. This was the name the right-wing military rebels gave themselves during the **Spanish Civil War** of 1936–1939. It was supposed to symbolize the fact that they considered themselves Spanish patriots fighting against the anti-Spanish forces of liberalism, communism, and freemasonry. *See also* FRANCO REGIME.

NAVARRE. Navarre (Navarra in **Castilian**, Nafarroa in **Basque**) is a small Spanish region (from 1978 an autonomous community) situated to the east of the **Basque Country**. In 2007, its **population** was 605,876 inhabitants. In the Middle Ages, the Kingdom of Navarre formed an independent territory, but in 1511, Alta Navarra (High Navarre) was forcibly incorporated into the **Crown of Castile**, while Baja Navarra (Low Navarre) would subsequently be incorporated into France. Like the Basque Country, through to the 19th century it retained a significant degree of administration autonomy (the so-called *fueros*). Up until the 1950s, it would remain a largely rural area, in which the **Catholic Church** was highly influential. For this reason, from the 1830s through to the 1930s, it would be the **Carlist** movement's strongest base of support. Nevertheless, in the 1930s, the **Partido Nacionalista Vasco** would begin to make some impact in northern Navarre, where the Basque language was widely spoken.

From the 1950s, the northern area around the capital, Pamplona, would rapidly industrialize. This produced a political divide between the north, in which the left began to make an impact, and the conservative Catholic rural south. In addition, divisions remained between the Basque-speaking north, and the center and south, whose inhabitants are monolingual **Castilian** speakers. This has, since the **transition to democracy**, produced bitter political and cultural conflict over the territory's future. Basque nationalists claimed that it was part of the greater Basque Country (which, since the 1990s, radicals have referred to as **Euskal Herria**), but the conservative majority wished to remain independent. Hence, when the **State of the Autonomies** was devised, Navarre became a separate autonomous region, though the **Constitution of 1978** did contemplate the possibility that in future it could join the Basque Country.

In 1979, the **Unión del Pueblo Navarro** (UPN) was set up to represent the conservative-Catholic Navarrese, while **Herri Batasuna** (HB) made a significant impact in the north and in Pamplona, and, during the 1980s and 1990s, was behind frequently violent agitation for incorporation into the Basque County. The regional branch of the **Partido Socialista Obrero Español** (Partido Socialista de Navarra [PSN]-PSOE), whose growth was based on the affiliation of the new working class in the 1970s, acts as a buffer between the two. Since 2000, politics in Navarre have evolved significantly. A new radical Basque nationalist movement called Aralar, which rejected **ETA** violence, quickly eclipsed HB. From 2004, it integrated into the Basque nationalist coalition Nafarroa Bai and gained a parliamentary seat in the 2004 and 2008 general elections. The UPN has governed the Basque autonomous government since 1996. In the May 2007 autonomous elections, the UPN failed to get an overall majority and the PSN-PSOE, Nafarroa Bai, and **Izquierda Unida** reached an agreement to govern the territory. This, however, was blocked by the leadership of the PSOE, which was afraid that the **Partido Popular** would use any alliance with radical Basque nationalists against it in the run-up to the March 2008 general elections.

NEGRÍN LÓPEZ, JUAN (1892–1956). Juan Negrín was prime minister of the Republican government between 16 May 1937 and March

1939 during the **Spanish Civil War**. He was born in Las Palmas into a wealthy middle-class family, studied medicine at university, and went on to occupy the chair of physiology at the University of Madrid. He joined the **Partido Socialista Obrero Español** (PSOE) during the 1920s and put his weight behind the democratic-republican sector of the party, captained by **Indalecio Prieto**. During the **Second Republic**, he represented the **Canary Islands** during the three legislatures. He did not, however, became a prominent force in Republican politics until the civil war, when he was made minister of finance in **Francisco Largo Caballero**'s **Popular Front** government. In common with Prieto, he argued that the only way to win the war was, on the one hand, to reconstruct state power and organize a disciplined army, and, on the other, to maintain good relations with the Western powers.

With the cabinet crisis of May 1937, he became the compromise candidate to take over the premiership, helped because he was on good terms with Prieto and with some pro-Communist Socialists (particularly Julio Álvarez del Vayo [1890–1975]). Over the next year, Negrín worked with the moderate Socialists, **republicans**, and the **Partido Comunista de España** (PCE). He disapproved of the PCE's Stalinist methods, but felt that given the importance of Soviet arms supplies it was inevitable that they would play a leading role in government. While therefore he made efforts to control operations by the Soviet secret police, the NKVD, he was not prepared for a showdown over the question. By May 1938, he was willing to reach a negotiated peace with the Francoists, but would not accept surrender at any price. For this reason, he was finally convinced of the need to try to maintain the war effort for as long as possible with the hope that a European war would break out and the Republic would receive Allied aid. This led to a break with his old friend Prieto, who was growing increasingly pessimistic and was less prepared to tolerate Communist influence. Negrín consequently dropped Prieto from the government on 4 March 1938 and personally took charge of Prieto's post of minister of defense. With the final **Nationalist** offensive on **Catalonia** at the beginning of 1939, Negrín was forced to cross the French frontier. He returned on 10 February to try to organize a last-ditch stand, but with the **Casado coup** of 4 March, he lost all control over the remaining Republican forces.

NEO-CORPORATISM. *See* CORPORATISM; PARTIDO SOCIAL-ISTA OBRERO ESPAÑOL; UNIÓN GENERAL DE TRABA-JADORES.

NEW SCHOOL. *See* ESCUELA NUEVA.

NIGHT OF SAN DANIEL. This name refers to a student protest brutally put down by the police in **Madrid** on 10 April 1865. It had its origin in an article written by the Madrid professor and **republican** politician **Emilio Castelar** called *"El rasgo"* ("The Cheat"), which criticized both the queen and government. An enquiry was ordered by the authorities, and when the rector of the university refused to carry it out, he was sacked. A serenade given by the students in honor of the rector on 8 April was then broken up by the police, and a protest against the new rector was again dispersed, this time with several deaths. The events of San Daniel further increased the unpopularity of the **Partido Moderado** administration under General **Ramón María Narváez**, given its authoritarian outlook.

NIN I PÉREZ, ANDREU. *See* MAY EVENTS; PARTIDO OBRERO DE UNIFICACIÓN MARXISTA.

NOCEDAL Y ROMEA, RAMÓN. *See* INTEGRISM.

NON-INTERVENTION. This was the official policy of the major European powers during the **Spanish Civil War** of 1936–1939. The Non-Intervention Pact was signed by 27 European states in August 1936. From the start, however, it was a farce, and was simply a means whereby the Western democracies could wash their hands of the **Second Republic.** The Germans and Italians supplied the military rebels with aid almost as soon as the war got under way (including, crucially, air support, allowing the **Nationalists** to transport the Army of Africa over to the mainland).

The French Popular Front government under Léon Blum sympathized with the Republic and, at the war's outset, had begun to supply arms. However, it was informed by the British that should this result in war with Germany, France would receive no help. It was at this point that the French first came up with the idea of a non-intervention pact. The Conservative British government quickly agreed. A non-intervention committee was set up in London under the chairmanship of the Conservative politician Lord Plymouth. Its principal trait was, however, its inactivity, with the committee taking no action against flagrant and continuous violation of the agreement by Germany and Italy. British policy was driven by two considerations. First, there was no sympathy for the Republican government, which was seen as revolutionary and a threat to British economic interests, and some support for General **Francisco Franco**, who was viewed as a conservative who could impose order and stability. Second, central to British foreign policy at this time was the appeasement of Adolf Hitler. It was in these circumstances that from November 1936 the Soviet Union was drawn into supplying arms to the Republic, both to live up to its name as the first workers' state and to halt the advance of Fascism. As a result, the civil war in Spain lasted almost three years, despite the fact that the non-intervention committee, to which all the European powers were signatories, was supposed to ensure no military supplies got through.

NORTH ATLANTIC TREATY ORGANIZATION (NATO). Because of the dictatorial nature of the **Franco regime**, Spain was not invited to enter NATO when it was founded in 1949. Instead, Spain was integrated into the Western bloc during the Cold War through the 1953 military bases treaty with the United States. However, during the **transition to democracy** in the mid-1970s, there was renewed interest in Spanish entry in the United States. Spain's strategic position was still very important and its accession would serve to strengthen the Atlantic Alliance considerably. In Spain, however, there was far less enthusiasm. The ruling **Unión del Centro Democrático** (UCD) government had affirmed in 1978 its support for NATO, but public opinion was hostile. Washington's tacit backing of the Franco regime had caused great resentment, and there was a strong anti-imperialist sentiment among the politically active youth. Yet in June 1980, the Spanish minister of foreign affairs, Marcelino Oreja (1935–), announced that the government intended to take Spain into NATO in the near future, and, after the attempted coup (the **Tejerazo**) of 23 February 1981, the new prime minister, Leopoldo Calvo Sotelo (1926–), quickly negotiated conditions for entry. Spain therefore became the organization's 16th member in December 1981. It seems that entry into NATO was aimed at putting pressure on France to allow Spain to join the **European Economic Community** (EEC). Moreover, it was hoped that in NATO the Spanish **military** would become more professionalized and interfere less in politics. Public opinion was, however, outraged, and the opposition **Partido Socialista Obrero Español** (PSOE) promised a referendum should they come to power, with the implication that they would favor withdrawal.

When the PSOE took office in October 1982, the anti-Atlanticist Fernando Morán (1926–) was appointed minister of foreign affairs, and it seemed that Spain's withdrawal from NATO would soon be consummated. Very soon, however, the Spanish prime minister, **Felipe González**, began to take a more pro-Western stance, stating on a visit to the United States in May 1983 that Spain might be willing to stay in NATO. The shift in government policy was confirmed at the PSOE's December 1984 congress. Behind this change of stance was the realization of the economic and political cost of not fully integrating within the Western bloc. In particular, it appears that it was made clear that Spain's bid to join the EEC would be prejudiced. Moreover, it has been suggested that the United States intimated that Spain would no longer receive support in maintaining the African enclaves of Ceuta and Melilla. The upshot of this was that when the referendum was finally called for 12 March 1986, the government backed continued membership under a certain number of conditions that it had negotiated, namely, "non-integration into the integrated military structure, prohibition of installing, housing or introducing nuclear weapons into Spain, and a progressive reduction of the U.S. military presence in Spain." Furthermore, Felipe González stated that if the vote was favorable to withdrawal, he would not implement it but resign. Hence, the referendum virtually became a plebiscite on González's continuance in power, and given the lack of a credible political alternative, there was fear of a power vacuum if the government lost. It was this that, despite a noisy campaign launched against membership by the **Partido Comunista de España** (PCE) and other leftist, pacifist, and antinuclear groups, turned a skeptical public around. On the day, 52.5 percent voted for continued membership and 40 percent against. The political effects were contradictory. Felipe González's stature on the international stage was enhanced, while much of the radical spirit generated by the anti-NATO campaign was dissipated because of the continued weakness of the PCE. Nevertheless, the campaign did provide a platform for the formation of a new coalition to the left of the PSOE, **Izquierda Unida** (IU).

During the 1990s, as Spain's international standing grew, it began to play a more active role in NATO. The former PSOE minister **Javier Solana** became NATO secretary general at the beginning of 1995, and Spain participated in the NATO bombing campaigns of Serbia in May and September–October of that year. Following the Dayton Peace Accords of November 1995, Spain then stationed about 1,500 troops in Mostar under a NATO mandate. Given the more Atlanticist position taken by the **Partido Popular** (PP) governments of **José María Aznar** between 1996 and 2004, this tendency was accentuated. In December 1996, Spain joined NATO's military structure. It participated in the bombing of Serbian troops in Kosovo in March–April 1999, and after Slobodan Milosevic had given way, sent a little over 1,000 troops into Kosovo. The PP's pro-U.S. stance subsequently led it to back the invasion of Iraq and commit troops. The PSOE in opposition, under **José Luis Rodríguez Zapatero**, was opposed to the **Iraq war**, and when it came to power in March 2004, quickly withdrew the troops. Yet Rodíguez Zapatero has been at pains to point out that his differences with the U.S. administration in no way means that he does not support NATO as a whole.

NOVA CANÇO. This was a folk-rock protest movement that grew up in **Catalonia** from the late 1950s, inspired by the likes of Pete Seeger and Bob Dylan and focused on Francoist oppression of Catalan freedoms and culture. Its leading early exponents were the singers Francesc Pi de la Serra (1942–) and the **Valencian** Raimon (Ramon Pelegero Sanchís, 1940–), whose song, *Al vent* (*To The Wind*, 1961), became an anti-Francoist anthem. In the 1960s, new figures, most notably the singer-songwriters Lluís Llach (1948–) and Joan Manuel Serrat (1943–), came to the fore, filling large concert halls and holding what were in effect anti-Francoist rallies. The former's song, *L'estaca* (*The Stake*), became a hymn to the pending fall of the **Franco regime**. At the same time, the movement began to spread to other parts of Spain.

NUNCA MÁIS. *See* PRESTIGE AFFAIR.

NÚÑEZ DE ARENAS, MANUEL (1886–1951). Best known as the founder of the **Escuela Nueva**, Núñez de Arenas was a member of the **Madrid** section of the **Partido Socialista Obrero Español** (PSOE) from 1909 to 1921. He was one of a new generation of young intellectuals who from the turn of the century wished to break with the party's "workerist" image and link up with the world of culture. Although at first more a **republican** democrat than a socialist, he soon became one of the country's leading Marxist theoreticians. Unlike most intellectuals affiliated with the PSOE, he advocated neutrality during **World War I**. From 1918, he then became one of the leading figures of the leftist opposition to the social-democratic party leadership and backed affiliation with the Third International. After the *terceristas'* defeat in 1921, he joined the breakaway **Partido Comunista de España** (PCE), though his work was more **educational** and journalistic than directly political. He was exiled in France during the **Primo de Rivera dictatorship** and again after the **Spanish Civil War**.

– O –

OCTOBER 1934 REVOLUTION. The October revolution was launched by the **Partido Socialista Obrero Español-Unión General de Trabajadores** (PSOE-UGT) in reaction to the entry of three members of the rightist **Confederación Española de Derechas Autónomas** (CEDA) coalition into government. The background to the revolt was the growing fear in PSOE circles that a CEDA government would signify the triumph of "Fascism" in Spain. The National Committee of the PSOE had already warned in January 1934 that revolutionary action would be taken if the CEDA joined the government, and in the following months a revolutionary committee was formed, which trained a Socialist militia and contacted military sympathizers. At the same time, through the **Alianzas Obreras**, there was an attempt to link the various working-class parties and unions together. Nevertheless, there was a good deal of bluff in the PSOE leadership's threats and reason to believe that the foremost voice of the Socialist left, **Francisco Largo Caballero**, hoped that saber rattling would be enough to convince the president of the **Second Republic, Niceto Alcalá Zamora**, not to allow CEDA deputies into government. But when it was announced in late September that three *cedistas* were to become ministers, the PSOE-UGT felt it had no choice but to go ahead.

The movement was extremely poorly organized. A general strike was called for 5 October, but, forewarned, the government had no problem rounding up most of the Madrid Socialist leadership. In **Catalonia** on the following day, the autonomous government (**Generalitat**) under **Lluís Companys** backed the revolt, but the uprising was easily put down by the army. Only among the Asturian coal miners did the strike turn into a full-blown insurrection. Here Socialists, **anarchists**, and the **Partido Comunista de España** (PCE) had united under the banner of the Alianzas Obreras. The miners were able to take over the **coal mining** towns and set up their own administration. The government then launched a counteroffensive, using elite troops from the **Legión Española**, and after two weeks of heavy fighting, they were finally able to quell the rebellion.

The results of the revolution were largely negative for the left. The PSOE leadership was decapitated and labor organization greatly weakened. Furthermore, left-wing fears that a "Fascist" takeover was imminent proved misplaced. More generally, it showed how polarized Spanish society had become. In some respects, October 1934 was a prelude to the **Spanish Civil War**, demonstrating the near impossibility of Spain's social and political tensions being settled by peaceful means. *See also* LABOR MOVEMENT.

O'DONNELL Y JORRIS, LEOPOLDO, COUNT OF LUCENA, FIRST DUKE OF TETUAN (1809–1867). Leopoldo O'Donnell was one of the leading soldier-politicians of the mid-19th century. He came from an absolutist family, but supported the **liberals** during the First **Carlist** War of 1833 to 1839. During these years, he gained a reputation for bravery and efficiency, reaching the rank of lieutenant general and being granted the titles of Count Lucena and Viscount of Aliaga. In 1840, he sided with the **Partido Moderado** against General **Baldomero Espartero**, but he was not a reactionary.

Consequently, by the late 1840s he had become strongly critical of *moderado* policies, in June 1854 he led the Vivalvarada *pronunciamiento*, and in the following month (under pressure to attract support, it must be said) issued the Manzanares Manifesto, which promised wide-ranging liberal reform and ushered in the **Progressive Biennium** of 1854–1856. He had, however, no sympathy for the radical left of liberalism, and was only lukewarm in his backing for the new Espartero administration. Hence, he played a key role in engineering the fall of the **Partido Progresista** in July 1856, and in September largely reinstated the **Constitution of 1845**.

Thereafter, O'Donnell tried to follow a middle course, forming a **Unión Liberal** that would incorporate moderate *progresistas* and progressive *moderados*. He had most success during his long administration of June 1858 to February 1863, during which he reinstated the *desamortización*, tried to modernize the **military**, pushed Spanish colonialization in Africa (he was particularly successful in the **Moroccan** war of 1859–1860 and was bestowed with the title of duke after the fall of Tetuán). But he was unwilling to do more than tinker with the regime, which remained a bastion of social elites. In any case, from 1863 Queen **Isabel II** once again turned to the *moderados*. He returned to power briefly between June 1865 and July 1866, but, faced by Partido Progresista conspiracies, launched a wide-ranging repression following the **San Gil revolt** of 22 June 1866. He was dismissed by the queen the following month and spent the last months of his life in self-imposed exile in France.

OLIVARES, COUNT-DUKE OF (GASPAR DE GUZMÁN Y PIMENTEL, 1587–1645). The count-duke of Olivares—a title he enjoyed from 1625—was the court favorite of **Felipe IV** between 1621 and 1643 and had virtual *carte blanche* to pursue his own policies. He was austere, hardworking, and probably the most far-sighted statesman in early modern Spain, but he was also a bully who tried to ram home his policies rather than negotiate. This weakness, along with the grave objective problems faced by the Spanish **Habsburg Empire**, resulted in the collapse of his entire project between 1640 and 1643.

The count-duke hailed from a family of Andalusian aristocrats of modest means. His uncle, Baltasar de Zúñiga, was a powerful figure under **Felipe III** and had introduced Gaspar de Guzmán into the court, where he gained increasing influence over the young prince. Hence, he was in an excellent position to take the lead in the formulation of policy when the latter came to power in 1621. This occurred in a context in which the **monarchy** was showing itself increasingly incapable of meeting its military commitments. The count-duke's response was to try to reassert Habsburg power on the basis of a more united and efficient Spain. He quickly attempted to reestablish control over the United Provinces, but soon faced hostilities from England and France. The situation became increasingly difficult in 1635 when a resurgent France declared war and launched an all-out attack.

There were two prongs to his reform project in the peninsula. First, influenced by the *arbitristas*, he sought to put state finances and the Spanish **economy** on a more solid footing, cutting back on court spending and putting a stop to the practice of debasing the currency. Second, he attempted to bring the various parts of the peninsula more closely together. At present, he believed, too much of the burden for defending the empire was placed on the **Crown of Castile**. Other territories—most notably the **Crown of Aragón** and Kingdom of **Portugal**—would have to do more, though in return the monarchy would have to lose its Castilian flavor, with posts and favors distributed more widely across the empire. During the 1620s, he put forward the proposal that all the states of the monarchy should contribute to a reserve army of 140,000 men, but the **Cortes** of Aragón and **Valencia** gave inadequate support and the Catalan Cortes refused to provide any finance.

In response, in 1639, he ensured that the war with France was centered on Catalan territory, announced that the Catalan constitution should be ignored whenever the well-being on the army was at stake, and billeted the army in **Catalonia**. This last move provoked peasant rebellions in Catalonia, culminating in the murder of the Spanish viceroy on 7 June 1640. A group within the standing committee of the Catalan Cortes (the Diputació) then broke with the monarchy, putting the territory under the protection of the French crown. Matters went from bad to worse in December, when rebellion then broke out in **Portugal**, with the duke of Braganza proclaimed João IV. The problem was that these territories were jealous of their traditional liberties, while there was little sympathy for military campaigns conducted in northern and central Europe. Furthermore, in Portugal there was disappointment that its integration into the Habsburg monarchy had done little to protect its possessions in the New World. Under intense pressure, in 1643 the king exiled Count Olivares to his estates in order to reach a compromise, allowing both Catalonia and Portugal to retain their *fueros*. He died two years later, a broken man.

OMINOUS DECADE. This is a term that was used by **liberals** to refer to the years between 1823 and 1833, when King **Fernando VII** tried to restore absolutist rule for the second time. *See also* FERNANDO RESTORATIONS.

OPUS DEI. The Opus Dei (full name, Prelature of the Holy Cross of Opus Dei) is a conservative lay religious order that was founded by the Aragonese priest José María Escribá de Balaguer (1902–1975) in 1928. It was Balaguer's intention that the association make it possible for ordinary Catholics to defend the **Catholic Church** within their daily lives (though the [male] leadership was expected to be single and celibate). The movement grew rapidly in **Francisco Franco**'s Spain, appealing to many within the elite who led busy professional lives, but who wished to propagate arch-conservative Catholicism. From the 1950s, it became closely associated with a new generation of technocrats, who wanted the regime to combine **corporatist** political structures with economic liberalization. Their rapid rise was propitiated by the fact that in the Cold War climate, the mix of liberal economics and staunch anticommunism appealed to U.S. administrations and also offered a way out of the economic mess produced by the regime's **autarkic** economic model. The Opus technocrats were strongly backed by the secretary of the presidency, **Luis Carrero Blanco**, and first entered government in 1957 in order to engineer economic liberalization. A short time before, in 1950, the status of the Opus Dei had been clarified by the Vatican, allowing it to operate internationally. In the following 20 years, it built up a large **educational** infrastructure both inside and outside Spain. In Spain, this included a prestigious business school in Barcelona (the Instituto de Estudios Superiores de la Empresa [IESE]) and an Opus Dei university in Pamplona.

However, during the 1960s, the organization's devotion to Francoism led it into conflict with the reforming clergy. In 1972, there was a direct confrontation between the Spanish primate **Vicente Enrique y Tarancón** (1907–) and the Opus Dei after it was revealed that newspaper reports aimed at discrediting his reforming stance, by claiming that the Vatican disapproved, emanated from Opus circles. The Opus Dei was very much out of step with the spirit of the Second Vatican Council and it was rumored that a papal offensive against the association was being planned. This was only dispelled with the election of the theologically very conservative Cardinal Wojtila as Pope John Paul II (1920–2005) in 1978, under whose papacy Escrivá de Balaguer was quickly beatified and the organization declared the first Personal Prelature (the equivalent of a diocese without geographical boundaries). The Opus, however, came to be distrusted by many Spaniards because of the secretive nature of its operations. Individual members were and are not at liberty to declare their affiliation. In this context, it became widely believed that Opus Dei members secretly aided the career advancement of their brethren, and references were even made to the Opus Dei as the Spanish Cosa Nostra. These claims have persisted. Many Spaniards see it as a shady organization able to pull strings for its sympathizers. It is estimated to have about 30,000 members in Spain and a presence in over 80 other countries. *See also* ECONOMY; FRANCO REGIME; LÓPEZ RODO, LAUAREANO.

ORGANIC DEMOCRACY. *See* FRANCO REGIME.

ORGANIZACIÓN SINDICAL ESPAÑOLA (OSE)/SPANISH SYNDICAL ORGANIZATION. The OSE was set up following the promulgation of the 1939 Labor Charter. In line with the **Franco regime**'s belief that the class struggle must be suppressed, all other unions were banned and both employers and workers were forced to join. Both were theoretically equal, though in reality employers were seen as the natural leaders in the workplace. The OSE itself was staffed by bureaucrats affiliated with the single party, the **Falange Española Tradicionalista y de las Juntas de Ofensiva Nacional Sindicalista** (FET y de las JONS), and its mission was at first to implement the wages and working conditions set by the Ministry of Labor. For the single party, the OSE became an important power base within the regime, and in order to maximize its strength it sought to tie workers to the organization in several ways. First, the OSE offered workers **welfare** benefits, recreational facilities, and a system of labor lawyers to help pursue claims with the Ministry of Labor. Second, it co-opted labor leaders and established networks of patronage. Those co-opted included some former members of the **Confederación Nacional del Trabajo** (CNT). Finally, the FET y de las JONS showed itself willing to make some concessions to labor by introducing reforms that permitted a degree of direct worker representation. In the 1940s, the post of *enlace* (shop steward) was created and *jurados* (factory committees) were established. These shop stewards could discuss plant-level working conditions and the organization of production with management. From 1953, the *jurados* were directly elected by the workforce. These local officials gained far greater power in 1958 when, in line with the regime's desire to lift some state controls and liberalize the Spanish **economy**, the Law of Collective Agreements was approved. For the first time, this allowed for local collective bargaining between workers' representatives and the management. Then, in 1962, "economic" strikes were—albeit ambiguously—decriminalized.

These changes were undertaken by the single party as it felt that they would bolster its working-class base and therefore strengthen its position within the regime. This was the policy followed by **José Solís**, minister general secretary of the FET y de las JONS (**Movimiento Nacional** from May 1958) between 1957 and 1969. It quickly caused problems. The OSE bureaucracy was still essentially an instrument of state control, and, given the chance to vote, many workers elected independents or even members of the clandestine opposition onto the factory committees. Moreover, workers also began to mobilize outside the structures of the OSE and set up semi-clandestine committees to organize protest and strike action. It was this effort that was behind the coalescence of the **Comisiones Obreras** (CC.OO), an independent **labor movement**, and the growth of strikes, especially from the late 1960s. By the early 1970s, the level of labor protest was beginning to call the whole regime into question. CC.OO representatives had, in some areas, colonized the lower levels of the OSE (at the higher levels the Falangists were protected by a complex system of indirect elections) and were even, in some cases, able to call strikes from the local OSE headquarters. The

Movimiento Nacional's response to this crisis was contradictory. On the one hand, hard-liners vainly hoped to turn the clock back to the 1940s. On the other hand, reformers tried to make the OSE more accountable. After Franco's death in November 1975, this all became academic. A coalition of regime reformers and the more moderate elements within the opposition agreed in the following year that some kind of transition to a liberal-democratic regime was necessary. The OSE was finally abolished in June 1977 at the same time as democratic unions were legalized. *See also* SINDICATO ESPAÑOL UNIVERSITARIO.

ORTEGA Y GASSET, JOSÉ (1883–1956). Ortega y Gasset was the most distinguished Spanish philosopher during the first half of the 20th century. He was born into a wealthy, intellectual family in **Madrid**, and studied philosophy in the Jesuit University of Deusto in **Navarre** and at the University of Madrid before going on to complete his studies in Germany between 1905 and 1908. On returning to Spain, he was appointed to the chair of metaphysics at the University of Madrid, and began a brilliant career as a journalist and essayist. He was a Europeanizer and like many of his contemporaries, his overriding concern was how to "modernize" Spain economically, politically, and culturally. Ortega y Gasset sympathized with the **Partido Socialista Obrero Español** (PSOE) when he returned to Spain, but never subscribed to the party's internationalism and advocacy of the class struggle. Hence, he joined the **republicans** in 1912 and began forcefully to criticize the PSOE thereafter. His worldview had, in fact, always been elitist and this elitism became more accentuated in the context of intensifying social and political conflict, especially between 1914 and 1923. In response, he defended rule by meritocracy, arguing in *España invertebrada* (*Spain Invertebrated*, 1921) that society cannot function when "the mass refuses to be a mass, that is to support the directing minority." He welcomed the coming of the **Second Republic** enthusiastically, participating in the foundation of a group of academic supporters called "At the Service of the Republic," but soon became disillusioned by the social and political strife it brought in its wake. This led him to retire from the political arena in 1932. During the **Spanish Civil War**, he moved to France, and at the end of the war went on to Buenos Aires. However, he returned to

Madrid in 1946, setting up the Institute of Humanities in an attempt to invigorate the mediocre intellectual climate.

OSORIO Y GARCÍA, ALFONSO. *See* TÁCITO; UNIÓN DEMOCRÁTICA ESPAÑOLA.

OSSORIO Y GALLARDO, ÁNGEL (1873–1946). Ossorio y Gallardo was an important political figure in the first half of the 20th century. He was the most significant element in the minority wing of Spanish Catholicism, which wished to move in a **Christian-democrat** direction. He was very close to **Antonio Maura**, acting as his civil governor in **Barcelona** between 1907 and 1909, where he had to deal with the **Tragic Week**, trying, unsuccessfully, to adopt a more conciliatory stance than that propounded by the minister of the interior, **Juan de la Cierva**. He fully shared Maura's vision of a "**revolution from above**," which would democratize the political system within the framework of the **monarchy**. After Maura lost his position as head of the **Partido Conservador** (PC) in 1913, he played a leading role in the construction of the **Maurista** movement. However, he was frustrated by Maura's timidity and by his continued links with PC *caciques*. Influenced by the Italian Partito Popolare, in June 1922 he founded his own **Partido Social Popular** (PSP). In consonance with his democratic ideals, he rejected the **Primo de Rivera dictatorship** (unlike a section of the PSP, which integrated into the new regime) and, disillusioned by King **Alfonso XIII**'s support for the dictator, in 1931 he backed the **Second Republic**. During the 1930s, he was (with the exception of **Niceto Alcalá Zamora**) the most distinguished former monarchist to take this stance. During the **Spanish Civil War**, he would represent the regime in the League of Nations and was named ambassador to Belgium, France, and Germany. After the end of the war, from his Argentinean exile he would become a member of the Republican government in exile.

OSTEND PACT. This was a pact signed by 45 members of the **Partido Progresista** and **Partido Demócrata** in the French town of Ostend on 16 August 1866. The aims of the pact were the overthrow of Queen **Isabel II**, the formation of a provisional government, and thereafter the celebration of elections to a constituent **Cortes** under universal male suffrage. After the death of **Leopoldo O'Donnell** in 1867, the **Unión Liberal** also joined the alliance. These events demonstrated the growing isolation of the **monarchy** and would culminate in the **Glorious Revolution** of September 1868.

OTEGI MONDRAGÓN, ARNALDO. *See* BASQUE COUNTRY; HERRI BATASUNA.

– P –

PABLISTA. This name refers to the supporters of the moderate and gradualist strategy advocated by **Pablo Iglesias**, the leader of the **Partido Socialista Obrero Español** (PSOE) between 1888 and 1925.

PAINTING. See DALÍ I DOMÈNECH, SALVADOR; EL GRECO; GOYA Y LUCIENTES, FRANCISCO DE; MIRÓ Y FERRÀ, JOAN; PICASSO, PABLO RUIZ Y; VELAZQUEZ, DIEGO RODRÍGUEZ DE SILVA Y.

PARLIAMENT. *See* BAYONNE CONSTITUTION; CONSTITUTION OF 1837; CONSTITUTION OF 1845; CONSTITUTION OF 1869; CONSTITUTION OF 1876; CONSTITUTION OF 1931; CONSTITUTION OF 1978; CORTES; CORTES OF CADIZ; ROYAL STATUTE; STATE OF THE AUTONOMIES.

PARLIAMENTARY ASSEMBLY MOVEMENT. *See* CÁNOVAS RESTORATION; CRISIS OF 1917; LLIGA REGIONALISTA.

PARTIDO COMUNISTA DE ESPAÑA (PCE)/SPANISH COMMUNIST PARTY. The PCE, like its sister parties in Europe, had its origins in the Bolshevik Revolution and the formation of the Communist Third International. During 1919–1920, the radical wing of the **Partido Socialista Obrero Español** (PSOE) pushed for the party to join the Third International. The party's youth, too impatient to await the outcome of the internal struggle within the PSOE, formed the PCE in January 1920. The rest of the leftist opposition, however, waited until after defeat at an extraordinary congress held in April 1921 before forming their own communist party, the Partido Comunista Obrero Español (Spanish Communist Workers' Party). There were, therefore, briefly two Communist parties in Spain, but after the intervention of the Third International, they merged under the name of PCE in November 1921.

The PCE remained only a very small organization until well into the 1930s. To the left of the PSOE, it faced strong competition from the powerful **anarchist**-syndicalist **Confederación Nacional del Trabajo** (CNT). Moreover, it was formed just as the revolutionary tide which had swept across Europe was receding, and following the coup by General **Miguel Primo de Rivera** in September 1923, it was illegalized and persecuted. The PCE therefore emerged from the dictatorship with only a few hundred activists. In addition, in 1931, its call for the formation of "workers' and peasants' soviets" at a time of great popular enthusiasm for the **Second Republic** meant that it was to remain marginalized. Nevertheless, with the social polarization of the early 1930s, the Communists' stock began to rise. Moreover, following Comintern instructions in 1935 the party shifted 180 degrees and began to support wide Popular Frontist alliances between the radical middle class, Communists, and socialists. This call for unity against **Fascism** struck a chord and was the basis of the PCE's growth in the months leading up to the **Spanish Civil War**. Its most spectacular gains were the result of the unification of the PSOE and PCE youth movements in May 1936, founding the Juventud Socialista Unificada (Unified Socialist Youth—JSU), which soon fell into Communist hands, and the organization in **Catalonia** in July of a sister party, the **Partit Socialista Unificat de Catalunya** (PSUC).

During the civil war, the PCE, along with the more moderate "reformist" wing of the PSOE (headed by **Indalecio Prieto**) and the **republicans**, opposed the collectivization drive launched by the CNT and left Socialists. In the PCE's case, this very much reflected Moscow's concern that it should not alienate the liberal democracies by appearing to sponsor proletarian revolution in Spain. Hence, the PCE became identified with central government attempts to rebuild state power and replace the fragmented militias by a disciplined **Popular Army** in order to effectively pursue the war effort. Because only the Soviet Union gave significant aid to the Republic, the PCE was rapidly to grow in strength between 1936 and 1938. Its base was still largely working class, but many of the new recruits were white-collar workers and members of the middle class who, ironically, came to see the party as a bulwark against revolution. The Communists set out to become the dominant force within the Republican coalition and used Stalinist methods to achieve their aims. This included the setting up of secret detention camps in collaboration with the Soviet secret police, the NKVD. They had to support the premiership of **Francisco Largo Caballero** in September 1936, but given his suspicion of Communist motives and determination to conserve the Socialist working-class base from Communist takeover, they were keen to get rid of him. The opportunity came after the **May Events** of 1937, when along with the "reformist" Socialists and republicans, they were able to engineer his fall and replacement by **Juan Negrín**.

The PCE emerged from the civil war with probably the largest number of activists among the opposition groups, though its Stalinist methods had gained it bitter enemies in the Republican camp. Over the next 20 years, a number of factors were to ensure that it would become the most powerful and active of General **Francisco Franco**'s enemies. Externally, the Allies' refusal to intervene in Spain after **World War II** undermined the position of the PSOE and republicans, who had looked to the Europeans and Americans for support. On the contrary, the PCE from the start took the battle to Spanish territory. From 1945, it supported a guerrilla campaign by the *maquis* against the regime. Its failure led the Communists to change tack. After a meeting with Joseph Stalin in October 1948, the party leadership decided that rather than try to destroy the regime through a frontal assault, it should move to undermine it from within. This led it to abandon the guerrilla struggle. The opportunity to penetrate the regime was provided by the election of workers' representatives onto factory committees within the framework of the single state union, the **Organización Sindical Española** (OSE). By the 1960s, in the major industrial conurbations, the Communists were able to get a large number of sympathizers elected onto the factory committees, thereby negotiating wages and working conditions on the workers' behalf, and had an important presence in the semi-clandestine branch, provincial, and regional committees that in the mid-1960s emerged to coordinate workers' demands. This decentralized protest coalesced into a national movement known as **Comisiones Obreras** (CC.OO), and it was the PCE that was to play the leading role in the organization's policy formulation. Through CC.OO, therefore, the PCE was able to gain a strong support base within the working class.

From the 1940s, through the Eastern Bloc, the PCE also enjoyed greater funding than other opposition groups. Furthermore, the party's cell structure and rigid hierarchy meant that it was difficult for the regime to totally dismantle. Indeed, even the regime's continual anti-communist propaganda aided the PCE in some respects, because for many it tended to conflate dissidence and pro-Soviet Communism. From the 1950s, the PCE also broadened its appeal as a result of the party's slow de-Stalinization. The origins of this process were to be found in the early 1950s, when a group of youngish "renovators"—the most important of whom were **Santiago Carrillo**, Fernando Claudín (1915–1990), and Jorge Semprún (1923–)—called for the party to democratize and accept parliamentary government and fashion a broad alliance (including discontented monarchists and **Catholics**) against the regime. This interclass alliance was supposed to usher in a bourgeois-democratic regime, which would be a prelude to socialism. At first it seemed that the PCE's general secretary, **Dolores Ibárruri**, would back the "old guard," but the situation was transformed following the death of Stalin in 1953 and Nikita Khrushchev's denunciation of his dictatorship at the 20th congress of the Communist Party of the Soviet Union (CPSU) in 1956. As a result, Soviet control over the strategy of the national Communist parties loosened considerably and Ibárruri swung around to support the renovators' new strategy, known as National Reconciliation.

Santiago Carrillo had become the director of the PCE's operational center in Paris in February of that year, and with Dolores Ibárruri in Moscow, to all intents and purposes he acted as general secretary. This was formalized at the party's sixth congress, held in January 1960. Under Carrillo, the policy of National Reconciliation was developed. The party hoped to use CC.OO as a battering ram to overthrow the **Franco regime** through a general strike, thus allowing the formation of a provisional government with representatives from all the opposition forces. At first, the party still remained strongly tied to Moscow, with Carrillo convinced that the Khrushchev reforms could provide a viable Communist model. With Khrushchev overthrown in

October 1964, relations became colder, and they erupted into open hostility after the Soviet Union invaded Czechoslovakia in 1968. The PCE had supported the Prague Spring, arguing that it showed liberty and socialism were compatible, and the invasion was, therefore, a great embarrassment. It was after these events that the PCE, along with the Partito Comunista d'Italia (PCI) in particular, fully developed the strategy of Eurocommunism: a pluralist model of socialist democracy, a peaceful and democratic means of obtaining it, willingness to respect religious and ideological differences, and even hostile verdicts by the electorate.

The strategy of National Reconciliation and the adoption of a pluralist conception of socialism helped the PCE attract many on the left, including large numbers of students and intellectuals. From the 1960s, the PCE further broadened its support by encouraging its members to become active in neighborhood associations, tenants' groups, and the like. Nevertheless, there was a contradiction between the PCE's ideological liberalization and the continued operation of autocratic party structures (democratic centralism). Carrillo used authoritarian means to modernize the party. This included the expulsion of members who did not support the party line, from hard-line Stalinists like Enrique Líster (1907–1995) to "liberal" intellectuals such as Claudín and Semprún. Nor, despite its strength, was the party ever able to launch a political general strike capable of bringing down the regime. The party called two one-day general strikes against the regime on 5 May 1958 (the day of national reconciliation) and 18 June 1959, but they were almost total flops. Even in the early 1970s, when CC.OO had become a mass movement and large area-wide strikes occurred at frequent intervals, political strikes with no base in economic demands received only limited support. For this reason when, in 1976, under **Adolfo Suárez**, the regime showed it was willing to negotiate a democratic transition, the PCE radically changed its policies, and combined the exercise of working-class pressure with discussions with Suárez in order to ensure full democratization. After the first general elections of June 1977, the Communists then cooperated with the ruling **Unión del Centro Democrático** (UCD) coalition government in trying to consolidate democracy.

However, the shift from street mobilization to smoke-filled rooms led to disillusionment among many party activists. This was coupled with growing discontent at the authoritarian leadership style of Carrillo and the team he brought back with him from exile, especially among many "interior" activists. This was compounded by the PCE's disappointing showing in the June 1977 and March 1979 elections (with 9.4 percent and 10.8 percent of the votes respectively). Three main tendencies came to the fore. First were the hard-line pro-Soviets (disparagingly referred to as "afghans" by their opponents because of their backing for the Soviet invasion of Afghanistan). These Communists received support from those who felt that Carrillo had made too many concessions during the transition, and particularly from some activists in CC.OO, who argued that the working class had borne the cost of the transition to democracy. Second, more reform-oriented Communists, often referred to as "renovators" or "super Eurocommunists," pushed for a democratization of the party's structures. Third were the unconditional supporters of Carrillo himself. Carrillo's authoritarian handling of the crisis ensured there could be no reconciliation. During 1981–1982, hard-liners broke off to form the Partido Comunista de los Pueblos de España (Communist Party of the Peoples of Spain–PCPE) and, in Catalonia, a sister party, the Partit dels Comunistes Catalans (Party of the Catalan Communists—PCC). Most of the renovators, for their part, either resigned or were expelled. The result was to be seen in the October 1982 general elections, when the PCE received only 4.04 percent of the vote.

In the aftermath of this result, Santiago Carrillo was forced to resign as general secretary and was replaced by the Asturian miner Gerardo Iglesias (1945–). Iglesias was at first widely seen as Carrillo's puppet, but was soon to prove more independent-minded than had been expected, and he began to try to open the party up to other forces on the left. This culminated in the celebration of an extraordinary conference in March 1985 to call for a "convergence of the left." The result was the decision, in April 1986, to form an electoral coalition called **Izquierda Unida** (IU) in which the PCE would be the dominant force. Carrillo opposed this shift but was marginalized, and he finally left the PCE. Iglesias was a worthy leader but lacked charisma. Hence, at the February 1988 party congress he was replaced by the former mayor of Córdoba, **Julio Anguita**. Over the next two years, in the context of growing trade union and working-class discontent at the PSOE's economic policies, Anguita was able to reestablish the PCE as a significant force in Spanish politics.

However, between 1989 and 1991, the PCE was again plunged into turmoil, first by the collapse of communism in eastern Europe, and then by the removal from power of the CPSU within the Soviet Union. A new critical current called Nueva Izquierda (New Left) emerged within the PCE under the auspices of the veteran Communist Nicolás Sartorius (1938–), which questioned whether a Communist party had a valid role to play in a seemingly postcommunist world, called for the PCE to be dissolved and IU to be reconstituted as a political party, and for contacts to be strengthened with the PSOE. This occurred in a context in which the PCI had disbanded in 1991 to form the Partito Democratico della Siniestra (Democratic Party of the Left). Such a strategy was, however, firmly rejected by Anguita and the majority of the PCE leadership. Matters came to a head during the June 1993 elections when three leading figures within the New Left, including Sartorius, withdrew from IU's electoral list. Because of these divisions, in the 1993 elections IU was not able to gain as much advantage as it had hoped from the difficulties of the ruling PSOE.

Subsequently, Anguita maintained the policy of implacable hostility to the Socialist prime minister, **Felipe González**, and was able to make some capital out of the growing crisis within the governing party. His aim was to undermine González's position and provoke a shift to the left in the PSOE. This led to continued discord within the PCE and IU. Members of the Nueva Izquierda now formed a political party, which briefly integrated into IU before Anguita had them expelled. The Catalan left-wing alliance **Iniciativa per Catalunya-Verds** left of its own accord. It can be argued that under Anguita's leadership the PCE did not adapt effectively to the new political landscape, with the result that in the 1996 elections IU—with 10.5 percent of the vote—did not perform as well as expected. After suffering a heart attack, Anguita was replaced as general secretary of the PCE by Francisco Frutos (1994–) at the party's 20th congress in December 1998, and with Anguita suffering further heart problems in the following year, Frutos briefly took over as IU coordinator. However, Frutos had spent his life in the PCE party apparatus and was not likely to come up with much new thinking. IU did very poorly in the 2000 general elections, leading to the replacement of Frutos as IU coordinator by the more conciliatory and open figure of **Gaspar Llamazares**. Under his leadership, IU has achieved a significantly higher profile. Frutos was reelected as secretary general of the PCE in 2002 and 2005, and under his leadership the PCE has opposed Llamarez, whom the party sees as too moderate and too willing to compromise with the PSOE. The poor showing of IU in the March 2008 general elections has given them the opportunity to remove Llamazares, but it is difficult to see how in the future the PCE can play a significant role in Spanish political life. *See also* TABLE 10.

PARTIDO COMUNISTA DE LOS PUEBLOS DE ESPAÑA (PCPE)/COMMUNIST PARTY OF THE PEOPLES OF SPAIN. *See* IZQUIERDA UNIDA; PARTIDO COMUNISTA DE ESPAÑA.

PARTIDO CONSERVADOR (PC)/CONSERVATIVE PARTY. The Partido Liberal Conservador (usually simply referred to as the Partido Conservador), founded by **Antonio Cánovas del Castillo**, was the major force around which the **Cánovas Restoration** was built. The party assumed the reins of power in January 1875 and remained in office until February 1881. During this time, the major building blocks of the regime were put in place. The **Constitution of 1876** ensured that the new king, **Alfonso XII**, was reserved a central role in Spanish political life, and gave the elitist Upper House (Senate) an important role in the decision-making process. These years were also to see a rigid control of political life, with heavy censorship and the illegalization of the nondynastic left, the approval of a highly restrictive suffrage law, and a further centralization of the administration. Nevertheless, the PC was not totally inflexible. Cánovas accepted the reforming program (including universal male suffrage) of the long **Partido Liberal** administration, which was in power between 1885 and 1890, in order to cement the *turno pacífico*. Indeed, from the 1890s, the PC tried to react to the growing signs of opposition to the system by making some effort to respond to public opinion and mollify left-wing opposition. Hence, it accepted the need for social reform, and after the "Disaster" of 1898—which, luckily for the Conservatives, caught the PL administration of **Práxedes Mateo Sagasta** in power—it adopted the **regenerationist** rhetoric of its political opponents. Yet the impact of the proposed reforms was limited. Following the death of Cánovas in 1897, the party was first led by **Francisco Silvela**, and, after his death, by his close collaborator **Antonio Maura** (between 1904 and 1913). Both these politicians called for a "**revolution from above**" and promised radical reforms. They maintained that in the future government would be based on "sound public opinion" rather than *caciquismo*. However, they were shocked when in the 1903 elections their decision not to use the traditional methods of electoral manipulation resulted in the **republicans** making significant gains. Henceforth, despite regenerationist rhetoric, Maura would (with the support of the arch election-fixer, **Juan de la Cierva**) "make" elections just like any other Restoration politician. Furthermore, it is doubtful whether Silvela and Maura's major legislative proposal, the decentralization of local government in order to ensure its independence, would have had the impact they claimed.

Until the end of the decade, unlike the PL, the PC had remained relatively united. This was to change with the events of 1909–1910. In July 1909, Maura carried out a harsh repression of anticlerical riots in **Barcelona** known as the **Tragic Week**. The PL reacted by supporting the republicans in a "Maura No!" campaign. King **Alfonso XIII**, fearful of the consequences of a simultaneous protest campaign in Europe for the stability of the monarchy, refused to renew his confidence in Maura in October 1909. From this date, Maura saw the Liberals as unfit to govern and refused to cooperate with them. The PC, however, wanted to get back into power, with the result that **Eduardo Dato** accepted the king's offer of government control in October 1913. These events resulted in a Conservative split, with the majority giving their support to Dato (the *idóneos*) and a minority supporting either Maura (the **Mauristas**) or **Juan de la Cierva** (the *ciervistas*). This would make the *turno* much more difficult to operate.

Under the leadership of Eduardo Dato, the PC's task became one of defending the Restoration regime, keeping the opposition at bay through a mixture of carrot and stick. The stick was used during the **crisis of 1917**, when Dato refused to give in to demands for a neutral government that would call elections to a constituent **Cortes** and then acted ruthlessly, calling in the **military** to crush the August general strike. Following this strike, Dato's government was brought down by the military, making it even harder to operate the *turno*. Antonio Maura, given the prestige he had acquired as a serious reformer, presided over two coalition governments during periods of major crisis (and a short-lived minority **Maurista** administration). Dato, on the other hand, along with the Liberal **Manuel García Prieto**, worked tenaciously to resurrect a bipolar political system. Dato's big chance came in 1920, when the king once again called on him to form a government, and in the December elections he was at least able to ensure that his followers formed easily the largest block in parliament. After his death in March 1921, the same policy would be followed by his successor, **José Sánchez Guerra**.

From 1919, the regime was also faced by spiraling social unrest. In this context, the king preferred the PC to their Liberal counterparts (who were in any case even more divided) between 1919 and 1922. Their response was mixed. Maura's reputation as a hard-liner was confirmed when, in April 1919, he was called upon by the king to form a government and dealt harshly with labor agitation, led by the **Confederación Nacional del Trabajo** (CNT) and centered on Barcelona and **Andalusia**. Dato's backers would play a key role in undermining his government in June, given that they feared Maura might once again take over leadership of the party. Similarly, during his second coalition government after the July 1921 **Annual** disaster, Maura was happy to maintain heavy repression in order to prevent any resurgence of labor unrest. Dato's wing of the party took a more conciliatory position. Joaquín Sánchez de Toca (1852–1942) (July–November 1919) and Dato himself (May–October 1920) tried to negotiate with the Catalan CNT and integrate it into state-sponsored arbitration machinery. The major departure from this policy came in November 1920 when, under pressure from the military and conservative Catalan circles (and, probably, the king), Dato appointed the tough general Severiano Martínez Anido (1862–1939) to be civil governor of Barcelona and allowed him to carry out a brutal repression. He was to pay with his life. The CNT responded by sending out a hit squad that gunned him down in Madrid in March 1921. Nevertheless, his successor as party leader, José Sánchez Guerra (March–December

1922), would once again contemplate allowing the CNT to resurface, removing Martínez Anido in October 1922.

Overall, the PC fought hard to retain a key role in Spanish political life. Without the September 1923 coup by General **Miguel Primo de Rivera**, its leaders could, no doubt, have operated the *turno* for some years to come. However, they faced massive problems. First, with Spain's urbanization and slow politicization, their *caciquista* networks were being eroded. Furthermore, in the age of mass politics, election fixing had become impossible to justify. Finally, the "regenerationist" alternative within the party, provided by Antonio Maura, had proved too timid and contradictory in its methods and strategy. In the aftermath of the coup, the *caciquista* glue that bound it together dissolved and the party quickly broke up. *See also* TABLES 7 AND 8.

PARTIDO CONSTITUCIONALISTA. *See* SAGASTA Y ESCOLAR, PRÁXEDES MATEO.

PARTIDO DE ACCIÓN SOCIALISTA (PASOC)/PARTY OF SOCIALIST ACTION. The origins of the PASOC are to be found in the **Partido Socialista Obrero Español-Histórico**, formed by the aging **Rodolfo Llopis** after the revolt of the "interior" in 1972. By the time it was reconstituted as the PASOC in 1983, however, its politics had totally changed. It was now largely the party of young socialists disgusted at the drift to the right of the **Partido Socialista Obrero Español** (PSOE) under **Felipe González**. From 1986, it has formed part of the left-wing coalition **Izquierda Unida** (IU). From the following year, **Pablo Castellano** became a key figure in the organization. He would be its president from 1989 to 2001. In the party's sixth congress, held in May 2001, the decision was made to leave IU. The PASOC has since become an increasingly marginal influence within Spanish political life.

PARTIDO DEMÓCRATA/DEMOCRATIC PARTY. The Partido Demócrata was founded in **Madrid** in 1849 by the left wing of the **Partido Progresista**. In order to stay within the political system, it accepted the **monarchy** and the confessionality of the Spanish state, though there were both convinced **republicans** and firebrand anticlerics within its ranks. All members had in common their desire for universal male suffrage and for an extension of civil liberties, but there were also important differences. On the right of the party were to be found constitutional monarchists, such as José Ordax y Avecilla (1813–1856), and "individualists" like **Emilio Castelar**, who would tolerate only limited state intervention to cure social ills. On the left of the party, figures like **Francesc Pi i Margall** and Fernando Garrido (1821–1883) called for wide-ranging tax reforms and state intervention to aid the lower classes. The left also showed an interest in the "utopian socialist" and cooperativist doctrines being discussed in France. For this reason, the first overtly socialist groups, the Fourierist followers of Joaquín Abreu in Cádiz and a Cabetian nucleus in Barcelona, operated within the party. The 1860s also saw left-liberal intellectuals like **Nicolás Salmerón**, inspired by **Krausism**, affiliate.

During the 1850s and 1860s, it was the party of the urban radicals and it was within its ranks that the activists behind the various popular uprisings would be drawn. Hence, it was to play an important role in the planning and execution of the 1868 **Glorious Revolution**. During 1868, however, the party itself would divide, with the more popular and populist left forming part of the republican **federalist** movement.

PARTIDO DEMÓCRATA CRISTIANO/CHRISTIAN DEMOCRAT PARTY. *See* UNIÓN DEMOCRÁTICA ESPAÑOLA.

PARTIDO GALEGUISTA/GALICIANIST PARTY. *See* GALICIA.

PARTIDO LIBERAL (PL)/LIBERAL PARTY. The Partido Liberal Fusionista or Partido Liberal, as it was finally called, along with the **Partido Conservador** (PC), were the two "official parties" of the **Cánovas Restoration**. The PL grew out of the Partido Constitucionalista (Constitutionalist Party), led by **Práxedes Mateo Sagasta**, which had acted as the "party of order" during the **Democratic Sexennium**. The party was founded in two stages. May 1880 saw a "fusion" between the Partido Constitucionalista and other elements within the liberal-dynastic camp. Between this date and 1885, it was, as a result, known as the Partido Fusionista. Then, in 1885, an agreement between the Partido Fusionista and the Izquierda Dinástica (Dynastic Left) led to the foundation of the Partido Liberal. It was made up by all those who had favored the **Constitution of 1869**, but who were now willing to work within the Cánovas Restoration. As in the case of the PC, it was not a mass party in the modern sense of the term, but a party of notables, with Sagasta, until his death in 1903, the undisputed leader.

The party first exercised power between February 1881 and October 1883, but it was during the so-called "long parliament," between November 1885 and June 1890, that it was to carry through an important legislative program, aimed at making the Restoration regime compatible with its **liberal** ideals. The most important laws were those guaranteeing freedom of the **press** in July 1883, the Associations Law of 1887, trial by jury in May 1888, and granting universal male suffrage in June 1890. This allowed a degree of freedom of expression heretofore only available during brief liberal interludes, while the Associations Law also made it possible for the **labor movement** to develop. However, from the start, the PL became enmeshed within the *caciquista* system of the regime, and therefore helped to falsify the very laws they had promulgated. In particular, in order to ensure the continued predominance of the two "official parties," elections were still "made" by the minister of the interior and the civil governors.

When faced with the growing crisis of the regime after 1898, the PL was torn between timid reform and defending the status quo. In the 1890s, the party very much stagnated as its more progressive measures, such as the move by the overseas minister, **Antonio Maura**, to give **Cuba** a measure of autonomy in 1892, were blocked by entrenched interests. Furthermore, as a new generation of politicians began to look for a place in the sun, the party's internal discipline began to fragment. The fact that Sagasta was in power during the **Spanish-American War** of 1898 was a heavy blow. With the death of Sagasta in 1903, divisions within the party further grew, with Eugenio Montero Ríos (1832–1914) and **Segismundo Moret** disputing the leadership. During these years, with the *caciquista* system of politics beginning to break down, first under Moret (between 1905 and 1909) and then under **José Canalejas** (between 1910 and 1912), the PL tried to widen its social base by following a policy of "attraction" of the **republicans**. The policy was finally to wean the Partido Reformista of **Melquiades Álvarez** from the Socialist-republican *conjunción*, but it was never radical enough to win over wide-ranging republican support. Moreover, the decision of Moret to align with the republicans to oust the prime minister, **Antonio Maura** (who had joined the PC), after his repression of the **Tragic Week**, would result in a growing crisis of the *turno pacífico*.

In the context of the growing social conflict and political tensions that accompanied **World War I**, the PL, like the PC, divided further and increasingly reacted to events rather than drawing up any long-term strategy. When Canalejas was assassinated in 1912, the **Count of Romanones** and **Manuel García Prieto** became the main rivals for political power within the party. García Prieto gained the upper hand after Romanones was removed from power by King **Alfonso XIII** in April 1917, for pursuing, in the view of the king (and that of the **military** and conservative Spanish society), too pro-Allied a **foreign policy**. Along with his Conservative counterpart, **Eduardo Dato**, García Prieto would try to overcome the difficulties facing the regime and reconstruct a bipolar political system from 1920. When he came to power in December 1922, he headed what was effectively a coalition of PL forces, including the party's rising star, **Santiago Alba**, and also managed to integrate the Partido Reformista. It promised significant liberal reforms, but, as the April 1923 elections showed, continued to "make" elections in alliance with the rural *caciques*.

With respect to escalating social conflict, Romanones followed a policy of trying to keep the lid on popular protest. Hence, during a one-day strike at the end of 1916, and again in the spring of 1917, he suspended constitutional guarantees when faced with worker protest. But this was combined with an attempt to take an even-handed approach to industrial strife, with governments headed by Romanones (December 1918–April 1919) and García Prieto (December 1922–September 1923) making an effort to find a negotiated solution to social conflict in **Barcelona**. This, however, exasperated military and conservative (especially business) opinion, which accused the party of weakness in the face of subversion. Military discontent intensified following the military disaster of **Annual** in July 1921, after which the colonial *africanista* army criticized the monarchist parties for trying to blame the military alone and for not following an aggressive enough policy in **Morocco**. García Prieto's 1923 Liberal coalition found itself in the eye of the storm. The major problem was that neither the PL in particular, nor the Restoration regime as a whole, had the prestige or support to overcome these challenges. Hence, when in September 1923 the government of García Prieto was confronted by the coup d'etat of General **Miguel Primo de Rivera** (which was tacitly backed by the king), it could not count on any popular backing. *See also* TABLES 7 AND 8.

PARTIDO LIBERAL CONSERVADOR/LIBERAL CONSERVATIVE PARTY. *See* PARTIDO CONSERVADOR.

PARTIDO LIBERAL DEMÓCRATA/LIBERAL DEMOCRATIC PARTY. *See* ÁLVAREZ GONZÁLEZ-POSADA, MELQUÍADES.

PARTIDO MODERADO/MODERATE PARTY. Between 1820 and 1868, the Partido Moderado or *moderados* represented the more conservative strand of the Spanish **liberal** tradition, which emerged in the **Cortes of Cádiz** during the revolutionary years of 1808–1814. At a political level, the *moderados* were concerned with maintaining a strong monarchy, a high property franchise, centralizing power, and ensuring social order through heavy-handed use of the security forces. Socially, they wished to effect a reconciliation between liberalism and the old order, by ensuring that the nobility should retain both its property and a powerful voice in the nation's affairs, and by weaning the **Catholic Church** away from **Carlism**.

The *moderado* tendency first made its appearance during the **Constitutional Triennium** during the death throes of absolutism in the 1820s and 1830s. The activists formed a political party after the promulgation of the **Constitution of 1837**, which they considered excessively radical. Over the next six years, they faced a serious challenge from more permissive liberals integrated within the **Partido Progresista**, who had a strong base among the urban middle and lower classes, but after playing a decisive role in the overthrow of General **Baldomero Espartero**'s regency in 1843, they were able to consolidate their power over the following decade. First under General Luis González Brabo (1811–1871) and then General **Ramón María Narváez**, they introduced a series of laws that tightened the elites' grip on the Spanish polity. Protest was ruthlessly suppressed, the *desamortización* of Church land halted, **press** freedoms restricted, a new, more centralist, local government law approved, and a new rural police, the **Civil Guard**, created. The *moderados'* power was institutionalized by the new **Constitution of 1845**, which increased the monarch's weight in the political process and created a largely noble Upper House or Senate. In the following year, the electorate was then reduced to 1 percent of the **population** and small electoral constituencies, which would be easier to control by local elites (soon to be known as *caciques*) were introduced.

The *moderados* were briefly marginalized from power during the **Progressive Biennium** of 1854 to 1856, but they were again to exert great influence in the decade that followed. Between 1856 and 1863, power was shared by the *moderados* and **Unión Liberal**, an amalgam of the more tepid *progresistas* and liberal *moderados*, but actual policies varied little, with new laws passed limiting the rights of association (in order to combat trade unions) and further centralize government. From 1863, moreover, with the support of Queen **Isabel II** and the figure of Narváez never far from center stage, the *moderados* once again dominated government. However, open **corruption** in government circles, combined with ever more repressive policies, led both to dissension within the *moderados'* own ranks and a determination within more liberal circles to both overthrow the government and force the queen into exile. This was to come to fruition with the **Glorious Revolution** of September 1868.

PARTIDO NACIONALISTA VASCO (PNV)/BASQUE NATIONALIST PARTY. The PNV is, at present, the dominant nationalist party in the **Basque Country**. It was founded in 1895 by the father of Basque nationalism, **Sabino de Arana**. The party's strength was at first based on the fear engendered in Basque society that the influx of "Spanish" migrants (*maketos*, as they were disparagingly known) that had accompanied industrialization would undermine Basque traditions and culture. It was strongly Catholic and conservative, and its adherents defended the racial superiority of the Basques over alien cultures, and had as their final goal the construction of an independent, confessional, Basque state. Its kernel of support was, in the 1890s, the small-town urban middle class, who were fearful of industrial development and social and cultural change. At an institutional level, it was also to gain the sympathy of sectors of the Basque **Catholic Church.** However, from the turn of the century, it also began to attract support among salaried classes more closely linked to the process of industrialization, such as shop workers, white-collar workers, and small and medium-sized industrialists (and the odd member of the Basque haute bourgeoisie, like the shipping magnate Ramón de la Sota [1852–1936]), who were frustrated at their marginalization from political power by the region's industrial and financial elite and saw the party as a vehicle for their grievances. This led to the development of two separate currents within the party. On the one hand, Sabino de Arana's unconditional supporters (known as *bizkaitarristas*) maintained their hero's original uncompromising separatist stance, and retained a populist, antiliberal, and vaguely egalitarian rhetoric. It was probably for this reason that the PNV was able to integrate an important number of ethnically Basque workers within the movement after the organization of the labor confederation Solidaridad de Obreros Vascos (Basque Workers' Solidarity) in 1911. The union was organizationally separate from the PNV, but its leadership was close to the *bizkaitarristas*. The more middle-class current, usually referred to as the *euskalerríacos*, on the other hand, wished to set up a probusiness party, rather like the Catalan **Lliga Regionalista**, whose aim was in part be to seek autonomy (not independence) for the Basque Country, but also to intervene in Spanish political affairs.

This current was, like the Catalan Lliga, to support **Antonio Maura**'s local government reforms between 1907 and 1909. Divisions within the PNV widened during **World War I** when the moderates linked up with the Lliga to push for a national policy more in line with business's perceived interests. This finally led the party (which had changed its name to Comunion Nacionalista Vasca [Basque Nationalist Communion] in 1916) to split, with the purists once again resurrecting the PNV. However, in 1930 the party was again reunited. This allowed it to become the most powerful political force in the Basque Country. Politically, it was torn between supporting the anticlerical but proautonomy left and the clerical but centralist right. After the 18 July 1936 **military** uprising, the Vizcaya and Guipúzcoa branches of the PNV finally sided with the Republican authorities in return for the granting of an autonomy statute and joined the wartime government. This earned the Basque nationalists heavy repression at the end of the **Spanish Civil War.**

During **World War II,** the PNV's leader, José Antonio Aguirre (1904–1960), participated in the Republican government in exile. In response, in March 1945, most of the Spanish democratic opposition signed a pact in Bayonne, which reaffirmed the legitimacy of the autonomous government formed in October 1936. At first, the government in exile pinned its hopes on Allied intervention. These hopes of Allied involvement began slowly to fade, and severe Francoist repression largely dismantled the PNV's interior organization from 1947. During the remainder of the **Franco regime,** the PNV posed little threat to the authorities. Indeed, a group of young nationalists, disgusted at the PNV's inaction, split with the organization to form **ETA** in 1959. Nevertheless, traditions of PNV affiliation were passed from generation to generation, and in the somewhat freer political climate of the 1960s, the PNV did much to foment a cultural revival of the **Basque language** through the setting up of language schools known as *ikastolas.*

During the transition to democracy, the PNV was to revive rapidly. In March 1977, it elected the charismatic leader from **Navarre,** Carlos Garaikoetxea (1938–), head of the party, and in the following year began setting up party branches (*batzokis*) throughout the Basque Country. This revival reflected the fact that much of the social base of Basque nationalism was socially conservative and feared the radicalism of ETA. The PNV's growing strength could be seen in the June 1977 elections, in which it polled 18.8 percent of the vote in the Basque Country, slightly behind the **Partido Socialista Obrero Español** (PSOE), but over the next two years it was to consolidate its position as the most powerful party in the territory. Henceforth, it would also be a key interlocutor for the **Adolfo Suárez** government, which, on the one hand, wished to diffuse political tension and offer autonomy, but, on the other, could not contemplate independence. The PNV was prepared to countenance autonomy rather than independence and accept a statute that did not include the province of Navarre (seen as a Basque province by nationalists, but by the 1970s largely against incorporation into the Basque Country). However, aware of the highly charged nationalism of much of its base, it took a tough line in other areas, refusing to back a **constitution** that did not incorporate the Basques' historic rights (*fueros*), above all, their right to collect their own taxes (the *concierto económico*). The PNV finally called for abstention in the referendum held to approve the constitution in December 1978, though it was tacitly prepared to recognize it. It then participated in negotiations over the Basque autonomy statute. Its position was strengthened because, although it rejected ETA violence, it could argue that only a generous statute could put an end to the strife. The result was that, in contrast to other autonomy statutes, the Guernika Statute gave the new autonomous government the power to collect taxes.

Between 1980 and 1984, the PNV was in control of the Basque regional parliament. This dominance was brought to an abrupt end in 1984 as the result of a fierce personal and political division between the PNV's current party president, **Xabier Arzallus**, and the former party president and current president (*lehendakari*) of the Basque parliament, Carlos Garaikoetxea, with the latter breaking away to form a new party, **Eusko Alkartasuna** (EA). In order to retain power, the PNV subsequently governed in coalition with the Basque Socialists, the Partido Socialista de Euskadi (PSE)-PSOE. From this date, the PNV took a moderate turn. Given the growing rejection of ETA within Basque society, in January 1988, along with the other "democratic" nationalist parties, EA and **Eskadiko Esquerra**, and countrywide parties with significant representation in the Basque parliament, it signed the Ajuria Enea Pact, which denounced **terrorist** violence and committed its signatories to working within the framework of the Guernika Statute. This was important because for the first time, the political representatives of the violent wing of Basque nationalism, **Herri Batasuna** and ETA, were completely isolated within the nationalist camp.

This strategy, however, was to change after 1996. Since the early 1990s, ETA, under growing pressure from the authorities, had begun to employ streets riots (Kale Borroka) and assassinate local politicians to force the government to negotiate. This had eroded support for the Basque nationalist cause. The right-wing Spanish party, the **Partido Popular** (PP), won the March 1996 elections and did surprisingly well in the Basque Country. These factors concentrated the mind of the PNV on the need to bring an end to ETA violence and reunify the nationalist camp. And between 1997 and 1998, under the leadership of its president, Xabier Arzallus, it developed a strategy that involved radicalizing its nationalist discourse while at the same time negotiating, through Herri Batasuna, an ETA cease-fire. The hope was that it could reunite Basque nationalism around a platform whose main component was the recognition of the Basques' right to independence (while not necessarily demanding total independence). Ideologically, this was not such a great step for the PNV, given that, although it had accepted autonomy, for many within the party the long-term goal remained an independent or semi-independent Basque homeland. This policy shift culminated in the 12 July 1998 Declaration of Lizarra (or Estella Pact), which reaffirmed the unity of all Basque territories (including Navarre and the French Basque provinces), called for a renegotiation of the Guernika Statute, and stated that the Basque Country's right to independence should be accepted. ETA declared a cease-fire four days later. The PNV's new strategy involved recasting its political alliances. In the spring of 1998, the Ajurea Enea Pact lapsed and in the summer, the PSE-PSOE, totally opposed to the PNV's new line, withdrew from the coalition government. As a result, after elections in October, the new PNV *lehendakari*, **Juan José Ibarretxe,** had to rely on the votes of the radical nationalists in **Euskal Herritarrok** (the name HB had temporarily adopted) for his investiture.

The strategy soon ran into difficulties. The PP government was implacably opposed to concessions and launched an offensive against the PNV, which it accused of objectively favoring ETA. In addition, frustrated that no political concessions were forthcoming, ETA broke the cease-fire in November 1999. Nevertheless, the PNV maintained its previous policy. From 2000, it once again worked for a new ETA cease-fire. Furthermore, in September 2002, in line with the Lizarra Pact, the *lehendakari* put forward his "Plan Ibarretxe" in the Basque parliament, which proposed that the Basque Country become a Free Associated State (Estado Libre Asociado) of Spain with a right to independence. Moreover, the text gave the Basque authorities the right to call a referendum on independence. In response, after winning an overall majority in the March 2000 general elections, the PP stepped up its offensive. In the Basque elections of May 2000, it hoped to inflict a historic defeat on Basque nationalism. However, in coalition with EA (and with many radical nationalists voting for this coalition), the PNV held on to power. The PP appealed to the Constitutional

Tribunal to declare the "Plan Ibarretxe" unconstitutional and introduced new legislation allowing for the imprisonment of anyone organizing an illegal referendum. Furthermore, the public prosecutor's office (*fiscalía*) brought an action against the PNV president of the Basque parliament, Juan María Atutxe, for not enforcing Spanish legislation and illegalizing Socialista Abertzaleak, as the HB parliamentary group briefly called itself. During 2003, the PP's leading Basque politician, **Jaime Mayor Oreja**, also insinuated that the Basque autonomy statute could be suspended.

The danger therefore existed that the PNV might be criminalized by the Spanish authorities, intensifying confrontation in the Basque Country. With the PSOE's victory in the March 2004 general elections, the political climate became significantly more congenial. The new prime minister, **José Luis Rodríguez Zapatero**, backed a negotiated reform of Spain's autonomy statutes, but would not countenance the "Plan Ibarretxe." He allowed it to be discussed in the Spanish parliament in February 2005, where it was overwhelmingly rejected. The PNV also began to take a more cautious line. Josu Jon Imaz (1963–) replaced Xabier Arzallus as PNV president in January 2004. He quickly showed himself to be a more moderate figure, stating that he would not support any compromise with the *abertzale* left until ETA renounced violence, stressing the need to work with the Spanish authorities and affirming that any reform of the autonomy statute had to achieve a broad consensus within the Basque Country itself. This very much represented a reversion to the position the PNV adopted between 1983 and 1996.

After ETA declared a cease-fire on 22 March 2006, he was the PNV representative in secret negotiations with the PSE-PSOE and HB over the future political status of the Basque Country and, along with the Socialists, rejected an HB proposal that a joint Basque-Navarre legislative body should operate within two years. This led to harsh attacks on Imaz from *abertzale* circles. Within his own party, there was also considerable opposition from more radical nationalists who backed the position of the party's former president, Xabier Arzallus. It was headed by the president of the PNV in Guipúzcoa, Joseba Egibar, and by Ibarretxe. After the ETA bombing of 30 December 2006 put an end to negotiations, Ibarretxe tried to revive his proposal, leading to serious tensions within the PNV. Imaz was finally defeated, announcing in September 2007 that he would not stand for reelection as PNV president. In the party's December 2007 congress, Iñigo Urkulla (1961–) was elected as the new president. He was a compromise candidate, but is much closer to Ibarretxe than his predecessor. The PNV did not perform well in the March 2008 general elections. The indication is that some moderate nationalists voted for the PSE-PSOE in order to prevent a PP victory. Nevertheless, the "Plan Ibarretxe" remains in place. *See also* TABLE 10.

PARTIDO OBRERO DE UNIFICACIÓN MARXISTA (POUM)/ UNITED MARXIST WORKERS' PARTY. The POUM, founded in September 1935, was an amalgamation of two anti-Stalinist communist parties, the **Bloc Obrer i Camperol** (BOC), headed by Joaquín Maurín (1896–1973), and Izquierda Comunista (Communist Left), whose principal figure was Andreu Nin (1892–1937). On the eve of the **Spanish Civil War**, its labor union, the Federación Obrera de Unificación Marxista (Workers' Federation of Marxist Unity) had the not inconsiderable figure of 60,000 affiliated workers.

Like the BOC, its center of strength would be **Catalonia**. With the outbreak of the civil war, the POUM supported the **anarchist** strategy of simultaneously waging war and pushing through a social revolution, though it did agree that its leader, Andreu Nin (Maurín had been caught in **Nationalist** territory at the start of the war), should join the **Generalitat** government. This brought it into conflict with the **Partit Socialista Unificat de Catalunya** (PSUC), the **Partido Comunista de España** (PCE), and the **republicans** (most notably, in Catalonia, **Esquerra Republicana de Catalunya** [ERC]), who aimed to reconstruct state power both in Catalonia and throughout the Republican zone.

Tensions were exacerbated in late 1936 and early 1937 by the POUM's attacks on Stalinism and denunciation of the Moscow show trials as a farce, and PSUC-PCE claims that the POUM "Trotskyists" were in reality counterrevolutionaries. In December, the PSUC managed to get Nin removed from the Generalitat government. Tensions finally exploded into violence during the **May Events** of 1937, when *poumistas* supported the rank-and-file of the anarchist **Confederación Nacional del Trabajo** (CNT) by engaging in street fighting against the PSUC, ERC, and the Republican police. The PCE-PSUC now denounced the POUM as agents in the pay of General **Francisco Franco** and Fascism, and demanded the party be suppressed. It was, in fact, as a result of **Francisco Largo Caballero**'s refusal to take this step that his enemies within the PSOE, PCE, and the republican parties were able to engineer his downfall and replacement by **Juan Negrín**. As a result, on 16 June, POUM offices were closed and its leaders arrested. The party's leader, Andreu Nin, was tortured and executed by Spanish Communists under the orders of the Soviet secret police, the NKVD.

PARTIDO POPULAR (PP)/POPULAR PARTY. Alianza Popular was renamed Partido Popular at its ninth congress in January 1989. At the end of the year, **Manuel Fraga** formally handed over the party's leadership to **José María Aznar** (while remaining honorary president). Under Aznar's leadership, the party presented a more centrist image. Hence, it pulled back from the campaign launched by Manuel Fraga against the abortion law approved by the government of the **Partido Socialista Obrero Español** (PSOE) and promised to protect pensions and unemployment benefits. However, it was strongly influenced by the legacy of Margaret Thatcher and took up the baton of neoliberalism, while its leadership and much of its activist base remained identified with traditional **Catholic** values. Moreover, while the party now accepted the **State of the Autonomies**, it emphasized the need to strengthen overarching Spanish identity, and showed some hostility toward Catalan and **Basque** nationalist identities. With respect to **foreign policy**, it took a less European federalist and a more Atlanticist stance.

The party was able to profit from the growing crisis of the PSOE government between 1993 and 1996. Nevertheless, the shrill tone adopted by Aznar and continued links between the party and the Catholic Church (especially **Opus Dei**) were a cause for concern among centrist electors. Hence, it was able seriously to challenge for power, but failed to take an unassailable lead in the opinion polls. It was helped by the fact that it built up a close alliance with sectors of the media (especially *El Mundo*, *ABC*, and the Correo media group), which were ruthlessly to exploit the **corruption** scandals engulfing the government and revelations that it had financed a dirty war against **ETA**. In the June 1993 general election, the party was narrowly defeated by the PSOE, but in June 1994 it won the elections to the European Parliament. It was finally victorious in the March 1996 general elections, but was disappointed not to achieve an overall majority. This reflected continued doubts over Aznar's personality and the party's policies.

This meant that the party had to reach pacts with the Catalan and Basque nationalist parties **Convergència i Unió** (CiU) and the **Partido Nacionalista Vasco** (PNV). This, subsequent experience was to show, to a degree moderated its policies and style. The abrasive minister of education and culture, **Esperanza Aguirre**, tried to reform secondary **education**, giving the government greater control over the curriculum, but her bill was defeated in the Spanish parliament. In other areas, it sought consensus, sponsoring agreements between unions and employers, and collaborating on reforms to the judiciary with the PSOE opposition. In the **economic** sphere, the government emphasized the need to achieve a balanced budget and speeded up the PSOE's program of **privatizations**. However, it was strongly criticized for placing businessmen close to the party in soon-to-be-privatized businesses. Most notably, its close links with the president of Telefónica, Aznar's boyhood friend Juan Villalonga (1953–), allowed it to create a large media group that backed the party. Once privatized, Telefónica helped set up the digital network Vía Digital and bought into private **television** and **radio** stations (especially Antena 3 and Onda Cero). At the same time, although it had accused the PSOE of using state television and radio as a propaganda tool, it ensured its subservience to the government line, while also getting conservative judges elected onto the major judicial tribunals.

Helped by the buoyant economic climate and by an ongoing crisis of succession within the PSOE, the PP won an overall majority in the March 2000 elections. It was henceforth to move to the right and adopt a much more forceful style. In the first place, its Spanish nationalist rhetoric became more strident. This was exacerbated by calls from the PNV, from 1998, for an autonomy statute that recognized the Basque Country's right to self-determination (which it linked to a process of negotiation with ETA), and demands from within **Catalonia** for a new, more generous, autonomy statute. Faced with what it saw as the danger of centrifugal forces undermining Spanish unity, in several areas the party tried to reassert central control, while also making clear that it would not reform the **State of the Autonomies.** This produced fierce polemic between the government and its supporters and the "peripheral nationalists" over the question of Basque and Catalonia autonomy, and over issues like the content of humanities teaching within the autonomous communities, the number of hours dedicated to the **Castilian language,** and whether the part of the Salamanca historical archive, which was confiscated from the **Generalitat** by the **Nationalists** at the end of the **Spanish Civil War,** should be returned to Catalonia.

In particular, the government launched a ferocious assault on the PNV, accusing it of helping to perpetuate **terrorism** in the Basque Country through the soft line it took with ETA. After the murder of a PP local councilor, Miguel Angel Blanco, in July 1997, the party had played a key role in mobilizing Spanish society against ETA violence, and during 2002 and 2003 it responded very effectively to an ETA offensive, dismantling much of its organization. The PP's tone was taken up in the Spanish right-wing press, producing significant ethnic and cultural tensions. The government also groomed two of its leading figures, **Jaime Mayor Oreja** and **Josep Piqué,** to capture (or a least take a share of) power in the Basque and Catalan governments themselves. Yet a Basque nationalist coalition won the crucial May 2001 elections in the Basque Country and in Catalonia the PP remained the third party.

In other areas, the PP also took a more aggressive line, making little or no attempt to consult and reach compromise agreements. During 2001, it forced its National Hydraulic Plan through parliament, despite heavy opposition in Catalonia and Aragón. It aimed above all to deal with water shortages on the southern Mediterranean coast, its controversial centerpiece being the transfer of water from the Ebro River to serve the needs of **Valencia** and Murcia. In the area of education policy, in 2001, its efforts to reform university education were opposed by both students and staff and produced a one-day strike in November. Then in 2003, as part of its educational reform package, it tried to increase the amount of religious education taught in state schools, producing fierce controversy and bringing the question of the role of the Church in Spanish society to the forefront of debate for the first time since the 1980s. In June 2002, the government also tried to impose labor reforms, which made it easier for employers to fire workers and made it harder to claim unemployment benefits (the so-called *decretazo*), leading to a one-day general strike. Under heavy pressure from the unions it subsequently backed down. In the area of foreign policy, given its Atlanticist perspective and Aznar's belief that "terror" must be combated wherever it lay (thus superimposing the United States' offensive against **al-Qaeda** on the government's struggle against ETA), it supported the U.S.-led invasion of **Iraq** in March 2003 despite heavy internal opposition. This led Aznar to link up with George W. Bush and Tony Blair in opposition to Jacques Chirac and Gerhard Schröder, a stance which very much contradicted the policies of the previous PSOE administration and was generally unpopular.

Between 2001 and 2003, the PP was rocked by a series of events. In 2001, the **Gescartera scandal** broke. This involved an investment firm that had illegally siphoned off clients' money. The difficulty for the government was the apparent collusion (or at the very least lack of action) by the regulatory body and the Ministry of the Economy. Then, in November 2002, an oil tanker, the ***Prestige***, sank off the Galician coast, causing a massive oil spill. This led to big demonstrations and accusations of incompetence. In May 2003, a Ukrainian transport plane, an aging Yakolev 42, crashed in Turkey, killing 62 Spanish servicemen returning from **Afghanistan**. There were claims that their lives had been put at risk because of cost-cutting measures by the Ministry of Defense, and matters were made worse when it transpired that little attempt was made to identify each soldier's remains before burial. In 2003, claims of incompetence were made with respect to the high-speed rail link (AVE) that was being built between **Madrid** and **Barcelona**. North of Zaragoza, the line traversed apparently unsound terrain.

From 2002, the PSOE, under its new leader, **José Luis Rodríguez Zapatero**, began to close ground on the PP. Yet the relatively good economic climate, Rodríguez Zapatero's inexperience, the Spanish nationalist mobilization that had accompanied the PP's struggle against the "peripheral" nationalisms, and the political capital gained from its effective offensive against ETA meant that PP maintained much of its support base. Its vote held up relatively well in the municipal elections and elections to the autonomous communities in May 2003. Hence, the government was still confident of winning general elections, to be held the following year. It was in this context that Aznar (who had stated that he would not run for office again) prepared his succession. The man chosen was **Mariano Rajoy**, probably because, unlike most of his fellow cabinet ministers, he exuded an air of quiet competence. Aznar's control over the party was indicated by the fact that he handpicked him at the end of August and that his decision was subsequently ratified at the party conference.

This was the background to the **Madrid train bombings** of 11 March 2004, three days before the elections, which left 151 people dead. The PP from the first claimed that ETA was to blame. This very much fitted into its offensive against the "terrorist gang" (*banda terrorista*). Yet on 12 March, information emerged that **Islamic** extremists were behind the attack. This was bad news for the PP because it shone a light on its unpopular support for the Iraq war. For this reason, it seems, the government continued to insist that ETA was behind the bombings until the day of the elections (though this is strenuously denied by the PP). This led to a big popular mobilization against the PP, led by Spain's more politicized youth. Dramatically, on 14 March it lost the elections. Commentators have since noted that the PSOE was already closing the gap on the PP before the bombings (although the PP was still in the lead). Nevertheless, the bombings clearly had a large impact, bringing the Iraq war to the forefront of people's minds and encouraging younger, culturally liberal Spaniards who opposed the war to vote.

After the elections, the PP tried to argue (rather unconvincingly in the view of many) that there were links between ETA and the Islamic extremists and even that the bombing was a deliberate ploy to undermine the government. Aggrieved that the PSOE, in its view, unfairly won the elections, it also launched a frontal assault on the new government's policies. This could be seen in three areas. First, it fiercely opposed "the peace process" with ETA. After ETA declared its cease-fire in on 22 March 2006, the PP stated that it would not oppose discussions regarding the end of terrorism with ETA, but was implacably against any political negotiations with **Herri Batasuna** (HB), which, it maintained, was simply an ETA front. Hence, when the Basque Socialists, the Partido Socialista de Euskadi (PSE)-PSOE, met HB in July, it withdrew support. Rajoy accused Rodríguez Zapatero of having "betrayed the dead and allowed ETA to recover"

(*Anuario El País 2006*, 11). Some media outlets close to the party, and even PP politicians, went so far as to claim that it was all part of a PSOE-Basque nationalist plot, hatched before the general elections with the connivance of elements within the security services, to oust the PP from power in return for the independence of the Basque Country. Second, it totally rejected the new Catalan autonomy statute, agreed upon in January 2006. Rajoy stated it would lead to the "break-up of Spain" (*Anuario El País 2006*, 80), and the PP collected signatures in favor of a Spanish-wide referendum (handing in the petition to parliament, with four million signatures, on 25 April) and referred it to Constitutional Tribunal. In some sectors of Spanish society, this campaign was accompanied by a boycott of Catalan *cava* wine. Third, with the support of the Church hierarchy, it rejected the government's legalization of gay marriage and reform of the education system, which made it possible to opt out of religious education in state schools. Large-scale street demonstrations were used to put pressure on the government. An anti–gay weddings march was held in Madrid on 18 July 2006 and the **Asociación de Víctimas del Terrorismo** held several big demonstrations, with PP support, against negotiations with ETA.

However, the problem for the PP was that, while these mobilizations had enthused its activists, they were frightening off more moderate electors. After ETA broke its cease-fire in December 2006, the PSOE and PP were neck and neck in the opinion polls, but during 2007, the PSOE reestablished a slender lead. Furthermore, Rajoy's approval ratings were low. He lacked charisma and centrist voters saw him as a prisoner of the PP hard right. The key figures on the right were the party heavyweights **Esperanza Aguirre**, **Eduardo Zaplana**, and **Ángel Acebes**, who were largely backed by the daily paper **El Mundo**, the digital newspaper **Libertad Digital**, and the radio station **COPE**. In **Catalonia**, the sense that the PP represented hard-right centralizing ideas was strengthened when the moderate Josep Piqué resigned as Catalan party president. Realizing the problem, during 2007 the PP moderated its tone somewhat. This strategy was maintained by Rajoy during the campaign in the run-up to the March 2008 general elections.

The party suffered an early setback in January when, under pressure from the party's right, Rajoy felt obliged to reject the petition of the well-liked centrist politician **Alberto Ruiz-Gallardón**, the mayor of Madrid, to stand for parliament. However, the rapidly deteriorating economic situation gave the PP ammunition, and Rajoy drafted in leading businessman Manuel Pizarro in order to give the party's economic program greater credibility. From February, the PP also launched a populist offensive against the government, accusing it of allowing an "avalanche" of **immigrants** to enter Spain. It stated that if elected, it would ensure immigrants signed a pledge to integrate into Spanish culture, that it would institute a points system for prospective immigrants, and that it would expel immigrants who failed to find work during one year. In a context in which the massive growth of immigration had worried many Spaniards, and in which these concerns were exacerbated by rapidly rising unemployment, these proposals had some impact on the electorate. The combined result of these factors was that during the campaign the PP closed the gap on the PSOE somewhat and prevented it from gaining an overall majority. Nevertheless, it still lost. Rajoy maintains that the result is good enough to justify his remaining as leader. *See also* ALIANZA POPULAR; TABLE 10.

PARTIDO PROGRESISTA/PROGRESSIVE PARTY. The Partido Progresista or *progresistas* (the term was first used in the elections of July 1836) made up the more radical wing of early 19th-century Spanish liberalism. The 1830s saw the emergence of two clear tendencies within **liberal** ranks: the Partido Progresista, which coalesced around the figure of **Juan Álvarez Mendizábal**, and the **Partido Moderado** (or *moderados*). In comparison with the more conservative *moderados*, the *progresistas* stood for greater restrictions on the powers of the monarch, a wider suffrage, an extension of civil liberties, a greater decentralization of the state, and a more resolute program of individualistic liberal reforms in order to undermine the social and institutional bases of the ancien regime. Hence it was the *progresistas* who were behind the *desamortización*, and the *progresista*-inspired **constitutions** of 1837 and of 1856 (the latter never put into effect) laid stress on national sovereignty.

Because their credentials were more democratic, the *progresistas'* power base was to be found among more radical officers recruited into the **military** during the **War of Independence**, and, in urban

Spain, among the middle-class merchants and manufacturers, the petty bourgeoisie, artisans, and workers. During most of the period of 1833–1868, they found themselves in opposition to the *moderados*, who captained a new amalgam of old and new social elites, with the backing of the queen regent, **María Cristina of Naples**, and then Queen **Isabel II**. Frozen out, the *progresistas* turned to the officers' *pronunciamiento* and the urban uprising to force the monarch to deliver power into their hands. Urban revolt played an important role in the assumption of power of Mendizábal in 1835 and in the birth of the **Espartero regency** of 1840–1843, the **Progressive Biennium** of 1854–1856, and the **Democratic Sexennium** of 1868–1874. Subsequently, grassroots urban committees (*juntas*) and militias were set up. However, the *progresista* leaders were men of substantial wealth and property, who still believed in the need for an enlightened elite to rule. After a revolution, they would, therefore, set about returning power to the center and call elections to a new constituent **Cortes**, which would promulgate a more democratic constitution. Moreover, they believed in the need for property qualifications and were doctrinaire liberals who rejected the need for social reform.

For this reason, the *progresistas* slowly lost the sympathy of the urban masses. Key moments in this process were the formation of the **Partido Demócrata** in 1849 and the rise of **federalist republicanism** in the 1860s. The Democratic Sexennium represented a time of crisis for the *progresistas*. From 1863, they refused to participate in elections under the ruling *moderados*, who adopted an increasingly authoritarian course (a policy referred to as the *retraimiento*), and entered into negotiations with the Partido Demócrata and **Unión Liberal** to overthrow the government. The main figure in this process was **Juan Prim**. This coalition of forces launched the so-called **Glorious Revolution** of September 1868, and over the next two years the *progresistas*, in coalition with the Unión Liberal and a fraction of the Partido Demócrata, dominated political life. However, the strains provoked by the rapid politicization of society and by the assassination of Prim in December 1870 provoked the division of the party into two. A more radical sector was led by Manuel Ruiz Zorrilla (1833–1895) while the conservatives grouped around **Práxedes Mateo Sagasta**. In the elections of April 1872, they formed two separate parties, the **Partido Radical** and Partido Constitucionalista

(Constitutionalist Party) respectively. Most supporters of the latter would subsequently, during the **Cánovas Restoration**, integrate into the **Partido Liberal** under Sagasta's leadership.

PARTIDO RADICAL/RADICAL PARTY. The Radical Party was set up in 1871 as a result of divisions within the **Partido Progresista** during the **Democratic Sexennium** (1868–1874), between the more conservative supporters of **Práxedes Mateo Sagasta**, who formed the Partido Constitucionalista (Constitutionalist Party), and the more left-wing supporters of Manuel Ruiz Zorrilla (1833–1895). It formed a government in June 1872 and after winning a large majority in the August elections, introduced a series of reforms, including the separation of Church and state and the extension of the state **education** system. However, the divisions between the victors of the 1868 **Glorious Revolution** were to lead the king, **Amadeo I**, to abdicate in February 1873. Initially, the Partido Radical accepted the **First Republic**, but, with power slipping from its hands, it tried to carry out a coup in April. Its failure forced it from the political stage. After the *pronunciamiento* staged by Manuel Pavia (1827–1895) in January 1874, Ruiz Zorrilla declared himself a **republican** and formed the **Partido Republicano Progresista**.

PARTIDO REFORMISTA/REFORMIST PARTY. *See* ÁLVAREZ GONZÁLEZ-POSADA, MELQUÍADES.

PARTIDO REPUBLICANO CENTRALISTA/REPUBLICAN CENTRALIST PARTY. *See* CASTELAR Y RIPOLL, EMILIO.

PARTIDO REPUBLICANO FEDERAL DEMOCRÁTICO/ FEDERAL DEMOCRATIC REPUBLICAN PARTY. Set up by **Francesc Pi i Margall** in 1880, the party was conceived as the heir of the **Partido Republicano Federalista**. It included all those left-wing **republicans** who supported the decentralization of the Spanish state. However, it never regained the former's position as a key force in Spanish political life and a fulcrum of republican politics. The popular and working-class base of federal republican politics fragmented with the growth of both the working-class left and **Catalanism** from the 1870s. Furthermore, from the first decade of the 20th century in particular, it was eclipsed by other republican formations for which the demand for decentralization was not incompatible with a more forceful **nationalist** discourse, and which were not afraid of adopting either a radical pseudo-**anarchist** discourse, which might appeal to the working-class left, or a more socially conservative rhetoric, aimed at bringing onboard the middle classes. The key figures in this respect would be **Alejandro Lerroux** on the republican left and **Nicolás Salmerón** on the republican right.

PARTIDO REPUBLICANO FEDERALISTA/FEDERAL REPUB-LICAN PARTY. This party was set up in October 1868 after a split between the **republican** and monarchist wings of the **Partido Demócrata**. With a large urban middle- and working-class base, it was the first mass party in Spanish history. Its program was calculated to appeal to those dispossessed of political power, stressing the need to democratize and decentralize political life, and guarantee civil liberties. Yet, in the turbulent political climate of the **Democratic Sexennium** (1868–1874), the party was pulled apart by a series of contradictory pressures. It was essentially a middle-class party dedicated to political reform, with only a mild social reform program. The arrival of Bakunist socialism in the shape of the **Federación Regional Española** (FRE), therefore, drew away some working-class support. At the same time, the party was hit by internal squabbles. Under the leadership of **Francesc Pi i Margall**, as against the criteria of the so-called "intransigent" republicans, who wished to launch an insurrection, the party maintained a peaceful opposition to the constitutional **monarchy**.

After the declaration of the **First Republic**, the party entered government for the first time, and then, after a failed coup by the **Partido Radical**, took over the reins of power. Pi i Margall tried to maintain an orderly process of reform, but was challenged by both the right and left of his party. On the one hand, the leftist intransigent republicans launched the **Cantonalist revolt** against the government; on the other, right-wing republicans, led by **Nicolás Salmerón** and **Emilio Castelar**, called for a more centralized "republic of law and order." Faced by the intensification of war with the **Carlists** and the Cantonalist uprisings, Pi i Margall was forced to relinquish power to Salmerón on 18 July. With the fall of the First Republic, the party was to disintegrate into a series of smaller parties representing its various internal currents.

PARTIDO REPUBLICANO PROGRESISTA/PROGRESIVE RE-PUBLICAN PARTY. Founded in 1880 by Manuel Ruiz Zorrilla (1833–1895), this party was distinguished by two main features. First, it was unitarian (i.e., opposed to a decentralizing, **federalist** Republic) and was to the right of the **Partido Republicano Federal Demócrata**. Second, it aimed for the overthrow of the **Cánovas Restoration** through an army coup or *pronunciamiento*. In the 1890s, however, the party divided into three groups, finally leading to its dissolution. First, there were those who wished to continue the strategy of provoking military coups. Second, given the failure of coups by **republican** army officers thus far attempted, a section of the party under the leadership of **Nicolás Salmerón** argued in favor of legal parliamentary opposition and split with the party in 1887 to form the Partido Republicano Centralista (Centralist Republican Party). Third, a group of young radicals emerged, under the leadership of **Alejandro Lerroux**, who adopted a more revolutionary discourse, aimed at linking up with the working class.

PARTIDO REPUBLICANO RADICAL (PRR)/RADICAL RE-PUBLICAN PARTY. This party was formed by **Alejandro Lerroux** in January 1908 after the split with the moderate **republicans** within the **Unión Republicana** in 1906. Despite the challenge posed by the **Solidaritat Catalana**, Lerroux was able to maintain most of the working-class support he had built up in **Barcelona** in previous years. Hence, though beaten in the 21 April 1907 general elections, the party defeated the **Lliga Regionalista** and the **Centre Nacionalista Republicà** in subsequent municipal elections and was thereby briefly able to take control of Barcelona municipal government. In order to appeal to the workers, the party at first maintained the demagogic, anticlerical, and seemingly socially radical ideology that had been Lerroux's trademark.

From 1910, however, its center of operations moved to **Madrid** and it became more moderate as it tried to attract a wider middle-class clientele and build a platform throughout Spain. The party largely lost its working-class base in Barcelona (where it was hit by a number of **corruption** scandals during 1910), but was able to establish new power bases, particularly in Madrid, Aragón, and **Valencia**. By the 1920s, it had very much become a party of the center. This led to a break with the more radical wing of the party, who in 1929 founded the Partido Radical Socialista (Radical Socialist Party) under Marcelino Domingo (1864–1939). However, with the founding of the **Second Republic** the party was handed the opportunity to grow rapidly. It could now become the depository of the votes of many in the middle classes and rural landowners who, in the context of a republic, saw the PRR as the surest bulwark against radical reform. Their hopes were to be confirmed. Alejandro Lerroux participated in the conspiracy to overthrow the **monarchy**, but he aimed to lead a coalition of republican forces that would put in place a conservative "republic of order." Following the massive **Partido Socialista Obrero Español** (PSOE)-republican victory in the June 1931 elections, the Radicals (as they were usually referred to) formed part of the republican-Socialist coalition government, but were unhappy at collaborating with the PSOE, finally leaving the coalition in December following the resignation of **Niceto Alcalá Zamora** as prime minister and his replacement by **Manuel Azaña**. Over the next two years, the PRR adopted an increasingly hostile stance toward the leftist coalition, trying to block much of its reforming legislation in the **Cortes**. Lerroux finally got his chance to govern after the resignation of Azaña in September 1933, but he could not count on the confidence of the Cortes, with the result that elections were called for November. In these elections, at a local level in many areas, the Radicals and the right-wing **Confederación Española de Derechas Autónomas** (CEDA) presented united candidatures. The PRR emerged as the second-largest party in parliament behind the CEDA with 102 seats. Nevertheless, because Alcalá Zamora did not trust the Republican credentials of the CEDA, the PRR ended up governing with CEDA support. The result was a series of cabinets (with CEDA participation from October 1934), which essentially served to put into reverse the reforms of the years 1931–1933. The party played an important role in limiting the impact of CEDA calls for repression following the **October 1934 revolution**, but it was always an organization low on ethics and was undermined by a series of **corruption** scandals during 1935. This opened the way for the elections of February 1936, when, with the PRR's credibility shattered and Spanish society increasingly polarized, the party's support collapsed. It gained only nine seats in the new parliament and Lerroux himself failed to get elected.

PARTIDO REPUBLICANO REFORMISTA/REFORMIST RE-PUBLICAN PARTY. *See* ÁLVAREZ GONZÁLEZ-POSADA, MELQUÍADES.

PARTIDO SOCIAL DEMÓCRATA/SOCIAL DEMOCRATIC PARTY. *See* BOYER SALVADOR, MIGUEL; FERNÁNDEZ ORDÓÑEZ, FRANCISCO; UNIÓN DEL CENTRO DEMOCRÁTICO.

PARTIDO SOCIAL POPULAR/PEOPLE'S SOCIAL PARTY. This was a social-**Catholic** party formed by **Antonio Maura**'s old follower **Ángel Ossorio y Gallardo** in June 1922. Ossorio y Gallardo had played a leading role in the creation of the **Maurista** movement in 1914, but he was increasingly alienated by the fact that it did not provide an unambiguous challenge to the **Cánovas Restoration**. From 1917, influenced by the Italian Partito Popolare, he also began to move in a **Christian-democratic** direction, emphasizing the need for social justice in order to deal with the left-wing revolutionary threat. However, the party was also to include more conservative—often antiliberal—Catholics who believed in the need for a unified Catholic front. Among these forces was the leading Catholic daily *El Debate*. This division came to the fore in the aftermath of the *pronunciamiento* by General **Miguel Primo de Rivera** in 1923. Ossorio y Gallardo opposed the dictatorship and wanted to turn the party into an unambiguously Christian-democratic force. However, others broke away, adopted an antiparliamentary **corporatist** discourse, and integrated into the dictatorship. Unlike in Italy and in central Europe, only a small minority of Spanish Catholics rallied to Christian-democracy.

PARTIDO SOCIALISTA DE ANDALUCÍA/ANDALUSIAN SOCIALIST PARTY. *See* ANDALUSIA; ISLAM AND SPAIN.

PARTIDO SOCIALISTA OBRERO ESPAÑOL (PSOE)/SPANISH SOCIALIST WORKERS' PARTY. The origins of the PSOE are to be found in a group of **Madrid** workers who formed part of the leadership of the Spanish branch of Karl Marx's International Working Men's Association, the **Federación Regional Española** (FRE). The FRE was predominantly **anarchist**, but these workers were converted to Marxism by Marx's son-in-law, Paul Lafargue, when he visited Madrid at the end of 1871. Soon after, they broke with the FRE and formed their own organization, the Nueva Federación Española (New Spanish Federation). The Spanish Marxists, however, remained only a small group, centered to a large degree on a circle of Madrid printers. The PSOE (at first referred to as the Partido Socialista) was founded in 1879, but it was not until August 1888, in a congress held in **Barcelona**, that it was put on a formal footing. In the same month, also in Barcelona, a labor confederation closely linked to the party, the **Unión General de Trabajadores** (UGT), was set up. In the following year, the PSOE then affiliated with the Second International at its founding congress in Paris. Thereafter, under the leadership of the Madrid printer **Pablo Iglesias**, the party began slowly to extend its influence in working-class circles, particularly among the workers of Madrid and the Asturian and Vizcayan miners. Nevertheless, in 1899, the PSOE was still a very small organization. It was only from the turn of the century that, aided by growing opposition to the **Cánovas Restoration** following the **Spanish-American War** of 1898, the party began to grow significantly, reaching about 13,000 members by 1913. This growth accelerated rapidly on the back of rising working-class discontent during **World War I**.

By the late 19th century, the party's ideology was a mixture of revolutionary rhetoric and moderate "reformist" practice. The leadership maintained that Spain was ripe for proletarian revolution, but, at the same time, they remained cautious trade unionists, trying not to put the UGT in jeopardy through rash strikes. In the early days, the party was also highly sectarian. It rejected the anarchists' insurrectionary tactics and strongly criticized the "bourgeois" **republicans** for leading the workers away from the path of socialism. From the turn of the century, however, it began to adopt a more realistic approach. It came to accept that revolution was a long way in the future and that the republicans were necessary allies against the right. This reappraisal culminated, after the events of the **Tragic Week**, in an alliance or *conjunción* with the republicans in October 1909. The alliance strengthened the party. In the May 1910 elections, it won its first seat in parliament, with the election of **Pablo Iglesias** for Madrid. From 1910, growing social unrest in the context of a more favorable economic climate also served to give the party greater weight in Spanish politics. This was particularly the case during the economic boom that followed the declaration of World War I. By 1917, the left, including the Socialists, felt it was strong enough to challenge the Cánovas Restoration. The **crisis of 1917** culminated in a Socialist-led revolutionary general strike on 9 August 1917. It was, however, bloodily repressed by the **military**. This had a dual effect. On the one hand, more moderate Socialists, like Pablo Iglesias and the Vizcayan leader **Indalecio Prieto**, shied away from further revolutionary action; on the other, anger among sectors of the rank-and-file intensified pressure to adopt a more revolutionary stance.

This division was intensified in postwar Spain by the experience of the Bolshevik Revolution in October 1917 and by an employer offensive that followed the onset of recession in 1920. The result was the emergence of a radical wing, the *terceristas*, who aimed to transform the party into a Communist organization. This was opposed by moderates within the party and union: in the first place, liberal Socialists like **Indalecio Prieto**, who wished to continue cooperating with the republicans in order to bring about democratic reform, and secondly, the UGT bureaucracy, represented by such figures as **Francisco Largo Caballero** and **Julián Besteiro**, who feared losing control of the organization. This led, between 1919 and 1921, to a struggle between the Socialist hierarchy and the radicals for control of the party. The conflict centered on whether the PSOE should join the Bolshevik Third International. At first it seemed that it would join, but by 1921, the revolutionary tide that had swept Europe had begun to ebb. Moreover, in the key extraordinary party congress called in April 1921 to make a decision, experienced Socialists like Largo Caballero were able to make their weight within the organization felt and concentrate large numbers of branch votes in their hands. The result was that the *terceristas* were defeated and went on to form the **Partido Comunista de España** (PCE).

Two years later, the military coup by **Miguel Primo de Rivera** swept away the Restoration regime. Almost immediately, the new authorities offered to do a deal with the Socialists. In return for restraining their criticism, they would become the privileged interlocutors of Spanish labor. This was rejected by liberal democrats in the party, horrified at the prospect of cooperating with a dictator. They were, however, overruled by the powerful UGT bureaucracy, who above anything else wished to maintain the organization's strength intact. Hence, the PSOE-UGT participated in the regime's arbitration boards, the *comités paritarios*, and in 1924, Largo Caballero joined the Council of State.

The Socialists were only to abandon tacit collaboration as the dictatorship declined between 1927 and 1929. Once Primo de Rivera had resigned in January 1930, **Alfonso XIII** engaged in a futile attempt to resurrect the discredited politics of the Restoration era. Consequently, the conjuncture became increasingly revolutionary and the PSOE joined a conspiracy led by the republicans to overthrow the regime and put in its place a democratic republic. The declaration of the **Second Republic** in April 1931 served enormously to enhance the Socialists' prestige. As a result, in the June 1931 elections, the PSOE won 114 seats and became the largest party in the new parliament. The new government was headed by the conservative republican **Niceto Alcalá Zamora**, while the party's strongman, Largo Caballero, became minister of labor. The fact that republicans were dominant in most areas of policy making reflected the Socialists' belief that it was the task of the liberal bourgeoisie to democratize Spain. Nevertheless, in order to content their supporters, they needed to carry out a thoroughgoing program of social reforms. Chief among their backers was the landworkers' union, the **Federación Nacional de Trabajadores de la Tierra**. A key Socialist goal therefore became the redistribution of part of the estates of the large landowners or *latifundistas* to the peasantry through the **Agrarian Reform Law**.

The reform program was, however, blocked by the right. This led to growing criticism of the Socialists' collaboration in government from sectors of the party and union's working-class base. Liberal democrats like Indalecio Prieto argued in favor of maintaining the Socialist-republican alliance, but Largo Caballero, backed by most of the UGT leadership, responded to this pressure by radicalizing his rhetoric, rejecting the coalition government, and implying that social revolution was now necessary. Unlike the situation between 1920 and 1923, he felt he had to take a more militant line in order to keep control of the organization. Largo Caballero and his backers proved the most powerful figures within the party, so when elections were held in November 1933, the PSOE fought them alone. The results were disastrous. The right-wing coalition, the **Confederación Espa-ñola de Derechas Autónomas** (CEDA), became the largest grouping in parliament, followed by the **Partido Republicano Radical** (PRR), while Socialist representation was cut to just 59 seats. The next 11 months saw the PRR govern with CEDA support. At a local level, employers took advantage of the new context to launch a counterof-fensive against the labor unions. International tensions also fed into the Spanish political scene. Two closely interrelated factors served further to radicalize the Socialist discourse: the rise of Fascism and the authoritarian right throughout Europe and the consolidation of Communism in the Soviet Union. Intensifying political and social conflict in Spain and Europe seemed to invalidate the optimistic social-democrat view that capitalism might be slowly reformed, while the western European economic crisis strengthened the view that the Soviet Union provided the alternative. After the elections, Largo Caballero talked of the need to "take power," and leftist intel-lectuals grouped around him drew parallels with Russia in 1917. The increasingly rarefied social and political climate culminated in the Socialist-inspired **October 1934 revolution**.

Despite the events of Asturias, the movement had no chance of success. This strengthened the position of the supporters of Indalecio Prieto, who wished to reestablish the republican-Socialist alliance of 1931. For many it now seemed that only through the ballot box could the right be defeated. Largo Caballero held out against this rapprochement until late 1935, but once elections had been called, the logic of the electoral arithmetic led him to desist. Nevertheless, in order to preserve his revolutionary image and to strengthen his hand vis-à-vis Prieto, he insisted that the alliance be limited to an electoral pact and that other working-class organizations, most notably the PCE, participate. This was the background to the February **Popular Front** left-wing coalition. Moderates could see it as a repeat of the June 1931 alliance, while radicals were encouraged by the participa-tion of leftist unions and parties. Everyone, however, subordinated his/her own particular demands to the need for victory. Yet victory at the polls, rather than signifying a return to the reforming adminis-tration of 1931–1933, was the prelude to the **Spanish Civil War**. In the run-up to the war, the PSOE-UGT remained totally divided. The growing strength of Prieto within the party was reflected in the fact that Largo Caballero was forced to resign from its National Executive in December 1935. Thereafter, he entrenched himself within the UGT, and from this vantage point the *caballeristas* maintained their revolutionary rhetoric, while also preventing Prieto and his followers from entering and strengthening the republican government. This was the worst of all possible worlds. Violent language frightened the right, yet nothing was actually done to prepare for armed conflict.

When the civil war began, the Socialist and anarchist working-class base pressed home a social revolution in much of Republican Spain. With the tide of proletarian revolution still riding high, Largo Caballero became prime minister on 4 September 1936 and presided over a true Popular Front government. He did not wish to alienate his working-class base, and so did not oppose the collectivizations. Yet he was convinced of the need to rebuild the state and create a regular army in order to win the war. This was not sufficient for the increasingly powerful PCE, which in 1937 was able to take advantage of the **May Events** in Barcelona to have Largo Caballero removed. Both the republicans and supporters of Indalecio Prieto, bitter at Largo Caballero's revolutionary posturing during the Republic, supported this move, and it was a *prietista* Socialist, **Juan Negrín**, who became prime minister. Yet over the following year, these democrats themselves became worried at growing Communist influence, and at the introduction of Stalinist practices into the Republican zone. Prieto and the president of the Republic, **Manuel Azaña**, also became despondent at the Republic's chances of victory, and began to consider the possibilities of a negotiated settlement. This pessimism was behind the dismissal of Prieto as minister of defense in April 1938. Negrín felt that there was no choice but to accept Communist influence, and he hoped to hold out until the start of a European war that might save the Republic.

The Republic, however, went down to defeat in March 1939. The PSOE found it difficult to come to terms with the conditions imposed by the **Nationalist** victory. At the end of the civil war, there were two main factions. A minority wing, led by Juan Negrín, favored continued cooperation with the PCE. However, the dominant current within the party, whose leading figure was Indalecio Prieto, reacted to its experience of Stalinism by adopting a virulently anticommunist stance. This predisposed it to seek help from the Allies in order to liberate Spain from the **Franco regime**. By the late 1940s, Prieto had managed to gain the support of the international Socialist organizations and impose his policies on the interior and exiled wings of the PSOE, while the *negrinistas* (who had themselves broken with the PCE in 1945) were a spent force.

Any satisfaction to be gained from this was, in the following years, undercut by a series of disastrous policy reverses. In 1945, the Socialists in exile had teamed up with the republicans to form a Republican **Cortes** in exile. However, at the end of the war, the United States and Great Britain suggested that they would only support a moderate coalition of democratic forces with monarchist participation. This tempted the Socialists to break with their republican allies in order to be better able to negotiate with the pretender Don **Juan de Borbón y Battenberg**. In August 1947, they left the Republican government in exile and in August 1948 signed the Pact of San Juan de Luz with the monarchists. This pact called for the installation of a democratic regime in Spain, the character of which would be decided by referendum. Yet, with the chance of an Allied intervention receding, Don Juan began negotiating a monarchist succession with General **Francisco Franco** and drew away from other opposition forces. This led the Socialists to break off the pact in 1951, but they were now left bereft of any coherent strategy. In the context of the Cold War, the United States now proved quite happy to support a staunchly anti-communist dictatorship, while the monarchists were unwilling to risk the possible succession by openly challenging Franco's rule.

In the late 1940s, the PSOE and UGT also tried to rebuild its organization in Spain. The party and unions' committees were, however, repeatedly broken up by the security forces. Consequently, both organizations decided to move their headquarters to Toulouse in July 1954. This was to be a mixed blessing for the PSOE. On the one hand, the party was put on a more stable footing, but it was placed in the hands of **Rodolfo Llopis**, a *caballerista* veteran who would find it hard to come to terms with rapidly changing social and political realities. During the 1950s and 1960s, the Socialists played only a secondary role in the opposition movement. In tune with their cautious past, the PSOE and UGT remained rather self-enclosed elitist organizations, which proved unable to take the lead in the fight against the regime. Their stance was justified by a belief that an economic and social crisis would soon result in the regime's collapse. In these circumstances, the PCE came to the fore, and by the early 1970s it was easily the most powerful among the opposition groups. The PSOE was only to revive during the transition years of 1973–1978. Criticism of Rodolfo Llopis's leadership began to surface in the Spanish "interior" from the late 1950s. Critics like the Basque Socialist Antonio Amat (1919–1979) attacked the Toulouse executive's passivity, argued that the civil war had to be forgotten and that a broad front of all opposition groups (including the Communists) needed to be established, and suggested that violence might have to be employed to overthrow the regime. As internal protest intensified, these Socialists grew in strength and began to push for the party's executive committee to be transferred back to Spain. By the late 1960s, critical nuclei had been established around **Felipe González** and **Alfonso Guerra** in Seville and **Enrique Tierno Galván** in Madrid. In **Catalonia**, meanwhile, an independent Socialist party, the **Moviment Socialista de Catalunya**, had eclipsed the official party branch. These "interior" Socialists were supported by a younger generation of exiles (often the sons of Spanish immigrants), who also saw the need for the party to be more active on the mainland. Their first success came in March 1970, when the executive of the Socialist youth (the Federación Nacional de Juventudes Socialistas de España [National Federation of Spanish Socialist Youth]) was moved back to Spain. The UGT followed suit in August 1971. This provoked an outright split between "interior" Socialists—who from 1970 became known as the "renewers" (*renovadores*)—and the aging Rodolfo Llopis leadership. The "renewers" called a congress of the PSOE for August 1972 to decide on future action. Llopis, however, maintained that it was illegal and called his own congress for December. As a result, from 1973, there were two parties, the PSOE-Renovador and Llopis's **Partido Socialista Obrero Español-Histórico**. But the former were stronger, and this encouraged the Socialist International to declare them the legitimate Socialist party in January 1974.

At first the party had a collegiate leadership, with the Madrid Socialist **Pablo Castellanos**, the Basque trade unionist **Nicolás Redondo**, and Felipe González as the leading figures. But the party's Suresnes congress in October 1974 saw Madrid marginalized as Felipe González was made first secretary with the support of Nicolás

Redondo and the Basque delegation. From this date, the Seville team, with González as spokesman and Alfonso Guerra as party organizer, took control. In the mid-1970s, verbally at least, the party seemed highly radicalized, but as the decade progressed, its practice became increasingly moderate. The dichotomy between theory and practice visible in the early 20th century was, therefore, once again to emerge. This was evident during the **transition to democracy**. At first, the party leadership had called for a "democratic break" with the Franco regime, which would involve the setting up of a provisional government of opposition figures, who would call elections to a constituent Cortes. However, when, from July 1976, under the presidency of **Adolfo Suárez** the regime showed itself willing to negotiate democratization, the Socialists (along with the PCE) agreed in return to drop their demands for a total dismantling of Francoist state structures and for the formation of a provisional government.

This was probably necessary, but it meant that a cabinet of regime reformers was able to call the first democratic elections since the Second Republic. In the run-up to these elections, the Socialists presented a fresh, young image, emphasizing the need to consolidate both democracy and social reform. Socialism was, however, very much pushed back into the indefinite future. Over the following five years, the PSOE further moderated its language, portraying itself as a national party rather than a party of organized labor. Notions of class struggle were marginalized and instead the PSOE's new image became that of the standard-bearer of an interclass program of modernization, the major elements of which were the construction of a **welfare state**, greater efficiency in **public administration**, and the transformation of the country's antiquated industrial base.

The program soon showed its potential. In the first elections, the PSOE achieved an easy second place, with 29 percent of the vote, and thereby established itself as the major party of the left. Moreover, in 1978 it incorporated a number of dissident Socialist organizations, including Tierno Galván's Partido Socialista Popular (People's Socialist Party), and the Catalan **Partit dels Socialistes de Catalunya** (Party of the Catalan Socialists—PSC). In order to make the party more electable, Felipe González also decided it was time to rein in the radical Socialist base. This in particular followed the party's rather disappointing showing in the March 1979 elections, when it failed to increase its share of the vote. On the eve of the elections, Suárez made a powerful attack on the PSOE in a television broadcast in which he accused it of being a hard-line Marxist organization. Party strategists argued that this had cost the party a large number of votes and it was, therefore, over the question of the need to remove the term Marxist from the party program that González launched his assault. In the party's 28th congress, held in May 1979, a motion sponsored by the Seville group toning down the party's definition of itself as Marxist was defeated, leading González temporarily to resign. But the congress also saw a resolution by the Seville branch to strengthen the party apparatus passed. This was then used by González's supporters (increasingly known as *filipistas*) to manufacture a largely compliant extraordinary congress in October, called finally to resolve the matter. González was, as a result, again reelected (significantly, now as "general secretary" rather than "first secretary") along with a loyal executive. Over the next three years, the *filipistas* were almost totally to impose themselves on the party. Their message of reform and modernization struck a chord with the electorate. In October 1982, aided by the breakup of the governing coalition, the **Unión del Centro Democrático** (UCD), and the crisis of the PCE, the Socialists swept to power, receiving 44 percent of the votes cast.

Once in power, the party moved further to the right. Spain faced a serious economic crisis, with high inflation and a large balance of payments deficit. Much of its heavy industrial base was also out of date. In order to deal with these problems, the government's economics and finance minister, **Miguel Boyer**, pursued what was in many respects an orthodox monetary policy, while attempting to modernize the country's productive structure through industrial restructuring (the so-called "industrial reconversion" plan) and a massive program aimed at transforming Spain's **transport** infrastructure. Like their social-democratic colleagues in central and northern Europe, the Socialists held tripartite discussions with management and unions and signed a series of social contracts between 1982 and 1985, but pursued the objective of moderating wage increases and increasing the "flexibility" of the **labor market**. This led to increasing tension with the trade unions. The Communist-influenced **Comisiones Obreras** (CC.OO) had from the start mobilized against the government. Given their close historical relationship, the UGT at first collaborated, but it became increasingly worried over continually rising unemployment and bitter that government promises to improve social benefits were not being fulfilled. As a result, the UGT signed no further social agreements with the government from 1985, and in 1988 declared a general strike in collaboration with CC.OO.

In other areas, the government also followed a moderate course, attempting to achieve reform by consensus and not overly antagonize established interests. In the field of **foreign policy**, the PSOE's 1982 electoral program was given a radical edge by its hostility toward Spanish membership in the **North Atlantic Treaty Organization** (NATO). Once in power, however, its stance on this issue was reversed. In the field of social reform, the government's performance was seen on the left as disappointing. The Socialists went about slowly building a welfare state, but in relative European terms, social security contributions by government and employers remained relatively low, the tax burden fell disproportionately on the salaried, and unemployment benefit covered only a minority. The PSOE's willingness to compromise with established interests could also be seen in the fields of abortion and **education**. It had promised abortion on demand, but the law finally approved only decriminalized abortion when the woman's life was in danger, she had been raped, or the fetus was badly deformed. The most serious clashes with the right occurred over the government's education reform law (the LODE), which forced private schools to take on nonpaying students and follow the state curriculum, but at the same time guaranteed them continued state subsidies.

The government's move away from the PSOE's left-wing origins led to tensions within the party. These were exacerbated by the result of the 1989 general election in which, although it remained in power, its share of the vote declined to 39 percent and it suffered a considerable hemorrhage of working-class support. Tensions centered on the neoliberal economic team now headed by Carlos Solchaga (1944–) and the followers of the government's vice president, Alfonso Guerra. Both these sectors agreed that the party should appeal to all social classes and not specifically to organized labor, but the *guerristas* believed it should remain within the social-democratic tradition and maintain cordial relations with the UGT. From 1990, public confidence was rocked by a series of scandals of **corruption** in high places, a number directly implicating the government. The first such scandal involved the use of official PSOE premises for private purposes by the brother of the deputy prime minister, Alfonso Guerra. This finally forced Guerra's resignation in January 1991. Even more serious, at the end of 1992 news broke that the judiciary was investigating illegal funding of the party through a holding company called **Filesa** after a police raid on the PSOE's offices in Madrid. These problems were briefly buried in time for the June 1993 general election, which the Socialists won while losing their overall majority in parliament, but in its aftermath the party remained divided between the dominant *filipista* current and the *guerristas*. Then, in April 1994, the former head of the **Civil Guard, Luis Roldán,** who was a PSOE activist, absconded in the face of allegations of massive corruption involving the adjudication of building contracts for Civil Guard barracks. This forced the resignation of the minister of the interior, Antoni Asunción (1951–). Moreover, from the end of the year the judge **Baltazar Garzón** began implicating the government in the actions of the anti-ETA terrorist group, the **GAL**. Finally, in June 1995, the prime minister was forced to accept the resignation of the vice president, Narcís Serra (1943–), along with the minister of defense, Julián García Vargas (1945–), following revelations of illegal phone tapping (of which among others King **Juan Carlos** was a victim) by the intelligence agency, the Centro Superior de Información de la Defensa (Higher Defense Intelligence Center—CESID). All of these scandals grievously damaged the reputation of the government. This became clear in the March 1996 general elections, in which the party went down to defeat, though González's continued high standing among sectors of the electorate and doubts regarding **José María Aznar** meant that the **Partido Popular** (PP) did not achieve an overall majority.

In opposition, the party found it difficult to regroup. Felipe González stepped down as general secretary at the party's 34th congress in June 1997. He was replaced by **Joaquín Almunia,** who had been an important figure in the Socialist government's economics team. His image was therefore that of the old guard's candidate and this led to considerable discontent in party ranks. Hence, he decided to give himself greater legitimacy by instituting a system of primary elections within the party to decide on its next candidate for prime minister, but he was defeated by the more charismatic and left-wing figure of **Josep Borrell**. There followed an awkward period in which the PSOE had a dual leadership, with Almunia as secretary general and Borrell the prospective Socialist prime minister. Borrell, under fire from the party hierarchy, resigned in May 1999, allowing Almunia to assume sole leadership, but the general election was only 10 months away and the instability of the previous year had cost the party credibility. In the run-up to the election, trailing behind the ruling PP, Almunia offered the leftist coalition **Izquierda Unida** (IU) an electoral pact, which, after negotiations, was limited to the Senate. However, it was not widely understood or welcomed and helped mobilize the right-wing vote. Following the electoral defeat, Almunia resigned as secretary general.

The party attained a much higher degree of stability with the election of **José Luis Rodríguez Zapatero** as general secretary in July 2000. His first move was to undertake a wide-ranging renewal of the party's leadership cadres. This was important because the new team now had few ties to the disappointments and corruption scandals of the past Socialist government. Rodríguez Zapatero was telegenic and his constructive style of opposition was generally well liked. He also began putting in place a set of viable alternative policies. He did not wish to break with the neoliberal economic consensus, but offered policy renewal on a number of fronts. First, he opposed Aznar's pro-American Atlanticist position, and in particular played an active role in the popular mobilization against the **Iraq war**. Second, he was open to suggestions—most notably advanced by the leading figure within Catalan Socialism, **Pascual Maragall**—that the **State of the Autonomies** needed reform and that the Senate should become a "Territorial House." This fitted in with the increasingly federalist nature of the Socialist party, in which leaders of the autonomous communities (the so-called "regional barons") had attained an important say in party policy. Third, as against the cultural conservatism of the PP, he advocated a more liberal approach in the spheres of education and personal freedoms. Fourth, he offered improvements in social provision. Finally, the party was very critical of the PP's control of the state-run media and he stated he wished to improve the "quality" of Spanish democracy.

As a result, Rodríguez Zapatero was able to offer a serious challenge to Aznar. Nevertheless, his inexperience raised doubts and the strength of the Spanish **economy** played in Aznar's favor. Hence, in the run-up to the March 2004 general elections, opinion polls indicated that while the PSOE was going to do better than in 2000, the PP would still win. This was changed by the **Madrid train bombings** of 11 March, three days before the general election, and the government's increasingly untenable claim that **ETA** was responsible. Most notably, it produced the mobilization of young culturally liberal voters, who were against the Iraq war.

As a result, the party came to power in a climate of, on the one hand, euphoria, and, on the other, bitter anger on the right that they had been "robbed." This was to set the tone for the legislature. The government's first moves were extremely popular. It quickly pulled Spanish troops out of Iraq and reestablished close ties with France and Germany. Second, it honored its commitment to reform the State of the Autonomies, but was careful not to give too much away (especially not to allow **Catalonia** power to raise all its own taxes). Third, it pushed through with what it saw as a modernizing cultural agenda, cracking down on violent assaults on **women** by their husbands, making divorce easier, legalizing gay civil weddings, and promulgating a new education law, which introduced a new citizenship course that would involve discussion of same-sex parenting, and made it possible to opt out of classes in religion. Most controversially, it passed a law that would compensate and improve the pensions of victims of the civil war and help local councils identify and excavate civil war burial sites. In all these respects, the government showed itself more willing to challenge the right than Felipe González had. Fourth, it loosened the government's grip on state **radio** and **television** (RTVB), by having its president elected by parliament rather than chosen by the prime minister. Finally, it established contacts with ETA during 2005 with the hope of securing the permanent end to violence in the **Basque Country**. ETA responded by declaring a "permanent" cease-fire in March 2006. Peace was now in sight, but was snatched away when ETA bombed Madrid Barajas airport in December 2006.

These measures produced a counteroffensive by the PP and the **Catholic Church**, which mobilized mass demonstrations against many of the PSOE's policies. The PSOE wanted to compromise with the Church, but this had little effect. The decision by ETA to break its cease-fire was a major blow to the government, laying it open to charges by the PP that it had been fooled by ETA. In the immediate aftermath of these events, for the first time since the March 2004 elections, the PP drew level in the opinion polls. However, during 2007, the government took a slim lead, which in July stood at 3.5 percent. Its strategy was to portray PP policies as extremist and attract center voters. This could be seen in the aftermath of a big meeting held by the Church "in defense of the Christian family" at the end of 2007. The PSOE accused the PP of supporting it and challenged it to include the Church's demands in its electoral program.

During the run-up to the March 2008 elections, the government promised increased social spending in areas like child care and housing subsidies for the young, and also used its budget surplus to give Spaniards a tax rebate of 400 euros. However, its position was weakened by the rapidly deteriorating economic situation, and, from February, by PP accusations that it had allowed an "avalanche" of **immigrants** to enter Spain. As a result, it lost a little ground and in the elections (despite the fact that it benefited from tactical voting by centrist and center-left voters determined to keep out the PP) failed to gain an overall majority. Nevertheless, it won relatively comfortably. This means that Rodríguez Zapatero will govern for a further four years. However, he will need to reach agreements with the minority parties, most notably the Catalan nationalist **Convergència i Unió**. *See also* LABOR MOVEMENT; TABLES 8, 9, AND 10.

PARTIDO SOCIALISTA OBRERO ESPAÑOL-HISTÓRICO (PSOE-H)/HISTORIC SOCIALIST PARTY. This party was formed in December 1972 by **Rodolfo Llopis** and the aging Toulouse leadership of the **Partido Socialista Obrero Español** (PSOE), after the "interior" had broken away to form its own party. From the start, it had less support, and the decision of the Socialist International to back its rival was a massive blow. Compared to the dynamism of the **Felipe González**-led PSOE, the PSOE-H seemed sluggish and out of touch. This was confirmed in the June 1977 elections, when it received just 112,000 votes. The party revived somewhat in the early 1980s when it became a home to a significant number of Socialists disgusted with the rightward drift of the PSOE. In 1983, it changed its name to **Partido de Acción Socialista** (PASOC).

PARTIDO SOCIALISTA POPULAR (PSP)/PEOPLE'S SOCIAL-IST PARTY. *See* PARTIDO SOCIALISTA OBRERO ESPAÑOL; TIERNO GALVÁN, ENRIQUE.

PARTIT DELS COMUNISTES CATALANS/PARTY OF THE CATALAN COMMUNISTS. *See* PARTIDO COMUNISTA DE ESPAÑA; PARTIT SOCIALISTA UNIFICAT DE CATALUNYA.

PARTIT DELS SOCIALISTES DE CATALUNYA-PARTIDO SO-CIALISTA OBRERO ESPAÑOL (PSC-PSOE)/PARTY OF THE CATALAN SOCIALISTS-SPANISH SOCIALIST WORKERS' PARTY). Two Catalan Socialist parties operated under the name PSC in the mid-1970s. The largest, the PSC-Congrés, captained by the experienced activist, Joan Reventós i Carner (1927–2004), was **federalist** and **Catalanist**, and at first did not wish to join what it considered the overly centralist Spanish Socialist party, the **Partido Socialista Obrero Español** (PSOE). From March 1976, it therefore integrated into a federation of regional Socialist parties. However, during this year, the PSOE tried to bring the Catalan parties onboard by federalizing its party structures. This was to prove almost totally successful. At the end of 1976, Reventós was brought into the fold. Then, in July 1978, the other major components of the Catalan social-ist family, the PSC-Renovació and the Federació Socialista Catalana (Catalan Socialist Federation), were integrated. As in the case of other "regional" Socialist parties, it was able to retain its name, PSC, as long as it tagged PSOE onto the end. More importantly, it main-tained the right to follow its own political strategy in **Catalonia**.

Reventós was elected general secretary, a post he retained until 1983 when he was replaced by Raimon Obiols i Germa (1940–), who held the post until 1996. He was in turn replaced by the former Social-ist minister **Narcís Serra**. The party has since 1979 gained the most Catalan votes in general elections and won the **Barcelona** municipal elections. Particularly successful was its management of the Barce-lona city council under the stewardship of **Pascual Maragall**. It was while Maragall was in charge that Barcelona held the Olympic Games in June 1992, which was a major component of the local administration's dynamic program to both regenerate the city and establish its reputation as one of Europe's leading cultural capitals and leisure destinations. However, between 1980 and 1995, it was beaten by the Catalan nationalist coalition **Convergència i Unió** (CiU) in elections to the autonomous Catalan parliament. In part, the problem was that much of its base was made up of migrant workers from southern Spain and that many of these workers abstained during regional elections. In addition, a sector of the liberal Catalan electorate voted PSOE-PSC in general elections and CiU in Catalan elections. In this respect, the party was damaged during 1981 when the PSOE supported the bill sponsored by the ruling **Unión del Centro Democrático** (UCD) coalition—the so-called LOAPA—to rein back the decentralization process that followed the enactment of the **State of the Autonomies**. Furthermore, it was dragged down by the growing unpopularity of the PSOE during the early 1990s.

From its inception, within the party there has been tension between a more middle-class-liberal Catalanist wing and a more pro-Spanish working-class wing. The Catalanists have generally held the upper hand, with Reventós, Obiols, and Maragall belonging to this tendency. Indeed, when Pascual Maragall left his post as mayor to lead the PSC-PSOE challenge in the 1999 autonomous elections, he not only traded on his reputation as mayor, but also hoped to galvanize the liberal Catalanist vote by demanding that the Catalan autonomy statute be renegotiated to give Catalonia more financial autonomy and that the Senate be reformed to represent the autonomous communities. The PSC-PSOE gained more votes than CiU (but less seats) in both the 1999 and 2003 elections to the Catalan parliament, and Maragall took over as president of the Catalan government (the **Generalitat**) in December 2003, after reaching a pact (the so-called *tripartit*) with the leftist Catalanist groupings **Esquerra Republicana de Catalunya** (ERC) and **Iniciativa per Catalunya-Verds**.

However, growing abstention among migrant workers from Barcelona's "red belt" in the 2003 elections, combined with Maragall's "Blairist" political outlook, led to criticism from the party's more left-wing and anti-Catalanist elements. Maragall's period in office proved very turbulent. He had supported quite a radical new Catalan autonomy statute (which was approved by the Catalan parliament in the autumn of 2003), but then had to compromise with the new PSOE government of **José Luis Rodríguez Zapatero**, which was unhappy with the financial arrangements. This led to division with the ERC, which refused to support the new statute. In the run-up to the 1 November 2006 autonomous elections, under fire from within his own party, Maragall announced he would not again run for the presidency. He was replaced by José Montilla (1955–), the PSC's first secretary since June 2000 and a figure close to Rodríguez Zapatero. In these elections the party lost votes, but in its aftermath the *tripartit* pact was reformed, allowing Montilla to take over from Maragall as president of the Generalitat. In the March 2008 general elections, the party gained a resounding victory (gaining 25 of the 47 Catalan seats), as many Catalans voted tactically in order to prevent the **Partido Popular**, associated with Spanish nationalist centralism, from coming to power.

PARTIT SOCIALISTA UNIFICAT DE CATALUNYA (PSUC)/ UNIFIED SOCIALIST PARTY OF CATALONIA. The PSUC was founded on 22 July 1936 after discussions involving several small Catalan socialist and communist parties and the Catalan branch of the **Partido Socialista Obrero Español** (PSOE). These parties had over the previous two years increasingly come under the influence of the **Partido Comunista de España** (PCE), with which the PSUC established close ties. It was largely a party of the skilled Catalan working-class and white-collar workers and as such developed a strong **Catalanist** identity. These twin elements of organizational independence and Catalanism were personified by Joan Comorera (1895–1960), the party's leader from 1936 until his expulsion in 1950. Thereafter, the party became more dependent on the PCE. Like the PCE, the PSUC adopted a Eurocommunist stance and, as in the rest of Spain, it established itself as the dominant leftist party in **Catalonia** during the 1960s.

After the death of General **Francisco Franco**, under the charismatic leadership of **Antoni Gutiérrez Díaz** ("El Guti"), it looked briefly as if it would become the territory's principal party. However, it was undermined by the polemics that followed its disappointing showing in the June 1977 elections. In the party's fifth congress in January 1981, hard-line pro-Soviets under Pere Ardiaca (1909–1986), strongly supported by **Comisiones Obreras** (CC.OO), were able to take over the party. The Eurocommunists, under "El Guti," made a comeback in the following year, but the pro-Soviets, as in the rest of Spain, then broke away and in Catalonia formed the Partit dels Comunistes de Catalunya (Party of the Catalan Communists—PCC). As in the case of the PCE, the result could be seen in the disastrous showing in the October 1982 elections. The PSUC nevertheless maintained its Eurocommunist identification. In 1986, the party elected Rafael Ribó (1945–) as its new secretary general, after which it made greater efforts to integrate "new social movements," such as the green movement and **feminism**. In the general elections of this year, it formed a coalition with the nationalist grouping Entesa de Nacionalistes d'Esquerra (Understanding of Left Nationalists). From 1987, the party then presented itself within a wider Catalan coalition, **Iniciativa per Catalunya** (IC), and from 1993 it also allied with the ecological confederation Els Verds. This has assured it a relatively modest but not insignificant place in the Catalan political spectrum. In the 2003 elections to the autonomous parliament, under Joan Saura (1950–) the coalition gained 7.3 percent of the vote, and after negotiations with **Pascual Maragall**'s **Partit dels Socialistes de Catalunya-Partido Socialista Obrero Español** (PSC-PSOE) and the separatist **Esquerra Republicana de Catalunya** (ERC) entered the Catalan government (the **Generalitat**).

Following the election of Ribó in 1986, it also distanced itself from the PCE, given what was seen as the latter's sectarian, intransigent stance under **Julio Anguita**. This divide intensified after the collapse of the Eastern Bloc, after which Ribó, like the so-called *críticos* with the PCE, called for the Spanish left to work together more effectively, in the future possibly leading to a reunification. Finally, in 1997, IC-Verds broke away from the PCE-dominated Spanish left-wing federation **Izquierda Unida**. In the same year, the PSUC dropped its long-term goal of the establishment of communism and fully integrated into IC-Verds. This meant that in reality it no longer existed as a separate party. In 2002, under the leadership of Saura, it was formally wound up and the coalition IC-Verds became a single party.

PEASANTRY. *See* AGRICULTURE; ANARCHISM; ASOCIACIÓN CATÓLICA NACIONAL DE PROPAGANDISTAS; CARLISM;

DESAMORTIZACIÓN; FEDERACIÓN NACIONAL DE TRA-
BAJADORES DE LA TIERRA; LATIFUNDIA; MINIFUNDIA;
RABASSAIRES.

PEIRÓ I BELIS, JOAN. *See* CONFEDERACIÓN NACIONAL DEL
TRABAJO; TREINTISTAS.

PENINSULARES. *See* JUNTAS DE DEFENSA; MILITARY.

PENINSULAR WAR. *See* WAR OF INDEPENDENCE.

PÉREZ GALDÓS, BENITO (1843–1920). Pérez Galdós is regarded
by many as the greatest Spanish novelist since **Miguel de Cervantes**.
His work was very much in the realist, naturalist tradition and gave a
vivid portrait of the Spain of his time, most especially **Madrid** urban
society. His work was informed by his progressive, **liberal** ideology,
which led him to mount a strong critique of traditional, aristocratic
society and to praise what he saw as the rationalist, democratic spirit
of the people. This led him directly into politics. He joined **Nicolás
Salmerón**'s **Unión Republicana** in 1906 and in 1910 he was elected
to parliament as a deputy for Madrid. His works also became more
overtly political from the turn of the century, with his anticlerical
play *Electra* (1901) opening to popular riots against the **Catholic
Church** in Madrid. His greatest work is usually regarded as *Fortu-
nata y Jacinta* (1886–1887).

PÉREZ RUBALCABA, ALFREDO (1951–). Rubalcaba is one of the
leading figures in the **Partido Socialista Obrero Español** (PSOE)
government. He was born in Santander and became a lecturer in
chemistry at the Complutense University of Madrid. After joining the
PSOE, from 1982 he took up a series of important posts in the area of
educational policy. Subsequently, he became minister of education
and science between 1992 and 1993, and minister of the presidency
between 1993 and 1996. With the PSOE victory in the March 2004
elections, he was made both government spokesman and head of the
Socialist group in the Lower House of parliament. This has made
him the most visible presence in the government behind **José Luis
Rodríguez Zapatero**. In April 2006, he took over as minister of

the interior. This put him in change of the failed attempt to bring a negotiated end to **ETA terrorism**. He is well liked on the left for his effective attacks on the opposition **Partido Popular**.

PHILIPPINES. The Philippines were occupied by Spain in 1563. This opened up a trade route for Chinese exports, most notably spices and silk. From 1593, a yearly connection was established between Manila and Veracruz in Mexico (the so-called "Manila run"). In 1871, an indigenous nationalist resistance movement (the *tagalog*) began to make its presence felt on the islands. With Spain also occupied with trying to pacify revolt in **Cuba**, a full-blown insurrection was ignited in the summer of 1896. It was controlled by the Spanish occupiers, but following the **Spanish-American War** of 1898, Spain was forced to renounce her sovereignty over the islands. *See also* COLONIES; DECOLONIZATION.

PI I MARGALL, FRANCESC (1824–1901). Pi i Margall rose to become one of the foremost leaders of Spanish **republicanism** in the late 19th century. He was born in **Barcelona**, the son of a textile worker, but soon stood out from those around him. He studied law in Barcelona, and went on to take a doctorate in **Madrid** in 1847. He came from a radical family background, and in Madrid he became involved in democratic politics. He was a central figure in both the uprising of 1854 and the **San Gil revolt** in 1864. Moreover, he quickly became a leading theoretical light within the Spanish republican movement and the outstanding personality within the **Partido Republicano Federalista** after its foundation in 1869. Strongly influenced by Pierre-Joseph Proudhon (a number of whose works he translated), he defended a decentralized vision of the republican future, in which the rights of the individual were inalienable.

Following the proclamation of the **First Republic** in February 1873, he first became minister of the interior and then, on 11 April, was elected prime minister. Over the following months he attempted to separate Church and state, decentralize the state administration, introduce social legislation, and set up arbitration boards to deal with labor disputes. His position was, however, undermined by divisions within his own party, and especially by the **Cantonalist revolt** launched by hard-line "intransigent" republicans, for whom the pace of reform was too slow. As a result, he was forced to resign on 18 July. During the **Cánovas Restoration**, unlike many of his erstwhile colleagues he remained faithful to his federalist beliefs, combating the regime in both parliament and in the **press**. He was a highly principled man who demonstrated great courage in his convictions, gaining him widespread respect in reforming and left-wing circles. Most notably, in the federal republican mouthpiece, *El Nuevo Régimen*, founded in Madrid in 1890, he supported the cause of **Cuban** independence and attacked Spain's entry into war with the United States in 1898, despite the harassment and censorship his paper and party suffered. Among his best known works are *La reacción y la revolución* (*Reaction and Revolution*, 1854) and *Las nacionalidades* (*The Nationalities*, 1875). *See also* SPANISH-AMERICAN WAR.

PICASSO, PABLO RUIZ (1881–1973). Pablo Picasso is probably the greatest Spanish artist of the 20th century. He was born in Málaga, moved on to La Coruña, and, in 1895, when his father was appointed professor of the Academy of Fine Arts, settled in **Barcelona**. From an early age, he showed exceptional talent and in 1899 he became acquainted with European trends through his association with several young *modernista* artists and, subsequently, his integration into the inner circle of the artistic *modernista* movement in the Els Quatre Gats café. During 1899, he also visited France for the first time, and moved there in 1904. Until 1939, he regularly returned to Spain, but with the installation of the **Franco regime** he vowed never again to set foot in the country until democracy had been restored.

His work is usually divided into a number of stages. In his Blue Period of 1901 to 1904, Picasso painted nudes, portraits, and scenes of social degradation and hardship in a naturalistic, expressionist style. After moving to Paris—during his so-called Rose Period—his work became lighter, centering on themes such as the circus and acrobats. Then, from 1907, Picasso became one of the founders—and perhaps the most distinguished practitioner—of the cubist movement, which was totally to revolutionize European art. His work in part drew inspiration from Spanish traditions (the **bullfight** was a constant theme) and from pre-Roman Iberian art. He was also influenced by African sculpture, and, during the 1920s and 1930s, took onboard the

European avant-garde movements such as Dada and surrealism. During the **Second Republic** and **Spanish Civil War**, Picasso strongly supported the Republican cause. His most remarkable contribution to that cause was his painting for the Spanish pavilion at the 1937 World Fair in Paris. Called "Guernica," it was inspired by the Nazi Condor Legion's bombing of the **Basque** market town of Guernika that spring. In order to show his opposition to General **Francisco Franco**, Picasso joined the Partie Communiste Francaise (French Communist Party) in 1944. He remained in self-imposed exile in France for the rest of his life.

PIDAL Y MON, ALEJANDRO (1846–1913). Alejandro Pidal would be a key figure linking the hierarchy of the **Catholic Church** with the **Cánovas Restoration** in the late 19th and early 20th centuries. He was born in **Madrid** into an elite aristocratic family from Asturias. He was a **Traditionalist**, but after the establishment of the Restoration regime led the more pragmatic wing of the movement, which wanted to reform the regime from within. In the 1870s, he established the Catholic party called the Unión Católica (Catholic Union) with the aim of forming a Catholic front that was doctrinally anti-**liberal**, but pragmatic in terms of strategy, and that would participate in the electoral process. He gained the support of Pope Leo XIII and the Spanish Catholic hierarchy, but his views were rejected by much of the Catholic right. Hence, he was expelled from the **Carlist** movement in 1883, leading him to integrate the Unión Católica into **Antonio Cánovas's Partido Conservador** in the following year. Henceforth, along with the **Second Marquis of Comillas**, he would be an influential voice on the right of the party, and would be close to both **Francisco Silvela** and, subsequently, **Antonio Maura**.

PIÑAR LÓPEZ, BLAS (1918–). Blas Piñar was the best known right-wing *ultra* during the 1970s, captaining a movement called Fuerza Nueva (New Force), which vociferously and violently combated the **transition to democracy**. *See also* BUNKER.

PIQUÉ I CAMPS, JOSEP (1955–). Piqué was the leading figure within the Catalan **Partido Popular** (PP) between 2000 and 2007. Born in the Catalan town of Vilanova i la Geltrú, he has a PhD in business and economics. Though linked to the **Partit Socialista Unificat de Catalunya** (PSUC) in his youth, he subsequently moved to the right, launching a successful career in business, establishing contacts with both **Convergència i Unió** (CiU) and the Catalan PP, and taking up the post of director general of industry in the **Generalitat**. When **José María Aznar** became prime minister in 1996, he was an independent but close to the Catalan PP. Because of his moderate image and competence he was promoted by Aznar, who hoped that under his leadership the party would make a greater impact in **Catalonia** than hitherto. He was made minister of industry, energy, and tourism, and then, after affiliating with the party, became its spokesperson in parliament in 1998. After the PP achieved an overall majority in March 2000, he became foreign minister, and in 2002—in the run-up to the November 2003 elections to the Catalan autonomous government, in which he would be the PP's candidate for president—he was given the less demanding post of minister of science and technology, while also taking over the presidency of the PP's Catalan branch.

Piqué attempted to break with the PP's anti-**Catalanist** image in Catalonia, trying to establish a link between the PP's ideology and practice and the more moderate, regionalist strand of Catalanism (which he saw as personified by **Francesc Cambó**). However, he was undermined by the increasingly vociferous Spanish nationalist discourse adopted by the Spanish PP and the polemics between the PP and Catalan and **Basque** nationalists. In the November 2003 elections, the PP got almost 12 percent of the vote (up from 9.5 percent in 1999), but this still left it in fourth place. In subsequent years he became estranged from the PP leadership, faced strong opposition within the Catalan PP, and received constant attacks from right-wing media outlets like **COPE** and *Libertad Digital*, which portrayed him as a Catalanist infiltrator. He finally resigned as president of the Catalan PP in July 2007.

PLATAFORMA DEMOCRÁTICA/DEMOCRATIC PLATFORM. *See* JUNTA DEMOCRÁTICA.

POLICE. During the 19th and early 20th centuries, the state's inability to create a civilian police force made it more difficult to establish democratic institutions. The main police force was the **Civil Guard**, which was put under **military** command. Furthermore, faced with civil disturbances, the state tended to declare states of emergency and call out the army. Between 1914 and 1923, as social strife grew, it was increasingly complemented by para-police forces (the most notorious of which was the Catalan Sometent), which, although nominally under military command, were in reality under the control of local social elites. During the **Franco regime**, this tradition of military control over much of the police was maintained, with the Civil Guard complemented by a new urban Policía Armada (Armed Police, or *grises* [greys] as they were known in opposition circles).

Change was slow after the dictator's death in 1975. In 1978, the Armed Police was renamed National Police (National Police Corps from 1986, when they were amalgamated with the plain-clothed police). However, the Civil Guard was maintained and given the lead role in the fight against **ETA** (a fact with had much to do with the appearance of the state-sponsored anti-ETA terrorist group, the **GAL**, in the 1980s). From the **transition to democracy**, the local police (Policía Municipal) has also been strengthened and an "autonomous" police has also begun to operate in the **Basque Country** and **Catalonia** (the Ertzaintza and Mossos d'Esquadra respectively). The operation of two parallel countrywide police forces has probably not helped improve efficiency. Though the police has shown it can operate very effectively in combating major crime (seen in drug busts and the growing success in fighting ETA), there are numerous complaints among the population that it does little to fight low-level street crime. These problems are exacerbated by the slow and cumbersome operation of the Spanish judiciary.

POLITICAL PARTIES. *See* ACCIÓ CATALANA; ACCIÓN NACIONAL; ACCIÓN POPULAR; ACCIÓN REPUBLICANA; ALIANZA POPULAR; BANDERA ROJA; BLOC OBRER I CAMPEROL; BLOQUE NACIONALISTA GALEGO; CARLISM; CENTRE NACIONALISTA REPUBLICÀ; CENTRO DEMOCRÁTICO Y SOCIAL; CHRISTIAN DEMOCRACY; CIUDADANOS DE CATALUÑA; COALICIÓN CANARIA; CONFEDERACIÓN ESPAÑOLA DE DERECHAS AUTÓNOMAS; CONVERGÈNCIA I UNIÓ; ESQUERRA REPUBLICANA DE CATALUNYA; ESTAT

CATALÀ; EUSKADIKO ESQUERRA; EUSKO ALKARTASUNA; FALANGE ESPAÑOLA; FALANGE ESPAÑOLA TRADICIONA-LISTA Y DE LAS JUNTAS DE OFENSIVA NACIONAL SINDI-CALISTA; FRENTE DE LIBERACIÓN POPULAR; FRONT OB-RER DE CATALUNYA; FUERZA NUEVA; HERRI BATASUNA; INICIATIVA PER CATALUNYA-VERDS; INTEGRISM; IZQUI-ERDA REPUBLICANA; IZQUIERDA UNIDA; LLIGA CATA-LANA; LLIGA REGIONALISTA; MAURISTAS; MOVIMENT SOCIALISTA DE CATALUNYA; MOVIMIENTO COMUNISTA DE ESPAÑA; PARTIDO COMUNISTA DE ESPAÑA; PARTIDO COMUNISTA DE LOS PUEBLOS DE ESPAÑA; PARTIDO CON-SERVADOR; PARTIDO CONSTITUCIONALISTA; PARTIDO DE ACCIÓN SOCIALISTA; PARTIDO DEMÓCRATA; PARTIDO DEMÓCRATA CRISTIANO; PARTIDO GALEGUISTA; PAR-TIDO LIBERAL; PARTIDO LIBERAL DEMÓCRATA; PARTIDO MODERADO; PARTIDO NACIONALISTA VASCO; PARTIDO OBRERO DE UNIFICACIÓN MARXISTA; PARTIDO POPULAR; PARTIDO PROGRESISTA; PARTIDO RADICAL; PARTIDO RE-FORMISTA; PARTIDO REPUBLICANO CENTRALISTA; PAR-TIDO REPUBLICANO FEDERAL DEMOCRÁTICO; PARTIDO REPUBLICANO FEDERALISTA; PARTIDO REPUBLICANO PROGRESISTA; PARTIDO REPUBLICANO RADICAL; PAR-TIDO SOCIAL DEMÓCRATA; PARTIDO SOCIAL POPULAR; PARTIDO SOCIALISTA DE ANDALUCÍA; PARTIDO SOCIAL-ISTA OBRERO ESPAÑOL; PARTIDO SOCIALISTA OBRERO ESPAÑOL-HISTÓRICO; PARTIDO SOCIALISTA POPULAR; PARTIT DELS COMUNISTES CATALANS; PARTIT DELS SOCIALISTES DE CATALUNYA-PARTIDO SOCIALISTA OBRERO ESPAÑOL; PARTIT SOCIALISTA UNIFICAT DE CATALUNYA; RENOVACIÓN ESPAÑOLA; SOLIDARITAT CATALANA; UNIÓ CATALANISTA; UNIÓ FEDERAL NA-CIONALISTA REPUBLICÀ; UNIÓN DE PROGRESO Y DE-MOCRACIA; UNIÓN DEL CENTRO DEMOCRÁTICO; UNIÓN DEL PUEBLO ESPAÑOL; UNIÓN DEL PUEBLO NAVARRO; UNIÓN DEMOCRÁTICA ESPAÑOLA; UNIÓN DO POBO GA-LEGO; UNIÓN LIBERAL; UNIÓN MONÁRQUICA NACIONAL; UNIÓN NACIONAL; UNIÓN PATRIÓTICA; UNIÓN REPUBLI-CANA; UNIÓN SOCIAL DEMÓCRATA ESPAÑOLA.

POPULAR ARMY. The Popular Army was formed by the **Popular Front** government of **Francisco Largo Caballero** in September 1936. It was set up on the initiative of the **Partido Comunista de España** (PCE) and modeled on the Soviet Red Army. The Communists argued that the revolutionary militias, which had sprung up after the July military uprising, were disorganized and had no chance of defeating General **Francisco Franco**'s Army of Africa. Only by setting up a disciplined regular army based on conscription, under the authority of trained officers and controlled from the Ministry of War, would it be possible to turn the tide. The ineffectiveness of these militias in halting Franco's advance when compared to the prestige attained by the PCE's **Fifth Regiment** certainly swung many, including Largo Caballero, behind the PCE's demand. Moreover, the creation of the Popular Army also had the advantage for the PCE that it would be centrally controlled and, given the key role of the Soviet Union in providing arms and supplies, be under Communist influence. The Communists' point was seemingly proved when, aided by the arrival of the first troops in the **International Brigades**, the new Popular Army was able to repulse the **Nationalist** assault on **Madrid** when it began on 7 November. The PCE exercised its power through the Soviet military advisors and large numbers of pro-Communist political commissars. Moreover, the PCE's discipline and growing strength attracted leading Republican army officers, such as the hero of the defense of Madrid, José Miaja (1878–1958). Hence, throughout the war the Popular Army, and in particular the Army of the Center, was strongly pro-Communist. This influence was only broken with the **Casado coup** in March 1939, when the Republic's military machine had largely been destroyed and an advance on Madrid by the Francoist forces was imminent.

POPULAR FRONT. Despite the fact that the name Popular Front was reminiscent of the strategy propounded by the Comintern from the autumn of 1934, the Spanish Popular Front was essentially an attempt to put back together the coalition of 1931–1933 between the **republicans** and the **Partido Socialista Obrero Español** (PSOE). The two most significant figures were **Manuel Azaña** and **Indalecio Prieto**. The need for the PSOE and republicans to join forces came

POPULAR FRONT • 525

back on the agenda after the defeat of the **October 1934 revolution.** The revolution's failure weakened the position of the Socialist left and its principal figure, **Francisco Largo Caballero,** because the only way the left could regain power now seemed to be through the ballot box, and that would only be possible if Socialists and republicans worked together. Since his release from prison in April 1934, Azaña had been seeking to woo Socialist support. His first move had been to unify the various left republican parties under his leadership. He was also in constant contact with the more moderate wing of the PSOE headed by Prieto. Prieto agreed in principle to an understanding, and a series of open-air meetings that attracted massive crowds were then held by Azaña in the summer of 1935 in order to publicize his program.

However, the main problem they faced was how to win over the *caballerista* wing of the PSOE and its labor confederation, the **Unión General de Trabajadores** (UGT). Largo Caballero, at least rhetorically, still aimed to "bolshevize" the PSOE and had developed close links with the **Partido Comunista de España** (PCE). He had revolted against the 1931–1933 coalition and during the summer and autumn of 1935 was in no mood to endorse a rerun. Matters were, however, to change drastically in November 1935. The **Partido Republicano Radical** had been undermined by a series of financial scandals and could no longer form a government. **Niceto Alcalá Zamora** did not trust the democratic credentials of the **Confederación Española de Derechas Autónomas** (CEDA) and so he reacted by calling elections. If the PSOE went into these elections alone, it would be defeated. Largo Caballero, therefore, finally agreed to a pact in a joint meeting of the committees of the PSOE, UGT, and Socialist Youth on 16 November. However, the *caballeristas* made two demands: first, that the pact should be circumscribed to the elections and that the republicans should then govern alone, and second, that all working-class parties and unions who wished to participate should be included. In the elections of 16 February 1936, the left won by a small number of votes, but this gave them a large advantage in terms of seats. Yet the republican government that emerged was in a weak position to counter military conspiracy and hence prevent the outbreak of the **Spanish Civil War.**

POPULATION. With an estimated 45.2 million inhabitants at the end of 2007, Spain is the fifth most populous nation within the **European Union**. However, in a western European context, it is still relatively sparsely populated, with 79 inhabitants per square mile in 2002, with a stark contrast between the heavily populated areas of Madrid and its surrounding area, the Mediterranean and Atlantic littorals, and (with the exception of Madrid) the sparsely populated central plain (*meseta*).

Between the 15th and 19th centuries, Spain's population did not grow at the same pace as those of its larger western European neighbors. During the 16th and 17th centuries, an underdeveloped manufacturing base and the low productivity of **agriculture**, combined with heavy taxes on the peasantry of the **Crown of Castile**, levied in order to fight the **Habsburg** rulers' continuous European wars, were to blame. In the 19th century, the uneven pattern of Spanish industrial development (limited to a significant degree to **Catalonia** and the **Basque Country**) was the key factor. As a result, Spain retained many of the features of a preindustrial society, with very high birth and death rates. In addition, the late 19th and early 20th centuries saw high levels of emigration to **Latin America** (three million between the 1880s and **World War I**).

From the 1900s through to the 1970s, as economic development gathered pace, new medical advances greatly reduced premature deaths, and the country slowly built a **welfare state**, Spain underwent what has often been referred to as a "first demographic transition," with death rates falling much more quickly than birth rates. As a result, the Spanish population rose from 18.6 million in 1900 to 37.7 million in 1980. With post-Francoist improvements to the welfare state, a benign climate, and relatively good diet, life expectancy in Spain is now among the highest in the world (in 2002, 75.6 years for men and 82.8 years for women).

During the 1980s, the "second demographic transition" kicked in, with a dramatic decline in fertility rates, from 2.8 children per woman in 1975 to 1.24 children per woman in 2001 (along with Italy, the lowest rate in the European Union). This was the key factor in the stagnation of Spanish population growth during the 1980s. In 1991, the Spanish population stood at 38.9 million inhabitants, only just over one million more inhabitants than in 1981. However, largely as a result of increased **immigration,** Spanish population growth began to rise significantly from the 1990s, a trend which has, since 2000, further accelerated. Between 2000 and 2007, it has grown by a little over four million inhabitants. *See also* TABLE 1.

PORTUGAL. Spain's relations with Portugal have very much been marked by the fact that the Kingdom of Portugal was integrated into the **Habsburg** dominions (at the heart of which was the **Crown of Castile**) between 1580 and 1640, but after an uprising in that year it was, with English and French aid, able to regain its independence. Even since, given Portugal's small size, there has been suspicion of Spain's expansionist pretensions (given credence during the "war of the oranges" in 1801, when, in alliance with France, Spain seized the Alentejo district of Olivença). This fact helps explain why, until the 1990s, the two countries lived with their backs to each other, with limited trade and cultural interchange. In Spain, on the other hand, for much of the modern age, the hope existed that the two countries might be reunited. On the authoritarian right, force was contemplated. In the early phase of **World War II,** between 1939 and 1941, the **Franco regime** discussed the possibility that if it entered the war on the side of a victorious Axis, while Great Britain (and therefore her ally Portugal) went down to defeat, Spain could, at the very least, achieve a dominant position within Portugal. Some liberals, for their part, hoped that Portugal would by her own voli-tion rejoin a democratic, decentralized Spain. This was the position taken by **Francesc Pi i Margall** and the **federal republicans** from the 1870s, and echoed by **Catalan** nationalists like **Enric Prat de la Riba** and **Francesc Cambó** in the 1900s. The latter maintained that with an end to Castilian domination and home rule for all of Spain's "nations," Portugal could be persuaded to rejoin a new, rejuvenated Iberian state.

Spain and Portugal's entry into the **European Economic Community** has meant that such ideas have subsided. However, from the mid-1990s, as the Spanish **economy** strengthened and several major international players emerged from within Spanish business, there has been a growth in **foreign trade** and surge of Spanish foreign direct investment in Portugal. Banco de Bilbao Vizcaya Argentaria (BBVA) and Banco Santander Central Hispano (BSCH) have targeted the

Portuguese **banking** sector, while the major banks, petrochemical and power companies, and the big telecommunications company, Telefónica, have bought up or into Portuguese business as a springboard for the Brazilian market. This has raised fears in Portugal that what Spain was unable to achieve politically it will now achieve economically.

PRAT DE LA RIBA I SERRA, ENRIC (1870–1917). Prat de la Riba was the foremost intellectual behind the construction of a conservative **Catalanist** political movement from the late 19th century. He was born in the rural town of Castellterçol in **Catalonia** into a prosperous conservative **Catholic** family and went on to study law in Barcelona and then **Madrid**. Strongly influenced by the Romantic writers of the **Renaixença**, he was attracted to Catalanism. In 1887, he joined the Center Escolar Catalanista (Catalanist Center for Schooling) and in 1891, he was elected secretary of the Unió Catalanista (Catalanist Union) and played a leading role in organizing the assembly that prepared a blueprint for Catalan autonomy, the Bases de Manresa (Manresa Demands), in 1892. In 1899, he led a breakaway from the Unió by a group of activists who favored participation in elections, setting up the Centre Nacionalista Català (Catalan Nationalist Center). Over the next two years, Prat de la Riba played a key role in forging a new major Catalanist party, which fused conservative Catalanists, rural Catholic traditionalists, and sectors of the urban middle class (in which manufacturing interests were to the fore). It was formed in 1901 and called the **Lliga Regionalista**.

Prat de la Riba was elected to the Barcelona Provincial Council (Diputació Provincial de Barcelona) in 1905. Two years later, he became president of the council and began working to achieve a measure of administrative autonomy for Catalonia through the fusion of the four Catalan provincial councils into a single body, to be known as the **Mancomunitat**. His demands were to a large extent granted by the Spanish parliament in December 1913, when it was agreed that a single body could take over many of the Catalan councils' functions. Prat de la Riba was elected president on 5 April 1914, a post that he was to retain until his death.

As the same time, he carried out a prodigious editorial task. His best-known work, *La nacionalitat catalana* (*Catalan Nationality*), published in 1906, outlined Prat's conservative, organicist vision of the Catalan nation. It has remained the key work in the Catalan nationalist cannon. In this and other works, he developed two further themes, which were to provide the blueprint for his colleague **Francesc Cambó**'s attempt to reform Spain, and which have remained influential in Catalanist thought to this day. First, he believed that if freed from the stifling control of Spanish central governments, Catalonia would be able to develop a dynamic economy and culture. Second, he argued that an autonomous Catalonia should play a leading role in modernizing Spain and turning it into a major imperialist power. Shortly before his death, in 1916 he wrote the Lliga's "Catalunya i L'Espanya gran" ("Catalonia and a Great Spain") manifesto, synthesizing these themes.

PRESS. Until the 1880s, the Spanish press had only been able to operate relatively openly during brief liberal interludes (the most important of which was the **Democratic Sexennium** between 1868 and 1874). The 1883 Press Law, introduced by the **Partido Liberal**, made possible the emergence of a lively press scene in urban areas, although, under the **Cánovas Restoration**, newspapers would still be heavily censored during the frequent states of emergency. The various parties (often factions of parties) had newspapers attached to them, but most popular were the independent papers. A number of best-selling publications were **liberal** or even **republican** in outlook. The latter included *El Heraldo de Madrid*. The highest quality left-liberal publication was, from 1917, *El Sol*, but because of its elite, intellectual content it did not have a wide audience. However, the Catholic right also had considerable influence. The **integrist** paper *El Siglo Futuro* sold well in the late 19th century, and from 1910 *El Debate* would become the major vehicle of conservative Catholic thought. From 1933, it would act as the mouthpiece of the **Confederación Española de Derechas Autónomas** (CEDA). From 1903, *ABC* also catered to conservative-monarchist tastes. The working-class left also had its own publications, most notably *El Socialista*, which was linked to the **Partido Socialista Obrero Español** (PSOE), and *Solidaridad Obrera*, which was the mouthpiece of the **Confederación Nacional del Trabajo** (CNT).

The **Franco regime** expropriated all left-wing newspapers, imposed strict press censorship, and set up its own press network under the control of the single party, the **Falange Española Tradiciona-lista y de las Juntas de Ofensiva Nacional Sindicalista** (FET y de las JONS). The most important of these was *Arriba*. The only newspapers to survive that maintained some degree of independence were linked to either the **Catholic Church** or **Bourbon** monarchism. The most important of the former was *Ya* (which the regime preferred to *El Debate*, which was unable to resume publication) and of the latter, the Madrid-based *ABC* and Barcelona-based *La Vanguardia*. The 1966 Press Law, promulgated by **Manuel Fraga**, eased press censorship somewhat. This made possible the appearance, in 1971, of the magazine *Cambio 16*, which was critical of the regime and quickly gained a large liberal middle-class audience. From the fall of the regime in 1975, a new press system quickly came into operation. Liberal-democratic dailies were set up, most notably *El País* and *Diario 16* in Madrid and *El Periódico* in Catalonia. *El País* and *ABC* became the major "national" newspapers, but large numbers of local and regional newspapers began to appear. These included non-Castilian newspapers, most notably **Avui** in Catalonia and the radical Basque nationalist publication **Egin**. The only newspapers that were popular under the Franco era and that were able to adapt to democratic times were *ABC*, which was the preferred read of conservative Spaniards who coalesced around Manuel Fraga's coalition **Alianza Popular** (AP), and *La Vanguardia*, which had maintained a conservative, but independent, editorial line, and had a loyal upper-middle-class Catalan following.

However, despite the new democratic freedoms, the number of Spanish adults who read a newspaper has remained disappointingly low, at about 25 percent. In Spain, there are no popular (and populist) tabloids, but the gap has been filled by daily newspapers that focus on sport and especially football (with *Marca*, *As*, *Sport*, and *El Mundo Deportivo* at the forefront), and gossip magazines (*prensa del corazón*), of which *Pronto* and *¡Hola!* are the most successful. The most important event in newspaper pushing over the last 30 years has been the publication of **El Mundo** from 1989. *El Mundo* catered to a younger, nonconformist, and right-wing audience, in a context in which *El País* was close to the ruling PSOE government and *ABC* still retained an old-fashioned conservative air. It played an important role in revealing and publicizing a whole series of **corrup-**

tion scandals, thereby playing a significant role in the 1996 electoral victory of the **Partido Popular** (PP). Since that date, it has remained quite close to the PP. Also significant is the appearance of Spain's first major digital newspaper, *Libertad Digital*, since 2000. It has operated as a right-wing ginger group, leading a Spanish **nationalist** offensive against the ruling PSOE government from 2004. In recent years, a whole series of free newspapers, which make money through advertising revenue, have also appeared. In 2007, more than million copies of *Gente*, *20 Minutos*, and *Compráctica* were given away.

PRESTIGE AFFAIR. The Prestige affair significantly damaged the **Partido Popular** (PP) government at the end of 2002. The *Prestige* was an oil tanker that was hit by a storm off the coast of **Galicia**, leaving it in danger of sinking. Rather than allow it ashore (which was the experts' preferred option), the government ordered it to be towed out of Galician waters. However, it sank in deep waters on 19 November and, despite government assurances to the contrary, large quantities of oil subsequently hit the Galician coastline. The government then made things worse because it denied any responsibility and because it was slow to react. By the time its own cleanup operation, led by the army, swung into action, from the beginning of December, around 150,000 volunteers had been mobilized by the localities hit. At the same time, a protest movement originally founded after a spillage in 1992, Nunca Máis, rapidly revived and led big demonstrations in Galicia and other parts of Spain. The only minister to emerge relatively unscathed was **Mariano Rajoy**, who showed himself a competent organizer when he was appointed to oversee the cleanup.

PRIETO TUERO, INDALECIO (1883–1962). Indalecio Prieto was the leading figure on the moderate wing of the **Partido Socialista Obrero Español** (PSOE) between the 1920s and 1940s. He was born in Oviedo but brought up in Bilbao. Prieto was strongly influenced by the liberal atmosphere of the city, working as a journalist in the progressive daily *El Liberal* during the first decade of the century. Nevertheless, he believed that the PSOE would be the most effective vehicle to bring about democratic change and joined the party in 1899, became a deputy in 1918, and was elected onto the party's executive committee in April 1921. It was the twin influence of liberalism and socialism that would guide Prieto throughout his life. He maintained that socialism was only attainable after a "democratic bourgeois" revolution, but he also attached great importance to the extension of civil liberties per se. Hence, he was a strong supporter of the republican-PSOE *conjunción*, signed in 1910, opposed Socialist collaboration with the **Primo de Rivera dictatorship**, and staunchly defended PSOE participation in the republican governments of the **Second Republic**.

Prieto was minister of finance and then minister of public works in the republican-Socialist coalition government of 1931–1933, and then pushed strongly for the coalition to be reformed during 1935. This led him to clash with the UGT bureaucracy and with **Francisco Largo Caballero** in particular, who was more concerned with preserving and extending the power of the Socialist labor confederation, the **Unión General de Trabajadores** (UGT). During the 1920s and early 1930s, the power of the UGT ensured that when Prieto crossed swords with Largo Caballero he would usually be at a disadvantage. However, the failure of the **October 1934 revolution** and the need to reform the republican-Socialist alliance of 1931–1933 to ensure the right did not retain power in the forthcoming elections put Prieto in a stronger position. He finally secured Largo Caballero's acquiescence to the formation of the **Popular Front** electoral coalition in November 1935, and from December he was able to dominate the PSOE executive, though Largo Caballero was able to veto his entering government as prime minister in May 1936.

The animus felt between Prieto and Largo Caballero added an extra dimension to the divisions in the Republican zone during the **Spanish Civil War**. Prieto had no choice but to acquiesce to Largo Caballero's designation as prime minister in September 1936, and he accepted the post of air force and navy minister. However, after the **May Events** in **Barcelona**, along with the **Partido Comunista de España** (PCE) and the republicans, Prieto and the more moderate "reformist" wing of the PSOE played a key role in engineering Largo Caballero's fall and his replacement by Prieto's close friend and political stablemate **Juan Negrín**. Prieto now became minister of defense. However, as the war progressed, he became increasingly disillusioned at the growing power exercised by the PCE and pessimistic regarding the Republic's chances of winning the war. This led to a break with Negrín and his exclusion from government on 5 April 1938.

At the end of the civil war, Prieto left for exile in Mexico. During the 1940s, the major division within the PSOE was between the *prietistas* and *negrinistas*. Given his experience during the war, Prieto became violently anticommunist, and argued that in order to liberate Spain, Allied support was needed and that this required them to form a broad coalition that included not only republicans and Socialists, but also the monarchist supporters of the Spanish pretender, **Juan de Borbón y Battenberg**. At first, the PSOE leadership called for the reestablishment of the Republic. However, when, during 1946–1947, the Allies made clear that they would only back an opposition alliance that included the monarchists, Prieto convinced the party that it should leave the Republican government in exile and enter negotiations with the representatives of Don Juan. Yet by 1950, it was clear that this strategy had ended in failure. Prieto reacted by resigning his posts in the party and returning to Mexico. He was to die in exile in Mexico in 1962.

PRIM Y PRATS, JUAN (1814–1870). Juan Prim was one of the archetypal **Partido Progresista** military personalities in 19th-century Spain and was a leading figure in the **Glorious Revolution** of 1868 and the attempt to consolidate a constitutional monarchy thereafter. He was born in Reus (Tarragona) in 1814, joining the **military** during the final crisis of absolutist rule in 1833. He was a **liberal**, militated in the Partido Progresista most of his adult life, and was a *progresista* deputy for a variety of Catalan constituencies. He achieved national acclaim when, in 1860, troops under his command in **Morocco** achieved important victories in Castillejos and Tetuan, for which he was made the marquis of Castillejos and a grandee. He played a leading role in the various *pronunciamientos* launched against the **Partido Moderado** authorities between 1865 and 1868. After the Glorious Revolution, he was made minister of war in the provisional government, and as prime minister in the government formed after the elections to the constituent **Cortes**, he led the negotiations that resulted in the coronation of **Amadeo** de Saboya as king of Spain. At the same time, with the outbreak of war in **Cuba**, he took a highly realistic position, recognizing the need for a process of negotiation and decolonization. His political career was, however, cut tragically short when he was assassinated by unknown assailants on 27 December 1870. Colonial interests were suspected, but this was never proved.

PRIMO DE RIVERA DICTATORSHIP. The Primo de Rivera dictatorship, which lasted from September 1923 to January 1930, was the first avowedly authoritarian regime in Spain since the **liberal** revolution in the 1830s. On seizing power on 13 September 1923, General **Miguel Primo de Rivera** claimed that his rule was simply a short-term response to the country's problems, and that once the nation was cleansed of corrupt politicians and *caciques* he would once again step into the background. Immediately after he assumed power, he set up a military directory and replaced provincial civil governors with **military** officers. At the same time, the **Cortes** were suspended, martial law was imposed, an offensive was launched against the **Confederación Nacional del Trabajo** (CNT) and **Partido Comunista de España** (PCE), and central control over **Catalonia** and the **Basque Country** was tightened.

From the spring of 1924, Primo de Rivera then went back on his promise to restore liberal-parliamentary rule and began to institutionalize his regime. He was strongly influenced by military values of order, discipline, and patriotism, and when he arrived in Madrid in September 1923, he came under the spell of right-wing **Catholic** thought. The major components of the regime's ideology became anti-liberal **corporatist** Catholicism, fierce Spanish nationalism, and economic interventionism. Regime ideologues declared that its main objective was to modernize Spain while (rather contradictorily) championing traditional rural values. It attempted to stimulate economic development by further raising **tariff** barriers on imports, encouraging industrial concentration, undertaking public works, and beginning an extensive road and **railway** building program. This was combined with populist, paternalist social-Catholicism. Hence, the regime extended **welfare** benefits in some areas, while the Socialist labor confederation, the **Unión General de Trabajadores** (UGT), was invited to participate in a system of arbitration boards, or *comités paritarios*, to negotiate industrial disputes.

In order to build a popular base, Primo de Rivera latched onto the provincial associations that were being set up by the major elite Catholic association, the **Asociación Nacional Católica de Propagandistas**, known as Uniones Patrióticas (Patriotic Unions), and turned them into the regime's single party. At the end of 1925, his military directory was replaced by a civilian directory made up of leading figures from the Unión Patriótica. It was to a significant degree staffed by former **Mauristas** and **Carlists**, though large numbers of opportunists intent on furthering their political careers also joined. Then, in September 1927, **King Alfonso XIII** approved plans to set up a National Assembly. This was a non-elected consultative body, charged with drawing up a new constitution (which was never to be promulgated).

From 1928, the regime's problems began to mount. Most importantly, Primo de Rivera began to lose the support of much of the military. From 1925, he had tried to modernize the armed forces, in part by extending the system of promotion by merit that existed in **Morocco** to the elite artillery corps. These moves provoked discontent in wide sections of the army and led to a strike among artillery corps officers. The regime's credibility was, at the same time, damaged by the economic downturn that swept the country during 1929. Matters were made worse because, given the dictatorship's reluctance to significantly increase taxes on the country's social elites, Primo de Rivera had largely funded his infrastructural program through borrowing. The results were a large government deficit, accelerating inflation, and a collapse in the value of the peseta (seen as a key element of national prestige). Even the business community, which had benefited under the regime, was disturbed by its unorthodox economic policies and resentful at the role the UGT played in collective bargaining. Moreover, the Unión Patriótica was too clerical and conservative to achieve genuine popular backing, and the Socialists had only aligned themselves with the dictatorship circumstantially. As its popularity waned, they distanced themselves. All of these factors played their part in the eventual fall of Primo de Rivera in January 1930.

Overall, the dictatorship represented an important milestone in Spain's political history. Repression had been low key, but antiliberal ideology had spread through important sections of the country's military and political elite. The civilian supporters of Primo de Rivera adopted a corporatist discourse, which equated democracy with chaos and revolution, and were subsequently determined to impose authoritarian models of political administration on Spain. They were to be found in Spain's rightist political associations during the **Second Republic**, and provided a bedrock of functionaries for the **Franco regime**.

PRIMO DE RIVERA Y ORBANEJA, MIGUEL, SECOND MARQUIS OF ESTELLA (1870–1930). Miguel Primo de Rivera was the dictator of Spain between September 1923 and January 1930. He was born into a **military** family from Jerez de la Frontera in January 1870. He soon joined the army and was able to rise rapidly in the ranks, both because he served in **Morocco** and because he enjoyed the patronage of his uncle, Fernando Primo de Rivera y Sobremonte (1831–1921), the marquis of Estella. On his uncle's death in 1921, he inherited the title and became a grandee.

Primo was bluff and outspoken, a fact that caused him not a few problems. He was to become increasingly disenchanted with the Spanish occupation of Morocco, and his suggestion in March 1917 that Spain should try to exchange Ceuta for **Gibraltar** led to his dismissal from the post of military governor of Cádiz. However, as the **Cánovas Restoration** entered into crisis, between 1917 and 1923, he was to play a key role in the country's political future. Like many army officers, he was outraged at what he saw as the **corruption** of Spanish political life, and the inability, as he saw it, of the weak and ineffectual Spanish politicians to solve the country's social problems. As captain general of **Madrid**, **Valencia**, and, finally, **Barcelona**, between 1920 and 1923, he was to experience firsthand the escalation of social conflict. In military circles, it was widely felt that only a strong government could solve Spain's problems and Primo de Rivera fully shared such views. Between 1922 and 1923, he was very close to conservative elites in Barcelona, totally supporting their assertions that the **anarchist**-syndicalist **Confederación Nacional del Trabajo** (CNT) was a **terrorist** organization that had to be destroyed in order for the revolutionary threat to be averted. Within the officer corps, anti-**Catalanist** sentiment was also intense and the radicalization of Catalanist agitation from 1918 would further stimulate discontent. However, while in Barcelona, Primo de Rivera declared himself in favor of regional decentralization and respectful of the

Catalan language. This was important because not only was he able to garner strong support from conservative-monarchist spokesmen, but also from the Catalanist **Lliga Regionalista**.

After 1921, discontent among officers based in Spain was mirrored by growing anger in the colonial *africanista* army in the aftermath of the military disaster of **Annual**. They believed that shifty politicians were trying to pin the blame on them and that the political elite was too pusillanimous to back an aggressive "forward policy" in Morocco. Primo de Rivera began to conspire with pro-*africanista* generals (the so-called *cuadrilatero*) in Madrid in June 1923. And in order to gain their support, he backtracked on earlier assertions that Spain should abandon Morocco. He was bolstered by the widespread backing he enjoyed in Catalan conservative milieus (with, it appears, business associations providing financial support) and by broad-based military sympathy for a coup. Furthermore, King **Alfonso XIII** also gave tacit support. This and the lack of popularity of the regime meant that there was little opposition to his *pronunciamiento* of 13 September 1923.

Primo de Rivera at first argued that his dictatorship would be a "brief parenthesis" necessary to cleanse Spain of corrupt politicians and lay the basis for a "purified" liberal-constitutional regime. However, from the outset there was a strong authoritarian thrust behind his coup. He moved against the anarchist and Communist left and "Catalan separatists." At first, in order to maintain order, he also intended to extend the Catalan bourgeois militia, the Sometent, to the whole of Spain. The idea was that it would henceforth play the same role as the *fascio di combattimento* in Mussolini's Italy. However, once he transferred from Barcelona to Madrid, he became influenced by right-wing Madrid-based **Catholic** ideologues. As a result, he abandoned the idea of turning the Sometent into the regime's supported base, choosing instead the provisional associations being set up by **Asociación Nacional Católica de Propagandistas** known as Uniones Patrióticas (Patriotic Unions). At the same time, he dropped his regionalist rhetoric, abolished the **Mancomunitat**, and reimposed the **Castilian language** on all aspects of public life in **Catalonia** and the **Basque Country**.

From the spring of 1924, he went back on early promises and began institutionalizing the regime. He was not without a populist touch. He regularly traveled around the country to keep in contact, as he saw it, with the masses. Under advice from his minister of labor, Eduardo Aunós (1894–1953), he implemented **welfare** reforms and allowed the Socialist **Unión General del Trabajo** (UGT) to participate in the arbitration boards set up to settle industrial disputes. At the height of his regime in 1925–1926, when with French cooperation he was for the first time able to pacify Spain's Moroccan Protectorate, he enjoyed considerable middle-class support and the tacit acquiescence of the country's major working-class organizations, the **Partido Socialista Obrero Español** (PSOE) and UGT. This did not, however, save him when the **economy** faltered and his credibility was called into question in the late 1920s. When his appeal to Spain's captains general for support in January 1930 elicited an unenthusiastic response, he resigned, dying in exile in Paris just two months later. *See also* PRIMO DE RIVERA Y SAÉNZ DE HEREDIA, JOSÉ ANTONIO.

PRIMO DE RIVERA Y SAÉNZ DE HEREDIA, JOSÉ ANTONIO, THIRD MARQUIS OF ESTELLA (1903–1936). José Antonio, the son of the Spanish dictator **Miguel Primo de Rivera**, was the founder of Spain's major Fascist party in the 1930s. Following his death in 1936, he was, at least on the surface, then revered by the early **Franco regime**, in order to provide it with ideological legitimacy. As the son of a wealthy southern landowning family, José Antonio enjoyed a privileged upbringing and education. He pursued a career in law in the 1920s, becoming strongly identified with his father's regime. It was from these roots that his visceral hatred of liberalism and support for a one-party state sprang.

After the fall of his father in January 1930, he became the vice secretary of the newly founded Unión Monárquica Nacional (National Monarchist Union), which was meant to inherit the mantle of the **Primo de Rivera dictatorship**'s ill-starred single party, the Unión Patriótica (Patriotic Union). It was, however, a total flop, and was wound up in the same year. José Antonio saw the coming of the **Second Republic** as a disaster for Spain and was at the same time inspired by the rise of Fascist movements in continental Europe. He collaborated with the fascistic newspaper *El Fascio* during 1933, and launched his own Fascist party, **Falange Española**, at the end of the year. It fused with another Fascist organization, the Juntas de Ofensiva

Nacional Sindicalista (Juntas of the National Syndicalist Offensive) in April 1934, but Primo de Rivera was able to assert his personal control over the new movement in October. The party's short-term aim was the violent overthrow of the Republic. José Antonio argued that its goal was to overcome the struggles between right and left, and the class divisions inherent in capitalism, through common national goals (the "unity of destiny" of the Spanish nation) within the framework of a **corporatist** organization of economy and society.

This supposed neutrality between right and left was, however, belied by José Antonio's own political maneuverings. Already in November 1933, he had sought *caciquista* support and formed part of a right-wing coalition in Cádiz in order to get elected (thereby ensuring himself parliamentary immunity until his defeat in the February 1936 elections). During 1934, he sought to establish an alliance with the **Alfonsoist monarchists** in return for monetary support, and despite his concern that a future **military** regime would subordinate the Falange to its agenda, he offered to back a military uprising. Until February 1936, the Falange remained a small, rather isolated group. Nevertheless, José Antonio's moneyed background and position as the former dictator's son did give the party a certain cachet in right-wing circles. This was enhanced by his elitist style, which seemed to distance the Falange from the more populist continental Fascist movements. Nevertheless, it was only after the **Popular Front** victory in February 1936 that the party was to grow rapidly. Primo de Rivera was not to enjoy the fruits of this success. After an attempt by Fascist gunmen to assassinate a Socialist law professor at the University of Madrid, on 14 March the Falange was banned and its leadership, including José Antonio, arrested. When the **Spanish Civil War** broke out, José Antonio found himself imprisoned behind Republican lines in Alicante. There were several attempts to negotiate his release as part of an exchange of prisoners but these came to nothing. Indeed, despite the deification of José Antonio by the **Nationalist** forces, evidence suggests that General **Francisco Franco** made little effort to gain his release. He was executed by firing squad on 20 November 1936.

PRISA GROUP. Under the stewardship of Jesús de Polanco (1929–2007), PRISA (Promotora de Informaciones, SA) has become Spain's leading media group. It was founded in 1972 by a number of liberal professionals, led by Polanco, who had already built up a personal fortune with the publishing house Santillana. Their intention was to set up a prodemocratic daily newspaper when conditions were right. This was achieved with the founding of *El País* in 1976, under the editorship of Juan Luis Cebrián (1944–), with whom Polanco developed a close friendship. Subsequently, PRISA bought a string of magazines (including Spain's second best selling sports daily, *AS*) and set up its own publishing house (Ediciones El País). In the mid-1980s, it then bought Spain's most popular radio station, Cadena **SER**, and in 1993, another radio station, Antena 3. In 1989, after the government began granting licenses for the operation of private **television** companies, it invested in Sogecable, which set up the pay-per-view channel Canal+. After 1996, its close links with the old **Partido Socialista Obrero Español** (PSOE) administration led it to clash with the **Partido Popular** (PP) government, which favored a group of businessmen who were in the process of setting up a media network friendly to the government (with the newly privatized phone company, Telefónica, the key player). This could be seen in the battle over digital television. PRISA supported the Sogecable satellite television station, Canal Satélite Digital, launched in January 1997. The government tried to block it, but the Constitutional Tribunal ruled in PRISA's favor. PRISA has in recent years expanded into the areas of music, advertising, and film production. It also holds a stake in the British daily *The Independent*, and has recently bought into a new terrestrial television station, Cuatro. In 2006, it also took a controlling stake in Sogecable.

PRIVATIZATIONS. At the end of the **Franco regime**, Spain had a large number of public sector companies under the wing of the holding company **Instituto Nacional de Industria** (INI). Their privatization began under the **Partido Socialista Obrero Español** (PSOE) administrations of the period between 1982 and 1996, when neoliberal economists within the Socialist administration (most notably **Miguel Boyer** and Carlos Solchaga [1944–]) convinced **Felipe González** of the potential benefits. At first, the impetus was above all the desire to liberate the exchequer from loss-making concerns and the need to deregulate in order to conform to the demands of integration into the **European Economic Community**. However, when the conservative **Partido Popular** (PP) government came to power in 1996, it was much more ideologically driven, and in subsequent years carried out a number of high-profile privatizations, including **Telefónica**, the petrochemical giant **Repsol**, the electrical goods manufacturer Endesa, and the bank Argentaria. The PP was criticized for ensuring that these companies were close to the government by appointing political friends in the run-up to their privatization. Once privatized, Telefónica then went on to play a key role in helping set up a large media group close to the party, which included the digital network Vía Digital and private **television** and **radio** stations (especially Antena 3 and Onda Cero). Nevertheless, the support they received prior to privatization has ensured that both Telefónica and Repsol have established themselves as important international players.

PROGRESISTAS. *See* PARTIDO PROGRESISTA.

PROGRESSIVE BIENNIUM. The term Progressive Biennium refers to the period between July 1854 and July 1856, during which the **Partido Progresista** played a key role in government. It was ushered in by the ***pronunciamiento*** at Vicalvaro (the Vicalvarada) by Partido Progresista officers led by **Leopoldo O'Donnell**, who were unhappy at the reactionary policies followed by the **Partido Moderado** in office. Although O'Donnell at first sought only a discreet liberalization (along with the post of prime minister), in order to gain popular support the officers had to radicalize their stance, issuing the Manzanares Manifesto on 7 July, which set out a typically *progresista* set of demands, such as the extension of civil liberties, widening of suffrage, and reestablishment of the **National Militia**. There followed insurrections in a number of urban centers, totally undermining the position of the government, and as a result, on 20 July, the most prestigious Partido Progresista general, **Baldomero Espartero**, took over the reins of power, though he had to accept O'Donnell as his minister of war.

Like the **Espartero regency**, the Progressive Biennium was once again to see a loosening of state controls. This was reflected in the blossoming of labor organization in the country's major industrial center, **Barcelona**. A constituent **Cortes** also met in November 1854 and drew up a new constitutional text (the "stillborn constitution").

Legislative power was to reside exclusively with the Cortes, civil liberties were extended, and for the first time religious toleration was accepted. However, it was never to be put into effect, in large measure because, as during the Espartero regency, serious divisions opened up within the *progresista* liberal camp. On the left, urban radicals called for the abolition of indirect taxes (*consumos*) and **military service** (the *quintas*), and a reduction in the price of basic necessities, and launched a number of popular revolts. More conservative elements were able to take advantage of this instability to regain power. O'Donnell became prime minister in July 1856 and ruthlessly put down the subsequent uprisings in **Madrid** and Barcelona. The biennium had come to an end, as symbolized by the reintroduction of the conservative **Constitution of 1845** later in the year.

PRONUNCIAMIENTO. This was the term used in Spain during the 19th and early 20th centuries to refer to military rebellions designed to force a change of government. The first *pronunciamientos* occured between 1814 and 1820 when the **liberals** turned to army officers in order to try to overthrow King **Fernando VII**. This signaled the entry of the **military** into Spanish politics. The first *pronunciamiento* to succeed was led by General Rafael de Riego (1785–1823) in January 1820, and from then until the outbreak of the **Spanish Civil War** in July 1936, the army *pronunciamiento* would become a common means of trying to overthrow the government of the day. After the demise of the **Franco regime**, on the other hand, the term for plots by discontented army officers to overthrow the new democratic institutions was *golpismo*, and the effort by **Antonio Tejero** to overthrow the regime was referred to as a *golpe* or *golpe de estado* (from the French, *coup d'état*).

PUBLIC ADMINISTRATION. Public administration was for a long time seen as one of Spain's Achilles' heels. In the mid-19th century, much of the bureaucracy rotated with their political masters. The **Cánovas Restoration** made civil servants permanent but there were serious problems of overstaffing. From 1918, the civil service was divided into a series of associations (*cuerpos*), such as engineers and tax inspectors. However, they were very hierarchical and promotion was largely based on seniority. The public administration retained a reputation for inefficiency through to the **Franco regime**. Since the **transition to democracy**, reform has been timid. There remains an overlap between the higher reaches of the civil service and the political elite, with political patronage a key factor in the appointment of figures like subdirectors general.

PUERTO RICO. *See* COLONIES; SPANISH-AMERICAN WAR.

PUJOL I SOLEY, JORDI (1934–). **Jordi Pujol** was the president of the Catalan **Generalitat** from the first elections to the autonomous Catalan parliament in 1980 through to 2003. He was born in **Barcelona** into a middle-class Catalan family and studied medicine at the University of Barcelona. From his student days, he was a leading figure in clandestine Catalan nationalist politics. He was one of the founders of the Christian-**Catalanist** student movement, Catòlics Catalans (Catalan Catholics), and, after a protest against the **Franco regime** at the famous *modernista* concert hall, La Palau de la Música, in May 1960, during which he sang the banned "Cant de la Senyera" in the presence of four Francoist ministers, he was sentenced to seven years in prison. This sparked off a widely supported protest campaign for his release. He was finally freed after two and a half years. After his release, he combined political and business activity. He was behind the creation of Banca Catalana (Catalan Bank) in 1959, which was meant to provide the impetus for Catalan industrial development while trying to build a unified Catalan nationalist opposition to Francoism. In 1974, he founded Convergència Democràtica de Catalunya (Catalan Democratic Convergence) and in the first free general elections in June 1977, he was elected to parliament, where he headed the so-called Minoria Catalana (Catalan Minority).

Between 1977 and 1979, he also became a minister (*conseller polític*) in the provisional Generalitat. In 1980, in the first elections to the Catalan autonomous parliament, he headed the coalition **Convergència i Unió** (CiU), winning a surprise victory. Between 1982 and 1986, Pujol faced an investigation into his activities at the head of Banca Catalana, with the decision made not to prosecute in 1986. Despite this, CiU established a stranglehold over Catalan politics through to the mid-1990s, with Pujol cementing his reputation as the father of the reborn Catalan nation and as an effective negotiator with

"Madrid" governments. He was also very active on the international plane, playing a leading role in the construction of the so-called "Europe of the Regions" within the **European Union**. In June 1992, he was elected president of the Assembly of the European Regions and, from its inception in 1994, was a key figure in the Committee of the Regions and Local Authorities.

During the 1990s, Pujol was also able to exercise greater influence on the Spanish political stage. After failing to win an overall majority in the June 1993 elections, the prime minister, **Felipe González**, turned to him. Pujol agreed to back the government from the wings without actually entering the cabinet, but in return demanded that central government cede 15 percent of Spain's tax on earnings, the Impuesto sobre la Renta de Personas Físicas (IRPF) to the autonomous communities. However, given the growing scandal surrounding the administration of the **Partido Socialista Obrero Español** (PSOE), Pujol withdrew his support in September 1995, forcing Felipe González to call new elections. Pujol followed a similar strategy after the **Partido Popular** (PP) failed to gain an overall majority in the general elections of 1996. The new prime minister, **José María Aznar**, now agreed to cede 30 percent of IRPF to the autonomous communities. Yet to counterbalance this image of cooperation with the Spanish political establishment, he also began to demand greater autonomy for **Catalonia**, with an emphasis on the need for the Generalitat to be better financed.

However, the tables were turned at the end of the decade. First, CiU performed poorly in the 1999 elections to the Catalan autonomous parliament, and then the PP achieved an overall majority in the 2000 general elections. Pujol's policy of wheeling and dealing had began to lose the support of more conservative Catalans, an increasing number of whom voted for the PP, and of more liberal and radical Catalanists, many of whom switched to either the Catalan Socialists, the **Partit dels Socialistes de Catalunya** (PSC)-PSOE, now led by **Pascual Maragall**, or **Esquerra Republicana de Catalunya**. Though still president of the Generalitat, Pujol's glory days were behind him. After the 1999 elections, he announced that he would not run for president again and began grooming Artur Mas (1955–) as his successor.

– Q –

QUEIPO DE LLANO Y SIERRA, GONZALO (1876–1951). General Queipo de Llano became famous (or infamous) for his brutal repression of the left in Seville during the **Spanish Civil War**. He was born in Tordesillas in the province of Valladolid, became a cadet in the Cavalry Academy, fought in **Cuba**, and rose rapidly through the ranks of the Army of Africa from the turn of the 20th century. Almost unique among the *africanistas*, he showed **republican** sympathies, and, after participating in the attempted Republican revolution in December 1930, had to go into exile until the proclamation of the **Second Republic**. During the Republic, he was to hold a series of important posts: captain general of Madrid and general inspector of the army in 1931, head of the military household of the president of the Republic between December 1931 and March 1933, and inspector general of the Carabineros (frontier police) between 1934 and 1936. However, he grew increasingly disillusioned with the Republic, and when **Niceto Alcalá Zamora**, a relative of his, was removed from the presidency in May 1936, he joined the rebellion being planned by General **Emilio Mola**. Mola put him in charge of organizing the insurrection in Seville, and despite limited resources, through a mixture of stealth and terror he was able to secure Seville for the **Nationalist** cause. From his base in Seville, during the first year of the war he converted the south of the Nationalist zone into something approaching his own personal fiefdom, imposing a reign of terror through the use of threats in his nightly radio broadcasts combined with summary executions.

From the start of the war, because of his early support for the Republic, relations with General **Francisco Franco** were cold. He opposed Franco's elevation to head of state in September 1936, and tension further grew as a result of Franco's attempts to limit his autonomy in the south. At the end of the war, in May 1939, Franco was informed that Queipo de Llano was plotting to set up a new military directory that would exclude him, take action against the **Falange Española Tradicionalista y de las Juntas de Ofensiva Nacional Sindicalista** (FET y de las JONS)—despised by many leading **military** officers—and place the monarchist pretender, **Juan de Borbón**

y Battenberg, on the throne. He finally decided to take action in June following an outburst by Queipo de Llano, who criticized Franco's decision to give Valladolid rather than Seville the military decoration of the Cruz Laureada de San Fernando. On 27 July, after a meeting in Burgos, Franco packed him off to Italy as head of a military mission, and in February 1942 placed him on the reserve. Queipo de Llano, nevertheless, continued to push for a monarchist restoration, supporting the memorandum signed by eight lieutenant generals asking Franco to step down in September 1943.

– R –

RABASSAIRES. In the 19th century, the name *rabassaire* was given to a class of Catalan peasants who rented land for the cultivation of vines under a system called the *rabassa morta* (dead roots), whereby the contract was valid until the death of two-thirds of the vines, subject to a maximum of 50 years. This system led to innumerable conflicts during the 19th century. These worsened in the 1890s as a result of the impact of phylloxera, because the new American vines that had to be planted lasted for only 25 years, and because the proprietors pressed to extend shorter tenant contracts. Moreover, from 1917, social tension was further heightened by a decline in the price of wine. In response, with the help of the left-wing **Catalanist** politician **Lluís Companys**, in 1922 the peasants formed the Unió de Rabassaires i Altres Cultivadors del Camp de Catalunya (Union of Rabassaires and other Cultivators of the Catalan Countryside), which was to have an important influence in Catalan social and political life over the next 17 years.

It grew rapidly after the proclamation of the **Second Republic**, reaching a total of 21,542 members in 1932. Politically, it was closely linked to the dominant party in **Catalonia, Esquerra Republicana de Catalunya** (ERC). In 1934, the Catalan parliament, the **Generalitat**, approved the Agricultural Contracts Law (Llei de Contractes de Conreu), which made it easier for the peasants to buy the land that they worked off the landowners, along with other provisions aimed at improving their working conditions. This led to a major conflict between the Catalan Generalitat and right-wing Spanish government.

The law was declared anticonstitutional by the Tribunal of Constitutional Guarantees in June 1934. An attempt was made to work out a compromise, but after the Generalitat's participation in the **October 1934 revolution** the law was annulled. However, it was again voted by the Catalan parliament after the **Popular Front** electoral victory of February 1936. Meanwhile, as social tensions escalated between 1933 and 1936, the Unió de Rabassaires moved to the left. It formed part of the **Alianzas Obreras** in 1934 and, as the political climate became ever more polarized, in 1936 it moved close to the newly formed **Partit Socialista Unificat de Catalunya** (PSUC). However, most members still wished to own the land they worked rather than see it collectivized. During the **Spanish Civil War**, therefore, the organization opposed the collectivizations proposed by the **Confederación Nacional del Trabajo** (CNT), supporting the stance in favor of the maintenance of private property advocated by the PSUC and ERC.

RADICALS. *See* PARTIDO RADICAL; PARTIDO REPUBLICANO RADICAL.

RADIO. Under the **Franco regime**, the only radio networks to operate were the state radio, Radio Nacional Española (RNE), and stations set up by organizations that supported the regime, most notably the **Catholic Church**. All had to take news from the state agency, Agencia EFE. Independent stations grew rapidly from the **transition to democracy**. Very important in this respect was the appearance of **SER**, which formed part of the **PRISA** media group (which publishes Spain's leading daily, *El País*). Onda Cero followed soon afterward. At the same time, the Church catered to more conservative listeners through **COPE**. The latter grew in popularity from the early 1990s in the context of the right-wing offensive against the government of the **Partido Socialista Obrero Español** (PSOE). However, the SER network remains in number one position. From the 1980s, the growth of FM also made possible an enormous proliferation of regional and local stations. Indeed, Spain has the highest per capita radio audience in western Europe. *See also* TELEVISION.

RAILWAYS. The first railway in Spain was built in 1848. However, it was not until the years of 1855–1865 that a great boom occurred in railway building. Almost all of this construction took place under the direction of foreign financial interests. In part (as in the case of **mining**), this was because indebted Spanish governments needed the support of European business houses in order to raise credit abroad. New government legislation, approved in 1856, was tailored to meet the demands of foreign and, in particular, French investors—with the Pereire brothers, Rothschilds, and Prost-Guilhou to the fore. Their credit companies were behind the great Spanish railway companies. The largest of these, Compañía Ferrocarriles del Norte (Northern Railway Company) and Madrid-Zaragoza-Alicante, had members of the Spanish elite on their boards in order to increase their power and influence. The size of the Spanish railway network increased rapidly. By 1865, Spain had about 4,800 kilometers of railway track. This went some way toward creating an internal market. Yet there were also penalties to be paid for having the railways controlled by foreign interests. In order to stimulate the companies to invest, from the start they were given subsidies, and between 1855 and 1865 they enjoyed a rebate on duties on imported capital goods, rolling stock, and fuel. The result was to stunt the development of the home-based **iron** and metal industries. Moreover, foreign investment responded to a colonial vision of Spanish economic development. Its aim was to facilitate the export of metals and minerals rather than link centers of manufacture and consumption. Hence, with the exception of **Catalonia** and **Valencia**, the lines radiated out from **Madrid** to the terminal points at Spain's sea ports.

When between 1914 and 1918, in the boom conditions created by **World War I**, the railways proved totally incapable of carrying the extra goods, it became clear that if Spain was to modernize, the network needed to be totally overhauled. Yet by this time the companies were financially weak and had to be bailed out by government loans. This led to calls in business circles for the railways to be nationalized and for a significant investment of state funds. From 1926, the **Primo de Rivera dictatorship** made an important start with the assignation of 2,000 million pesetas, out of a total budget of 3,539 million, for infrastructural improvements to the railways. However, during the **Second Republic**, government's efforts to balance the budget meant that the companies received little aid, and during the **Spanish Civil War** a large part of the rolling stock was destroyed.

In 1941, as part of the **Franco regime**'s **autarkic economic policies,** Spanish railways were nationalized and integrated within RENFE. Like much of Spanish nationalized industry, RENFE was overbureaucratic and had heavy losses, and the postwar years were to witness an extremely slow and uneven reconstruction and modernization. Only from the 1980s has there been a considerable investment in the railways, though until recently the industry has played second fiddle to the massive program of road building. In 1988, the key decision was made to convert Spanish railways to the European gauge and to put in place a high-velocity train network (AVE). This was correctly seen as the best way of generating revenue and winning back passengers from the road network and air travel. The first high-velocity service covering **Madrid** and Seville began to operate in April 1992. It was built to coincide with the **Barcelona** Olympics and Seville Expo and its rapid completion was seen very much as responding to political rather than commercial imperatives. There then followed a long time lag until the **Partido Popular** (PP) government gave the go-ahead for new AVE links between Madrid and Valladolid, Córdoba and Málaga, and Madrid and Barcelona. The first two lines opened at the end of 2007. Unfortunately, because of poor planning and construction, the Barcelona line was subject to long delays, with the final stretch (Barcelona-Tarragona) not opening until March 2008. It will subsequently link up with the French high-speed rail network at Perpignan. The line through northern Catalonia and tunnel under the Pyrenees are already under construction. Work has also begun on a line linking Madrid and Lisbon, and lines between Madrid and Valencia, and Seville and Cádiz, are also planned. The aim is to have 10,000 kilometers of high-speed track by 2020. *See also* TRANSPORT.

RAJOY BREY, MARIANO (1955–). Rajoy is the leader of the opposition **Partido Popular** (PP). He was born in Santiago de Compostela and studied law at the local university. He rose through local and regional PP politics before joining the party's national executive in 1989. He became minister of public administration of **José María Aznar**'s first government in 1996, and was made minister of education and culture in 1999. During this period, he gained a reputation for competence, composure, and an ability to dialogue and reach compromises (a quality of which the PP was in short supply). His reputation for competence was enhanced when he effectively managed the party's 2000 election campaign. Hence, in Aznar's second legislature, he was further promoted. Despite not forming part of Aznar's inner circle, he became party vice president and minister of the interior and from 2002 took over as the government spokesperson. During this year, he further strengthened his position when he effectively coordinated the cleanup operation in the aftermath of the sinking of the oil tanker, the *Prestige*, off the Galician coast. It was these qualities that led Aznar to anoint him as his successor in August 2003 (a decision subsequently ratified at the PP's party conference).

At this point, the PP expected to win the forthcoming general elections. The **Madrid train bombing** just three days before these elections, on 11 March 2004, and the PP's insistence that **ETA** was to blame, changed all that. In opposition, the PP, believing it had been robbed, launched an implacable offensive against the new **Partido Socialista Obrero Español** (PSOE) government, centered on its decision to enter into a dialogue with ETA, its **education** policy, and its reform of the Catalan autonomy statute. Rajoy maintained a calmer tone than some of his front bench team, but his words were just as violent. Thus, he accused the prime minister, **José Luis Rodríguez Zapatero**, of betraying the dead during the ETA negotiations and stated that the new Catalan statute would lead to the breakup of Spain. As in the past, a fiery Spanish nationalist rhetoric was at the heart of much PP policy. This helped mobilize the PP's core support and attracted considerable sympathy, especially in central Spain.

In the aftermath of ETA's decision to break the cease-fire in December 2006, the PP drew level with the PSOE in the opinion polls and it looked as if Rajoy was in a strong position to win the next elections. However, during 2007, the PSOE reestablished a slender lead. A problem with the PP's radical discourse was that it frightened off moderate voters, with Rajoy seen by some as a prisoner of the hard right of his party (represented by **Esperanza Aguirre**, **Eduardo Zaplana**, and **Ángel Acebes**). To counter this, Rajoy did not attend any antigovernment demonstrations from March 2007. Furthermore, while he retained an air of professional competence, he remained a rather distant figure, lacking in charisma. During 2007, this was reflected in low personal ratings in the opinion polls. The rapidly deteriorating economic climate from the end of 2007 gave Rajoy new hope during the February–March 2008 election campaign. He centered his attacks on the PSOE on their supposed economic incompetence and also connected with fears among the Spanish population that **immigration** was running out of control, promising far stricter controls. The PP performed better than in 2004 but was unable to defeat the PSOE. Nevertheless, Rajoy is arguing that the rise in the number of votes and seats justifies his staying on as party leader.

RATIONALIST EDUCATION. This was a system of **education** that emphasized self-enquiry by students rather than indoctrination, and all-round intellectual and physical development. The system became popular with the Spanish left at the end of the 19th century because it was seen as a progressive and scientific alternative to the reactionary teachings of the **Catholic Church**. Its foremost practitioners in Spain were Francisco Giner de los Ríos (1839–1915) and the **Institución Libre de Enseñanza** (ILE), but it was also advocated by **anarchists**, the **Partido Socialista Obrero Español**, and **republicans**.

RATO FIGAREDO, RODRIGO. Rato is best known as the minister of the economy and as one of the two vice presidents of the **Partido Popular** (PP) between 1996 and 2000 (the other was **Francisco Álvarez Cascos**). He studied law at the Complutense University of Madrid and did an economics doctorate at Berkeley. Subsequently, he embarked on a successful career in business before entering politics. His father was close to **Manuel Fraga** and this eased his passage into the upper echelons of the party in the 1980s. At one point, he was strongly tipped as a possible successor to Aznar, but there was some tension between the two men and Rato was also weakened by the 2001 **Gescartera** scandal. After the 2000 elections, he had a somewhat lower profile, and with the electoral defeat of 2004 he took up the post of managing director of the International Monetary Fund. He stepped down in October 2007 for "personal reasons" and was touted as a possible compromise candidate for PP president should **Mariano Rajoy** lose the March 2008 elections. Such talk subsided in the aftermath of the elections. Despite suffering a narrow defeat, it appears that Rajoy will remain leader.

REAL MADRID FC. Founded in 1902, Real Madrid is Spain's most successful football team and, indeed, the most successful of all European football clubs. The greatest team in its history, led in the 1950s by Alfredo Di Stéfano and Ferenc Puskás, won the European Cup for an unrivalled five consecutive seasons. However, during this period it gained something of a reputation as the regime team (**Francisco Franco** was a known supporter and the final of the Spanish cup, the Copa del **Generalísimo**, was played in its home stadium, the Bernabéu). From **Barcelona**, dark mutterings were heard regarding match fixing and referees favoring Madrid (which, one suspects post-Franco with little foundation, have continued up till this day). At the same time, the fact that **Barcelona FC** was identified with **Catalanist** opposition to the regime, meant that matches between these two clubs acquired strong political overtones. Though less marked, this political dimension still remains, with the link often drawn (above all in **Catalonia** and the **Basque Country**) between Real Madrid and conservative Spanish **nationalism**.

RECONQUEST. In the eighth century, Muslim forces crossed from North Africa and began to conquer the Iberian Peninsula. By the 10th century, over three quarters of the peninsula was in Moorish hands. However, from the 10th century onward, the Christian kingdoms began to reconquer Muslim lands. The process was completed under the **Catholic Monarchs** with the fall of Granada in 1492. The image of the so-called "reconquest" (a debatable term, given that by the time most of the land was retaken by the Christian forces, **Moors** had lived on it for many generations) has played an important role in the construction of Spanish national identity. For conservative **Catholic** ideologues, in particular, it was seen, from the 19th century, as the first manifestation of Spain's rise to greatness, under divine inspiration, during the Middle Ages. The medieval noble El Cid Campeador (1044–1099) became a mythical figure in this respect.

REDONDO URBIETA, NICOLÁS (1927–). Nicolás Redondo was the strongman of the Socialist trade union **Unión General de Trabajadores** (UGT) between the early 1970s and early 1990s. He was born in Barracaldo, an industrial suburb of Bilbao, into a Socialist working-class family. In the 1940s and 1950s, his father was a leading anti-Francoist labor activist. Nicolás followed in his father's footsteps. He found work in the shipbuilding plant La Naval, joined the **Partido Socialista Obrero Español** (PSOE) and UGT in 1945, and over the next two decades became intensively involved in the clandestine political and union struggle against the dictatorship. By the early 1970s, as de facto leader of the party and the union's most powerful regional organization, he was the most influential figure in the Socialist movement. He strongly supported the "renewers" (*renovadores*) against the exiled PSOE leadership and with the transfer of the UGT and PSOE back to Spain between 1971 and 1972, he joined the leadership teams of both organizations. Redondo believed that he was returning the party to its socialist roots, but he saw himself as a trade union organizer and not a politician. For this reason, at the Suresnes congress of October 1974 he turned down the offer of the post of first secretary, and instead supported **Felipe González**'s candidature. Redondo's specialization in union work was confirmed in 1978 when he resigned his post on the PSOE's executive committee in order to integrate part of the independent labor confederation **Union Sindical Obrera** into the UGT.

Relations between Redondo and Felipe González were, however, to deteriorate after the PSOE came to power in 1982. Under Redondo, the UGT participated in several institutional pacts between employers, government, and trade unions, but from 1985 the UGT became increasingly critical of the PSOE's failure, as it saw it, to defend the interests of the working class. Divisions culminated in 1988, when Redondo, who had been elected to parliament on the Socialist ticket in 1982, resigned his seat and led the UGT (with the support of **Comisiones Obreras** [CC.OO]) into a one-day general strike against government economic policy. He felt increasingly betrayed by his old friends, arguing that while he had remained faithful to the party's social-democratic tradition, it had been abandoned by the government. Once crossed, he proved a tenacious foe, maintaining links with CC.OO and pressing the government to pursue more prolabor policies. He was able to marginalize progovernment voices in the UGT itself and was not without friends within the PSOE. In 1993, he retired as general secretary of the UGT and was replaced by his protégé, Candido Méndez. However, over the next three years, he remained a thorn in Felipe González's side, sympathizing with the attempts of the PCE's general secretary, **Julio Anguita**, to undermine Gonzalez's position and calling for his replacement as PSOE general secretary.

REGENERATIONISM/REGENERACIONISMO. Regenerationism is the name given to a movement for the reform of Spain's polity that developed in the 1890s and came to a head after Spain's defeat in the **Spanish-American War** of 1898. The movement first came into prominence through a series of writers who developed a withering critique of the **Cánovas Restoration**. The major regenerationists were Lucas Mallada (1841–1921), Ricardo Macías Picavea (1847–1899), Damían Isern (1845–1914), Angel Ganivet (1865–1898), and **Joaquín Costa**. All of these authors lamented what they perceived as Spain's economic and moral decline, and they all, at least in part, blamed Spain's corrupt political institutions and in particular the oligarchic *caciquista* system of government. They often, however, came from **Catholic** backgrounds and were not social revolutionaries. The solutions they proposed for Spain's malaise varied, but they concentrated on the need to radically overhaul the political system and modernize **industry** and **agriculture**.

Politically, their ideas could appeal to the urban middle classes, growing numbers of which felt marginalized from the Restoration regime. The movement gathered political steam under the leadership of Joaquín Costa and Basilio Paraíso (1849–1930), who founded the **Unión Nacional** in 1900. Internal squabbling and an inability to reach out to the most disadvantaged sectors of society meant that the Unión was soon to founder. However, the moral critique of the Restoration regime was to have a far more long-term impact, with even some Restoration politicians, at least publicly, accepting the need for reform. The most farsighted announced their intention to carry out a "revolution from above."

REGENTIALIST/REGENCIALISTA. The name Regentialist was used in the 1960s to describe a group within the Francoist establishment who would prefer a nonmonarchist successor to **Francisco Franco**. The Regentialists were largely members of, or sympathized with, the **Movimiento Nacional**. The major figures were General **Agustín Muñoz Grandes**, **José Solís**, and **Manuel Fraga**. They feared that the **Bourbon** successor, **Juan Carlos**, at this time strongly backed by Admiral **Luis Carrero Blanco**, would maintain Spain's authoritarian political structures but dismantle the Movimiento. The argument was lost when, in 1969, Juan Carlos was appointed Franco's successor, but in any case by the early 1970s debate had moved on, with some former Regentialists, like Fraga, now demanding far-reaching political reform.

REGIONALISM. *See* NATIONALISM.

RELIGION. *See* CARLISM; CATHOLIC CHURCH; INTEGRISM; ISLAM AND SPAIN; JEWS; MOORS; TRADITIONALISM.

RENAIXENÇA. The Renaixença was a literary and cultural movement that developed in **Catalonia** from the 1830s and reached its peak between 1870 and 1880. Its founding work is seen as Bonaventura Carles Aribau's poem, *La pàtria* (*The Motherland*, 1833). It was strongly influenced by European Romanticism and sought Catalonia's identity or "spirit" in its historical past and in its language. Above all, the movement propagated an idealized vision of the Middle Ages, during which the **Crown of Aragón** developed a Mediterranean empire. It also heralded the revival of **Catalan** as a literary language. The movement was strongest in the field of poetry and reached a wider audience through poetry competitions called Jocs Florals instituted in 1859, and in campaigns to revive the Catalan language. The elitism and social conservatism of the movement led to criticism from more progressive **republican** circles, and from the 1880s its Romanticism was rejected by a new generation of intellectuals under the impact of realism and positivism. The Renaixença is usually seen as of key importance in laying the groundwork for the birth of Catalan **nationalism** in the late 19th and early 20th centuries. However, recent researchers have emphasized that it was regionalist in tone and that its authors did not question the fact that Catalonia formed part of the Spanish nation.

RENOVACIÓN ESPAÑOLA/SPANISH RENOVATION. *See* ALFONSOIST MONARCHISTS; CALVO SOTELO, JOSÉ; FRANCO REGIME.

REPSOL. In 1999, Repsol was Spain's third largest business and came in at number 136 in the Forbes list of the world's 500 leading companies. It began life as a nationalized petrol refiner under the **Franco regime**, but in the early 1990s it was encouraged to expand and diversify prior to **privatization**. As with the majority of major Spanish companies, the key to its expansion has been investment in **Latin America** during the 1990s. The key move was its takeover of the Argentinean oil and gas company YPF in 1999 (after which it became Repsol-YPF). It was badly hit by the Argentinean economic crisis of 2002 but has since recovered. Since 2000, it has also moved into the European market, buying a chain of petrol stations in Great Britain.

REPUBLIC. *See* FIRST REPUBLIC; REPUBLICANS; SECOND REPUBLIC.

REPUBLICANS. The republicans were a powerful force in Spanish politics between the 1860s and 1930s. At the outset they represented the Spanish **liberal** left. The first republican clubs were founded in Spain at the beginning of the 19th century under the impact of the **French Revolution**. They were supported by those social groups largely dispossessed of political power. Key elements of their creed were the economic modernization and political democratization of Spain and they looked to western Europe (especially France and Great Britain) for models from which Spain could profitably learn. They saw the **monarchy** as an insurmountable block to social and political progress. Only under a republic, they believed, would it be possible to democratize the country's political structures and extend civil liberties. Furthermore, though only a minority of republicans would regard themselves as atheists, they also viewed the **Catholic Church** as holding back cultural modernization and the dissemination of knowledge because of its outmoded scholastic doctrines and antiliberal ideology. Hence, the republican movement became very much bound up with the anticlerical milieus of the Masonic societies, freethinking clubs, and "**rationalist**" educational reforms.

The republicans formed an important current within the **Partido Demócrata**, set up in 1849, but in 1868 they split away to organize their own **Partido Republicano Federalista**. Briefly during the

Democratic Sexennium of 1868 to 1874, republicans were to play a key role in Spanish political life. They were driven underground with the establishment of the **Cánovas Restoration** in 1875, but a number of republican parties emerged during the 1880s, and with the granting of universal male suffrage in 1890, they began to grow. At a political level, the movement was handicapped by divisions between its leading figures. These divisions went back to the Democratic Sexennium and pitted revolutionaries against parliamentarians, the socializing left against the individualist right, and federalists against more centralist unitarians. These differences were reflected in the various republican organizations such as the **Partido Republicano Progresista**, Partido Republicano Centralista (Centralist Republican Party), **Partido Republicano Federal Democrático**, and the Partido Republicano Posibilista (Possiblist Republican Party). Despite these differences, at a local level in Spain's urban centers, republicanism was still the preferred political option of the working and lower middle classes (the *pueblo*, or people, in the vocabulary of the day). Hence, republicans were able to take control of a number of urban local councils (including **Madrid**) from 1892, and gain between one and three dozen seats in the national elections during the decade.

The crisis of the Restoration regime from 1898 allowed the republicans to further extend their influence. In **Barcelona** and **Valencia**, mass republican organizations were formed under **Alejandro Lerroux** and Vicente Blasco Ibañez (1867–1928) respectively. Efforts were also made through the **Unión Republicana** to unify the various republican forces. The impact of **World War I** was mixed. On the one hand, as the Restoration regime entered its final death throes, the opportunity to install a republic grew. However, the rapid growth of the working-class left from 1914 heralded the rise of class-based politics and an erosion of the republicans' working-class support. By the **Second Republic**, therefore, republicanism was seen as largely a lower-middle- and middle-class movement, though the republican left, represented by the **Esquerra Republicana de Catalunya** (ERC) in **Catalonia** and **Manuel Azaña**'s Izquierda Republicana (Republican Left), still attracted considerable working-class sympathy. The Republic represented an opportunity to undertake a thorough overhaul of the authoritarian Spanish state, but the efforts of republicans and the **Partido Socialista Obrero Español** was cut short by the **Spanish Civil War**. During the **transition to democracy** in the 1970s, republicanism was not significantly to revive. The major reason was that the only viable path toward democracy was a constitutional monarchy. Nevertheless, the **Constitution of 1978** incorporates the essential democratic aspirations of the early twentieth-century republican movement. *See also* TABLES 7, 8, AND 9.

RESTORATION. *See* CÁNOVAS RESTORATION; FERNANDO RESTORATIONS.

RETAIL SECTOR. Over much of the 20th century, Spain was slow to develop large-scale retail businesses. Between the 1900s and 1970s, the structure of the sector remained atomized, characterized above all by small shops with one or two assistants. But since then, rising incomes and car ownership, combined with the growth of female employment, have encouraged the growth of, first, supermarkets, then hypermarkets and out-of-town shopping malls. This is a trend that has greatly accelerated since the 1990s. Foreign companies have played a leading part in this transformation, with the French giant, Carrefour España, becoming Spain's largest retailer. However, Spanish firms have done better in the clothing industry, helped by the growing international profile of the country's fashion industry. Spanish clothing firms have, since the 1970s, reestablished the putting-out system in order to keep down costs, taking advantage of cheap female labor in poor rural areas. This has been the key to the success of the Galician-based clothing chain Zara, which undertook a major expansion abroad in 2000. El Corte Inglés has also established itself as the country's leading departmental store chain, with clothing the key to its success. On the other hand, as in other Mediterranean countries, food markets, located in major towns and cities, retain their importance, and Spaniards continue to buy some products (especially bread) in smaller retail outlets. As the population's spending power has risen, the transformation of the sector has also been matched by growing employment opportunities, especially for **women** workers. By 2000, over two million people were employed in retailing, with its sales accounting for 12.5 percent of Spanish gross domestic product.

REVOLUTION. *See* FRENCH REVOLUTION; GLORIOUS REV-OLUTION; OCTOBER 1934 REVOLUTION; REVOLUTION FROM ABOVE; SPANISH CIVIL WAR.

REVOLUTION FROM ABOVE. The slogan "revolution from above" was adopted by the official parties of the **Cánovas Restoration** after being defeated in the **Spanish-American War** of 1898. In its aftermath, **regenerationist** calls for the moralization of political life came to the fore, and more farsighted Restoration politicians sought to maintain their dominant position by integrating elements of regenerationist rhetoric into their programs. First off the mark was the **Partido Conservador**, through **Franciso Silvela** and, subsequently, **Antonio Maura**. Both Silvela and Maura argued that in the future the Conservatives would govern not through the operation of *caciquismo*, but with the support of "healthy public opinion." However, neither of these politicians could come to grips with the possibility that urban public opinion was not generally conservative, with the result that despite the rhetoric, they continued to manipulate elections. Furthermore, the Conservatives continued to rely for legitimacy on the arch-reactionary **Catholic Church**, and the increasingly authoritarian characteristics of **Antonio Maura**'s 1904–1909 administration led to wide-ranging left-wing and liberal protest. Maura then rejected a golden opportunity to democratize the Restoration regime when he refused to back calls by the **Lliga Regionalista** for a constituent **Cortes** during the **crisis of 1917**.

The **Partido Liberal**, on the other hand, tried to attract the moderate **republican** left to the regime and thereby strengthen its power base. This was the policy followed by **Segismundo Moret**, while the Liberals were in opposition, between 1908 and 1910, and also during the administration of **José Canalejas** between 1909 and 1912. Yet their policies proved too timid to gain significant backing among the urban middle classes. By 1914, as a result, the essential features of the Restoration regime were the same as they had been in 1901, and "revolution from above" can be seen as ending in failure.

REYES CATÓLICOS. *See* CATHOLIC MONARCHS.

REXURDIMENTO. *See* CASTRO Y MURGUÍA, ROSALÍA DE; GALICIA.

RIDRUEJO, DIONISIO (1912–1975). The poet-cum-politician, Dionisio Ridruejo, became strongly identified with the **Fascist** cause in the early 1930s. During the **Spanish Civil War** and early years of the **Franco regime**, in collaboration with **Ramón Serrano Suñer** he played a key role in extending the propaganda network of the regime's single party, the **Falange Española Tradicionalista y de las Juntas de Ofensiva Nacional Sindicalista** (FET y de las JONS). In 1937, he was promoted to the post of chief of the National Propaganda Service, and in August 1939, he became FET y de las JONS director general of propaganda. Ridruejo, however, soon became disillusioned when his dreams of converting the Franco regime into a full-blown Fascist regime were unrealized. In 1940, his plans for the **Organización Sindical Española** (OSE) were modified because they were seen as too radical. Then on 8 May 1941, after an article appeared in the Falangist daily *Arriba*—probably written by Ridruejo himself—criticizing the recent appointment of a conservative army general to the post of minister of the interior, he was dismissed from his post.

Ridruejo's immediate reaction was to reaffirm his Fascist identity by enlisting in the recently created **Blue Division** to fight on the Russian front. At the same time, he was becoming increasingly critical of Franco's rule, especially after the dismissal of his friend and ideological companion **Ramón Serrano Suñer** from the post of foreign secretary in September 1942. Like Serrano Suñer himself, by the 1950s, Ridruejo had thrown off his Fascist cloak, joining forces with the democratic opposition, and in the 1960s he was behind the foundation of the small semi-clandestine social-democratic party Uníon Social Democrática Española (Spanish Social Democratic Union). During the **transition to democracy**, most of its members would join the **Unión del Centro Democrático** (UCD).

RIEGO PRONUNCIAMIENTO. *See* CONSTITUTIONAL TRIENNIUM.

ROCA I JUNYENT, MIQUEL. Miquel Roca was a leading figure in Catalan politics between the 1970s and 1990s. Between 1976 and 1996, he was effectively number two to **Jordi Pujol** in the reforming, centrist, Catalanist party Convergència Democràtica de Catalunya, holding the posts of deputy general secretary between 1976 and 1988 and general secretary between 1988 and 1996. Between 1977 and 1994, he was also the leader of the **Convergència i Unió** (CiU) coalition in the Spanish parliament. In 1995, he turned to municipal politics, but was defeated by **Pascual Maragall** in that year's **Barcelona** mayoral elections. Through to 1999, he then held the post of leader of the opposition in the Barcelona town hall. Unlike Pujol, following in the footsteps on **Francesc Cambó**, Roca believed that **Catalanists** should play a leading role on the Spanish political stage, reforming Spain while extending Catalan autonomy. His most ambitious undertaking in this respect was the so-called "operación reformista" in 1986. This was an attempt to forge a centrist Spanish political party from **Catalonia**, the Partido Reformista Democrático (Democratic Reformist Party). It, however, proved a total failure, with Spanish voters unwilling to support someone linked to Catalan nationalist politics. Between 1993 and 1999, he also attempted, to no avail, to convince Pujol to enter the governments of the **Partido Socialista Obrero Español** (PSOE) and **Partido Popular** (PP), which were dependent on the support of CiU in the Spanish parliament. In 2002, as part of a strategy to co-opt sectors of the CiU, **José María Aznar** offered him the post of foreign secretary. Roca i Junynet turned him down.

RODRÍGUEZ ZAPATERO, JOSÉ LUIS (1960–). Rodríguez Zapatero is the current Spanish prime minister. He was born in Valladolid, studied law, and went on to teach constitutional law in the University of León. He came from an anti-Francoist family. His grandfather was an army captain who was shot for refusing to participate in the 1936 **Nationalist** uprising against the **Second Republic**. This no doubt influenced his decision to join the **Partido Socialista Obrero Español** (PSOE) at the age of 29. He quickly made a mark in the local and provincial party and was first elected as Socialist deputy for León in the 1986 general elections. Over the next decade and a half, he built a reputation for common sense and tact, joining the party's Federal Committee in 1990 and its Federal Executive Commission—the key decision-making body between elections—in 1997. Importantly, though after 1996 he believed in the need for party renewal, he did not ally with any particular sector of the party. His chance came at the party's July 2000 congress, in which he narrowly beat **José Bono** in the election for party leader.

Rodríguez Zapatero subsequently undertook a wide-ranging renewal of the party's leadership cadres. This was a crucial step because the new team now had few ties to the disappointments and **corruption** scandals of the past PSOE government. His thoughtful, open manner and willingness to enter into a constructive dialogue with the government (backing, for example, an antiterrorist pact in 2000) also contrasted positively with Prime Minister **José María Aznar**'s much more aggressive style. In terms of policy, he offered change on a number of fronts. First, he opposed Aznar's Euroskeptic Atlanticist position and in particular played an active role in the popular mobilization against the **Iraq war**. Second, he was open to suggestions—most notably advanced by the leading figure within Catalan Socialism, **Pascual Maragall**—that the **State of the Autonomies** needed reform and that the Senate should become a "Territorial House." This would take Spain in a **federalist** direction. Third, as compared to the cultural conservatives of the **Partido Popular** (PP), he advocated a more culturally liberal approach in the spheres of **education** and personal freedoms. Fourth, he offered the introduction of further **welfare** reforms. Finally, he was critical of the PP's control of the state-run media and affirmed his intention to improve the "quality of Spanish democracy."

These factors meant that Rodríguez Zapatero was able to offer a serious challenge to Aznar. Opinion polls became more favorable during 2002, yet he failed to make a decisive breakthrough in the May 2003 municipal and regional elections. His inexperience raised doubts and the strength of the Spanish **economy** played in Aznar's favor. Hence, in the run-up to the March 2004 general elections, opinion polls indicated that while the PSOE was going to do better than in 2000, the PP would still win. This was changed by the **Madrid train bombings** of 11 March and the government's increasingly untenable claim that **ETA** was responsible. Most notably, it produced the mobilization of young culturally liberal voters, who were against the Iraq war.

As a result, Rodríguez Zapatero came to power in a climate of, on the one hand, euphoria on the left, and, on the other, bitter anger on the right that they had been "robbed." This was to set the tone for the legislature. Rodríguez Zapatero delighted his supporters by quickly pulling Spanish troops out of Iraq and announcing his intention to "return Spain to the heart of Europe." This, in reality, meant reestablishing close links with the French and German governments. At the United Nations he then announced in September—implicitly rejecting the idea that there was a "clash of civilizations" between **Islam** and the Western world—that an "alliance of civilizations" was needed to combat **terrorism** (*Anuario El País 2005*, 130–31). His key policy initiatives—reforming the State of the Autonomies, introducing changes in state education (and reducing the importance of religious teaching), sanctioning gay marriage and making divorce easier, along with his effort to try to bring ETA terrorism to an end through negotiation—produced a right-wing countermobilization. The decision by ETA to break its cease-fire by bombing Madrid Barajas airport in December 2006 was a big blow. Critics, probably correctly, criticized Rodríguez Zapatero for becoming too directly implicated and too obsessed with the issue. The theme of government "concessions" to ETA became a stick with which the PP and right-wing media could effectively beat the government, backed up by massive demonstrations organized by the **Asociación de Víctimas del Terrorismo**. This offensive continued into 2007. In March, when the government allowed the ETA hunger striker who was on the point of death, Iñaki de Juana Chaos, to serve out the rest of his prison sentence under house arrest, Rodríguez Zapatero's poll ratings were hit, and a demonstration in Madrid on 11 March attracted several hundred thousand protestors.

However, Rodríguez Zapatero's position subsequently improved. He made clear that there would be no further discussions with ETA or the *abertzale* left. The PP-inspired offensive also had the effect of frightening some more moderate voters and its attack on the reform of the State of the Autonomies went down very badly in **Catalonia**. Furthermore, Rodríguez Zapatero's culturally liberal agenda was popular among wide sectors of Spanish youth and in much of the professional middle class. And during 2007, he also stressed the strong performance of the Spanish economy and that he intended, if successful in the March 2008 general elections, to introduce new social reforms aimed at working families. His own poll ratings were relatively high: in July his acceptance rating stood at 5.1 (out of 10), compared to **Mariano Rajoy**'s rating of 3.8. This was just as well. During the election campaign, the PSOE was hit by the rapidly deteriorating economic climate and also put on the defensive by Rajoy's claim that Spain had suffered an "avalanche" of **immigrants** in recent years, which had to be curbed. Nevertheless, though the Socialists failed to gain an overall majority, they won a narrow victory. This will allow Rodríguez Zapatero to govern for another four years, but he will need to reach agreements with the minority parties, especially the Catalan nationalists, **Convergència i Unió**.

ROLDÁN IBÁÑEZ, LUIS (1943–). Roldán was the figure at the center of one of the most damaging **corruption** scandals to hit the **Partido Socialista Obrero Español** (PSOE) government during the 1990s. He had been a PSOE activist since the 1970s. After being appointed director general of the **Civil Guard**, he set about amassing an illicit fortune by charging construction companies commission for the building of Civil Guard barracks. Under suspicion, he was removed from office in December 1993. In April of the following year, he then fled to Laos, but was tracked down and extradited. In February 1998, he was sentenced to 28 years. He was released on parole in 2002, but most of the money is still missing.

ROMANONES, COUNT OF. ÁLVARO DE FIGUEROA Y TORRES (1863–1950). The count of Romanones was, along with **Manuel García Prieto**, the leading **Partido Liberal** (PL) politician between 1912 and 1923. He was born in **Madrid** into a wealthy landowning family, which also had important **mining** interests. His power base was the large *caciquista* support network he built up, based on the family's estates in the province of Guadalajara. After the death of **José Canalejas** in 1912, he vied for power within the party with García Prieto. It appeared he had come out on top in December 1915 when King **Alfonso XIII** chose him as prime minister and allowed him to call elections (and therefore "make" a majority in parliament). However, his pro-Allied **foreign policy** during **World War I** increasingly antagonized the king (along with **military** and conservative opinion), who brought him down in April 1917 and handed over power to his archrival, García Prieto (an advocate of strict neutrality).

The PLwas subsequently split, with Romanones controlling only a minority of Liberal deputies in the **Cortes**.

In the aftermath of the Allies' victory, his pro-Allied stance briefly came in handy and he was chosen by the king to take over as prime minister in December 1918, even though he had only a small group of Liberal deputies behind him. During this ministry, he took a conciliatory stance with respect to the major political issues of the day. He tried seriously to resolve the Catalan "problem," setting up an extraparliamentary commission to draft a Catalan autonomy statute. However, it was undermined by both the **Partido Conservador** opposition and the **Catalanist** left. Subsequently, as labor agitation in **Barcelona** escalated, he attempted to integrate the **anarchist**-syndicalist **Confederación Nacional del Trabajo** (CNT) into state-sponsored arbitration machinery. This, however, enraged the Barcelona military garrison, along with conservative (especially business) opinion in the Catalan capital, provoking his fall in April 1919. He would never again hold the post of prime minister. In 1930–1931, he participated in the attempt to resurrect the Restoration regime, becoming minister of the state in the government of Juan Bautista Aznar (1860–1933). However, in the aftermath of the 12 April 1931 municipal elections, he played an important role in ensuring a peaceful transition to the **Second Republic**.

ROMERO ROBLEDO, FRANCISCO (1838–1906). Nicknamed the "pollo de Antequera" (Antequera peacock), Romero Robledo rose to become a key figure in the construction of the *caciquista* underpinnings of the **Cánovas Restoration**. He was born in Antequera (Málaga), and, like almost all ambitious young men, went on to study law. He first joined the **Unión Liberal** and then during the **Democratic Sexennium** (1868–1874) formed part of **Práxedes Mateo Sagasta**'s Partido Constitucionalista (Constitutionalist Party). As subsecretary in the Ministry of the Interior in 1871, he began to learn the art of electoral manipulation. From 1873, he moved over to the **Alfonsoist monarchist** camp, captained by **Antonio Cánovas del Castillo**. He occupied the post of interior minister in Cánovas's first administration between 1875 and 1879, ensuring that although the December 1875 elections were held under universal suffrage, the government would attain a large majority. He was again to hold this position between

1880 and 1881 and between 1884 and 1885. From this vantage point, he would take the lead in forging the **Partido Conservador**'s (PC) *caciquista* base. In 1885, however, he fell out with Cánovas over the latter's decision to hand over power to the **Partido Liberal**, and for a time formed part of a small Partido Liberal Reformista (Liberal Reformist Party). This was the first serious dissidence within the PC.

Through marriage to the daughter of Salvador Zulueta y Sama (second marquis of Álava from 1875), Romero Robledo acquired extensive interests in **Cuba**, and in 1898 was one of the most vocal supporters of war with the United States at all costs. He reintegrated into the PC in 1890 and after the death of Cánovas in 1897 he hoped to take over the leadership. He represented the "continuist" option. **Regenerationist** winds were, however, blowing, and the post went to **Francisco Silvela**. Thereafter, he formed his own Conservative group in parliament, briefly holding the reins of power in 1902. *See also* SPANISH-AMERICAN WAR.

ROVIRA I VIRGILI, ANTONI. *See* ACCIÓ CATALANA; CENTRE NACIONALISTA REPUBLICÀ.

ROYAL STATUTE/ESTATUTO REAL. The Royal Statute was a constitutional text produced by the **Martínez de la Rosa** administration and sanctioned by the queen regent, **María Cristina of Naples**, on 10 April 1834. Its aim was to permit a timid liberalization of Spanish society, while trying to reconcile the forces of **Carlism** and maintain political power firmly in the hands of social elites. This was reflected in its restrictive provisions. It was the prerogative of the sovereign to choose the representatives of a noble Upper House (*próceres del reino*), while property qualifications were needed to elect representatives to the Lower House (*procuradores del reino*). A royal decree that accompanied the statute limited the electors to the Lower House to well under 1 percent of the population. However, the statute failed to mollify the Carlists and was opposed by **Partido Progresista** liberals, leading to its replacement by the **Constitution of 1837**.

RUIZ-GALLARDÓN JIMENEZ, ALBERTO (1958–). Ruiz-Gallardón has made his name as the major representative of the minority centrist wing of the **Partido Popular** (PP). He was born in **Madrid** and studied law at the Complutense University of Madrid. He first made his mark when he led the PP to an impressive victory in the elections to the Madrid regional government in May 1994. However, he was unhappy at the direction in which **José María Aznar** was taking the party after 1996 and the latter came to regard him as his enemy. He was forced to abandon the presidency of the Madrid regional assembly (Comunidad de Madrid) in early 2003 to make way for Aznar's close ally, **Esperanza Aguirre**, and ran for the post of mayor of Madrid in the March 2003 local election. In these elections, he was spectacularly successful.

Since the March 2004 general election, he has been at daggers' drawn with right-wingers in the PP (most notably Esperanza Aguirre, **Eduardo Zaplana**, and **Ángel Acebes**) and has tried to present himself as representing a more liberal, centrist alternative (outraging the **Catholic** right by officiating over a gay wedding in June 2006). In August 2007, he announced that he wished to form part of the PP list of candidates for the March 2008 general elections in Madrid. This was, however, blocked by the right, who feared that as a parliamentary deputy he would be in a strong position to challenge Rajoy should the PP perform very poorly. His future prospects are now complex. The hard right (most notably Zaplana and Acebes) has been weakened by the election defeat. Rajoy looks likely to remain as party president, and will in the future probably try to take the PP toward the political center. Esperanza Aguirre is, however, still a powerful foe.

RUIZ-GIMÉNEZ CORTÉS, JOAQUÍN (1913–). Joaquín Ruiz-Giménez was the only member of a Francoist cabinet who was subsequently to move into direct opposition to the regime. He was born into an upper-class **Madrid** family on 2 August 1913. His father had been a minister under King **Alfonso XIII** and mayor of Madrid. He became a leading figure in the **Catholic** Youth and during the **Spanish Civil War** he fought for the **Nationalist** cause. During the **Franco regime**, he was strongly identified with Catholic interests and was one of a group of members of the **Asociación Católica Nacional de Propagandistas** (ACNP) who attained cabinet office (others were **Alberto Martín Artajo** and **Fernándo María Castiella**) and who from the 1950s began to push for a greater degree of cultural freedom. None, however, were to go as far as Ruiz-Giménez. He was made minister of **education** in the cabinet reshuffle of 19 July 1951. From this position, he tried to modernize Spanish universities, and appointed a number of culturally more liberal **Falangists** to university chairs. This provoked a backlash among the Francoist right, who by 1954 had virtually blocked his reforms. His final downfall came in February 1956, when he was sacked following serious student protests at the University of Madrid.

Henceforth, along with a group of "progressive Catholics," he adopted a **Christian-democratic** outlook and broke with Francoism. A number of "critical Falangists," most notably **Dionisio Ridruejo**, also severed their ties with the regime. The importance of these splits lay in the fact that for the first time, elements within the Franco elite had moved into opposition. In 1963, Ruiz-Gimenez founded the influential journal *Cuadernos para el diálogo*, in which Christian-democratic, social-democratic, liberal, and socialist intellectuals all participated. This was to be an important precedent of the cooperation that underlay the **transition to democracy** between 1976 and 1978. He also founded a semi-tolerated political party, Izquierda Democrática Cristiana (Left Christian Democracy), renamed Izquierda Democrática (Democratic Left) in April 1976. His party joined Plataforma Democrática (Democratic Platform), led by the **Partido Socialista Obrero Español** (PSOE), in 1975, and then participated with the left in negotiations with the government of **Adolfo Suárez** that made possible the transition. In the June 1977 elections, Izquierda Democrática formed part of a Federación Demócrata-Cristiana (Christian-Democratic Federation). Yet without a mass base, neither Izquierda Democrática nor the coalition as a whole made an impact. In 1982, the PSOE government appointed him to the post of Defender of the People (Defensor del Pueblo), a position he retained until 1987.

RUIZ ZORRILLA, MANUEL. *See* DEMOCRATIC SEXENNIUM; PARTIDO RADICAL; PARTIDO REPUBLICANO PROGRESISTA.

– S –

SAGASTA Y ESCOLAR, PRÁXEDES MATEO (1825–1903). Together with **Antonio Cánovas de Castillo**, Sagasta was the major politician of late 19th-century Spain. He was born in the province of Logroño into a **liberal** family of modest circumstances. He soon showed himself to be academically able, and on moving to **Madrid** in the 1840s to study engineering, he joined the **Partido Progresista**. Over the next 20 years, he was to be at the forefront of the *progresista*-inspired revolts against the **Partido Moderado**. By the 1860s, he had become a leading figure within the party and was to play a key role in the plot to overthrow Queen **Isabel II**. With the success of the **Glorious Revolution**, he moved into government, and over the following four years he held a series of high offices, including the post of prime minister. However, between 1871 and 1872, in the context of growing political and social agitation, the coalition behind the September Revolution began to fall apart. Sagasta captained the more conservative supporters of constitutional monarchy, who formed the Partido Constitucionalista (Constitutionalist Party) and outlawed the pro-**anarchist** labor confederation, the **Federación Regional Española** (FRE), in January 1872. With the radicalization of the regime after the resignation of King **Amadeo I**, in February 1873 he was forced out of office and he determined that in the future liberal reform should be made compatible with order and stability.

For this reason, after the fall of the **First Republic**, Sagasta acted as a focus for those former *progresistas* who were willing to participate in the **Cánovas Restoration**, agreeing to head a new **Partido Liberal** in return for a constitution that accepted a degree of religious toleration and that allowed the possibility of slowly legislating the civil rights guaranteed in the **Constitution of 1869**. In this way, in power in the 1880s, he was able to enact, in an orderly fashion, many of the rights he had fought for as a young man. And yet it was also during these years that Sagasta's party showed its limitations. It was a party of notables, which participated in the construction of the regime's undemocratic *caciquista* foundations, and which had limited popular backing. The regime's failings were fully exposed by the **Spanish-American War** of 1898. Sagasta, as prime minister, bore the brunt of the criticism. Discredited in more reforming circles, he would die five years later.

SALMERÓN ALONSO, NICOLÁS (1838–1908). Salmerón was the leading figure on the moderate wing of Spanish **republicanism** between 1873 and 1908. He was born in the province of Almería and went on to study law and humanities at the University of Madrid, where he was strongly influenced by **Krausism**. From the 1850s, he became involved in democratic politics and journalism, helping to found the **Partido Republicano Federalista** in 1868. With the coming of the **First Republic**, however, he made clear his determination to ensure republicanism would be compatible with order. Hence, after replacing **Francesc Pi i Margall** as president of the Republic on 20 July following the onset of the **Cantonalist revolt**, he did not hesitate to use the army against the insurgents.

This preoccupation with the need to maintain discipline and central control led Salmerón to break with the federalists after the fall of the Republic. He helped to found the **Partido Republicano Progresista**, went on to set up his own Partido Republicano Centralista (Centralist Republican Party), and thereafter attempted to unify the fragmented republican movement around his person. In 1903, it seemed he had achieved success with the formation of the **Unión Republicana**, but over the following three years dissensions between right and left once again tore republicanism apart. Salmerón was concerned to build an interclass alliance against the **Cánovas Restoration**, and so after the *Cu-Cut!* **incident** he proved willing to ally with the **Lliga Regionalista** in a coalition known as **Solidaritat Catalana**. However, the most powerful figure of Catalan republicanism, **Alejandro Lerroux**, refused to back what he saw as the reactionary Catalan bourgeoisie, founding his own **Partido Republicano Radical**. When Salmerón died in September 1908, therefore, he had not achieved his major goal. His greatest accomplishment was to help keep the flame of republicanism alive among the country's progressive urban middle classes, but, imbued by 19th-century patrician politics, he proved unable to weld the organizations he led into mass parties with efficient electoral machines.

SAMARANCH I TORELLÓ, JUAN ANTONIO, MARQUIS OF SAMARANCH (1920–). Samaranch was president of the International Olympic Committee (IOC) between 1980 and 2001. He was born in **Barcelona** into a family with important business interests. From an early age, he was attracted to right-wing politics, and during 1936 suffered a police interrogation for belonging to the youth wing of the **Confederación Española de Derechas Autónomas** (CEDA). He was also a keen sportsman, and during the **Franco regime** would rise to the top in sports administration. He affiliated with the single party, the **Falange Española Tradicionalista y de las Juntas de Ofensiva Nacional Sindicalista** (FET y de las JONS), began to train the national Spanish hockey team, and, in 1954, became the provincial head of sport of the FET y de las JONS in Barcelona and a local councilor in the Barcelona town hall. The following year he would become a member of the Spanish Olympic Committee. At the same time, he continued his rise up the Francoist hierarchy and was chosen as government secretary for sports in 1966. He subsequently established himself as a leading figure within the IOC. He was vice president between 1974 and 1978 before finally being elected president of the IOC on 16 July 1980.

During his time as head of the IOC, Samaranch presided over the professionalization of Olympic sport and showed himself to be both a skillful diplomat and good organizer. However, he has been criticized for doing little to stem drug use and for his lavish personal tastes. Although it is officially denied, the fact he was president no doubt helped Barcelona's bid to stage the Olympic Games in 1992. For this reason, despite his Francoist past, he is treated with respect in Catalan political circles.

SÁNCHEZ GUERRA, JOSÉ (1859–1935). Born in Córdoba, Sánchez Guerra became a leading figure in the **Partido Conservador** between 1914 and 1923. He was very close to **Eduardo Dato** and, as his interior minister in the **crisis of 1917**, played a key role in thwarting the regime's enemies. He took over as leader of the party after the assassination of Dato in March 1921 and continued Dato's efforts, along with his **Partido Liberal** adversary, **Manuel García Prieto**, to reconstruct the *turno* system. When he came to power in March 1922 in the aftermath of the **Annual** disaster, he faced a strong left-wing campaign for those responsible to be tried and for the reestablishment of constitutional guarantees (suspended throughout Spain since March 1919). He responded by pursuing a moderate course. He restored constitutional guarantees on 31 March and in October he tried to reassert civilian control over the army, removing the civil governor of **Barcelona**, General Martínez Anido (1868–1939), who had established a virtual **military** fiefdom in the province. But, with several members of his cabinet in office during Annual, his government split and fell in December when the responsibilities question was discussed in parliament. After the fall of the **Primo de Rivera dictatorship** in 1930, like several leading Restoration politicians he broke with King **Alfonso XIII**, migrating to the conservative **republican** camp. In the June 1931 elections, he was elected as deputy for **Madrid** as part of an association called Agrupación al servicio de la republica (Grouping in the Service of the Republic), but as his health was poor, he would play no further active role in politics.

SAN GIL REVOLT. The revolt at the San Gil barracks in **Madrid** was part of a *pronunciamiento* launched by General **Juan Prim** on 22 June 1866. After its failure, the government of **Leopoldo O'Donnell** carried out a wide-ranging repression, executing 66 of those involved (including some sergeants who had not wished to take part).

SAN SEBASTIÁN PACT. This was an agreement reached between a number of **republican** groups, along with disillusioned former monarchists, in the Republican Center in San Sebastián on 17 August 1930, to bring down the monarchy and install a republic. **Indalecio Prieto** was present in a personal capacity and the **Partido Socialista Obrero Español** (PSOE) was, thereafter, to participate in the movement. A central revolutionary committee was formed and charged with making preparations for an uprising against the **monarchy**. Unlike events during the **crisis of 1917**, support for the movement encompassed an extremely wide political spectrum. Of the committee members, the president, Niceto Alcalá Zamora, and Miguel Maura had been important figures in the **Cánovas Restoration**; Marcelino Domingo (1864–1939), Álvaro de Albornoz (1879–1954), and **Manuel Azaña** were republicans; and **Francisco Largo Caballero** and Fernando de los Ríos (1879–1949) represented the PSOE. Meanwhile, a parallel committee was also set up in **Catalonia**. The committee tried to develop contacts with the **military** in order to organize a *pronunciamiento*, while the **Unión General de Trabajadores** (UGT), in alliance with the **Confederación Nacional del Trabajo** (CNT), prepared a general strike in support. The date was finally set for 15 December. It was, however, badly coordinated. On 12 December, a regiment led by captains Fermín Galán (1899–1930) and Angel García Hernández (1900–1930) rose up in Jaca and marched on Huesca only to be defeated in battle on their arrival. They were executed on 14 December. From 13 December, the government also began detaining members of the revolutionary committee, and although general strikes were declared in northern Spain on 15 December, in **Madrid** itself all remained quiet. The following months were, however, to see an enormous groundswell of support in urban Spain for a republican regime. Hence, when the revolutionary committee was put on trial on 20 March it was, in reality, the monarchy that was in the dock. Three days later, its members were sentenced by a military court to just six months and a day in prison, and the following day they were provisionally released. Less than one month later, following the republican victory in the 12 April municipal elections, they would form the **Second Republic**'s provisional government.

SANJURJADA. *See* SANJURJO Y SACANELL, JOSÉ.

SANJURJO Y SACANELL, JOSÉ (1872–1936). General Sanjurjo is best known for his attempted coup against the **Second Republic**, the so-called *Sanjurjada*, in September 1932. He was born in Pamplona, and like his father (a **Carlist** colonel), he chose a career in the **military**. He fought in **Cuba**, then played a leading role in the **Moroccan** war and was made a lieutenant general after having overseen the amphibious landing at Alhucemas Bay in September 1925. Sanjurjo was a close friend of General **Miguel Primo de Rivera** and, as captain general of Zaragoza, had closely cooperated in the Primo de Rivera coup of September 1923. Hence, the decision by King **Alfonso XIII** to sacrifice Primo de Rivera in January 1930 in the face of mounting protest lost him the support of Sanjurjo, then the director general of the **Civil Guard**. For this reason he refused to guarantee the loyalty of the Civil Guard after the municipal election results of 12 April 1931, opening the way to the proclamation of the Second Republic.

The new authorities left Sanjurjo in charge of the Civil Guard, from where he maintained a vigorous policy of maintaining law and order at all costs. This resulted in a large number of clashes between Civil Guards and peasants and workers. In one incident in the village of Arnedo in January 1932, Civil Guards opened fire, killing a number of workers. In response, the prime minister, **Manuel Azaña**, replaced Sanjurjo and moved him on to the post of head of the Carabineros (frontier police). Sanjurjo not only took this as a personal insult but also believed it would lead to anarchy and disorder, and responded by heading a military plot to overthrow the Republic. The date was set for 10 September. However, it was poorly organized and easily suffocated. Sanjurjo was arrested and condemned to death. The sentence was at first reduced to life, and then, with the rise to power of the right in November 1933, he was amnestied on condition that he live in exile. He chose the neighboring state of **Portugal**, and when a new military conspiracy, coordinated by General **Emilio Mola**, took shape in 1936, he agreed, as the most senior commander implicated, to head an interim junta after the coup. He made a trip to Berlin in March to seek German support, but achieved little in the way of concrete results. He died in an air crash on 20 July 1936, when taking off from Portugal to become the figurehead of the rebellion.

SAURA ATARES, CARLOS (1932–). Saura was the Spanish film director who enjoyed greatest international recognition between the 1960s and 1980s. His films comprised an often complex series of overlapping themes. He was interested in Spanish cultural and artistic traditions and directed a series of adaptations, the best known of which were his flamenco trilogy, *Bodas de Sangre* (*Blood Wedding*, 1981), *Carmen* (1983), and *El amor brujo* (*Love, the Magician*, 1985). In common with most serious artists of his period, he chartered the negative impact of the **Franco regime** on Spanish society in films like *Ana y los lobos* (*Ana and the Wolves*, 1972), but his interest in universal themes and the human condition gave his works a broader, international appeal.

SECCIÓN FEMININA (SF)/WOMEN'S SECTION. This body was originally created in 1934 as the **women**'s front of the Fascist **Falange Española**. When the **Franco regime** created its single party, the **Falange Española Tradicionalista y de las Juntas de Ofensiva Nacional Sindicalista** (FET y de las JONS) in April 1937, it was charged with the task of socializing women in the new conservative, Catholic, patriarchic culture of the regime and grew massively. Unmarried women under the age of 35 and childless widows were required to undertake six months of "social service." They undertook courses on topics like religion, the family, and child care, and also did voluntary work in schools, hospitals, and the like. In schools, the SF ran courses on motherhood and it also provided a rural health service. There was some tension between the Sección Feminina and the **Catholic Church**. Because of the former's Fascist heritage, it envisaged young women playing a more active role than that approved of by the Church. The members' relatively short skirts and sporting activities sometimes drew the condemnation of local clergy. Nevertheless, it put across a similar message, stressing that married women should limit themselves to bringing up children within the private sphere. It was wound up in 1977. Since its inception in 1934, it was run by Pilar Primo de Rivera (1907–1991), the sister of **José Antonio Primo de Rivera**.

SECOND INTERNATIONAL. *See* IGLESIAS POSSE, PABLO; PARTIDO SOCIALISTA OBRERO ESPAÑOL; TRES CLASES DE VAPOR.

SECOND MARQUIS OF COMILLAS. *See* COMILLAS, SECOND MARQUIS OF.

SECOND REPUBLIC. The Second Republic was born following the municipal elections of 12 April 1931 and is usually seen as ending with the **military** insurrection of 17–18 July 1936. During the **Spanish Civil War**, a Republican government continued to function in part of Spain, but its authority was contested by the forces of General **Francisco Franco**. It was a period of acute political and social strife. It began as an attempt by the political representatives of a part of the organized **labor movement** and the radical middle classes to fundamentally reform Spain's polity and the balance of social forces in the country. A countermobilization by the right then produced an increasingly polarized political climate, culminating in civil war.

The Republic can roughly be divided into three main phases. During the Bienio Reformista (Reforming Biennium) of 1931–1933, an alliance between the various **republican** groupings and the **Partido Socialista Obrero Español** (PSOE) attempted to carry through a number of fundamental political and social reforms. In December 1931, a new, more democratic **constitution** was approved by the constituent **Cortes**. Then, four major reform projects were undertaken. First, measures were taken to make the army more efficient and politically neutral. Second, new laws were passed reducing the power and influence of the **Catholic Church** in Spanish life. Third, an attempt was made to solve the "Catalan problem" by promulgating an autonomy statute for **Catalonia**—a similar statute was to be approved for the **Basque Country** during the civil war. Fourth, the **Agrarian Reform Law** was drawn up, with the object of transferring some of the land held by the southern estate owners to the land-hungry peasantry.

These reforms quickly ran into difficulty. In the first place, workers' and peasants' expectations had been raised enormously and there was disappointment at the slow pace of reform. The anarchist-syndicalist **Confederación Nacional del Trabajo** (CNT) was able to take advantage of this to mobilize against the Republic. Second, the slow pace of change also led to disillusionment within the PSOE and its labor confederation, the **Unión General de Trabajadores** (UGT), and led to talk of the need to break with the republicans (who were lukewarm in their support for social reform) and take power themselves. Third, the right began rapidly to mobilize against the reforms, forming a powerful coalition, the **Confederación Española de Derechas Autónomas** (CEDA), in February 1933.

When new elections were held in November 1933, because of divisions within the leftist camp the republicans and PSOE presented separate candidatures. The right, however, was far more united. As a result, the CEDA emerged as the largest party in parliament, followed by the conservative republican party **Partido Republicano Radical** (PRR). The period between November 1933 and February 1936 forms the next broad period into which the Republic can be divided. In leftist circles, it was to be known as the Bienio Negro (Black Biennium). Throughout this period, the right was in power. First the PRR governed with CEDA backing, and then, from October 1933, with the participation of CEDA ministers. The reforms of the

Bienio Reformista were put into reverse. The PSOE, which feared that once in power the CEDA would try to set up an authoritarian **corporatist** state, warned that if CEDA members entered government, it would carry out a revolutionary general strike. This was the background to the **October 1934 revolution**. It was, however, put down by the **military**. The PRR held out against the wide-ranging repression demanded by the CEDA, and this gave the left an opportunity to reorganize. In the February 1936 elections, the left did not make the same mistake as in November 1933, forming a united **Popular Front** coalition. The left won and a new republican government took power. It became clear to the right that it would not be able to stop leftist reforms through victory at the polls, and so a conspiracy to overthrow the Republic began to take shape.

The slide to war between February and July 1936 may be seen as the third phase of the Republic. It was marked by the decline of the CEDA and the transfer of right-wing support to those parties that favored a coup, the Fascist **Falange Española**, along with the **Carlists** and **Alfonsoist monarchists**. However, the main burden of preparing the conspiracy fell on the shoulders of rightist officers. Many in the military were dismayed at what they saw as the lack of order and the threat to the unity of Spain posed by the autonomy statutes. Their conspiracy culminated on 17–18 July 1936 with a military uprising in most Spanish cities and in **Morocco**. It was only partially successful, and so what was planned as a swift military coup ended in civil war. *See also* TABLE 9.

SEGUÍ I RUBINAT, SALVADOR (1887–1923). Salvador Seguí was the greatest leader of the **Confederación Nacional del Trabajo** (CNT) during the years in which the **Cánovas Restoration** entered into crisis between 1917 and 1923. He was born in Reus but soon moved to **Barcelona**, where he became a painter's apprentice. He was quickly taken in by the libertarian atmosphere of the Catalan capital and during the first decade of the century led a bohemian lifestyle and frequented an individualist anarchist group known as the Hijos sin Nombre (Sons with no Name). However, from 1907, he became more seriously involved in union politics. He attended the founding congress of the CNT in 1910, and in 1915 was elected head of the Federation of Barcelona Construction Workers. Over the next four years, he emerged as the leading light on the syndicalist or possibilist wing of the Catalan CNT, and was elected its general secretary at the Sants Congress in the summer of 1918. He was not averse to using militant tactics, but believed unions should not be drawn into suicidal general strikes that could only benefit the bourgeoisie. He was a committed **anarchist** but also argued that the revolution could not come before the workers were organizationally prepared and well enough educated. Finally, he was not so virulently "anti-political" as his hard-line anarchist-syndicalist colleagues and was willing to cooperate with other leftist groups in order to bring about a more democratic republican regime.

All of these elements were to be seen in Seguí's strategy between 1916 and 1919. He allied with the **Unión General de Trabajadores** (UGT) to put pressure on the government to take action against price rises during 1916, and during the **crisis of 1917**, he supported the attempt to overthrow the Cánovas Restoration and put in place a more democratic regime. At the same time, he aimed to strengthen the Catalan unions through the formation of local industrial unions (Sindicats Unics). His concern with strengthening the organization could also be seen in 1919 following the great La Canadenca strike in Barcelona. Radicals within the CNT were hoping to turn the strike in the electrical power-generating company into a general strike. However, in a triumph of oratory at the Las Arenas bull ring on 19 March, Seguí managed to convince the strikers to return to work in return for the release of those strikers held.

What seemed like a victory for Seguí was, however, undone three days later when the **military** authorities in Barcelona, in what looked like a deliberate provocation, refused to release some of the strikers, leading to the calling of a general strike against his advice. This highlights the great problems Seguí and his "team" faced in imposing their strategy. As the CNT grew at a vertiginous rate and strikes escalated, employers struck back in order to reimpose social control in their factories, and to achieve this end were not adverse to using hired gunmen and allying with the local military establishment. As a result, between 1919 and 1923, a dirty war was fought against the CNT, with gunmen used to assassinate labor leaders and the military and police used to break up the CNT trade unions. In these circumstances, after the La Canadenca strike, Seguí and those who thought like him found it almost impossible to operate, finding themselves in prison for much of the time and in constant danger of physical annihilation from the employers' gunmen. This was the fate of Salvador Seguí. Between November 1920 and April 1922, he was incarcerated in a prison on Mahón Island, and a year after his release, on 10 March 1923, he was shot down on the streets of Barcelona. It is not unreasonable to suppose that had Seguí and his collaborators been able to operate with relative freedom, the Catalan CNT might slowly have evolved in a moderate "reformist" direction. The events of 1919–1923, however, were to ensure that the hard-line anarchist insurrectionists were in the future to play a key role within the confederation.

SENDER GARCÉS, RAMÓN JOSÉ (1901–1981). Sender is one of the best and most widely read Spanish novelists of the 20th century. He was born in the province of Huesca and spent a brief period at law school before undertaking **military service** in **Morocco** in 1923. His time in the **military** radicalized him and led his early writing to take on a distinctly political content. This was brought out in his first novels such as *Iman* (*Magnet*, 1930) and his favorable portrait of Spanish **anarchism**, *Siete domingos rojos* (*Seven Red Sundays*, 1932). Sender fought on the Republican side during the **Spanish Civil War**, but his experience of the barbarity and horrors of war (including the murder of his wife behind **Nationalist** lines) led him to recoil from radical politics and take a far more pessimistic view of the human condition. Hence, subsequent works, most notably *Requiem por un campesino español* (*Requiem for a Spanish Peasant*, 1960), centered on the civil war and were personalized accounts of struggle, sacrifice, and grief. Before the civil war, he had earned his living as a journalist on the prestigious **Madrid** daily *El Sol*. He subsequently went into exile and took up teaching posts in the universities of Albuquerque and Los Angeles.

SEÑORÍOS. *Señoríos* or lordships had their origin in the "**Reconquest**" of Spain from the **Moors**. They were privileges granted by the crown to the nobility on newly reconquered land in order to build up alliances with the major aristocratic families. At the outset, most of these were so-called *señoríos territoriales*, which gave the nobles not only possession of the land, but also power to administer justice, collect taxes, nominate officials, and raise armies. Later, an increasing number of *señoríos jurisdiccionales* were granted, through which the nobles did not actually own the land, but they enjoyed the privileges outlined above. This was the origin of the great *latifundia* estates that were to dominate much of La Mancha and **Andalusia**. They were, moreover, greatly extended in the 16th and 17th centuries, as the **Habsburg** monarchs sold off crown and Church lands in order to raise revenue, with the result that much of rural and small-town Spain came under *señorío* jurisdiction. During the 19th century, nobles benefited from confusion between the two types of *señorío* and used their power within local communities to extend their landholdings. This was one of the factors that fueled peasant discontent with the **liberal** transition, leading many to mobilize behind either **Carlism** or **republicanism**.

SEPTEMBER REVOLUTION. *See* GLORIOUS REVOLUTION.

SER. Cadena SER is Spain's most popular **radio** network. Originally created in the 1920s, in the late 1980s the **PRISA** group (which also owns *El País*) took a key stake in the business. This has meant that, while it can by no means be regarded as a propaganda outlet, it tends to be favorably inclined toward the **Partido Socialista Obrero Español** (PSOE). In 1996, it had 9.6 million listeners, over double that of its nearest rival, **COPE**.

SERRA I SERRA, NARCÍS (1943–). Serra was a leading figure in **Felipe González**'s **Partido Socialista Obrero Español** (PSOE) governments of the 1980s and 1990s. He gained a reputation for competence as mayor of **Barcelona** between 1979 and 1982. He then became minister of defense between November 1982 and March 1991, playing a key role in Spain's integration into the **North Atlantic Treaty Organization**. He was subsequently given the post of government vice president, but was forced to resign in June 1995 following revelations by *El Mundo* that the for the previous 10 years the Spanish intelligence agency, the Centro Superior de Información de la Defensa (CESID), had been involved in illegal phone tappings of businessmen, journalists, politicians, and even King **Juan Carlos**.

He then returned to Catalan politics and took over as general secretary of the Catalan Socialists, the **Partit dels Socialistes de Catalunya-Partido Socialista Obrero Español** (PSC-PSOE) (though **Pascual Maragall** became the candidate for presidency of the **Generalitat**), but stepped down after the party's poor showing in the March 2000 general elections. He was seen by González as loyal and a safe pair of hands in the sensitive area of relations with the **military**, but lacked the charisma and flair necessary to become a party leader. In 2005, he was appointed president of the mutual savings bank La Caixa Catalana.

SERRANO Y DOMÍNGUEZ, FRANCISCO (1810–1885). Francisco Serrano was one of a number of **military** figures who were to play a key role in 19th-century Spanish politics. He was born in Cádiz into a military family and joined the cavalry. Politically, he was somewhat of an opportunist, very much blowing with the prevailing wind. He was involved in the execution of **liberals** following the abortive Torrijos *pronunciamiento* of 1830, but with the collapse of absolute monarchy, he quickly moved over to the liberal camp. After Queen **Isabel II** acceded to the throne in 1843, he became a favorite at court (and was rumored to be her lover), but after he was pushed out in 1847, he became more critical. He favored **Baldomero Espartero**'s rule between 1854 and 1856, and then during the 1860s played a leading role in the consolidation of the **Unión Liberal**. He put down the **San Gil revolt** of 1865, but after the death of **Leopoldo O'Donnell** in the following year, he led the **Unión Liberal** into an alliance with the **Partido Progresista** and **Partido Demócrata**, with the result that he now formed part of a coalition of forces trying to overthrow the dynasty. Along with **Juan Prim**, he organized the **Glorious Revolution** of 1868. After its success, he headed the first provisional government, and after the elections of January 1869 he was made regent.

Following the coronation of King **Amadeo I**, he presided over the government on two more occasions and took command of the government forces fighting the **Carlists** in the **Basque Country**. He was not, however, willing to countenance the proclamation of the **First Republic**. He tried to organize a countercoup, and when this failed, he went into exile in Biarritz. He returned just before the Manuel

Pavia (1827–1895) coup against the Republic on 4 January 1874, and subsequently tried to consolidate a right-wing republic under his presidency. His efforts were undone by the groundswell of support for a **Bourbon** restoration and he could do little to counter the *pronunciamiento* of General Arsensio Martínez Campos (1831–1900) in favor of Isabel's son Alfonso. Typically, however, he soon reconciled himself to the new authorities and became the nominal head of the new liberal dynastic camp. Yet, when in 1881 the **Partido Liberal** came to power, the king called for **Práxedes Mateo Sagasta**, and in the last years of his life a disappointed Serrano was left to head a critical faction within the party known as the Izquierda Dinástica (Dynastic Left).

SERRANO SUÑER, RAMÓN (1901–2003). Like many future rightwing politicians, Serrano Suñer came from a traditional, **Catholic** family. He studied law at the University of Madrid and spent some time doing postgraduate work in Italy, where he developed an admiration for Fascism. He married Zita Polo, the sister of **Francisco Franco**'s wife, in 1931, and established a friendship with the future **Caudillo**. During the **Second Republic**, he became a deputy in the **Confederación Española de Derechas Autónomas** (CEDA), though he was also on close terms with the Fascist leader **José Antonio Primo de Rivera**. Like many rightists, he abandoned the CEDA in 1936 when it seemed clear that only a violent assault on the Second Republic would halt social reform.

Serrano Suñer was taken prisoner by the Republican forces during the **Spanish Civil War**. Two of his brothers were executed, but he was released in a prisoner exchange in February 1937. Immediately upon his arrival in the **Nationalist** zone, he began to stand out among the Franco entourage for his sharp mind, political acumen, and legal training. He therefore quickly replaced Franco's brother Nicolás as his most trusted advisor, and was over the next three years able to concentrate a vast amount of political power in his hands. His most important task in the first months was to institutionalize the new regime and give it a mass base. He showed Fascist leanings, but was somewhat more clerical and conservative than many in the pro-Fascist camp. In consonance with his beliefs, he came up with the plan to amalgamate the **Falange Española** and **Carlists**—the only Nationalist parties with a mass base—to form a new single party, the **Falange Española Tradicionalista y de las Juntas de Ofensiva Nacional Sindicalista** (FET y de las JONS), while ensuring that it was firmly subordinate to his person and that of the Caudillo.

His preeminent position under Franco (he quickly became known as the Cuñadísimo, or super brother-in-law, a play on Franco's title of Generalísimo) was confirmed by a number of key appointments over the next two years. In Franco's first cabinet of 30 January 1938, he was given the post of interior minister. He then became the head of the FET y de las JON's executive committee, the Junta Política, on 31 July 1939, running its day-to-day policy. Finally, on 16 October 1940, he was made foreign secretary. Moreover, because no one was appointed minister of the interior to replace him, he effectively controlled both departments. Along with Franco, he played the part of a Fascist dictator with gusto. He was strongly pro-German and during 1940 took the lead in negotiating the conditions under which Spain would enter **World War II**. Both he and Franco were at this time keen for Spain to join the Axis and therefore receive a cut of the imperial spoils following what they saw as the inevitable defeat of the Allies, but negotiations broke down as a result of Adolf Hitler's unwillingness to accept Franco's territorial demands.

During 1941, he continued to pursue a strongly pro-Axis **foreign policy** while also seeking to enhance the position of the FET y de las JONS within the regime. It is unlikely that he wished to challenge Franco. Rather, he aimed to build a more clearly fascistic state, with Franco as the leader and he himself as Franco's lieutenant. This provoked the strong opposition of conservative **military** men, who believed that both the single party and Serrano Suñer were becoming too powerful, and it appears that Franco was becoming alarmed that he might be trying to establish an independent power base. In order to cut him down to size, on 5 May 1941 Franco made a series of ministerial and administrative changes, including, most spectacularly, the appointment of the monarchist sympathizer Colonel Valentín Galarza (1882–1951) as minister of the interior. A crisis then ensued when the FET y de las JONS's mouthpiece, *Arriba*, which was staffed by Serrano Suñer sympathizers, indirectly criticized Galarza's appointment. This led to calls for revenge in military circles. Franco responded with one of his proverbial balancing acts, but the overall result was to tie the single party more securely to his person. Most significantly, the acting minister secretary general of the FET y de las JONS, Pedro Gamero del Castillo (1910–), and the controllers of party's **press** and propaganda, the independent-minded "old shirts" **Dionisio Ridruejo** and Antonio Tovar (1911–1985), all close collaborators of Serrano Suñer's, were removed from their posts. Serrano Suñer offered to resign as foreign secretary. This was refused, but his position was greatly weakened.

During 1942, Serrano Suñer's standing deteriorated further. The realization that Germany might not win the war led many military men to call for the regime to take a more genuinely neutral stance. In addition, Franco, ever suspicious, still believed that Serrano Suñer might be a threat. The opportunity to take action came with an incident on 16 August during a memorial mass at the sanctuary of the Virgin of Bergoña in Bilbao in memory of Carlists fallen during the war, in which a group of disaffected Falangists threw two hand grenades at the crowd. Both Galarza and the army minister, General Enrique Varela (1891–1951), were present and demanded that action be taken. In a cabinet reshuffle on 3 September, both were to lose their jobs for informing the captains general of the military regions without Franco's permission, but, more importantly, Serrano Suñer was replaced as foreign secretary and Franco himself became head of the party's Junta Política. Serrano Suñer never again held high office. This led him to become increasingly hostile toward Franco. Ironically, from the 1950s, the man most closely identified with the "fascistization" of the early **Franco regime** put his weight behind those who called for political liberalization.

SERVICE SECTOR. As in other advanced Western countries, in Spain the service sector makes the greatest contribution to gross domestic product (GDP) and employment. Over the last three decades, it has expanded extremely rapidly. It grew from employing around 25 percent of the labor force in 1960 to 63.5 percent in 2006. It overtook industry as the main employer during the economic recession that followed the first oil price hike of 1973 and by 2001 close to eight million people worked within the sector. It has, at the same time, rapidly restructured and modernized, aided by the fact that the early

1990s saw a boom in foreign direct investment, over half of which was directed at services.

In terms of employment, **retail** is the largest sector, providing work for over two million people in 2000. Close behind is **tourism**, which provided direct employment for around 10 percent of the Spanish workforce in 2002 (860,000 people directly employed, and another 650,000 in related industries), but whose contribution to GDP is actually greater. These areas also provide much of the employment of Spain's **women** workers. The problem is that pay and working conditions tend to be poor and employment (especially in the tourist industry) seasonal. As a result, a significant sector of Spain's working population is locked into a low-wage economy. Conditions are much better in the public sector, which grew rapidly in size as the **welfare state**, which was underdeveloped under the **Franco regime**, subsequently expanded (most notably in the areas of health and **education**). In addition, the construction of the **State of the Autonomies** has necessitated a rapid growth in the number of regional administrators. Other parts of the service sector also provide well-qualified jobs. Both **banking** and **telecommunications** have developed rapidly in recent years, with the rapid growth of business and Internet services in particular. *See also* LABOR MARKET.

SEXENIO DEMOCRÁTICO. *See* DEMOCRATIC SEXENNIUM.

SEXUAL DIVISION OF LABOR. *See* LABOR MARKET.

SILVELA Y DE LA VILLEUZE, FRANCISO (1843–1905). Born in **Madrid**, like most aspiring politicians Franciso Silvela studied law at university before entering politics. He formed part of the **Unión Liberal** in the 1860s, but during the **Democratic Sexennium** (1868–1874) came to support the **Alfonsoist monarchists** headed by **Antonio Cánovas del Castillo**, and when he became minister of the interior under Cánovas in 1890, he was regarded by many as his deputy. However, Silvela was becoming increasingly disillusioned with the *caciquista* roots of Spanish politics, epitomized in the **Partido Conservador** by the figure of **Francisco Romero Robledo**. As a result, he came to oppose the manipulation of elections, resigning his post in 1891 and breaking with the party in the following year. Between 1894 and 1896, he set forth his program, arguing that conservatism should be based on "sound" public opinion. In 1898, after the death of Cánovas, he returned to the party and was able to put his project into practice in the wake of the **regenerationist** clamor following the **Spanish-American War**.

Silvela came to power in March 1899, claiming that it was his task to carry through "radical reforms" and a "real **revolution from above**." He attempted to enlist the support of the discontented middle classes and especially the **Catalan** bourgeoisie, shocked at the loss of its valuable export markets in **Cuba**. Hence, he made General Camilo Polavieja (1838–1914), who was close to Catalan bourgeois circles, his war minister, and the conservative Catalan regionalist and lawyer Manuel Duran i Bas (1823–1907) his minister of justice. However, Silvela's "revolution from above" soon ran into difficulties. The attempt by the finance minister, Fernández Villaverde (1848–1905), to reduce the huge budget deficit run up during the war through new taxes on industry and commerce antagonized Catalan opinion. This finally led to a taxpayers' strike in **Barcelona**, known as the *tancament de caixes*, and the withdrawal of Duran i Bas. Moreover, proposed cuts in defense spending provoked the resignation of Polavieja. Silvela's government had disintegrated, and he resigned on 21 October 1900. Between December 1902 and July 1903, he led a second attempt at reform along with **Antonio Maura**. Again, however, he ran into difficulties when the attempt to "wipe out the *caciques*" (*descuajar el cacique*) in the April 1903 general elections led to **republican** gains in urban Spain, thereby provoking the anger of King **Alfonso XIII**. In October 1903, after the failure of his second ministry, Silvela retired from politics, having "lost faith and hope."

SINDICATO ESPAÑOL UNIVERSITARIO (SEU)/SPANISH UNIVERSITY SYNDICATE. The SEU was a branch of the **Franco regime**'s single party, the **Falange Española Tradicionalista y de las Juntas de Ofensiva Nacional Sindicalista** (FET y de las JONS). Rather like the **Organización Sindical Española** (OSE), it was slowly undermined from within by opposition pressure. Student protest, against the regime in general and against the undemocratic SEU in particular, began in the 1950s. In order to try to incorporate this discontent, like the OSE the SEU allowed for elections of student representatives onto the lower echelons of the organization from 1958, and again like the OSE, the result was the infiltration of the SEU by opposition political groupings. The 1960s were to see a massive upsurge in student protest, fueled by rapidly growing numbers, and the growth of liberal and libertarian cultural values in the universities. By the mid-1960s, as a result, anti-Francoist student groups felt they were strong enough to ignore the SEU. Its redundancy was recognized by the Francoist authorities, who wound it up in 1965 and tried to put in its place an Asociación Professional de Estudiantes (Professional Association of Students), which, however, had absolutely no influence.

SINDICATOS LIBRES/FREE TRADE UNIONS. The Sindicatos Libres or Libres, as they were usually called, were the brainchild of a Dominican priest based in Jerez, Pedro Gerard. Up until the end of the first decade of the century, **Catholic unions** had had little impact in Spain because they had made virtually no attempt to address workers' material demands. It was Gerard's intention, based on European experience, to found Catholic unions that would actually defend workers' interests. The first such Sindicato Libre was set up among the Jerez vineyard workers in 1912, sponsored by the vineyard and bodega owner Patricio Garvey. The Libres then spread to northern and central Spain. In 1916, a national congress was held in Pamplona at which about 10,000 workers were represented, and which founded a Federación Nacional de Sindicatos Libres Católicos (National Federation of Catholic Free Unions).

The Libres showed more vitality than the Catholic unions, proving attractive to more conservative workers, who were willing to cooperate with their employers and opposed to the social and political radicalism of the **Unión General de Trabajadores** (UGT) and **Confederación Nacional del Trabajo** (CNT). This was especially the case in **Barcelona**, where Sindicatos Libres were set up independently by a group of **Carlist** workers in October 1919 in order to compete with the CNT. The history of the Libres in the Catalan capital over the next three years is complex. On the one hand, from November 1920 they established a reactionary alliance with the Barcelona military garrison—with financial backing from the employers—in order to annihilate the CNT.

From the ranks of the Libres were to come the gunmen who were to assassinate much of the local CNT leadership—including, it seems, **Salvador Seguí**—during these years. This earned them the undying hatred of libertarian circles. On the other hand, unlike the Catholic unions, they were prepared to push for improvements in working conditions, leading them to break with the Catalan Employers' Federation in 1922. This, together with the fact that they were the only union confederation able to operate openly between 1921 and 1922, and that (like their CNT counterparts) they often forced workers to join, meant that considerable numbers of workers affiliated. In 1921, they claimed a membership of 100,000.

Their position was seemingly consolidated during the **Primo de Rivera dictatorship** because, with the benefit of official sponsorship, in **Catalonia** they largely took control of the arbitration boards (*comités paritarios*) set up to mediate labor disputes. However, their underlying weakness was demonstrated between 1930 and 1931 when, in the face of the rapid CNT reorganization, the Libres' organization largely collapsed. Organizational disintegration was followed by physical annihilation for prominent Libres who did not flee Catalonia quickly enough following the commencement of the **Spanish Civil War**, but after General **Francisco Franco**'s victory they were once again to be found in prominent positions within the single regime union, the **Organización Sindical Española** (OSE). *See also* LABOR MOVEMENT.

SOCIAL REFORM. See AZCÁRATE MENÉNDEZ, GUMERSINDO DE; DATO IRADIER, EDUARDO; INSTITUTO DE REFORMAS SOCIALES; KRAUSISM; PARTIDO SOCIALISTA OBRERO ESPAÑOL; WELFARE STATE.

SOCIALIST PARTY. *See* PARTIDO SOCIALISTA OBRERO ESPAÑOL.

SOLANA MADARIAGA, JAVIER (1942–). Solana is the Spanish politician who, over the past 20 years, has made the most impact on the international political stage. The grandson of the **republican** diplomat and historian Salvador de Madariaga (1886–1972), Javier Solana at first combined a career in academia with intense political agitation. He studied physics at university, spent a period as a doctoral student in the United States between 1965 and 1971, and subsequently took up a post in the Autonomous University of Madrid. As a student, he clandestinely joined the **Partido Socialista Obrero Español** (PSOE) and was heavily involved in anti-Francoist student politics. On returning to Spain, he then played an important role in the reform of the PSOE, establishing a close friendship with **Felipe González.** He became minister of culture in González's first cabinet in 1982, and minister of education in 1988. It was, however, as foreign minister from 1992 that he began to make his mark as a major European political figure. He is seen, above all, as a skilled diplomat, adept at finding common ground.

It seems that during 1995, González planned to step down and support Solana's candidacy for party general secretary. However, when a stalemate was reached over who was to be general secretary of the **North Atlantic Treaty Organization** (NATO), he put his name forward as the compromise candidate with widespread backing. It was a post he was to hold from December 1995 through to October 1999, during which time Spain was to play a much more active role than had hitherto been the case in both NATO and in United Nations operations. Solana subsequently moved into **European Union** (EU) politics, taking over as general secretary of the Council of the European Union and High Representative for Common Foreign and Security Policy. As such, when the EU has held a common position in **foreign policy**, Solana has acted as its foremost advocate. This is a post he still holds in early 2008.

SOLBES MIRA, PEDRO (1942–). Solbes has become a key figure in the development of the economic policy of the **Partido Socialista Obrero Español** (PSOE) since the 1990s. He was born in Pinoso (Alicante) and studied economics and politics at the Complutense University of Madrid. He then made a career in the civil service, working especially on Spain's efforts to enter the **European Economic Community**. For this reason, in 1985 he was brought into the PSOE government economics team with the post of secretary of state for the European communities. He only actually joined the PSOE a year after his appointment and shortly before becoming parliamentary deputy for Alicante. He then went on to hold the posts of minister of agriculture and fisheries (1991–1993) and minister of economy and finance (1993–1996). After the PSOE's defeat in 1996, he moved into **European Union** politics, becoming commissioner for economic and monetary affairs in September 1999. With the PSOE's victory in March 2004, he was then appointed minister of economy and finance and second government vice president. Given his ample experience in economic policy making, his presence has been important for the government. In the context of rapid economic expansion in recent years, he is generally viewed by the Spanish public as a safe pair of hands. This was shaken somewhat by the sharp economic downturn that has hit Spain since the end of 2007, but Solbes was able relatively successfully to argue during the March 2008 election campaign that this was due to international factors.

SOLIDARIDAD DE OBREROS VASCOS/BASQUE WORKERS' SOLIDARITY. *See* BASQUE COUNTRY; CATHOLIC UNIONS; PARTIDO NACIONALISTA VASCO.

SOLIDARIDAD OBRERA (SO)/WORKER SOLIDARITY. SO was a local labor confederation set up in **Barcelona** in August 1907. It was formed by an amalgam of **anarchists** or anarchist-syndicalists, members of the Catalan **Partido Socialista Obrero Español** (PSOE) and **Unión General de Trabajadores** (UGT), and **republican** and nonpolitical workers. From the outset, it also brought out a weekly newspaper under the same name. Its ideology was syndicalist, but in its first two years its leaders tried to steer a moderate course and unite the entire unionized working class. In February 1908, it became a regional confederation and attempted to affiliate workers throughout **Catalonia**. From this date, divisions within the organization grew as committed anarchist-syndicalists grew in strength. On the one hand, a dispute broke out with the **Partido Republicano Radical** (PRR), led by **Alejandro Lerroux**, who feared that an autonomous labor confederation would call into question his party's dominance of working-class politics in the city of Barcelona. On the other hand, members of the PSOE and UGT were increasingly antagonized by the "anti-political" stance of leading figures within SO. The anarchist-syndicalist line pursued by SO was confirmed in 1910 when the Catalan members of the PSOE withdrew their support and the confederation held a national congress in September to form a national labor confederation, the **Confederación Nacional del Trabajo** (CNT). However, the confederation's mouthpiece retained the name *Solidaridad Obrera*. This tradition has continued into the 21st century. In 2007, the publication was the online mouthpiece of the CNT of Catalonia and the Balearic Islands. *See also* LABOR MOVEMENT.

SOLIDARITAT CATALANA/CATALAN SOLIDARITY. Solidaritat Catalana was an electoral coalition, formed in **Catalonia** in January 1906 in the wake of the *Cu-Cut!* incident, whose main demands were the restoration of constitutional guarantees and the repeal of the **Jurisdictions Law**. The coalition was formed by what was, in many respects, a disparate set of parties and organizations, bound together loosely by the wish to defend civil liberties against the central state. From right to left, its main supporters were the Catalan **Carlists**, the **Lliga Regionalista**, **republicans** affiliated with **Nicolás Salmerón**'s **Unión Republicana** (with the exception of the followers of **Alejandro Lerroux**), the republican-Catalanist **Centre Nacionalista Republicà**, and Catalan **federalist** republicans. At first Solidaritat Catalana proved a very effective mobilizing force, winning 40 of the 44 Catalan seats in the 21 April 1907 general elections. This was a devastating blow to the monarchist *caciques*, who had heretofore dominated rural Catalonia, and, even though the "official" **Partido Conservador** (PC) and **Partido Liberal** were still easily able to maintain a majority in parliament, it represented a serious challenge to the **Cánovas Restoration**.

This was, however, to be the high point of the Solidarity movement. It soon became clear that because of its superior organization and more abundant resources the Lliga was the dominant force behind the coalition, and the party used this to extend its influence. This led to growing criticism from the republican elements within the coalition. Conflict sharpened in 1908 when the Lliga supported a local government bill sponsored by the PC government of **Antonio Maura**, which though giving the municipalities more autonomy vis-à-vis central government, also curtailed universal suffrage. As a result, by the beginning of 1909, Solidaritat Catalana was little more than a name and was formally wound up after the **Tragic Week**.

SOLÍS RUIZ, JOSÉ (1915–1990). José Solís was, during the second half of the **Franco regime**, the most influential figure within the single party, the **Movimiento Nacional**. He was born in Córdoba on 27 September 1915, and went on to study law at university. During the **Spanish Civil War**, he fought in the **Nationalist** militia and subsequently became an official in the single state union, the **Organización Sindical Española** (OSE). He soon established his reputation as an efficient and populist organizer, rising rapidly through the ranks. Finally, in the cabinet reshuffle of February 1957, he was made minister secretary general of the **Falange Española Tradicionalista y de las Juntas de Ofensiva Nacional Sindicalista** (Movimiento Nacional from May 1958). During the 1960s, he and **Manuel Fraga** became the leading figures of a current of Falangist reformers, who accepted the need for some cultural liberalization, and who sought to reform the Movimiento in order to make it somewhat more representative and thereby shore up its position within the regime. Solís operated within the sphere of the OSE, promoting a number of reforms that gave workers a greater say over their representatives and allowed collective bargaining between labor and capital at factory level. However, the result was not to regenerate the Movimiento but to allow the dissident union movement **Comisiones Obreras** (CC. OO) growing influence within the OSE. It was discontent at these consequences among the most *continuista* sectors of the regime that led to Solís's removal from his post in 1969.

SOMETENT. *See* MAURISTAS; POLICE; PRIMO DE RIVERA Y ORBANEJA, MIGUEL.

SPANISH-AMERICAN WAR. With defeat at the hands of the United States in the Spanish-American War (or the "Disaster" as it was popularly known) of 1898, Spain lost the colonial possession of **Cuba** and Puerto Rico in the Antilles, and the **Philippines**, Guam, the Mariana and Caroline Islands, and Palau in the Pacific. A number of factors led to a growing determination in the United States to bring Cuba above all within its sphere of influence. First, the United States was the rising imperial power in America and the Pacific, and Cuba—Spain's prize colony—was an important market for the export of U.S. goods and capital. Second, with the construction of the Panama Canal, the Caribbean had a newly found strategic importance. Finally, given its economic and military weakness, Spain had shown itself incapable of controlling a strongly backed insurrection that had spread rapidly through Cuba from February 1895, and that was followed by a Tagalog (indigenous Filipino) revolt in the summer of 1896 in the Philippines.

In April 1896, the U.S. government offered its good offices to find a negotiated settlement to the conflict in Cuba, and in September 1897 secretly offered to buy the island. The Spanish government, however, refused any compromise. While Spanish political elites were aware that the Spanish fleet would be no match for the Americans, there was a fear that the reaction to any climb down by the ultranationalist Spanish **military** would be such as to put the regime in jeopardy. Hence, it was agreed by both the **Partido Conservador** and **Partido Liberal** that a heroic and honorable defeat at the hands of the United States was the only dignified way out. The road to war was sparked by the sinking of an American battleship, the USS *Maine*, while it was on a "courtesy visit" to La Havana. It seems that the bomb was planted by Cuban insurrectionaries in order to precipitate an armed intervention by the United States. This is exactly what it did. In the United States, a press campaign calling for war with Spain got under way. War was declared on 25 April. Thereafter, two rapid naval confrontations sealed Spain's fate: on 1 May, the Spanish Pacific fleet was destroyed at Cavite off the Philippines, then on 3 July, Spanish naval forces in Cuba were sent to the bottom in Santiago Bay. This made impossible the continuation of the war. An armistice was, therefore, agreed to on 18 July, and Spain signed away her **colonies** at the **Treaty of Paris** on 10 December 1898.

SPANISH ARMADA. Growing tension between England and Spain developed when Elizabeth I became queen of England in 1558, broke with the papacy, and, from 1665, supported the Dutch Protestants, who had rebelled against Spanish **Habsburg** rule. Elizabeth initiated hostilities against Spain in 1585 after **Felipe II** had seized all English ships in Spanish ports. As a result, Felipe resolved to build up an invasion force (*la armada invincible*) in order to invade England and restore the **Catholic** faith. The plan was for the Spanish fleet to pick up 19,000 soldiers from the army of Flanders, who would then march on London. However, the English navy prevented the army from being taken onboard and forced the Spanish galleons to retreat into the North Sea. As a result, in appalling weather conditions they had to return to Spain via the coasts of Scotland and Ireland. In all, 40 of the 68 Spanish ships were destroyed and about 15,000 men lost. The mission's failure very much marked a turning point in European history, with the pretension of the Spanish Habsburg Empire, under **Castilian** leadership, to maintain a hegemonic role in European affairs, being dealt a decisive blow.

SPANISH CIVIL WAR. The Spanish Civil War raged across the country between July 1936 and March 1939. It began in an attempted **military** coup against the **Second Republic** on 17–18 July. However, the strength of the working-class response and the fact that in strongly Republican areas part of the army, the **Civil Guard** and Assault Guard remained loyal, meant that it was only partially successful. The Republicans retained much of urban and southern Spain (including, crucially, **Barcelona** and **Madrid**), while the uprising was successful in **Morocco**, points in the south, and in rural **Catholic** northern and central Spain. From the start, the **Nationalist** forces called on assistance from Germany and Italy, the major Fascist powers. The elitist Army of Africa, under the command of General **Francisco Franco**, had, as expected, risen up, but because most of the navy had remained loyal to the Republic, it could not cross the straits of **Gibraltar**. This problem was solved by Italian and German planes, which transported the troops over to the mainland. Henceforth, Franco's army was able to drive up through Extremadura and then toward Madrid, annihilating all leftist opposition in its wake. The systematic execution of prisoners and imposition of terror on captured territories would, indeed, from the start be official policy in Nationalist Spain.

On 21 September, the Nationalists made Franco their commander in chief, and henceforth would largely unite under his leadership. On 21 April 1937, the **Carlists** and the **Falange Española** were united in a single party, the **Falange Española Tradicionalista y de las Juntas de Ofensiva Nacional Sindicalista** (FET y de las JONS), and in a collective letter in July almost the entire Church episcopate gave its blessing to the Francoist cause. The political history of the

Republican zone would be far more turbulent. In much of Republican Spain, the military uprising unleashed a social revolution, with the formation of working-class militias, committees to run local affairs, and industrial and agrarian collectives. During these first months of the war, leftist militias were also to carry out attacks on known rightists and on the Church hierarchy, though the government attempted to stamp the practice out. A **Popular Front** government was formed under **Francisco Largo Caballero** on 4 September and gradually began to reassert state power. This would lead to enormous tension within the Republic, for while the **Confederación Nacional del Trabajo** (CNT), **Partido Obrero de Unificación Marxista** (POUM), and left-wingers within the **Partido Socialista Obrero Español** (PSOE), and Unión General de Trabajadores (UGT) called for the social revolution and war to be pursued simultaneously, **republicans**, moderate "reformist" PSOE-UGT Socialists, and the **Partido Comunista de España** (PCE) argued that the war had to be won before any social revolution could be carried through.

Within a revolutionary context it might be thought that the leftists would prevail. However, the republicans and moderate Socialists were an important counterweight. Furthermore, despite the **nonintervention** pact signed by the European powers, the Germans and Italians continued supplying the Nationalists with men and armaments. From November 1936, the Soviet Union did the same in the Republican zone. This was to ensure that the PCE would grow rapidly in power and help swing the balance of power away from the social revolutionaries. In some respects, the PCE's state-building centralist strategy was effective. This could be seen when, fearing its fall, the Republican government left Madrid for **Valencia** on 6 November. The defense of the city was left largely in the hands of the Communists. Over the previous two months, they had been welding the Republican militias into a more coherent, disciplined fighting force called the **Popular Army**. And, reinforced by the **International Brigades**, they were able to beat off the Nationalist assault when it began on 7 November.

However, the PCE's repressive Stalinist policies also served to alienate part of the Republic's working-class and peasant base and sap enthusiasm. Following the **May Events**, together with the "reformist" Socialists and republicans, they were able to force the awkward Largo

Caballero to resign and replaced him with **Juan Negrín**, who was more willing to compromise with the PCE. Henceforth, the state's offensive against the social revolution was intensified and the leftist opposition emasculated. Actions included the illegalization of the POUM and the secret murder of its leader, Andreu Nin (1892–1937), and the dismantling of the anarchist **Council of Aragón**.

Yet, despite the greater effectiveness of the Republican army from the end of 1936, it could still not in the long run match the better-equipped Nationalist forces. Hence, between the springs of 1937 and 1939, the Nationalists slowly but relentlessly expanded the territory under their control. In the spring and summer of 1937, they drove through northern Spain, capturing Bilbao on 19 June, Santander on 26 August, and Gijón on 19 October. This would allow the National-ists to use the **Basque** steel and Asturian **mining** industries to aid the war effort, and increased the population under their control by about two million. The following March they pushed through Aragón to the sea, cutting **Catalonia** off from the rest of the Republic, and finally, from December 1938, Franco launched an offensive on Catalonia. Juan Negrín wished to fight to the bitter end, hoping that a European war would internationalize the Spanish conflict. But his efforts were cut short on 4 March when anticommunist republicans launched the **Casado coup** in Madrid. General Franco would march into the Span-ish capital virtually unopposed 23 days later.

SPANISH COMMUNIST PARTY. *See* PARTIDO COMUNISTA DE ESPAÑA.

SPANISH INQUISITION. The pope had begun granting the power to establish religious commissions (or inquisitions) to root out "heresy" in particular areas from the 13th century, above all in France but also in the **Crown of Aragón**. It was within this tradition that the Span-ish Inquisition began to operate at the end of 15th century. However, unlike its predecessors, it would be directly controlled by the **mon-archy** (rather than the local bishops) and would build permanent statewide structures.

Its origins were to be found in the growing religious intolerance toward other faiths within the **Crown of Castile** during the 15th century. As a result, many **Jews** converted to Christianity. However, there was considerable suspicion as to whether these so-called *conversos* (or "New Christians") were in reality practicing Christians. It was in this atmosphere that, after Queen Isabel I had been informed by the Church authorities of the supposed activities of false Jewish converts, in 1478 the **Catholic Monarchs** applied to the pope for a bull establishing an inquisition into heresy (whose official title was the "Tribunal del Santo Oficio"). The bull was issued and it began to operate from 1480. At first its objective was to establish whether *converso* Jews were adhering to the Christian faith. Although nominally headed by the pope, it was under the direct control of the monarchs, who appointed an Inquisition Council (Consejo de la Inquisición) to advise them on policy and an inquisitor general to oversee operations.

In its early years, it set in motion a campaign of terror against *converso* Jews, ordering 2,000 executions and punishing a further 15,000 between 1480 and 1490. From the 1520s, the appearance of the Lutheran "heresy" breathed new life into the institution. Not only did it look for evidence of Protestant penetration into Spain, it also took action against reforming **Catholic** currents, which it viewed as incubating the Protestant virus. Most important in this respect was the attack on the followers of the Dutch theologian Desiderius Erasmus, because of the important position they held in the political and cultural elite. The climate became even more intolerant after the appointment of Fernando de Valdés (1483–1568) as inquisitor general in 1546, in a context in which the strength of Protestantism in the Germanic lands, and the advance of the Huguenots in France, convinced the aging **Carlos I** and then his son **Felipe II** of the need to suppress the spread of "heresy" in their dominions at all costs. Furthermore, the growing threat of the Ottoman Empire also led to the Inquisition to take a growing interest in the religious practices of the *moriscos* during the 1550s. Most shocking for Felipe II was the discovery of two Protestant sects in Spain itself at the end of the decade, which resulted in over 40 executions. In response, in order to isolate Spain, in 1551–1552 the Inquisition published its first index of prohibited books, which was subsequently greatly extended, and in 1559 (with the exception of some universities in Portugal and Italy) Spanish students were prevented from studying in foreign universities.

Nevertheless, after the assault on the *converso* Jews, the numbers affected were not large (over the 16th and 17th centuries an average of three persons a year were executed in the Spanish **Habsburg Empire**), and from the 1540s it aimed above all to impose religious conformity on Catholic Spaniards themselves (arresting people for blasphemy, for disrespecting marriage vows, and the like). By the 18th century, it was directing its attention at keeping the most radical voices of the **Enlightenment** out of Spain, forming part of a coalition of forces within the Catholic Church (led by the Jesuits) who were concerned that modern ideas in philosophy and the sciences might undermine the country's Catholic values. Their suspicion was confirmed by the **French Revolution**, in the immediate aftermath of which the Inquisition gained considerably more power.

Nevertheless, it is important not to exaggerate the extent to which the Inquisition stifled public debate in Spain. If one was careful not to broach matters of religion and morality it was quite possible to comment on and criticize government policy. This can be seen in the example of the *arbitristas* in the 16th century and moderate pro-Enlightenment writers, who had the ear of the new **Bourbon** dynasty, in the 18th century. The Inquisition was finally abolished in 1834 following the compromise between absolutism and moderate liberalism in the aftermath of the death of **Fernando VII**.

SPANISH LANGUAGE. *See* CASTILIAN LANGUAGE.

SPANISH LEGION. *See* LEGIÓN ESPAÑOLA.

SPANISH SOCIALIST WORKERS' PARTY. *See* PARTIDO SOCIALISTA OBRERO ESPAÑOL.

STABILIZATION PLAN. The Stabilization Plan was the centerpiece of the strategy pursued by General **Francisco Franco**'s **Opus Dei** ministers to liberalize the Spanish **economy**. The plan came into effect in 1959. Its short-term aim was to deflate the economy and squeeze inflation out of the system, but it was accompanied by a devaluation of the peseta, the abandonment of import and export licenses, and the encouragement of foreign investment for up to 50 percent of the capital invested in any particular enterprise. This whole package was backed up by a $554 million loan from the United States. Its immediate effect was to produce a sharp recession, but it laid the basis for the economic boom of the 1960s. *See also* AUTARKY; FRANCO REGIME; LÓPEZ RODÓ, LAUREANO.

STATE OF THE AUTONOMIES/ESTADO DE LAS AUTONOMÍAS. The new decentralized model of Spanish government put in place by the **Constitution of 1978**—the so-called Estado de las Autonomías—was a response to demands for devolution from the older, culturally specific areas (**Catalonia**, the **Basque Country**, and **Galicia**), along with other regions critical of overbureaucratized, corrupt administration from the center. The constitution laid the basis for the formation of autonomous governments in the Spanish "regions and historic nationalities," setting out a number of guidelines outlining the minimum powers the autonomous governments might have, and a further series of powers to which they might aspire. The actual shape of the new autonomy statutes would, therefore, be a matter of negotiation. It was envisaged that the "historic nationalities" would be able to obtain a high degree of autonomy rather rapidly, while other regions would have to travel at a slower pace. The tough negotiating stance taken by the **Partido Nacionalista Vasco** (PNV) and the threat of **ETA** ensured that the Basque statute would be the most generous, incorporating a large measure of financial autonomy—a *concierto económico* or flat-rate tax, which would be raised by the autonomous government—while other areas were dependent on the central state distributing taxes to them. Among the "regions," during 1980–1981 **Andalusia** ensured through popular mobilization that its autonomy statute would be upgraded to the "fast track" along with the "historic nationalities."

The speed at which the territorial map of Spain was transformed produced a fear in right-wing circles (especially important in this respect was the **military**) that it would result in a breakup of Spain. After the attempted coup of 1981 (the so-called **Tejerazo**), the ruling **Unión del Centro Democrático** (UCD) government and the main opposition party, the **Partido Socialista Obrero Español** (PSOE), reached an accord and passed a law called the Ley Orgánica de Armonización del Proceso Autonómico (Fundamental Law to Harmonize the Autonomy Process—**LOAPA**), aimed at limiting the scope of the decentralization. This led to fierce protest by the Catalan and Basque nationalist parties and the LOAPA was finally declared unconstitutional by the Constitutional Tribunal.

The 1980s and 1990s saw a slow transfer of competencies to the autonomous communities. It was completed with the transfer of the state health service, Insalud, during 2001, with the result that they accounted for over 40 percent of public spending at the beginning of 2002 (greater than the central administration). However, as the State of the Autonomies has leveled up, with the "regions" attaining many of the same competencies as the "historic nationalities," the latter, above all, have voiced demands for further transfers of power. Catalonia, in particular, has complained at heavy financial constraints. Between 1993 and 1996, in negotiations with first the PSOE and then the **Partido Popular** (PP)—both of whom had failed to win an overall majority in the general elections and needed support from the Catalan nationalist coalition **Convergència i Unió** (CiU)—its leader, **Jordi Pujol**, attained the concession that in future the central government would cede 15 percent and then 30 percent of all Spain's earnings tax, the Impuesto sobre la Renta de las Personas Físicas (IRPF) to the autonomous communities.

However, in subsequent years "peripheral" nationalist and regionalist parties voiced demands that the plurinational nature of Spain be explicitly recognized. This was ratified in the "Barcelona Pact" between CiU, the PNV, and the **Bloc Nacionalista Galego** (BNG) in July 1998. Catalan parties (with the exception of the PP) demanded that the Catalan Statute be renegotiated, allowing it greater financial autonomy; that the Senate be turned into a "Territorial House" (rather like the German Bundesrat); and that the autonomous governments have representatives on the council of the **European Union** (as in the case of the German Länder and Belgian Regions). In this, they received support from Galician BNG and other regionalist parties. Under *lehendakari* **Joan José Ibarretxe**, from 1998 the PNV went further, calling for the Basque Country to become a "Free Associated State" with the right to succeed. This approach was fleshed out in the so-called "Plan Ibarretxe" of September 2002. Explicit in all these demands was the vision of an asymmetrical development of the State of the Autonomies, in which the historic "nations" and "nationalities" would retain a higher level of home rule.

The PP government opposed all these moves, affirming that the State of the Autonomies negotiated in 1978 should represent the end point, and blocked any major reform of the Senate. The opposition PSOE was, on the other hand, willing to make concessions, but it saw the process in terms of a symmetrical evolution of the State of the Autonomies and the Senate, which would create a more **federal** Spain (mirroring the increasingly federalized structure of the party itself). Hence, the Socialists' victory in the March 2004 elections totally changed the political climate. Already in the autumn of 2003, a commission formed by the Catalan parliament, with representatives from all the Catalan parties, had produced a new statute (with only the Catalan PP in opposition). **José Luis Rodríguez Zapatero** hoped this would be the model for the reform of the entire State of the Autonomies and held meetings with the heads of all the autonomous communities to reach a consensus.

There were, however, problems on the horizon. The PNV pushed on with the "Plan Ibarretxe," which was rejected by the PSOE both because it had not achieved a high degree of consensus in the Basque parliament and because it questioned the unity of Spain. It was approved by the Basque parliament, but then rejected by its Spanish counterpart in February 2005. At the same time, in Socialist circles there was opposition to the proposed Catalan statute, most notably its reference to Catalonia as a "nation" and the tax-raising powers it gave the Catalan autonomous government, the **Generalitat**. This was seen as undermining the model established by the 1978 Constitution (with the exception of **Navarre** and the Basque Country). For the first time in many years there was also saber rattling in some military circles. There followed three months of tough negotiations between November 2005 and January 2006 until the new statute was agreed upon (relegating the term Catalan nation to the preamble and cutting back on the proposed tax-raising powers in return for guarantees regarding the level of state spending). The PP launched a fierce campaign against the statute, which, it claimed, would undermine Spanish unity. However, other autonomy statutes were thereafter reformed on the Catalan model. In the Basque Country, in early 2008 Ibarretxe still insists on his proposed reforms and wants to call a plebiscite. Reform of the Senate has been put off until the next legislature by the PSOE. *See also* MAP 2.

STEEL INDUSTRY. *See* IRON AND STEEL INDUSTRY.

SUÁREZ GONZÁLEZ, ADOLFO (1932–). Adolfo Suárez is the person who did most to steer Spain through the **transition to democracy** between 1976 and 1979. He was born in 1932 in Cebreros in the province of Ávila and studied law at the University of Madrid. After having obtained a doctorate, he began work within the Francoist administration, rising rapidly within the **Movimiento Nacional.** His first key appointment came in 1965, when he was made director of Spanish **television** (TVE) and **radio** (RNE). Then, in the cabinet reshuffle carried out by **Carlos Arias Navarro** in March 1975, he was appointed vice secretary of the Movimiento.

Suárez was at first seen as a protégé of **Luis Carrero Blanco.** But by the early 1970s he, like many in the regime, was convinced that political reform was necessary and from his position as director of television he began to develop close contacts with the heir, Prince **Juan Carlos.** For many Movimiento figures at the time, the path to reform was through the establishment of political associations within the Movimiento itself. During 1975, once given the go-ahead by the minister secretary general of the Movimiento, Fernando Herrero Tejedor (1920–1975), a number of such associations were set up. Suárez began work on the largest of these, the "centrist progressive" Union del Pueblo Español (Union of the Spanish People—UDPE). The intention seems to have been to build the UDPE into a hegemonic party within a somewhat more open political system.

With the death of **Francisco Franco,** however, it became clear that this was insufficient, and Juan Carlos, along with many regime figures, including Suárez, realized the need for further democratization. King Juan Carlos, unhappy at the pace of reform under Arias Navarro, moved to have him replaced by Adolfo Suárez in July 1976. This was a great surprise in political circles, for Suárez was still a relative unknown. But the king wanted a man who knew the regime well from within, and favored the relatively young Suárez because his oratorical gifts and suave good looks could attract a mass following.

Suárez was quick to promise far-reaching democratic change, including Spain's first free general elections since 1936, by June 1977. He was, however, determined that the elections should be held under his government rather than a provisional government as the opposition wished. His position was greatly strengthened after he won a referendum called to vote on his reforms on 15 December 1976. Thereafter, the opposition was brought to the negotiating table, and parties legalized in the run-up to the election. Suárez fought the election at the head of a coalition of forces called the **Unión del Centro Democrático** (UCD), shedding his Francoist past and now presenting himself as a democratic man of the center. The image fitted well with a large part of the electorate's desire for change, but fear of disorder. Hence, the UCD was able to win the elections with 34.5 percent of the vote.

In the following two years, Suárez, in collaboration with the opposition, laid the foundations of the new democratic regime in Spain. However, his star began to wane after the March 1979 elections when the UCD, riven by internal strife, began to fall apart. Suárez in particular found himself the target of criticism by conservative **Christian-democrats**, who wished to turn the UCD into a right-wing confessional party. By late 1979, Suárez seemed, as a result, to be drawing into his shell, and becoming detached from the day-to-day business of government. Faced with constant attacks, he finally resigned as prime minister on 29 January 1981, and was replaced by a compromise candidate, Leopoldo Calvo Sotelo (1926–).

Over the next few months, Suárez's supporters tried to reinstall him. They failed, but by the second half of the year the UCD was in any case imploding. Suárez's response was to leave and form his own party, the Centro Democrático y Social (Social and Democratic Center – CDS). The CDS benefited from the considerable prestige Suárez still maintained. He presented the party as somewhat left of center with a program of social reform and democratic renewal. The CDS was the third largest party in the general elections of 1986 and 1989, but it had to battle over the center ground with the **Partido Socialista Obrero Español** (PSOE) and the centrist nationalist formations **Partido Nacionalista Vasco** (PNV) and **Convergència i Unió** (CiU). Suárez retired from active politics in 1990. And when a rejuvenated Partido Popular (PP), under the leadership of **José María Aznar**, shook off its Francoist image in the run-up to the 1993 elections and also began to dispute the center ground, his party's days were also numbered.

SYNDICALISM. *See* ANARCHISM; CONFEDERACIÓN NACIO-
NAL DEL TRABAJO; SOLIDARIDAD OBRERA.

– T –

TÁCITO. Tácito was the name of a group of youngish **Madrid**-based
professionals from upper-class families closely identified with the
Franco regime, who played a key role in the **transition to democracy**.
The group was formed in May 1973. Its importance lay in the fact that
its members were very well-connected. They were on friendly terms
with Prince **Juan Carlos** and saw themselves as destined, by social
standing and training, to play a key role in the state apparatus and government. The key figures in the group were Alfonso Osorio (1923–)
(who, however, was more conservative than most of the group and
estranged from Tácito during much of 1974–1976), Marcelino Oreja
(1935–), Landelino Lavilla (1927–), Juan Antonio Ortega y Díaz Am-
brona, and José Manuel Otrero Novas (1940–). Tácito was founded in
reaction to the imminent appointment of the *continuista*, **Luis Carrero
Blanco**, as prime minister. Its members were linked to the Catholic
association, the **Asociación Católica Nacional de Propagandistas**
(ACNP), sectors of which had taken an increasingly reforming stance
during the 1960s. However, they went further than most of the 1960s'
aperturistas. Though their families were allied to the regime, few of
them had as yet held posts within the administration and, as the regime
weakened in the early 1970s, inspired by **Christian-democratic** ideals,
they became convinced of the need for some kind of democratic opening, and realized that only if people from within the establishment took
the lead could they safeguard their political careers and guard against
radical political and social reforms.

For this reason, the *tácitos* agreed to collaborate with the first
Carlos Arias Navarro government of January 1974. The lack of
reform led most of them to withdraw following the sacking of Pío
Cabanillas (1923–1991) in October. Alfonso Osorio, however, dis-
agreed with this decision and set up his own **Unión Democrática
Española**. The *tácitos* were relieved when **Francisco Franco** died
in November 1975, and, sensing that the gates of reform were now
open, they joined the second Arias Navarro government of January

1976. Once Arias Navarro had been replaced by **Adolfo Suárez** in July, the *tácitos* played a key role in government. By this time, they were convinced of the need to establish of a full-blown parliamentary democracy "from above" and, in tandem with the King Juan Carlos and Suárez, they were to successfully pursue this course. Alfonso Osorio was appointed vice president in Suárez's first government of July 1976 and helped him choose the cabinet, with the result that seven of the 20 ministers had links with Tácito. At the same time, they began constructing a new party of the center to fight the first democratic elections. In December 1976, they founded the Partido Popular (Popular Party) and in January the broader Centro Democrático (Democratic Center), reuniting with Alfonso Osorio. Two months later they agreed to integrate into a new coalition, the **Unión del Centro Democrático** (UCD), under Suárez's leadership. *See also* TRANSITION TO DEMOCRACY.

TANCAMENT DE CAIXES. The *tancament de caixes* (shutting of the tills) was the name given to a tax strike by shopkeepers and small businessmen in **Barcelona** between July and November 1899 to protest new taxes levied on trade and industry by the finance minister, Raimundo Fernández Villaverde (1848–1905). The strike failed in its primary aim, but further alienated the Catalan middle classes from central government. This would be seen in the strong support these groups gave to **Catalanism** during the first decade of the 20th century. *See also* LLIGA REGIONALISTA; SILVELA Y DE LA VILLEUZE, FRANCISCO.

TARIFF POLICY. Between 1833 and the late 1860s, Spain was for most of the time governed by conservative liberals. Their tariff policy was twofold. On the one hand, they had no hesitation in affording tariff protection to the agrarian elite, their most powerful backers. On the other hand, in order to maintain the support of the **Catalan** industrial bourgeoisie, they were willing to put high tariffs on imported **cotton textiles**. Yet these governments were in constant budgetary difficulty and in frequent need of loans. This gave foreign financiers a high degree of leverage over government **economic policy**. The upshot of this situation was that where powerful national interests were not adversely affected, facilities were given for foreign business to import quite freely. Hence, Spanish governments allowed massive import of rails and rolling stock to construct the Spanish **railways** and permitted virtually duty-free imports of coal and machinery. The growth of indigenous **coal** and **iron** industries was to alter this policy balance from the 1880s.

More progressive liberals, on the other hand, were in favor of more generalized tariff reductions. This was the policy pursued after the **Glorious Revolution** of 1868. This was reversed with the overthrow of the **First Republic**. From 1875, **Partido Conservador** administrations led by **Antonio Cánovas del Castillo** defended agrarian and textile interests. When the **Partido Liberal** came to power, from 1881 it once again tried to follow a policy of reducing tariffs. The most important agreement reached was with France in February 1882, which allowed a rapid growth of Spanish wine exports. However, this led to a virulent campaign by both the **Castilian** wheat and Catalan textile interests (and from the late 19th century the **Basque** iron and steel industrialists and Asturian coal owners also became increasingly vociferous). Agrarian interests were being hit by the influx of cheap grain from Russia and the United States, while businessmen and flour producers redoubled efforts to further raise tariff barriers following the loss of the American **colonies** after the **Spanish-American War** of 1898. Conservative administrations responded to this pressure by drastically raising duties in 1891 and 1906. From this date, Spain had the highest tariff barriers in Europe. At the same time, Spanish governments began to intervene in the **economy** far more decisively to aid Spanish **industry**. The system of corporative state intervention was extended during the **Primo de Rivera dictatorship** and reached its zenith with the policy of **autarky** instituted by the **Franco regime**.

Only with the economic liberalization that began from the late 1950s by the new team of **Opus Dei** ministers were state controls reduced (though the 1960 tariff still afforded Spanish business significant protection). From 1986, Spain has formed part of the **European Economic Community** (now European Union) and has brought her tariff policy into line with other Community members.

TEJERAZO. The term *Tejerazo* (also known as *23-F*) refers to the attempted coup on 23 February 1981, when a detachment of **Civil**

Guards, under the command of **Antonio Tejero Molina,** stormed parliament and held the nation's deputies hostage for the night. This was the culmination of a year-long conspiracy. It comprised two rather different components. On the one hand, far-right officers planned a hard-line so-called *golpe a la turca* (Turkish coup). On the other hand, General Alfonso Armada (1920–), the former secretary of the royal household and tutor of King **Juan Carlos I,** was aiming for a *golpe blando* (soft coup), which would involve the substitution of the governing party, the **Unión del Centro Democrático** (UCD), by a government of national salvation under his presidency.

The two plots came together in the Tejerazo. Armada had convinced the plotters that his plan for a government of national salvation had the tacit approval of the king. It was, therefore, agreed that the parliamentary deputies should be captured, the army take to the streets, and Armada then offer himself as president. The first part of the projected coup worked perfectly, with Antonio Tejero securing the Moncloa palace. However, the king resolutely opposed the operation, with the result that only the captain general of **Valencia,** Jaime Milans del Bosch (1915–1997), ordered tanks onto the streets. Other captains general (some perhaps reluctantly) fell into line behind the king, and Milans del Bosch was finally persuaded to desist in the early hours. By morning, therefore, Tejero was isolated and forced to surrender.

The coup had a significant effect on Spanish politics. It stimulated greater cooperation between the major parties, but the desire to placate the **military** also played a large role in molding policy. Hence, the fight against **terrorism** was intensified; the UCD and opposition **Partido Socialista Obrero Español** (PSOE) agreed to put a brake on the autonomy process through the Ley Orgánica de la Armonización del Proceso Autonómico (Fundamental Law to Harmonize the Autonomy Process—**LOAPA**); and Spain rapidly entered the **North Atlantic Treaty Organization.** This would be the last time the army would significantly influence Spanish politics. In the following years, more liberal officers acceded to key posts, and from 1982 the army was effectively subordinated to civilian rule. *See also* BUNKER; GALAXIA OPERATION.

TEJERO MOLINA, ANTONIO (1932–). Colonel Antonio Tejero gained instant international fame as the commander of a detachment of **Civil Guards** who stormed the Spanish parliament on 23 February 1981 as part of a plot (the so-called **Tejerazo**) to overthrow the democratically elected government and install a military dictatorship. Like many men socialized within the Spanish **military** establishment during the **Franco regime**, Tejero held extreme right-wing views. These were confirmed during a period of service in the **Basque Country**, where he participated in the counterinsurgency campaign against **ETA**.

Tejero, who blamed weak politicians for not smashing ETA, mixed in *ultra* circles, in which talk centered on the need for a military government of order. He was briefly arrested and then posted to Málaga in January 1977 after having sent an impertinent telegram to the minister of the interior, Rodolfo Martín Villa (1934–), in which he criticized the flying of the Basque **flag**, the *Ikurriña*. Once in Málaga, he was soon in trouble again for ordering his forces to attack a legally authorized demonstration in favor of **Andalusian** autonomy. His punishment was light. He was sent to a desk job in **Madrid**, where he mixed with *ultra* rightists, who encouraged his increasingly messianic belief that he had to save Spain from chaos and disintegration. During 1978, he was involved in a plot to kidnap the cabinet, known as the **Galaxia Operation**. After it was discovered, Tejero was, once again, let off lightly, serving only seven months' arrest before being put in charge of a transport unit in the capital.

From this vantage point he continued to conspire. He was, finally, to play a leading role in the Tejerazo, storming the Moncloa Palace on the night of the 23rd with a detachment of Civil Guards and holding the Spanish deputies hostage throughout the night. Yet as the hours progressed, it became increasingly clear that he was largely isolated, leading him finally to surrender the following morning. *See also* BUNKER.

TELECOMMUNICATIONS. The major telecommunications company is Telefónica, which in 2002 was Spain's largest company and one of the world's 50 largest businesses. It started out life as a state-run telephone monopoly during the **Franco regime**. This all changed following the 1996 **privatization** legislation, sponsored by the new **Partido Popular** (PP) government of **José María Aznar**. This coincided with the boom in the use of mobile phones (whose usage expanded extraordinarily rapidly in Spain), the growth of private **television** companies, and the appearance of digital television, allowing the emergence of a powerful new business. Telefónica was able to a large degree to keep its dominant position in the Spanish phone market (allowing it to maintain relatively high prices) and rapidly expand into **Latin America** (in which it invested $10 billion between 1991 and 1999), followed by Africa and Australasia. From 2000, it also began investing more heavily in Europe, purchasing the Dutch television company Endermol, Austria's European Telecom International, and, in 2006, the British company O_2. In Spain, it has also successfully pursued a policy of diversification and acquisitions: it is now the parent company of a mobile-phone division (Movistar), an Internet company (Terra Lycos), and a **media** group. Its only big rival in the Spanish phone market is the holding company Auna (formed in 2000), backed by the power companies Endesa and Unión Fenosa along with Telecom Italia, and which owns Retevisión (which competes with Telefónica in the area of fixed-line telephone services), Amena (the third largest mobile operator in Spain), regional cable companies, and set up Spain's first terrestrial digital television service, Quiero TV (which, however, only operated between 2000 and 2002). Telefónica now operates its own terrestrial digital television service, Idearium.

Telefónica's decision to buy into television and **radio** caused considerable controversy in the 1990s. Aznar ensured that the heads of soon-to-be-privatized companies were politically close, and brought in his boyhood friend, Juan Villalonga (1953–), as chief executive of Telefónica. Once privatized, Telefónica helped set up the digital network Vía Digital and bought into private television and radio stations (most notably Antena 3 and Onda Cero). All these media outlets were strongly progovernment. In 2003, it sold its shares in Antena 3 and also largely pulled out of the Spanish cable satellite market, leaving the **PRISA**-controlled Sogecable in a dominant position.

TELEFÓNICA. *See* TELECOMMUNICATIONS.

TELEVISION. Between its foundation in 1956 and the end of the **Franco regime**, Spanish television was a centralized, state-run operation in the service of the government. In 1980, the attempt was made to bring state-owned public broadcasting into the modern era with the creation of Radio Televisión Española (RTVE), which incorporated both television (TVE) and **radio** (RNE) stations. The problem was that the director general was elected by the government of the day, and this led to biased reporting under both the **Partido Socialista Obrero Español** (PSOE) and, to an even greater degree, **Partido Popular** (PP) administrations. This has only changed (to a degree) under the PSOE administration of **José Luis Rodríguez Zapatero**, which has placed the election of the director general in the hands of parliament. Other problems have raised their heads. Relatively low government subsidies of TVE combined with an inefficient over-manned bureaucracy means that program quality has not been high (and ad breaks very long), while it has also run up large debts (over six million euros in 2003). The exception to this rule has been public television's second channel, La-2 which has put greater effort into producing documentaries and dramas.

After the formation of the **State of the Autonomies**, from 1982 "regional" television channels, supported by the territory's autonomous governments, also began to appear. The first was the **Basque** network Euskal Telebista (ETB), which from 1986 has consisted of two major channels (ETB-1 and ETB-2), as well as satellite services for the rest of Spain and America. Between 1982 and 1986, it won two important battles with the government, conducted in the Constitutional Tribunal, allowing it to operate free from central control and also to set up both **Basque** and **Castilian language** channels. Subsequently, the Catalan **Generalitat** set up TV3 (1984) and Canal 33 (1988). Both are broadcast in **Catalan**. TV3 has done particularly well, through an eclectic mix of higher-quality programs and popular soaps (*telenovel·les*). TV3 is also beamed to the other Catalan-speaking areas of Spain, **Valencia**, and the Balearic Islands, though, in 2007, the Valencian autonomous government tried to stop this practice in its territory.

Legislation in 1988 allowed for the operation of three private television channels, Antena 3, Telecinco, and the pay television channel, Canal+. The latter was owned by Sogecable, founded in 1989, in which the **PRISA** group had an important stake (and in 2006 took a controlling interest). The 1990s then saw the emergence of the cable satellite companies Canal Satélite Digital (owned by Socecable) and

Vía Digital (owned by Telefónica), along with small local television stations. The former fused in 2003 to form Digital+, which is run by Sogecable. In 2005 and 2006, two new open-view private television channels appeared, Cuatro (a rebranding of the pay-per-view channel Canal+) and La Sexta. TVE responded to the appearance of private television companies by being more aggressively commercial itself, but this served to question whether it deserved government subsidies. Moreover, it still lost market share, worsening its deficit. In 2006, Antena 3 (which since 2003 has been owned by the Planeta group) had a 26 percent audience share, TV-5 (part of Silvio Berlusconi's media empire) 21 percent, TVE-1 21 percent, and La-2 3 percent. The Autonomous communities' television channels got 19 percent of the total audience.

TEN YEARS' WAR. This refers to the war between Spain and the **Cuban** insurrectionaries that lasted from 1868 to 1878. It was brought to an end by the **Zanjón Peace**.

TERCERISTA. This was the name given to the left-wingers in the **Partido Socialista Obrero Español** (PSOE), who, between 1919 and 1921, tried to get the party to join the Bolshevik Third International. After defeat in the extraordinary party congress held in April 1921, most left to constitute a new Communist party, called the **Partido Comunista de España** (PCE), from November 1921.

TERRA LLIURE/FREE LAND. *See* CATALONIA.

TERRORISM. Modern Spain has a long history of terrorist groups. From the late 19th century, an individualist terrorist wing developed within the **anarchist** movement. The 1890s witnessed a number of major terrorist outrages, including the bomb attacks on the Liceo Opera House and the Corpus Christi processions in **Barcelona** in November 1893 and June 1896 respectively, and the assassination of the Spanish prime minister, **Antonio Cánovas del Castillo**, in August 1897. The Corpus Christi bombings led to a roundup of anarchists and left-wing sympathizers, followed by the **Montjüic Trial**, in which torture was used to extract confessions. The Italian anarchist Michelle Angiolillo shot Cánovas in revenge.

There then followed a period in the 1900s in Barcelona in which bombs were frequently simply left in the street. Anarchists were no doubt involved, but the waters were muddied when the former anarchist Joan Rull gained the confidence of the authorities and was paid by the civil governor to stop bombs being planted. He was able to keep his part of the bargain because his gang was planting at least some of them. Alerted, the authorities executed him in August 1908. The period also saw further attempts to assassinate leading political figures. Most notably, a teacher in **Francisco Ferrer**'s **Escuela Moderna**, Mateo Morral, caused carnage when he tried to assassinate King **Alfonso XIII** on his wedding day on 31 May 1906. Ferrer was suspected of involvement but cleared at his trial.

After the formation of the anarchist-syndicalist labor confederation **Confederación Nacional del Trabajo** (CNT) in 1910, terrorist outrages were more closely linked to industrial disputes, with, from 1916 in particular, employers and foremen gunned down during strikes and lockouts in Barcelona. From 1919, a sector within the Catalan Employers' Federation, with the support of the local **military** garrison and police, adopted counterterrorist measures, employing policemen and elements within the criminal underworld to intimidate and, on occasion, assassinate CNT activists. This policy was greatly extended between November 1921 and October 1922, when General Severiano Martínez Anido (1862–1939) became civil governor and operated a virtual military dictatorship in the city. Gunmen close to the **Sindicatos Libres** were now paid to murder CNT activists. Over 100 were murdered between November 1921 and September 1923, including the CNT's leading figure, **Salvador Seguí**. The CNT struck back. Most spectacularly, a CNT hit squad assassinated the Spanish prime minister, **Eduardo Dato**, in Madrid on 8 March 1921.

During the 1960s, terrorism reemerged in the context of the struggle against the **Franco regime**. In the late 1950s, a new group, called **ETA**, was born within the **Basque** nationalist movement. From the late 1960s, ETA took up the "armed struggle." Its most spectacular action was the assassination of General **Francisco Franco**'s right-hand man, **Luis Carrero Blanco**, in December 1973. ETA continued to operate during and after the **transition to democracy**. During the 1980s, elements within the security forces, with the tacit backing of the government, set up their own terrorist organization, the **GAL**, which targeted ETA members in the south of France. In terms of its military objectives, it could be considered a success. However, the investigative magistrate **Baltasar Garzón** was able to shed light on the operations of the movement. This led several high-ranking figures to be prosecuted, including the minister of the interior between 1982 and 1988, **José Barrionuevo**.

ETA still operates, though it is much weakened in comparison to its heyday in the late 1970s and early 1980s. It has been joined by a new threat from **Islamic** terrorism. This was first tragically revealed with the **Madrid train bombings** on 11 April 2004. It later transpired that the terrorists involved were ideologically inspired by **al-Qaeda**, but that there was no organizational link. Despite large numbers of arrests, Islamic terrorist networks have continued to operate in Spain, and militants in Barcelona at the very least have established contacts with terrorist training camps on the Pakistan-**Afghanistan** border.

THIRD INTERNATIONAL. *See* BESTEIRO FERNÁNDEZ, JULIÁN; ESCUELA NUEVA; LARGO CABALLERO, FRANCISCO; NUÑEZ DE ARENAS, MANUEL; PARTIDO COMUNISTA DE ESPAÑA; PARTIDO SOCIALISTA OBRERO ESPAÑOL; TERCERISTA.

TIERNO GALVÁN, ENRIQUE (1918–1986). Tierno Galván was born in **Madrid** in 1918, entering law school in 1934. During the **Spanish Civil War**, he fought on the Republican side, and spent several months in a concentration camp at the end of the war. On his release, he was able to continue studying, and gained a chair in constitutional law in Murcia in 1948, before moving on to Salamanca in 1953. Over the next 15 years, he combined political activism with the development of his Marxist humanist ideas. In 1965, he was expelled both from the university for his support for student protest and from the **Partido Socialista Obrero Español** (PSOE) because of his opposition to the exiled party leadership. He believed that the "interior" should play a greater role in formulating party policy, and in order to overthrow the regime was far more prepared to cooperate with the **Partido Comunista de España** (PCE) than the party hierarchy.

Tierno Galván reacted by forming his own party, the Partido Socialista del Interior (Socialist Party of the Interior) in 1968, which became the Partido Socialista Popular (People's Socialist Party) in 1974. However, its disappointing showing in the first democratic elections in June 1977 led him to negotiate its integration into the PSOE during 1978. He was treated with reverence within his new home, but remained significantly on the left of the PSOE leadership. Hence, in the party's 23rd congress, held in May 1979, he opposed **Felipe González**'s bid to tone down the Marxist element within the party program, though he refused to openly challenge González's leadership. His most successful period of political activity followed when, in the same year, with Communist support he was elected mayor of **Madrid**, a post he retained until his death in January 1986. He encouraged the arts and manifestations of youth culture in particular (the so-called *movida madrileña*), with the result that his period in office saw something of a cultural renaissance in the Spanish capital.

TORRES I BAGES, JOSEP (1846–1916). Torres i Bages was an important religious and cultural figure in late 19th-century **Catalonia**. He studied humanities at the University of Barcelona in the 1860s, where he came into contact with Romantic literary currents (the so-called **Renaixença**). He subsequently studied for the priesthood and was ordained in 1871. Over the following two decades, he became the most influential personality among a group of intellectuals, linked to the **Catholic Church**, known as the "Vic School" (which also included the poet Jacint Verdaguer [1845–1902]). These men developed an anti-**liberal** regionalist/**Catalanist** ideology, which stressed Catalonia's religious roots. However, Torres i Bages and the "Vic School" did not take such an extreme position as the **Traditionalists**. They did not reject industrialization and wished to link up with the territory's social elites and urban middle classes. Hence, in the 1880s, they supported the protectionist campaigns of Catalan **industry**. For this reason, they were important in laying the foundations of the early 20th-century conservative Catalanist movement. Torres i Bages participated in the Unió Catalanista in the 1890s and, subsequently, sympathized with the **Lliga Regionalista**. From 1899, he was the bishop of the Vic diocese. His most important work was *La tradició catalana* (*Catalan Tradition*, 1892).

TOURISM. Tourism to Spain was a minority pursuit in the 19th and early 20th centuries, to preserve the haute bourgeoisie and aristocracy of continental Europe. It was only with the post-1945 consumer boom in the West and the liberalization of the Spanish **economy** in the late 1950s that the tourism sector boomed. The number of tourists, which was three million in 1958, had reached 34 million by the early 1970s, attracted above all to the Mediterranean littoral and the Balearic and **Canary Islands**. This influx of tourists had massive economic, social, and cultural consequences during the **Franco regime**. The tourists provided much-needed foreign currency for Spain's industrial development. The coast of Mediterranean Spain was transformed as great hotels were put up to take advantage of the demand. And, as a result of the lack of adequate regulation, the environment was seriously blighted. Tourists brought with them secular Western lifestyles and cultural values. The Franco regime had in previous years attempted to reverse Spain's early 20th-century cultural liberalization and impose a set of traditionalist, **Catholic** values. It may be doubted whether the effort was ever successful in working-class circles and within middle-class families in which there was a Republican tradition, but the impact of tourism and growing contact with the democratic West further undermined the dominant culture.

Since the dictator's death, the number of tourists has continued to rise. In 2002, Spain received 49 million tourists, defined as persons who spent at least one night in the country, together with an additional 25 million day-trippers, and the industry's earnings accounted for just over 12 percent of gross domestic product. The only countries in the world to attract more tourists were the United States and France. The industry has also become more segmented. In the early 1970s, the typical tourist holiday in Spain was the relatively cheap package tour. Despite growing competition (though devaluations of the peseta in the early 1990s helped to keep prices down), Spain's location, mass advertising campaigns, the construction of major theme parks (most notably Port Aventura and Terra Mítica), and the "anything goes" reputation of many resorts, have buoyed up this sector of the market. Nevertheless, from the 1980s attempts were made to encourage more up-market package tours, cultural, eco and sports tourism (with golf a firm favorite).

The sector has been aided by the expansion of low-cost travel, which has led to a boom in weekend tourism to the major Spanish cities, and provided additional incentives for northern Europeans to either buy second homes in or retire to Spain. The major cultural attractions to be found in Madrid (especially the Prado and Reina Sofia Museums) has ensured that the Spanish capital is a relatively popular destination, but **Barcelona** has established itself as Spain's premier tourist center, while the construction of the Guggenheim Museum in 1997 has transformed Bilbao's status. Success, however, has brought serious problems, most notably the saturation of the Mediterranean coast (which at times has the appearance of one long urbanized ribbon) and water shortages. There have also been complaints by locals that certain areas have become foreign ghettos and at the strains foreign nationals of retirement age place on the health service.

Though the structure of much of the industry is small scale (and therefore dependent on powerful foreign tour operators), major multinational operations have begun to emerge, above all Sol Meliá and Barceló. The industry has also become a major employer. In 2002, 860,000 people were employed in the industry directly, and another 650,000 worked in related industries. It has provided much work for **women** workers, but much of this is low paid and seasonal. For this reason, since the mid-1990s, a growing percentage of the workforce has been filled by **immigrant** labor, especially from **Latin America**.

TRADE. *See* FOREIGN TRADE.

TRADE UNIONISM. *See* ALIANÇA SINDICAL OBRERA; CATHOLIC UNIONS; COMISIONES OBRERAS; CONFEDERACIÓN NACIONAL DEL TRABAJO; FEDERACIÓN DE TRABAJADORES DE LA REGIÓN ESPAÑOLA; FEDERACIÓN NACIONAL DE TRABAJADORES DE LA TIERRA; FEDERACIÓN REGIONAL ESPAÑOLA; FEDERACIÓN REGIONAL ESPAÑOLA DE SOCIEDADES DE RESISTENCIA; HERMANDAD OBRERA DE ACCIÓN CATÓLICA; JUVENTUD OBRERA CATÓLICA; LABOR MARKET; LABOR MOVEMENT; ORGANIZACIÓN SINDICAL ESPAÑOLA; SECOND INTERNATIONAL; SINDICATO ESPAÑOL UNIVERSITARIO; SINDICATOS LIBRES; SOLIDARIDAD DE OBREROS VASCOS; SOLIDARIDAD OBRERA;

THIRD INTERNATIONAL; TREINTISTAS; TRES CLASES DE VAPOR; UNION GENERAL DE TRABAJADORES; UNIÓN SINDICAL OBRERA.

TRADITIONALISTS. This was the name given to anti-**liberal Catholics** who sympathized with the **Carlist** movement during the 19th and early 20th centuries. In 1919, the leading theorist of Carlism, **Juan Vázquez de Mella**, split with the Carlist pretender, Jaime de Borbón y Borbón-Parma (1870–1931), who he regarded as too liberal, to form his own separate Partido Tradicionalista (Traditionalist Party).

TRAFALGAR, BATTLE OF. This battle was fought in the seas between Cádiz and **Gibraltar** on 21 October 1805, and pitted the French and Spanish forces, led by Admiral Pierre Charles Villeneuve and Lieutenant General Federico Gravina (1756–1806), against the British fleet under Lord Horatio Nelson. The Spanish were drafted, in a subordinate position, into the French war effort because of the policy of alliance with France pursued by **Manuel de Godoy.** Losses were heavy on both sides but—despite his own death—Nelson won a decisive victory. The result was drastically to weaken the Spanish fleet, the cream of which had been involved in the battle. The invasion of Spain by France in 1808, and then the penury of the Spanish exchequer from 1813, meant that Spain was not able to effectively rebuild and would not, therefore, be in a position to reconquer its American **colonies.** Trafalgar can, as a result, be seen as inaugurating a long period of Spanish maritime decadence.

TRAGIC WEEK. The events of the Tragic Week unfolded in **Barcelona** between 26 and 30 July 1909. The catalyst was the decision by the Spanish prime minister, **Antonio Maura**, to call up reservists to fight in **Morocco** after a railway line in the Spanish colony had been attacked by Riff clansmen on 9 July 1909. This caused great bitterness in working-class circles because many reservists now had wives and children, and their call-up would leave their families destitute. This was compounded by the fear (especially strong because of the debacle of the **Cuban** wars) that the troops would suffer heavy casualties. The result was street protests throughout much of urban Spain. These went furthest in Barcelona, where there were clashes between protestors and security forces. It was in this bitter and anguished atmosphere that the regional labor confederation, **Solidaridad Obrera**, decided to call a general strike to begin on Monday 26 June. On the first day, all was peaceful, but from Tuesday groups of men, women, and children began to burn down the city's religious institutions. Barricades were also put up, leading to fierce fighting between the working-class rebels, **Civil Guards**, and troops. By Friday, the uprising had been put down, but Maura now called for an exemplary repression. Wide-scale arrests followed, and, after military trials, five people were executed, including the founder of the **Escuela Moderna**, **Francisco Ferrer**, who (despite the lack of evidence) was accused of being the organizer of the rebellion. There followed a protest movement throughout much of western Europe against reactionary "Black Spain." In Spain itself, the **Partido Liberal** participated, along with **republicans** and the **Partido Socialista Obrero Español**, in a "Maura No!" campaign. In response, King **Alfonso XIII**, fearing the **monarchy** might be in danger, forced Maura's resignation on 20 October 1909.

TRANSITION TO DEMOCRACY. The phrase "transition" or "transition to democracy" usually refers to the period between the death of General **Francisco Franco** in November 1975 and the establishment and attempted consolidation of liberal democracy in Spain between 1977 and 1979. The transition process began when King **Juan Carlos I** took over the reins of state from Franco. Juan Carlos had already established himself as a reform-minded figure. He had to tread warily in order not to antagonize the Francoist old guard (or **Bunker** as they were widely known), and so chose to retain the previous prime minister, **Carlos Arias Navarro**. A number of *aperturistas* (foremost among which was the **Tácito** group), known for their reforming views, were also appointed to the government. Nevertheless, Arias Navarro proved too wedded to his Francoist past to carry out far-reaching reform, at a time when protest from workers, students, nationalists, and intellectuals for democratic reform was escalating.

In response, in July 1976, Juan Carlos forced Arias Navarro's resignation, and then pushed for the Council of the Realm (whose job it was to choose a successor under the guidance of the head of state) to replace him with the former **Movimiento Nacional** bureaucrat

Adolfo Suárez. This was at first seen as a disaster by the left, but Suárez soon showed he was prepared to dismantle the structures of Francoism and initiate the democratization of Spanish political life. More farsighted former Francoists, like Suárez, realized that in order to maintain their political careers and guard against radical social and political upheaval, they would have to make democratic concessions. In order for this strategy to work, it would be necessary to control the democratization of Spanish political life from above. When Suárez came to power, therefore, he pledged to hold free elections before 30 June 1977, but insisted that these elections be held under his government, and not a provisional government of opposition forces as the **Partido Socialista Obrero Español** (PSOE) and **Partido Comunista de España** (PCE) demanded.

This strategy was to prove highly successful, with Suárez able to force his reform proposals through the old Francoist institutions. The key moment came in November 1976 when the deputies (or *procuradores*, as they were known) of the **Cortes** committed political hara-kiri and approved democratization, in part out of an ingrained respect for authority, and in part because many were promised posts within the new regime. It proved more difficult to tame the left, which continued to mobilize its base for faster change. Yet the extent of the reform offered by Suárez meant that leftist forces had to accept that their call for a total break with the old regime (the *ruptura democrática* or democratic break) was unrealistic, and that they would have to negotiate the contours of the new regime with the Suárez government (the so-called *ruptura pactada* or pacted break).

Suárez gained the upper hand when a strike called by the emerging leftist trade unions against the government on 12 November 1976 proved a less than total success. He had already called a referendum on his reforms for 15 December. The left called for abstention because opposition political parties and unions had not yet been legalized. Nevertheless, the referendum was a victory for the government, with 77 percent of Spaniards voting, and of these, 94 percent voting in favor. Thereafter, the opposition, allied from October 1976 in the Plataforma de Organismos Democráticos (Platform of Democratic Bodies—POD), came to the negotiating table. The left accepted that the new regime would be a constitutional monarchy; that the elections, called for 15 June 1977, would be held under Suárez; and that some kind of social contract was needed to deal with the economic crisis. However, it was able to ensure that all political parties and unions, without exception, were legalized.

In the run-up to these elections, former regime reformers turned their mind to constructing new political parties. First off the mark was **Manuel Fraga**, who did not wish to join the Suárez government, and who in September 1976 had already founded the distinctly right-wing **Alianza Popular** (AP). Suárez then put together a centrist coalition of former regime reformers and bureaucrats, which was called the **Unión del Centro Democrático** (UCD). As elections approached, the government had in its favor control of the state **media** and the massive funding it received from the **banks**. Many middle-class Spaniards also greatly respected Suárez for his success in steering Spain toward its first democratic elections since 1936, and feared the possible destabilizing consequences of a left-wing victory. In these circumstances, the UCD won the elections with 34.5 percent of the votes, though the coalition did not achieve an overall majority of seats in parliament. The PSOE obtained 29.3 percent of the votes, and the PCE and AP a disappointing 9.3 percent and 8.2 percent respectively.

The following two years saw a high degree of cooperation between the government and the democratic opposition in order to lay the foundations of a new democratic regime. This could be seen in the October 1977 **Moncloa Pacts**, signed by all the major political parties, which were designed to tackle the economic crisis. Then in 1978 the major parties participated in the deliberations of a constitutional committee appointed to draw up the new constitution, which was ratified by both houses of parliament on 31 October 1978 (though a part of the PP and the Basque nationalist **Partido Nacionalista Vasco** refused to give their support). A referendum followed on 6 December. The turnout was 67.7 percent, with 87.8 percent of the votes in favor. Very importantly, the **constitution** contemplated the decentralization of the Spanish political system through the construction of a new **State of the Autonomies**. However, the new democracy still faced the threat of a backlash from pro-Francoists within the **military** and a high level of discontent in the **Basque Country**.

The transition is usually seen as coming to an end with new elections held on 1 March 1979. They were called by the Suárez government in order to gain an overall majority in parliament (which he failed to achieve). Nevertheless, the attempted military coup, the so-called **Tejerazo**, of 23 February 1981 demonstrated that Spain's democratic political structures were still at risk. Only after the victory of the PSOE in the 1982 general elections was democracy fully consolidated.

TRANSPORT. From the 17th century, advocates of Spanish modernization (the *arbitristas*) saw the relatively poor transport system as a significant impediment to economic development. A **railway** network grew up from the mid-19th century, but it lagged behind those of the major Western powers. The **Primo de Rivera dictatorship** made some effort to improve the transport system in the 1920s. However, the country's political vicissitudes meant that a sustained push to bring the system up to European standards was only effectively undertaken by the **Opus Dei** economics team during the second half of the **Franco regime** in the 1960s.

Since the 1980s, the modernization of the country's transport infrastructure has accelerated decisively. The major transformation has been that of the country's road network. Motorway (*autopista*) construction began in the 1960s, with the major work undertaken by private companies who charged tolls. However, from the 1980s, the central Spanish state and regional authorities have played a more active role, above all developing a network of fast dual carriageways (*autovías*). In the poorer south of Spain, the process has been encouraged by **European Union** subsidies (indeed, there have been accusations that some road building in sparsely populated areas has been excessive).

Rail transport has failed to keep pace. Local railways have improved greatly and are now generally fast and efficient, but intercity services tend to be slow by western European standards (not helped by the large number of single-track lines). However, the quality of the trains themselves has improved greatly. Moreover, Spain is also developing its own high-speed (AVE) network. In addition, the air transport industry has grown quickly since the 1980s. By the late 1990s, there were over 40 million domestic flights and 60 million international flights.

TREATY OF PARIS. Through this treaty, signed by Spain and the United States on 10 December 1898 following the **Spanish-American War**, Spain renounced her last remaining **colonies** in American and the Pacific: **Cuba** and Puerto Rico in America, and the Philippines, the Mariana and Caroline Islands, Palau, and Guam in the Pacific.

TREINTISTAS. The *treintistas* were a syndicalist current which broke from the **Confederación Nacional del Trabajo** (CNT) in 1932 because of the growing control exercised by the hard-line **anarchist** or anarcho-communist Federación Anaquista Ibérica (Anarchist Iberian Federation) within the organization. They were known as *treintistas* because of the manifesto signed by 30 leading syndicalists, including Joan Peiró (1887–1942) and Angel Pestaña (1886–1936), in January 1932. They finally left the CNT in April 1932 after the Sabadell branch had been expelled. During the year, they formed their own trade union confederation, the Sindicatos de Oposición (Opposition Trade Unions), and in the following year a political federation, the Federación Sindicalista Libertaria (Libertarian Syndicalist Federation). At the root of the split was the *treintistas*' greater emphasis on the need to build CNT strength rather than be carried away by revolutionary adventures, along with their willingness to work within the institutions of the **Second Republic**. This was reflected in their refusal to campaign against the vote at election time, and in their agreement to participate in the arbitration boards set up by the labor minister, **Francisco Largo Caballero**, and administered from 1933 in **Catalonia** by the **Generalitat**. This greater flexibility could also be seen in their collaboration in the **Alianzas Obreras** set up by the dissident-communist **Bloc Obrer i Camperol** (BOC) during 1933, despite the fact this meant working with political parties. All these elements indicate that the *treintistas* were moving away from anarchist "antipoliticism."

The *treintistas* took a significant slice of the CNT trade union base with them in Catalonia, were dominant in **Valencia**, and enjoyed some sympathy in Asturias. Their greater caution and realism meant that they were able to maintain their membership intact between 1933 and 1936 even though that of the CNT fell significantly (the Sindicatos de Oposición had 26,000 members in Catalonia in 1933, but by 1936 this figure had risen to 42,000 members in Catalonia and 70,000 throughout Spain). Some *treintistas* took this slow integration within the political system to its ultimate consequences in 1936 and joined the **Unión General de Trabajadores** (UGT) and, in Catalonia, the **Partit Socialista Unificat de Catalunya** (PSUC). Others were not prepared to make such a drastic break with their past, and feeling threatened by the growing influence of Marxist political parties, retreated back into the CNT in May 1936. They were encouraged to do this by the more moderate position adopted by the CNT itself during the year. As a result, during the **Spanish Civil War** men like Joan Peiró, who were essentially trade unionists prepared to intervene within the state apparatus and political institutions, again took up positions of responsibility within the CNT. *See also* LABOR MOVEMENT.

TRES CLASES DE VAPOR (TCV)/THREE STEAM CLASSES. The TCV was a large **cotton textile** labor federation that operated in **Catalonia** between 1868 and 1913. It was founded in 1868 shortly after the **Glorious Revolution**, growing rapidly to reach 8,000 members in December 1870. In these early years, it collaborated with the **anarchist**-led union confederation, the **Federación Regional Española** (FRE). However, the TCV was under the influence of **republicans** and cooperatists. This was confirmed when, with the revival of the **labor movement** in 1881, the TCV refused to join the FRE's anarchist successor, the **Federación del Trabajadores de la Región Española** (FTRE), and instead for a time collaborated with the Madrid-based **Partido Socialista Obrero Español** (PSOE) and attempted, during 1882, to form a rival labor confederation to the FTRE.

Nevertheless, it soon became clear that its ideology was more "reformist" than Marxist. Its main aim was to develop stable labor relations with employers, as indicated by its willingness to work with business leaders in order to pressure central government to increase duties on imported textile goods. This led to a break with the PSOE in the late 1880s. The TCV's reformism was confirmed when its representatives attended the Brousist or Possibilist congress held in Paris in 1889 (rather than, like the PSOE, participating in the founding congress of the Second International), and when, in 1891, it tried to form a rival political formation, the Partido Socialista Oportunista (Opportunist Socialist Party). During the 1880s, the TCV was the strongest labor organization in Catalonia, reaching 21,000 members in 1890. However, it was undermined by a joint state-employer offensive between 1891 and 1892 as, in the context of economic recession, the cotton textile industrialists attempted to reduce costs. The TCV would, henceforth, be a pale shadow of its former self. It would finally be wound up in 1913 when a new, leftist, national textile federation refused to allow it to join.

TRIENIO BOLCHEVIQUE. *See* BOLSHEVIK TRIENNIUM.

TRIENIO CONSTITUCIONAL. *See* CONSTITUTIONAL TRIENNIUM.

TURNO PACÍFICO/NONVIOLENT CHANGEOVER. The term *turno pacífico* was coined to describe the practice whereby the two "official" parties of the **Cánovas Restoration**, the **Partido Conservador** and **Partido Liberal**, alternated in power. Its key features were that the government would first be chosen by the king and would then "make" the election (the so-called *encasillado*), ensuring victory. After a period in office, it would then be the turn of the opposition. The key to the system was the link between the minister of the interior, the provincial civil governors, and local *caciques*. It worked effectively until 1898, but then became more difficult to operate because of divisions within the major parties and the growing mobilization of sectors of the electorate. Growing opposition was first apparent, above all in **Catalonia**, after Spain's defeat in the **Spanish-American War**. The years 1918 and 1919 saw a period of grave instability, but between 1920 and 1923 a serious attempt was made to reconstruct the *turno*. It was brought to an end by the military coup by General **Miguel Primo de Rivera** in September 1923. *See also* CACIQUISMO; TABLES 7 AND 8.

– U –

ULTRAS. *See* BUNKER.

UNAMUNO Y JUGO, MIGUEL DE (1869–1936). Unamuno is probably the best known figure of the **"Generation of 1898."** He was born in Bilbao into a pious **Catholic** family, studied in **Madrid**, and then in 1891 got a chair at the University of Salamanca, where he was to spend most of his life. Unamuno's private and public life were dedicated to the attempt to reconcile the apparently irreconcilable. Between 1894 and 1897, he belonged to the **Partido Socialista Obrero Español** (PSOE) and wrote copiously for the Basque Socialist weekly *La Lucha de Clases*. However, he was frustrated by the Socialists' sectarianism and was still strongly influenced by his Catholic upbringing. This led him to break with the PSOE. Thereafter, Unamuno would be torn by several ideological contradictions. One of the main torments of Unamuno's life would be the struggle between a will to believe in God and his rationalist skepticism. A second source of tension was Unamuno's belief in the positive role the people played in the historical process (his concept of "intrahistoria") and his unease at the eruption of mass politics from the turn of the century. Finally, it was not easy to reconcile Unamuno's desire to modernize Spain with his belief the country should conserve its Hispanic roots. In the literary sphere, these stresses manifested themselves in the anguished intensity of his main characters. In political terms, his doubts resulted in a certain ambiguity. From the turn of the century he showed strong **republican** sympathies, and, in 1931, was elected to parliament on the republican slate, but he criticized the **Second Republic**'s Church reforms, and at first seemed to support the July 1936 **Nationalist** uprising. However, his sense of individual freedom soon reasserted itself, and, after a clash with the Francoist authorities during the celebrations of the Day of the Race in Salamanca on 12 October 1936, he was placed under virtual house arrest until his death in December.

UNEMPLOYMENT. *See* LABOR MARKET.

UNIÓ CATALANISTA/CATALANIST UNION. *See* ALMIRALL I LLOZER, VALENTÍ; PRAT DE LA RIBA, ENRIC.

UNIÓ FEDERAL NACIONALISTA REPUBLICÀ/FEDERAL NATIONALIST REPUBLICAN UNION. This was a **republican Catalanist** party, founded in **Barcelona** in April 1910. Its main component parts were the left of the old **Solidaritat Catalana**, made up of the **Centre Nacionalista Republicà** (CNR), **Nicolás Salmerón**'s **Unión Republicana**, and the **Partido Republicano Federal Democrático**. During 1907–1909, these forces had been drawn closer together by opposition to **Antonio Maura**'s local government bill. In the May 1910 general elections, the party became the second force in Barcelona politics, a little behind the **Partido Republicano Radical** (PRR), but comfortably in front of the **Lliga Regionalista**. The years 1911–1914 were, however, to see a slow decline in its fortunes. It was riven by divisions between the more conservative former members of the Unión Republicana, harder-line Catalan nationalists, and younger leftist radicals. Moreover, like the CNR, the party was not radical enough to capture a significant working-class vote and lost middle-class support to the more compact Lliga, which was able to negotiate the foundation of the **Mancomunitat** with central government in 1913. It became totally divided after its leader, Pere Coromines (1870–1939), decided to ally with the PRR in 1913, finally disintegrating in 1916.

UNIÓN CATÓLICA. *See* PIDAL Y MON, ALEJANDRO.

UNIÓN DEL CENTRO DEMOCRÁTICO (UCD)/UNION OF THE DEMOCRATIC CENTER. The UCD coalition was a key political force during the **transition to democracy**. Its leading light was the former **Movimiento Nacional** bureaucrat **Adolfo Suárez**, who had taken over as prime minister from **Carlos Arias Navarro** in July 1976. After Suárez had announced his government's intention to dismantle Francoism, he needed a vehicle to win the elections set for June 1977. His supporters came from within the ranks of former Francoists who now recognized the need for reform and regime bureaucrats looking for a new home. Already in late 1976, regime reformers had begun to organize in expectation of the need to fight elections. In January 1977, a broad grouping of **Christian-democrats**, most of whom had belonged to **Tácito**, founded the Centro Democrático (Democratic Center), and in the following month they formed a coalition with the Partido Social Demócrata (Social Democratic Party), led by **Francisco Fernández Ordóñez**, and the liberal Partido Demócrata (Democratic Party), headed by Joaquín Garrigues Walker (1933–1980). Then, in the spring, Suárez took the coalition over and also brought in a large number of former regime bureaucrats, who were coalescing around Rodolfo Martín Villa (1934–). The UCD coalition was finally launched at the beginning of May, shortly before the 15 June 1977 elections. Suárez's positive image, along with control of the official **media** and large-scale funding from the financial and business world, ensured the party would win the elections (though not achieve an overall majority in parliament), with 34.5 percent of the vote. Over the next two years the governing coalition, in collaboration with the democratic opposition, would go a long way toward laying the foundations of democratic government in Spain. Suárez tried to develop the image of the UCD as a progressive, centrist coalition. However, there were serious ideological divisions between the various component groups, along with increasingly fierce squabbles over power and office. There was particular resentment among Christian and social democrats that under Suárez the former Movimiento bureaucrats (often referred to as *azules* because of the blue **Falange** shirts they had worn) formed a majority of the parliamentary deputies and members of the cabinet.

Divisions came into the open after the 1 March 1979 elections. These had been called by Suárez in order to gain an overall majority. In this, he was not successful, but the UCD slightly increased its percentage of the vote and was subsequently able to govern comfortably. Yet it was from this date that the coalition began to break up. In part, this was because of policy differences, with **Christian-democrats** unhappy at the divorce law that Fernández Ordóñez was piloting through parliament. Christian-democrat attacks on Suárez himself also grew in strength from 1980. Furthermore, between 1981 and 1982, the Spanish employers' confederation, the **Confederación Española de Organizaciones Empresariales** (CEOE), under Carles Ferrer Salat (1931–1998), launched an offensive against the government because of what it saw as its prolabor social and economic policies. All this occurred within a context in which the economic crisis, along with the government's efforts to slow down the pace of political decentralization, was making it highly unpopular. The latter point was dramatically demonstrated in the referendum on **Andalusian** autonomy held on 28 February 1980. It was called because the government had tried to stop the Andalusians from taking the fast track to autonomy provided by Article 151 of the **Constitution of**

1978. The result was a dramatic rebuff for the UCD, with 54 percent of the electorate voting in favor of accelerated autonomy.

The sense of crisis was further heightened by the knowledge that parts of the **military** were conspiring, and the intensification of **ETA**'s **terrorist** offensive. Tired of Christian-democrat attacks, Adolfo Suárez resigned on 29 January 1981 and was replaced by Leopoldo Calvo Sotelo (1926–). Calvo Sotelo was a compromise candidate, but this did not stop the UCD from continuing to fall apart. Politicians' minds were concentrated by the coup attempt (the so-called **Tejerazo**) of 23 February 1981, which led to renewed cooperation between the UCD and the opposition **Partido Socialista Obrero Español** (PSOE) on the question of decentralization. But the disintegration of the UCD, fueled by unpopularity at the polls, was now unstoppable. Social democrats left in October 1981 to form a new party, the Partido de Acción Democrática (Party of Democratic Action). Meanwhile, so-called Christian-democrat *críticos*, led by Oscar Alzaga (1942–) and Miguel Herrero Rodríguez de Minón (1940–), threatened to team up with the rightist **Alianza Popular** (AP) in the next elections, while the Suárez supporters maneuvered to get their man reelected president. In the end, Calvo Sotelo was replaced by a little-known Christian-democrat, Landelino Lavilla (1927–), in July 1981.

Nevertheless, conservative Christian-democrats still broke away, with followers of Oscar Alzaga forming their own Partido Demócrata Popular (Democratic Popular Party) and those grouped around Miguel Herrero Rodríguez del Miñón directly joining AP. Liberals followed suit to form the Partido Demócrata Liberal (Popular Liberal Party), and even Suárez left to organize his own new party, the Centro Democrático y Social (Social and Democratic Center). Landelina Lavilla quickly called elections in an attempt to prevent the new parties from consolidating. It was to no avail. The PSOE was victorious, with a landslide 48.3 percent of the vote. The UCD achieved just 6.8 percent. It was the greatest defeat to befall a governing party in postwar Europe, and was followed by the UCD's rapid demise. *See also* TABLE 10.

UNIÓN DEL PUEBLO ESPAÑOL/UNION OF THE SPANISH PEOPLE. *See* SUÁREZ GONZÁLEZ, ADOLFO.

UNIÓN DEL PUEBLO NAVARRO (UPN)/UNION OF THE NA-VARRESE PEOPLE. This is right-wing party that operates in the autonomous community of **Navarre**. It was set up in 1979 to voice the opposition of the Spanish-speaking, conservative **Catholic** electorate to integration into the **Basque Country**. It is closely allied with the **Partido Popular** (PP), with which it formed a "pact of association" in 1991. From this date, though it has operated independently within Navarre, its deputies have formed part of the PP group in the Spanish parliament. Its president, Miguel Sanz Sesma (1952–), has presided over the autonomous government since 1996.

UNIÓN DEMOCRÁTICA ESPAÑOLA (UDE)/DEMOCRATIC SPANISH UNION. This was an association of Francoist reformists set up in 1974 by Alfonso Osorio (1923–). Its foundation was the culmination of a split within the group known as **Tácito**, between the majority, who had resigned their posts in government after Pío Cabanillas (1923–1991) had been sacked from the administration of **Carlos Arias Navarro** (and who continued to use the name Tácito), and a more conservative group, under Osorio, who maintained their positions. They were close to the **Catholic Asociación Católica Nacional de Propagandistas** (ACNP) and professed a **Christian-democrat** ideology. In 1976, the UDE itself then split between a more rightwing faction, led by the former Francoist minister of public works Federico Silva Muñoz (1923–1996), which joined **Alianza Popular** (AP), and a more centrist grouping, including Alfonso Osorio, which merged with the more progressive Partido Popular Demócrata Cristiano (Popular Christian Democrat Party) under Fernando Álvarez de Miranda (1924–) to form the Partido Demócrata Cristiano (Christian Democratic Party), and which then rejoined the *tácitos* in January 1977 under the name Centro Democrático (Democratic Center). Soon after, the new party integrated into **Adolfo Suarez**'s **Unión del Centro Democrático** (UCD).

UNIÓN DE PROGRESO Y DEMOCRACIA. This is the name adopted by **Basta Ya** in September 2007 after it decided to turn itself into a political party in order to fight the March 2008 general elections. It chose as its candidate for prime minister a former member of the **Partido Socialista Obrero Español** (PSOE), Rosa Díez

(1952–). In these elections, Díez performed very well in Madrid, gaining a seat in parliament. This showed that there were significant numbers of center-left and centrist voters in the Spanish capital unhappy with the protagonism of the "peripheral nationalist" parties in Spanish political life and concerned that further doses of autonomy would jeopardize Spanish unity. However, the party performed very poorly in **Catalonia** and the **Basque Country**.

UNIÓN DO POBO GALEGO (UPG)/UNION OF THE GALICIAN PEOPLE. This was a left-wing nationalist party set up in **Galicia** in 1964, which, like **ETA**, combined Marxism-Leninism and Third-Worldist anticolonialism, demanding the creation of an independent, socialist, Galician state. However, the UPG never adopted **terrorist** methods. During the **transition to democracy**, it became the major nationalist force in Galician politics, gaining some peasant support through the creation of a peasants' trade union, the Comisiones Labregas (Landworkers' Commissions) and also building a small base in the industrial working class by setting up a nationalist union, the Sindicato do Obreros Galegos (Galician Workers' Trade Union). Nevertheless, it was never able to seriously challenge the major Galician parties, the **Unión del Centro Democrático** (UCD), **Alianza Popular** (AP), and the **Partido Socialista Obrero Español** (PSOE). During the 1980s, the party began to evolve in a more moderate, social-democratic direction. In 1989, it integrated into a new left-wing nationalist coalition, the **Bloque Nacionalista Galego** (BNG) and, thereafter, the Galician nationalism movement was to grow rapidly.

UNIÓN GENERAL DE TRABAJADORES (UGT)/GENERAL WORKERS' UNION. The UGT has over most of the last 100 years been one of the two most important labor confederations in Spain. It was founded in **Barcelona** in August 1888, and from the first, though theoretically independent, it was closely associated with the **Partido Socialista Obrero Español** (PSOE). This link was reinforced from 1899 when the union moved to **Madrid**, where the PSOE's central committee was located. From this date until his death in 1925, **Pablo Iglesias** was president of both organizations.

At first the UGT was a tiny organization. It was only to grow significantly in the more open and critical climate that followed

Spain's defeat in the **Spanish-American War** of 1898. By 1913, it had 147,729 members, the majority of whom were to be found in Madrid, Asturias, and the **Basque Country**. The favorable economic climate that followed the outbreak of **World War I** allowed the union to expand rapidly from 1917 and extend its influence to the rural proletariat of southern Spain. This growth was accompanied by the emergence of a paid union bureaucracy to run the new nationwide industrial labor federations the union had built. By the end of the decade, it had become the stronger half of the PSOE-UGT alliance. This was demonstrated during 1919–1920, when UGT bureaucrats, most notably **Francisco Largo Caballero** and **Julián Besteiro**, headed off the left Socialists' attempt to get the party and union to ally with Moscow. It was confirmed after General **Miguel Primo de Rivera**'s coup in September 1923 when, despite opposition from the liberal-democratic wing of the PSOE, headed by **Indalecio Prieto**, the UGT ensured that the Socialist movement adopted its policy of tacit collaboration with the regime in order to preserve its organization.

However, when the **Primo de Rivera dictatorship** weakened during 1929, the UGT split. A section led by Julián Besteiro wanted to maintain collaboration, while the followers of Largo Caballero wished to break with the dictatorship and seek an understanding with the **republicans**. Largo Caballero's supporters realized that a left-wing alliance could engineer the proclamation of a republic, and were mindful that in such circumstances, the UGT would further strengthen its position within state and society. The latter were to get their way. After the proclamation of the **Second Republic**, they went further and backed the entrance of PSOE-UGT ministers into the Republican government, with the result that Largo Caballero became minister of labor. The birth of the Republic was followed by a massive growth of the UGT. By 1932, it had over one million members.

However, resistance put up by employers and the right to social reform was leading the union to reconsider whether ministerial participation was in its best interests. In 1933, under pressure from a frustrated and angry union base, the *caballeristas* forced the Socialist movement to break with the republicans. At the same time, they talked of the need for a dictatorship of the proletariat in order to fully realize the workers' aspirations. Revolutionary talk intensified after the right took power in the November 1933 elections. Finally, in October 1934, the PSOE-UGT led a revolutionary general strike in response to the entrance of three ministers of the right-wing **Confederación Española de Derechas Autónomas** (CEDA) into government. The strike proved a disastrous failure, leading the UGT's *caballerista* leadership to recognize that only through elections would they retake power. As a result, in November 1935, Largo Caballero agreed to endorse the **Popular Front** alliance forged by Prieto and **Manuel Azaña**. But the UGT executive, dominated by Largo Caballero's supporters, and the PSOE executive, in which the *prietistas* had a majority, were at total loggerheads over the question of ministerial collaboration. After the Popular Front electoral victory, Prieto wished to reestablish the 1931–1933 coalition government, but he was blocked by the *caballeristas*, who hoped that the Socialists might govern alone in the foreseeable future. The result was that during the final months of the Republic, weak republican governments faced the threat of a **military** coup alone.

The dispute carried over into the **Spanish Civil War**. The aftermath of the attempted military coup of 17–18 July was a social revolution in much of the Republican zone, in which the UGT base participated. Hence, a "revolutionary" leader was needed, with the result that Largo Caballero became prime minister in September. Yet the next two years were to see the state roll back this union revolution. Largo Caballero himself participated in this reconstruction of the state, and once he had been removed from office in May 1937 the reassertion of the state power accelerated.

During the **Franco regime**, the UGT played only a secondary role in labor protest. This was in large measure due to its isolationism. Between 1945 and 1947, with the Franco regime fearing an Allied invasion, the UGT was able to begin to rebuild its organization. But as the regime grew more confident, it struck back viciously, and in 1947 it largely dismantled the UGT's skeletal union organization and arrested many of its leading activists. This demonstrated that independent unions would not be able to operate under the dictatorship. It was not until the 1960s that a viable alternative strategy was found, when workers' representatives began to colonize the lower echelons of the state union, the **Organización Sindical Española** (OSE), and use this base to launch an independent **labor movement**,

Comisiones Obreras (CC.OO). The UGT, however, refused to participate in the official syndical elections, arguing that to do so would only strengthen the regime, and continued in its efforts to build factory committees independent of the OSE. Consequently, the UGT was marginalized from the main developments in labor organization during the 1960s. It only retained significant support in Asturias and Vizcaya, areas in which there were tight-knit working-class communities and a strong Socialist tradition. But, over most of Spain, CC.OO grew apace, and by the late 1960s it was dominated by the **Partido Comunista de España** (PCE). Matters were made worse because from 1954, the UGT was totally subordinate to the PSOE leadership installed in Toulouse under **Rodolfo Llopis** and shared the leadership's visceral anticommunism and its extremely cautious practice. This led the UGT to maintain a rather elitist organization, reluctant to proselytize among workers who were not from a Socialist milieu for fear of infiltration.

For the reasons outlined above, the UGT emerged in the early 1970s with only a very small union base. Following the Socialist revolt against the Toulouse leadership, the UGT executive committee was transferred back to Spain after its 11th congress, held in August 1971. Thereafter, it began to play a more active role with the anti-Francoist opposition. The anticommunist phobia of the Llopis group was replaced by a willingness to cooperate with CC.OO. However, it was not until the revival of the PSOE under the dynamic team of **Felipe González** and **Alfonso Guerra** that the UGT began significantly to grow. Under the leadership of the Basque trade unionist **Nicolás Redondo**, the UGT had 6,500 members at the end of 1976, but by the end of 1977 it claimed 500,000 members.

During the **transition to democracy**, the UGT adopted a largely moderate stance. The transition had been possible because of an understanding between the various democratic forces. Between 1977 and 1982, this model was maintained by the ruling **Unión del Centro Democrático** (UCD) coalition in the field of labor relations. Tripartite talks between government, union representatives, and management were held in an attempt to reach agreements, which would then be binding. This was a similar system to the one that had been adopted by social democrats in northern and central Europe (often referred to as neocorporatism) and was looked upon very favorably by the UGT. The UGT's stance differentiated it from CC.OO, which was more skeptical of pacts, and was more prepared to mobilize its working-class base in protest. This gave the UGT a protagonism not enjoyed by CC.OO, and its high profile and moderation at a time of mounting economic crisis helped it to close the membership gap on CC.OO.

With the election of a PSOE government in October 1982, the UGT continued this policy, and the years 1982–1984 were to see several agreements signed by all sides. It remained very close to the PSOE; it had played a major role in the elaboration of the PSOE's political program, and several of its activists were PSOE parliamentary deputies. However, it grew increasingly concerned that the government's economic policies were exacerbating unemployment and it became angry that government promises to improve social benefits were not being fulfilled. The UGT also had to look over its shoulder at CC.OO, which by the mid-1980s was having considerable success in mobilizing workers against what it described as the government's right-wing economic policies. Relations between the UGT and the government began to deteriorate from 1984, and from 1986, the UGT refused to sign any more tripartite pacts. At the same time, it moved closer to CC.OO.

The final split between party and union occurred in 1988. The background was the government's amendments to the 1981 Workers' Statute in 1984, which made it easier to employ workers on temporary contracts; its refusal to extend unemployment benefits to the long-term unemployed under 45 years of age; and its youth employment scheme, which provided employers with subsidies to take on unemployed youngsters on a short-term basis. The UGT saw all of these elements as interrelated, aimed at lowering labor costs by reducing numbers of permanent posts and using the young as a cheap labor force. After negotiations with the government broke down, in the summer of 1988 it allied with CC.OO and jointly called a one-day general strike for 14 December. It proved a great success, leading the government to withdraw its youth scheme.

The historic link was now severed. Over the next five years, relations were not to improve, with the UGT and CC.OO calling further one-day general strikes in May 1992 and January 1994. In 1993, Nicolás Redondo finally retired as the union's general secretary, to be replaced by his protégé, Cándido Méndez (who has since been reelected on several occasions). After Felipe González stepped down as PSOE general secretary in 1997, relations between party and union have become significantly more cordial. Since 2000, Cándido Méndez and **José Luis Rodríguez Zapatero** have been on very good terms. In the run-up to the March 2008 general elections, the UGT suggested that the PSOE incorporate a union activist into its list of Madrid candidates, and indicated they would like an input into social and labor legislation. This was not accepted by the PSOE. Nevertheless, although both parties agreed relations cannot be the same as prior to 1988, the UGT's views are seriously taken into account by PSOE policy makers.

UNION OF THE CROWNS. This term refers to the union between the **Crown of Aragón** and **Crown of Castile** in 1479, giving birth to the new composite Spanish **monarchy**. It followed the marriage of Fernando of Aragón and Isabel of Castile (subsequently to be known as the **Catholic Monarchs**) in 1469. Both belonged to the same Castilian Trastámara dynasty.

UNIÓN LIBERAL/LIBERAL UNION. The Unión Liberal was formed in April 1856 during the **Progressive Biennium**. Under the leadership of General **Leopoldo O'Donnell** it was meant to be a centrist force equidistant between the **Partido Moderado** and **Partido Progresista**. In reality, however, it was closer to the *moderados*. O'Donnell and the Unión Liberal played a key role in undermining the Progressive Biennium, and during the periods of Unión Liberal rule between 1858 to 1863 and 1865 to 1866, the party showed itself as prepared to suppress Partido Progresista agitation as the *moderados*, and made very little effort to extend civil liberties. However, after the death of O'Donnell in 1867, the party joined the Partido Progresista and **Partido Demócrata** in their conspiracy to overthrow the reactionary *moderado* government of General **Ramón María Narváez** and force **Queen Isabel II** into exile. During the **Democratic Sexennium**, former *unionistas* were to be found on the more conservative wing of the monarchist-constitutionalist coalition, and, after the experience of the **First Republic**, they were almost to a man happy to welcome the **Cánovas Restoration**.

UNIÓN MILITAR DEMOCRÁTICA (UDM)/DEMOCRATIC MILITARY UNION. This was a liberal pressure group that began to operate in the Spanish **military** during the mid-1970s. It was repressed by the intelligence services in 1975 and its leaders jailed. They were amnestied after the first democratic elections in June 1977, but not reincorporated into the army.

UNION MILITAR ESPAÑOLA (UME)/SPANISH MILITARY UNION. The UME was a conspiratorial monarchist organization that functioned within the Spanish **military** from late 1933 through to the beginning of the **Spanish Civil War.** It was founded by Lieutenant Colonel Emilio Rodríguez Tarduchy and Captain Bartolomé Barba Hernández, while Lieutenant Colonel Valentín Galarza (1882–1951) coordinated its operations. It was to be at the forefront of the various military plots against the **Second Republic,** and was put at the disposal of General **Emilio Mola** in the run-up to the uprising of 17–18 July 1936.

UNION MONÁRQUICA NACIONAL/NATIONAL MONARCHIST UNION. *See* PRIMO DE RIVERA Y SAÉNZ DE HEREDIA, JOSÉ ANTONIO.

UNIÓN NACIONAL/NATIONAL UNION. The Unión Nacional was a political party formed in March 1900 by members of the Chambers of Agriculture and Chambers of Commerce under the auspices of **Joaquín Costa, Santiago Alba,** and Basilio Paraíso (1849–1930). It was formed in reaction to the **Spanish-American War** and represented the grievances of modest landowners, the petty bourgeoisie and commercial classes, who were marginalized from the political system and felt their economic interests had been ignored. However, despite a temporary rush of enthusiasm, the party proved ephemeral and was wound up in 1904. There were a number of reasons. In the first place, disagreements flared between Costa and Paraíso, the latter wishing to launch a taxpayers' strike. More important in the long run, the social base of the party was too narrow. Much of rural Spain was still under *caciquista* influence and so politically inactive, while in **Catalonia** the **Lliga Regionalista** was mobilizing the urban middle classes. Moreover, the party was socially conservative and so never able to attract industrial workers.

UNIÓN PATRIÓTICA/PATRIOTIC UNION. *See* ASOCIACIÓN CATÓLICA NACIONAL DE PROPAGANDISTAS; PRIMO DE RIVERA DICTATORSHIP.

UNIÓN REPUBLICANA/REPUBLICAN UNION. This is the name given to a coalition of **republican** forces that operated between 1893 and 1896 and, again, between 1900 and 1903, and to a new republican party founded on 23 March 1903 under the leadership of **Nicolás Salmerón.** The new party incorporated Salmerón's Partido Republicano Centralista (Centralist Republican Party), much of the **Partido Republicano Progresista** (including **Alejandro Lerroux**), some members of the **Partido Republicano Federal Democrático**, and a large number of independents, making it the major force in republican politics. Given the growing disaffection toward the **Cánovas Restoration** following the **Spanish-American War** of 1898, it did very well in its first electoral outing in the general elections of 26 April 1903. However, as hopes of the regime's demise faded, its fortunes began to wane, and it was fatally divided at the beginning of 1906 when Salmerón decided to support the **Solidaritat Catalana** coalition after the *Cu-Cut!* **incident.** In **Catalonia, Alejandro Lerroux** refused to join the coalition and formed his own **Partido Republicano Radical**, while outside Catalonia many republican nuclei broke away and regained their independence.

UNIÓN SINDICAL OBRERA (USO)/WORKERS' SYNDICAL UNION. The USO was an independent trade union that emerged during the **Franco regime** and that, like **Comisiones Obreras** (CC. OO), worked within the structures of the official state union, the **Organización Sindical Española** (OSE). It was founded in 1960 by left-wing **Catholics** affiliated with the **Hermandad Obrera de Acción Católica** (HOAC) and **Juventud Obrera Católica** (JOC). During the 1960s, it operated as a small but significant current within the opposition movement, proclaiming as its ultimate goal a socialist society based on worker self-management. In the early and mid-1960s, it worked within CC.OO, but abandoned the organization in 1967, arguing that it had become too subordinate to the **Partido Comunista de España** (PCE). During the period of union-building following the legalization of independent unions in April 1976, it was approached by the **Unión General de Trabajadores** (UGT) to form a single union. A minority of USO activists refused to join, but most of its best cadres (including its leading figure, José María Zafiaur), joined the UGT in 1978. In return, in deference to their concern at the UGT's subordination to the PSOE, **Nicolás Redondo** resigned from the party's executive committee. The remnants of the organization then gravitated to the right and became closely linked to the governing party, the **Unión del Centro Democrático** (UCD). *See also* LABOR MOVEMENT.

UNIÓN SOCIAL DEMÓCRATA ESPAÑOLA/SPANISH SOCIAL DEMOCRATIC UNION. *See* RIDRUEJO, DIONISIO.

UNIVERSITIES. *See* EDUCATION.

– V –

VALENCIA. The autonomous community of Valencia (Comunitat Valenciana) is located on the Mediterranean coast between **Catalonia** to the north and Murcia to the south. In 2007, its **population** was 4,885,029. Its capital city, Valencia (València in the autochthonous **Valencian language**) is Spain's third largest, with 810,064 inhabitants in this year.

It was "reconquered" from the **Moors** by Jaume I of Aragón (1208–1276) between 1232 and 1245 and integrated into the **Crown of Aragón**. Under Moorish rule, wide-scale irrigation had been introduced to the Valencian littoral, which developed a prosperous **agriculture** based on citrus fruits and horticulture, and the expulsion of the Moors from Spain in 1609 was a serious blow to the region. In the 19th century, Valencian agriculture was unique in that from the 1870s it made rapid strides in improving productivity and became highly export-oriented. It still remains a key component of the **economy**. From the 1960s, **tourism** has also boomed, with Benidorm the archetypal mass-market tourist destination. The city of Valencia has found it difficult to compete with the cultural attractions of **Barcelona** and **Madrid**, but with the construction of the Ciutat de les Arts i les Ciències (City of the Arts and Sciences), designed by the renowned Valencian architect **Santiago Calatrava**, it has attracted larger slice of the weekend-break market.

The local variant of the **Catalan language** spoken in Valencia came to be known as Valencià. After the privileges (*fueros*) of the Crown of Aragón were stripped away by **Felipe V** during the **War of Succession**, its political development was rather different from its northern neighbor. Though a strong regional identity was forged, no significant nationalist movement developed from the late 19th century. Hence, the majority of the population has rejected attempts by Catalan nationalists to forge a common identity. Indeed, there is some hostility to what is seen as Barcelona "imperialism."

Politically, in the early 20th century, there was a great divide between the **anarchist**, Socialist, and **republican** left and the agrarian right. Valencian landowning interests integrated into countrywide parties, such as the **Confederación Española de Derechas Autónomas** (CEDA) in the 1930s, and strongly supported the **Franco regime**. Since the **transition to democracy**, the big statewide parties have vied for political control over the region. Between 1982 and 1995, the **Partido Socialista Obrero Español** (PSOE) was dominant, but since this date the **Partido Popular** (PP) has controlled the Valencian autonomous government (the **Generalitat**), its popularity boosted by its plans to transfer water from the Ebro River to Valencia and Murcia (a scheme the PSOE blocked when it came to power in 2004). **Eduardo Zaplana** was president of the Generalitat between 1995 and 2002 and the present incumbent is his local rival, Francesc Camps (1962–).

VALENCIAN LANGUAGE. Valencian (valencià) in the name given to the variant of the **Catalan language** spoken in the autonomous community of **Valencia** (València). Because no powerful pan-**Catalanist** nationalist current emerged in Valencia, from the late 19th century the language has been viewed very differently than in **Catalonia**. Most of Valencia's inhabitants see themselves as Spaniards and Catalan as a regional language. The result has been that the usage of Valencian has declined since the early 20th century. It is little spoken in the interior and south of the territory and is the minority language in the city of Valencia. In a study by the Valencian **Generalitat** in 2005, 48 percent of the population stated that they spoke only **Castilian** at home and 32 percent only Valencian. Moreover, the rejection of Catalan nationalism (and the claims by many Catalan nationalists that Valencia forms part of a larger Catalan cultural community, which they refer to as the Països Catalans) has led some people in Valencia (with the support of the Spanish right) to argue that they speak a separate language. Such assertions are based on the fact that because no common grammatical rules have been established throughout the Catalan-speaking territories, there are some grammatical differences. In 1998, the Valencian autonomous government set up its own Acadèmia Valenciana de la Llengua (Valencian Language Academy), which, in 2005, recognized that Catalan and Valencian were the same language, while stating that there are significant variants that should be maintained. Likewise, almost all philologists maintain that Catalan and Valencian are the same language.

VALLE INCLÁN, RAMÓN MARÍA DEL (1866–1936). Valle Inclán was one of Spain's leading novelists during the early 20th century. He was born into an aristocratic family in the village of Villanueva de Arosa in **Galicia**. He came into contact with the "**Generation of 1898,**" but his first works were strongly influenced by **modernism**. During the first decade of the century, like the members of the "Generation of 1898," his novels were critical of the social and political realities of Spain, but his concerns for the plight of rural Spain were channeled into support for a rather romanticized rendition of **Carlism**. However, after 1910, his rebellious spirit and sympathy for popular protest developed in a more leftist direction. With the publication in 1920 of *Luces de Bohemia* (*Lights of Bohemia*), Valle Inclán initiated his most famous literary style, known as *esperpento*.

VÁZQUEZ DE MELLA, JUAN (1861–1928). Vázquez de Mella was the leading **Carlist** ideologue of the late 19th and early 20th centuries. His most notable achievement was to provide a detailed blueprint for the **Traditionalist-corporatist** society of the future. This proved more convincing than the 19th-century Carlist goal of returning to (an idealized rendition of) the Spanish composite **monarchy** of the Middle Ages. Vázquez de Mella was also important in that, in the face of growing social strife and political agitation, post-

1913 he frequently coincided with the **Maurista** right in parliament. This anticipated the rapprochement between the various sectors of the antiliberal right from the 1920s onward. In 1919, unhappy at the "liberal" stance of the new Carlist pretender, Jaime de Borbón y Borbón-Parma (1870–1931), he set up his own Partido Tradicionalista (Traditionalist Party).

VELAZQUEZ, DIEGO RODRÍQUEZ DE SILVA Y (1599–1660). Velazquez was Spain's greatest 16th-century painter. He was born in Seville, where he learned his trade in the studio of Francisco Pacheco. It was through Pacheco's contacts with the **count-duke de Olivares** that he was brought to the attention of King **Felipe IV**, becoming his court painter in 1623. His rise was made easier in a context in which Spain's imperial role had produced a great demand for public buildings and palaces and for their decoration. His horizons were broadened by his trip to Italy between 1629 and 1631 and it was after his return that he painted his greatest works.

VERA LÓPEZ, JAIME (1859–1918). Jaime Vera was one of the few intellectuals to join the **Partido Socialista Obrero Español** (PSOE) in the late 19th century. A doctor by profession, Vera was to enter into contact with the small group of Madrid Socialists in the 1870s. He is particularly well known for his 1884 *Informe a la Comisión de Reformas Sociales* (*Report to the Commission of Social Reforms*), which showed a deeper grasp of Marxist theory than was current in Spain at the time and became a key text of early Spanish socialism. However, like **Miguel Unamuno**, he was critical of the PSOE's isolationism and briefly withdrew his membership in 1886 over the party's refusal to establish alliances with the **republicans**. Nevertheless, he still supported the Socialist cause, and after an alliance (*conjunción*) was finally established with the republicans in 1910, despite deteriorating health, he spent the last years of his life actively involved in party work.

VERGARA PACT. The Vergara Pact brought an end to the First Carlist War in August 1839. It was signed by General **Baldomero Espartero** and the **Carlist** general Rafael Maroto (1783–1847), who agreed to abandon the armed struggle so long as the **Basques'** historic laws (*fueros*) were respected and Carlist officers were incorporated into the Spanish **military** with the same grade.

VERTICAL SYNDICATES. *See* ORGANIZACION SINDICAL ESPAÑOLA.

– W –

WAR OF INDEPENDENCE. The War of Independence was fought between 1808 and 1814 to liberate Spain from the occupying army of Napoleon Bonaparte. French troops entered Spain in late 1807 under Marshall Joachim Murat and captured **Madrid** on 23 March 1808. In May, the former king **Charles IV**, along with his son, King **Ferdinand VII**, met Napoleon in Bayonne, where they were forced to renounce their claims to the throne. Napoleon then proceeded to name his own brother Joseph as **José I**, king of Spain. In the following month, an acquiescent **Cortes**, called by José I, then ratified the Napoleonic **Bayonne Constitution**. Spain's administrative elite and part of its intellectual elite acquiesced to the new monarchy (and therefore became known as the *afrancesados*).

This left a power vacuum, which was filled by a popular protest movement. In **Madrid** on 2 May, an urban revolt against French rule was savagely put down by Murat's forces. The painting by **Francisco de Goya** of the ringleaders' execution on the following day was in the future to become a powerful symbol of Spanish nationhood. In urban areas not under French control, provincial committees or *juntas* were subsequently set up to run local affairs and coordinate the military campaign against Napoleon. During the summer, they were to elect a central junta (Junta Suprema Central Administrativa), which first met in Aranjuez on 25 July. These so-called "patriots" then summoned the **Cortes of Cádiz** in 1810, which would produce the first (excluding the Bayonne Constitution) **liberal** constitution in Spanish history.

Their sphere of action was widened by early setbacks for the French forces. After defeat in the battle of Bailén on 19 July 1808, José I was forced to retreat from Madrid to Vitoria. Napoleon's response was to reenter the peninsula with a force of 250,000 men, many veterans of the Grande Armée. An expeditionary force under

Sir Arthur Wellesley, the future duke of Wellington, was sent out by Great Britain to help the Spanish in August 1808, but after the battle of Talavera in July 1809 he prudently retreated to **Portugal**. Given the superior forces at its disposal, France was over the next two years able to capture most Spanish territory, allowing José I to return to Madrid. Yet most of the Spanish army dispersed rather than being defeated in open battle. This made it possible, for the first time in history, to launch a guerrilla campaign that was to keep occupied an average of four-fifths of the French troops at any one time. It was to an important degree this guerrilla campaign that was finally to make continued occupation of the peninsula impossible. By 1812, Napoleon was also occupied on the Russian front and began to withdraw his forces from Spain. This allowed the British troops, under Wellesley, to sweep in from Portugal and defeat the French at Arapiles (July 1812) and Vitoria (June 1813). The last French troops crossed the border at the beginning of 1814. Napoleon then accepted the return to Spain of Ferdinand VII, after trying to extract the promise that he would not join a coalition of forces against him.

WAR OF SUCCESSION. The War of Succession was provoked by the opposition to the accession of the French **Bourbon** dynasty to the Spanish throne by an alliance of England and Holland (both under William of Orange) and the German **Habsburg** emperor, Leopoldo I. Their alternative candidate was Archduke Charles of Austria, the emperor's son.

The allies' cause was helped by the fact that the new king, **Felipe V**, was little more than a puppet of the king of France. Their base became the **Crown of Aragón**, in which they enjoyed considerable support, above all in **Catalonia**. Merchants and manufacturers were attracted by the commercial advantages they were promised, while there was suspicion that the new Bourbon king would follow the centralizing policies of the French monarchy. At first the allies were in the ascendancy, but they suffered key defeats in the battles of Almansa in April 1707 and Villaviciosa in December 1710. Holland and Great Britain then abandoned the Habsburg cause at the end of 1711, when, following the death of Leopoldo I, Charles of Austria ascended to the Habsburg throne. Their chief concern now became Habsburg rather than French dominance of western Europe.

A deal was then reached at the March 1713 Treaty of Utrecht. Felipe V was confirmed as ruler of Spain (the Crowns of Aragón and Castile and the American colonies), but lost the rest of the Spanish Habsburg Empire. **Gibraltar** and Menorca—which had been captured during the war—remained in British hands (though Menorca was returned to Spain in 1783). The Catalan rebels fought on until 11 September 1714, when **Barcelona** fell to the forces of Felipe V. As feared, between 1707 and 1714 the new monarch did abolish the *fueros* of the Crown of Aragón and imposed a more centralized model of rule, inspired by the French political system.

WELFARE STATE. The Spanish welfare state developed slowly in comparison to those of the major western European powers of the 20th century. At the turn of the century, only 9.4 percent of Spanish national income was spent by the state, and about 50 percent of that went on to servicing the public debt and on defense spending. Its first social legislation, accompanied by the formation of the **Instituto de Reformas Sociales**, was the work of the **Partido Conservador** politician **Eduardo Dato** at the beginning of the 20th century. However, the new legislation was only patchily enforced. Similarly, though the 1857 Moyano Law established the principle of state responsibility for **education**, until the early 20th century, resources were scarce and there was wide-scale absenteeism. It was not until the **Second Republic** that a serious effort was made to put in place the rudiments of a welfare state, but progress was held up by an insistence on maintaining a balanced budget. Under the **Franco regime**, taxes were held down and the new welfare states of the democratic West were not copied.

This changed with the **transition to democracy**. Important in this respect was the decision by the **Unión del Centro Democrático** (UCD) to introduce a personal earnings tax, the Impuesto sobre la Renta de las Personas Físicas (IRPF) in 1979, as part of the **Moncloa Pacts**. This made possible an increase in government spending from 18 percent to 30 percent of gross domestic product between 1975 and 1986. During the long period of government by the **Partido Socialista Obrero Español** (PSOE), between 1982 and 1996, a state health care system was put in place that by 1993 covered 99 percent of the population (the other 1 percent was excluded because of its high income). In addition, social security systems improved, but employer and state contributions remained low by European standards. In particular, the government continued to severely restrict numbers who could claim unemployment benefit. In 1985, only 32 percent of the unemployed were covered. The number of persons covered by pensions increased, but at the cost of a decline in purchasing power.

Overall, in 1998 the Spanish welfare state still remained one of the weakest in western Europe, with social expenditure representing 21.6 percent of gross domestic product, compared to the western European average of 27.6 percent. The amount spent on policies to support families remains particularly low (only 1.3 percent of gross domestic product as compared to the Organization of Economic Cooperation and Development-24 average of 2.4 percent in 2007). Family structures are relatively stable in Spain and the family is expected to take the strain in supporting children who cannot find work, the long-term unemployed, and aged family members. Nevertheless, the 2004–2008 PSOE government increased state support for the disabled and unemployment benefits, and in 2007 announced measures to support newborn babies (with 2,500 euros for the family upon the birth of the child) and subsidize low-paid youngsters trying to rent a flat. *See also* TABLE 4.

WOMEN. The changing place of women in Spanish society is often, in rather simplistic terms, viewed as a two-stage process. First, in the **Catholic**-conservative Spain of the **Franco regime**, women held "traditional" values and were confined to the private domestic sphere. The end of the regime then saw women adopting more "modern" secular ideas and increasingly integrating into the world of work.

Matters were, in reality, rather more complex. In the late 19th century, patriarchal attitudes were dominant within middle- and upper-class circles and the dichotomy was firmly established between the male public and female private sphere. Such attitudes were staunchly defended by the **Catholic Church**, which from the 1880s became the predominant provider of **education** for these social groups. This perspective was ratified in the 1889 Civil Code, which affirmed that when a woman got married she lost her legal and property rights and was dependent on the male head of household. Women themselves internalized these attitudes. In well-to-do circles, it was taboo for all women, whether single or married, to undertake paid labor, and even poorer lower-middle-class women, who worked from home to make ends met, did so in secret. These factors help explain the slow development of a middle-class **feminist** movement.

On the other hand, working-class women had little choice but to work in manufacturing and domestic labor when young, given low family income. Once of childbearing age, they would often retire to the domestic sphere but continue working from home. Despite the strength of the Church in rural northern and central Spain, within peasant families female labor was also the norm. Girls either helped on the land or worked as domestic servants, and peasant women would continue to supplement their husbands' work in the fields throughout their lives.

Middle-class attitudes began to change in the 1920s and 1930s and young women from such backgrounds started entering service sector professions in increasing numbers. These changes were given a great boost by the establishment of the **Second Republic** in 1931. The regime was committed to the legal equality of women, introducing a divorce law and giving women the right to the vote for the first time. However, the triumph of the **Nationalists** in the **Spanish Civil War** signified a brutal cultural counterrevolution. The Franco regime, in league with the Church, attempted to impose conservative, patriarchal, Catholic values on the population. At the same time, through its policy of economic and cultural **autarky**, it isolated Spain from what it saw as decadent Western influences. The regime announced in the 1938 Labor Charter that it was "liberating married women from the workshop and factory," and in 1941, married women were prohibited from working. It also reintroduced the 1889 Civil Code, which it integrated into its 1945 People's Charter, the Fuero de Los Españoles.

Meanwhile, divorce became impossible and abortion and the use of contraceptives were banned. Married couples were encouraged to have large families (seen by the regime as both morally right and of key importance in laying the foundation for a resurgent Spanish nation) through a "family subsidy" for families with over two children. Its message was not only propagated within the classroom. Through the women's front of the regime's single party, the **Sección Feminina**, young women undertaking six months of "social service" would also be exposed to the regime's cultural agenda and expected to promote it.

These measures certainly reversed the nascent incorporation of middle-class women into the **labor market** and led female participation rates to decline. However, given the dire poverty faced by many working-class households during the "hunger years" of the 1940s, large numbers of women remained in paid employ. The 1950 census indicated that 16 percent of women worked but the real figure was much higher. No doubt regime propaganda made a big impact on many women within the middle classes. However, it had less of an impact within working-class circles (where many, it should be recalled, had been schooled in left-wing anticlerical socialist and **anarchist** political parties and **trade unions**), though everyone had to conform outwardly. Similarly, there was tacit resistance in urban middle-class families in which there was a tradition of **republicanism**.

The regime's attitude began to change in the late 1950s. The new brand of **Opus Dei** technocrats was culturally very conservative, but also wanted to stimulate economic development by opening Spain up to international markets. This required more flexibility with respect to female labor. Accordingly, in 1962, new legislation once again allowed married women to work, though this was subject to the husband's permission. In addition, foreign **tourism** was encouraged as it provided much-needed jobs and foreign currency. However, this occurred at a time when the democratic West was undergoing an antitraditional cultural revolution, with the result that in coastal areas Spaniards were confronted by new, less formal dress codes and more sexually liberated attitudes. The impact of democratic Western norms and ideas was also stimulated by the relaxation of censorship, especially after the 1966 Press Law.

Consequently, the 1960s were to see the growing incorporation of women into the labor market. By 1969, women made up 26.7 percent of the labor force. After the death of Franco in 1975, even among conservative Catholic families the stigma attached to women working outside the home rapidly evaporated. This incorporation was slowed by the economic recession that hit Spain between 1973 and 1989 and by the escalating unemployment rate. In 1992, women made up 34 percent of the labor force. However, the economic boom of the period 1995–2006, which from 1998 was accompanied by rapidly declining unemployment, saw this trend accelerate, with women reaching 42.3 percent of the labor force by 2006.

Most women went into the **service sector**, a trend that accelerated in the 1990s. They frequently found themselves in the lowest-paid, least-regarded jobs. From the 1990s, increasing numbers of women have attained posts in the better-paid professions, like the judiciary, and numbers of women in public administration and the education sector have increased rapidly. However, they tend to be concentrated at more junior levels. Moreover, a disproportionate number of women work in the black market. Finally, the problem of the proliferation of temporary contracts has particularly affected women along with young people generally, with many facing no prospect of progressing from temporary to permanent employment. From the 1990s, the worst-paid jobs in which women's labor had predominated—especially domestic service and the tourist industry—have increasingly been undertaken by **immigrant** workers. The problems facing women with partners and children have been compounded because women still do most of the housework, because demand for preschool places outstrips supply, and because grown-up children frequently remain at home until they are in their late twenties. Relatively strong family networks often take up the strain.

Women's legal status changed dramatically after the death of Franco. The **Constitution of 1978** specifically stated that women were equal to men. Divorce and the use of contraceptives were legalized in 1981, and an abortion law, albeit very restrictive, was approved in 1985. The foundation of the **Instituto de la Mujer** by the government of the **Partido Socialista Obrero Español** (PSOE) in 1983, and the subsequent institutionalization of sectors of the feminist movement, has ensured that women's issues have remained high on the political agenda. There has been a slow increase in the number of women in politics. In the 1977 general elections, 6.3 percent of the deputies elected to the Lower House were women. The 1989 elections saw a significant increase, to 15 percent, and this change was subsequently reflected in local and regional elections. By the 2004 elections, the figure was up to 36.3 percent. From the late 1980s, left-wing parties also introduced minimum quotas for the number of women in party posts. From the 1990s, "big hitting" women politicians also emerged. At present the most important are, on the right,

Esperanza Aguirre, and on the left, **María Teresa Fernández de la Vega.**

WORLD WAR I. The economic, social, and political history of Spain between 1914 and 1923 was very much conditioned by the impact of World War I. The war contributed to the growing polarization of Spanish society between 1914 and 1918 by dividing liberals and conservatives into two clearly differentiated groups. The left and liberals tended to support the Allies (hence the name *aliadófilos*), while right-wing Spain tended to line up behind the Germans (the *germanófilos*). Toward the end of the war, the growing likelihood of an Allied victory encouraged hope on the left that in its aftermath, democratization would sweep through Europe. And President Woodrow Wilson's support for the rights of the "small nations" of central and eastern Europe stimulated **Catalanist** agitation for an autonomy statute.

The war also provoked far-reaching economic and social changes. When the war began in August 1914, the resulting dislocation of Spain's traditional markets led to a temporary economic crisis. Spanish **industry** was, however, soon to benefit. The countries at war had to concentrate production on the war effort, and this allowed Spanish manufactures into previously inaccessible foreign markets. Moreover, Spain could also supply the warring nations with equipment, such as clothing and weaponry, badly needed to conduct the war. The result was a great growth in the profitability of Spanish industry. This tended to strengthen the position of urban manufacturing interests within Spain. At the same time, the buoyant industrial climate allowed the organizations of the working class to grow rapidly, and this resulted in an escalation of strike action. Strikes were, moreover, given a bitter edge because of galloping inflation caused by the undersupply of the home market that resulted from the redirection of goods into profitable export markets. In consequence, membership in both the **Confederación Nacional del Trabajo** (CNT) and the **Unión General de Trabajadores** was to take off from 1917.

The overall result of the war was to strengthen those urban middle- and working-class forces that wished either to reform or overthrow the **Cánovas Restoration.** Key in this respect would be the working-class left, the **republicans**, and the Catalan **Lliga Regionalista.** This was at the root of the **crisis of 1917**. *See also* FOREIGN TRADE; LABOR MOVEMENT.

WORLD WAR II. At the beginning of World War II, the **Franco regime** adopted a strongly pro-Axis stance. German submarines were allowed to refuel in Spanish ports, Spanish raw materials were exported to Germany (including, most importantly, wolfram), and through the propaganda machine of the single party, the **Falange Española Tradicionalista y Juntas de Ofensiva Nacional Sindicalista** (FET y de las JONS), the virtues of the Axis and its military exploits were extolled. **Francisco Franco** regarded the Fascist powers as authoritarian sister states and saw it as his task to ensure that Spain should receive a share of the spoils in the new world order that would follow what he saw as the inevitable Fascist military victory. As a result, Franco wanted to enter the war if possible and spent 1940 negotiating acceptable terms of entry with Germany. Franco had two main concerns: first, that Spanish territorial acquisitions should be guaranteed, and second, that Germany should offer Spain sufficient protection from British retaliation.

In June 1940, the chief of the General Staff, General Juan Vigón (1880–1955), was sent to Berlin to negotiate. The Germans were presented with a shopping list of Spanish demands. Spain wanted the annexation of the Oran district of western Algeria, the incorporation of all of **Morocco** into its empire, the extension of the Spanish Sahara southward to the 20th parallel, and the addition of French Cameroon to Spanish Guinea. Spain also demanded German heavy artillery and aviation to help conquer **Gibraltar**, and German submarine support to assist in the defense of the **Canary Islands**, along with large amounts of food, ammunition, fuel, and other raw materials. **Ramón Serrano Suñer**, Franco's most trusted advisor, was then sent to Berlin and Rome to discuss the matter further. Finally, on 20 October, Franco met Adolf Hitler at Hendaye. Hitler, however, felt that given what Spain could contribute, the price was too high. In particular, he did not wish to antagonize the Vichy regime in France by giving Spain territory in Africa that he did not think that it could hold.

The only agreement reached was that Spain should sign a secret protocol pledging to join the Tripartite Pact (the defensive alliance between Germany, Italy, and Japan) and to enter the war at some unspecified date in the future after consultation with Germany and Italy. Spain nevertheless continued to maintain a strongly pro-Axis stance and elements within the FET y de las JONS and the **military** still pushed for Spain to enter. Germany's invasion of the Soviet Union on 22 June 1941 produced anxiety, but also the desire, especially among Falangists, to participate in the struggle against communism. This was the background to the decision to form the **Blue Division**, to fight alongside Nazi Germany on the Russian front.

Franco's pro-Axis stance was maintained until the autumn of 1942, when growing doubts regarding whether Germany would win the war began to surface. Within the Francoist establishment, a number of leading military figures in particular, afraid of the consequences of an Allied victory, pushed for the regime to take a more neutral stance. Following the fall of Serrano Suñer in 1942, these included the new foreign secretary, General Francisco Gómez-Jordana (1876–1944), and Franco's new confidant, Admiral **Luis Carrero Blanco**. Franco, ever mindful of his political (and probably physical) survival, took note. He still hoped Germany would win the war, but at the beginning of 1943 launched a failed attempt at mediation. Then, in order to distance himself from the Axis, Franco developed his theory that there were in fact two wars, the conflict between Germany and the Allies in which Spain was neutral, and the struggle with the Soviet Union, in which Spain favored Germany.

As the Allies' position strengthened, so their pressure on Spain grew. Early in 1944, they announced a total suspension of oil shipments to Spain until the export of Spanish raw materials to Germany ended. Franco soon capitulated and in August he issued orders that the Spanish press be more neutral in their reporting. Great Britain was willing to try to bring Spain into the fold, but the United States took a harder line. As a result, the Allies' Potsdam Conference, held in July 1945, recommended that Spain be excluded from the new United Nations and support be given to the country's "democratic forces." This step was effectively taken in the first meeting of the United Nations, held in the same month. Thus, by the end of 1945, because of its authoritarian regime and previous support for the Axis, Spain found itself ostracized from the international community and excluded from the U.S.-sponsored reconstruction of western Europe.

– Y –

YAGÜE BLANCO, JUAN (1891–1952). General Yagüe was one of **Francisco Franco**'s staunchest supporters during the early years of the **Franco** regime. He was born in San Leonardo (Soria), and after joining the army became an *africanista*, rising through the ranks in **Morocco**. He had already made friends with Franco in the Toledo Infantry Academy between 1907 and 1910, and was placed in charge of the African troops who brutally put down the Asturias uprising in **October 1934** by Franco. From his post as head of the **Legión Española**'s Second Battalion (Segunda Bandera), he then played a key role in preparing the **military** uprising against the **Second Republic** in Morocco, and once the Army of Africa had been transferred to Spain in August 1936, Franco put Yagüe in overall field command as the army swept through Extremadura, up toward Talavera and then Maqueda. Under Franco's orders, Yagüe conducted the campaign in the same fashion as he had fought Spain's **colonial** war in Morocco, with mass executions of prisoners, looting, and the rape of women. In the most infamous incident, after the capture of Badajoz on 14 August, nearly 2,000 people were shot.

After being incorporated into Franco's personal entourage, Yagüe then played an important role in engineering the elevation of Franco to head of state in September, but during the following year, he became increasingly disillusioned at the path taken by the new regime. He was one of the few army officers who had joined the **Falange Española** during the Second Republic, and was apparently disappointed at the decision made by Franco in April 1937 to fuse the Falange and the **Carlists** into a single party. He was also critical of the slowness of the Nationalist military advance, finally speaking out in a Falangist banquet held in Burgos on 19 April 1938.

Yagüe was relieved of his command of the Moroccan army corps for a few weeks. However, Franco did not want an open conflict with a man who was extremely popular with his troops and soon reinstated him. Then, with Spain's **foreign policy** becoming increasingly pro-Axis during 1939, in a cabinet reshuffle on 9 August Yagüe was made air force minister. Nevertheless, he continued to criticize Franco, and after being informed by the intelligence services that Yagüe was scheming with Falangist radicals to have him replaced, Franco decided to act, sacking him on 27 June and having him confined to the village of his birth. Yagüe continued to maintain a strongly pro-German stance, and in November 1941 was packed off to Morocco as commander of the 10th Army Corps in Melilla to keep him out of trouble. Yet once the tide of **World War II** began to turn against Germany, he was bought back into the picture to act as a counterweight to the increasingly powerful promonarchist generals. Faced with this threat, he now showed himself loyal to Franco. He was made captain general of Burgos in October 1941 and promoted to lieutenant general in October of the following year. He was then made commander of the Melilla garrison in November 1942, and from September 1943 coordinated the fight against the *maquis* from his new post of captain general of the Burgos military region.

YUGOSLAVIA. Spain was involved in both humanitarian missions and military action, under the auspices of the United Nations (UN) and **North Atlantic Treaty Organization** (NATO), following the breakup of Yugoslavia. Between 1993 and 1995, during the final phase of the premiership of **Felipe González**, about 1,000 Spanish troops operated in Bosnia-Herzegovina under the UN flag, distributing humanitarian aid. Spain participated in the NATO bombing campaigns of Serbia in May and September–October 1995. Following the Dayton Peace Accords of November 1995, Spain then stationed about 1,500 troops in Mostar under a NATO mandate, and in March 1997 agreed to send troops into Albania in support of the UN's humanitarian mission. Under **José María Aznar**'s **Partido Popular** government, Spain then participated in the bombing of Serbian troops in Kosovo in March–April 1999, and after Slobodan Milosevic had given way, sent a little over 1,000 troops into Kosovo. At the end of 2001, Spain had over 2,000 troops on the ground, split between Bosnia and Kosovo. By 2008, numbers had fallen to 800 men (550 in Kosovo and 250 in Bosnia). In February 2008, the government of **José Luis Rodríguez Zapatero** opposed the decision by the United States and most **European Union** (EU) countries to recognize Kosovo's independence. Nevertheless, it backed the EU proposal that it should become a "European protectorate" and will keep troops on the ground. *See also* FOREIGN POLICY.

– Z –

ZANJÓN PEACE. The Zanjón Peace was a pact signed by the general of the Spanish armies, Arsensio Martínez Campos (1831–1900), and the **Cuban** insurrectionaries in February 1878, bringing to an end the Ten Years' War on the island. The Cubans were granted an amnesty and slaves fighting in the Cuban army were made free men. Thereafter, the Cubans would be able to form their own parties and hold local and provincial elections. However, promises of greater autonomy were to prove meaningless. This was finally to produce a new insurrection in 1895, which would culminate in the **Spanish-American War** of 1898.

ZAPLANA HERNANDEZ-SORO, EDUARDO (1956–). Zaplana could, until the March 2008 elections, effectively be considered as the joint number two (along with **Ángel Acebes**) within the **Partido Popular** (PP) behind **Mariano Rajoy**. He did a degree in law at the University of Alicante and subsequently built a power base in local and regional politics. He began his political career within the **Unión del Centro Democrático** (UCD) and moved across to the PP when it collapsed. He was mayor of Benidorm between 1991 and 1994, and between 1995 and 2002 was president of the **Valencian** autonomous government, the **Generalitat**. During this period, he gained a reputation as a ruthless and effective politician. In 2002, he was brought into government by **José María Aznar**, who made him minister of labor. After the general strike of 20 June 2002, he did a good job negotiating modifications to the government's decree imposing reform of the **labor market**. He was promoted in 2003 when he became the government's spokesperson. After defeat in the 2004 elections, he then took up the post of spokesperson for the PP opposition in parliament. He has taken a highly combative stance, fiercely criticizing the **Partido Socialista Obrero Español** (PSOE) government for its supposed "concessions" to **ETA**. This has helped mobilize the right, but it also alienated some centrist voters. Along with Acebes and **Esperanza Aguirre**, he forms part of a triumvirate of right-wing heavyweights in the party. However, in the run-up to the March 2008 elections, with the party leader, Mariano Rajoy, trying to present a more moderate image, he was somewhat marginalized.

Appendixes

The following maps and tables are designed to provide the reader with a number of key indicators of Spain's changing economic, social, and political structures over the past two centuries.

Map 1 outlines the administrative structure established by the new liberal administration in 1833. Spain was divided into provinces, and in each province a civil governor represented central authority. This remained in place until 1978 (with the exception of the autonomy statutes granted Catalonia in 1932 and the Basque Country in 1936 respectively). After the Constitution of 1978, however, autonomous communities were superimposed on the provinces. These are outlined in map 2.

Table 1 emphasizes Spain's transition to a "modern" demographic structure over the past century. Thus, average life expectancy has increased enormously, both birth and death rates have fallen, and the population has aged significantly.

Tables 2 and 3 indicate Spain's changing economic structure. The story they tell is in many ways a similar one. As table 2 shows, until the decade of the 1960s, agriculture was the largest employer within the economy. From that date, rapid industrialization produced a massive transfer of labor to industry and services. Then, from the 1970s, in line with other "postindustrial" countries, services have eclipsed industry as the major generator of employment within the economy. Table 3 indicates the growth of industrial production was slow from the mid-19th century until the 1930s. It went into reverse during the Spanish Civil War and early years of the Franco regime, but accelerated vertiginously from the 1950s.

In table 4 attention is turned to the key role of the state in economy and society. Not only was Spain a relatively poor country in the early 20th century, but state spending as a percentage of national income,

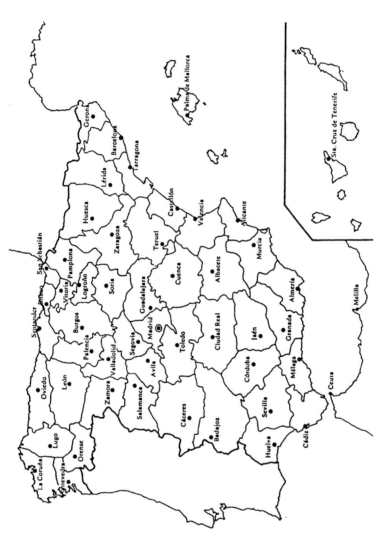

Map 1. Spain's Provincial Structure from 1833

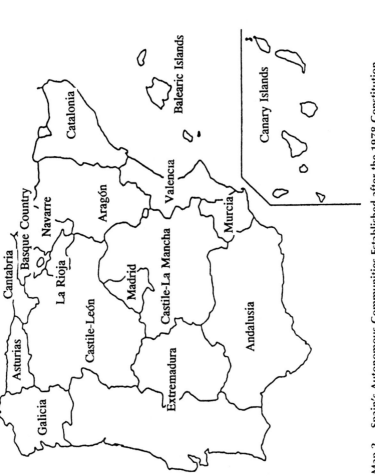

Map 2.   Spain's Autonomous Communities Established after the 1978 Constitution

Table 1. Various Demographic Indicators, 1900–2004.

Year	1900	1950	1990	2004
Total population (in millions)	18.59	27.98	39.4	42.3
Crude birth rate (per 1000)	34	21.1[1]	12	10.7
Crude death rate (per 1000)	28.4	10.7	8.5	8.7
Infant mortality rate (under 1 year, per 1000)	185.9 (1901)	64.2	7.6	4
Life expectancy	35	62	77	83.8
Chidren per woman	4.7	2.5	1.4	1.3

[1]Five-year average, 1945–1950.
Sources: Francisco Bustelo, *Historia económica: Introducción a la historia económica mundial, Historia económica de España, siglos XIX–XX* (Madrid: Universidad Complutense, 1994), 359; Gabriel Tortella, *The Development of Modern Spain: An Economic History of the Nineteenth and Twentieth Centuries* (Cambridge, Mass.: Harvard, 2000), 242–43; Joseph Harrison and David Corkill, *Spain: A Modern European Economy* (Aldershot: Ashgate, 2004), 24 and 31; Anuario Estadístico de España, 2006 (Madrid: INE, 2006).

Table 2. Spain's Active Population by Sectors, 1877–2004 (percentages).

Year	Agriculture	Industry[1]	Services
1877	70	11	19
1900	70	15	15
1910	66	17	17
1920	59	22	19
1930	54	24	22
1940	52	24	24
1950	50	25	25
1960	42	32	26
1970	29	37	34
1980	19	36	45
1990	11	35	54
2000	7	29	59
2004	6	30	62

[1]Includes construction.
Sources: *Censos de Población*, 1877; Instituto Nacional de Estadistica, www.ine.es/inebase. The data for 2000, and 2004 does not add up to 100 percent because it does not include those seeking their first job and those unemployed for three or more years, and who are not ascribed to any particular economic sector (who are regarded as forming part of the active population).

Table 3. Index of Spanish Industrial Production, 1861–1990 (1930 = 100).

1861	21	1910	64	1960	178
1870	23	1920	65	1970	493
1880	33	1930	100	1980	750
1890	44	1940	77	1990	987
1900	55	1950	98		

Source: Francisco Bustelo, *Historia económica: Introducción a la historia económica mundial, Historia económica de España, siglos XIX XX* (Madrid: Universidad Complutense, 1994), 185 (based on figures compiled by Albert Carreras).

Table 4. The Share of Public Expenditure in National Income in Various Countries, 1900–1902 through to 1970–1972 (percent).

Country	1900–1902	1935–1938	1956–1960	1970–1972
United States	6.8	21.3	31.3	34.1
France	14.4	30.5	51.7	49.0
United Kingdom	14.4	23.4	36.3	50.3
Germany	16.2	42.2	44.4	35.6
Italy	7.1	13.6	28.1	37.8
Spain[1]	9.4	13.5	11.2	17.3
Spain[2]	N/A	N/A	14.8	21.3

[1]Central government expenditure as a fraction of national income.
[2]All public expenditures (including those of regional governments) as a fraction of national income.
Source: Gabriel Tortella, *The Development of Modern Spain: An Economic History of the Nineteenth and Twentieth Centuries* (Cambridge, Mass.: Harvard, 2002).

Table 5. Trade Union Densities in Spain, 1900–2001.

Year	No. Members	No. Wage Earners	Union Density
1904	171,791	4,169,535	4.1
1919–1920	932,203	4,530,575	20.6
1931	1,494,016	5,467,931	27.3
1980	2,796,000	N/A	33.8
1989	1,881,000	N/A	16.4
2001	2,537,000	14,014,000	18.1

Sources: Instituto de Reformas Sociales, *Estadística de la asociación obrera en 1 de noviembre de 1904* (Madrid: Suc de M. Minuesa de los Ríos, 1907); *Censos de Población de España, 1900, 1920, 1930* (Madrid: 1907, 1929, 1941); Victor Perez Díaz, *El retorno de la sociedad civil* (Madrid: Instituto de Estudios Económicos, 1987), 234; Richard Gillespie, "The Break-up of the 'Socialist Family': Party-Union Relations in Spain, 1982–1989," *West European Politics* 13, no. 1 (January 1990): 54; José M. Magone, *Contemporary Spanish Politics* (London: Routledge, 2004), 196; Instituto Nacional de Estadistica, www.ine.es/inebase. Additional data from trade union sources.

Table 6. Strikes, Strikers, and Working Days Lost in Spain, 1905–1934 and 1966–2006.

Year	Strikes	Strikers	Working Days Lost
1905–1910	1,025	168,493	N/A
1911–1916	1,539	330,589	7,714,584
1917–1922	3,795	1,041,012	25,598,333
1923–1928	1,064	378,433	9,451,901
1929–1934	3,634	2,392,560	37,047,145
1966–1971	3,799	N/A	3,173,029
1972–1977	N/A	7,832,803	30,123,099
1978–1983[1]	N/A	N/A	63,358,199
1984–1989[2]	7,243	14,516,840	32,212,200
1990–1995	6,880	9,804,722	22,226,500
1996–2001	4,009	6,501,700	11,133,600
2002–2006[3]	3,270	6,483,700	11,584,500

[1]Data for 1981–1983 do not include Catalonia.
[2]Data for 1984–1985 do not include Catalonia, data for 1986–1989 do not include the Basque Country.
[3]Data for 2006 only refer to January–November.
Sources: Instituto de Reformas Sociales, *Estadística de huelgas, 1905–1922* (Madrid: 1906–1923); Ministerio de Trabajo, Comercio e Industria, *Estadística de huelgas,1923–1929* (Madrid: 1924–1930); Ministerio de Trabajo y Previsión Social, *Estadística de huelgas, 1930–1934* (Madrid: 1934–1936); Josep Lluís Martín Ramos, "Analisi del moviment vaguístic a Barcelona, 1914–1923," *Recerques* 20 (1988): 110; Sebastian Balfour, *Dictatorship, Workers and the City: Labor in Greater Barcelona Since 1939* (Oxford: Clarendon Press, 1989), 143; J. A. Sargadoy Bengoechea and D. León Blanco, *El poder sindical en España* (Barcelona: Planeta, 1982); *El País*, 23 May 1993; *Anuario El País, 1993–2007* (Madrid: Ediciones El País, 1994–2008).
In order to improve the statistics, the official figures for Barcelona City for the years 1914–1923 has been replaced by those compiled by Martín Ramos. The *Anuario El País* data for 1993–2007 has been rounded up.

Table 7.   General Election Results in Spain, 1876–1910: Seats Obtained by the Major Parties.[1]

Year	Partido Conservador	Partido Liberal	Republicans[2]	Lliga Regionalista	Others
1876	333	27	6	-	25
1879	293	56	7	-	36
1881	39	297	0	-	56
1884	318	31	5	-	38
1886	56	278	22	-	36
1891	253	74	31	-	41
1893	44	281	47	-	28
1896	269	88	1	-	43
1898	68	266	14	-	53
1899	222	93	18	-	58
1901	79	233	19	6	64
1903	234	102	36	5	26
1905	115	229	30	7	23
1907	252	69	17	14	52
1910	102	219	38	8	37

[1]Only MPs who accepted party discipline are included under the headings "Partido Conservador" and "Partido Liberal." Dissidents and independents are included under "Others."

[2]With the exception of Emilio Castelar's Possibilistas, other republican groups boycotted the elections until 1886.

Sources: María Carmen García Nieto and Esperanza Ylán, *Historia de España, 1808–1978*, Vol. 3, *Teoría y práctica del parlamentarismo, 1874–1914* (Barcelona: Critica, 1986), 203; Albert Balcells, et al., *Les eleccions generals a Catalunya, 1901–1923* (Barcelona: Fundació Jaume Bofill, 1923).

Table 8.   General Election Results in Spain, 1914–1923: Seats Obtained by the Major Parties.[1]

Year	Partido Conservador	Partido Liberal	Republicans and Reformists	Lliga Regionalista	Partido Socialista Obrero Español	Others[2]
1914	214	121	33	12	1	27
1916	113	230	30	13	1	26
1918	155	167	23	20	6	38
1919	202	133	24	14	6	30
1920	232	103	25	14	4	31
1923	108	223	11	19	7	41

[1]The headings Partido Conservador and Partido Liberal include both deputies who accepted party discipline and monarchist dissidents.

[2]This column is made up of all other parties and groups who opposed the Cánovas Restoration.

Source: María Carmen García Nieto and Esperanza Ylán, *Historia de España, 1808–1*,Vol. 4, *Crisis social y dictadura, 1914–1923* (Barcelona: Critica, 1987), 125; Miguel Martínez Caudrado, *La burguesía conservadora, 1874–1931* (Madrid: Alianza Editorial/Alfaguara), 444; Albert Balcells, et al., *Les eleccions generals a Catalunya, 1901–1923* (Barcelona: Fundació Jaume Bofill), 1923.

Table 9. General Election Results in Spain, 1931–1936: Seats Obtained by the Major Parties.

Parties	June 1931	November 1933	February 1936
LEFT			
Partido Socialista Obrero Español	114	59	88
Esquerra Republicana de Catalunya	36	22	22
Partido Radical Socialista	55	3	-
Acción Republicana	30	5	-
Izquierda Republicana	-	-	79
Unión Republicana	-	-	34
Organización Republicana Gallega Autónoma	16	3	-
Federals and other left-wing republicans	14	-	-
Partido Comunista de España	-	1	14
Others			26
Total Left	265	93	263
CENTER			
Partido Republicano Radical	89	102	9
Derecha Liberal Republicana/Partido Republicano Conservador	22	16	3
Agrupación al Servicio de la República	16	-	-
Partido Liberal Demócrata	4	10	1
Partido Progresista	-	3	6
Others	-	-	18
Total Center	131	131	37
RIGHT			
Confederación Española de Derechas Autónomas	-	115	101
Partido Agrario	21	32	11
Partido Nacionalista Vasco and Basque Traditionalists (PNV from 1933)	13	12	5
Traditionalists	-	21	15
Renovación Española	-	15	13
Lliga Regionalista/Catalana	2	26	12
Monarchists	2	-	2
Other right-wing groups	3	28	4
Total Right	41	249	163
Others	3	-	10

There is a serious problem with contradictory electoral data for this period. I have largely compiled this table using data from *Historia de España del Siglo XX*, ed. Ángel Bahamonde (Cátedra: Madrid, 2000), 556–57, 598–99, and 629–30, but have compared it with other sources.

Table 10. General Election Results in Spain, 1977–2008. Seats and the Percentage of the Votes Obtained by the Major Parties/Coalitions.

Party/Coalition	1977	1979	1982	1986	1989	1993	1996	2000	2004	2008
Partido Socialista Obrero Español	110 (29.3%)	121 (30.4%)	202 (48.3%)	184 (44.1%)	175 (39.6%)	159 (38.8%)	141 (37.6%)	125 (34.2%)	164 (42.6%)	169 (43.6%)
Alianza Popular/ Partido Popular	16 (8.2%)	10 (6.1%)	107 (26.5%)	105 (26%)	107 (25.8%)	141 (34.8%)	156 (38.8%)	183 (44.5%)	148 (37.7%)	153 (40.1%)
Unión del Centro Democrático	166 (34.5%)	168 (34.9%)	11 (6.8%)	-	-	-	-	-	-	-
Partido Comunista de España/ Izquierda Unida	19 (9.3%)	23 (10.8%)	4 (4%)	7 (4.6%)	17 (9.1%)	18 (9.6%)	21 (10.5%)	8 (5.5%)	5 (5%)	2 (3.8%)
Centro Democrático y Social	-	-	2 (2.9%)	19 (9.2%)	14 (7.9%)	-	-	-	-	-
Convergencia i Unió[1]	11 (2.8%)	8 (2.7%)	12 (3.7%)	18 (5%)	18 (5%)	17 (4.9%)	16 (4.6%)	15 (4.2%)	10 (3.2%)	11 (3.1%)
Partido Nacionalista Vasco	8 (1.6%)	7 (1.7%)	8 (1.9%)	6 (1.5%)	5 (1.2%)	5 (1.2%)	5 (1.3%)	7 (1.5%)	7 (1.6%)	6 (1.2%)
Herri Batasuna[2]	-	3 (1%)	2 (1%)	5 (1.2%)	4 (1.1%)	2 (0.9%)	2 (0.7%)	-	-	-

Eukadiko Esquerra	1 (0.3%)	1 (0.3%)	1 (0.5%)	2 (0.5%)	2 (0.5%)	-	-	-	-	-
Esquerra Republicana de Catalunya[3]	1 (0.8%)	1 (0.5%)	1 (0.7%)	0	0	1 (0.8)	1 (0.7%)	1 (0.8%)	8 (2.5%)	3 (1.2%)
Eusko Alkartasuna	-	-	-	-	2 (0.7%)	1 (0.6%)	1 (0.5%)	1 (0.4%)	1 (0.3%)	0
Coalición Canaria	-	-	-	-	-	4 (0.9%)	4 (0.9%)	4 (1.1%)	3 (0.9%)	2 (0.7%)
Bloque Nacionalista Galego	-	-	-	-	-	0	2 (0.9%)	3 (1.3%)	2 (0.8%)	2 (0.7%)
Others	12	4	0	4	5	1	1	3	2	2

[1]The 1977 election results are for the forerunner of Convergència i Unió, the Pacte Democràtic de Catalunya.
[2]Euskal Herritarrok in 1996.
[3]Coalició Electoral Esquerra de Catalunya in 1977.
I have only included the percentage of votes if the party won seats in parliament.
Sources: www.electionresources.org/es; www.elpais.com/especial/elecciones-generales.

when compared to other industrializing countries, was also low. This pattern was maintained during the Franco regime, which very much served the interests of social elites and did relatively little to develop a welfare state. Only after this date would Spain build a welfare state on western European lines.

Tables 5 and 6 provide information on the role of the labor movement in Spain. As table 5 indicates, the number of workers unionized generally remained low before 1914. From this date, however, organized labor was to have a far more powerful voice. Hence, in 1920, during the Second Republic and during the transition to democracy, over 20 percent of all workers were unionized. As table 6 shows, this was also reflected in the escalation of strike activity during these periods. From the 1980s, however, there has been a marked decline in both union membership and strikes.

Tables 7 to 10 analyze Spain's changing political circumstances. Table 7 shows the *turno pacífico* operating quite comfortably between 1875 and 1910, with the Partido Conservador and Partido Liberal alternating in government. Table 8 indicates that opposition increased from 1914, and that in 1918 (under a coalition government with Lliga Regionalista representation) the *turno* failed to operate. However, between 1919 and 1923, the "official" parties attempted to resurrect it. Table 9 reflects the transformation of this situation during the Second Republic when competition between right and left became a central feature of the political system. It points to the particularly polarized situation in February 1936 when left and right formed large electoral blocs and the center vote collapsed. Table 10 outlines the new political map after the parenthesis of the Franco regime. It indicates a more fluid political situation, with the centrist Unión del Centro Democratico holding power between 1977 and 1982, a long Partido Socialista Obrero Español (PSOE) administration between 1982 and 1986, and a shorter period of rule by the Partido Popular between 1996 and 2004, before the PSOE retook power in the latter year.

Bibliography

The bibliography that follows should not be seen as an exhaustive catalog of publications on Spain. This would require a work spanning several volumes. Two criteria have been followed. As the book is largely directed at an English-language readership, more emphasis has been given to works in English than would be the case if the selection were made solely on grounds of merit. However, publications in Spanish have not been overlooked. Since the death of General Francisco Franco in 1975, in particular, the overwhelming majority of works on modern Spain have been published in the Castilian-Spanish (and to a lesser extent Catalan) language, and in a whole series of areas serious study is not possible without a reading knowledge of the Castilian-Spanish tongue. In general—especially in the case of Spanish publications—emphasis has been placed on material published since the late 1970s. Only works of particular importance published before that date are included. This reflects, on the one hand, the fact that existing reading lists and bibliographical guides make it possible to consult books published beforehand more easily, and, on the other, that many of the highest-quality studies have appeared since those years. References have also been limited to academics and scholars working in the field and have not extended to firsthand sources such as memoirs and reminiscences.

Having said this, at more than 60 pages in length the bibliography is likely to be rather daunting for the nonspecialist reader who wishes to know more about Spain and its history. There therefore follows a brief selection of major publications. Of course, what the reader sees as a key text will depend on his or her reason for approaching the subject and the level of depth to which he or she wishes to delve. To try to tackle this problem, I first give a brief description of a series of essential introductory works for readers in English, and then go on to outline paths for the reader who wishes to look at one or more areas in somewhat greater detail. Finally, I will give a brief introduction to Spanish authors. There are a number of good short introductions to the history of Spain. In the first place, Pierre Vilar's *Spain: A Brief History*, first published in French in the 1940s, is still a stimulating read. Second, Richard Herr's interpretative piece, *An Historical Essay on Modern Spain*, is another fine introduction, though rather difficult to obtain. The cultured tourist is well served by Juan Lalaguna's *A Traveller's History of Spain*. A more recent introduction, which includes a number of excellent essays, is the book edited by Raymond Carr, *Spain: A History*. Finally, John Lynch is the general editor of an excellent 14-volume *History of Spain*, produced by Blackwell, of which nine volumes have so far appeared.

For those wishing to focus more on the society and politics of modern Spain, the works by Gerald Brenan, the former Bloomsbury group member who emigrated to Spain in the 1930s, are an enjoyable read. His analysis of the origins of the Spanish Civil War, *The Spanish Labyrinth*, though originally published in 1943, contains many insights. Those who wish a broader understanding of Spain's recent history and its roots in the 19th century can then progress to Carr's monumental *Spain: 1808– 1975*, which, though at times a difficult read, is indispensable for the serious student. A briefer up-to-date introduction is Francisco J. Romero Salvado's *Twentieth-Century Spain*. More in-depth coverage is to be found in the book edited by José Álvarez Junco and Adrian Shubert, *Spanish History since 1808*, which takes onboard recent advances in historical knowledge and debates within the historical profession.

For those who wish to focus more on the Spanish cultural scene, the book edited by Helen Graham and Jo Labanyi, *An Introduction to Spanish Cultural Studies*, provides a series of stimulating chapters on major aspects of 20th-century Spanish history and culture. More focused on Spain since the 1980s is the work edited by Barry Jordan and Rikki Morgan-Tamosunas, *Contemporary Spanish Cultural Studies*. An entertaining and well-written book on contemporary Spain, written from a historical perspective, is John Hooper's *The New Spaniards*. The reader who is looking for a broader introduction to Spanish history, literature, and the arts can consult the comprehensive book edited by P. E. Russell, *A Companion to Spanish Studies*, which is aimed at the undergraduate market.

Treatment in English of specific historical periods is uneven. Spain's rise to great power status in the early modern period has, not surprisingly, attracted much attention. The best-written introduction is still John Elliott's *Imperial Spain, 1469–1716*, though aspects of his interpretation are now regarded as outdated. More recent is Henry Kamen's *Spain 1469–1714: A Society in Conflict*, though it is more a discussion of the state of the debate among historians than an introduction. An easier read, centered on the 16th century, is John Lynch's *Spain 1516–1598: From Nation State to World Empire*.

There is much less written on the 18th century, though John Lynch's *Bourbon Spain, 1700–1808* is a detailed introduction. For the 19th century, there are several histories of modern Spain, which in part deal with the period. Adrian Shubert's *A Social History of Modern Spain* is good on the social backdrop and on state institutions. Charles Esdaile's *Spain in the Liberal Age, 1808–1939*, offers an up-to-date account and is particularly strong on the military. There are also a number of high-quality studies of particular periods. The most important of these are Carlos Marichal's *Spain 1834–1844: A New Society*, Victor Kiernan's *The Revolution of 1854 in Spanish History*, and the broader studies by C. A. M. Hennessy and Richard Kern, *The Federal Republic in Spain* and *Liberals, Reformers and Caciques in Restoration Spain* respectively. For the early 20th century, an elegant overview of the growing crisis of Spain's liberal monarchy is Sebastian Balfour's *End of Spanish Empire: Spain, 1898–1923*. Also important is Joan Connelly Ullman's excellent *Tragic Week*, which centers on the politics of clericalism and anticlericalism (a much expanded version has also been published in Spanish). Much new research on the final crisis of Spanish liberalism has been incorporated into the volume edited by Francisco J. Romero Salvadó and Angel Smith, *The Agony of Spanish Liberalism: From Revolution to Dictatorship, 1914–1923*.

In the English language there is at present only one major study of the Primo de Rivera dictatorship of the 1920s, Shlomo Ben-Ami's *Fascism from Above: The Dictatorship of Primo de Rivera in Spain*. This relative scarcity is replaced by abundance once one turns to look at the Second Republic and Spanish Civil War. A good short introduction to the entire period is Martin Blinkhorn's *Democracy and Civil War in Spain*. The classic liberal account remains Gabriel Jackson's *The*

Republic and Civil War in Spain, which, despite being published in the mid-1960s, is still required reading. The best account of the struggles between right and left during the Second Republic is Paul Preston's *The Coming of the Spanish Civil War*, while Edward Malefakis provides a powerful account of the failure of agrarian reform in his *Agrarian Reform and Peasant Revolution in Spain*. Nigel Townson has, for his part, dealt with a previously under-researched area, the crisis of the political center, in his *The Crisis of Democracy in Spain: Centrist Politics under the Second Republic*. These works can be supplemented by detailed studies in books edited by, above all, Blinkhorn and Preston, and the more recent work edited by Chris Ealham and Michael Richards, *The Splintering of Spain*.

Brief but accomplished introductions to the civil war are provided by Sheelagh Ellwood, Helen Graham, and, from a very different perspective, Andy Durgan. Weightier is Paul Preston's *The Spanish Civil War*, which also includes a wide-ranging overview of the early 20th century in the first three chapters. Another full recent account is George Essenwein and Adrian Schubert'a *Spain at War*. The best interpretative essay is perhaps Raymond Carr's *The Spanish Tragedy*. These works can be supplemented by Hugh Thomas's *The Spanish Civil War*, which includes a wealth of detail on military operations. Given the emotional appeal of the anti-Fascist struggle in Spain to liberal and left-wing European and North American intellectuals in the 1930s, the study of the Republic during the civil war has, not surprisingly, become a growth area. The latest incarnation of the work by Burnett Bolloten on the Spanish Communist Party and the Republic (which began life as *The Grand Camouflage* in 1961) is *The Spanish Civil War: Revolution and Counterrevolution*. A life of research makes this a key work, though it is marred by the author's visceral anticommunism. More objective is Helen Graham's excellent study of the Socialists in government during the war, *Socialism and War: The Socialist Party in Power and Crisis*, and her more wide-ranging *The Republic at War*. There has been much stirring writing from a leftist perspective on the social revolution in the Republican zone, starting, of course, with George Orwell's *Homage to Catalonia*. The most scholarly work has, however, been undertaken by Julián Casanova, most notably in his book *Anarchism, the Republic and Civil War in Spain, 1931–1939*.

It has, however, been in the field of international intervention, and especially the role of the International Brigades, that most has been written in the English-speaking world. Alexander Bill, Jim Fyrth, and John Gerassi have undertaken important studies, though the single most significant work on the International Brigades remains that of the Catalan author Andreu Castells. The international climate during the civil war is studied by Michael Alpert in *A New International History of the Spanish Civil War*. An introduction to Great Britain's role in the war is to be found in Jill Edwards's *Britain and the Spanish Civil War*, though the book has been superseded by the first-rate studies of Enrique Moradiellos. John Coverdale provides an analysis of Italian intervention, David Cattell looks at the role of the Soviet Union, Robert Wheatley discusses Nazi intervention, and Douglas Little charts changing attitudes in the United States and Great Britain.

The Franco regime and transition to democracy is covered by a first-rate overview, Raymond Carr and Juan Pablo Fusi's *Spain: Dictatorship to Democracy*. There are several important works on the regime itself. Jean Grugel and Tim Rees's *Franco's Spain* is a good introduction. Stanley Payne's *The Franco Regime* is a detailed account of the politics of Francoism. Juan José Linz has produced a number of penetrating articles on the regime and opposition, while the early chapters of Carr and Fusi are good on social and cultural change during Franco's rule. For the major impact on the regime of the changing international climate, the edited volume by Christian Leitz and David Dunthorne, *Spain in an International Context*, is excellent. There are a number of biographers of General Franco. Two short recent works by Juan Pablo Fusi and Sheelagh Ellwood are fine introductions, but in many respects the definitive work is Paul Preston's blockbuster *Franco: A Biography*. The controversial topic of the growth of Fascism in the 1930s and the place of the fascistic single party is discussed in Stanley Payne's *Fascism in Spain*, in the articles by Martin Blinkhorn and Paul Preston in the book edited by Martin Blinkhorn, *Fascists and Conservatives*, and in Sheelagh Ellwood's work *Spanish Fascism in the Franco Era*.

Spain's surprisingly painless transition to democracy has also been the focus of considerable debate. As noted previously, the best overall work is probably Carr and Fusi, though Paul Preston's *The Triumph of Democracy in Spain* is an engrossing account of the politics of the transition, and Coverdale, Gilmour, and Graham have all produced informative accounts. There has been a steady stream of works on society and politics in the 1980s and early 1990s. Of key importance are the edited works by Christopher Abel and Nissa Torrents, David Bell, Robert Clark, and Michael Haltzel and Richard Gunther. Peter Donaghy and Michael Newton's *Spain: A Guide to Political and Economic Institutions* is highly informative, while the new posttransition political system is dissected in Richard Gunther, et al., *Spain after Franco: The Making of a Competitive Party System*. A comprehensive overview of the Spanish political system is Paul Heywood's work *The Government and Politics of Spain*. This can be supplemented with the book by T. Lawler and M. Rigby, *Contemporary Spain*, which contains more information on culture and society. Up-to-date guides to Spanish politics are José M. Magone's *Contemporary Spanish Politics* and the first-rate collection of essays edited by Sebastian Balfour, *The Politics of Contemporary Spain*. Finally, a stimulating analysis of social and cultural change since the death of Franco can be found in Víctor Pérez Díaz's *The Return of Civil Society*.

As regards more specific aspects of modern Spanish history, the key work of economic history is Gabriel Tortella's *The Development of Modern Spain: An Economic History of the Nineteenth and Twentieth Centuries*. Joseph Harrison has also written a number of accessible works on 19th- and 20th-century Spanish economic history and, with David Corkill, has recently written an account of the contemporary Spanish economy, *Spain: A Modern European Economy*. These can be supplemented, for the transition to democracy and the present-day Spanish economy, by the very full introduction by Keith Salmon, *The Modern Spanish Economy*, William Chislett's *Spain Going Places*, and the more analytical studies by Charles Anderson, Eric Baklanoff, and Sima Lieberman.

The 1970s and 1980s saw a boom in studies on the working class. For the pre-Franco years Benjamin Martin has produced an extremely thorough account, *The Agony of Modernization: Labor and Industrialization in Spain*. There is no such general account of the Franco and post-Franco years, but Sebastian Balfour's *Workers and the City* is not only a fine analysis of labor in Barcelona, but also offers a wide-ranging and stimulating discussion of the place of the labor movement in the transition from dictatorship to democracy. This should be complemented by

Robert Fishman's important sociological study of the attitudes of labor activists during the transition, *Working-Class Organization and the Return of Democracy to Spain*. There are also a large number of more specific studies on the pre-Franco years. Paul Heywood has produced a challenging interpretative account of the history of the Socialist Party (Partido Socialista Obrero Español, PSOE), *Marxism and the Failure of Organised Socialism in Spain*. There is nothing comparable on the anarchists, but the works by Richard Kern and Murray Bookchin can be read in conjunction with the more specific studies by Temma Kaplan, Jerome Mintz, Angel Smith, Chris Ealham, and Julián Casanova.

For the Franco and post-Franco years, Paul Preston, Paul Heywood, and Richard Gillespie have written articles on the Socialists and Communists (Partido Comunista de España, PCE). Eusebio Mujal-Leon's *Communism and Political Change in Spain* is an account of the PCE during the transition, while Jorge Semprun's *Communism in Spain during the Franco Era* is an insightful and highly critical political commentary by a former activist. There are two major studies on the PSOE in English: Richard Gillespie's detailed political analysis, *The Spanish Socialist Party: A History of Factionalism*, and Donald Share's study of the Socialists in power, *Dilemmas of Social Democracy*.

Recent years have also seen a growing interest in questions of nationalism and national identity. There is no general study in English, though Carolyn Boyd's *Historia Patria* is an ambitious account of the construction of Spanish national identity. The volume edited by Clare Mar-Molinero and Angel Smith, *Nationalism and the Nation in the Iberian Peninsula*, contains a number of important articles, and Daniele Conversi's *The Basques, the Catalans and Spain* is a controversial analysis of the development of Basque and Catalan nationalism. There are two general works in English on the major anti-Spanish nationalist movements, Stanley Payne's *Basque Nationalism* and Albert Balcell's *Catalan Nationalism: Past and Present*. For those interested in further delving into the Basque question, there has been a proliferation of studies on Basque nationalist movements in Francoist and the post-Francoist Spain. Among the best of these are the book edited by A. Douglas Williams, *Basque Politics: A Case Study in Ethnic Nationalism*, and, from an anthropological perspective, Marianne Heiberg's *The Making of the Basque Nation*. There are also two particularly fine studies of the terrorist group ETA, Robert P. Clark's *The Basque Insurgents* and John Sullivan's *ETA and Basque Nationalism*. These works are, however, at least 20 years old. For a much more recent analysis of the conflictive political situation in the Basque Country see Ludger Mees's *Nationalism, Violence and Democracy: The Basque Clash of Identities*. For an analysis of national idenity in Catalonia from the Franco era see Maria Montserrat Guibernau's *Catalan Nationalism: Francoism, Transition and Democracy*.

With respect to gender relations, Mary Nash has over the last 40 years written a large number of studies covering varying aspects of the relation between women, the world of work, and the political Left. Temma Kaplan has focused her attention on women, popular protest, and the anarchist movement. In recent years, more general overviews have been produced, most notably Anny Brooksbank-Jones's *Women in Contemporary Spain* and the edited volume by Victoria Engers and Pamela Radcliffe, *Constructing Spanish Womanhood*.

There are three excellent analyses of the Spanish Church: William Callahan's *Church, Society and Politics in Spain*, Frances Lannon's *Privilege, Persecution and Prophecy*, and Audrey Brasloff's work, focused on Francoist and post-Francoist Spain, *Religion and Politics in Spain: The Spanish Church in Transition, 1962–1996*. There are also a number of good studies on the military by Eric Christiansen, Stanley Payne, and Carolyn Boyd (which is also of key importance for the breakup of the Cánovas Restoration), along with the edited volume by Thomas Barker and Rafael Banón Martínez, *Armed Forces and Society in Spain*.

Spanish foreign policy before the 1930s has attracted little interest. Given the growing involvement of the major Western powers, post-1936 Spain has, however, been the subject of far more scrutiny. The civil war has already been dealt with. For the 20th century as a whole, the work edited by Sebastian Balfour and Paul Preston, *Spain and the Great Powers in the Twentieth Century*, is essential reading. The only general study of foreign policy under Franco and democracy is Benny Pollack's *The Paradox of Spanish Foreign Policy*, but, as noted in the section on Franco, the several chapters in Leitz and Dunthorne discuss the international context of Francoism in great depth. With respect to post-1960s Spain, Denis Smyth and Paul Preston wrote a good account of the politics of Spain's entry into the European Economic Community and North Atlantic Treaty Organization, which has recently been supplemented by the edited work by Federico Gil and Joseph Tulchin, *Spain's Entry into NATO*. For an analysis of present-day foreign policy see the edited volume by Richard Gillespie and M. Youngs, *Spain: The European and International Challenges*. Much of the analysis of the arts in Spain has focused on painting and architecture. With respect to painting, volume 1 of John Richardson's *A Life of Picasso* evokes the *modernista* revolution in fin-de-siècle Barcelona. The genesis of Dalí and Miró's work is dealt with in C. B. Morris's *Surrealism in Spain*. For architectural modernism, see E. Casanelles's study *Antonio Gaudí*. The revival of Spanish architecture post-Franco is the subject of A Zabalbeascoa's *The New Spanish Architecture*, while there is a short study of the prize-winning Valencian architect, Santiago Calatrava, by P. Jodidio. For Spanish literature, the works written by Donald Shaw in the 1970s offer a reliable guide. A more up-to-date overview is Christopher Perriam's *A New History of Spanish Writing*. Catherine Davies has written extensively on Spanish women writers. With respect to Spanish cinema, the Franco era is dealt with in Virginia Higginbotham's *Spanish Cinema under Franco*. Peter William Evans provides an excellent analysis of Luis Buñuel's films and their cultural impact. The present-day scene is the subject of a wide-ranging recent overview, Barry Jordan and Rikki Morgan-Tamosunas's *Contemporary Spanish Cinema*, while the key figure of Pedro Almodovar has been analyzed from different angles by Paul Julian Smith and Mark Allison.

A similarly detailed account of Spanish bibliography would take us outside the scope of this dictionary. What, therefore, follows is simply a cursory outline which will hopefully serve to set the reader on the right course. A detailed reference guide was edited by Miguel Artola in the 1990s, the seven-volume *Enciclopedia de historia de España*. There are several multivolume histories. The most comprehensive, begun by Ramón Menéndez Pidal in 1935, is now in its 41st volume, and has covered Spain up to the Franco years. Many of the earlier volumes are, not surprisingly, now largely out of date. However, on the death of Menéndez Pidal, the task of editing was taken over by José María Jover Zamora in 1981, and under his guidance the later volumes provide a detailed analysis of modern Spain. Of the other multivolume histories the best are those edited by Miguel Artola, Manuel Tunón de Lara, and Antonio Domínguez Ortiz. Required reading for early 19th-century

Spain are the works by Miguel Artola and Josep Fontana. The doyen of Spanish social history is Manuel Tunón de Lara. For the late 19th and early 20th centuries, José María Jover Zamora has written with not a little sensitivity on the themes of nationalism and cultural change. Spain now has a talented crop of economic historians, though the beginner could start with the work of the pioneering economic and social historian Jaume Vicens Vives and one of his foremost disciples, Jordi Nadal. José Luis García Delgado has also written widely on the 20th-century Spanish economy and organized a series of generally excellent symposiums on Spanish history, which have been published by Siglo XXI.

The best work on the Spanish Socialist Party has probably been undertaken by Santos Juliá, Manuel Pérez Ledesma, and Santiago Castillo, while José Álvarez Junco has written fruitfully on anarchism and republicanism. Recently, questions of nationalism and national identity have attracted a great deal of attention. José Alvarez Junco has produced a major study of Spanish national identity focused on the 19th century, *Mater Dolorosa*. With respect to the Basque Country, José Luis de la Granja has written widely and fruitfully.

The most prolific writer on the Franco years has been Javier Tusell. José Felix Tezanos, Salvador Giner, and Amando de Miguel have written productively on social trends in post-Francoist Spain, while José Oneto, Ismael Fuente, and Juan Luis Cebrián have provided pungent political commentaries. Finally, less academic perhaps, but excellent for the "feel" of the transition, are the works by Manuel Vázquez Montalbán. Javier Tusell also provided an interesting commentary on the years in government of José Mará Aznar between 1996 and 2004. On the Spanish social and political scene, *El País* produces an annual guide, entitled *Anuario El País*, which includes a lot of statistical data.

ORGANIZATION

A. General
  1. Bibliographical and Reference Guides
  2. Encyclopedias, Dictionaries, and Directories
  3. Statistical Abstracts, Maps, and Yearbooks
B. History (Pre-1982)
  1. Multivolume Spanish Histories

A. GENERAL

1. Bibliographical and Reference Guides

Amell, S. *The Contemporary Spanish Novel: An Annotated Critical Bibliography, 1936–1994.* Westport, Conn.: Greenwood, 1996.

Anderson, James M. *The Spanish Civil War: A History and Reference Guide.* Westport, Conn.: Greenwood, 2003.

Capel, Rosa María, and Julio Iglesias de Ussel. *Mujer española y sociedad: Bibliografía, 1900–1984.* Madrid: Instituto de la Mujer, 1984.

Cortada, James W. *A Bibliographic Guide to Spanish Diplomatic History.* Westport, Conn.: Greenwood, 1977.

García Duran, Juan. *La guerra civil española: fuentes (archivos, bibliografía y filmografía).* Barcelona: Crítica, 1985.

Jordan, Barry, ed. *Spanish Culture and Society: The Essential Glossary.* London: Arnold, 2002.

Lamberet, Renée. *Mouvements ouvriers et socialistes: Chronologie et bibliographie: L'Espagne, 1700–1936.* Paris: Editions Ouvriers, 1953.

Levine, Linda Gould, Ellen Engleson Marson, and Gloria Feinan Waldman. *Spanish Women Writers: A BioBibliographical Source Book.* Westport, Conn.: Greenwood, 1993.

Monteath, Peter, ed. *The Spanish Civil War in Literature, Film and Art: An International Bibliography of Secondary Literature.* Westport, Conn.: Greenwood, 1994.

Rodgers, Eamonn, ed. *Encyclopedia of Contemporary Spanish Culture.* London and New York: Routledge, 1999.

Shields, Graham. *Spain.* World Bibliographical Series. 2nd revised edition. Oxford: Clio Press, 1994.

2. Encyclopedias, Dictionaries, and Directories

Aldea Vaquero, Q. T. Marín, and J. Vives. *Diccionario de historia eclesiástica de España.* 5 vols. Madrid: Consejo Superior de Investigaciones Científicas, 1972–1982.

Artola, Miguel, ed. *Enciclopedia de historia de España.* 7 vols. Madrid: Alianza Editorial, 1989–1993.

Bleiberg, German. *Diccionario de historia de España.* 3 vols. 2nd edition. Madrid: Alianza, 1979.

Bleiberg, German, Maureen Ihrie, and Janet Pérez. *Dictionary of the Literature of the Iberian Peninsula.* 2 vols. Westport, Conn.: Greenwood, 1993.

Borau, J., ed. *Diccionario del cine español.* Madrid: Alianza Editorial, 1998.

Cortada, James W. *Historical Dictionary of the Spanish Civil War, 1936–1939.* Westport, Conn.: Greenwood, 1982.

Enciclopedia universal ilustrada Europea-Americana. Madrid: Espasa Calpe, 1906–present.

Gerlie, E. Michael, ed. *Medieval Iberia: An Encyclopedia.* New York/London: Routledge, 2003.

Kern, Robert W. *Historical Dictionary of Modern Spain.* New York: Greenwood Press, 1990.

Mestre i Campi, Jesús, ed. *Dictionari d'història de Catalunya.* Barcelona: Edicions 62, 1992.

Olson, James S., ed. *Historical Dictionary of the Spanish Empire, 1402–1975.* Westport, Conn.: Greenwood, 1992.

Rubio Cabeza, M. *Diccionario de la guerra civil española.* 2 vols. Barcelona: Planeta, 1987.

3. Statistical Abstracts, Maps, and Yearbooks

Anuario El País, 1980-2008. Madrid: Ediciones El País, 1982–2008.

Carreras, Albert, ed. *Estadísticas históricas de España, siglos XIX y XX.* Madrid: Fundación Banco Exterior, 1989.

Estadísticas básicas de España, 1900–1970. Madrid: Confederación Española de Cajas de Ahorros, 1975.

Instituto Nacional de Estadística. *Anuario estadístico de España, 1858–2008*

Vicens Vives, Jaume. *Atlas histórico de España.* 6th ed. Barcelona: Teide, 1969.

B. HISTORY (PRE-1982)

1. Multivolume Spanish Histories

Artola, Miguel, ed. *Historia de España.* 7 vols. Madrid: Alianza Editorial-Alfaguara, 1973.

Domínguez Ortiz, Antonio, ed. *Historia de España.* 12 vols. Barcelona: Planeta, 1987–1992.

Historia de España. Vols. edited by Angel Bahamonde, Jesús A. Martínez, and Ricardo Cárcel García. Madrid: Cátedra, 1999–present.

Jover Zamora, José María, ed. *Historia de España, fundada por Ramón Menéndez Pidal.* 41 vols. Madrid: Espasa-Calpe, 1935–present.

Lynch, John, ed. *A History of Spain.* 14 vols. (9 vols. published). Oxford: Blackwell, 1989–present.

Menéndez Pidal, Ramón. *See* Jover Zamora, José María.

Suárez Fernández, Luis, et al., eds. *Historia general de España y América.* 19 vols. Madrid: Rialp, 1981–1992.

Tuñón de Lara, Manuel, ed. *Historia de España.* 13 vols. Barcelona: Labor, 1980–1984.

Vicens Vives, Jaume, ed. *Historia de España y América social y económica.* 5 vols. 2nd ed. Barcelona: Vicens Vives, 1971.

2. General Works

i. All Periods

Carr, Raymond, ed. *Spain: A History.* Oxford: Oxford University Press, 2000.

Lalaguna, Juan. *A Traveller's History of Spain.* Windrush: Aldestrop, 1990.

Ledesma, Pérez. *Estabilidad y conflicto social: España de los Iberos al 14 D.* Madrid: Narea, 1990.

Tuñón de Lara, Manuel, Julio Valdeón Baruque, and Antonio Domínguez Ortiz. *Historia de España.* Barcelona: Labor, 1991.

Vicens Vives, Jaume. *Approaches to the History of Spain.* 2nd ed. Berkeley: University of California Press, 1970.

Vilar, Pierre. *Spain: A Brief History.* Oxford: Pergamon Press, 1977.

ii. Medieval and Early Modern Spain

Casey, James. "Spain: A Failed Transition." In *The European Crisis of the 1590s: Essays in Comparative History*, ed. Peter Clark. London: Allen and Unwin, 1985.

Chejne, Anwar G. *Islam and the West: The Moriscos, a Cultural and Social History*. Albany: State University of New York Press, 1983.

Domínguez Ortiz, Antonio. *The Golden Age of Spain*. London: Weidenfeld and Nicolson, 1971.

Edwards, John. *The Spain of the Catholic Monarchs, 1475–1520*. Oxford: Blackwell, 2000.

Elliott, John H. *Imperial Spain, 1469–1716*. London: E. Arnold, 1963.

———. *The Revolt of the Catalans: A Study in the Decline of Spain*. Cambridge: Cambridge University Press, 1963.

———. *The Count-Duke of Olivares: The Statesman in an Age of Decline*. New Haven and London: Yale University Press, 1988.

———. *Spain and Its World, 1500–1700: Selected Essays*. London: Yale University Press, 1989.

Fernández Alvarez, M. *Charles V: Elected Emperor and Herditary Ruler*. London: Thames and Hudson, 1975.

Fernández-Armesto, Felipe. *Ferdinand and Isabela*. New York: Taplinger, 1975.

———. *The Spanish Armada: The Experience of War in 1588*. Oxford: Oxford University Press, 1988.

Haliczer, Stephen. *The Comuneros of Castile: The Forging of a Revolution, 1475–1521*. Madison, Wisc.: University of Wisconsin Press, 1981.

Hilgarth, J. N. *The Spanish Kingdoms*. 2 vols. Oxford: Clarendon Press, 1975 and 1978.

Kamen, Henry. *Spain 1469–1714: A Society in Conflict*. 2nd ed. London and New York: Longman, 1991.

———. *Philip II of Spain*. London: Yale University Press, 1997.

———. *The Spanish Inquisition: An Historical Revision*. London: Weidenfeld and Nicolson, 1997.

Lovett, A. W. *Early Habsburg Spain, 1517–1598*. Oxford: Oxford University Press, 1986.

Lynch, John. *Spain under the Habsburgs*. 2 vols. 2nd ed. Oxford: Basil Blackwell, 1981.

———. *Bourbon Spain, 1700–1808*. Oxford: Blackwell, 1989.

———. *Spain 1516–1598: From Nation State to World Empire*. Oxford and Cambridge, Mass.: 1991.

Martin, Colin, and Geoffrey Parker. *The Spanish Armada*. 2nd ed. Manchester: Mandolin, 1999.

Parker, Geoffrey. *Philip II*. London: Hutchingson, 1979.

———. *The Grand Strategy of Philip II*. New Haven: Yale University Press, 1998.

Rawlings, Helen. *Church, Religion and Society in Early Modern Spain*. London: Palgrave Macmillan, 2002.

Rodríguez Salgado, M. J. *The Changing Face of Empire: Charles V, Philip II and Habsburg Authority*. Cambridge: Cambridge University Press, 1989.

Roth, Norman. *Conversos, Inquisition and the Expulsion of the Jews from Spain*. Madison, Wisc.: University of Wisconsin Press, 1995.

Stradling, R. *Europe and the Decline of Spain: A Study of the Spanish System, 1580–1720*. London: Allen and Unwin, 1981.

Thomas, Hugh. *Rivers of Gold: The Rise of the Spanish Empire*. London: Weidenfeld and Nicolson, 2003.

Thompson, I. A. A. *War and Government in Habsburg Spain, 1560–1620*. London: Atlone Press, 1976.

iii. The 19th and 20th Centuries

Brenan, Gerald. *The Spanish Labyrinth: An Account of the Social and Political Background of the Civil War*. 2nd ed. Cambridge: Cambridge University Press, 1950.

Carr, Raymond. *Modern Spain, 1875–1980*. Oxford: Oxford University Press, 1980.

———. *Spain, 1808–1975*. 2nd ed. Oxford: Clarendon Press, 1982.

Cortada, James W. *Spain in the Twentieth Century World: Essays on Spanish Diplomacy, 1898–1978*. Westport, Conn.: Greenwood Press, 1980.

———. *Spain in the Nineteenth Century World: Essays on Spanish Diplomacy, 1789–1898*. Westport, Conn.: Greenwood Press, 1994.

Esdaile, Charles. *Spain in the Liberal Age, 1808–1939*. Oxford: Blackwell, 2000.

Graham, Helen, and Jo Labanyi, eds. *Spanish Cultural Studies: An Introduction*. Oxford: Oxford University Press, 1995.

Herr, Richard. *An Historical Essay on Modern Spain*. Berkeley: University of California Press, 1971.

Jackson, Gabriel. *Costa, Azaña, el Frente Popular y otros ensayos*. Madrid: Turner, 1976.

Jover Zamora, José María. *El siglo XIX en España: Doce estudios*. Barcelona: Planeta, 1991.

Junco, José Álvarez, and Adrian Shubert, eds. *Spanish History since 1808*. London: Arnold, 2000.

Lannon, Frances, and Paul Preston, eds. *Elites and Power in Twentieth Century Spain*. Oxford: Clarendon Press, 1989.

Madariaga, Salvador. *Spain*. London: Benn, 1930.

Martínez Cuadrado, Miguel. *La burguesía conservadora, 1874–1931*. Vol. 6, *Historia de España, dirigida por Miguel Artola*. Madrid: Alianza Editorial/ Alfaguara, 1976.

Payne, Stanley. *A History of Spain and Portugal*. 2 vols. Madison: University of Wisconsin Press, 1973.

Payne, Stanley, ed. *Politics and Society in Twentieth-Century Spain*. New York: New Viewpoints, 1976.

Preston, Paul. "Spain, 1945–1985." In *Government and Economies in the Postwar World*, ed. A. Graham and A. Seldon. London: Routledge, 1990.

Ramos Oliveira, Antonio. *Politics, Economics and the Men of Modern Spain*. London: Victor Gollancz, 1946.

Romero Salvadó, Francisco. *Twentieth-Century Spain: Politics and Society in Spain, 1898–1998*. Basingstoke: Macmillan, 1999.

Shubert, Adrian. *A Social History of Modern Spain*. London: Unwin Hyman, 1990.

Tortella, Gabriel, et al. *Revolución burguesa, oligarquía y constitucionalismo (1834–1923)*. Vol. 8, *Historia de España, dirigida por Manuel Tuñón de Lara*. Barcelona: Labor, 1983.

Tuñón de Lara, Manuel. *Estudios sobre el siglo XIX*. Madrid: Siglo XXI, 1971.

———. *La España del siglo XX*. 3rd ed. 3 vols. Barcelona: Laia, 1974.

———. *La España del siglo XIX*. 8th ed. 2 vols. Barcelona: Laia, 1976.

Vicens Vives, Jaume. *Industrials i politics (segle XIX)*. 3rd ed. Barcelona: Vicens Vives, 1980.

Vincent, Mary. *Modern Spain, 1833 to the Present: The Problem of the State*. Oxford: Oxford University Press, 2007.

3. Regional and Local Studies

Balcells, A., N. Salas, and M. Ardit. *Història dels països Catalans*. 2 Vols. Barcelona: Edhasa, 1980.

Balcells, Albert. *Historia contemporánea de Cataluña*. Barcelona: Edhasa, 1983.

Domínguez Ortiz, Antonio, ed. *Historia de Andalucía*. 8 vols. Barcelona: Cupsa-Planeta, 1980.

Hughes, Robert. *Barcelona*. London: Harvill, 1982.

Ruiz, David, et al. *Asturias Contemporánea, 1808–1975*. Madrid: Siglo XXI, 1981.

Sánchez, Alejandro. *Memoria de las ciudades: Barcelona, 1888–1929*. Madrid: Alianza Editorial, 1992.

Ugalde, Martin de, ed. *Historia de Euskadi.* 6 vols. Barcelona: Cupsa-Planeta, 1981.

Valdeón, Julio, ed. *Historia de Castilla y León.* 10 vols. Valladolid: Ambito, 1982–1984.

Vilar, Pierre, ed. *Història de Catalunya.* 7 vols. Barcelona: Edicions 62, 1987–1989.

Villares, Ramón. *Historia de Galicia.* Madrid: Alianza Editorial, 1985.

4. Economic and Agrarian History

i. General Works

Anes, Gonzalo, ed. *Historia económica de España: siglos XIX y XX.* Barcelona: Galaxia Gutenberg, 1999.

Baklanoff, Eric N. *The Economic Transformation of Spain and Portugal.* New York: Praeger, 1978.

Carreras, Albert. *Industrialización española: Estudios de historia cuantitativa.* Madrid: Espasa-Calpe, 1990.

Catalán, Jordi. *La economía española en la segunda guerra mundial.* Barcelona: Ariel, 1995.

Comín, F., M. Hernández, and E. Llopis, eds. *Historia económica de España: Siglos X–XX.* Barcelona: Crítica, 2002.

Comín Comín, Jordi. *Hacienda y economía en la España contemporánea, 1800–1936.* Madrid: Ministerio de Economía y Hacienda, 1988.

Fontana, Josep, and Jordi Nadal. "Spain 1914–1970." In *The Fontana Economic History of Europe: Contemporary Economies,* ed. Carlo M. Cipolla, vol. 6, pt. 2. London: Collins/Fontana, 1976.

Fradera, Josep María. *Indústria i mercat: Les bases comercials de la indústria catalana moderna.* Barcelona: Critica, 1987.

Fraile, Pedro. *Industrialización y grupos de presión en España, 1900–1950.* Madrid: Alianza Editorial, 1991.

García Delgado, José Luis, ed. *Economía española de la transición a la democrácia, 1973–1986.* Madrid: CIS, 1990.

Harrison, Joseph. *An Economic History of Modern Spain.* Manchester: Manchester University Press, 1978.

———. "The Failure of Economic Reconstruction in Spain, 1916–1923." *European Studies Review* 13, no. 1 (January 1983): 63–68.

———. *The Spanish Economy in the Twentieth Century.* London: Croom Helm, 1985.

———. "The Economic History of Spain since 1800." *Economic History Review* 43 (February 1990): 79–89.

——. "Towards the Liberalization of the Spanish Economy, 1951–1959." In *Economy and Society: European Industrialization and Its Social Consequences*, ed. Colin Holmes and Alan Booth. Leicester: Leicester University Press, 1991.

——. *The Spanish Economy from the Civil War to the European Community.* London: Macmillan, 1993.

Lieberman, Sima. *The Contemporary Spanish Economy: A Historical Perspective.* London: Allen and Unwin, 1982.

——. *Growth and Crisis of the Spanish Economy, 1940–1993.* London: Routledge, 1995.

Maluquer de Motes, Jordi. *Història econòmica de Catalunya: Segles XIX y XX.* Barcelona: Edicions de la Universitat Oberta/Proa, 1998.

Maluquer de Motes, Jordi, and Carles Sudria, eds. *Història econòmica de la Catalunya contemporània.* 5 vols. Barcelona: Enciclopèdia Catalana, 1989–1990.

Martín Aceña, Pablo, and James Simpson, eds. *The Economic Development of Spain since 1870.* Aldershot: Edward Elgar, 1995.

Nadal, Jordi. "Spain, 1830–1914." In *The Fontana Economic History of Europe: The Emergence of Industrial Societies*, ed. Carlos M. Cipolla, vol. 4, pt. 2. London: Collins/Fontana, 1973.

Nadal, Jordi, ed. *Atlas de la industrialización de España, 1750–2000.* Barcelona: Crítica, 2003.

Nadal Jordi, Albert Carreras, and Carles Sudrià. *La economía española en el siglo XX: Una perspectiva histórica.* Barcelona: Ariel, 1987.

Prados de Escosura, L., and J. Sanz. "Growth and Macroeconomic Performance in Spain, 1939–93." In *Economic Growth in Europe since 1945*, ed. M. Crafts and N. Toniolo. Cambridge: Cambridge University Press, 1996.

Prados de Escosura, Leandro. *De imperio a nación: Crecimiento y atraso económico en España, 1780–1930.* Madrid: Alianza Editorial, 1991.

Ringrose, David R. *Madrid and the Spanish Economy, 1560–1850.* Berkeley: University of California Press, 1983.

——. *Spain, Europe and the "Spanish Miracle," 1700–1900.* Cambridge: Cambridge University Press, 1996.

Sánchez Albornoz, Nicolás., ed. *La modernización económica de España, 1830–1930.* Barcelona: Alianza Editorial, 1987.

Tamames, Ramón. *The Spanish Economy: An Introduction.* London: Hurst, 1986.

Tortella, Gabriel. *The Development of Modern Spain and Economic History of the 19th and Twentieth Centuries.* Cambridge: Harvard University Press, 2000.

Vicens Vives, Jaume. *Economic History of Spain.* Princeton: Princeton University Press, 1969.

Wright, Alison. *The Spanish Economy, 1959–1976*. Basingstoke: Macmillan, 1977.

ii. Economic Policy

Aguirre, José Antonio. *La política económica de la transición española, 1975–1980*. Madrid: Union Editorial, 1981.

Anderson, Charles W. *The Political Economy of Modern Spain*. Madison: Wisconsin University Press, 1970.

Arana Pérez, Ignacio. *La liga vizcaína de productores y la política económica de la Restauración, 1894–1914*. Bilbao: Caja de Ahorros Vizcaína, 1988.

Lancaster, T. D. *Political Stability and Democratic Change: Energy in Spain's Transition*. University Park and London: The Pennsylvania State University Press, 1989.

Pelecha Zozaya, Francisco. *El proteccionismo industrial en España, 1914–1931*. Barcelona: PPU, 1987.

Richardson, H. W. *Regional Development Policy and Planning in Spain*. Farnborough: Saxon House, 1975.

Ros Hombravella, J. *Política económica española, 1959–1973*. Barcelona: Blume, 1979.

Serrano Sanz, José María. *El viraje proteccionista de la Restauración: La política comercial Española, 1875–1895*. Madrid: Siglo XXI, 1987.

Viñas. Angel. *Guerra, dinero, dictadura: Ayuda fascista y autarquía en la España de Franco*. Barcelona: Crítica, 1984.

iii. Mining, Industry, and Transport

Bahamonde Magro, Angel, et al. *Las comunicaciones en la construcción del estado contemporáneo en España, 1700–1936*. Madrid: Ministerio de Obras Publicas, 1993.

Checkland, S. G. *The Mines of Tharsis: Roman, French and British Enterprise in Spain*. London: George, Allen & Unwin, 1967.

Ringrose, David R. *Transportation and Economic Stagnation in Spain, 1750–1850*. Durham: Duke University Press, 1970.

iv. Agriculture

Aceves, Joseph B., and William A. Douglas, eds. *The Changing Face of Rural Spain*. Cambridge Mass.: Halstead Press, 1976.

García Sanz, Angel, and Ramón Garrabou, eds. *Historia agraria de la España contemporánea*. Vol. 1, *Cambio social y nuevas formas de propiedad, 1850–1900*. Barcelona: Critica, 1985.

———. *Historia agraria de la España contemporánea*. Vol. 2, *Expansión y crisis*. Barcelona: Critica, 1985.

Garrabou, Ramón, Carlos Barciela, and Ignacio Jimenez Blanco. *Historia agraria de la España contemporánea*. Vol. 3, *El fin de la agricultura tradicional*. Barcelona: Critica, 1986.

Harrison, Joseph. "The Agrarian History of Modern Spain 1800–1960." *Agrarian History Review* 37 (1989): 180–87.

Simpson, J. "Spanish Agricultural Production and Productivity, 1890–1936." In *The Economic Development of Spain since 1870*, ed. P. Martín Aceña and J. Simpson. Aldershot: Edward Elgar, 1995.

———. *Spanish Agriculture: The Long Siesta, 1765–1965*. Cambridge: Cambridge University Press, 1995.

v. Demography and Migration

Nadal, Jordi. *La población española: Siglos XVI al XX*. 2nd ed. Barcelona: Ariel, 1984.

Pérez Moredo, Vicente, and David-Sven Reher, eds. *Demografía histórica de España*. Madrid: El Arquero, 1988.

Ródenas. C. *Emigración y economía en España, 1960–1990*. Madrid: Civitas, 1994.

Sánchez Alonso, B. "Those Who Stayed and Those Who Were Left Behind: Explaining Emigration from the Regions of Spain, 1880–1914." *Journal of Economic History* 60 (2000): 730–55.

5. Social Structure

i. General Works

Bennassar, Bartolomé. *The Spanish Character: Attitudes and Mentalities from the Sixteenth to the Nineteenth Century*. Berkeley: University of California Press, 1989.

Domínguez Ortíz, Antonio. *La sociedad española en el siglo XVII*. 2 vols. Madrid: Consejo Superior de Investigaciones Científicas, 1963.

Fernández Alvarez, Manuel. *La sociedad española en el siglo de oro*. Madrid: Editorial Nacional, 1983.

Jover Zamora, José María, ed. *Los comienzos del siglo XX, 1898–1931: La población, la economía, la sociedad*. Vol. 37, *Historia de España, fundada por Menéndez Pidal*. Madrid: Espasa-Calpe, 1984.

Miguel, Amando de. *Recursos humanos, clases y regiones en España*. Madrid: Edicusa, 1977.

Shubert, Adrian. *A Social History of Modern Spain*. London: Unwin Hyman, 1990.

ii. Social Elites

Amelang, James. *Honored Citizens of Barcelona: Patrician Culture and Class Relations, 1490–1714*. Princeton: Princeton University Press, 1986.

Cruz, Jesús. *Gentlemen, Bourgeois and Revolutionaries: Political Change and Cultural Persistance among the Spanish Dominant Groups, 1750–1850*. Cambridge: Cambridge University Press, 2002.

Fraile, Pedro. *Industrialización y grupos de presión en España, 1900–1950*. Madrid: Alianza Editorial, 1991.

Glass, Eduardo Jorge. *Bibao's Modern Business Elite*. Reno: University of Nevada Press, 1997.

Harrison, Joseph. "The Catalan Industrial Elite, 1898–1923." In *Elites and Power in Twentieth Century Spain*, ed. P. Preston and F. Lannon. Oxford: Clarendon Press, 1989.

Herr, Richard. "Spain." In *European Landed Elites in the Nineteenth Century*, ed. David Spring. Baltimore: Johns Hopkins University Press, 1977.

Molinero, Carme, and Pere Ysàs. *Els industrials Catalans durant el Franquisme*. Vic: Eumo, 1991.

Wray, McDonogh. *Good Families of Barcelona: A Social History of Power in the Industrial Era*. Princeton: Princeton University Press, 1986.

iii. Landowners and Peasants

Aceves, Joseph B., and William A. Douglas, eds. *The Changing Face of Rural Spain*. Cambridge, Mass.: Halstead Press, 1976.

Artola, Miguel, A. M. Bernal, and J. Contreras. *El latifundio*. Madrid: Servicio de Publicaciones Agrarias, 1978.

Banks, Stanley H. *Migration, Kinship and Community: Tradition and Transition in a Spanish Village*. New York: Academic Press, 1975.

Brenan, Gerald. *South from Granada*. London: Hamish Hamilton, 1957.

Carrion, Pascual. *Los latifundios en España*. 2nd ed. Barcelona: Ariel, 1975.

Gilmore, David D. *The People and the Plain: Class and Community in Lower Andalusia*. New York: Columbia University Press, 1980.

Martínez Alier, Juan. *Laborers and Landowners in Southern Spain*. London: George Allen and Unwin, 1971.

Pitt-Rivers, Julián. *People of the Sierra.* 2nd ed. Chicago: University of Chicago Press, 1971.

Rodríguez Labandeira, José. *El trabajo rural en España, 1876–1936.* Barcelona: Anthropos, 1991.

Sevilla Guzman, Eduardo. *La evolución del campesinado en España.* Barcelona: Península, 1979.

Sevilla Guzman, Eduardo, ed. *Sobre agricultores y campesinos: Estudios de sociología rural de España.* Madrid: Servicio de Publicaciones Agrarias, 1984.

Uria, Jorge. "The End of the Friendly Peasantry in the North of Spain. Asturias, 1898–1914." *International Labor and Working-Class History* 67 (2005).

Vassberg, David E. *Land and Society in Golden Age Castile.* Cambridge: Cambridge University Press, 1984.

iv. Industrialists

Arana Pérez, Ignacio. *La Liga Vizcaína de Productores y la política económica de la Restauración, 1894–1914.* Bilbao: Caja de Ahorros Vizcaína, 1988.

Bengoechea, Soledad. *Organització patronal y conflictivitat social a Catalunya.* Barcelona: Publicacions de la Abadia de Montserrat, 1994.

Cabrera, Mercedes, and Fernando del Rey. *The Power of Entrepreneurs: Politics and Economy in Contemporary Spain.* Oxford: Berghahn, 2007.

Rey Reguillo, Francisco. *Propietarios y patronos: La política de las organizaciones económicas durante la Restauración, 1914–1923.* Madrid: Ministerio de Trabajo y Seguridad Social, 1992.

Serrano Sanz, José María. *El viraje proteccionista de la Restauración: La política comercial española, 1875–1895.* Madrid: Siglo XXI, 1987.

v. Urban Workers

Borderías, Cristina, Cristina Carrasco, and Carme Alemanys. *Las mujeres y el trabajo: Rupturas conceptuales.* Barcelona: Icaria, 1994.

Nash, Mary. *Mujer, familia y trabajo en España, 1875–1936.* Barcelona: Anthropos, 1983.

Soto Carmona, Álvaro. *El trabajo industrial en la España contemporánea, 1874–1936.* Barcelona: Anthropos, 1989.

vi. Local Studies

Behar, Ruth. *Santa María del Monte: The Presence of the Past in a Spanish Village.* Princeton: Princeton University Press, 1986.

Brenan, Gerald. *South from Granada.* London: Hamish Hamilton, 1957.

Fraser, Ronald. *The Pueblo: A Mountain Village on the Costa del Sol*. London: Allen Lane, 1973.

Gilmore, David D. *The People and the Plain: Class and Community in Lower Andalusia*. New York: Columbia University Press, 1980.

Lisón Tolosana, Carmelo. *Belmonte de los Caballeros: A Sociological Study of a Spanish Town*. Oxford: Clarendon Press, 1966.

Pike, Ruth. *Aristocrats and Traders: Sevillian Society in the Sixteenth Century*. Ithaca: Cornell University Press, 1972.

Pitt-Rivers, Julian A. *The People of the Sierra*. 2nd ed. Chicago: University of Chicago Press, 1971.

6. Labor, Republican and Socialist Movements in Spain, 1808–1936

i. General Works

Bernal, Miguel. *La lucha por la tierra en la crisis del antiguo régimen*. Madrid: Taurus, 1979.

Blinkhorn, Martin. "Spain." In *The Working Class and Politics in Europe and America, 1929–1945*, ed. Stephen Salter and John Steverson. London/New York: Longman, 1990.

Forcadell, Carlos. *Parlamentarismo y Bolshevización: El movimiento obrero español, 1914–1918*. Barcelona: Critica, 1978.

Fusi, Juan Pablo. "El movimiento obrero en españa, 1876–1914." *Revista de Occidente* 131 (1974): 204–37.

Heywood, Paul. "The Labor Movement in Spain before 1914." In *Labor and Socialist Movements in Europe before 1914*, ed. Richard Geary. Oxford: Berg, 1989.

Jackson, Gabriel, et al. *Octubre 1934: 50 años para la reflexion*. Madrid: Siglo XXI, 1985.

Martin, Benjamin. *The Agony of Modernization: Labor and Industrialization in Spain*. Ithaca: ILR Press, 1990.

Meaker, Gerald. *The Revolutionary Left in Spain, 1914–1923*. Stanford: Stanford University Press, 1974.

Ruiz, David. *Insurrección defensiva y revolución obrera: El octubre español de 1934*. Barcelona: Labor Universitaria, 1988.

Smith, Angel. "Spain." In *The Force of Labor: The Western European Labor Movement and the Working Class in the Twentieth Century*, ed. Stefan Berger and David Broughton. Oxford: Berg, 1995.

Tuñón de Lara, Manuel. *El movimiento obrero en la historia de España*. 2 vols. Madrid: Taurus, 1972.

ii. Anarchism

Ackelberg, Martha A. *Free Women of Spain: Anarchism and the Struggle for the Liberation of Women.* Bloomington and Indianapolis: Indiana University Press, 1991.

Álvarez Junco, José. *La ideología política del anarquismo español, 1868–1911.* 2nd ed. Madrid: Siglo XXI, 1991.

Bookchin, Murray. *The Spanish Anarchists: The Heroic Years, 1868–1936.* New York: Harper, 1978.

Boyd, Carolyn. "The Anarchists and Education in Spain, 1868–1909." *Journal of Modern History* 48, no. 4 (December 1976): 125–72.

Brademas, John. *Anarcosindicalismo y revolución en España, 1930–1937.* Barcelona: Ariel, 1974.

Casanova, Julián. *Anarchism, the Republic and Civil War in Spain, 1931–1939.* London: Routledge, 2004.

Duncan, Martha Grace. "Spanish Anarchism Refracted: Theme and Image in the Millenarian and Revisionist Literature." *Journal of Contemporary History* 23, no. 3 (July 1988): 315–46.

Ealham, Chris. *Class, Culture and Conflict in Barcelona, 1898–1937.* London: Routledge, 2005.

Esenwein, George. *Anarchist Ideology and the Working-Class Movement in Spain, 1868–1898.* Berkeley: University of California Press, 1989.

Kaplan, Temma. "Other Scenarios: Women and Spanish Anarchism." In *Becoming Visible: Women in European History*, ed. R. Bridenthal, C. Koonz, and S. Stuard, 2nd ed. Boston: Houghton Mifflin, 1977, 401–21.

Kern, Richard. *Red Years, Black Years: A Political History of Spanish Anarchism, 1911–1937.* Philadelphia: Institute for the Study of Human Issues, 1978.

Lida, Clare. *Anarquismo y revolución en la España del siglo XIX.* Madrid: Siglo XXI, 1972.

Mintz, Jerome R. *The Anarchists of Casas Viejas.* Chicago: Chicago University Press, 1982.

Núñez Florencio, Rafael. *El terrorismo anarquista, 1888–1909.* Madrid: Siglo XXI, 1983.

Oyón, José Luis, and Juan José Gallardo. *El cinturón rojo: Radicalismo cenetista y obrero en la periferia de Barcelona, 1918–1939.* Barcelona: Ediciones Carena, 2004.

Paz, Abel. *Durruti: The People Armed.* Montreal: Black Rose, 1976.

Peirats, José. *The CNT in the Spanish Revolution.* Ed. Chris Ealham. Vol. 1, Hastings: Metzer, 2001; vol. 2, Hastings: ChristieBooks, 2005; vol. 3, Hastings: ChristieBooks, 2006.

Smith, Angel. *Anarchism, Revolution and Reaction: Catalan Labour and the Crisis of the Spanish State, 1898–1923.* Oxford: Berghahn, 2007.

Termes, Josep. *Anarquismo y sindicalismo en España: La primera internacional, 1864–1881.* Barcelona: Ariel, 1972.

iii. Socialism

Castillo, Santiago. *Historia del socialismo español.* Vol. 1, *1870–1909.* Barcelona: Conjunto, 1989.

Graham, Helen. *Socialism and War: The Spanish Socialist Party in Power and Crisis, 1936–1939.* Cambridge: Cambridge University Press, 1989.

Heywood, Paul. *Marxism and the Failure of Organised Socialism in Spain.* Cambridge: Cambridge University Press, 1990.

Juliá, Santos. *Historia del socialismo español.* Vol. 3, *1931–1939.* Barcelona: Conjunto, 1989.

Juliá, Santos, ed. *El socialismo en España: Desde la formación hasta 1975.* Madrid: Pablo Iglesias, 1986.

Juliá, Santos, ed. *El socialismo en las nacionalidades y regiones.* Madrid: Pablo Iglesias, 1988.

Pérez Ledesma, Manuel. *El obrero consciente: Dirigentes, partidos y sindicatos en la segunda internacional.* Madrid: Alianza Editorial, 1987.

Preston, Paul. "The Struggle against Fascism in Spain: Leviatan and the Contradictions of the Spanish Left." *European Studies Review* 9, no. 1 (January 1979): 81–103.

iv. Communism

Alba, Victor. *The Communist Party in Spain.* New Brunswick, N.J.: Transaction, 1983.

Cruz, Rafael. *El Partido Comunista en la España de la Segunda República.* Madrid: Alianza Editorial, 1987.

Durgan, Andrew. "Revolution and Counter-Revolution in Spain during the Comintern Period." In *The Communist International and its National Sections, 1919–1943,* ed. J. Orgen Rojahn. Amsterdam: Internationaal Instituut voor Sociale Geschiendis, 1994.

v. Social Protest by Region

Aviv, Aviva, and Isaac Aviv. "The Madrid Working-Class, the Spanish Socialist Party and the Collapse of the Second Republic, 1934–36." *Journal of Contemporary History* 16, no. 2 (April 1981): 229–50.

———. "Ideology and Political Patronage: Workers and Working Class Movements in Republican Madrid, 1931–1934." *European Studies Review* 11, no. 4 (October 1981): 487–515.

Barrio Alonso, Angeles. *Anarquismo y anarcosindicalismo en Asturias, 1890–1936.* Madrid: Siglo XXI, 1988.

Calero, Antonio M. *Movimientos sociales en Andalucía, 1820–1936.* Madrid: Siglo XXI, 1976.

Castells, Luis. *Los trabajadores en el País Vasco, 1876–1923.* Madrid: Siglo XXI, 1993.

Collier, George. *Socialists of Rural Andalusia: Unacknowledged Revolutionaries of the Second Republic.* Stanford: Stanford University Press, 1987.

Díaz del Moral, Juan. *Historia de las agitaciones campesinas Andaluzas: Córdoba (antecedentes para una reforma agraria).* Reprint of 1928 edition. Madrid: Alianza Editorial, 1967.

Ealham, Chris. "Anarchism and Illegality in Barcelona, 1931–1937." *Contemporary European History* 4, no. 2 (July 1995): 133–51.

Fusi, Juan Pablo. *Política obrera en el País Vasco, 1880–1923.* Madrid: Turner, 1975.

Hobsbawm, Eric. *Primitive Rebels: Studies in Archaic Forms of Social Protest in the Nineteenth and Twentieth Centuries.* 3rd ed. Manchester: Manchester University Press, 1971.

Juliá, Santos. *De la fiesta popular a la lucha de clases: Madrid, 1931–1934.* Madrid: Siglo XXI, 1984.

Kaplan, Temma. *Anarchists of Andalusia, 1868–1903.* Princeton: Princeton University Press, 1977.

———. "Women's Communal Strikes in the Crisis of 1917–22." In *Becoming Visible: Women in European History*, ed. R. Bridenthal, C. Koonz, and S. Stuard. 2nd ed. Boston: Houghton MiMin, 1977.

———. "Female Consciousness and Collective Action: The Case of Barcelona, 1900–1918." *Signs* 7, no. 3 (1982): 545–66.

———. *Red City, Blue Period: Social Movements in Picasso's Barcelona.* Berkeley: University of California Press, 1992.

Kelsey, Graham. *Anarcho-Syndicalism, Libertarian Communism and the State: The CNT in Zaragoza and Aragón, 1930–1937.* Amsterdam: Kluwer Academic, 1991.

Maurice, Jacques. *El anarquismo Andalaz: Campesinos y sindicalistas, 1868–1936.* Barcelona: Crítica, 1990.

Rider, Nick. "The Practice of Direct Action: The Barcelona Rent Strike of 1931." In *Anarchism: History, Theory and Practice*, ed. David Goodway. London: Routledge, 1989.

Seidman, Michael. *Workers against Work: Labor in Paris and Barcelona during the Popular Fronts.* Berkeley: University of California Press, 1991.
Shubert, Adrian. *The Road to Revolution in Spain: The Coal Miners of Asturias, 1860–1936.* Urbana: University of Illinois Press, 1987.
Smith, Angel. "Social Conflict and Trade-Union Organization in the Catalan Cotton Textile Industry, 1890–1914." *International Review of Social History* 36, no. 3 (1991): 331–76.

vi. Catholic and Yellow Unionism

Castillo, Juan José. *El sindicalismo amarillo en España: Aportación al estudio del Catolicismo social en España.* Madrid: Cuadernos para el Dialogo, 1977.
Winston, Colin. *Workers and the Right in Spain, 1900–1936.* Princeton: Princeton University Press, 1985.

vii. Republicanism, Anticlericalism, and Freethought

Álvarez Junco, José. *The Emergence of Mass Culture in Spain: Populist Demagoguery and Republican Culture, 1890–1910.* Brighton: Sussex Academic Press, 2002.
Avilés Farré, Juan. *La Izquierda burguesa en la Segunda República.* Madrid: Espasa-Calpe, 1985.
Connelly Ullman, Joan. *Tragic Week: A Study of Anticlericalism in Spain.* Cambridge, Mass.: Harvard University Press, 1968.
———. *La Semana Trágica: Estudio sobre las causas socioeconomicas del anticlericalismo en España, 1898–1912.* Barcelona: Ariel, 1972.
———. "The Warp and the Woof of Parliamentary Politics in Spain, 1808–1939: Anticlericalism versus 'NeoCatholicism.'" *European Studies Review* 13, no. 2 (April 1983): 145–76.
Duarte, Angel. *Història del republicanisme a Catalunya.* Barcelona: Pagès, 2004.
Ferrer Benimeli, José A. *Masonería española contemporánea.* 2 vols. Madrid: Siglo XXI, 1980.
Hennessy, C. A. M. *The Federal Republic in Spain, 1868–74.* Oxford: Clarendon Press, 1964.
Juliá, Santos. "Fieles y martires: Raices religiosas de algunas prácticas sindicales en la España de los años treinta." *Revista de Occidente* 23 (1983): 60–75.
———. *Manuel Azaña: Una biografía política: Del ateneo al palacio nacional.* Madrid: Alianza Editorial, 1990.

Romero Maura, Joaquín. *La rosa del fuego: El obrerismo barcelonés de 1899 a 1909.* Barcelona: Gribaljo, 1975.

Suárez Cortina, Manuel. *El reformismo en España: Republicanos y Reformistas bajo la monarquía de Alfonso XIII.* Madrid: Siglo XXI, 1986.

Townson, Nigel, ed. *El Republicanismo en España, 1830–1970.* Madrid: Alianza Editorial, 1994.

Ucelay de Cal, Enric. *La Catalunya populista: Imatge, cultura i política en l'etapa republicana, 1931–1939.* Barcelona: La Magrana, 1982.

7. Language, Nationalism, and National Identity

i. General Works

Anguera, Pere, Justo Beramendi, and José Luis de la Granja. *La España de los nacionalismos y autonomías.* Madrid: Síntesis, 2001.

Balfour, Sebastian, and Alejandro Quiroga. *The Reinvention of Spain: Nation and Identity since Democracy.* Oxford: Oxford University Press, 2007.

Beramendi, Justo G., and R. Maiz, eds. *Los nacionalismos en la España de la II República.* Madrid: Siglo XXI, 1981.

Beramendi, Justo G., Ramón Maiz, and Xosé M. Núñez. *Nationalism in Europe: Past and Present.* 2 vols. Santiago de Compostela: Universidade de Santiago de Compostela, 1994.

Blinkhorn, Martin. "Spain, the Spanish Problem and the Imperial Myth." *Journal of Contemporary History* 15, no. 1 (January 1980): 5–25.

Conversi, Daniele. *The Basques, the Catalans and Spain: Alternative Routes to Nationalist Mobilization.* London: C. Hurst, 1997.

Cortazar, Guillermo, ed. *Nación y estado en la España liberal.* Madrid: Noesis, 1994.

Fusi, Juan Pablo. "Center and Periphery 1900–1936: National Integration and Regional Nationalism Reconsidered." In *Elites and Power in Twentieth Century Spain*, ed. P. Preston and F. Lannon. Oxford: Oxford University Press, 1989.

Linz, Juan José. "Early State Building and Late Peripheral Nationalism against the State: The Case of Spain." In *Building States and Nations*, ed. S. Eisenstadt and S. Rokkan. London and Beverly Hills: Sage, 1973.

———. "From Primordialism to Nationalism." In *New Nationalisms of the Developed West: toward Explanation*, ed. E. A. Tiryakian and R. Rogowski. Boston: Allen & Unwin, 1985.

Marfany, Joan-Lluís. "'Minority Languages' and Language Revivals." *Past and Present* 184 (2004): 137–68.

Mar-Molinero, Clare, and Angel Smith, eds. *Nationalism and the Nation in the Iberian Peninsula: Competing and Conflicting Identities.* Oxford: Berg, 1996.

Nash, Mary. "Social Eugenics and Nationalist Race Hygiene in Early Twentieth Century Spain." *History of European Ideas* 15, nos. 4–6 (August 1992): 741–48.

Núñez Seixas, Xosé M. *Historiographical Approaches to Nationalism in Spain.* Saarbrucken/Fort Lauderdale: Verlag Breitenbach, 1993.

Payne, Stanley. "Nationalism, Regionalism and Micro-Nationalism in Spain." *Journal of Contemporary History* 26, nos. 3–4 (1991): 479–91.

ii. Spanish Nationalism

Álvarez Junco. José. *Mater dolorosa: La idea de España en el siglo XIX.* Madrid: Taurus, 2001.

Blas Guerrero, Andrés. *Sobre el nacionalismo español.* Madrid: Centro de Estudios Constitucionales, 1989.

Boyd, Caroline P. *Historia Patria: Politics, History and National Identity in Spain, 1875–1975.* Princeton, N.J.: Princeton University Press, 1997.

Burdiel, Isabel. "Myths of Failure, Myths of Success: New Perspectives on 19th-Century Spanish Nationalism." *Journal of Modern History* 70, no. 4 (1998): 892–912.

Carr, Mathew. "Spain: The Day of the Race." *Race and Class* 33 (January–March 1992): 89–95.

Cirujano Marin, P., T. Elorriaga Planes, and J. S. Pérez Garzón. *Historiografía y nacionalismo español 1834–1868.* Madrid: Consejo Superior de Investigaciones Científicas, 1985.

Díaz-Andreu, Margarita. "Theory and Ideology in Archaeology: Spanish Archaeology under the Franco Regime." *Antiquity* 67, no. 254 (March 1993): 74–82.

Holguín, Sandie. *Creating Spaniards: Culture and National Identity in Republican Spain.* Madison: University of Wisconsin Press, 2002.

Mar Pozo, María, and J. F. A. Braster. "The Re-Birth of the Spanish Race: State, Nationalism, and Education in Spain, 1875–1931." *European History Quarterly* 29, 1 (January 1999): 75–107.

Quiroga, Alejandro. *Making Spaniards: Primo de Rivera and the Nationalization of the Masses.* Basingstoke: Macmillan, 2007.

Riquer i Permanyer, Borja. "La debil nacionalización española del siglo XIX." *Historia Social* 20 (1994): 97–114.

iii. Catalanism

Acevedo, M. "The Establishment of Catalan as a Language of Culture." *Hispanic Linguistics* 1, no. 2 (1984): 305–30.

Balcells, Albert. *Catalan Nationalism: Past and Present*. London: Macmillan, 1995.

Conversi, Daniel. "Language or Race? The Choice of Core Values in the Development of Catalan and Basque Nationalisms." *Ethnic and Racial Studies* 13, no. 1 (January 1990): 50–70.

———. *The Basques, the Catalans and Spain: Alternative Routes to Nationalist Mobilization*. Reno: University of Nevada Press, 1997.

Díez Medrano, Juan. *Divided Nations: Class, Politics and Nationalism in the Basque Country and Catalonia*. Ithaca: Cornell University Press, 1995.

Guibernau i Berdún, Maria Montserrat. *Catalan Nationalism: Francoism, Transition and Democracy*. London: Routledge, 2004.

Harrison, Joseph. "Big Business and the Rise of Right-wing Catalan Nationalism, 1901–1923." *The Historical Journal* 19, no. 4 (1976): 901–18.

Johnson, H. *Tales of Nationalism: Catalonia, 1939–1979*. Newark, N.J.: Rutgers University Press, 1991.

Llobera, J. M. "The Idea of Volkgeist in the Formation of Catalan Nationalist Ideology." *Ethnic and Racial Studies* 6, no. 3 (1983): 332–50.

———. "Catalan National Identity: The Dialectics of the Past and the Present." In *Foundations of Nationalism: From Catalonia to Europe*, ed. Elizabeth Tonkin, Maryon McDonald, and Malcolm Chapman. Oxford: Berghahn, 2004.

Marfany, Joan-Lluis. *La llengua maltractada: El castellà i el català a Catalunya del segle XVI al Segle XIX*. Barcelona: Empúries, 2001.

Payne, Stanley. "Catalan and Basque Nationalism." *Journal of Contemporary History* 6, no. 1 (January 1971): 15–51.

Riquer, Borja de. *Lliga regionalista: La burguesia catalana i el nacionalisme (1898–1904)*. Barcelona: Edicions 62, 1977.

Sole Tura, Jordi. *Catalanismo y revolución burguesa*. 2nd edition. Madrid: Edicusa, 1974.

Ucelay Da-Cal, Enric. *El imperialismo catalán: Prat de la Riba, Cambó, d'Ors y la conquista moral de España*. Barcelona: Edhasa, 2003.

iv. Basque Nationalism

Ben-Ami, Shlomo. "Basque Nationalism between Tradition and Modernity." *Journal of Contemporary History* 26, nos. 3–4 (September 1991): 493–521.

Blinkhorn, Martin. "The Basque Ulster: Navarra and the Basque Autonomy Question under the Spanish Second Republic." *Historical Journal* 17, no. 3 (1974): 595–613.

Clark, Robert P. *The Basques: The Franco Years and Beyond*. Reno: University of Nevada Press, 1979.

———. *The Basque Insurgents: ETA, 1952–1980*. Madison: University of Wisconsin Press, 1984.

Conversi, Daniel. "Language or Race? The Choice of Core Values in the Development of Catalan and Basque Nationalisms." *Ethnic and Racial Studies* 13, no. 1 (January 1990): 50–70.

———. *The Basques, the Catalans and Spain: Alternative Routes to Nationalist Mobilization*. Reno: University of Nevada Press, 1997.

Corcuera Atienza, Javier. *Origins of Basque Nationalism*. Reno: University of Nevada Press, 2001.

Díez Medrano, Juan. *Divided Nations: Class, Politics and Nationalism in the Basque Country and Catalonia*. Ithaca: Cornell University Press, 1995.

Douglas, William A., ed. *Basque Politics: A Case Study in Ethnic Nationalism*. Reno: University of Nevada Press, 1985.

Elorza, Antonio. *Un pueblo escogido: Génesis, definición y desarrollo del nacionalismo vasco*. Barcelona: Crítica, 2001.

Fusi, Juan Pablo. *El País Vasco: Pluralismo y nacionalidad*. Madrid: Alianza Universidad, 1984.

———. *El País Vasco, 1931–1937: Autonomía, revolución, guerra civil*. Madrid: Biblioteca Nueva, 2002.

Granja Sanz, José Luis de la. *El nacionalismo vasco, 1876–1975*. Madrid: Arco, 2000.

Harrison, Joseph. "Big Business and the Rise of Basque Nationalism." *European Studies Review* 7, no. 4 (October 1977): 371–91.

Heiberg, Marianne. *The Making of the Basque Nation*. Cambridge: Cambridge University Press, 1979.

Linz, Juan José. *Conflicto en Euskadi*. Madrid: Espasa-Calpe, 1986.

Mees, Ludger. *Nationalism, Violence and Democracy: The Basque Clash of Identities*. London: Macmillan, 2003.

Payne, Stanley. *Basque Nationalism*. Reno: University of Nevada Press, 1975.

Sullivan, John. *ETA and Basque Nationalism: The Fight for Euskadi, 1890–1986*. London: Routledge, 1988.

v. Galician Regionalism Nationalism

Cabrera Varela, Julio. *La nación como discurso: La estructura del sistema ideológico nacionalista: El caso gallego*. Madrid: Siglo XXI, 1992.

Díaz López, C. "Disglosia and Social Cleavage: The Case of Galicia." In *Language Attitudes and Language Conflict*, ed. P. Nelde. Bonn: Duemmler, 1980.

Maiz, Ramón. "The Open Ended Construction of a Nation: The Galician Case in Spain." In *Nationalism in Europe: Past and Present*, ed. Justo G. Beramendi, Ramón Maiz, and Xosé M. Núñez, vol. 2. Santiago de Compostela: Universidade de Santiago de Compostela, 1994, 173–208.

vi. Other Regionalist and Nationalist Movements

Archilés, Ferran, and Manuel Martí. "Ethnicity, Region and Nation: Valencian Identity and the Spanish State." *Ethnic and Racial Studies* 24, no. 5 (2001): 779–97.

Cucó, Alfons. *El valencianismo político, 1874–1939*. Barcelona: Ariel, 1974.

Gari Hayek, Domingo. *Historia del nacionalismo canario*. Las Palmas/Santa Cruz: Benchomo, 1992.

Lacomba, Juan Antonio. *Regionalismo y autonomía en la Andalucía contemporánea, 1835–1936*. Granada: Caja de Ahorros y Monte de Piedad, 1988.

Peiró Arroyo, Antonio, and Vicente Pinilla Navarro. *Nacionalismo y regionalismo en Aragón, 1868–1942*. Zaragoza: Unal, 1982.

8. Gender History

Ackelberg, Martha A. *Free Women of Spain: Anarchism and the Struggle for the Liberation of Women*. Bloomington and Indianapolis: Indiana University Press, 1991.

Alcalde, Carmen. *Mujeres en el franquismo: Exiliadas, nacionalistas y opositoras*. Barcelona: Flor de Viento Ediciones, 1996.

Borderías, Cristina. *Entre líneas: Trabajo y identidad femenina en la España contemporánea: La compañía Telefónica*. Barcelona: Icaria, 1993.

Borreguera, Concha. *La mujer española: De la tradición a la modernidad, 1960–1980*. Madrid: Tecnos, 1986.

Brooksbank-Jones, Anny. *Women in Contemporary Spain*. Manchester: Manchester University Press, 1997.

Capel, Rosa María, et al. *Mujer y sociedad en España, 1700–1975*. Madrid: Dirección General de Juventud y Promoción Socio-Cultural, 1982.

Charnon-Deutsche, Lou, and Jo Labanyi, eds. *Culture and Gender in 19th-Century Spain*. Oxford: Clarendon Press, 1995.

Cleminson, Richard, and Francisco Vázquez García. *"Los Invisibles": A History of Male Homosexuality of Spain, 1850–1940*. Cardiff: University of Wales Press, 2007.

Enders, Victoria, and Pamela Radcliffe, eds. *Constructing Spanish Womanhood: Female Identity in Modern Spain*. Albany, N.Y.: University of New York Press, 1999.

Folguera, Pilar, ed. *El feminismo en España: Dos siglos de historia.* Madrid: Editorial Pablo Iglesias, 1988.

Fyrth, Jim, and Sally Alexander, eds. *Women's Voices from the Spanish Civil War.* London: Lawrence and Wishart, 1991.

Graham, Helen. "Gender and the State: Women in the 1940s." In *Spanish Cultural Studies: An Introduction,* ed. Helen Graham and Jo Labanyi. Oxford: Oxford University Press, 1995.

Grunell, Marianne. "Joining Anti-Fascism with Feminism: Women's Studies in Spain." *Journal of Women's Studies* 1, no. 2 (Autumn 1994): 247–56.

Kaplan, Temma. "Other Scenarios: Women and Spanish Anarchism." In *Becoming Visible: Women in European History,* ed. R. Bridenthal, C. Koonz, and S. Stuard, 2nd ed. Boston: Houghton Mifflin, 1977.

———. "Women's Communal Strikes in the Crisis of 1917–22." In *Becoming Visible: Women in European History,* ed. R. Bridenthal, C. Koonz, and S. Stuard, 2nd ed. Boston: Houghton Mifflin, 1977.

———. "Female Consciousness and Collective Action: The Case of Barcelona, 1900–1918." *Signs* 7, no. 3 (1982): 545–66.

Mangini, Shirley. *Memories of Resistance: Women's Voices from the Spanish Civil War.* New Haven: Yale University Press, 1995.

Morcillo, Aurora G. *True Catholic Womanhood: Gender Ideology in Franco's Spain.* Illinois: Northern Illinois University Press, 2000.

Nash, Mary. *Mujer, familia y trabajo en España, 1875–1936.* Barcelona: Anthropos, 1983.

———. "Pronatalism and Motherhood in Franco's Spain." In *Maternity and Gender Politics: Women and the Rise of the European Welfare States,* ed. Gisela Bock and Pat Thane. London: Routledge, 1991.

———. *Defying Male Civilization: Women in the Spanish Civil War.* Denver: Arden Press, 1995.

Perinat, Adolfo, and María Isabel Marrades. *Mujer, prensa y sociedad en España, 1800–1939.* Madrid: Centro de Investigaciones Sociológicas, 1980.

Preston, Paul. *Doves of War: Four Women of the Spanish Civil War.* London: HarperCollins, 1999.

Richmond, Kathleen. *Women and Spanish Fascism: The Women's Section of the Falange, 1934–1939.* London: Routledge, 2003.

Scanlon, Geraldine M. *La polémica feminista en la España contemporánea, 1868–1974.* Madrid: Siglo XXI, 1976.

Threlfall, Monica. "The Women's Movement in Spain." *New Left Review* 151 (1985): 44–73.

Vincent, Mary. "The Martyrs and the Saints: Masculinity and the Construction of the Francoist Crusade." *History Workshop Journal* 47 (1999): 68–98.

9. The Church

Brasloff, Audrey. *Religion and Politics in Spain: The Spanish Church in Transition, 1962–1996*. London: Macmillan, 1998.

Callahan, William J. *Church, Society and Politics in Spain, 1750–1874*. Cambridge, Mass. and London: Harvard University Press, 1984.

———. "Was Spain Catholic?" *Revista Canadiense de Estudios Hispanos* 8, no. 2 (Winter 1984): 160–181.

———. *The Catholic Church in Spain, 1875–1998*. Washington, D.C.: Catholic University of America Press, 2000.

Casanova, Julián. *La iglesia de Franco*. Madrid: Temas de Hoy, 2001.

Christian, William Jr. *Local Religion in Sixteenth Century Spain*. Princeton: Princeton University Press, 1981.

Cooper, Norman. *Catholicism and the Franco Regime*. Beverly Hills: Sage, 1975.

Estruch, Joan. *Santos y pillos: El Opus Dei y sus paradojas*. Barcelona: Herder, 1994.

Foard, Douglas W. "The Spanish Fichte: Menéndez y Pelayo." *Journal of Contemporary History* 14, no. 1 (January 1979): 83–97.

Haliczer, Stephen. *Inquisition and Society in the Kingdom of Valencia, 1478–1834*. Berkeley: University of California Press, 1990.

Hermet, Guy. *Los Católicos en la España de Franco*. 2 vols. Madrid: Centro de Investigaciones Sociológicas, 1985–1986.

Kamen, Henry. *The Spanish Inquisition: An Historical Revision*. London: Weidenfeld and Nicolson, 1997.

Lannon, Frances. *Privilege, Persecution and Prophecy: The Catholic Church in Spain, 1875–1975*. Oxford: Clarendon Press, 1987.

Martí Gilabert, Francisco. *Política religiosa de la Restauración, 1875–1931*. Madrid: Rialp, 1991.

Martin Descalzo, José Luis. *Tarancón, el cardenal del cambio*. Barcelona: Planeta, 1982.

Payne, Stanley. *Spanish Catholicism: An Historical Overview*. Madison: University of Wisconsin Press, 1984.

Raguer, Hilari. *Gunpowder and Incense: The Catholic Church and the Spanish Civil War*. London: Routledge, 2006.

Robles Muñoz, Cristóbal. *Insurrección o legalidad: Los Católicos y la Restauración*. Madrid: Consejo Superior de Investigaciones Cientificas, 1988.

Yetano, A. *La enseñanza religiosa en la España de la Restauración, 1900–1920*. Barcelona: Antropos, 1988.

10. The Military

Alpert, Michael. *La reforma militar de Azaña, 1931–1933*. Madrid: Siglo XXI, 1982.

Balfour, Sebastian. *Deadly Embrace: Morocco and the Road to the Spanish Civil War*. Oxford: Oxford University Press, 2002.

Ballbé, Manuel. *Orden público y militarismo en la España constitucional, 1812–1983*. Madrid: Alianza Editorial, 1983.

Barker, Thomas M., and Rafael Bañón Martínez, eds. *Armed Forces and Society in Spain: Past and Present*. Boulder: Social Science Monographs, 1988.

Boyd, Carolyn P. *Praetorian Politics in Liberal Spain*. Chapel Hill: University of North Carolina Press, 1979.

Busquets, Julio. *El militar de carrera en España*. 2nd ed. Barcelona: Ariel, 1984.

Cardona, Gabriel. *El poder militar en la España contemporánea hasta la guerra civil*. Barcelona: Siglo XXI, 1983.

Christiansen, Eric. *The Origins of Military Power in Spain, 1800–1854*. Oxford: Oxford University Press, 1967.

Fernández, Carlos. *Los militares en la transición política*. Barcelona: Argos Vergara, 1982.

———. *Tensiones militares durante el franquismo*. Barcelona: Plaza y Janes, 1985.

Fernández Bastarreche, Fernando. *El ejército español en el siglo XIX*. Madrid: Siglo XXI, 1978.

Headrick, Daniel R. *Ejército y política en España, 1868–1898*. Madrid: Tecnos, 1981.

Lleixá, Joaquim. *Cien años de militarismo en España: Funciones estatales confiadas al ejercito en la Restauración y el franquismo*. Barcelona: Anagrama, 1986.

López Garrido, Diego. *La guardia civil y los orígenes del estado liberal*. Barcelona: Critica, 1982.

———. *El aparato policial en España: Historia, sociología e ideología*. Barcelona: Ariel, 1987.

Payne, Stanley. *Politics and the Military in Modern Spain*. Stanford: Stanford University Press, 1967.

Preston, Paul. *The Politics of Revenge: Fascism and the Military in Twentieth-Century Spain*. London: Unwin Hyman, 1990.

Romero Maura, Joaquín. *The Spanish Army in Catalonia: The "Cu Cut!" Incident and the Law of Jurisdictions*. Sage Research Papers in the Social Sciences 5. Beverly Hills/London: Sage Publications, 1977.

Seco Serrano, Carlos. *Militarismo y civilismo en la España contemporánea.* Madrid: Instituto de Estudios Económicos, 1984.

11. Foreign Policy

Armero, José Mario. *La política exterior de Franco.* Barcelona: Planeta, 1978.

Balfour, Sebastian, and Paul Preston, eds. *Spain and the Great Powers in the Twentieth Century.* London: Routledge, 1999.

Bernacker, Walther L., ed. *España y Alemania en la edad contemporánea.* Frankfurt: Vervuart, 1992.

Cortada, James W. *Two Nations over Time: Spain and the United States.* Westport, Conn.: Greenwood, 1978.

Hill, George. *Rock of Contention: A History of Gibraltar.* London: Robert Hale and Co., 1974.

Morris, D. S., and R. H. Haigh. *Britain, Spain and Gibraltar, 1945–1990: The Eternal Triangle.* London: Routledge, 1992.

Pollack, Benny. *The Paradox of Spanish Foreign Policy: Spain's International Relations from Franco to Democracy.* London: Pinter, 1987.

Portero, Florentino. *Franco aislado: La cuestión española, 1945–1950.* Madrid: Aguilar, 1989.

Preston, Paul, and Denis Smyth. *Spain, the EEC and NATO.* London: Routledge, 1984.

Rein, Raanan. *The Franco-Perón Alliance: Relations between Spain and Argentina, 1946–1955.* Pittsburgh: Pittsburgh University Press, 1993.

Rubottom, R. Richard, and J. Carter Murphy. *Spain and the United States since World War Two.* New York: Praeger, 1984.

Smyth, Denis. *Diplomacy and Strategy for Survival: British Foreign Policy and Franco's Spain, 1940–1941.* Cambridge: Cambridge University Press, 1975.

Tusell, Javier. *Franco y los Católicos: La política exterior española entre 1945 y 1957.* Madrid: Alianza Editorial, 1984.

Tusell, Javier, et al. *El régimen de Franco: Política y relaciones exteriores.* 2 vols. Madrid: Universidad Nacional de Educación a Distancia, 1993.

12. The Impact of the French Revolution, 1789–1814

Artola, Miguel, *Los afrancesados.* Madrid: Sociedad de Estudios y Publicaciones, 1953.

Artola, Miguel, ed. *Las Cortes de Cádiz.* Madrid: Pons, 1991.

Artola, Miguel, and Enrique Moral Sandoval, eds. *España y la revolución francesa*. Madrid: Pablo Iglesias, 1989.

Aymes, Jean-Rene, ed. *España y la revolución francesa*. Barcelona: Critica, 1989.

———. "Spain and the French Revolution." *Mediterranean Historical Review* 6 (June 1991): 62–85.

Cruz, Jesús. *Gentlemen, Bourgeois and Revolutionaries: Political Change and Cultural Persistance among the Spanish Dominant Groups, 1750–1850*. Cambridge: Cambridge University Press, 2002.

Esdaile, Charles. "War and Politics in Spain, 1808–1814." *Historical Journal* 31 (June 1988): 295–317.

———. *The Spanish Army in the Peninsular War: The Causes, Experience, and Consequences of Military Humiliation*. Manchester: Manchester University Press, 1988.

Fraser, Ronald. *To Die in Spain: The Experience of Popular Resistance during the Peninsular War, 1808–1814*. London: Verso, 2006.

Glover, Michael. *The Peninsular War, 1807–1814: A Concise Military History*. London: David and Charles, 1974.

Hilt, Douglas. *The Troubled Trinity: Godoy and the Spanish Monarchs*. Alabama: University of Alabama Press, 1987.

Lovett, G. H. *Napoleon and the Birth of Modern Spain*. 2 vols. New York: New York University Press, 1965.

Tone, John Lawrence. *The Fatal Knot: The Guerilla War in Navarre and the Defeat of Napoleon in Spain*. Chapel Hill: University of North Carolina Press, 1994.

13. Colonial Crisis and Liberal Revolution, 1808–1874

Anna, Timothy E. *Spain and the Loss of America*. Lincoln: University of Nebraska Press, 1983.

Artola, Miguel. *Antiguo régimen y revolución liberal*. Barcelona: Ariel, 1978.

Bernal, Miguel. *La lucha por la tierra en la crisis del antiguo régimen*. Madrid: Taurus, 1979.

Costeloe, Michael P. *Response to Revolution: Imperial Spain and the American Revolutions, 1810–1840*. Cambridge: Cambridge University Press, 1986.

Fontana, Josep. *La quiebra de la monarquía absoluta, 1814–1820: La Crisis del Antiguo Régimen*. Rev. ed. Barcelona: Crítica, 2002.

Gil Novales, Alberto, ed. *La revolución burguesa en España*. Madrid: Universidad Complutense de Madrid, 1985.

Griffin, Charles C. *The United States and the Disruption of the Spanish Empire, 1800–1822.* New York: Columbia University Press, 1937.

Hennessy, C. A. M. *The Federal Republic in Spain: Pi y Margall and the Federal Republican Movement, 1868–1874.* Oxford: Clarendon Press, 1962.

Jover Zamora, José María. *Realidad y mito de la Primera Republica: Del "gran miedo" meridional a la utopía de Galdós.* Madrid: Espasa Calpe, 1991.

———. *La civilización española a mediados del siglo XIX.* Madrid: Espasa Caspe, 1992.

Jover Zamora, José María, ed. *La era Isabelina y el Sexenio Democrático, 1834–1874.* Vol. 34, *Historia de España, fundada por Ramón Menéndez Pidal.* Madrid: Espasa-Calpe, 1981.

Kiernan, Victor G. *The Revolution of 1854 in Spanish History.* Oxford: Clarendon Press, 1966.

Lida, C. E., and L. Zavala. *La revolución de 1868: Historia, pensamiento, literatura.* New York: Las Americas Publishing Co., 1970.

Lynch, John. *The Spanish-American Revolutions, 1808–1826.* London: Weidenfeld and Nicolson, 1973.

Marichal, Carlos. *Spain 1834–1844: A New Society.* London: Tamesis, 1977.

Piqueras Arenas, José Antonio. *La revolución democrática (1868–1874): Cuestión social, colonialismo y grupos de presión.* Madrid: Ministerio del Trabajo y Seguridad Social, 1992.

Rueda, German. *La desamortización de Mendizábal y Espartero en España.* Madrid: Catedra, 1986.

Schmidt-Nowara, Christopher. *Empire and Anti-Slavery: Spain, Cuba and Puerto Rico, 1833–1874.* Pittsburgh: University of Pittsburg Press, 1999.

Tomás y Valiente, Francisco. *El marco político de la desamortización en España.* Barcelona: Ariel, 1989.

Van Aken, Mark J. *Pan-Hispanism: Its Origins and Development to 1866.* Berkeley: University of California Press, 1959.

14. Carlism

Barahona, Renato. *Vizcaya on the Eve of Carlism: Politics and Society, 1800–1833.* Reno: University of Nevada Press, 1989.

Blinkhorn, Martin. *Carlism and Crisis in Spain 1931–1939.* Cambridge: Cambridge University Press, 1975.

Carles Clemente, J. *Historia del Carlismo contemporáneo.* Barcelona: Gribaljo, 1977.

Coverdale, John F. *The First Phase of Spain's First Carlist War.* Princeton: Princeton University Press, 1984.

Fradera, Josep María, ed. *Carlisme i moviments absolutistes a la Europa de la primera meitat del segle XIX*. Vic: Eumo, 1990.

Garmendia, V. *La segunda guerra Carlista*. Madrid: Siglo XXI, 1976.

Real Cuesta, Javier. *El Carlismo Vasco, 1876–1900*. Madrid: Siglo XXI, 1985.

Torras, Jaime. *Liberalismo y rebeldía campesina, 1820–1823*. Barcelona: Ariel, 1976.

15. The Cánovas Restoration, 1875–1923

Balfour, Sebastian. "Riot, Regeneration and Reaction: Spain in the Aftermath of the 1898 Disaster." *The Historical Journal* 38, no. 2 (June 1995): 405–23.

———. *The End of Spanish Empire, 1898–1923*. Oxford: Clarendon Press, 1997.

Beck, Earl R. *A Time of Triumph and Sorrow: Spanish Politics during the Reign of Alfonso XII, 1874–1885*. Carbondale: Southern Illinois University Press, 1979.

Bengoechea, Soledad. *Organització patronal y conflictivitat social a Catalunya*. Barcelona: Publicacions de la Abadia de Montserrat, 1994.

Boyd, Carolyn P. *Praetorian Politics in Liberal Spain*. Chapel Hill: University of North Carolina Press, 1979.

Castells, L. *Modernización y dinámica política en la sociedad guipuzcoana de la Restauración, 1876–1915*. Madrid: Siglo XXI, 1987.

Chandler, James A. "Spain and Her Moroccan Protectorate, 1898–1927." *Journal of Contemporary History* 10, no. 2 (April 1985): 301–22.

Cheyne, George J. G. *Bibliographical Study of the Writings of Jouquín Costa*. London: Tamesis, 1972.

Connelly Ullman, Joan. *La semana trágica: Estudio sobre las causas socioeconomicas del anticlericalismo en España, 1898–1912*. Barcelona: Ariel, 1972.

Costa, Joaquín. *Oligarquía y caciquismo como forma actual de gobierno en España. Estudio introductorio de Alfons Ortí*. 2 vols. First published 1902. Madrid: Revista del Trabajo, 1975.

Espadas Burgos, Manuel. *Alfonso XIII y los orígenes de la Restauración*. 2nd ed. Madrid: Consejo Superior de Investigaciones Cientificas, 1990.

García Delgado, José Luis, ed. *La España de la Restauración: Política, economía, legislación y cultura*. Vol. I, *Coloquio de Segovia sobre historia contemporánea de España*. Madrid: Siglo XXI, 1985.

———, ed. *La crisis de la Restauración: España entre la Primera Guerra Mundial y la Segunda República*. Vol. II, *Coloquio de Segovia sobre historía contemporánea de España*. Madrid: Siglo XXI, 1986.

———, ed. *España entre dos siglos, 1875–1931*. Vol. VII, *Coloquio de historia contemporánea de España*. Madrid: Siglo XXI, 1990.

——, ed. *Las ciudades en la historia de España: Los descenios intersecu-
lares.* Vol. VIII, *Coloquio de historia contemporánea de España.* Madrid:
Siglo XXI, 1992.

Harrison, Joseph. "Catalan Business and the Loss of Cuba, 1898–1914." *Economic History Review,* 2nd series, 27, no. 3 (1974): 431–41.

——. "The Regenerationist Movement in Spain after the Disaster of 1898."
European Studies Review 9, no. 1 (January 1979): 1–27.

Harrison, Joseph, and Alan Hoyle. *Spain's 1898 Crisis: Regeneration, Modernism, Postcolonialism.* Manchester: Manchester University Press, 2000.

Kern, Richard. *Liberals, Reformers and Caciques in Restoration Spain.* Albuquerque: University of New Mexico Press, 1974.

Linz, Juan José. "Parties, Elections and Elites under the Restoration monarchy
in Spain, 1875–1923." *VII World Congress of International Political Science.* Brussels: 1967.

Luzón, Javier Moreno. *Romanones, caciquismo y política liberal.* Madrid:
Alianza, 1998.

——. "Political Clientelism, Elites and Caciquismo in Restoration Spain
(1875–1923)." *European History Quarterly* 37, no. 3 (July 2007): 417–41.

Moradiellos, Enrique. "1898: A Colonial Disaster Foretold." *Journal of the Association for Contemporary Iberian Studies* 6, no. 2 (1993): 33–38.

Porte, Pablo La. "From Cuba to Annual: Spain's Colonial Policy in Morocco
and Its Impact in the Crisis of the Liberal System, 1898–1923." *International
Journal of Iberian Studies* 13, no. 1 (2000): 14–24.

Rey Reguillo, Francisco. *Propietarios y patronos: La política de las organizaciones económicas durante la Restauración, 1914–1923.* Madrid: Ministerio
de Trabajo y Seguridad Social, 1992.

Romero Maura, Joaquín. "Terrorism in Barcelona and Its Impact on Spanish
Politics, 1904–1909." *Past and Present* 41 (December 1968): 131–83.

——. "El caciquismo: Tentativa de conceptualización." *Revista de Occidente*
127 (1973): 15–44.

Romero Salvadó, Francisco J. "Spain and the First World War: The Structural
Crisis and the Liberal Monarchy." *European History Quarterly* 25, no. 4
(October 1995): 529–54.

——. *Spain, 1914–18: Between War and Revolution.* London: Routledge,
1999.

——, *The Foundations of Civil War: Revolution, Social Conflict and Reaction
in Liberal Spain, 1916–1923.* New York: Routledge, 2008.

Romero Salvador, Francisco J., and Angel Smith, eds. *The Agony of Spanish
Liberalism: From Revolution to Dictatorship, 1913–1923.* Basingstoke:
Palgrave Macmillan, 2009.

Serrano, Carlos. *Fin del imperio: España 1895–1898.* Madrid: Siglo XXI, 1984.

Serrano, Carlos, and Serge Salauen, eds. *1900 en España*. Madrid: Espasa Calpe, 1991.

Serrano, Carlos, and Jacques Maurice. *Jonquín Costa: Crisis de la Restauración y populismo, 1875–1911*. Madrid: Siglo XXI, 1977.

Smith, Angel. *Anarchism, Revolution and Reaction: Catalan Labour and the Crisis of the Spanish State, 1898–1923*. Oxford: Berghahn, 2007.

———. "The Catalan Counter-revolutionary Coalition and the Primo de Rivera Coup, 1917–23." *European History Quarterly* 37, no. 1 (January 2007): 7–34.

Smith, Angel, and Emma Dávila-Cox, eds. *The Crisis of 1898: Nationalist Mobilization and Colonial Redistribution*. Basingstoke: Macmillan, 1999.

Tuñón de Lara, Manuel. "La burguesia y la formación del bloque de poder Oligárquico, 1875–1914." In *Estudios sobre el siglo XIX Español*, ed. Manuel Tuñón de Lara. Madrid: Siglo XXI, 1981.

Tusell, Javier. "El funcionamiento del sistema caciquil en Andalucia." In *Política y sociedad en la España del siglo XX*, ed. Stanley Payne. Madrid: Akal, 1978.

———. *Antonio Maura: Una biografía política*. Madrid: Alianza Editorial, 1994.

Tusell, Javier, and Juan Farre Avilés. *La derecha española contemporánea: Sus orígenes: El Maurismo*. Madrid: Espasa Calpe, 1986.

Varela Ortega, José. *Los amigos políticos: Partidos, elecciones y caciquismo en la España de la Restauración, 1875–1900*. Madrid: Alianza Editorial, 1977.

———. "Aftermath of Splendid Disaster: Spanish Politics before and after the Spanish-American War of 1898." *Journal of Contemporary History* 15, no. 2 (April 1980): 317–44.

Woolman, David S. *Rebels in the Rif: Abd El Krim and the Rif Rebellion*. Stanford: Stanford University Press, 1969.

16. The Primo de Rivera Dictatorship, 1923–1930

Ben-Ami, Shlomo. "The Forerunners of Spanish Fascism: Unión Monárquica and Unión Patriótica." *European Studies Review* 9, no. 1 (January 1979): 49–79.

———. *Fascism from Above: The Dictatorship of Primo de Rivera in Spain, 1923–1930*. Oxford: Clarendon Press, 1983.

Fleming, Shannon E., and Ann K. Fleming. "Primo de Rivera and Spain's Moroccan Problem, 1923–1927." *Journal of Contemporary History* 12, no. 1 (January 1977): 85–99.

Gómez Navarro, José L. *El régimen de Primo de Rivera*. Madrid: Catedra, 1991.

González Calbet, María Teresa. *La dictadura de Primo de Rivera: El directorio militar*. Arquea: El Arquero, 1987.

González Calleja, Eduardo. *La España de Primo de Rivera: La modernización autoritaria, 1923–1930*. Madrid: Alianza Editorial, 2005.

Queipo de Llano, Genoveva García. *Los intelectuales y la dictadura de Primo de Rivera*. Madrid: Alianza Editorial, 1988.

Quiroga, Alejandro. *Making Spaniards: Primo de Rivera and the Nationalization of the Masses*. Basingstoke: Macmillan, 2007.

Tusell, Javier. *Radiografía de un golpe de estado: El ascenso del al poder del General Primo de Rivera*. Madrid: Alianza Editorial, 1987.

17. The Second Republic and Civil War, 1931–1939

i. General Works

Balfour, Sebastian. *Deadly Embrace: Morocco and the Road to the Spanish Civil War*. Oxford: Oxford University Press, 2002.

Ben-Ami, Shlomo. *The Origins of the Second Republic in Spain*. Oxford: Clarendon Press, 1978.

Blinkhorn, Martin, ed. *Spain in Crisis, 1931–39: Democracy and Its Enemies*. London: Sage, 1986.

Blinkhorn, Martin. *Democracy and Civil War in Spain, 1931–1939*. London: Routledge, 1988.

Broue, Pierre, and Emile Temime. *The Revolution and Civil War in Spain*. London: Faber & Faber, 1972.

Carr, Raymond, ed. *The Republic and Civil War in Spain*. London: Macmillan, 1971.

Carr, Raymond. *The Spanish Tragedy: The Spanish Civil War in Perspective*. 2nd ed. London: Weidenfeld and Nicolson, 1986.

Casanova, Julián. *Anarchism, the Republic and Civil War in Spain, 1931–1939*. London: Routledge, 2004.

Cunningham, Valentíne, ed. *Spanish Front: Writers on the Civil War*. Oxford: Oxford University Press, 1978.

Durgan, Andrew. *The Spanish Civil War*. Basingstoke: Palgrave Macmillan, 2007.

Ealham, Chris, and Michael Richards. *The Splintering of Spain: Cultural History of the Spanish Civil War, 1936–1939*. Cambridge: Cambridge University Press, 2002.

Ellwood, Sheelagh. *The Spanish Civil War*. Oxford: Blackwell, 1991.

Essenwein, George R. *The Spanish Civil War: A Modern Tragedy*. London: Routledge, 2005.

Essenwein, George, and Adrian Shubert. *Spain at War: The Spanish Civil War in Context*. London: Longman, 1995.

Fraser, Ronald. *Blood of Spain: The Experience of Civil War, 1936–1939.* London: Allen Lane, 1979.

Graham, Helen. *The Spanish Civil War: A Very Short Introduction.* Oxford: Oxford University Press, 2005.

García Delgado, José Luis, ed. *La Segunda República: El primer bienio.* Vol. III, *Coloquio de Segovia sobre historia contemporánea de España.* Madrid: Siglo XXI, 1986.

———. *La Segunda Republica española: Bienio rectificador y Frente Popular, 1934–1936.* Vol. VI, *Coloquio de Segovia sobre historia contemporánea de España.* Madrid: Siglo XXI, 1987.

———. *Los orígines culturales de La Segunda Republica.* Vol. IX, *Coloquio de historia de España.* Madrid: Siglo XXI, 1993.

Graham, Helen. *The Spanish Republic at War, 1936–1939.* Cambridge: Cambridge University Press, 2002.

Jackson, Gabriel. *The Republic and Civil War in Spain, 1931–1939.* Princeton: Princeton University Press, 1965.

———. *A Concise History of the Spanish Civil War.* London: Thames and Hudson, 1974.

Malefakis, Edward. *Agrarian Reform and Peasant Revolution in Spain: The Origins of the Spanish Civil War.* New Haven: Yale University Press, 1977.

Mangini, Shirley. *Memories of Resistance: Women's Voices from the Spanish Civil War.* New Haven: Yale University Press, 1995.

Maurice, Jacques. *La reforma agraria en España en el siglo XX, 1900–1936.* Madrid: Siglo XXI, 1975.

Nash, Mary. *Defying Male Civilization: Women in the Spanish Civil War.* Denver: Arden Press, 1995.

Payne, Stanley. *Spain's First Democracy: The Second Republic, 1931–1936.* Madison: Wisconsin University Press, 1993.

———. *The Spanish Civil War, the Soviet Union and Communism.* New Haven: Yale University Press, 2004.

Preston, Paul. *The Coming of the Spanish Civil War.* 2nd ed. London: Methuen, 1983.

———. *The Spanish Civil War, 1936–1939.* London: Weidenfeld and Nicolson, 1986.

———. *Doves of War: Four Spanish Women and the Spanish Civil War.* London: HarperCollins, 2002.

Preston, Paul, ed. *Revolution and War in Spain.* London: Methuen, 1984.

Preston, Paul, and Anne Mackenzie, eds. *The Republic Besieged.* Edinburgh: Edinburgh University Press, 1996.

Robinson, Richard A. H. *The Origins of Franco's Spain: The Right, the Republic and Revolution, 1931–1936.* Newton Abbot: David and Charles, 1970.

Sánchez, José M. *The Spanish Civil War as a Religious Tragedy*. Notre Dame, Ind.: University of Notre Dame Press, 1987.

Seidman, Michael. *Republic of Egos: A Social History of the Spanish Civil War*. Madison, Wisc.: Wisconsin University Press, 2002.

Southworth, Herbert. *Guernika! Guernika! A Study of Journalism, Diplomacy and Propaganda*. Berkeley: University of California Press, 1977.

Thomas, Hugh. *The Spanish Civil War*. 3rd ed. Harmondsworth: Penguin, 1977.

Tisa, John. *The Palette and the Flame: Posters of the Spanish Civil War*. New York: International Publishers, 1979.

Townson, Nigel. *The Crisis of Democracy in Spain: Centrist Politics under the Second Republic, 1931–1936*. Brighton: Sussex Academic Press, 2000.

Tuñón de Lara, Manuel. *Tres claves de la Segunda República: La cuestión agraria, los aparatos del estado, Frente Popular*. Madrid: Alianza Editorial, 1985.

Tuñón de Lara, Manuel, et al. *La guerra civil española 50 años después*. Barcelona: Labor, 1985.

Vernon, Kathleen, ed. *The Spanish Civil War and the Visual Arts*. Ithaca, Cornell University Press, 1974.

Vincent, Mary. *Religion and Politics in Salamanca, 1930–1936*. Oxford: Clarendon Press, 1995.

ii. The Spanish Left, 1931–1936

Brademas, John. *Anarcosindicalismo y revolución en España, 1930–1937*. Barcelona: Ariel, 1974.

Casanova, Julián. *Anarchism, the Republic and Civil War in Spain, 1931–1939*. London: Routledge, 2004.

Cruz, Rafael. *El Partido Comunista en la España de la Segunda República*. Madrid: Alianza Editorial, 1987.

Graham, Helen, and Martin Alexander. *The French and Spanish Popular Fronts: Comparative Perspectives*. Cambridge: Cambridge University Press, 1989.

Graham, Helen, and Paul Preston, eds. *The Popular Front in Europe*. Basingstoke: Macmillan, 1987.

Jackson, Gabriel, et al. *Octubre 1934: 50 años para la reflexion*. Madrid: Siglo XXI, 1985.

Juliá, Santos. *Los orígenes del Frente Popular en España*. Madrid: Siglo XXI, 1979.

———. *Historia del socialismo español*. Vol. 3., *1931–1939*. Barcelona: Conjunto, 1989.

Preston, Paul. "The Struggle against Fascism in Spain: Leviatan and the Contradictions of the Spanish Left." *European Studies Review* 9, no. 1 (January 1979): 81–103.

Ruiz, David. *Insurrección defensiva y revolución obrera: El octubre español de 1934*. Barcelona: Labor Universitaria, 1988.

iii. The Spanish Right, 1931–1936

Blinkhorn, Martin. *Carlism and Crisis in Spain 1931–1939*. Cambridge: Cambridge University Press, 1975.

———. "Conservatism, Traditionalism and Fascism in Spain, 1898–1937." In *Fascists and Conservatives: The Radical Right and the Establishment in Twentieth Century Europe*, ed. Martin Blinkhorn. London: Unwin Hyman, 1990.

Gibson, Ian. *En busca de José Antonio*. 2nd ed. Barcelona: Planeta, 1980.

Jimenez Campo, Javier. *El Fascismo en la crisis de la Segunda Republica Española*. Madrid: Centro de Investigaciones Sociológicas, 1979.

Montero, José Ramón. *La CEDA: El Catolicismo social y político en la Segunda Republica*. 2 vols. Madrid: Ediciones de la Revista del Trabajo, 1977.

Morodo, M. *Los orígines ideológicos del franquismo: Acción Española*. 2nd ed. Madrid: Alianza Universidad, 1985.

Payne, Stanley. *Fascism in Spain, 1923–1977*. Madison: University of Wisconsin Press, 1999.

Preston, Paul. "Alfonsoist Monarchism and the Coming of the Spanish Civil War." *Journal of Contemporary History* 7, nos. 3–4 (July–October 1972): 89–114.

———. *The Politics of Revenge: Fascism and the Military in Twentieth-Century Spain*. London: Routledge, 1995.

Thomas, Hugh. "The Hero and the Empty Room: José Antonio Primo de Rivera and Spanish Fascism." *Journal of Contemporary History* 1, no. 1 (1966): 174–82.

iv. The Republican Zone during the Civil War

Bolloten, Burnett. *The Spanish Civil War: Revolution and Counterrevolution*. New York/London: Harvester Wheatsheaf, 1991.

Bolloten, Burnett, and George Esenwein. "Anarchists in Government: A Paradox of the Spanish Civil War." In Paul Preston and Frances Lannon, eds. *Elites and Power in Twentieth-Century Spain*. Oxford: Clarendon Press, 1989.

Casanova, Julián. "Anarchism and Revolution in the Spanish Civil War: The Case of Aragón." *European History Quarterly* 17, no. 4 (October 1987): 423–51.

Cattell, David T. *Communism and the Spanish Civil War*. Berkeley: University of California Press, 1955.

Chomsky, Noam. *American Power and the New Mandarins*. London: Chatto and Windus, 1969.

Dolgoff, Sam, ed. *The Anarchistic Collectives: Workers' Self-Management in the Spanish Revolution, 1936–1939*. Montreal: Black Rose, 1974.

Graham, Helen. "The Spanish Socialist Party in Power and the Government of Juan Negrín, 1937–1939." *European History Quarterly* 18, no. 2 (April 1988): 175–206.

———. *Socialism and War: The Spanish Socialist Party in Power and Crisis, 1936–1939*. Cambridge: Cambridge University Press, 1989.

Juliá, Santos, ed. *Socialismo y guerra civil*. 2 vols. Madrid: Pablo Iglesias, 1987.

Kern, Robert W. "Anarchist Principles and Spanish Reality: Emma Goldman as a Participant in the Spanish Civil War, 1936–1939." *Journal of Contemporary History* 11, nos. 2–3 (July 1976): 237–59.

Leval, Gaston. *Collectives in the Spanish Revolution*. London: Freedom Press, 1975.

Orwell, George. *Homage to Catalonia*. London: Secker and Warburg, 1938.

Peirats, José. *Anarchists in the Spanish Revolution*. London: Freedom Press, 1990.

———. *The CNT in the Spanish Revolution*. Ed. Chris Ealham. Vol. 1, Hastings: Metzer, 2001; vol. 2, Hastings: ChristieBooks, 2005; vol. 3, Hastings: ChristieBooks, 2006.

Preston, Paul. *Comrades! Portraits from the Spanish Civil War*. London: HarperCollins, 1999.

Seidman, Michael. *Workers against Work: Labor in Paris and Barcelona during the Popular Fronts*. Berkeley: University of California Press, 1991.

Thomas, Hugh, "Anarchist Collectives in the Spanish Civil War." In *A Century of Conflict, 1850–1950: Essays for A. J. P. Taylor*, ed. Martin Gilbert. London: H. Hamilton, 1966.

v. The Nationalist Zone during the Spanish Civil War

Fleming, Shannon E. "Spanish Morocco and the Alzamiento Nacional, 1936–1939." *Journal of Contemporary History* 18, no. 1 (January 1983): 27–42.

Jensen, R. Geoffrey. "José Millán Astray and the Nationalist 'Crusade' in Spain." *Journal of Contemporary History* 27, no. 3 (July 1992): 425–27.

Monteath, Peter. "Guernica Reconsidered: Fifty Years of Evidence." *War and Society* 5, no. 1 (May 1987): 79–104.

Raguer, Hilari. *Gunpowder and Incense: The Catholic Church and the Spanish Civil War.* London: Routledge, 2006.

Southworth, Herbert. *El mito de la cruzada de Franco.* Paris: Ruedo Iberico, 1963.

———. *Antifalange: Estudio crítico de "La falange en la guerra civil española" de M. García Venero.* Paris: Ruedo Iberico, 1967.

Tusell, Javier. *Franco en la guerra civil: Una bibliografía política.* Barcelona: Tusquetts, 1992.

vi. Foreign Intervention

Alexander, Bill. *British Volunteers for Liberty.* London: Lawrence and Wishart, 1982.

Algate, Anthony. *Cinema and History: British Newsreels and the Spanish Civil War.* London: Scolar Press, 1979.

Alpert, Michael. "Humanitarianism and Politics in the British Response to the Spanish Civil War, 1937–1939." *European History Quarterly* 14, no. 4 (October 1984): 423–40.

———. *A New International History of the Spanish Civil War.* London: Macmillan, 1994.

Buchanan, Tom. *The Spanish Civil War and the British Labor Movement.* Cambridge: Cambridge University Press, 1991.

Castells, Andreu. *Las brigadas internacionales en la guerra civil española.* Barcelona: Ariel, 1974.

Cattell, David T. *Soviet Diplomacy and the Spanish Civil War.* Berkeley: California University Press, 1957.

Coverdale, John F. *Italian Intervention in the Spanish Civil War.* Princeton: Princeton University Press, 1975.

Edwards, Jill. *Britain and the Spanish Civil War, 1936–1939.* London: Macmillan, 1979.

Fleay, C., and M. L. Sanders. "The Labor Spain Committee: Labor Party Policy and the Spanish Civil War." *Historical Journal* 28 (March 1995): 187–97.

Fyrth, Jim. *The Signal Was Spain: The Spanish Aid Movement in Britain, 1936–1939.* London: Lawrence and Wishart, 1986.

Gerassi, John. *The Premature Anti-Fascists: An Oral History: North American Volunteers in the Spanish Civil War, 1936–1939.* New York: Praeger, 1986.

Hywel, Francis. *Miners against Fascism: Wales and the Spanish Civil War.* London: Lawrence and Wishart, 1984.

Kent, Peter C. "The Vatican and the Spanish Civil War." *European History Quarterly* 16, no. 4 (October 1986): 441–64.

Landis, Arthur. *The Abraham Lincoln Brigade*. New York: Citadel, 1967.

Little, Douglas. *Malevolent Neutrality: The United States, Great Britain and the Origins of the Spanish Civil War*. Ithaca: New York, 1985.

——. "Red Scare, 1936: Anti-Bolshevism and the Origins of British Non-Intervention in the Spanish Civil War." *Journal of Contemporary History* 23, no. 2 (April 1988): 291–311.

Merriman, Marrion, and Warren Lerude. *American Commander in Spain: Robert Hale Merriman and the Abraham Lincoln Brigade*. Reno: University of Nevada Press, 1986.

Moradiellos, Enrique. "The Origins of British Non-Intervention in the Spanish Civil War: Anglo-Spanish Relations in early 1936." *European History Quarterly* 21, 3 (July 1991): 441–64.

——. "British Political Strategy in the Face of the Military Rising of 1936 in Spain." *Contemporary European History* 1, no. 2 (1992): 123–37.

——. "Appeasement and Non-Intervention: British Foreign Policy during the Spanish Civil War." In *Britain and the Threat to Stability in Europe, 1918–1945*, ed. Peter Catterall and C. J. Morris. Leicester: Leicester University Press, 1993.

Pike, David Wingeate. *Conjecture and Deceit and the Spanish Civil War*. Stanford: Stanford University Press, 1970.

Proctor, Raymond L. *Hitler's Luitwaffe in the Spanish Civil War*. Westport, Conn.: Greenwood, 1983.

Puzo, Dante A. *Spain and the Great Powers, 1936–1941*. New York: Columbia University Press, 1962.

Richardson, R. Dan. *Comintern Army: The International Brigades and the Civil War*. Lexington: University of Kentucky Press, 1982.

Southworth, Herbert. *Conspiracy and the Spanish Civil War*. London: Routledge, 2001.

Traina, Richard P. *American Diplomacy and the Spanish Civil War*. Bloomington: Indiana University Press, 1968.

Veatch, Richard. "The League of Nations and the Spanish Civil War, 1936–1939." *European History Quarterly* 20, no. 2 (April 1990): 181–207.

Viñas, Angel. *La alemania Nazi y el 18 de Julio*. 2nd ed. Madrid: Alianza Editorial, 1977.

——. "Gold, the Soviet Union and the Civil War." *European Studies Review* 9, no. 1 (January 1979): 105–28.

Whealey, Robert H. "How Franco Financed His War: A Reconsideration." *Journal of Contemporary History* 12, no. 1 (January 1977): 133–52.

——. *Hitler and Spain: The Nazi Role in the Spanish Civil War, 1936–1939*. Lexington: University of Kentucky Press, 1989.

18. The Franco Regime, 1939–1975

i. General Works

Abella, Rafael. *La vida cotidiana en España bajo el régimen Franquista*. Barcelona: Argos Vergara, 1985.

Alcalde, Carmen. *Mujeres en el Franquismo: Exiliadas, nacionalistas y opositoras*. Barcelona: Flor de Viento Ediciones, 1996.

Amodia, José. *Franco's Potitical Legacy: From Dictatorship to Facade Democracy*. London: Allen, 1977.

Ben-Ami, Shlomo. *La revolución desde arriba: España, 1936–1979*. Barcelona: Riopiedras, 1980.

Blaye, Edouard de. *Franco and the Politics of Spain*. Harmondsworth: Penguin, 1976.

Brenan, Gerald. *The Face of Spain*. London: Turnstile Press, 1950.

Carreras Ares, J. J., and M. A. Ruiz Carnicer. *La universidad española bajo el franquismo: 1939–1975*. Zaragoza: IFC, 1991.

Díaz, Elias. *Pensamiento español en la era de Franco, 1939–1975*. Madrid: Tecnos, 1983.

Fontana, Josep, ed. *España bajo el franquismo*. Barcelona: Critica, 1986.

Gallo, Max. *Spain under Franco: A History*. London: Allen and Unwin, 1973.

Grugel, Jean, and Tim Rees. *Franco's Spain*. London: Arnold, 1997.

Leitz, Christian. *Nazi Germany and Francoist Spain*. Routledge: London, 2006.

Leitz, Christian, and David J. Dunthorne, eds. *Spain in an International Context, 1939–1959*. Oxford: Berghahn, 1999.

Linz, Juan José. "An Authoritarian Regime: Spain." In *Cleavages, Ideologies and Party Systems*, ed. E. Allardt and Y. Littunen. Helsinki: Transactions of the Westermaark Society, 1964.

Miguel, Amando de. *Sociología del franquismo*. Barcelona: Euros, 1975.

Morcillo, Aurora G. *True Catholic Womanhood: Gender Ideology in Franco's Spain*. Illinois: University of Illinois Press, 2000.

Nash, Mary. "Pronatalism and Motherhood in Franco's Spain." In *Maternity and Gender Politics: Women and the Rise of the European Welfare States*, ed. Gisela Bock and Pat Thane. London: Routledge, 1991.

Payne, Stanley. *The Franco Regime*. Madison: Wisconsin University Press, 1987.

———. *Fascism in Spain, 1923–1977*. Madison: University of Wisconsin Press, 1999.

Preston, Paul. *The Politics of Revenge: Fascism and the Military in Twentieth-Century Spain*. London: Routledge, 1995.

Preston, Paul, ed. *Spain in Crisis: Evolution and Decline of the Franco Regime.* Brighton, Sussex: Harvester, 1976.

Saz Campos, Ismael. *España contra España: Los nacionalismos franquistas.* Madrid: Marcial Pons, 2003.

Shaw, Duncan. "The Politics of Football." *History Today* 35 (August 1985): 38–42.

———. *Futbol y franquismo.* Madrid: Alianza, 1987.

Tusell, Javier. *La dictadura de Franco.* Madrid: Alianza Editorial, 1988.

———. *La España de Franco: El poder, la oposición y la política exterior durante el franquismo.* Madrid: Historia 16, 1989.

Tusell, Javier, and Genoveva García Queipo de Llano. *Carrero: La eminencia gris del régimen de Franco.* Madrid: Temas de Hoy, 1993.

Tusell, Javier, et al. *El régimen de Franco: Política y relaciones exteriores.* 2 vols. Madrid: Universidad Nacional de Educación a Distancia, 1993.

Wigg, Richard. *Churchill and Spain: The Survival of the Franco Regime, 1940–1945.* London: Routledge, 2005.

ii. Biographies and Works on General Franco

Cierva, Ricardo de La. *Francisco Franco: Un siglo de España.* 2nd ed. Barcelona: Planeta, 1986.

Ellwood, Sheelagh. *Franco (Profiles in Power).* London: Longman, 1994.

Franco Salgado, Araujo. *Mis conversaciones con Franco.* Barcelona: Planeta, 1976.

Fusi, Juan Pablo. *Franco: A Biography.* London: Unwin Hyman, 1987.

Hills, George. *Franco: The Man and His Nation.* London: Hale, 1967.

Preston, Paul. "Franco: The Patient Dictator." *History Today* 35 (November 1985): 8–9.

———. *Franco.* London: HarperCollins, 1993.

Tusell, Javier. *Franco en la guerra civil: Una biografía política.* Barcelona: Tusquets, 1992.

iii. FET y de Las Jons and the Francoist Bureaucracy

Balfour, Sebastian. "From Warriors to Functionaries: The Falangist Syndicalist Elite, 1939–1976." In *Elites and Power in Twentieth-Century Spain*, ed. Paul Preston and Frances Lannon. Oxford: Clarendon Press, 1989.

Chueca, Ricardo. *El fascismo en los comienzos del régimen de Franco: Un estudio sobre FET-JONS.* Madrid: Centro de Investigaciones Sociológicas, 1983.

Ellwood, Sheelagh. *Spanish Fascism in the Franco Era: Falange Española de las Jons*. Basingstoke: Macmillan, 1987.

——. "Falange Española and the Creation of the New State." *European History Quarterly* 20, no. 2 (April 1990): 209–25.

Gallego Méndez, María Teresa. *Mujer, falange y franquismo*. Madrid: Taurus, 1983.

Linz, Juan José. "From Falange to Movimiento Organización." In *Authoritarian Politics in Modern Society: The Dynamics of Established One-Party Systems*, ed. S. Huntington and C. Moore. New York: Basic Books, 1970.

Pérez Montfort, Ricardo. *Hispanismo y falange: Los suenos imperiales de la derecha española*. Mexico D.F.: Fondo de Cultura Económica, 1992.

Preston, Paul. "Populism and Parasitism: The Falange and the Spanish Establishment, 1939–1975." In *Fascists and Conservatives: The Radical Right and the Establishment in Twentieth-Century Europe*, ed. Martin Blinkhorn. London: Unwin Hyman, 1990.

Richmond, Kathleen. *Women and Spanish Fascism: The Women's Section of the Falange, 1934–1959*. London: Routledge, 2003.

iv. Postwar Spain, 1939–1953

Abella, Rafael. *Por el imperio hacia Dios: Crónica de una postguerra, 1939–1959*. Barcelona: Planeta, 1978.

Beaulac, Willard L. *Franco: Silent Ally in World War Two*. Cardondale: Southern Illinois University Press, 1986.

González Portilla, Manuel, and José María Garmendia. *La posguerra en al País Vasco: Política, acumulación, miseria*. San Sebastián: Donostia, 1988.

Graham, Helen. "Gender and the State: Women in the 1940s." In *Spanish Cultural Studies: An Introduction*, ed. Helen Graham and Jo Labanyi. Oxford: Oxford University Press, 1995.

Kleinfeld, Gerald R., and Lewis A. Tames. *Hitler's Spanish Legion: The Blue Division in Russia*. Carbondale: Southern Illinois University Press, 1979.

Leitz, Christian, and David J. Dunthorne, eds. *Spain in an International Context, 1939–1959*. Oxford: Berghahn, 1999.

Moradiellos, Enrique. *Franco frente a Churchill: España y Gran Bretaña en la Segunda Guerra Mundial*. Barcelona: Ediciones Península, 2005

Preston, Paul. "Franco and Hitler: The Myth of Hendaye 1940." *Contemporary European History* 1, no. 1 (March 1992): 1–16.

Richards, Michael. *A Time of Silence: Civil War and the Culture of Repression in Franco's Spain*. Cambridge: Cambridge University Press, 1996.

Ruhl, Klaus-Jorg. *Franco, Falange y Tercer Reich: España durante la Segunda Guerra Mundial*. Madrid: Akal, 1986.

Smyth, Denis. "Franco and World War Two." *History Today* 35 (November 1985): 10–15.

Tuñón de Lara, Manuel, ed. *Primer franquismo: España durante la Segunda Guerra Mundial*. Vol. V, *Coloquio de Segovia sobre historia contemporánea de España*. Madrid: Siglo XXI, 1989.

Tusell, Javier, and G. G. Quiepo de Llano. *Franco y Mussolini: La política española durante la Segunda Guerra Mundial*. Barcelona: Planeta, 1985.

Vinas, Angel. *Guerra, dinero y dictadura: Ayuda fascista y autarquía en la España de Franco*. Barcelona: Critica, 1984.

Wigg, Richard. *Churchill and Spain: The Survival of the Franco Regime*. London: Routledge, 2005.

Wingeate Pike, David. "Franco and the Axis Stigma." *Journal of Contemporary History* 17, no. 3 (July 1982): 369–407.

v. Desarrollismo and Crisis, 1954–1975

Aguirre, Julen. *The Execution of Admiral Carrero Blanco*. New York: New York Times, 1975.

Fuente, Ismael, et al. *Golpe mortal: Asesinato de carrero y agonía del franquismo*. Madrid: Aguilar, 1988.

Gunther, Richard. *Public Policy in a No-Party State: Spanish Planning and Budgeting in the Twilight of the Francoist Era*. Berkeley: University of California Press, 1980.

Miguel, Amando de. *40 millones de españoles 40 años después*. Barcelona: Gribaljo, 1976.

Oneto, José. *Arías entre dos crisis, 1973–1975*. Madrid: Temas/Cambio 16, 1975.

vi. The Opposition

Alberola, Octavio, and Ariane Gransac. *El anarquismo español y la acción revolucionaria, 1961–1974*. Paris: Ruedo Iberico, 1975.

Amsden, J. *Collective Bargaining and Class Conflict in Spain*. London: Weidenfeld and Nicolson, 1972.

Balfour, Sebastian. *Workers and the City: Labor in Greater Barcelona, 1939–1975*. Oxford: Clarendon Press, 1989.

Claudín, Fernando. *The Communist Movement from Cominturn to Cominform*. Harmondsworth: Penguin, 1975.

Cowan, Andrew. "The Guerilla War against Franco." *European History Quarterly* 20, no. 2 (April 1990): 227–53.

Gillespie, Richard. *The Spanish Socialist Party: A History of Factionalism.* Oxford: Clarendon Press, 1989.

Giner, Salvador. "Spain." In *Students, University and Society*, ed. M. S. Archer. London: Heinemann, 1972.

Heine, Harmut. *La oposición política al franquismo: De 1939 a 1952.* Barcelona: Critica, 1983.

Hermet, Guy. *The Communists in Spain: Study of an Underground Political Movement.* Farnborough, Hants: Saxon House, 1974.

Ibarra Guell, Pedro. *El movimiento obrero en Vizcaya, 1967–1977: Ideología, organización y conflictividad.* Bilbao: Universidad del Pais Vasco, 1987.

Jauregui, Fernando, and Pedro Vega. *Crónica del antifranquismo.* 3 vols. Barcelona: Argos Vergara, 1982–1985.

Linz, Juan José. "Opposition in and under an Authoritarian Regime: The Case of Spain." In *Regimes and Oppositions*, ed. R. A. Dahl. New Haven: Yale University Press, 1974.

Lizcano, Pablo. *La generación del 56: La universidad contra Franco.* Barcelona: Gribaljo, 1981.

Maravall, José María. *Dictatorship and Political Dissent: Workers and Students in Franco's Spain.* London: Tavistock, 1978.

Martin Ramos, José Luis. *Historia del socialismo español.* Vol. 4, *1939–1977.* Barcelona: Conjunto, 1989.

Mateos, Abdón. *El PSOE contra Franco: Continuidad y renovación en el socialismo español, 1953–1974.* Madrid: Pablo Iglesias, 1993.

Morán, Gregorio. *Miseria y grandeza del PCE, 1939–1985.* Barcelona: Planeta, 1986.

Preston, Paul. "The Dilemma of Credibility: The Spanish Communist Party, the Franco Regime and After." *Government and Opposition* 11, no. 1 (Winter 1976): 440–62.

———. "The PCE's Long-Road to Democracy, 1954–1977." In *In Search of Eurocommunism*, ed. R. Kindersley. London: Macmillan, 1981.

———. "The Decline and Resurgence of the Spanish Socialist Party during the Franco Regime." *European History Quarterly* 13, 2 (April 1988): 207–24.

Ruiz, David, ed. *Historia de comisiones obreras, 1958–1988.* Madrid: Siglo XXI, 1993.

Semprun, Jorge. *Communism in Spain in the Franco Era: The Autobiography of Federico Sánchez.* Brighton: Harvester Press, 1980.

Stein, Louis. *Beyond Death and Exile: The Spanish Republicans in France, 1939–1955.* Cambridge, Mass.: Harvard University Press, 1979.

Tcharh, Cesar, and Carmen Reyes. *Clandestinidad y exilio: Reorganización del sindicato socialista (1939–1953)*. Madrid: Pablo Iglesias, 1986.

Tusell, Javier. *La oposición al régimen franquista*. Madrid: Rialp, 1987.

Tusell, Javier, ed. *La oposición al régimen de Franco: Estado de la cuestión y metodología*. Madrid: UNED, 1990.

Wingeate Pike, David. *In the Service of Stalin: The Spanish Communists in Exile, 1939–1945*. Oxford: Clarendon Press, 1993.

19. The Transition to Democracy in Spain, 1975–1982

i. General Works

Abel, Christopher, and Nissa Torrents, eds. *Spain: Conditional Democracy*. London: Croom Helm, 1984.

Arango, Ramón. *The Spanish Political System: Franco's Legacy*. Boulder, Colorado: Westview Press, 1978.

Bell, David S., ed. *Democratic Politics in Spain: Spanish Politics after Franco*. London: Frances Pinter, 1983.

Carr, Raymond, and Juan Pablo Fusi. *Spain: Dictatorship to Democracy*. 2nd ed. Oxford: Oxford University Press, 1982.

Cebrián, Juan Luis. *La España que bosteza: Apuntes para una historia crítica de la transición*. Madrid: Taurus, 1980.

Coverdale, John F. *The Political Transformation of Spain after Franco*. New York: Praeger, 1979.

Díaz, Elias. *La transición democrática: Claves ideológicas, 1976–1986*. Madrid: Eudema, 1987.

Gagigao, José L., John Crispin, and Enrique-Pupo-Walker. *Spain 1975–1980: The Conflicts and Achievements of Democracy*. Madrid: José Porrua Turanzas, 1982.

Gilmour, David. *The Transformation of Spain: From Franco to Constitutional Monarchy*. London: Quartet, 1985.

Giner, Salvador, and Eduardo Sevilla Guzman. "From Despotism to Parliamentarianism: Class Domination and Political Order in the Spanish State." In *The State in Western Europe*, ed. R. Scase. London: Croom Helm, 1980.

———. "Spain from Corporatism to Corporatism." In *Southern Europe Transformed*, ed. A. Williams. London: Harper & Row, 1984.

Graham, Robert. *Spain: Change of a Nation*. London: M. Joseph, 1984.

Huneeus, Carlos. *La Unión del Centro Democrático y la transición a la democracia en España*. Madrid: Gribaljo, 1985.

Maravall, José María. *The Transition to Democracy in Spain*. London: Croom Helm, 1982.

Maravall, J. M., and J. Santamaria. "Political Change in Spain and the Prospect for Democracy." In *Transitions from Authoritarian Rule*, ed. P. C. Schmitter and L. Whitehead. Baltimore: Johns Hopkins University Press, 1986.

Maxwell, Kenneth. *The Spectacle of Democracy: Spanish Television, Nationalism, and the Political Transition*. Minneapolis: University of Minnesota Press, 1995.

McDonough, Peter, Antonio López Pina, and Samuel H. Barnes. "The Spanish Public in Political Transition." *British Journal of Political Science* 11, no. 1 (January 1981): 49–79.

Medhurst, K. "Spain's Evolutionary Pathway from Dictatorship to Democracy." *West European Politics* 7, no. 2 (April 1994): 30–49.

Melia, Josep. *Así cayó Adolfo Suárez*. Barcelona: Planeta, 1981.

Morán, Gregorio. *El precio de la transición*. 2nd ed. Barcelona: Planeta, 1992.

Ortuño Anaya, Pilar. *European Socialists and Spain: The Transition to Democracy, 1959–77*. Palgrave: Basingstoke, 2002.

Palomares, Cristina. *The Quest for Survival under Franco: Moderate Francoism and the Slow Journey to the Polls, 1964–1977*. Brighton: Sussex Academic Press, 2003.

Penniman, Howard R., and Eusebio M. Mujal-Leon. *Spain at the Polls: 1977, 1979 and 1982*. Durham: Duke University Press, 1985.

Pollack, B. "Spain: From Corporate State to Parliamentary Democracy." *Parliamentary Affairs* 31 (1978): 52–66.

Pollack, B., and J. Taylor. "The Transition to Democracy in Portugal and Spain." *British Journal of Political Science* 13, no. 2 (April 1983): 209–42.

Powell, Charles T. *El piloto del cambio: El rey, la monarquía y la transición a la democracia*. Barcelona: Planeta, 1991.

Preston, Paul. *The Triumph of Democracy in Spain*. London: Methuen, 1986.

———. *Juan Carlos: A People's King*. London: HarperCollins, 2001.

Share, Donald. *Making Spanish Democracy*. London: Praeger, 1986.

Soto, Álvaro. *La transición a la democracia: España, 1975–82*. Madrid: Alianza, 1998.

Tezanos, José Félix, et al. *La transición democrática española*. Madrid: Sistema, 1989.

Tuñón de Lara, Manuel, et al. *Transición y democracia, 1973–1985*. Vol. 10/2, *Historia de España, dirigida por Manuel Tunón de Lara*. Barcelona: Labor, 1991.

Tusell, Javier, and Álvaro Soto Carmona, eds. *Historia de la transición, 1975–1986*. Madrid: Alianza, 1996.

Vazquez Montalban, Manuel. *Crónica sentimental de la transición*. Barcelona: Planeta, 1985.

Wiarda, H. J. *The Transition to Democracy in Spain and Portugal.* Washington, D.C.: American Enterprise Institute for Public Policy, 1989.

ii. The Left

Díaz, Elias. *Socialismo en España: El partido y el estado.* Madrid: Mezquita, 1982.

Fishman, Robert M. "The Labor Movement in Spain: From Authoritarianism to Democracy." *Comparative Politics* 14, no. 3 (April 1982): 281–305.

———. *Working Class Organization and the Return to Democracy in Spain.* Ithaca: Cornell University Press, 1990.

Foweraker, Joseph. *Making Democracy in Spain: Grass Roots Struggle in the South, 1955–1975.* Cambridge: Cambridge University Press, 1989.

Gillespie, Richard. *The Spanish Socialist Party: A History of Factionalism.* Oxford: Clarendon Press, 1989.

Heywood, Paul. "Mirror-Images: The PCE and PSOE in the Transition to Democracy in Spain." *West European Politics* 10, no. 2 (April 1987): 193–210.

Ibarra Guell, Pedro. *El movimiento obrero en Vizcaya, 1967–1977: Ideología, organización y conflictividad.* Bilbao: Universidad del Pais Vasco, 1987.

Maravall, José María. "Spain: Eurocommunism and Socialism." *Political Studies* 27, no. 2 (1979): 218–35.

Martin Ramos, José Luis. *Historia del socialismo español.* Vol. 4, *1939–1977.* Barcelona: Conjunto, 1989.

Martínez Lucio, Miguel. "Trade Unions and Communism in Spain: The Role of CC.OO in the Political Project of the Left." *Journal of Communist Studies* 6 (December 1990): 80–99.

Morán, Gregorio. *Miseria y grandeza del PCE, 1939–1985.* Barcelona: Planeta, 1986.

Mujal-León, Eusebio. *Communism and Political Change in Spain.* Bloomington: Indiana University Press, 1983.

Preston, Paul. "The Dilemma of Credibility: The Spanish Communist Party, the Franco Regime and After." *Government and Opposition* 11, no. 1 (Winter 1976): 440–62.

———. "The PCE's Long-Road to Democracy, 1954–1977." In *In Search of Eurocommunism,* ed. R. Kindersley. London: Macmillan, 1981.

———. "The PCE and the Struggle for Democracy in Spain." In *National Communism in Western Europe,* ed. H. Machin. London: Methuen, 1983.

Ruiz, David, ed. *Historia de comisiones obreras, 1958–1988.* Madrid: Siglo XXI, 1993.

Share, Donald. "Two Transitions: Democratization and Evolution of the Spanish Socialist Left." *West European Politics* 8, no.1 (1985): 82–103.

iii. ETA and Terrorism

Clark, Robert P. *The Basque Insurgents: ETA, 1952–1980.* Madison: University of Wisconsin Press, 1984.
———. *Negotiating with ETA: Obstacles to Peace in the Basque Country, 1975–1988.* Reno: University of Nevada Press, 1990.
Muñoz Alonso, Alejandro. *El terrorismo en España.* Barcelona: Planeta, 1982.
Pinuel, J. L. *Terrorismo en la transición política española, 1972–1982.* Madrid: Fundamentos, 1986.
Sullivan, John. *ETA and Basque Nationalism: The Fight for Euskadi, 1890–1986.* London: Routledge, 1988.

iv. The Military and the Far Right

Ellwood, Sheelagh M. "The Extreme Right in Post-Francoist Spain." *Parliamentary Affairs* 45, no. 3 (July 1992): 373–85.
Izquierdo, Antonio. *Claves para un día de Febrero.* Barcelona: Planeta, 1982.
Oneto, José. *La verdad sobre el caso Tejero.* Barcelona: Planeta, 1982.
Preston, Paul. "Francoism's Last Stand: The Military Campaign against Democracy." In *The Politics of Revenge: Fascism and the Military in Twentieth Century Spain*, ed. Paul Preston. London and New York: Routledge, 1990.
Urbano, Pilar. *Con la venia . . . yo indagué el 23-F.* Barcelona: Argos Vergara, 1984.

C. THE ECONOMY

1. General Works

Catalán, J. "Spain." In *The National Economies of Europe*, ed. D. Dyker. London: Longman, 1995.
Chislett, William. *The Internationalization of the Spanish Economy.* Madrid: Real Instituto Elcano, 2001.
———. *Spain at a Glance 2001.* Madrid: Banco Santander Central Hispano, 2001.

——. *Spain Going Places: Economic, Social and Political Progress, 1975–2008.* Madrid: Telefónica, 2008.

Cuadrado Roura, J. R. "Structural Changes in the Spanish Economy: Their Regional Effects." In *Industrial Change and Regional Economic Transformation: The Experience of Western Europe,* ed. L. Rodwin and H. Sazamani. New York: HarperCollins, 1991.

Economist Intelligence Unit. *Spain: EIU Country Profile 2001.* London: Economist Intelligence Unit, 2001.

García Delgado, José Luis, ed. *España económica.* 6th ed. Madrid: Espasa-Calpe, 1993.

——, ed. *España, economía. Ante el siglo XXI.* Madrid: Espasa, 1999.

Harrison, Joseph. *The Spanish Economy: From Civil War to the European Community.* Basingstoke: Macmillan, 1993.

Harrison, Joseph, and David Corkill. *Spain: A Modern European Economy.* Aldershot: Ashgate, 2004.

Kleinman, J., and P. Sington. *Spain: The Internationalisation of the Economy.* London: Euromoney Books, 1989.

Lieberman, S. *Growth and Crisis in the Spanish Economy, 1940–1993.* London: Routledge, 1995.

Martín, C. *The Spanish Economy in the New Europe.* Basingstoke: Macmillan, 2000.

Prados de Escosura, L., and J. Sanz. "Growth and Macroeconomic Performance in Spain, 1939–93." In *Economic Growth in Europe since 1945,* ed. M. Crafts and N. Toniolo. Cambridge: Cambridge University Press, 1996.

Salmon, Keith. *The Modern Spanish Economy: Transformation and Integration into Europe.* 2nd ed. London: Pinter, 1995.

Scobie, H. M., et al. *The Spanish Economy in the 1990s.* London: Routledge, 1998.

Tortella, Gabriel. *The Development of Modern Spain: An Economic History of the Nineteenth and Twentieth Centuries.* Cambridge: Harvard University Press, 2000.

2. Economic Policy

Fuentes Quintana, E., and J. Requeijo. "La larga marcha hacia una política económica inevitable." *Papeles de Economía Española* 21 (1984): 3–39.

Kennedy, P. "Europe or Bust? Integration and Its Influence on the Economic Policy of the PSOE." *International Journal of Iberian Studies* 9 (1996): 87–97.

Maravall, F., ed. *Economía y política industrial en España*. Madrid: Pirámide, 1987.

Montes Gan, V. J., and Juan A. Petitò. "The Privitization of State Enterprizes in the Spanish Economy." In *Privitization in the European Union: Theory and Policy Perspectives*, ed. D. Parker. London: Routledge, 1998.

Murphy, B. "European Integration and Liberalization: Political Change and Economic Policy Continuity in Spain." *Mediterranean Politics* 4 (1999): 53–78.

Pérez, S. A. "From Labor to Finance: Understanding the Failures of Socialist Economic Policies in Spain." *Comparative Political Studies* 32 (1999): 659–89.

Rand Smith, W. *The Left's Dirty Job: The Politics of Industrial Restructuring in France and Spain*. Pittsburgh: University of Pittsburgh Press, 1998.

Recio, A., and J. Roca. "The Spanish Socialists in Power: Thirteen Years of Economic Policy." In *Social Democracy in Neo-Liberal Times: The Left and Economic Policy since 1980*, ed. A. Glyn. Oxford: Oxford University Press, 2001.

Royo, S. *From Social Democracy to Neoliberalism in Spain, 1982–1996*. Basingstoke: Macmillan, 2000.

Villaverde, J., and B. Sánchez Robles. "The European Union and Regional Convergence in Spain: A New Approach." In *Economic Policy in the European Union: Current Perspectives*. Cheltenham: Edward Elgar, 1999.

Youngs, R. "The Domestic Politics of Spanish European Economic Policy, 1986–94." *South European Society and Politics* 4 (1999): 48–70.

3. Foreign Investment, Trade, and the European Union

Baiges, J., K. Olsen, and R. Tornabell. "Catalonia in the 1990s: A European Investment Region." *London: Economist Intelligence Unit Special Report*, No. 2097 (December 1991).

Baklanoff, E. N. "Spain's Economic Strategy towards the 'Nations of its Historic Community': The 'Reconquest' of Latin America?" *Journal of Inter-American Studies and World Affairs* 1 (1996): 105–27.

Closa, C. "The Domestic Basis of Spanish European Policy and the 2002 Presidency." *Notre Europe* (December 2001).

Crespo MacLennan, J. *Spain and the Process of European Integration, 1957–1985*. Basingstoke: Palgrave, 2000.

Farell, M. *Spain and the EU: The Road to Economic Convergence*. Basingstoke: Palgrave, 2001.

Haywood, Paul, ed. *Spain and the European Dimension: The Integrated Market, Convergence and Beyond*. Glasgow: University of Strathclyde, 1994.

Holman, O. *Integrating Southern Europe: EC Expansion and the Transnationalization of Spain*. London: Routledge, 1996.

Jones, R. *Beyond the Spanish State: Central Government, Domestic Actors and the EU*. Basingstoke: Palgrave, 2000.

Salmon, Keith. "Spanish Foreign Direct Investment, Transnationals and the Redefinition of the Spanish Business Realm." *International Journal of Iberian Studies* 14 (2001): 95–109.

Tondl, G. "EU Regional Policy in the Southern Periphery: Lessons for the Future." *Southern European Society and Politics* 3 (1998): 93–129.

Toral, P. *The Reconquest of the New World: Multinational Enterprizes and Spanish Direct Investment in Latin America*. Aldershot: Ashgate, 2001.

4. Agriculture and Industry

Benton, L. *Invisible Factories: The Informal Economy and the Industrial Development of Spain*. Albany: State University of New York, 1990.

Fariñas, J. C., and J. Jaumandreu. *La empresa industrial en la década de los noventa*. Madrid: Fundación Argentaria, 1999.

Lamo de Espinosa, J. *La década perdida, 1986–96: La agricultura española en Europa*. Madrid: Mundi-Prensa, 1997.

Martín, C. "La industria española: problemas estructurales y coyuntura actual." *Papeles de Economía Española* 62 (1995): 188–210.

Navarro Arancegui, M. *Crisis y reconversión de la siderurgia española, 1978–1988*. Bilbao: Junta del Puerto de Pasajes/Ministerio de Obras Públicas y Urbanismo, 1989.

Sumpsi, J. M., ed. *Modernización y cambio estructural en la agricultura Española*. Madrid: Ministro de Agricultura, Pesca y Alimentación, 1994.

Sumpsi, J. M. "La modernización de la agricultura y el desarrollo económico." *Papeles de Economía Española* 73 (1997): 149–59.

5. The Service Sector

Antón Clavé, S. "The Port Aventura Theme Park and the Restructuring of Coastal Tourism Areas in Catalonia." *European Urban and Regional Studies* 4 (1997): 257–69.

Balaguer, J., and M. Cantevalla-Jordá. "Tourism as Long Run Economic Growth Factor: The Spanish Case." *Applied Economics* 34 (2002): 877–84.

Bueno Campos, E. "El Corte Inglés: Sixty Years of Business Success." *European Retail Digest* 23 (2000): 26–28.

Caminal, R., J. Gual, and X. Vives. "Competition in Spanish Banking." In *European Banking in the 1990s*, ed. J. Dermine, 2nd ed. Oxford: Blackwell, 1993.

Corkill, D. "Cross-Border Banking Mergers: The Case of Spain's BSCH and Portugal's Champalimaud Group." *International Journal of Iberian Studies* 12 (1999): 173–84.

González Benito, O. "Geodemographic and Socio-Economic Characteristics of the Retail Attraction of Leading Hypermarket Chains in Spain." *International Review of Retail, Distribution and Consumer Research* 12 (2002): 81–103.

Howard, E. "Global Ambitions for Zara." *European Retail Digest* 25 (2000): 24–6.

Maiztegui-Oñate, C., and M. T. Areito Bertolín. "Cultural Tourism in Spain." In *Cultural Tourism in Europe*, ed. G. Richards. Wallingford: CAB International, 1996.

Priestley, G. K. "City Tourism in Spain." In *Tourism in Major Cities*, ed. C. M. Law. London: International Thompson Business Press, 1996.

Valenzuela, M. "Spain: From the Phenomenon of Mass Tourism to the Search for a More Diversified Model." In *Tourism and Economic Development: European Experiences*, ed. A. Williams and G. Shaw. Chichester: Wiley, 1998.

Verbeek, E. "Retailing in Spain: Sector Trends and Company Strategies." *European Retail Digest* 8 (1995–1996): 33–39.

6. The Labor Market

Argandoña, A. "Spain and the European Social Charter: Social Harmonization with Unemployment and High Wage Growth." In *Labour Markets in Europe: Issues of Harmonization and Regulation*, ed. J. T. Addison and W. S. Siebert. London: Dryden Press, 1997.

Bover, O., O. García Perea, and P. Portugal. "Labour Market Outliers: Lessons from Portugal and Spain." *Economic Policy* 31 (2000): 379–428.

Castro, A., et al. "The Portuguese and Spanish Labour Markets: So Alike Yet So Different." In *Working Europe: Reshaping European Employment Systems*, ed. J. Christiansen, P. Koistinen, and A. Kovalainen. Aldershot: Ashgate, 1999.

Dolado, J. J., F. Felgueroso, and J. F. Jimeno. "Youth Labour Markets in Spain: Education, Training and Crowding Out." *European Economic Review* 44 (2000): 943–56.

———. "Drawing Lessons from the Boom in Temporary Jobs in Spain." *Economic Journal* 112 (2002): 270–95.

Encarnación, O. "The Casualty of Unemployment: The Breakdown of Social Concertation in Spain." *South European Society and Politics* 4 (1999): 32–59.

Glatzer, M. "Rigidity and Flexibility: Patterns of Labour Market Policy Change in Spain and Portugal, 1981–96." *South European Society and Politics* 4 (1999): 90–110.

Jimeno, J., and K. Toharia. *Unemployment and Labour Market Flexibility: Spain.* Geneva: International Labour Organization, 1994.

Laparra, M., and M. Aguilar. "Social Exclusion and Minimum Income Programmes in Spain." *South European Society and Politics* 3 (1996–1997): 87–114.

Martínez, Lucio, and Paul Blyton. "Constructing the Post-Fordist State? The Politics of Labor Market Flexibility in Spain." *West European Politics* 18, no. 2 (1995): 340–60.

Rhodes, M. "Spain." In *The New Politics of Unemployment: Radical Policy Initiatives in Western Europe*, ed. H. Compton. London: Routledge, 1997.

Threlfall, M. "Comparing Unemployment in the UK and European Union: A Gender and Working Time Analysis." *Policy and Politics* 28 (2000): 309–29.

Toharia, L., and M. A. Malo. "The Spanish Experiment: Pros and Cons of Flexibility at the Margin." In *Why Deregulate Labour Markets?* ed. G. Esping-Anderson and M. Regini. Oxford: Oxford University Press, 2000.

Viñals, J. "Job Creation in Spain: A Macroeconomic View." In *The Social Challenge of Job Creation: Combating Unemployment in Europe*, ed. J. Gula. Cheltenham: Edward Elgar, 1996.

7. Demography and Migration

Pujol, R., ed. *Dinámica de la población española: Cambios demográficos en el último cuarto del siglo XX.* Madrid: Síntesis, 1997.

Ródenas, C. *Emigración y economía en España, 1960–1990.* Madrid: Civitas, 1994.

Romero González, J., and J. M. Albertos Puebla. "Spain: Return to the South. Metropolitan Concentration and New Migration Flows." In *Population Migration in Western Europe*, ed. P. Reece, et al. Chichester: Wiley, 1996.

D. SOCIETY

1. General Works

Cabrera, Mercedes, and Fernando del Rey. *The Power of Entrepreneurs: Politics and Economy in Contemporary Spain.* Oxford: Berghahn, 2007.

Chislett, William. *Spain Going Places: Economic, Social and Political Progress, 1975–2008*. Madrid: Telefónica, 2008.

Fishman, Robert M. *Democracy's Voices: Social Ties and the Quality of Public Life in Spain*. Ithaca: Cornell University Press, 2004.

Gascón, A. Ramos, ed. *Spain Today: In Search of Modernity*. Madrid: Cátedra, 1991.

Giner, Salvador, ed. *España: Política y sociedad*. Madrid: Espasa Calpe, 1990.

Gunther, Richard, ed. *Politics, Society and Democracy: The Case of Spain. Essays in Honour of Juan José Linz*. Boulder: Westview Press, 1993.

Hooper, John. *The New Spaniards*. Harmondsworth: Penguin, 1995.

Lawlor, Teresa, and Mike Rigby, eds. *Contemporary Spain: Essays and Texts on Politics, Economics, Education, Employment and Society*. London: Longman, 1998.

Linz, Juan José, ed. *España: Un presente para un futuro*. Vol. 1, *La sociedad*. Madrid: Instituto de Estudios Económicos, 1984.

Macdonald, I. R. "The Police System in Spain." In *Police and Public Order in Europe*, ed. J. Roach and J. Thomaneck. Beckenham: Croom Helm, 1985.

Mangen, Stephen P. *Spanish Society after Franco: Regime Transition and the Welfare State*. London: Palgrave Macmillan, 2001.

Miguel, Amando de. *La sociedad española, 1994–95*. Madrid: Universidad Complutense, 1995.

Miguel, J. de. *Estructura y cambio social en España*. Madrid: Alianza Editorial, 1998.

Pérez Díaz, Víctor. *The Return of Civil Society: The Emergence of Democratic Spain*. Cambridge, Mass.: Harvard University Press, 1999.

Ross, Christopher J. *Contemporary Spain: A Handbook*. London: Arnold, 1997.

Shaw, D. "The Politics of Football." *History Today* (August 1985): 38–42.

Tezanos, José Félix. *Estructuras de clase y conflictos de poder en la España post-Franquista*. Madrid: Edicusa, 1978.

Vazquez Montalban, Manuel. *Crónica sentimental de España*. Madrid: Espasa-Calpe, 1986.

2. Class Structure, Trade Unionism, Business, and Industrial Relations

Cabrera, Mercedes, and Fernando Rey Reguillo. *El Power of Entrepreneurs: Politics and Economy in Contemporary Spain*. Oxford: Berghahn, 2007.

Espina, Alvaro. *Concertación social, neocorporativismo y democracia*. Madrid: Ministerio de Trabajo y Seguridad Social, 1991.

Estivill, J., and J. M. de la Hoz. "Transition and Crisis: The Complexity of Spanish Industrial Relations." In *European Industrial Relations: The Challenge of Flexibility*, ed. G. Baglioni and C. Crouch. London: Sage, 2000.

Lawlor, Teresa, and Mike Rigby. "Spanish Trade Unions, 1986–1993." *Industrial Relations Journal* 25, no. 4 (1994): 258–71.

Longhurst, C. A. "Calculating the Incalculable: Reflections on the Changing Class Structure of Contemporary Spain." *Journal of the Association for Contemporary Iberian Studies* 8., no. 2 (1995): 2–18.

Magone, José M. *Iberian Trade Unionism: Democratization under the Impact of the European Union*. New Brunswick, N.J.: Transaction Publishers, 2001.

Martínez Lucio, M. "Spain: Regulating Employment and Social Regulation." In *Changing Industrial Relations in Western Europe*, ed. A. Ferner and R. Hyman. Oxford: Blackwell, 1998.

Miguelez, F., and C. Prieto, eds. *Las relaciones laborales en España*. Madrid: Siglo XXI, 1991.

Zaragoza, Angel, et al., eds. *Pactos sociales, sindicatos y patronal en España*. Madrid: Siglo XXI, 1988.

3. Gender Roles and Family Structure

Enders, Victoria, and Pamela Radcliffe, eds. *Constructing Spanish Womanhood: Female Identity in Modern Spain*. Albany, N.Y.: State University of New York Press, 1999.

García-Osuna, Carlos. *La mujer Española hoy*. Madrid: Nuer, 1993.

Matsell, C. "Spain." In *The Politics of the Second Electorate: Women and Public Participation*, ed. J. Lovenduski and J. Hills. London: Routledge and Kegan Paul, 1981.

Meil, G. "Changing Domestic Roles in the New Urban Family in Spain." *South European Society and Politics* 3 (1998): 75–97.

Ortiz Corulla, Carmen. *La participación de las mujeres en la democracia, 1979–1986*. Madrid: Instituto de la Mujer, 1987.

Reher, D. S. *Perspectives on the Family in Spain, Past and Present*. Oxford: Clarendon Press, 1997.

Threlfall, Monica. "The Women's Movement in Spain." *New Left Review* 151 (1985): 44–73.

Threlfall, Monica, Christine Cousins, and Celia Valiente. *Gendering Spanish Democracy*. London: Routledge, 2005.

Twomey, L., ed. *Women in Contemporary Culture: Roles and Identities in France and Spain*. Bristol: Intellect Books, 2000.

4. Youth Culture

Allison, Mark. "The Construction of Youth in Spain in the 1980s and 1990s." In *Contemporary Spanish Cultural Studies*, ed. Barry Jordan and Rikki Morgan-Tamosunas. London: Arnold, 2000.

5. Immigration

Azurmendi, M. *Estampas de El Ejido: Un reportaje sobre la integración del inmigrante.* Madrid: Taurus, 2001.

Corkill, David. "Race, Immigration and Multiculturalism in Spain." In *Contemporary Spanish Cultural Studies*, ed. B. Jordan and R. Morgan-Tamosunas. London: Arnold, 2000.

———. "Economic Migrants and the Labour Market in Spain and Portugal." *Ethnic and Racial Studies* 24, no. 5 (2001): 828–44.

———. "Immigration, the Ley de Extranjería and the Labour Market in Spain." *International Journal of Iberian Studies* 12, no. 3 (2001): 148–56.

Izquierdo Escribano, A. *La imigración inesperada: La población extranjera en España, 1991–1995.* Madrid: Trotta, 1996.

6. The Church

Brassloff, A. *Religion and Politics in Spain: The Spanish Church in Transition, 1962–1996.* London and New York: Macmillan, 1998.

Callahan, William. *The Catholic Church in Spain, 1875–1998.* Washington, D.C.: Catholic University of America Press, 2000.

7. Education

González Anleo, J. *El sistema educativo español.* Madrid: Instituto de Estudios Económicos, 1985.

McNair, J. M. *Education for a Changing Spain.* Manchester: Manchester University Press, 1984.

8. The Media

Bernández, A. "The Mass Media." In *Spain Today: In Search of Modernity*, ed. Ramon Gascón, 431–54. Madrid: Cátedra, 1991.

Bustamente, E. "Spain's Interventionist and Authoritarian Communications Policy: Telefónica as Political Battering Ram of the Spanish Right." *Media, Culture and Society* 22, no. 4 (2000): 433–45.

Deacon, Philip. *The Press as Mirror of the New Spain*. Bristol: Department of Hispanic, Portuguese and Latin American Studies, University of Bristol, 1995.

Jordan, Barry. "Redefining the Public Interest: Television in Spain Today." In *Spanish Cultural Studies: An Introduction*, ed. Helen Graham and Jo Labanyi. Oxford: Oxford University Press, 1995.

Kinder, Marsha, ed. *Refiguring Spain: Cinema/Media/Representation*. Durham, N.C., and London: Duke University Press, 1997.

Mateo, R., and J. M. Cobella. "Spain." In *The Media in Western Europe*, ed. B. S. Ostergaard. London: Sage.

Maxwell, R. *The Spectacle of Democracy: Spanish Television, Nationalism and Political Transition*. Minneapolis, Minn.: University of Minnesota Press, 1995.

Smith, Paul Julian. *Contemporary Spanish Culture: Television, Fashion, Art and Film*. Oxford: Polity, 2002.

———. *Spanish Visual Culture: Cinema, Television, Internet*. Manchester: Manchester University Press, 2006.

Villagrasa, J. M. "Spain." In *The Emergence of Commercial Television*, ed. A. Silj. London: John Libbey, 1992.

E. POLITICS

1. General Works

Abel, Christopher, and Nissa Torrents, eds. *Spain: Conditional Democracy*. London: Croom Helm, 1984.

Balfour, Sebastian, ed. *The Politics of Contemporary Spain*. Routledge: London, 2005.

Balfour, Sebastian, and Alejandro Quiroga. *The Reinvention of Spain: Nation and Identity since Democracy*. Oxford: Oxford University Press, 2007.

Bell, David S., ed. *Democratic Politics in Spain: Spanish Politics after Franco*. London: Frances Pinter, 1983.

Cebrián, Juan Luis. *Crónicas de mi país*. Madrid: Promotora de Informaciones, 1985.

Clark, Robert P., and Michael H. Haltzel, eds. *Spain in the 1980s: The Democratic Transition and a New International Role*. Cambridge, Mass.: Ballinger, 1987.

García de Enterria, E. *España: Un presente para un futuro*. Vol. 2., *Las Instituciones*. Madrid: Instituto de Estudios Economicos, 1984.

Gibbons, John. *Spanish Politics Today*. Manchester: Manchester University Press, 1999.

Gillespie, Richard. "The Continuing Debate on Democratization in Spain." *Parliamentary Affairs* 46, no. 4 (October 1993): 534–48.

Giner, Salvador, ed. *España: Política y sociedad*. Madrid: Espasa Calpe, 1990.

Gunther, Richard. *Política y cultura en España*. Madrid: Centro de Estudios Constitucionales, 1992.

Gunther, Richard, ed. *Politics, Society and Democracy: The Case of Spain. Essays in Honour of Juan José Linz*. Boulder: Westview Press, 1993.

Heywood, Paul. "Governing the New Democracy: The Power of the Prime Minister in Spain." *West European Politics* 14 (April 1991): 97–115.

———. *The Government and Politics of Spain*. Basingstoke: Macmillan, 1995.

———. "From Dictatorship to Democracy: Changing Forms of Corruption in Spain." In *Democracy and Corruption in Europe*, ed. D. Della Porta and Y. Ménys. London: Pinter, 1997.

Heywood, Paul, ed. *Politics and Policy in Democratic Spain: No Longer Different?* London: Frank Cass, 1999.

Hooper, John. *The New Spaniards*. Harmondsworth: Penguin, 1995.

Lancaster, Thomas D. "A New Phase of Spanish Democracy? The General Election of 1993." *West European Politics* 17, no. 1 (January 1994): 183–90.

Lawlor, T., and M. Rigby. *Contemporary Spain*. London: Longman, 1998.

Llera Ramo, José. *Postfranquismo y fuerzas políticas en Euskadi: Sociología electoral del País Vasco*. Bilbao: Universidad del Pais Vasco, 1985.

Magone, José M. *Contemporary Spanish Politics*. London: Routledge, 2004.

Montero Gibert, José R. *Sobre la democracia en España: Ligitimidad, apoyos instituciónales y significados*. Madrid: Instituto Juan Marc de Estudios e Investigaciones, 1992.

Montero Gibert, José R., and Mariano Torcal. *Value Change, Generational Replacement and Politics in Spain*. Madrid: Centro de Estudios Avanzados en Ciencias Sociales, 1994.

Newton, Michael T., with Peter J. Donaghy. *Institutions of Modern Spain: A Political and Economic Guide*. Cambridge: Cambridge University Press, 1997.

Powell, Charles. *Juan Carlos of Spain: Self Made Monarch*. London: Macmillan, 1996.

———. *España en democracia, 1975–2000*. 2nd ed. Barcelona: Plaza y Janés, 2001.

Pérez Díaz, Víctor. *The Return of Civil Society: The Emergence of Democratic Spain*. Cambridge Mass.: Harvard University Press, 1999.

Preston, Paul. *Juan Carlos: A People's King*. London: HarperCollins, 2001.

Rodríguez Ibañez, José Enrique. *Después de una dictadura: Cultura autoritaria y transición política en España.* Madrid: Centro de Estudios Constitucionales, 1987.

Ross, C. J. *Contemporary Spain: A Handbook.* London: Arnold, 1997.

Tezanos, José Felix, and Alfonso Guerra. *La década del cambio: Díez años de gobierno socialista.* Madrid: Sistema, 1992.

Woodworth, Paddy. "The War against Terrorism: The Spanish Experience from ETA to al-Qaeda." *International Journal of Iberian Studies* 12, no. 3 (2004): 169–82.

2. The Party System

Bar, A. "The Emerging Spanish Party System: Is There a Model?" *West European Politics* 7, no. 4 (October 1984): 128–55.

Cagiari, Mario. "Spain: Parties and the Party System in Transition." *West European Politics* 7, no. 2 (April 1984): 84–98.

Ellwood, Sheelagh M. "The Extreme Right in Post-Francoist Spain." *Parliamentary Affairs* 45, no. 3 (July 1992): 373–85.

Gunther, Richard, Giacomo Sani, and Goldie Shabad. *Spain after Franco: The Making of a Competitive Party System.* Berkeley: University of California Press, 1986.

Linz, Juan José, and José R. Montero. *Crisis y cambio: Electores y partidos en la España de los años 80.* Madrid: Centro de Estudios Culturales, 1986.

3. The Left, Socialism, and Social Democracy

Amodia, José. "Requiem for the Spanish Communist Party." In *Western European Communists and the Collapse of Communism*, ed. David Bell. Oxford: Berg, 1993.

Camiller, Patrick. "Spanish Socialism and the Atlantic Order." *New Left Review* 156 (1986): 5–36.

Fuente, Ismael. *El caballero cansado: El largo adios de Felipe González.* Madrid: Temas de Hoy, 1991.

Gallagher, T., and A. M. Williams. *Southern European Socialism: Parties, Elections and the Challenge of Government.* Manchester: Manchester University Press, 1986.

Gillespie, Richard. "The Break-Up of the Socialist Family: Party-Union Relations in Spain, 1982–989." *West European Politics* 13, no. 1 (January 1990): 47–62.

———. "Programa 2000: The Appearance and Reality of Socialist Renewal in Spain." *West European Politics* 16, no. 1 (January 1993): 78–96.

Gutiérrez, José Luis, and Amando de Miguel. *La ambición de César.* Madrid: Temas de Hoy, 1989.

Heywood, Paul. "Spanish Communists in Crisis." *Journal of Communist Studies* 1, nos. 3–4 (1985): 167–70.

———. "The Socialist Party in Power, 1982–1992: The Price of Progress." *Journal of the Association for Contemporary Iberian Studies* 5, no. 2 (1992): 4–15.

———. "The Spanish Left: Towards a Common Home?" In *Western European Communist Parties after the Revolutions of 1989,* ed. Martin Bull and Paul Heywood. Basingstoke: Macmillan, 1994.

Jauregui, Fernando. *La metamorfosis: Los últimos años de Felipe González: De la crisis de Suresne a la crisis del XXXIII congreso.* Madrid: Temas de Hoy, 1993.

Maravall, José María, et al. *Socialist Parties in Europe.* Barcelona: ICPS, 1992.

Martínez Lucio, Miguel. "Trade Unions and Communism in Spain: The Role of CC.OO in the Political Project of the Left." *Journal of Communist Studies* 6 (December 1990): 80–99.

Mujal-León, Eusebio. "Decline and Fall of Spanish Communism." *Problems of Communism* 35, no. 2 (1986): 1–27.

Petras, James, and Rita Carroll-Seguín. *El socialismo español: Camino a Marbella.* Madrid: Revolucion, 1990.

Pollack, Benny. "The 1982 Spanish General Election and Beyond." *Parliamentary Affairs* 36, no. 2 (Spring 1983): 201–17.

Share, Donald. *Dilemmas of Social Democracy: The Spanish Socialist Workers' Party in the 1980s.* New York: Greenwood Press, 1989.

Sotelo, Ignacio. *Los socialistas en el poder.* Madrid: El Pais, 1986.

Tusell, Javier, and Justino Sinova. *La década socialista y el ocaso de Felipe González.* Madrid: Espasa Calpe, 1992.

4. Alianza/Partido Popular

Balfour, Sebastian. "The Reinvention of Spanish Conservatism: The Popular Party since 1989." In *The Politics of Contemporary Spain,* ed. Sebastian Balfour. London: Routledge, 2005.

Davila, Carlos, and Luis Herrero. *De Fraga a Fraga: Crónica secreta de Alianza Popular.* Barcelona: Plaza y Janes, 1989.

Jauregui, Fernando. *La Derecha después de Fraga.* Madrid: El Pais, 1987.

López Nieto, Lourdes. *Alianza Popular: Estructura y evolución de un partido conservador.* Madrid: Centro de Investigaciones Sociologicas, 1988.

Montero, J. "More Than Conservatism, Less than Neo-Conservatism." In *The Transformation of Contemporary Conservatism,* ed. B. Girvin, London: Sage, 1988.

Tusell, Javier, ed. *El gobierno de Aznar: Balance de una gestión, 1996–2000.* Barcelona: Crítica, 2000.

Tusell, Javier. *El aznarato: El gobierno del Partido Popular, 1996–2003.* Madrid: Santillana Editiones Generales, 2004.

5. Foreign Policy

Armero, José Mario. *La política exterior de España en democracia.* Madrid: Espasa Calpe, 1988.

Balfour, Sebastian, and Paul Preston, eds. *Spain and the Great Powers in the Twentieth Century.* London: Routledge, 2000.

Barbé, E. *La política Europea de España.* Barcelona: Ariel, 1999.

Closa, Carlos, and Paul M. Heywood. *Spain and the European Union.* Basingstoke: Palgrave Macmillan, 2004.

Gil, Federico G., and Joseph S. Tulchin, eds. *Spain's Entry into NATO.* Boulder: Westview Press, 1988.

Gillespie, Richard. *Spain and the Mediterranean: Developing a European Policy towards the South.* Basingstoke and New York: Macmillan, 2000.

Gillespie, Richard, F. Rodrigo, and J. Story, eds. *Democratic Spain: Reshaping External Relations in a Changing World.* London: Routledge, 1995.

Gillespie, Richard, and M. Youngs, eds. *Spain: The European and International Challenges.* London: Frank Cass, 2001.

Gold, P. *A Stone in Spain's Shoe: The Search for a Solution to the Problem of Gibraltar.* Liverpool: Liverpool University Press, 1994.

Marks, M. P. *The Formation of European Policy in Post-Franco Spain: The Role of Ideas, Interests and Knowledge.* Aldershot: Avebuty, 1997.

Maxwell, Kenneth, ed. *Spanish Foreign and Defense Policy.* Boulder: Westview Press, 1991.

Pollack, Benny. *The Paradox of Spanish Foreign Policy: Spain's International Relations from Franco to Democracy.* London: Pinter, 1987.

6. The State of the Autonomies, the National Question, and ETA

Clark, Robert P. "The Question of Regional Autonomy in Spain's Democratic Transition." In *Spain in the 1980s,* ed. Robert P. Clark and Michael H. Haltzel. Cambridge, Mass.: Ballinger Publishing, 1987.

———. "'Rejectionist' Voting as an Indicator of Ethnic Nationalism: The Case of Spain's Basque Provinces, 1976–1986." *Ethnic and Racial Studies* 10, no. 4 (October 1987): 427–47.

———. *Negotiating with ETA: Obstacles to Peace in the Basque Country, 1975–1988.* Reno: University of Nevada Press, 1990.

Díaz López, Cesar. "Centre-Periphery Structures in Spain: From Historical Conflict to Territorial-Consociational Accommodation?" In *Centre-Periphery Relations in Western Europe*, ed. Yves Mény and Vincent Wright. London: Unwin and Allen, 1985.

Douglass, William A. *Basque Politics and Nationalism on the Eve of the Millennium.* Reno: University of Nevada Press, 1999.

Elorza, Antonio. *Historia de ETA.* Madrid: Temas de Hoy, 2000.

Fusi, Juan Pablo, ed. *España.* Vol. 5, *Autonomías.* Madrid: Espasa Calpe, 1989.

Giner, Salvador. "Ethnic Nationalism, Centre and Periphery in Spain." In *Spain: Conditional Democracy*, ed. Christopher Abel and Nissa Torrents. London: Croom Helm, 1984.

Guibernau, Maria Montserrat. "Nationalism and Intellectuals in Nations without States: The Catalan Case." *Political Studies* 48, no. 5 (2000): 989–1005.

———. "Spain, Catalonia and the Basque Country." *Parliamentary Affairs* 53, no. 1 (2000): 55–68.

———. *Catalan Nationalism: Francoism, Transition and Democracy.* London: Routledge, 2004.

Hargreaves, John. *Freedom for Catalonia? Catalan Nationalism, Spanish Identity and the Barcelona Olympic Games.* Cambridge: Cambridge University Press, 2000.

Herr, R., and J. H. R. Holt, eds. *Iberian Identity: Essays on the Nature of Identity in Portugal and Spain.* Berkeley: Institute of International Studies, 1989.

Keating, M. "The Minority Nations of Spain and European Integration: A New Framework for Autonomy?" *Journal of Spanish Cultural Studies* 1 (2000): 29–42.

———. *Nations against the State: The New Politics of Nationalism in Quebec, Catalonia and Scotland.* 2nd ed. Basingstoke: Palgrave, 2001.

Kirakzadeh, Cyrus Ernesto. *A Rebellious People: Basque Protest and Politics.* Reno: University of Nevada Press, 1991.

Llera, Francisco J., José M. Mata, and Cynthia L Irvin. "ETA: From Secret Army to Social Movement. The Post-Franco Schism of the Basque Nationalist Movement." *Terrorism and Political Violence* 5, no. 2 (1993): 106–43.

Mansvelt Beck, Jan. "Ethnic Minorities and Post-Francoist Territorial Administration in Spain: Changes in the Linguistic Landscape." *History of European Ideas* 19, nos. 4–6 (July 1994): 637–45.

Mar-Molinero, Clare. "Language Policies in Post-Franco Spain: Conflict of Central Goals and Local Objectives?" In *Language and Power*, ed. Romey Clark, et al. London: Silt, 1990.

———. *The Politics of Language in the Spanish-Speaking World.* London and New York: Routledge, 2000.

McDonough, Gary W., ed. *Conflict in Catalonia: Images of an Urban Society.* Gainesville: University of Florida Press, 1986.

McRoberts, K. *Catalonia: Nation Building without a State.* Oxford: Oxford University Press, 2001.

Mees, Ludger. *Nationalism, Violence and Democracy: The Basque Clash of Identities.* Basingstoke: Macmillan, 2003.

Moreno, L. *The Federalization of Spain.* London: Frank Cass, 2001.

Núñez, Xosé Manuel. "What Is Spanish Nationalism Today? From Legitimacy Crisis to Unfulfilled Renovation, 1975–2000." *Ethnic and Racial Studies* 24, no. 5 (2001): 828–44.

Ross, C. "Party-Nation and Region-State. The Reorientation of Basque Nationalist Ideology in the 1980s." In *The Resurgence of Nationalist Movements in Europe*, ed. José Amodia. Bradford: Bradford University Press, 1993.

———. "Nationalism and Party Competition in the Basque Country and Catalonia." *West European Politics*, 19, no. 3 (1996): 488–504.

Shabad, G., and R. Gunther. "Language, Nationalism and Political Conflict in Spain." *Comparative Politics* 14, no. 4 (1982): 443–47.

Siguan, M. *Multilingual Spain.* Amsterdam: Swets and Zeitlinger, 1993.

Squires, J. "Catalonia, Spain and the European Union: A Tale of Regional 'Empowerment.'" *International Journal of Iberian Studies* 12 (1999): 34–42.

Sullivan, John. *ETA and Basque Nationalism: The Fight for Euskadi, 1890–1986.* London: Routledge, 1988.

Urla, Jacqueline. "Ethnic Protest and Social Planning: A Look at the Basque Language Revival." *Cultural Anthropology* 3, no. 4 (1988): 379–94.

Woodsworth, P. *Dirty War, Clean Hands: ETA, the GAL and Spanish Democracy.* Cork: Cork University Press, 2001.

———. "The War against Terrorism: The Spanish Experience from ETA to al-Qaeda." *International Journal of Iberian Studies* 12, no. 3 (2004): 169–82.

Woolard, Kathryn A. *Double Talk: Bilingualism and the Politics of Ethnicity in Catalonia.* Stanford: Stanford University Press: 1989.

F. CULTURE

1. General Works

Gascón, A. Ramos, ed. *Spain Today: In Search of Modernity.* Madrid: Cátedra, 1991.

Gibson, Ian. *Fire in the Blood: The New Spain.* London: Faber and Faber/BBC Books, 1992.

Gies, D., ed. *The Cambridge Companion to Modern Spanish Culture.* Cambridge: Cambridge University Press, 1999.

Graham, Helen, and Jo Labanyi, eds. *Spanish Cultural Studies: An Introduction*. Oxford: Oxford University Press, 1995.

Hooper, J. *The New Spaniards*. Harmondsworth: Penguin, 1995.

Jordan, Barry, and R. Morgan-Tamosunas, eds. *Contemporary Spanish Cultural Studies*. London: Arnold, 2000.

Rodríguez Ibanez, José Enrique. *Después de una dictadura: Cultura autoritaria y transición política en España*. Madrid: Centro de Estudios Constitucionales, 1987.

Russell, P. E. *A Companion to Spanish Studies*. London: Routledge, 1983.

Sieburth, Stephanie. *Inventing High and Low: Literature, Mass Culture, and Uneven Modernity in Spain*. Durham: Duke University Press, 1994.

Smith, Paul J. *Contemporary Spanish Culture: Television, Fashion, Art and Film*. Oxford: Polity, 2002.

——. *Spanish Visual Culture: Cinema, Television, Internet*. Manchester: Manchester University Press, 2006.

Tuñón de Lara, Manuel. *Medio siglo de cultura española, 1885–1936*. Madrid: Tecnos, 1970.

2. Intellectual and Cultural Trends and Institutions

Cacho Viu, Vicente. *La Institución Libre Enseñanza. de* Madrid: Rialp, 1962.

Díaz, Elíaz. *Pensamiento español en la era de Franco, 1939–1975*. Madrid: Tecnos, 1983.

Dobson, A. *An Introduction to the Politics and Philosophy of José Ortega y Gasset*. Cambridge: Cambridge University Press, 1989.

Johnson, Roberta. *Crossfire: Philosophy and the Novel in Spain, 1900–1934*. Lexington, Ky.: University of Kentucky Press, 1993.

López Morillas, Juan. *The Krausist Movement and Ideological Change in Spain, 1854–1874*. Cambridge: Cambridge University Press, 1981.

Mermall, T. *The Rhetoric of Humanism: Spanish Culture after Ortega y Gasset*. New York: Bilingual Press, 1976.

Ramsden, H. *The 1898 Movement in Spain: Towards a Reinterpretation*. Manchester: Manchester University Press, 1974.

Shaw, Donald. *The Generation of 1898 in Spain*. London: E. Benn, 1975.

3. Architecture, Painting, and the Arts

Ades, D. *Dalí*. London: Thames and Hudson, 1982.

Berger, J. *The Success and Failure of Picasso*. New York: Vintage International, 1989.

Bergos, J., and M. Llimargas. *Gaudí—the Man and his Works*. Boston: Little Brown, 1999.

Casanelles, E. *Antonio Gaudí*. Greenwich, Conn.: New York Graphic Society, 1965.

Dent Coad, E. *Spanish Design and Architecture*. London: Studio Vista, 1990.

Deschames, Robert. *Salvador Dalí*. London: Thames and Hudson, 1985.

Harris, Derek, ed. *The Spanish Avantguard*. Manchester: Manchester University Press, 1995.

Jodidio, P. *Santiago Calatrava*. Cologne: Taschen Verlag, 1997.

Marco, T. *Spanish Music in the Twentieth Century*. Cambridge, Mass.: Harvard University Press, 1993.

Marfany, Joan Lluís. *Aspectes del modernisme*. Barcelona: Curial, 1975.

Mitchel, T. *Flamenco Deep Song*. New Haven and London: Yale University Press, 1994.

Moffit, John F. *The Arts in Spain*. New York: Thames and Hudson, 1999.

Moldoveanu, Mihail. *Barcelona: Architects of Exhuberance*. Barcelona: Lunwerg, 1996.

Morris, C. B. *Surrealism in Spain, 1920–1936*. Cambridge: Cambridge University Press, 1992.

Penrose, R. *Miró*. London: Thames and Hudson, 1995.

Raeburn, Michael, ed. *Salvador Dalí: The Early Years*. London: South Bank Center, 1984.

Richardson, John. *A Life of Picasso*. Vol. 1., *1886–1906*. New York: Random House, 1991.

Rispa, R., ed. *Birkhäuser Architectural Guide: Spain, 1920–1999*. Basil, Berlin, Boston: Birkhäuser Publishers, 1998.

Zabalbeascoa, A. *The New Spanish Architecture*. New York: Rizzoli, 1992.

4. Literature, Literary Trends, and Literary Critism

Brown, Gerald. *The Twentieth Century (A Literary History of Spain)*. London: Benn, 1972.

Chandler, Richard E., and Kessek Schwartz. *A New History of Spanish Literature*. Rev. ed. Louisiana: Louisiana State University Press, 1992.

Charlebois, L. *Understanding Camilo José Cela*. Columbia: University Presses of South Carolina, 1998.

Davies, Catherine. *Women Writers in Twentieth-Century Spain and Spanish America*. Lewiston: Edwin Mellon Press, 1993.

———. *Contemporary Feminist Fiction in Spain: The Work of Montserrat Roig and Rosa Montero*. Oxford: Berg, 1994.

Davies, Catherine, ed. *Spanish Women's Writing, 1894–1996*. London: Athlone, 1998.

Debicki, A. P. *Spanish Poetry of the Twentieth Century: Modernity and Beyond.* Lexington: Kentucky University Press, 1994.

Gibson, Ian. *Federico García Lorca: A Life.* London: Faber, 1989.

Jiménez Fajardo, S. *Multiple Spaces: The Poetry of Rafael Alberti.* London: Tamesis, 1985.

Jongh-Rossel, Elena M. de. *El krausismo y la generación de 1898.* Valencia: Albatros, 1985.

Jordan, Barry. *British Hispanism and the Challenge of Literary Theory.* Warminster: Aris & Philips, 1990.

———. *Writers and Politics in Franco's Spain.* London: Routledge, 1990.

Juretschke, Hans, et al. *La época del romanticismo, 1808–1874.* Vol. 35, 1, *Historia de España, fundada por Ramón Menéndez Pelayo.* Madrid: Espasa-Calpe, 1989.

Labanyi, Jo. *Myth and History in the Contemporary Spanish Novel.* Cambridge: Cambridge University Press, 1989.

Labanyi, Jo, ed. *Galdós.* London: Longman, 1993.

Laín Entralgo, Pedro, et al. *La edad de plata de la cultura española, 1898–1936.* Vol. 39, 2, *Historia general de España, fundada por Menéndez Pelayo.* Madrid: Espasa-Calpe, 1994.

Lee Six, A. *Juan Goytisolo: The Case for Caos.* New Haven: Yale University Press, 1990.

Pérez, J. *Miguel Delibes.* Boston: Twaine, 1971.

———. *Contemporary Woman Writers of Spain.* Boston: Twain, 1988.

———. *Camilo José Cela Revisited: The Later Novels.* Boston: Twain, 2000.

Perriam, Christopher, M. Thompson, S. Frenck, and V. Knights. *A New History of Spanish Writing, 1939 to the 1990s.* Oxford: Oxford University Press, 2000.

Rix, Robert, ed. *Thrillers in the Transition: Novela Negra and Political Change in Spain.* Leeds: Trinity and All Saints College, 1992.

Schneider, M. J., and I. Stern, eds. *Modern Spanish and Portuguese Literatures.* New York: Continuum, 1988.

Shaw, Donald F. *The Twentiteth Century (A Literary History of Spain).* London: E. Benn, 1972.

———. *The Generation of 1898 in Spain.* London: E. Benn, 1975.

Smith, Paul Julián. *The Body Hispanic: Gender and Sexuality in Spanish and Spanish American Literature.* Oxford: Clarendon Press, 1989.

———. *The Law of Desire: Questions of Homosexuality in Spanish Writing and Film.* Oxford: Clarendon Press, 1990.

———. *Representing the Other: Race, Text and Gender in Spanish and Spanish American Narrative.* Oxford: Clarendon Press, 1992.

Thomas, Gareth. *The Novel of the Spanish Civil War (1936–1975)*. Cambridge: Cambridge University Press, 1990.

5. Film Studies

Allison, Mark. *A Spanish Labyrinth: The Films of Pedro Alomóvar*. London and New York: I.B. Tauris, 2001.
Besas, P. *Behind the Spanish Lens: Spanish Cinema under Fascism and Democracy*. Denver: Arden Press, 1985.
Capards-Lera, J. M., and Rafael de España. *The Spanish Cinema: An Historical Approach*. Spain: Center for Cinematic Research Film Historia, 1987.
D'Lugo, M. *The Films of Carlos Saura: The Practice of Seeing*. Princeton, N.J.: Princeton University Press, 1991.
Evans, Peter William. *The Films of Luis Buñuel: Subjectivity and Desire*. Oxford: Oxford University Press, 1995.
Higginbotham, Virginia. *Spanish Cinema under Franco*. Austin, Tex.: University of Texas Press, 1988.
Hopewell, J. *Out of the Past: Spanish Cinema after Franco*. London: BFI, 1986.
Jordan, Barry, and Riki Morgan-Tamosunas. *Contemporary Spanish Cinema*. Manchester and New York: Manchester University Press, 1998.
Kinder, Marsha. *Blood Cinema: The Reconstruction of National Identity in Spain*. Berkeley and Los Angeles: University of California Press, 1993.
Molina Foix, Vicente. *New Cinema in Spain*. London: British Film Institute, 1977.
Smith, Paul Julián. *Desire Unlimited: The Cinema of Pedro Almodóvar*. 2nd ed. London: Verso, 2000.

6. Popular Culture

Allison, Mark. "Alaska: Star and Stage on Screen and Optimistic Punk." In *Identity in Twentieth Century Spain: Theoretical Debates and Cultural Practice*, ed. Jo Labanyi. Oxford: Oxford University Press, 2001.
Burns, J. *Barça: A People's Passion*. London: Bloomsbury, 1999.
Carnon-Deutsch, Lou. *The Spanish Gypsy: The History of a European Obsession*. University Park: Pennsylvania State University Press, 2004.
Shubert, Adrian. *Death and Money in the Afternoon: A History of the Spanish Bullfight*. New York: Oxford University Press, 1999.
Vázquez Montalban, Manuel. *Crónica sentimental de España*. Barcelona: Bruguera, 1980.
———. *Crónica sentimental de la transición*. Barcelona: Planeta, 1985.

About the Author

Angel Smith is reader in modern Spanish history at the University of Leeds. He has worked extensively in the areas of social and labor history, the crisis of early 20th-century Spanish liberalism, and nationalisms and national identities in Spain. His works include: Clare Mar-Molinero and Angel Smith, eds., *Nationalism and Nation Identity in the Iberian Peninsula: Competing and Conflicting Identities* (Oxford: Berg, 1996); Angel Smith and Emma Dávila-Cox, eds., *The Crisis of 1898: Colonial Redistribution and Nationalist Mobilization* (Basingstoke: Macmillan, 1999); Stefan Berger and Angel Smith, eds., *Nationalism, Labour and Ethnicity, 1870–1939* (Manchester: Manchester University Press, 1999); Angel Smith, ed., *Red Barcelona: Social Mobilization and Labour Conflict in the Twentieth Century* (London: Routledge, 2002); and Angel Smith, *Anarchism, Revolution and Reaction: Catalan Labour and the Crisis of the Spanish State* (Oxford: Berghahn, 2007). At present he is coediting a volume on the crisis of the Cánovas Restoration between 1913 and 1923 together with Francisco J. Romero-Salvadó, and preparing a book on the origins and rise of Catalan nationalism between the 1880s and 1930s.

Breinigsville, PA USA
11 May 2010
237787BV00004B/1/P